Grindhouse Nostalgia
Memory, Home Video and Exploitation Film Fandom

David Church

EDINBURGH
University Press

© David Church, 2015, 2016

Edinburgh University Press Ltd
The Tun – Holyrood Road
12 (2f) Jackson's Entry
Edinburgh EH8 8PJ
www.euppublishing.com

First published in hardback by Edinburgh University Press 2015

This paperback edition 2016

Typeset in Monotype Ehrhardt by
Servis Filmsetting Ltd, Stockport, Cheshire,
and printed and bound in Great Britain by
CPI Group (UK) Ltd, Croydon CR0 4YY

A CIP record for this book is available from the British Library

ISBN 978 0 7486 9910 0 (hardback)
ISBN 978 1 4744 0900 1 (paperback)
ISBN 978 0 7486 9911 7 (webready PDF)
ISBN 978 1 4744 0354 2 (epub)

The right of David Church to be identified as author of this
work has been asserted in accordance with the Copyright,
Designs and Patents Act 1988 and the Copyright and
Related Rights Regulations 2003 (SI No. 2498).

Contents

List of Figures vi
Acknowledgements viii

    Introduction 1
1 A Drive-in Theatre of the Mind: Nostalgic Populism and the Déclassé Video Object 29
2 42nd Street Forever? Constructing 'Grindhouse Cinema' from Exhibition to Genre to Transmedia Concept 73
3 Paratexts, Pastiche and the Direct-to-video Aesthetic: Towards a Retrosploitation Mediascape 119
4 Dressed to Regress? The Retributive Politics of the Retrosploitation Pastiche 176
    Conclusion 243

Appendix: Selected Filmography and Videography of Retrosploitation Media 258
Selected Bibliography 264
Index 278

Figures

I.1	Modelling reductive reception: *The Touch of Satan* (1971) receives plenty of historically chauvinistic mockery.	15
1.1	Japanese import *Destroy All Monsters* (1968) receives marginal billing below general-interest Hollywood films in a *Milwaukee Journal* newspaper advertisement.	36
1.2	In John Waters's *Polyester* (1980), the humorous incongruity of a dusk-to-dawn drive-in triple feature of erudite Marguerite Duras art films.	47
1.3	Mill Creek Entertainment's fifty-film *Drive In Movie Classics* box set.	55
2.1	42nd Street by night, c. October 1970, featuring a sexploitation double bill at the Victory.	89
2.2	Marquee for the hard-core feature film *Sometime Sweet Susan* (1975) and quasi-hardcore 'white coater' documentary *Swedish Marriage Manual* (1969).	89
2.3	In Bette Gordon's *Variety* (1983), Christine (Sandy McLeod) flips through a magazine in a Times Square adult bookstore.	90
2.4	BCI's 'Welcome to the Grindhouse' DVD menus.	108
3.1	DVD/VHS combo pack for Justin Russell's retro-styled slasher film *The Sleeper* (2012).	120
3.2	The evocation of a battered and degraded pulp paperback cover in the poster design for *Black Snake Moan* (2006).	129
3.3	A title card as seen in Robert Rodriguez's original *Machete* trailer that opened *Grindhouse* (2007).	131
3.4	The frame abruptly jumps and a horizontal splice appears for a split second as a zombie smashes a cop's head open in *Planet Terror* (2007).	153
3.5	Poster for the American double-feature theatrical release of *Grindhouse* in April 2007.	155
3.6	Cover for the late-2007 US DVD of Quentin Tarantino's disjoined *Death Proof*.	157

FIGURES

4.1	In *The Minstrel Killer* (2009), the titular minstrel dances along to a country boy playing 'Dixie' on the banjo, just before killing him.	188
4.2	Black Dynamite (Michael Jai White) teams with a group of black revolutionaries to stop a governmental plan to emasculate the African American community.	193
4.3	Original promotional poster for Rob Zombie's *The Devil's Rejects* (2005).	198
4.4	Part-time projectionist Tyler Durden (Brad Pitt) self-reflexively points out the emulsion scrapes signalling *Fight Club*'s (1999) approaching reel change.	206
4.5	In *Viva* (2007), writer/director/actor Anna Biller's starring credit appears while her protagonist reads middlebrow *Viva* magazine.	213
4.6	Valerie (Geneviere Anderson) is sprayed down by a female prison guard in *Sugar Boxx* (2009).	231
C.1	The *Machete* trailer's image of machete-wielding Latino immigrants raised white supremacist paranoia.	251

Acknowledgements

No doubt I shall be kicking myself in the future over accidental omissions from the following acknowledgements so, if your name does not appear here and justifiably should, please consider me thoroughly and pre-emptively kicked. First of all, thanks to my dissertation committee, including Joan Hawkins, Matt Guterl, Barbara Klinger, and Gregory Waller. The principal writing of this study roughly coincided with the illness and passing of Joan's husband but, as my adviser, she remained my main interlocutor throughout, reliably offering her keen feedback across multiple drafts. If any project of this length requires a certain measure of patience and perseverance, my own pales in comparison with hers under the difficult circumstances. For their constructive criticism of various lengthy pieces of this study, my thanks as well to fellow members of Joan's dissertation reading group, especially Mark Hain, Laura Ivins-Hulley, Will Scheibel, and Joshua Vasquez. The last two comrades in cinematology served as my sounding board for early ideas, vented frustrations, and shared navigation of the woolly world of doctoral studies. They were also admirably polite in turning down my repeated efforts to foist questionable films into their hands. In addition, Jon Vickers of the Indiana University Cinema invited me to programme several film series growing out of this research project, which kept spirits running high while allowing me to inflict my tastes on a wider audience.

Many other people contributed to this project in ways large and small, whether it was a useful research recommendation or simply a welcome vote of confidence: Peter Bondanella, Roger Corman, Steffen Hantke, I. Q. Hunter, Russ Hunter, James Kendrick, Jerry Kovar, William Lustig, Ernest Mathijs, Jimmy McDonough, James Naremore, Richard Nowell, and Eric Schaefer. The same can be said of the following people who, additionally (and very generously), provided me with early or unpublished versions of articles, chapters, or conference papers that have proven invaluable to my thinking on this topic: Caetlin Benson-Allott, Scott Herring, Katrin Horn, Elena Gorfinkel, Mark Jancovich, Tim Snelson, Jason Sperb, and Will Straw. Ernest Mathijs kindly offered access to the anonymised survey results cited in Chapter 3. Charles Bruss allowed me to reprint scans from his extensive collection of drive-in theatre newspaper advertisements, while Greg Waller also opened his files of drive-in theatre clippings to me. My thanks as well to Michael Fredianelli and Wild Dogs Productions for generously supplying me with a copy of their film *The Minstrel Killer*; and to Margaret DeWolf and Steve Lundeen for permission to reproduce Nick DeWolf's beautiful photos of 42nd Street in its heyday.

Gillian Leslie, Richard Strachan, Kate Robertson, Eddie Clark and all the people at Edinburgh University Press were wonderful to work with as this project transitioned into a *real live book* – and, of course, I owe a debt to the individuals who took the time to anonymously review the typescript. Parts of Chapter 2 were first published as the article 'From Exhibition to Genre: The Case of Grind-house Films', *Cinema Journal* 50, no. 4 (2011): 1–25; copyright © 2011 University of Texas Press; all rights reserved. I thank the publishers for graciously allowing me to reprint it.

Finally, I have to thank my family for their love and support, even if I sometimes struggled to describe to them what exactly this project was all about. And my heartfelt gratitude to Stephanie for understanding the necessity of investing long hours with strange and sometimes smutty materials (not that she wasn't invited to join in).

Introduction

Our film opens with an old farmer leading his cow into the barn for the night, where an assailant brutally stabs him to death with a pitchfork. Meanwhile, Jodie is a young man travelling alone in search of himself during a cross-country road trip. Stopping beside a small pond in the California countryside, he meets Melissa, a captivating young woman who invites him back to her family's farmhouse. Melissa's parents are not pleased to play host to a stranger, especially once senile but murderous grandmother Lucinda begins leaving her room. To his horror, Jodie soon discovers that Melissa and Lucinda are actually witchcraft-practising sisters hundreds of years old. Melissa had made a satanic pact to save Lucinda from being burned alive by angry townspeople, allowing the former to remain eternally youthful while the latter ages horribly and becomes increasingly homicidal. Such is the bizarre story of *The Touch of Satan* (1971), a minor exploitation film distributed by Futurama International Pictures in an attempt to capitalise on the earlier success of *Rosemary's Baby* (1968).

At first glance, this is not an instance of a film that would seem to be a likely candidate for cultural remembrance but, like many other low-budget exploitation films, it has proven remarkably resilient against the forces of obsolescence, in part because it has moved across a range of material sites – from theatrical exhibition to VHS to television to DVD – and garnered a variety of uses by fans along the way. These different material sites include not only a shift from theatrical to non-theatrical spaces but also encompass each distinct video format as well, since each can be invested with mnemonic value. Though, for example, *The Touch of Satan* would have probably played at drive-in theatres and urban grind houses upon its initial release, the film's continuing fan following today derives largely from having featured in a 1998 episode of *Mystery Science Theater 3000* (1988–99), the cult television series that features hosts offering sardonic running commentary on the perceived aesthetic shortcomings of substandard genre pictures.

At the same time, however, not all contemporary fans of the film necessarily want to keep its memory alive through the reductively ironic lens of mockable 'badness', instead tempering an awareness of the film's datedness with a straight-faced appreciation of its relative effectiveness even today. Indeed, the overlapping, or even conflicting, sources of pleasure that fans may derive from the historical pastness of a film like *The Touch of Satan* are suggested by discussion-board postings on the film's Internet Movie Database page. One user, for example, identifies him/herself as a loyal fan of *Mystery Science Theater 3000* but also complains about the tendency for some fans merely to follow the show's lead in finding the film an object of derision:

> I love MST3K. I have most episodes on tape. But if you want to spit out heckels [*sic*] from the show then do so on the MST3K page. Don't waste everyone else's time. I love the *Touch of Satan* episode of MST, but I also own a VHS original copy of the actual movie *The Touch of Satan*, not the edited and censored version that made it to the comedy show's broadcast. While there are some inherent problems in the film, pacing being one of them, I actually enjoy the movie itself and have gone back to it several times.

This fan's claims to more faithful devotion are figured through the ability to enjoy the film (despite its faults) without a thick slathering of ironic humour, plus ownership of a more 'complete' version of the film on an increasingly outmoded video format. Another fan concurs with this sentiment, declaiming at length:

> Thousands of young fans are wasting their time, and I'm talking about tens of thousands of hours in front of the DVD screen, watching what they have been told is disreputable entertainment, the lousier the better. It might be softcore sex films (take your pick from Column A reading Joe D'Amato and Jess Franco or Column B featuring Joe Sarno and the Something Weird brigade) or horror films (same guys plus the hundreds of no-budget videomakers and their favorite low-rent scream queens). But they are missing the point. We older film buffs (and I admit to plenty of mileage) were ALWAYS attracted to unusual/exotic/B movies. [. . .] [F]ilm buffs from the '30s through '70s (PRE-VHS, PRE-BETA, PRE-DVD, PRE-BLU-RAY) paid our dues. We traveled to remote or disreputable cinemas to catch rare films. We sifted through miles of celluloid in search of a GREAT, UNSUNG movie, not to find the worst. [. . .] I don't recall wasting much of my time arguing the demerits of crap or making fun of it the way Ghoulardi or other chiller theater horror hosts used to do, or parasitically making one's own programming out of it as MST3K did.[1]

This second commenter suggests that a generational divide has made younger audiences not only more inclined towards ironic distance but also more passive consumers than the pre-video film connoisseur. According to this logic, the sheer *quantity* of hours intentionally spent watching 'bad' movies through an ironic default mode is outweighed by the *quality* of interpretive labour once necessary both to track down and to find more than just unintentional humour in exploitation films. Of course, this commenter also plays down the fact that fans of D'Amato, Franco, Sarno, or Something Weird Video releases can and do interpret those films with earnest appreciation, not just ironic derision; and that, for some viewers, *Mystery Science Theater 3000* could also trigger fond memories of the horror hosts who brought exploitation films to local UHF television stations during the pre-video era. As Something Weird's founder Mike Vraney put it, 'The older you get, the more nostalgic you get – the more you hate today. And the more you just want to revel in your youth and your parents' youth and all this time period that came and went. [. . .] I just want to take the wayback machine and go there.'[2]

What these examples of fan discourse indicate, then, is the extent to which the residual value of a film like *The Touch of Satan* is linked to its uneven mnemonic use by fans as a means of nostalgically recalling past times and spaces of consumption. Where one fan considers possession of the original VHS release a source of nostalgia and fan-cultural privilege, another celebrates the days before home video made once-obscure films easily available to fans who can write a cheque but are supposedly incapable of non-ironic appreciation. These seemingly insignificant quibbles over the *who* and *how* of interpretation bespeak a deeper concern with the *where* and *when* of consumption, especially as the audiences and venues that theatrically screened these films increasingly recede into the past, making it more difficult to separate the lived places and symbolic spaces of exploitation film consumption in the home video era. Furthermore, accounting for the mnemonic desires that exploitation fans feel towards past texts and sites illuminates how culturally neglected cinematic artefacts are remembered and revalued during a period of unprecedented textual abundance and accessibility. That is, in response to industrial and technological shifts that might seem to equalise the cultural histories of specific films, fans increasingly reflect upon the *historicity* of these texts as objects whose value becomes inseparable from inflection by nostalgia.

Exploitation fandom is especially relevant in this regard because the exploitation film, as more of a broad mode or sensibility than a distinct genre in its own right, echoes the diffusion and mobility of contemporary fandom itself, having arguably become a cinematic corpus tied together by a sense of pastness. Much as James Naremore says of film noir, *exploitation cinema* is a discursively constructed idea projected on to the past, which helps account for its various uses as a genre, a mode, a style, a sensibility, a set of politically convoluted viewing practices, and so on. Indeed, 'depending on how it is used, it can describe a dead period, a nostalgia for something that never quite existed, or perhaps even a vital tradition'.[3] Yet, unlike film noir, the exploitation film has also existed as an industrial set of practices before being taken up by critics and fans with diverse reasons for identifying a given film as such. In fact, the cyclical qualities of exploitation cinema as a mode of production have proven remarkably conducive to fans' memorialisation of these films, despite the often short-sighted economic objectives of their original producers and distributors.

At its heart, this is a book about nostalgia as not only a common form of cultural memory (memory that transcends the individual) but, more particularly, a 'structure of feeling' upholding a 'positive evaluation of the past in response to a negatively evaluated present' which supposedly threatens sources of agency, identity, and community.[4] In terms of agency, identity, and community, media fandom has often been described as a subcultural formation. There is, however, an increasing awareness among film producers and scholars alike that fans are not 'a manifestation of a spectacular subculture' but rather 'fixtures of the mass cultural landscape'. This is especially true as media convergence hails all users as potential fans by spreading content across multiple platforms, and as film consumption becomes primarily centred within the home.[5]

This does not mean, however, that subcultural ideologies of alleged authenticity, connoisseurship and transgression cease to operate within increasingly mobile and diffuse fan cultures. Even if some fans may seldom interact in person, 'through repeated acts of imagination', they construct images of themselves that are 'fundamentally caught up in nostalgia for a specific absent community' that might seem threatened by cultural and technological shifts in consumption – despite that imagined community also potentially coming into view through technological platforms such as blogs, websites and social media.[6] Different nostalgic valences – sometimes conflicting, sometimes complimentary – play out in the minds of viewers whose once-obscure media choices are revived in the marketplace in ways that seem less confined to niche fan groups than ever before. This increased accessibility spurs longing for a sense of subcultural community that *perhaps never truly existed* but which persists as an object of nostalgia in itself. Consequently, nostalgia's affective qualities mediate between *intra*personal and *inter*personal aspects of fan identity that are subtended by broader changes in media industries, technologies and ongoing histories of social inequality.

Throughout this book, then, I argue that, when the material sites of film consumption change over time, nostalgia arises as a spatio-temporal structure of feeling that accommodates multivalent responses to the remediation of not only past films but also the structure of fandom itself.[7] For fans, a film can operate as a desirable *object of textual nostalgia* in its own right as a beloved artefact, as a *vehicle for contextual nostalgia* that triggers associated memories of a past time/place/audience, or as some combination thereof. In other words, nostalgia grounds the subcultural ideologies and capitals of film fandom by providing an imagined time and space in relation to which one's fandom can be mnemonically located. Much as nostalgia allows past time periods to be envisioned like spaces that can be imaginatively inhabited, past spaces of consumption can be nostalgically linked to particular time periods and audiences (for example, the 'grindhouse era'). Likewise, past periods of fandom can be envisioned as a particular time and space, a sort of territory arising as a locus for nostalgia, especially when the acceleration of format transitions in the home video market allows the shape of contemporary film fandom seemingly to grow more nebulous. As a means of distorting the past, nostalgia thus mediates between individual and more collective memories of the past, potentially offering both a buffer against, and source of anxieties over, perceived (sub) cultural and technological change. And as a key technology for juxtaposing different temporalities, home video constructs and mediates these cultural memories connecting the lived places and symbolic spaces of fan consumption. In this regard, home video has inherited the longer-lived significance of *media distributors* as key players in shaping the reception of potentially marginal films. Hence, this study explores fan practices more invested in imagined territories of pastness than in the latest technological advances, allowing us to better account for how cultural memory shapes the contours and pleasures of fandom in general.

Before proceeding, it is important to foreground the mnemonic connections between *place* and *space* as a means of understanding how cultural memory abstracts the loci of film consumption into what Pierre Nora calls *lieux de mémoire*, or material sites to which collective memory attaches and condenses, 'invest[ing] [them] with a symbolic aura'.[8] For Nora, 'every social group' must 'redefine its identity through the revitalization of its own history', and *lieux de mémoire* help serve this purpose as mnemonically charged locations for identity-building processes.[9] Yet, I would argue that these *lieux de mémoire* include not only physical buildings such as theatres but also the physical video formats that allow the replaying of memories at home. Specific drive-in theatres, for example, are lived places that individual audience members can visit, with each theatre offering unique variations on the general drive-in exhibition concept. Yet, the spatio-temporal idea of *the drive-in theatre* as an exhibition site also operates more broadly as a 'generic place' categorised on the basis of 'comparable scale, social similarities, [and] institutional relationships'.[10] As my first two chapters will elaborate, nostalgia for generic places such as the drive-in theatre or the grind house remains an important factor in the self-image of contemporary fans, particularly when cues for nostalgia are encoded into the video formats that deliver remediated exploitation films into the home.

As Cornel Sandvoss notes, 'Places of media fandom are of such particular importance to fans . . . because they offer the rare opportunity to relocate in place a profound sense of belonging which has otherwise shifted into the textual space of media consumption'.[11] With niche-interest texts so readily available today on home video and online, imagined fan communities are united more by ideologically charged ideas about privileged sites of consumption than by simply acquiring access to a specific text itself. This seems all the more true if the physical places where fandom most commonly occurs, such as the domestic sphere, are under a special burden to 'accommodate the imagined symbolic content of such communities'.[12] Indeed, for Giuliana Bruno, films and their consumption sites can become *lieux de mémoire* since film spectatorship commodifies the audiovisual experience of imaginatively travelling through space and time. Spatial consumption becomes linked to the spaces *of* consumption, with one's attendant experiences of subjectivity and temporality affected by changes in the film/viewer's cultural location. Much as places can be invested with memories of spectatorship, viewers can read their own memories as inhabitable spaces that can be revisited in new contexts, unleashing a sense of desire that inflects the viewing experience over time.[13]

According to Sandvoss, the self becomes a performed object in fan performances of identity because fandom both 'reflects *and* constructs the self' through the recognition of part of oneself in one's fan object (and vice versa). Consequently, public performance of fandom is not necessary under this logic because 'the first and foremost audience for the performance of fans is the fan him- or herself'.[14] As Will Brooker argues, fans experience a sort of spiritual connection with the fan text itself, pleasurably reuniting with a familiar textual universe upon repeated viewings, which is not necessarily dependent on feelings of connection with an imagined, wider fan community – and may, in fact, be antithetical to it if one wants to preserve the text's personal significance as a mnemonic trigger for other recollections. Regardless of whether or not it actually existed at one time, an imagined sense of community seems 'now lost in nostalgic memory', occupying the spatio-temporal realm of the past.[15] Holding and sharing particular nostalgias for select films and their means of consumption thereby become a way of situating oneself within a given fandom's imagined territory, especially through one's degree of imagined identification with past fans. Indeed, fan cultures develop through a shared sense of pastness that is cultivated over time by embracing myths about subcultural resistance and belonging, and by becoming part of the cultural history of their chosen objects.

To avoid unnecessary oppositions between history, memory and nostalgia, I adopt Pam Cook's model of these terms as

> a continuum, with history at one end, nostalgia at the other, and memory as a bridge or transition between them. The advantage of this formulation is that it avoids the common hierarchy in which nostalgia and some 'inauthentic' forms of memory are relegated and devalued in order to shore up notions of history 'proper'. Instead, it recognises that the three terms are connected: where history suppresses the element of disavowal or fantasy in its re-presentation of the past, nostalgia foregrounds those elements, and in effect lays bare the processes at the heart of remembrance.[16]

This model thereby allows us to account for the intertwining of 'real' historical context, appeals to nostalgia, and the overall mediation of memory in fans' consumption practices. Indeed, as Andreas Huyssen suggests, 'The real can be mythologized just as the mythic may engender strong reality effects', so there can be 'no pure space outside of commodity culture' for evaluating a concrete distinction between history and memory. Consequently, 'opposing serious memory to trivial memory . . . would only reproduce the old high/low dichotomy of modernist culture in a new guise'.[17]

José van Dijck's concept of *mediated memories* is my guiding principle in understanding how these memory objects can be both personal and cultural, since cultural frameworks influence what and how we remember, while our individual choices jointly influence those cultural frameworks in turn. Mediation 'comprises not only the media tools we wield in the private sphere but also the active choices of individuals to incorporate parts of culture into their lives'. We may, for example, have 'unconscious preferences for a particular mode of inscription' via technologies that privilege 'particular sensorial perceptions over others', as is arguably true of different video formats. Overall, then, mediated memories encompass *'the activities and objects we produce and appropriate by means of media technologies, for creating and re-creating a sense of past, present, and future of ourselves in relation to others'*.[18] Notably, these can include not only the use of technology to record one's own memories but also the commercial acquisition of pre-recorded media artefacts invested or investible with memory. Encompassing the use of films as objects of textual nostalgia and vehicles for contextual nostalgia, these performances of self-formation blur into wider forms of sociality, producing struggles over which memories should be inscribed for oneself and which should be shared with wider audiences under certain conditions.[19]

Sandvoss, for instance, argues that fandom involves a projection of self-identity on to the collective group that reinforces one's spatially imagined sense of belonging by offering a sense of security and 'emotional warmth' – but this process 'always involves an evaluation and categorisation of others', implying 'a sharp division between "us" and "them" in the form of a constructed "Other"'.[20] In this sense, a fandom can continue to use visions of pastness in policing its imagined borders and building its fan-cultural competencies, despite – or, perhaps more appropriately, because of – the diffusion and mobility of texts that render shared images of the past all the more open to contestation. If our consumption choices contingently perform our senses of belonging to multiple social groups, then the more groups we occupy, the more multivalent are the nostalgias about our own and others' prior engagements with films claimed as markers of belonging. In this respect, 'the more "collective" the medium (that is, the larger its potential or actual audience), the less likely it is that its representation will reflect the collective memory of that audience'.[21] The remembered spaces of film consumption thus potentially become all the more important in maintaining one's nostalgia for texts that otherwise gain wider circulation. Tensions between differently inflected nostalgias about past forms of culturally marginalised cinema consequently animate a commingling of desire for, and reluctance towards, fan-cultural belonging as niche films increasingly move from the margins to mainstream accessibility.

Exploitation films permit an appropriate cluster of case studies in this regard, not only because of their cult reputations sustained through home video but also because the tensions between ironic distance and sincere appreciation in their contemporary reception echo the tensions generated between the perceived fragmentation and coalescence of fan-cultural memories as films are remediated across different video formats and reach broader taste publics. As suggested by the aforementioned *Touch of Satan* example, an exploitation film's contested status as a mockably 'bad' atrocity, an underrated gem, or some variation between can depend upon the fan's historical distance from the text's original spatio-temporal reception context, the technological means of presently accessing the film, and how much accumulated film-historical knowledge the fan possesses at the time of viewing. As ways of making claims to authenticity, connoisseurship and nonconformist tastes, these factors all share a common concern with memories of film history's material sites – memories that help construct affectively charged relationships to texts which have become part of one's own personal history as a fan. Consequently, they can all factor into a fan's feelings of (sincere) closeness to, or (ironic) distance from, the broader groups of viewers that may crystallise as home video mobilises nostalgia by allowing its objects to better move through time and space in the marketplace.

Irony and nostalgia are often socially coded as opposed to one another but viewers do not necessarily experience these as binary positions; nor do these aspects of the reception experience cleanly map on to arbitrary distinctions between so-called 'high' and 'low' culture. As Svetlana Boym observes, some forms of nostalgia may regressively attempt to revive the past unchanged whereas others invoke a far more ironic and critical approach to past objects presently perceived as cultural ruins.[22] Accordingly, different valences of nostalgia – some more ironic or sincere than others – can contingently shift and recombine depending on the fan's respective level of historical proximity to the text or fandom in question. Likewise, nostalgia is not inherently conservative, even if it has often been deployed for politically conservative purposes; rather, it can serve very different political aims depending on the user and the reception context.[23] Moving past the simple equation of nostalgia with reactionary politics broadens our focus on how appeals to pastness may be unevenly successful in targeting consumers who have their own reasons for recovering texts that have often been overlooked by conventional film histories. Even as nostalgic valences may be used as a means of gaining imagined refuge from present industrial demands and cultural shifts, these selective visions of the past are always subject to suspicion as mythic falsifications of a history which is perpetually debated in fan discourse – hence the ambivalent blend of ironic distance and retrospective longing potentially felt towards past and present periods of fandom themselves.

Existing fan studies have too often focused on the technological advances that are quickly appropriated by fan cultures but have paid less attention to fandoms rooted in media-implanted memories of a desired distance from the contemporary moment. This is certainly not to say that exploitation fans share a Luddite sensibility but that their stance towards emergent technologies is often infused with a longing to occupy the past – even as they may nevertheless take advantage of the increased access to once-obscure texts and fellow viewers that complicate their assumed claims to exclusivity and nonconformity. Taking fuller account of cultural memory's role in structuring both the personal and collective dimensions of fandom thus allows us to understand better how and why the past is distorted by media producers/distributors and everyday users, indexing social and economic inequalities that cannot be merely reduced to ironic mockery or distanced contemplation. Likewise, while most cultural memory studies have focused on collective forms of trauma, national forgetting and public commemoration, this book focuses on more private, individualistic uses of memory objects which allow us to challenge the presumption that fan cultures possess a uniformly collective subcultural consciousness.

Though the following chapters attempt to provide a backdrop of historical facts behind the changing material sites of exploitation films, it is more crucial to observe *how* and *why* media producers and fans alike distort the past for various purposes. In other words, because historically erroneous or oversimplified cultural memories may play a large role in informing subcultural ideologies, analysing the contemporary form and function of such memories is more vital than correcting their potential distortions of historical 'truth'. After all, as Sandvoss observes, 'facts become relative within the meta-narrative of the myth [built up around a fan text], which in turn is reflective of the fan's values, beliefs, and image of self'.[24] Personal memories and more collective forms of group memory may insulate themselves from historical criticism by dissolving memory into mythology but this dynamic is more important with forms of cultural memory that (by definition) transcend the individual in making shared claims about the past. Whereas the assemblages of formative memories held by an individual may be rather idiosyncratic, the common past shared by a social group is more likely to overlap with the broader domain of history, and thus make more hegemonic appeals to consensual interpretation – even if that consensus remains inevitably contested.[25]

Exploitation Cinema between History and Memory

To begin exploring the selective contours of the corpus of films under consideration in this study, we should allow that a concrete definition of *exploitation film* would merely prove a moving target for analysis, given the term's historically shifting connotations. As it is commonly known today, the exploitation film encompasses a mode of low-budget film-making that emphasises sensationalism, spectacle and direct appeals to the viewer's body. Often read as such during the process of reception, it seems closer to a style or sensibility that can be recognised in a broad range of genres and subgenres, particularly when films are marked by visible signs of budgetary restriction, deliberate excess, sleaziness and apparent 'bad taste'. It is particularly worth noting that 'bad taste' is often seen as a symptom of budgetary impoverishment, since higher-budgeted or more prestigious productions are perhaps less likely to be accused of pandering to 'lower' tastes. That is, exploitation films tend to 'offend not only because they show grisly violence, but also because in their grainy, low-lighting shaky-cam amateurism they transgress notions of filmic decorum as they do so'.[26]

Yet, despite the auteurist emphasis often placed by critics and fans upon the romanticised role of low-budget film-makers, this book finds the role of *distributors* key to understanding the propagation of exploitation cinema, because distributors often suggested and assembled lurid publicity materials, strategised where and how to exhibit films, retitled or recut prints for different regions and periods and, in later years, licensed these films for home video release. Then, as now, garish advertising and ballyhoo are longstanding trademarks of the exploitation film, so much of a film's initial and continued framing as 'exploitation' derives from its paratexts, including trailers, posters, lobby displays, newspaper advertisements and so on.

Eric Schaefer describes classical exploitation films as a distinct category and market of independently produced and distributed films that formed by the 1920s, paralleling the rise and fall of classical Hollywood's studio era by offering lurid sights and subject matter forbidden under the Production Code. Barred from playing in studio-affiliated theatres, classical exploitation films, such as *Marihuana* (1936), *Mom and Dad* (1945) and *Because of Eve* (1948), were more likely to be screened to adults-only audiences at independently owned theatres. Though they may have been made to capitalise quickly on timely social problems, such as drug abuse or vice scandals, the films often played for many years on the American exploitation circuit, even over a decade after their initial release as they circulated through travelling roadshows and the states' rights market. For Schaefer, the Hollywood film industry tried to construct its public image in opposition to the disreputability of exploitation films, while exploitation film-makers accepted their otherly social position as a mark of pride and distinction.[27]

As the studio system crumbled during the 1950s, films addressing once-taboo subject matter could be made and shown much more openly, heralding the end of market demand for classical exploitation films. Schaefer notes that the far more diverse range of later films dubbed 'exploitation', such as titles from mainstays like American International Pictures (AIP), may have relied heavily on hyperbolic publicity and gimmickry but were typically more technically polished than classical exploitation films had been, and were more directly targeted at teen/youth viewers.[28] These post-classical films generally turned to exploitation techniques to overcome their low budgets, lack of star power, and uncertain viewer demographics. Imitating the formulas of successful major-studio genre films while spicing up their substandard offerings with juicier titles and promotional imagery became key components of exploitation film-making ever since. With the titles and posters for exploitation films often developed long before scripts, these films were effectively low-budget, 'high-concept' productions that developed into cycles by formulaically imitating the most sensational (para)textual aspects of major-studio successes.[29] Yet, independents also sometimes initiated cycles that were subsequently picked up by the major studios, as with the science fiction films *Rocketship X-M* (1950) and *Destination Moon* (1950), so major-studio influence was not a one-way street.[30] Indeed, the post-1950s era saw many different industries embracing how

> the counterculture seemed to be preparing young people to rebel against whatever they had patronized before and to view the cycles of the new without the suspicion of earlier eras. Its simultaneous craving for authenticity and suspicion of tradition seemed to make the counterculture an ideal vehicle for a vast sea-change in American consuming habits,

eschewing the thriftiness and brand loyalty of older, 'conformist' parent generations in favour of the contingently 'hip' products connoting 'rebellion'.[31]

A series of changes during the 1970s and 1980s dramatically altered the American marketplace for exploitation cinema. Taking inspiration from independent successes such as *Billy Jack* (1971), Hollywood's increasing adoption of exploitation subject matter and marketing/distribution strategies for big-budget spectaculars such as *Jaws* (1975) eventually squeezed many independent exploitation companies out of the market.[32] Higher production values became the new norm for sensational genre material while less reputable exhibition sites (drive-ins, subsequent-run theatres) became targeted by the majors' newfound penchant for saturation booking and advertising. As Roger Corman recalls, 'when the majors saw they could have enormous commercial success with *big-budget* exploitation films, they gave them loftier terms – "genre" films or "high concept" films'.[33]

One of the most crucial changes during this period was the rise of home video, which may have had a negative impact on the long-standing theatrical venues for exploitation films but succeeded in tangibly placing decades' worth of low-budget genre pictures at audiences' fingertips for the first time. Though celluloid copies of theatrically released films had been available as 8 mm prints for home film collectors for years, the easier duplicability and circulation of films on analogue video formats made far more titles distributable on VHS, relegating 8 mm collecting to greater obsolescence. Some exploitation distributors initially benefited from releasing both older and newer titles on VHS (introduced in 1976) but many were eventually driven out by the home video market's consolidation in the late 1980s and early 1990s. Nevertheless, the sudden ability to choose from a wide range of exploitation titles, and to apply a variety of reading strategies to them over subsequent re-viewings, encouraged the growth of fan cultures that became fresh markets for the films as cult objects. Ironically, many of these films became patronisingly labelled 'trash cinema' at the very time they were being not only economically revalued for the first time in years but also becoming incorporated into the lived spaces of fan identity at home. Whether circulating bootlegs of hard-to-find titles or buying official releases as video sell-through prices dropped during the 1990s, these fan cultures took up the mantle of researching, archiving and assigning value to a wide swathe of cinema history that had been overlooked or deliberately ignored by film historians, high-minded critics and various arbiters of cultural taste.

Cultism and Subcultural Capital

Sarah Thornton convincingly argues that subcultures do not form organically but, rather, develop through fans' relation to media industries from the start. The fanzines which sprang up around home video, for example, tended to be infused with nostalgia for past points in subcultural history, such as times with different censorship restrictions or times when exploitation films were exhibited in theatres. Some of these publications even supported themselves by offering mail-order sales of the very VHS bootlegs that helped construct their readership. Yet, Thornton argues that supposed distinctions between subcultures and the nebulously imagined 'mainstream' that they define themselves against routinely blur. Even if the shape of a given subculture does not conform to its ideal self-image as an 'underground' cultural formation, certain hip ideologies and competencies (*subcultural capital*) remain relevant to the policing of imagined subcultural boundaries. This even occurs at the risk of reproducing wider social inequalities (such as gender-based exclusions) that uphold dominant ideological values.[34] Thus, even if fans may continue to latch on to subcultural ideologies to (erroneously) imagine their social position as special or unique, it is impossible to pinpoint subcultures themselves as internally coherent or ideologically resistant entities.

A central subcultural ideology expounded by exploitation fans celebrates these films as the 'authentic' product of rebels working outside, or on the margins of, the Hollywood industry, combating budgetary impoverishment with shocking, inventive or boundary-pushing attempts to thrill audiences with depictions of sex and violence that violated the tastes of bourgeois, conformist society. Whether heralded as glorious failures or hailed for making more money than their Hollywood-spawned kin, exploitation films play into a thoroughly romantic mythology of excess, hedonism and transgression that has since been mapped on to the broader notion of the 'independent film' as well. One fan, for example, describes the 1970s exploitation world as 'something renegade, outlaw. The beginning of a new cinema where anyone could do it for any reason at all. A cinema that would spiral away into the current day and age of modern digital video and computerized editing.'[35] Still, even as he laments digital shifts in film production, the changing shape of post-1970s film distribution had more to do with exploitation cinema's own shifting sense of time and space as it entered the home as collectible, replayable video objects.

Within academic considerations of exploitation cinema, these subcultural ideologies have been most notably raised through Jeffrey Sconce's influential concept of 'paracinema' which he associates with the fan-cultural practices of trading and selling exploitation films on home video in the 1980s and 1990s. For Sconce, the 'so bad it's good' reading strategy, which privileges wild moments of excess, continuity errors, and other symptoms of film-making desperation, can be raised to the level of political critique by ironically celebrating the aesthetically 'worst' films as masterpieces of the medium. Exploitation cinema's tendency towards unintentional textual disruptions which expose the profilmic means of production allows viewers to champion these films as a 'counter-cinematic' practice on a par with the work of more celebrated avant-gardists. A paracinematic reading strategy thus allows one to resist the reified canons of legitimate film culture by asserting one's 'bad taste' as a valid rival to the 'good tastes' of film aesthetes.[36]

Yet, I would argue that Sconce's (over)emphasis on the 'badness' of some exploitation films plays down more traditional viewing pleasures that uneasily coexist with the profound negativity of paracinematic reading strategies. In my estimation, scholars have too often overextended Sconce's argument by neglecting that paracinema as a *reading strategy* does not always dominate the corpus of films upon which such readings focus.[37] Indeed, it has been far more common to find subsequent scholars quoting Sconce's laundry list of films that might be clumped under the umbrella of 'paracinema' than heeding his all-important caveat that the term describes

Figure I.1 Modelling reductive reception: *The Touch of Satan* (1971) receives plenty of historically chauvinistic mockery in a 1998 episode of *Mystery Science Theater 3000* (1988–99). (Source: DVD.)

'less a distinct group of films than a particular reading protocol' that the films' textual traits certainly cannot guarantee. Hence, as undeniably useful as Sconce's concept is, it offers only partial explanation for the fan appeal of these films. By his own admission, Sconce's paracinephile is much like the commentator–hosts of *Mystery Science Theater 3000*, actively seeking textual sources of unintentional humour wherever they can be found (Figure I.1).[38] Yet, as the aforementioned *Touch of Satan* example indicates, there are many fans for whom paracinematic irony may not be the preferred mode of exploitation film consumption. There are, after all, many exploitation films that are least competently made within their respective budgetary constraints, and many are not just critically championed by fans as inverted 'great works'.

Alternatively, I find it more common for fans to view exploitation cinema with a degree of paracinematic irony that recognises the datedness of a film's sensational appeals and the technical/artistic limitations placed upon the production but without those elements necessarily overwhelming more moderated reading strategies that attempt to take the film on its own terms. One film might encourage a different array of reading strategies than another, some veering more strongly towards irony or earnestness. While more casual observers might primarily mock the cheap film-making of an early Roger Corman creature feature or the over-the-top excesses of a Harry Novak sexploitation production, devoted fans are more likely to use their accumulated knowledge to contextualise these films within production trends, censorship histories and the publicity strategies of their respective eras. A fan-scholar's DVD review of *Malibu High* (1979), for example, notes that '[t]he script jumps all over the place, the photography is dark and amateurish, and the dialogue provides plenty of [unintentional] belly laughs' – but he also describes Crown International Pictures' 'everything but the kitchen sink' approach to making successful drive-in fodder, the film's 'surprising social commentary on the American class system', and its 'cheap thrills and anything-goes attitude that continue to entertain and enthral viewers bored with the mainstream'.[39]

Nostalgia's dialectical relationship between a celebrated past and devalued present permits a tension between the presentism of our historical distance from films that may seem quaint, primitive or silly in their exploitative appeals, and a more serious retrospective appreciation when these films seem successfully to transcend their historical context by still working their sleazy or sensational magic even today. This is not unlike how more traditional cinephiles commonly recognise the artistry of studio-era Hollywood films in ways that contemporary viewers with less cultural capital may not appreciate. In this sense, I find that the undergraduate film student who sees unintentional humour in the datedness of an established Hollywood 'classic' from the 1930s is little different from the scholar who recognises but does little to move beyond the exploitation film's perceived 'to-be-laughed-at-ness'. The ramshackle exploitation text may comparatively exhibit more obvious deficiencies from a contemporary aesthetic or political standpoint but, for viewers with a lack of knowledge about such films (and, at worst, an unwillingness to learn), this is less a difference in kind than in degree.

Often treating the terms *cult* and *subculture* as synonymous, academic attention to exploitation cinema has also resonated with the study of cult films, which are generally associated with select but devoted groups of fans who engage in repeated screenings, ritualistic viewing behaviours and specific reading strategies. Yet, in our contemporary media landscape, most fan practices are not visible subcultural behaviours but situational (though not casual) affective affinities with a range of cinematic texts.[40] Sconce suggests that 'cult cinema' belonged to the historical period of 1970s midnight movies when repeated 'access to certain films remained somewhat limited' to niche theatrical exhibition whereas, today, the term is commonly associated with the connoisseurship of exploitation films readily available on DVD, 'providing a few extra inches of critical distance that help better protect said cultist from the implications of simply enjoying exploitation for what it is – *obsolescent sex and violence*'.[41] He thus nostalgically positions 'true' cult fandom in past times and places while arguing that today's 'cult' has been emptied of meaning as a marketing label applied to all manner of media texts with fan followings.

Yet, Thomas Elsaesser views labels like 'cult film' as a way of 'coping with the sudden distance *and* proximity in the face of a constantly re-encountered past' made possible by the huge number of titles available on DVD (introduced in 1997).[42] Similarly, Elena Gorfinkel argues that '[c]ultism may have been more attuned to and defined by the shift to video than cinephilia, which still sustained the prestige of the art cinema and international festival circuit to anchor it in specific locations and to the primacy of theatrical exhibition'. The cultist and the cinephile who similarly search for fleeting, fragmentary moments of excess and profilmic revelation may have begun to blur during the midnight-movie era but have since become increasingly indistinguishable in the home video era, with cultism operating as a historical subcategory of cinephilia when films can be endlessly replayed.[43] Like the nostalgic idea of coherent or visible subcultural sociality, then, 'cult' shares with 'exploitation' a certain association with culturally outmoded practices and dynamics that may nevertheless remain important to a fan's self-image, despite the latter-day easy accessibility of texts that are no longer restricted to the niche audiences who have increasingly become foci for contemporary fans' nostalgia.

Many of fandom's *intra*personal pleasures hinge upon personal or cultural memories of times and spaces of past consumption while others centre upon *inter*personal dynamics that generally arise over competitive investments in one's perceived level of 'authenticity' or connoisseurship as a fan. This also reflects some viewers' ambivalence over self-application of the term 'fan', suggesting different degrees of performing a fan identity, which do not always correlate with different levels of intensity or involvement with media texts. After all, one's investment in a media text need not take the form of stereotypically 'fannish' behaviour but may be no less powerful even if it remains largely private and invisible. Matt Hills, for example, posits a continuum between *actual subcultural capital*, which circulates through fan cultures in the form of active participation directly recognised by other fans (for example, convention attendance or online discussion), and *potential subcultural capital* which does not circulate beyond the lone viewer or close friends/family. Neither fan performance is more 'authentic' than another but each side of the continuum simply activates subcultural capital in different ways.[44] Because one's tastes cannot be completely divorced from one's sociality, however, even our most seemingly idiosyncratic consumption choices remain fluid and shifting openings to wider social groups. A simple web search, for example, will yield dozens of online retailers specialising in exploitation films, many of which would have previously been accessible only through mail-order catalogues, advertisements in specialist fan magazines, booths at fan conventions, and other venues accessible by viewers 'in the know'. Individualism is thus tempered by the fact that today's viewer of even the most obscure texts can potentially locate fellow fans online, perpetually situating even wildly distinctive tastes in relation to a wider community, regardless of whether one actualises this potential subcultural capital by interacting with other fans.

Rooted in both individual and shared tastes and pleasures, the interpretive field provided by cultural memory mediates between the singular fan and the open, unstable groups that he/she situationally occupies. That is, the structures of feeling provided by cultural memory, including nostalgia, motivate *intra*personal performances of fandom by serving as partial justification for tastes set against the backdrop of *inter*personal sociality. Furthermore, the continued circulation of marginal texts can also confer a valuable sense of pastness upon the very fan audiences who continue to support films that have been otherwise forgotten or minimised in traditional media histories. The films' ongoing consumption generates nostalgic myths about a sense of community that 'perhaps never really existed' within these ephemeral social groups but which 'nevertheless create a state of mind that . . . seems called upon to last'.[45] The pleasures of fan identity thus hinge upon not only one's own formative memories of media consumption but also one's degree of access to the affective affinities of other viewers actively recalling these texts.

But, even as these myths provide a shared mnemonic territory for fans, communal consensus remains elusive because subcultural capital is still primarily actualised and negotiated on an individual basis. The symbolic territory represented by any given fandom is perhaps less about an authentic nostalgia for community than about the individual fan's need to manage competing interpretations that could diminish his/her claims to subcultural capital. Though '[t]he interpretation of the cult text in the future is made to appear as the extension of a supposedly consensual and objective view of the past',[46] interpersonal antagonisms perpetually threaten to fragment fan cultures when cultural memory provides links to the participation and interpretation of others beyond the self. Nostalgically positioning oneself in relation to past audiences who encountered the same films earlier in their reception tails (by, for example, privileging older theatrical or residual video modes of circulation) allows contemporary fans to imagine themselves connected across time to supposedly more 'authentic' and sincerely affected audiences than the more casual viewers who might encounter these films on mass-produced DVD editions. Fan cultures may thereby demand enough investment in subcultural capital to make social use of the past but the past's increased commodification, via remediation on to commercially accessible home video formats, can threaten the supposed exclusivity of existing fan-cultural participants.

Mediated Memories and Home Video

Much as lurid paratexts can frame a film's status as part of the exploitation tradition, technologically embedded frames of meaning have arguably become more significant in influencing how films are remembered when encountered away from special sites (such as certain types of theatres, specific video-store shelves, and so on) and, thus, how they can potentially appeal to various market segments – including those beyond long-time fan communities. If shared consensus about the meanings of a technology can fragment and open up when social groups themselves shift and open up,[47] then digital video formats' increased garnering of access to niche texts might be productive of new meanings that both threaten the stability of fan cultures but also force them to rework themselves to accommodate potential new members. Though fans may feel threatened by the ostensible 'mainstreaming' of their memory objects via widely available formats, memory has *always* seemed to be under threat because technologies of memory are always changing.[48]

Andreas Huyssen suggests that the explosion of information technologies has made memory objects more available to us than ever before; yet, 'many of the mass-marketed memories we consume are "imagined memories" to begin with, and thus more easily forgotten than lived memories'. Consequently, 'the more we are asked to remember in the wake of the information explosion and the marketing of memory, the more we seem to be in danger of forgetting and the stronger the need to forget'.[49] When exploitation film fans today recall the urban grind house as a nascent site of 'rebellious' subcultural tastes, for example, the latterly mass-marketed memory of this distinctive exhibition context is more probably rooted in retrospective fantasies than in fans' personal experiences of such bygone sites. Rather than seeing the nostalgias described in this book as, say, symptoms of cultural crisis over changing mores,[50] they are more likely to be symptoms of technological changes in degrees of textual access. Though technological transition may unsettle *how* we remember, *what* is remembered will nevertheless tend to be films that could remain potentially profitable when marketed to a new generation of viewers via a new generation of media formats. Hence, fans affectively invest in texts that allow them to recall past times and places of media consumption (even if not personally experienced), potentially sharing these experiences with other fans who might have similar memories – particularly if wider society does not share this remembrance of film history's overlooked sites and artefacts. The nostalgia that exploitation fans often have for outdated exhibition contexts or marketing tactics may thus be a sort of 'imagined' or 'implanted' memory of a time and place not personally lived through, but we should not assume outright that nostalgic discourses merely dupe fans into being unable to see through a capitalist ruse, because this assumption would play into the same all-too-familiar taste hierarchies that associate 'passive' and 'unthinking' audiences with the cultural dregs. After all, 'If nostalgia appears as the antithesis of enlightenment, the low status it often receives amongst contemporary theorists and critics is in its own right a paradoxical instance of nostalgia' for a supposedly less mediated past.[51] As this book will demonstrate, fans may have rather ambivalent responses to the marketing of nostalgia so, even as remediation may selectively stabilise cultural memories in some ways, not all appeals to pastness will be effective with all viewers.

Indeed, home video is a replayable technology of memory that has proven particularly generative for what Lucas Hilderbrand calls 'a shift in collecting practices from seeking out various forms of *objects related to* the production or promotion of a film to collecting *the film itself*'. Video objects become not only a way in which media history is kept in circulation indefinitely but also a means for people to save or seek out memories that shaped them.[52] Barbara Klinger similarly observes that possessing a film on video allows the viewer to commingle his/her personal history with that of the text itself while encouraging successive viewings that make 'the personal flashback a primary feature of reception', especially when triggered within the private space of the home.[53] The word 'nostalgia', after all, etymologically means a painful desire to return home – often to some more 'authentic' experience from a historical past *felt as if* overlapping with one's lived past (regardless of whether this overlap truly existed or is an 'implanted' nostalgia). In this sense, 'the trace of all those readings remains as a sedimentation in which the layers of past engagement inflect every new one, comparing, assessing, remembering, quoting'.[54]

This sedimentation of memories associated with the fan's repeated viewings of the mediated memory object is linked to the sedimentation of such objects in the marketplace. Video produced 'a wholesale collapsing of horror and exploitation production history' since films from many different historical periods and cultural contexts suddenly appeared on store shelves within the span of a few years.[55] Will Straw identifies the video store as a force slowing the cultural obsolescence of older film titles by allowing texts to accumulate spatially, instead of being replaced temporally, thus allowing people to navigate through these artefacts in idiosyncratic ways. Historical chronologies are muddied as viewers can follow intertextual links back and forth across older and newer films of all types.[56] Attempting to differentiate themselves from other viewers, fan cultures often carry out shared lines of unconventional travel through these dense mazes of video spatiality. As one fan recalls, 'You drifted, in the aisles, picking at boxes, scoping, digging bins, trying to keep track, agog at incongruous juxtapositions. You could be dithered by the box auras[;] your taste in movies – your filtration and rationality – were now victims of the postmodern clusterfuck.'[57] Furthermore, the very pastness of technologies such as VHS can be romanticised to help justify a romanticised view of fan cultures themselves. As such, moments of format transition are particularly productive of mediated memories because the coexistence and co-influence of emergent and residual media encourage us to alter our personal and cultural mnemonic processes.[58] Therefore, fans often retain format-specific memories of media consumption (such as a fetishisation of image grain and artefacting) that remain in tension with the nostalgias officially encoded into emergent formats by media producers and distributors – as seen, for example, in the retro-styled exploitation pastiches explored in my final chapters.

From DVD's inclusion of trailers and advertisements from across a film's reception tail to the Internet's annotated display of retro-coded goods for sale, a sense of loss has become commodified during a historical period paradoxically filled with textual (over)abundance. Klinger, for instance, notes that DVD reissues of older films invite the viewer to nostalgically re-experience history through bonus features and special packaging that allow one seemingly to gain some small measure of access to the films' own textual pasts – albeit through digital technologies 'modernising' the films' appeal to contemporary audiences.[59] As a means of imagining past times and spaces, such appeals to nostalgia reassert the semblance of historical distance as an attempt to assuage anxieties over cultural or technological change, 'help[ing] to constitute the uncommon, sought-after media object, [and] suggesting that the collector's trade has found a way to construct the categories of authenticity and rarity for mass-produced film artifacts'.[60] Yet, media technologies can only ever be unevenly successful in implanting certain memories, engendering continuing conflicts between the past-as-past and the past-preserved-as-present. After all, these modernised ('complete, uncut, restored') editions of historic films often displace the older textual iterations that may fondly linger in one's memory but increasingly become lost chunks of film history, complicating one's imagined connection to past audiences.

Futhermore, the rise of emergent video technologies over the past two decades has accelerated the turnover rate of older formats, compressing the temporal delay through which past delivery systems are nostalgised. These format transitions have thereby created a more acute tension between, on the one hand, the push towards personal/group fragmentation as access to niche texts becomes more open through remediation, rendering fandom inevitably open and unstable; and, on the other, the nostalgic desire for subcultural coalescence imagined to exist somewhere in the past. Cultural memory's resulting importance arises as a means of not only maintaining potential and actual subcultural capital through the accumulation of past knowledge and experience but also inspiring the affective pleasures of engaging with outmoded texts as a meaningful part of one's self-image. From desiring the text itself to desiring remembered experiences associated with the text, these pleasures are manifest in the retrospective celebration of exploitation cinema's past material sites of consumption – and, by extension, the past fans who inhabited the lived places and symbolic spaces that share mnemonic echoes in the present. Yet, the very name 'exploitation' additionally suggests that the films under consideration here reflect a range of social and technological inequalities that nostalgia's dialectical friction between past and present can invoke but not necessarily resolve, raising the political implications of living in our own time and space.

As a scholar-fan of exploitation films, this book reflects a certain unavoidable degree of nostalgia on my own part, because I do not assume to speak from a wholly rational, academic remove from my objects of study. When writing about the early years of VHS rental, for instance, how can I not flash back to my own childhood memories of wandering through video store aisles and sneaking into the horror section to peruse the lurid box art with imagination aflame? Thus, despite the discomfort I have often felt when peripherally engaged in struggles for subcultural capital, and my consequent feelings of distance from traditionally 'subcultural' fan practices, this remains a personal project in many ways. It would be naive to assume, for example, that presenting my own work to a public readership is not, in some small way, motivated as an intervention into wider bids for subcultural capital.

To avoid the shortcomings of an approach rooted exclusively in critical readings, historical reception study, or cultural theory, I mobilise those lenses in methodologically impure ways befitting the conflicted fan responses to widely circulating memory objects. Some of the following chapters are weighted more towards one critical lens than another – but, like the valences of nostalgia itself, these approaches need not be seen as contradictory or mutually exclusive. Likewise, much as exploitation cinema's development is a non-linear process building from memories of prior cycles, these chapters are not arranged as a historical chronology; instead, they offer multiple ways to approach nostalgia's importance in film consumption. As a means of exploring how the past is used or distorted by nostalgia, each chapter briefly engages with the industrial or cultural history behind the material sites of exploitation film consumption, and then moves into analysis of the juxtaposed temporalities offered by home video. Setting historical data against theories about memory and fandom shows how individuals and communities can alternately frame nostalgia as the desired recollection of a more 'authentic' past but also as a threatening mystification of history. If my own experiences as a fan animate my initial approach to the case studies under consideration here, then historical data and discourse analysis allow such observations to be grounded in wider patterns of market demand and fan reception. Discursive data also temper the generalising claims offered by critical theories about fandom, taste and cultural memory, preventing the theorist's individual experiences from becoming reified as universal.

Across this study, markets and fans often frame the tastes and values associated with one's degree of access to exploitation films in classed and gendered ways. Class disparities loom in the background of my first two chapters, reflecting the question of who has the ability to materially access these films as they shift sites over the decades; while gender inequalities increasingly come into play in subsequent chapters, especially when masculine fantasies of exploitation film consumption are complicated by home video's transition towards the broader demographics and feminine connotations of domestic viewership. The final two chapters also move further afield by focusing on the development of contemporary films that nostalgically simulate the look and feel of archival exploitation texts.

In Chapter 1, I explore the drive-in theatre as a *lieu de mémoire* that has become increasingly obsolete as a lived place, yet persists as a symbolic space invested with multiple class-inflected nostalgias. Exploring the historical mobility and diffusion of drive-in theatres and their patrons provides an explanatory lens for the shift from theatrical to non-theatrical exhibition of exploitation films, even as the populist appeal of both exhibition site and screened content potentially conflict with present-day fans' claims to subcultural capital. Examining populism's central but paradoxical role in exploitation fandom, I demonstrate how fans and media distributors alike can mnemonically abstract a generic place such as the drive-in theatre, with contested control over access still echoing historical class inequalities.

In similarly tracing the discursive history of a specific locale that has attained mythic proportions in the remembrance of exploitation cinema, Chapter 2 argues that the term 'grindhouse' has transitioned from a specific exhibition context, to a generic label synonymous with exploitation cinema, to a transmedia concept, owing to a tendency for non-normative exhibition sites to be coded generically to normalise Hollywood films and exhibition practices. Specific urban spaces, such as New York City's 42nd Street at Times Square, may be symbolic sites of unfulfilled cinephiliac fantasies among exploitation fans – yet the flexibility of 'grindhouse' as a commodity across different media formats illustrates how nostalgia for an exhibition site can spawn deeply ambivalent responses when revived for easy consumption through the economic forces that have similarly refashioned areas like Times Square itself.

Accompanying the remediation of archival exploitation films on home video, the historical weight of the past upon more recent films has increased as cultural memories of the grind house have come home. Accordingly, Chapter 3 looks at a recent cycle of nostalgia-driven, retro-styled exploitation (or 'retrosploitation') films which internalise the coexistence of irony and sincerity found in the fan reception of archival exploitation texts. It can be difficult, however, to discern these latter-day pastiches' evaluative tone towards their historical referents. Consequently, fans express divergent reactions when these creative rewritings of exploitation film history seem not only too closely associated with the 'feminised' domestic sphere but also subject to the wider film industry's recent and ongoing blurring of lines between direct-to-video and theatrically released films.

If Chapters 2 and 3 describe fans' ambivalent reactions towards exploitation cinema's retro-stylised revival, Chapter 4 focuses squarely on the political implications of this ambivalence. While some viewers excuse the anachronistic political incorrectness of retrosploitation films as an escape from contemporary attitudes, others maintain their fan-cultural connoisseurship by remaining critically attuned to the political work that these ostensibly regressive films do. Much as exploitation cinema has today reached broader audiences than the straight white men who were often its original intended viewers, the selective use of particular genres and cycles as retrosploitation's historical referents demonstrates both opportunities and limitations in using the cinematic past as raw material for addressing contemporary political concerns that extend beyond the traditional interests of socially dominant demographics.

Overall, then, this book addresses the affective and social importance of cultural memory in structuring contemporary film fandom. None of us is immune to the forces of cultural memory but there are, perhaps, those of us who choose to live with tastes more attuned to the outdated and nostalgic, feeling themselves out of step with the present day even as they make use of contemporary video technologies to keep one foot planted in the past. Highlighting the reciprocal influences between remembered times and spaces of consumption thus allows us better to account for the territorial skirmishes in which fans may engage as new material formats come and go. This study does not make sweeping predictions about the continuing place of exploitation films as their reception tails grow ever longer but it does argue for the need to understand how culture industries are increasingly mining obscure corners of film history for 'new' products to market as commodified objects of nostalgia. As older filmic styles are reworked for contemporary consumption, we at least find fans envisioning the times and spaces of their own futures through residual and emergent lenses of the past, intervening in the work of cultural memory to negotiate the terms of their own potential exploitation.

Notes

1. Comments from the discussion thread 'These boards are a joke', *The Touch of Satan* (1971) IMDb boards, The Internet Movie Database, http://www.imdb.com/title/tt0066476/board/nest/98243500 (accessed 22 March 2012).
2. Mike Vraney, interviewed in BigPoppaOnline, *Third Eye Cinema* podcast, 6 May 2012, http://www.blogtalkradio.com/bigpoppaonline/2012/05/06/third-eye-cinema-5612-with-mike-vraney (accessed 12 February 2014).
3. James Naremore, *More Than Night: Film Noir in its Contexts* (Berkeley: University of California Press, 2008), p. 39.
4. Stuart Tannock, 'Nostalgia Critique', *Cultural Studies* 9, no. 3 (1995): 454, 456.
5. Barbara Klinger, *Beyond the Multiplex: Cinema, New Technologies, and the Home* (Berkeley: University of California Press, 2006), p. 13 (quoted); and Henry Jenkins, *Convergence Culture: Where Old and New Media Collide* (New York: New York University Press, 2006).
6. Rick Altman, *Film/Genre* (London: British Film Institute, 1999), p. 161.
7. On the reciprocally repurposed influences between older and newer media, see Jay David Bolter and Richard Grusin, *Remediation: Understanding New Media* (Cambridge, MA: MIT Press, 2000).
8. Pierre Nora, 'Between Memory and History: *Les Lieux de Mémoire*', *Representations*, no. 26 (1989): 19, 22, 24.
9. Ibid., pp. 15–16.
10. Anna McCarthy, *Ambient Television: Visual Culture and Public Space* (Durham, NC: Duke University Press, 2001), p. 19.
11. Cornel Sandvoss, *Fans: The Mirror of Consumption* (Cambridge: Polity Press, 2005), p. 64.

12. Ibid., pp. 54, 58.
13. Giuliana Bruno, *Atlas of Emotion: Journeys in Art, Architecture, and Film* (New York: Verso, 2002), pp. 45, 62, 66, 223, 352–3.
14. Sandvoss, *Fans*, pp. 48, 97–8.
15. Will Brooker, 'A Sort of Homecoming: Fan Viewing and Symbolic Pilgrimage', in *Fandom: Identities and Communities in a Mediated World*, eds Jonathan Gray, Cornel Sandvoss and C. Lee Harrington (New York: New York University Press, 2007), pp. 158–60. Quote at p. 158.
16. Pam Cook, *Screening the Past: Memory and Nostalgia in Cinema* (London: Routledge, 2005), pp. 3–4.
17. Andreas Huyssen, 'Present Pasts: Media, Politics, Amnesia', *Public Culture* 12, no. 1 (2000): 26, 29.
18. José van Dijck, *Mediated Memories in the Digital Age* (Stanford, CA: Stanford University Press, 2007), pp. 7, 12–14, 19–21, 23 (original italics).
19. Ibid., pp. 12–13, 24–5.
20. Sandvoss, *Fans*, pp. 64–5.
21. Wulf Kansteiner, 'Finding Meaning in Memory: A Methodological Critique of Collective Memory Studies', *History and Theory* 41, no. 2 (2002): 193.
22. Svetlana Boym, *The Future of Nostalgia* (New York: Basic Books, 2001), pp. 41, 49.
23. Tannock, 'Nostalgia Critique', pp. 455–6.
24. Sandvoss, *Fans*, p. 135.
25. Ross Poole, 'Memory, History, and the Claims of the Past', *Memory Studies* 1, no. 2 (2008): 158.
26. Stephen Thrower, *Nightmare USA: The Untold Story of the Exploitation Independents* (Godalming: FAB Press, 2007), p. 27. Also see Joan Hawkins, *Cutting Edge: Art-Horror and the Horrific Avant-Garde* (Minneapolis: University of Minnesota Press, 2000), p. 195.
27. Eric Schaefer, *'Bold! Daring! Shocking! True!' A History of Exploitation Films, 1919–1959* (Durham, NC: Duke University Press, 1999), pp. 2–6, 39, 96–105, 156.
28. Ibid., pp. 327–37, 340.
29. Thomas Doherty, *Teenagers and Teenpics: The Juvenilization of American Movies in the 1950s* (Philadelphia: Temple University Press, 2002), pp. 30, 57, 62, 127. On 'high-concept' film-making, see Justin Wyatt, *High Concept: Movies and Marketing in Hollywood* (Austin: University of Texas Press, 1994), pp. 1–22.
30. Blair Davis, *The Battle for the Bs: 1950s Hollywood and the Rebirth of Low-Budget Cinema* (New Brunswick, NJ: Rutgers University Press, 2012), pp. 28–32, 85–6.
31. Thomas Frank, *The Conquest of Cool: Business Culture, Counterculture, and the Rise of Hip Consumerism* (Chicago: University of Chicago Press, 1997), pp. 27–8, 122. Quote at pp. 27–8.

32. See Justin Wyatt, 'From Roadshowing to Saturation Release: Majors, Independents, and Marketing/Distribution Innovations', in *The New American Cinema*, ed. Jon Lewis (Durham, NC: Duke University Press, 1998), pp. 64–86.
33. Roger Corman with Jim Jerome, *How I Made a Hundred Movies in Hollywood and Never Lost a Dime* (New York: Random House, 1990), p. 34. Original italics.
34. Sarah Thornton, *Club Cultures: Music, Media, and Subcultural Capital* (Middletown, CT: Wesleyan University Press, 1996), pp. 8, 10–12, 93, 96–9, 111, 117, 139–40.
35. Stephen Romano, *Shock Festival* (San Diego: IDW Publishing/RAW Entertainment, 2008), p. 23.
36. Jeffrey Sconce, '"Trashing" the Academy: Taste, Excess, and an Emerging Politics of Cinematic Style', *Screen* 36, no. 4 (1995): 383–5, 387, 391–3.
37. Among others, see, for example, Ian Olney's *Euro Horror: Classic European Horror Cinema in Contemporary American Culture* (Bloomington: Indiana University Press, 2013), ch. 4, which takes the blatantly paracinematic following of Claudio Fragasso's notoriously 'bad' *Troll 2* (1990) as emblematic of European horror reception in general – a case study that does a tremendous disservice to the complexity of European horror's far more earnest Anglo-American reception which I instead outline in my article 'One on Top of the Other: Lucio Fulci, Transnational Film Industries, and the Retrospective Construction of the Italian Horror Canon', *Quarterly Review of Film and Video* 32, no. 4 (2015), forthcoming.
38. Sconce, '"Trashing" the Academy', pp. 372, 373. Quote at p. 372.
39. Casey Scott, '*Malibu High/Trip With the Teacher*' (review), DVD Drive-In, http://www.dvddrive-in.com/reviews/i-m/malibuhightripteacher7579.htm (accessed 26 January 2012).
40. Matt Hills, *Fan Cultures* (London: Routledge, 2002), p. 30; and Sandvoss, *Fans*, p. 29.
41. Jeffrey Sconce, in Joe Bob Briggs, et al., 'Cult Cinema: A Critical Symposium', *Cineaste* 34, no. 1 (2008): 48. Original italics.
42. Thomas Elsaesser, 'Cinephilia or the Uses of Disenchantment', in *Cinephilia: Movies, Love, and Memory*, eds Marijke de Valck and Malte Hagener (Amsterdam: Amsterdam University Press, 2005), p. 38. Original italics.
43. Elena Gorfinkel, 'Cult Film, or Cinephilia by Any Other Name', *Cineaste* 34, no. 1 (2008): 38.
44. Matt Hills, 'Attending Horror Film Festivals and Conventions: Liveness, Subcultural Capital, and "Flesh-and-Blood Genre Communities"', in *Horror Zone: The Cultural Experience of Contemporary Horror Cinema*, ed. Ian Conrich (London: I. B. Tauris, 2010), pp. 92–3.
45. Michel Maffesoli, *The Time of the Tribes: The Decline of Individualism in Mass Society*, trans. Don Smith (London: Sage, 1996), pp. 16, 22, 26, 66–7, 148. Quote at p. 148.

46. Derek Johnson, 'Fan-tagonism: Factions, Institutions, and Constitutive Hegemonies of Fandom', in *Fandom*, p. 291.
47. Joshua M. Greenberg, *From Betamax to Blockbuster: Video Stores and the Invention of Movies on Video* (Cambridge, MA: MIT Press, 2008), p. 115.
48. Marita Sturken, *Tangled Memories: The Vietnam War, the AIDS Epidemic, and the Politics of Remembering* (Berkeley: University of California Press, 1997), p. 17.
49. Huyssen, 'Present Pasts', pp. 27–8.
50. For this crisis model of nostalgia, see Fred Davis, *Yearning for Yesterday: A Sociology of Nostalgia* (New York: The Free Press, 1979).
51. Jeffrey Pence, 'Postcinema/Postmemory', in *Memory and Popular Film*, ed. Paul Grainge (Manchester: Manchester University Press, 2003), p. 243.
52. Lucas Hilderbrand, *Inherent Vice: Bootleg Histories of Videotape and Copyright* (Durham, NC: Duke University Press, 2009), pp. xiv, 62, 97.
53. Klinger, *Beyond the Multiplex*, pp. 65, 177.
54. Sean Cubitt, *Timeshift: On Video Culture* (London: Routledge, 1991), p. 157.
55. Kate Egan, *Trash or Treasure? Censorship and the Changing Meanings of the Video Nasties* (Manchester: Manchester University Press, 2007), p. 51.
56. Will Straw, 'Embedded Memories', in *Residual Media*, ed. Charles R. Acland (Minneapolis: University of Minnesota Press, 2007), pp. 5–6, 8–9, 11.
57. Jacques Boyreau, *Portable Grindhouse: The Lost Art of the VHS Box* (Seattle: Fantagraphics Books, 2009), p. 6.
58. Van Dijck, *Mediated Memories*, p. 50.
59. Klinger, *Beyond the Multiplex*, pp. 86–7, 122.
60. Ibid., p. 67.

CHAPTER 1

A Drive-in Theatre of the Mind: Nostalgic Populism and the Déclassé Video Object

[T]he revaluing of space is correlative to the revaluing of more restricted entities (groups, 'tribes'). Symbolic and spatial proxemics encourage the desire to leave one's mark, that is, to bear witness to one's durability. This is the true aesthetic dimension of a given spatial affiliation: to serve the collective memory that defined it.
                         Michel Maffesoli, *The Time of the Tribes*[1]

We are drive-in mutants.
We are not like other people.
We are sick.
We are disgusting.
We believe in blood,
In breasts,
And in beasts.
We believe in Kung Fu City.
If life had a Vomit Meter,
We'd be off the scale.
As long as one single drive-in
Remains on the planet Earth,
We will party like jungle animals,
We will boogie till we puke.
Heads will roll.
The drive-in will never die.
Amen.
                         Joe Bob Briggs, 'The Drive-In Oath'[2]

Though its number of screens continues to dwindle across the American landscape, the drive-in theatre has retained a place of particular celebration in the annals of popular Americana, often associated with the postwar 'baby boom' generation that came of age in the 1950s and 1960s. Indeed, it would probably be hard for white, middle-class Americans of a certain age to imagine a nostalgically prelapsarian 1950s without picturing the drive-in as a mythic site for teenage pleasures outside the home. Recently equipped with cars for their nocturnal excursions, hormonal adolescents were temporarily freed from parental oversight, and perhaps afforded the opportunity for couplings in their coupés. Yet, this selective nostalgia, linked to visions of a relatively innocent past, overlaps with another popular (if less prevalent) mythology of the drive-in: as a notorious site for the exhibition of exploitation films, especially as post-1950s censorship erosion allowed content to veer sharply towards the violent, sexual, and sleazy.[3] Meanwhile, cheap admission and the populist appeal of these films drew in many working-class viewers of various ages, not just middle-class teenagers, commingling multiple class strata within the shared viewing experience of the cheap genre fare that eventually became dubbed 'drive-in movies'.

Suburban and rural drive-in theatres are fondly regarded today as originary spatio-temporal sites for a wide variety of films that have since been deemed cult texts not only by the fan cultures who avidly consume them as demonstrations of supposedly nonconformist taste but also through marketing discourses aiming to remediate these older films on home video to audiences too young to have experienced them at the drive-in. Even if, for example, exploitation fans have never personally attended a drive-in theatre, the exhibition site still circulates as a powerful abstraction in this fandom's articulations of self, offering a historical context for the emergence of disparate films that can be united under the broad label 'exploitation'.

As at their height of their popularity in the 1950s, today's surviving drive-ins remain predominantly attended by teenagers and families, and typically play double features of first- and second-run major-studio films, not the lurid and outlandish texts championed by exploitation fans. The latter were among the first wave of films released on pre-recorded video cassettes in the early 1980s – a platform shift that accelerated the decline of the drive-in as an alternative exhibition market while simultaneously giving rise to fan cultures embracing videos as mediated memory objects. Indeed, the initial dispersion of drive-ins across the American landscape in the 1940s and 1950s was not unlike the VHS-enabled dispersion of niche films beyond metropolitan areas in the 1980s; like the rise of drive-ins, the adoption of home video was also a rather slow process at first, eventually accelerating into a highly profitable boom. If exploitation films are 'like the uncultivated American landscape, where weeds and flowers alike grow more freely',[4] then the springing up of drive-ins and video stores similarly represents the decentralisation of exploitation cinema towards more dispersed and private consumption. Accordingly, this chapter examines home video as a vehicle for *contextual nostalgias* about the drive-in experience, with the mobility and diffusion of drive-in audiences offering a lens for exploring the mobility and diffusion of home video, contemporary fans, and their tastes.

Unlike the individual drive-in theatres visitable during one's lifetime, the drive-in as a *generic place* is a more abstract and categorical site signifying larger spatial dynamics. The very fact that contemporary drive-in theatres are still vanishing as lived places has allowed the drive-in as generic place to become all the more abstracted into a polysemic *lieu de mémoire* that fans can uphold as an apparent reflection of their own values. Hence, viewers from different generations and socio-economic classes may situationally embrace different nostalgias for the drive-in experience, regardless of whether they attended the same specific theatres or even attended drive-ins at all. Yet, if the tenor of nostalgia for past times and places is more often associated with collective memories of social milieux than individual memories,[5] then the existence of multiple, overlapping nostalgias for the drive-in suggests a tendency towards remembering drive-ins as less an elite marker of fan identity than as a populist entertainment site fostering shared affective responses among diverse audiences – even to the detriment of fans who might today privilege subcultural exclusivity over the dearth of subcultural prestige traditionally associated with populist media forms.

As implied in the first epigraph above, material sites like the drive-in can take on powerful spatial meanings when fan cultures use them as markers of their own enduring significance in the cultural history of their chosen texts. Sarah Thornton notes how subcultural capital may have 'built-in obsolescence' within a particular social group to 'maintain its status not only as the prerogative of the young, but the "hip"'. Many exploitation fans, however, intentionally turn towards 'lost and almost forgotten' cinematic texts and exhibition sites that have stubbornly resisted obsolescence and re-acquired a sense of hipness owing to being out of the contemporary public eye.[6] Yet, the very ability of fans to imaginatively identify with historical drive-in audiences from different socio-economic classes – who are alternately figured as naive-but-sincere dupes and rebellious-but-discerning precursors to today's aficionados – complicates some fans' attempts to maintain the scarcity of subcultural capital. If the drive-in's connotations of disreputability are a major source of celebration by exploitation fans today, these connotations derived not only from the films they played but also from the diversity of their historical patrons – including a populist contingent whose supposedly 'naive' pleasures potentially overlap with present-day fans' earnest, non-ironic readings of archival exploitation texts. Of course, marked class stratification can be observed in rural, suburban and urban areas alike, much as working-class viewers' reactions to exploitation films are not necessarily more naive than connoisseurial. Rather, I believe that the *cultural memories* of rurality and suburbanity circulating in popular media are more heavily infused with binaristic class connotations than reality tends to bear out – and therein sits cultural memory's power to mythologise visions of the past in ways that remain open to contestation by fans from different socio-economic statuses.

In this chapter, I argue that, even if exploitation films and the drive-in theatres where they played often appealed to forms of populism which could undercut present-day fans' claims of subcultural exclusivity and aesthetic discernment, the very pastness of the drive-in as a generic place still provides a degree of temporal/historical distance and abstraction within which class tensions can be *contained but never fully resolved*. That is, although contemporary fans may take advantage of the textual proliferation and interpersonal sociality afforded by newer technologies, the very ideological incoherence of the drive-in theatre as a nostalgically contested *lieu de mémoire* permits a modicum of imagined refuge from the populist appeals of contemporary consumerism. Furthermore, these multivalent appeals to the drive-in's pastness are reproduced in the different video formats that coexist in the marketplace, repackaging exploitation films for present-day consumption without altogether removing the echoes of class tension that some fans may paradoxically see as threats to their nostalgic visions of subcultural cohesion.

Today's commercial video distributors play a large role in creating mobile/digital archives of exploitation-related artefacts that official archives tend to neglect. While the discourses attached to emergent video formats have generally carried higher cultural values than residual ones, I will show that the contemporary repurposing of exploitation films has not necessarily followed a one-way path of linear development towards greater respectability. Rather, different methods of remediation have drawn upon different nostalgias to confer a sense of legitimacy that may be only unevenly recognised by fans. That is, the same film can be released on DVD, Blu-ray or other video formats in differently classed editions that offer dissimilar cultural values and viewing pleasures through different appeals to pastness. This cross-class viability helps to account for the symbolic territory that drive-ins continue to hold within fan cultures, because fans of various class backgrounds may nostalgically uphold a particular vision of the past as a time when exploitation films could more probably seem to be 'rebelliously' controversial amid a media landscape of greater textual scarcity. By tracing a history of the so-called 'drive-in movie' as it travelled from theatrical exhibition to home video, we can thereby see how nostalgia's tendency towards populism remains a central tension within the historical viewing contexts imaginatively drawn upon to support contemporary fan identities.

A Brief History of the American Drive-in Theatre

Offering a 'quick and dirty' history of the drive-in theatre's rise and fall admittedly threatens to collapse into a nostalgic mode of its own, positing these theatres as heroic and misunderstood outsiders eventually consigned to cultural twilight – which may well echo the self-image of exploitation fans for whom this brief historical narrative would not be unfamiliar. Nevertheless, a brief historical overview is necessary for appreciating how the drive-in has become such a powerful locus of nostalgia for various fan groups. Mary Morley Cohen suggests that scholars have tended to neglect drive-in theatres because they proved an especially liminal exhibition site, organised around contradictory discourses about the relative benefits and hazards of public and private space.[7] The academic neglect of drive-ins may additionally reflect what Robert C. Allen identifies as film historiography's bias towards a 'determinative connection between the experience of metropolitan urbanity and the experience of cinema',[8] which has also been reproduced in high-minded dismissals of home video as an inferior technology good only for those unfortunate enough to live in the hinterlands beyond the festival/repertory circuits.

The first drive-in theatre opened in New Jersey in 1933 but drive-ins did not become a widespread phenomenon in the United States until the post-war baby boom created greater demand for family entertainment, alongside increased prosperity which translated into greater car ownership among white, middle-class, increasingly suburban households. As a Los Angeles zoning administrator reported in 1949, 'it has been found that the drive-in theater is a decided benefit to families with small children who cannot afford or obtain "baby sitters" and also to families with crippled or partially infirm members who cannot attend the regular theaters'.[9] Yet, widespread car ownership was more crucial for everyday transport in rural areas than in cities or even suburbs, helping reinforce the eventual connections between rurality and drive-in patronage. Morley Cohen argues that 'while cars allowed for greater personal mobility, they also brought previously isolated communities together and allowed others to flee from each other', creating a safety buffer of semi-privacy from other viewers. Aside from families, drive-ins also specifically advertised to audiences who might not be comfortable in some indoor (aka 'hardtop') theatres, such as working-class, obese, non-white, female, teenage or disabled viewers. In the process, the intermingling of these less conventional demographics with white suburban families, in an exhibition site blurring the boundaries between public and private space, reinforced lingering cultural discourses about drive-ins as disreputable 'passion pits'.[10]

At various points in drive-in history, surveys suggested that audiences were attracted to the novelty, convenience, privacy and lower cost of watching films in one's car – including the ability to pursue less disciplined behaviours that would have been impermissible at indoor theatres – and less interested in which films were actually playing.[11] This novelty value was profitable for drive-in operators (many of whom were independent entrepreneurs) because distributors initially restricted first-run studio films to indoor theatres because of fears that conventional Hollywood product would be cheapened by its showing to drive-ins' less conventional audiences – at least until the major studios' belated divorce from their affiliated theatre chains in 1956 allowed drive-ins to bid competitively for first- or second-run films.[12] Yet, first-run films were generally offered to drive-ins on terms that gave distributors up to 70 per cent of total returns, discouraging many drive-in operators from extending their programming beyond the B or exploitation movies that could often be rented for a flat rate.[13] Major theatre chains would also occasionally build a limited number of their own drive-ins 'as a self-defense measure adjacent to towns where they had local theaters'.[14]

Drive-in operators sometimes emphasised their different clientele, attempting to stymie complaints by indoor theatre owners that drive-ins were siphoning their audiences away. Anthony Downs suggests that, if drive-ins stole audiences from indoor theatres, it was mostly from the 'local theaters which specialize in Westerns, war movies, or other "action" cinema',[15] because these films would already be inexpensive for drive-in operators to acquire. If drive-in owners could prove they were not a substantial threat to the indoor theatres that garnered major-studio sympathies, then they could perhaps lobby studio-affiliated distributors for better films to show. Though these lobbying efforts might have been successful at the peak of drive-in popularity in the late 1950s, Kerry Segrave notes that efforts at organisation did not occur, because drive-in profits remained high during that period, no matter what was screened.[16] The fact that drive-ins screened films for fewer months of the year than indoor theatres also limited the amount of influence they held with major distributors. Yet, the rise of the drive-in may actually have benefited the overall film industry by substantially buffering against the total number of viewers lost to television.[17]

Surveying a range of newspaper advertisements for drive-ins across the United States between the late 1930s and early 1980s, we find that, both during and after the studio era, Hollywood films made up a larger amount of drive-in programming than exploitation fans often assume. As Downs noted in 1953, 'Some drive-ins now show only first-class pictures as a part of the second-run group of theaters, lagging behind the downtown first-run theaters by roughly four weeks. Others still specialize in action shows, but the majority combine both kinds of cinema in a weekly schedule calling for three picture-changes.'[18] Drive-ins would also revive popular moneymakers as much as a decade after their original release, sometimes in conjunction with a studio-sanctioned theatrical re-release or even to capitalise on a film's television broadcast by screening theatrical versions shown on network television only in censored form, as was the case with Hitchcock's *Psycho* (1960).

It has often been suggested that drive-ins tended to make do with exploitation films from independent producers and distributors, such as American International Pictures (AIP), and would generally acquire Hollywood studio films late in their subsequent runs, after the films had already exhausted their appeal at indoor theatres. Yet, my broad survey of newspaper advertisements suggests that subsequent-run Hollywood films actually remained the main draw for many drive-ins. Many ads visually privilege a particular film – often a mainstream or critically acclaimed film appealing to a wide audience, not just the 'action shows' geared towards genre aficionados – by prominently foregrounding its publicity images and taglines while relegating the second (or more) 'co-hit' to the ad's margins with little more than the title and stars listed (Figure 1.1). Given Hollywood's belated crossover between indoor and outdoor theatres, this advertising strategy suggests that audiences may have been more interested in what drive-ins actually screened than is often presumed. Though some drive-ins would offer special programmes (such as dusk-to-dawn horror shows one night a week or 'action shows' during weekends), daily offerings tended to be of mixed appeal. When exploitation films appeared, they were often double-billed with another exploitation film of an adjacent genre, with the resulting programme appealing to different, but overlapping, youth audiences – though advertisements also indicate that single exploitation films would occasionally support a major-studio film.[19]

While '[t]he complaint most often mentioned by drive-in patrons was that the films shown were too old', drive-ins were also making their highest profits during the summer season, when 'conventional theater grosses are at their lowest point' – hence more reason for animosity between indoor and drive-in theatres.[20] Indeed, the break-up of the studio system led to fewer major-studio releases (including B movies), leaving most local indoor theatres desperate for product – especially during the summer months when release schedules became particularly lean – so exploitation film companies formed to fill the market gap with their quick and cheap genre films.[21] Indeed, as Roger Corman told me, AIP was so dependent on

Figure 1.1 Japanese import *Destroy All Monsters* (1968), distributed by American International Pictures, receives marginal billing below general-interest Hollywood films in a *Milwaukee Journal* (19 June 1970) newspaper advertisement for the 41 Twin Outdoor Theater drive-in, Franklin, Wisconsin. (Source: Charles Bruss/ www.drive-inthruwisconsin.com)

the drive-in market that all of their release prints were deliberately underexposed by the processing laboratory, giving the prints an overall lighter look that would help compensate for drive-ins' substandard brightness in projection (much to the detriment of the films' quality of cinematography when the same prints were also shown at indoor theatres).[22] When directed towards drive-in audiences, exploitation films could sometimes rival Hollywood films in per-screen box-office receipts, because both types of films were generally distributed on a region-by-region basis.[23] Apart from obvious factors, such as friendlier weather conditions, summer months could thus be especially profitable for drive-ins because major-studio films released earlier in the year would finally be trickling down to them at the end of their runs, while summer-released exploitation films would offer a supplemental amount of programming. This does not mean that drive-ins never played new films concurrently with first-run houses but that such cases were relatively uncommon, though the few organised drive-in chains (such as Pacific Drive-In Theatres and the Walter Reade Organization) seemed to have more luck in this regard.[24] Some newspaper advertisements will occasionally (and misleadingly) refer to their programming as 'first run', even if the film being shown had already been in general release for several months, suggesting the exceptional nature of such relatively early acquisitions. Overall, then, an accurate history of drive-in theatres must avoid overemphasising the ratio of exploitation films to mainstream product, as these exhibition sites were not always the contra-Hollywood hotbeds that exploitation fan cultures have often claimed.

By the early 1960s, the initial novelty of drive-in theatres had begun to wear off. Drive-in revenues peaked in the mid-1960s, and the construction boom in new screens slowed by the mid-1970s as the number of available drive-ins eventually outstripped audience demand.[25] While family-friendly and general-interest fare (such as Sunn Classic Pictures' 1970s frontier-adventure films and historical/paranormal docudramas) still proved profitable when it became available, many drive-ins attempted to draw declining audiences with the more violent and risqué films made possible by the Production Code's disintegration. Consequently, civic groups and moral watchdogs began legal action against some drive-ins – potentially adding to the drive-in theatre's 'outlaw' associations that more recent fan cultures have embraced. From sexploitation to European art films, the increasingly permissive adult films of the 1960s generally launched in urban areas but faced rural resistance from regional theatre-owner organisations and citizen boycotts in small towns and southern parts of the country.[26] Popular associations between drive-ins, exploitation films, and youth audiences meant that some moralists unearthed obscure local zoning statutes to prevent drive-in construction within city limits – another reason (in addition to lower property taxes) why many drive-ins were built just outside these jurisdictions.[27] Still, after the Motion Picture Association of America (MPAA) ratings system was established in 1968, R-rated and X-rated films out-grossed most other films by large margins, so some drive-in owners were not quick to change their programming after such complaints. Segrave argues that most drive-ins' bills would have been relatively tame and acceptable for the whole family during the theatres' 1950s heyday but, in later years, amenities for families had been neglected and the majority of drive-in films catered to teen or adult audiences. 'Nobody went to the drive-in to see the movie in the fifties and sixties', he suggests (with some overstatement), 'but, ironically, by the 1980s that was all the drive-ins had left to offer patrons.'[28]

Yet, recounting his own experiences working at a midwestern drive-in, Andrew Horton suggests that fluctuating attendance meant audiences did, indeed, come to see specific films, with 'soft pornography', 'hot car movies', horror, and disaster films cited as the most popular genres in the summer of 1976.[29] A modest upswing in 1970s drive-in attendance coincided with the rise of teen-oriented, R-rated films mixing mild sexploitation, countercultural or youth interest, and comedy – a combination exemplified by Crown International Pictures releases such as *Superchick* (1973) and *The Pom Pom Girls* (1976).[30] Such films were described in the trade press as '[o]bviously made to titillate farm boys in small towns and for fast playoffs at drive-ins'.[31] Drive-ins occasionally figure as settings in exploitation films from this period as well, helping cement the link between film and exhibition site; examples include *The Adventures of Lucky Pierre* (1961), *Teenage Mother* (1967), *Targets* (1968), *The Toy Box* (1971), *Deathdream* (1972), *Hollywood Boulevard* (1976), *Kiss of the Tarantula* (1976), and *Drive-In Massacre* (1977). Still, we should consider that major Hollywood films continued to play at drive-ins during this time, so it is more likely that the programming of adult-oriented films (eventually including hardcore pornography at some theatres) which seemed better suited for niche or private viewing environments tainted the drive-in's reputation as an accessible public place for general audiences.

As audiences gradually dwindled, many exploitation producers and distributors moved into other venues, such as UHF television, cable television, and home video, able to reach greater numbers of viewers and generate larger profits by bypassing drive-ins altogether.[32] It had been common practice for exploitation companies, such as New World Pictures and Dimension Pictures, to inexpensively pick up art films for distribution in urban markets during the lean winter months when their capital was already depleted by the autumn and winter production of the following summer's releases. When more temperate seasons approached, the newly produced films were released to drive-ins in a '"follow the sun" distribution pattern: start in the south in the spring and move north as the weather gets warmer'.[33] Producer–distributors could also afford this strategy because they generally avoided union contracts on their films. During the 1970s, it was advantageous to shoot on location in southern 'right-to-work' states that were hostile towards organised labour. To avoid alienating locals or prospective audiences, this practice encouraged filmmakers to depict elements of southern rurality in romanticised ways (for example, the 'good ole boy' as outlaw hero), spawning a number of film cycles appealing to the high concentration of drive-in viewers in that part of the country – films that have since been tellingly rebranded as 'hixploitation'.[34] Indeed, the industrial decline of drive-in theatres was generally slower in the midwestern and southern United States than elsewhere, and regional newspaper advertising suggests that exploitation films were more regularly billed together at southern drive-ins than at northern ones.

But, as the major Hollywood studios began marketing their own genre films into drive-ins, several of these independent companies (including AIP, New World, and Dimension) bankrupted themselves by producing programmes of higher-budgeted films to compete with the majors.[35] Meanwhile, faced with both the shrinking exploitation market and facilities that had fallen into disrepair, it was often more advantageous for drive-in owners to sell off their property – in some cases, to construct shopping-mall multiplexes – as land values increased than to invest in costly renovations.[36] Other drive-in owners remained afloat by diversifying the use of their property during daylight hours as a site for flea markets – ironically enough, a grassroots marketplace also devoted to the used and repurposed (eventually including residual media such as early VHS cassettes). Furthermore, the rise of flea markets was part of a growing 1970s nostalgia industry devoted to 1950s Americana, with the widespread turn towards 1950s nostalgia often attributed to a conservative reaction against the subsequent decades of social turmoil.[37]

Drive-ins themselves began turning towards 1950s nostalgia in the early 1980s, sometimes holding special events with classic car clubs and screenings of 1950s films. Yet, this period also saw the development of fan cultures dedicated to films from the later, less family-friendly years of drive-in history. By this time, 'drive-in movies' had become a generic epithet virtually synonymous with exploitation films. Much as companies like American International Television (AIP's television subsidiary), Allied Artists, and Embassy Pictures assembled large packages of exploitation films for television syndication in the 1950s and 1960s, distributors such as Cinema Shares and World Northal created packages for sale to local UHF television affiliates during the 1980s. These packages spurred drive-in-themed, late-night and weekend movie blocks as a cost-effective means of filling up undervalued airtime, such as World Northal's *Kung Fu Theater* package or the *Drive-In Movie* showcase that played during Saturday afternoons on New York's WNEW-TV from 1981 to 1988.[38] 'Drive-in movie' as a popular classification thereby served not only as a tool for marketing such films to television and the burgeoning home video market but also freed remaining drive-in theatres from some of their associations with such potentially disreputable films. In other words, by segregating exploitation films into a niche market as 'drive-in movies', surviving drive-in theatres benefited by effectively clearing these films off the historical slate to make way for the more general-interest fare that has once again become the dominant variety of drive-in programming.

For drive-ins that have continued to operate to this day, their relative scarcity restores a sense of novelty in the age of the multiplex and home video. Families and teens remain the dominant demographics served, but nostalgia has become the dominant tenor even if first-run Hollywood films are now their featured entertainment. Some drive-ins, for example, bookend their double features with 1950s–60s pop hits played over the short-range FM radio signal used to transmit film sound, while others screen vintage promotional and concession advertisements before or after the first feature – effectively 'Fifties-ising' the experience. As in the 1950s, convenience, affordability, and family-friendly fun remain major selling points in drive-in theatres' self-promotion, as theatre operators attempt to recall the 'healthy' period of drive-in history while still catering to current cinematic tastes.

Yet, we can also see small concessions to other nostalgias in the occasional drive-in event catering specifically to exploitation fans. The cult film website DVD Drive-In, for example, organises semi-annual dusk-to-dawn horror shows of archival 35 mm prints at a Pennsylvania drive-in as a means of bridging the gap between the home DVD experience of exploitation films and the hallowed drive-in experience itself. These types of exceptional screenings suggest that the drive-in theatre continues to exist not just as an abstract generic place imaginatively occupied by different generations and segments of audiences but also as actual physical places of pilgrimage where fan nostalgias continue to play out in person. At the time of writing, however, the major studios' turn towards eliminating 35 mm film prints and mandating the projection of Digital Cinema Packages (DCP) threatens to make many of the nation's remaining drive-in screens ineligible for first-run Hollywood films without digital technological conversions that, even when partially subsidised by the Hollywood studios, are beyond the financial capacities of many independent operators.[39] Whether this industry shift will herald a final death knell for many drive-ins after eight decades of service or a desperate return to the programming of independently produced genre films remains to be seen.

Irony, Classism and the DVD Viewer

The division between differently appraised visions of drive-in history has reinforced supposed distinctions between the 'cult' reputation of exploitation films and the 'mainstream' cinema from which it is often distinguished within fan discourse. Though urban exhibition sites, such as art theatres and grind houses, have been mythologised as originary sites for cult film – especially through the post-1950s, pre-video phenomenon of midnight movies which can be linked to the artistic pedigree of 1960s underground cinema[40] – I would suggest that examining the lower class connotations of rural drive-ins allows us to reconsider why such sites constitute a mythical location in exploitation film history that has received relatively little critical or academic attention.

Contradictorily positioned as 'occupying a capitalist-class position by virtue of their domination of the working class [or those with less cultural and economic capital, such as students], even as they are located in a working-class position due to the fact that they do not own and control the means of production', many academics occupy a professional-managerial class within the knowledge industries whose 'deployment of cultural capital not only serves to distinguish it from the working class but also frequently functions to establish its prerogatives against those of capital'. Even though they may espouse anti-capitalist sentiments, they can also help uphold ideological superstructures through the educational system's reproduction of cultural capital.[41] This tendency can lead to the classic hypocrisy of the middle-class academic who loftily champions socialist ideals or equality for the working classes but who secretly (or not so secretly) harbours a distrust of, or disgust towards, working-class culture. In their mission to educate and, therefore, uplift those lacking cultural capital, 'distinctions are going to be erased ... by the working class moving in the direction of middle-class manners rather than the other way around'.[42] The spatial dimensions of this conflict historically emerged in the gradual sacralisation of public entertainment sites in nineteenth-century American society. With the rise of industrialisation and the increased stratification of social class, some theatres became privileged over others, fit only for the exhibition of 'legitimate' cultural forms. But 'while there was never a total monopoly of access, there was a tight control over the terms of access', with supposedly 'higher' cultural forms requiring properly tasteful reception strategies seemingly removed from the crassness of populist market demands.[43]

As Jeffrey Sconce rightly observes, however, the strictures of 'good taste' that once dominated academic film studies have also been challenged by students-turned-professors who rose from working-class roots, uneasily importing their own tastes for exploitation cinema and other forms of so-called 'low culture' as objects of legitimate study. He therefore sees paracinema's ironic celebration of culturally devalued exploitation films as 'a site of "refuge and revenge"' for 'exiles from the legitimizing functions of the academy'.[44] Since cultural capital 'cannot be passively bequeathed to one's offspring', but must be 're-earned with each generation through education and professional training', Derek Nystrom argues that 'the failure or refusal to acquire and embrace the fruits of this training reads as a kind of "class treason"'.[45] As an academic who is reading ostensibly low-cultural texts as avant-garde, Sconce's vision of paracinematic irony may thus seem a rebellious 'misuse' of the formalist reading strategies acquired through the cultivation of cultural capital (such as polemical comparisons between Jean-Luc Godard's distanciation devices and the inadvertent textual ruptures in Edward D. Wood films). Yet, critics who fall back on ironic reading strategies as the *overwhelming* lens for interpreting exploitation films also threaten to play into the paternalistic tradition of artists who develop a fascination for popular culture and privilege the naivety of the 'common people' who supposedly 'have none of the pretensions to art (or power) which inspire the ambitions of the "petit bourgeois"'.[46] Playing down the role of affect – including his own heartfelt nostalgia for earlier periods of film history associated with his personal past (as discussed below) – therefore allowed Sconce to defend himself against potential criticism that his recuperation of exploitation films was rooted in the more visceral, and supposedly unsophisticated, sensations traditionally associated with low culture.

This overemphasis on ironic formalism spurs Mark Jancovich's accusation that Sconce sees the ironic celebration of exploitation films as primarily accessible to viewers with enough cultural capital to use paracinema's formalist reading strategies. He argues that 'what Sconce calls "paracinema" is a species of bourgeois aesthetics, not a challenge to it', since paracinematic reading strategies focus so much on formal issues typically deemed above the mass film-goer's purview. For Jancovich, then, 'paracinema is at least as concerned to assert its superiority over those whom it conceives of as the degraded victims of mainstream commercial culture as it is concerned to provide a challenge to the academy and the art theatre'.[47] Yet, because Sconce is interested in mounting an institutional critique by claiming *academically justifiable* lenses for exploitation cinema's study, these arguments over the classed dimensions of formalism say little about the pleasures of contemporary working-class fans who may have increased access to such films on DVD but who still potentially possess lower levels of 'legitimate' cultural capital.

In other words, Jancovich's criticism holds water only if bourgeois critics and fans predominantly fall back on irony as a source of derisory pleasure when watching such films. But if, as I would argue, the affective potential of nostalgia allows irony and sincerity to coexist as multivalent pleasures that are not exclusive to any class position, then we can increasingly restore questions of affect to the study of exploitation cinema. In the years since Sconce's 1995 article first appeared, exploitation films have, indeed, become academically viable enough to admit the potential for affective and non-ironic appreciation back into scholarly consideration. Overlapping or conflicting nostalgias for exploitation cinema's texts and contexts are especially significant in this regard because they cannot be clearly claimed by one class position over another, and thus remain open to cultural contestations haunted by class conflict.

In my estimation, the pleasures of paracinematic irony do not require a great deal of legitimate cultural capital (such as formalist training); rather, the popularity of a family-friendly television programme such as *Mystery Science Theater 3000* – which Sconce dismisses as 'prepackaged' irony for implicitly passive viewers[48] – attests to the wide range of audiences who can, even with middling levels of cultural capital, still recognise and laugh at a film's technical ineptitude or exploitative excesses. Meanwhile, some working-class fan-scholars, who value exploitation films for more than ironic laughs, may accumulate greater knowledge about specific films or directors than possessed by formally trained academics – but that fan knowledge is typically dismissed as mere 'trivia' if it does not conform to scholarly rigour.[49] In this sense, ironic reading strategies and the accumulation of knowledge do not necessarily correspond to levels of legitimate cultural capital (and vice versa) despite common assertions to the contrary. Merely focusing on the ironic reading of exploitation films, then, explains only part of their appealing datedness for contemporary fans, foreclosing the more earnest appreciation that nostalgia also permits.

Fans currently occupying a working-class position may not have the years of formalist training to academically interpret exploitation films on a par with avant-garde art, nor as much disposable income for building an extensive Blu-ray collection or travelling to participate in fan-related activities, but they have as much right to *cultural memories* about exploitation cinema as anyone else. Attention to style may indeed be a 'class privilege' rooted in a 'double access' to the formal comprehension of both high and low culture[50] but we should not underestimate the capacity of viewers from many class standings and educational levels to locate these strange films in some alternate or faulty film-making mode from the past. After all, if paracinema's apparent 'badness' is largely measured by its perceived deviance from dominant Hollywood film-making norms, then so-called 'mass' audiences should already be intuitively familiar with the mainstream conventions from which exploitation films seem to depart by virtue of their apparent aesthetic/economic impoverishment. Approaching these films with a multivalent blend of irony and sincerity is thus as open to working-class fans as to middle-class cult movie aficionados, because no class can stake a definitive claim upon the cultural memories that influence one's performances of identity.

Though DVD has generally helped to mainstream the high-cultural standards and paratextual bonus features (for example, correct aspect ratios, remastered audiovisual quality, commentary tracks) that cinephiles once associated with a high-end format such as laserdisc, DVD has also allowed video collecting to move beyond the realm of elitist collectors, owing to the economic growth of a DVD sell-through market that far outpaces the rental market once associated with VHS.[51] In this sense, the tension that Barbara Klinger identifies between DVD's digital presentism and its yearning for access to the past helps account for the nostalgic mix of irony and sincerity that many contemporary fans bring to the exploitation text, in turn offering partial explanation for the various video editions on the market at the same time. As Klinger points out, if relatively affluent men are the biggest early adopters of emergent video technologies, and, if potential video sales are increasingly factored into the film industry's production decisions, then gendered and classed preferences in home video consumption may influence the types of films that continue to be distributed.[52] Klinger's argument, however, is grounded in the early years of DVD during the late 1990s, and is thus problematised now that DVD usage has extended far beyond the professional-managerial class that largely comprised the format's early adopters. DVD market penetration reached over 76 per cent of television-owning American households by late 2005, becoming 'the fastest-selling technology in the history of consumer electronics', and easily outpacing the former market penetration rate of VHS.[53]

As DVD's life cycle as a video format has grown ever longer and its heady early days have receded into the past, the technology has gradually acquired its own sense of historical span, in part through its increased acceptance by more and more viewers across different class strata. In effect, the technology's historical significance has opened up not only temporally but also spatially as access to it has spread throughout the United States and world populations. At the time of writing, DVD has reached widespread market penetration, even if facing competition from Blu-ray, a newer format dating from 2006, whose present prestige is linked to its higher price and smaller user base. But, as the price of a new video format falls to accommodate increased economies of scale, a film's reception tail can extend even longer, because greater numbers of potential buyers can help the text gain greater cultural longevity as it is (re)introduced to older and younger generations on video. With this expansion of access to a video format, it is more probable that a particular film and technology alike will be mnemonically (re)valued by diverse groups of viewers who can afford to adopt said technology into their everyday lives. Yet, though market penetration by video technologies encourages a democratisation of access to mediated memory objects, we must ask to what extent this democratisation also impinges upon fans' competition for the subcultural capital that accrues around material scarcity, producing interpersonal antagonisms that can privilege elitism over egalitarianism.

Because 'one can now use DVDs to reconstruct the entire exhibition history of a long defunct Alabama drive-in',[54] the celebration of a *lieu de mémoire*, such as the drive-in theatre, as a symbolic territory for exploitation film consumption is a prime example of a culturally implanted memory mediated by video technologies, because most contemporary fans seldom personally viewed those films in drive-ins. Nevertheless, if 'many such locales of memory are artificial constructions, the imprinting on space of the memory of the group', then the drive-in's slow disappearance from the nation's physical landscape has encouraged a nostalgia linked to the transformation of 'spatial shelters of memory . . . in their physical properties and in the hearts of their denizens'.[55] Indeed, the nostalgic reappraisal of drive-ins falls within the proliferation of memory culture since the 1970s and 1980s which includes the rise of home video as a key technology of cultural memory.[56] Yet, it is quite ironic that a decidedly 'low-tech' exhibition site such as the drive-in theatre has become championed by exploitation fans at a time when high-end home cinema technologies are challenging older assumptions that the 'big-screen performance is marked as authentic' while video is coded as 'inauthentic and ersatz'.[57] If we believe Paul Willemen that 'we unconsciously re-translate the perceived television image back onto a screen in the cinema' in our imaginations,[58] then the drive-in screen remains one of the primary locations to which fans imaginatively project exploitation films when watching them at home. In fact, the very specificity of this *lieu de mémoire* complicates how convergence-era media producers may encourage viewers to 'consciously eliminate that part of the message that is medium specific and to retain only that part of the movie that can be translated from medium to medium'.[59]

Furthermore, the very nature of the drive-in experience also helps explain exploitation films' transition from theatrical exhibition to home video. Mary Morley Cohen, for example, compares drive-in spectatorship and television spectatorship, as the car represented the extension of the private living room into public space – a sort of 'mobile privatisation' permitting viewers to disregard rules of etiquette that they would not have to follow at home.[60] Similarly, as indoor theatre behaviour became more disciplined during the 1950s and 1960s, drive-ins inherited some of the more actively sociable aspects of earlier theatre-going, which also later extended to places such as the video store. Drive-ins and home video, for example, offered viewers the ability to freely make derogatory comments during viewing, à la *Mystery Science Theater 3000*.[61] Given the range of behaviours permitted in and around cars, drive-ins could potentially create the sort of 'distracted' spectatorship often (if erroneously) associated with home viewing.[62] Like the home television screen, the drive-in screen is typically smaller than one's field of vision, offering softer and dimmer image resolution and more potential obstructions than an indoor theatre screen. At drive-ins and at home, the individual viewer is also permitted a certain degree of control over the speaker volume transmitting the film's audio, though the sound is usually below par compared with an indoor theatre. Obviously, one can only extend this metaphor so far – the drive-in patron lacks the time-shifting abilities of the home video viewer, for example – but the video store's opening of affordable access to niche texts nevertheless recalls the drive-in's general appeal to viewers of many different class backgrounds and geographical areas, potentially destabilising presumed class associations between certain texts, audiences, and theatre locations.

Drive-ins, Class Tensions and Competing Populisms

As nostalgias for the drive-in theatre mnemonically lurk in the background of exploitation film consumption within the home, fan reception remains haunted by ambivalence over the long-standing class diversity associated with the drive-in as a generic place. Research suggests that working-class

Figure 1.2 In John Waters's *Polyester* (1980), the humorous incongruity of a dusk-to-dawn drive-in triple feature of erudite Marguerite Duras art films depends on audience familiarity with drive-in theatres' generalised low-cultural connotations by the late 1970s. (Source: DVD.)

and less educated audiences – 'the cold-beer-and-greaseburger gang', in producer David F. Friedman's words[63] – became more prevalent at drive-in theatres over time, particularly from the early 1960s to the early 1980s, the same period when exploitation films seemed to increasingly dominate their screens (Figure 1.2).[64] Yet, this apparent 'winning' of social space for culturally marginalised audiences was not necessarily a resistant or rebellious process, because 'places are "won" when social groups are recognized as profitable markets'.[65] By the 1970s, the supposed white, conservative, blue-collar patron of rural drive-ins had become, in Derek Nystrom's words, 'a figure that inspired both attraction and antipathy – an ambivalent structure of feeling that spoke to both the [professional-managerial class]'s then current anxieties and the more long-standing and more fundamental contradictions of its own class position' as neither working-class labourers nor industry owners.[66]

Urban film critics, for example, assumed that the audience for 'Southerns', or so-called 'redneck movies', such as *Walking Tall* (1973), *White Line Fever* (1975) and *The Great Texas Dynamite Chase* (1976), were viscerally moved by vulgar exploitation elements to the extent that their working-class bodies became threateningly unmanageable by an educated middle class increasingly shifting towards the management of rural southern industry. 'Furthermore, their revulsion at the films' ostensibly conservative values often served as a cover for the discomfort they felt over the Southerns' more populist elements.' Yet, even if these films tended to open in southern drive-ins, they also sometimes worked their way north to urban areas, where larger numbers of middle-class viewers could engage in a 'cross-class identificatory desire ... motivated by the familiar, homosocial impulse to remasculinize themselves through an affective connection with laboring bodies'.[67] Similarly, middle-class fans today may situationally identify with past drive-in audiences in some ways but the apparent datedness of exploitation films can also engender a historical chauvinism that distances present-day fans from associations with the films' initial, supposedly less savvy audiences who can be denigrated as having been horny teenagers or rural folk so unsophisticated as to be sincerely fooled by the lurid appeals of 'bad' movies.

On the one hand, then, past drive-in patrons were (and still are) potentially seen as ignorant, feminised and easily manipulated – all cultural associations similarly applied to many television viewers during this period. On the other hand, working-class drive-in patrons could also be seen as unruly, hypermasculine and even potentially dangerous in their collective power. (Beyond common stereotypes of television viewers, many of these ambivalent connotations have been applied to media fans in general.) Indeed, the working classes may be coded as feminised masses in some contexts but '[t]hese men [sic] are hardly feminized in their subordination; in fact, their manner and smell reveal the feminization of the men above them': the highly educated and even effete professional-managerial class.[68]

If exploitation films were seen as culturally low because their appeals to populist thrills seemingly stimulated the body more than the mind, then it makes sense why many critics and academics occupying a professional-managerial class position have been hesitant to revalue the rural exhibition sites reputedly home to such films. Much as nostalgia for the prelapsarian 1950s drive-in experience takes a primarily conservative tenor by idealising drive-ins as a relatively innocent space for white middle-class youth, the possibility of a class-inflected nostalgia for politically conservative populism may undergird professional-managerial class anxieties about the spatial dynamics of drive-ins.[69] Yet, I would argue that fans' latter-day enjoyment of these same thrills – which paracinematic reading strategies could, through the relative safety of intellectual/aesthetic distance, attempt to recode as unintentionally humorous excess – means exploitation cinema's continuing affectivity cannot be wholly subsumed by professional-managerial ideals of bourgeois self-management. In other words, even beneath the 'loving yet subtle smirk' of ironic distance engendered by nostalgia's disjuncture between past and present – beneath, that is, the 'gentle ribbing at how far we've come from this earlier stage of development'[70] – historically transcendent thrills still commingle with this ironic potential.

As such, fans' nostalgia potentially remains politically problematic by 'ironically elevat[ing] texts that often exhibit a naive disregard for sexism, misogyny, racism, and other pre-enlightenment sins', thus championing straight white males' 'reassertion of the right to look, to make anything the object of the knowing, sardonic, ironising, and frankly excited gaze'.[71] Fans, for example, tend to reproduce mainstream distributors' ill-informed belief that drive-ins were 'passion pits' showing indecent films,[72] as this image of the drive-in as immoral space seemingly justifies their choice to view films that may have violated normative taste standards upon their initial release but which often reinforce what today seem retrograde depictions of women, people of colour, the queer community and so on. As Sconce rhetorically asks, '[I]s the "ironic" reading of a "reactionary" text necessarily a "progressive" act?'[73] If exploitation films were solely consumed through paracinema's ironic reading strategies, then I might answer in the affirmative – but, because the regressive aspects of these films continue to be read at least partly 'straight' as historically dated but viscerally transcendent pleasures, their contemporary consumption retains more troubling dimensions. As a particularly disturbing example, Nazisploitation films, such as *SS Experiment Love Camp* (1976) and *Gestapo's Last Orgy* (1977), have found continuing followings among not only exploitation fans but also various groups of white supremacists and other Nazi sympathisers. While viewers in the latter groups do not need high levels of legitimate cultural capital to recognise and enjoy the campy or over-the-top excesses of such films, the more earnest dimension of their reception can also position these films as reinforcing past and present hatreds. Or, to use a more prevalent example, consider how the '[v]alorization of bad movies also seems to go hand-in-hand . . . with an unreconstructed, distinctly non-ironic appreciation of B-movie female flesh'.[74] Whether attending older texts remediated in new ways or more recent texts deploying deliberate archaism (see Chapter 3), nostalgia's multivalence allows irony to serve as a cover for non-ironic pleasures, belying fans' defensive protests that these films are just excusably 'mindless entertainment' or 'great politically incorrect fun'.[75]

Hence, nostalgia for past consumption sites like the drive-in may not *explicitly* idealise our more politically conservative past as a 'better' time. Rather, it implicitly longs for an era of lessened consumer choices and greater opportunities for those historical texts to seem 'rebellious' by provoking scandal through affective impacts that can potentially still be experienced today in politically unreconstructed ways. Imagining oneself linked across time to the glut of drive-in patrons who allegedly jammed highways in long lines to see a notoriously boundary-pushing gore film like Herschell Gordon Lewis's *Blood Feast* (1963) upon its premiere in Peoria, Illinois, offers today's fans the fantasy of occupying a nonconformist, niche viewership – even if a DVD or Blu-ray of said film can be easily picked up in the 'Cult' section of the local book/video megastore, scarcely capable of generating controversy amid a flood of more recent films. On the one hand, then, exploitation fans who imaginatively place themselves in the shoes of past drive-in patrons may implicitly uphold a more conservative past to a certain degree but primarily challenge *past* taste constraints and thereby claim an imagined sense of historical distance from present-day consumer culture's increasingly blurred taste hierarchies. On the other hand, the potential controversy these historical texts could have once evoked has passed from former constraints on screen content (which have since been thoroughly surpassed) to the unreconstructed pleasures they can still engender in violation of latter-day associations between mainstream 'political correctness' and 'good taste'. For present-day fans to celebrate exploitation films (and by extension, their preference for such films) as 'transgressive', they often imaginatively resurrect cultural prohibitions associated with the past's moralising censors but which are more accurately rooted in the latter-day politics of representation advanced by various post-1950s activists such as feminists and civil rights proponents.[76]

Consequently, empirical facts about films' production and distribution histories merge with mythical beliefs about original drive-in audiences who are alternately figured as rebellious outsiders or passive dupes, providing a range of ways for present-day fans to situationally claim or disclaim cultural memories of the drive-in experience. Indeed, such shared memories can be upheld as signifiers of supposed exclusivity and authenticity as easily as they can be considered a 'colonization of consciousness' and 'a mechanism of subjection'.[77] Hence, fans, critics, and scholars often share a (differently inflected) rejection of populist consumerism because consumerism has few presumed associations with (sub)cultural capital's valuation of the exclusive and the 'authentic'. Some exploitation fans, for example, may reject the conservative middle-class populism within an earlier generation's memories of the drive-in as quintessentially innocent 1950s Americana, even as some professional-managerial class members may similarly reject the working-class populism associated with later drive-in audiences. As Elizabeth Guffey says, one person's signifiers of 1950s innocence – such as drive-ins, leather jackets and rock 'n' roll – can be another person's signifiers of working-class rebellion, juvenile delinquency and a fledgling counter-cultural ethos.[78]

In this sense, despite fans' ambivalent identification with historical drive-in patrons, recognising the pastness of exploitation films often means recognising oneself as not (or no longer) part of the audience originally meant to be *exploited by* these films – a possibility made more complicated for present-day viewers who still partly respond to these films' affectivity in earnest or sincere ways. Yet, it makes no more sense to assume that past audiences passively absorbed exploitation cinema's ideological premises than to assume that viewers today can approach the same films only with ironic distance. Rather, we might imagine both past and present viewers activating a multivalent mixture of irony and sincerity during the viewing experience, depending on relative factors such as their historical distance from the text's moment of origin and their degree of accumulated subcultural capital at the time of the viewing. More historical distance or greater subcultural capital can potentially increase *both* the irony and sincerity felt when approaching an exploitation text, because these impulses are not mutually exclusive.

The coexistence of these reception qualities, however, does not fully resolve the class inequalities long attached to drive-ins and exploitation films alike. While exploitation films are still popular with rural and working-class audiences on home video, some middle-class fans tend to treat such audiences with mocking disdain – unless, for example, appearing in the critical vein of 'redneck' drive-in guru Joe Bob Briggs, a tongue-in-cheek persona created by film critic John Bloom. Briggs is a notable figure in the remediation of exploitation films, using his newspaper columns, books, DVD commentary tracks and website to lament the drive-in theatre's decline while also hosting several cable television shows and home video series dedicated to extending the afterlives of 'drive-in movies'. Launched at the *Dallas Times Herald* in 1982, his syndicated column 'Joe Bob Goes to the Drive-In' focused on exploitation films, while his television hosting duties included The Movie Channel's *Joe Bob Briggs's Drive-In Theater* (1987–96) and TNT's *MonsterVision* (1996–2000). His host segments on the early-1990s VHS series 'Sleaziest Movies in the History of the World' saw Briggs walking around abandoned drive-in theatres while promising the preservation of films such as *Two Thousand Maniacs!* (1964) and *Bad Girls Go to Hell* (1965). He has also been interviewed in Americana-fuelled documentaries such as *After Sunset: The Life & Times of the Drive-In Theater* (1995) and *Drive-In Movie Memories* (2001), in addition to hosting a drive-in movie festival honouring Roger Corman's career.

Briggs's criticism generally blends tongue-in-cheek appreciation of a film's excesses and failings while also cataloguing 'the Three B's: Blood,

Breasts, and Beasts' – those exploitable elements that should hypothetically appeal to a populist (male) audience and continue to make the films highly watchable today. Moments of datedness or ineptitude become privileged alongside genuinely affective genre thrills. His review of the Australian exploitation film *Escape 2000* (1982), for example, offers the following 'drive-in total':

> We're talking exploding heads. We're talking recreational vehicle crash-and-burns. We're talking bimbo meat factories. Twenty-one breasts, including two stunt breasts. Thirty-four dead bodies. Six pints blood. One beast (gonzo werewolf). Four motor vehicle chases, two crash-and-burns. Heads roll. Hands roll. Stomachs roll. Little toe rolls. Three stars. Joe Bob says check this baby out.[79]

Like an ersatz working-class fan-scholar who has somehow infiltrated the professional-managerial class of professional film critics, Briggs positions himself as a 'good ole boy' who relishes the populist appeal and 'bad taste' of exploitation cinema's entertaining spectacle. (In actuality, John Bloom is a Vanderbilt University honours graduate who loved foreign films and 'wrote essays on the *nouvelle vague*', whereas alter ego Briggs was introduced to readers as a self-taught authority who had seen over 6,800 drive-in flicks.)[80] For Briggs and his fans, then, the classed rurality of the 'redneck' serves as the basis for a classed rebellion against mainstream and middlebrow tastes. Depending on one's interpretation, his ambivalent tone can be read as either a satire or celebration of the type of machismo-laden Texan men left out of Dallas's early-1980s economic boom.[81] At the same time, his writing also retains an acute knowledge of genre history, inseparable from a nostalgic celebration of drive-ins as an endangered species allegedly threatened by the forces of consumerism – even as those same forces have allowed Briggs to make a career for himself as a self-appointed steward of remediated drive-in movies in the home video era. Thus, even the 'redneck' fan-scholar retains appeals to connoisseurship, helping avoid the suggestions of passive consumption that the populist appeal of drive-ins and exploitation cinema threatens to raise. Yet, this tongue-in-cheek performance of a redneck persona is also a means of internalising and pre-emptively deflecting a 'common fear that elevating "inferior" tastes above their stations can only render one foolish'.[82]

Accordingly, Briggs is a pivotal figure because his performance of working-class rurality positions him at the nexus of a class tension lurking beneath much of exploitation cinema's contemporary consumption. Put simply: how does one reconcile the original populist appeal of these films with their latter-day subcultural appropriation as non-mainstream, 'outsider' texts? There is a glaring contradiction between, on the one hand, celebrating the 'mindless fun' supposedly offered by films that are (in one fan's words) 'made with a micro budget, and exploitative, politically incorrect, rude, crude, filled to the brim with blood, breasts and beasts'; and, on the other hand, rejecting the present-day populist appeals of Hollywood films appearing 'at your neutered, spineless local googaplex [sic] which offers us nothing but mindless, million-dollar, brain-meltingly useless pop culture turd smears which do nothing more than recycle the same old shit, whether it's a remake of a beloved franchise or an adaptation of a Hasbro toy line'.[83]

To manage this paradox effectively, mnemonically abstracting the drive-in into an antiquated symbolic site associated with outdated (but not completely obsolete) tastes has helped fans explain and excuse the populist appeals of dated exploitation texts by locating those appeals in a generic symbol of the cultural past. Fans from different socioeconomic standings can thereby use their affective closeness to, and historical distance from, the nostalgically remembered drive-in as a means of situationally positioning themselves in relation to this historical consumption site's differently classed audiences. Yet, even if helping distance fans from the populist appeals of present-day 'mainstream' cinema and the scarcity of (sub)cultural capital associated therewith, nostalgia for the drive-in as generic place can never fully resolve the classed ambivalence that exploitation cinema's populism retrospectively garners among fans.

Déclassé DVDs and the Non-teleology of Value

The overlapping or even competing nostalgias associated with exploitation cinema as populist entertainment help account for the sheer range of DVD editions readily available on the market, because each edition can evoke pastness differently: from those offering pristine, remastered transfers dressed up like art objects and accompanied by specific historical paratexts; to those offering grainy, misframed and occasionally mutilated transfers of films in the public domain, such as Elite Entertainment's series of 'Drive-In Discs' that simulate

> not merely the visual experience of the typical double feature . . . but the extras as well: concession stand ads, the countdown clock, cartoons, vintage ads, previews, and 'Distorto' sound. (This makes the film's soundtrack available only through the front left speaker, enhanced by the ambient surround sound of other speakers, crickets, and laughter.)[84]

The films most likely to be retrospectively repackaged as budget-priced 'drive-in'-themed DVDs often feature below-par transfers (sometimes from an earlier VHS release) of pictures whose indeterminate copyright status was caused by the proliferation of different titles and versions of the same film, as if the democratising populism associated with the drive-in has also extended to texts whose current legal ownership is more democratic or decentralised than the copyrighted works owned by huge corporations. In early 2013, for instance, the exploitation video label Vinegar Syndrome released *The Lost Films of Herschell Gordon Lewis*, a combined Blu-ray/DVD set of three newly discovered sexploitation films restored from the original 35 mm negatives, while the label concurrently released a series of 'Drive-In Collection' double-feature DVDs sourced from unrestored theatrical prints – the latter DVDs listed at a reduced price reflecting this more déclassé condition/context. Other examples include Mill Creek Entertainment's fifty-film *Drive In Movie Classics* (2009) and thirty-two-film *Drive-In Cult Classics* (2010) box sets; Image Entertainment's seven-film *Drive-In Classics Collection* (2009); and Pop Flix's ten-film *Roger Corman Drive-In Collection* (2010).

By privileging economic affordability and easy accessibility as justification for their déclassé quality, drive-in-themed DVD sets thus seem to internalise the lower-class, populist associations of drive-in theatres, while the recurrent epithet 'classic' aims to restoratively bestow cultural value upon texts too neglected to have retained proper copyright ownership (Figure 1.3). A marketably 'retro' sense of pastness is also evoked by the relatively unprofessional, no-frills look of these DVD packages and their poorly transferred films, recalling the 'trashy' primitivism and inferior audiovisual quality of the drive-in as an exhibition site.[85] Because cultural memories far less often associate mainstream Hollywood films with drive-in exhibition, their remediated video editions are less likely to intentionally evoke the drive-in experience, instead presuming a much broader, less site-specific viewership than the exploitation film audiences who have been consciously written into the afterlives of so-called 'drive-in movies'.

Like the coexistence of irony and sincerity in the exploitation viewing experience, then, the various DVD editions commingling in the marketplace offer multivalent appeals to the different class positions associated with this historical exhibition site. As Will Straw argues, these budget-priced box sets 'enact the reduction of hundreds of films to virtually indistinguishable products of equal value, in a market where competition is based almost exclusively on the offering of greater and greater abundance for ever lower prices'. Much as exploitation films were often screened at drive-ins as programme filler but have since been rediscovered

Figure 1.3 Mill Creek Entertainment's fifty-film *Drive In Movie Classics* box set repackages public-domain exploitation films within a package visually suggesting how the marketing of 1950s nostalgia is generated through drive-ins' latter-day destruction as lived places. (Source: author's collection.)

as specifically collectible titles on home video, exploitation texts continue to offer appeals to 'both hip cinephiles and to the [populist] audiences for cheap genre films – [which] is often signaled in the different titles they carried at different points in their commercial lives'. Since 1970s exploitation films figure prominently in these box sets owing to their indeterminate copyright status when quickly released under various titles across different territories, Straw suggests that these mobile DVD archives reinforce the notion of the 1970s as a period of generic decline. The turn towards more exploitative genres becomes visually reflected in the historical degradation of the public-domain transfers themselves: faded colours, scratches, alternative titles, shabby sound, inadvertent jump cuts caused by missing frames, and tired stylistic clichés.[86] Yet, as I will explain in later chapters, the multivalent appeals of nostalgia can also allow these seemingly negative signifiers of archaism and decay to become retrospectively privileged by fans as positive marks of the archival text's auratic 'authenticity'.[87]

This polysemy is further suggested by how fans themselves repackage grey-market drive-in texts in similar ways as independent DVD distributors. Here, however, the free distribution of these texts seems motivated more by affectionate memories than by profit, becoming accessible by anyone with the technology to do so. On the non-profit Internet Archive website, for example, the fan-assembled 'Shocker Internet Drive-In' series of free video downloads simulates a drive-in experience by pairing public-domain exploitation films with cartoons, shorts and drive-in concession ads, while another fan's 'Drive-In Madness' YouTube series compiles exploitation film trailers with intermission and concession stand ads. Finally, public-domain exploitation films continue to appear on drive-in-themed public-access television shows – including one airing late at night in Bloomington, Indiana, at the time of writing, which features a neon-lit 'Drive-In Theatre' proscenium framing the filmic image throughout.

At the same time, however, these déclassé examples of remediation must vie with more upmarket DVD and Blu-ray editions that less often aim to simulate 'the drive-in experience' with concession ads and random trailers. The upmarket editions, from companies such as Anchor Bay Entertainment and Blue Underground, are more likely to offer 'uncensored director's cuts' of a single film, supplemented by specifically curated paratexts from selected points in the film's reception tail – all of which offer a different means of cumulatively evoking pastness than the more populist, downmarket editions. Vinzenz Hediger argues that the notion of an 'original' version is typically propagated by a modern film industry that generates much of its profits from its copyright holdings. A single iteration of a film becomes elevated as 'the original' – a lost paragon of wholeness that must be reconstructed via emergent video technologies – while playing down the many other versions that inevitably existed across its lifespan (including alternative versions in the public domain).[88] By asserting a remedial version that appears to restore and correct the damage that time and neglect have potentially done to the text, the discursive construction of 'the original' thereby creates cultural visibility and (economic) value at the expense of an attention to historical nuance (including physical wear and tear) that has increasingly shifted to the film's paratexts in these upmarket editions.

The remedial edition can thus become a privileged node of consumption despite the historical and mnemonic value attached to the pastness of budget-priced, downmarket versions that potentially circulate more widely in the marketplace (see the DVD 'bargain bins' in filling stations or any big-box retailer such as Walmart or Target) than their more expensive and prestigious kin. Yet, even as they may celebrate the uncensored, authored 'original' as a highly desirable object, fans can also complicate such dubious claims of originality by archiving alternative textual iterations for the sake of completism. In this sense, the different connotations of historicity evoked by differently classed video editions and formats – some more explicitly populist than others – fragment any clear sense of subcultural coherence. Through their video consumption choices, fans can situationally claim the 'authenticity' of one means of evoking pastness over another, much as they can situationally position their own values in relation to the historical drive-in theatre's differently classed audiences.

Hence, we should not assume that a teleological flow of cultural value necessarily follows the progression of newer video technologies. Raiford Guins, for example, argues that Italian horror films, among the most popular of exploitation variants, have experienced an upward cultural trajectory, moving from apparently unauthored, heavily cut 'gore-objects' on VHS to a new presentation as uncut, restored, authored 'art-objects' on DVD. In this way, technological remediation has supposedly allowed Italian horror's once-lowbrow cultural value to be restored to a greater state of highbrow respectability through traditional appeals to auteurism and formalism.[89] Yet, I would argue that this alleged one-way flow of value is an oversimplification of the complexity seen in the past and present home video marketplace, especially since DVD is no longer considered a prestigious 'new' technology. While it may be true that the name of the auteur is trumpeted on box covers, as with the 'Dario Argento Collection' and 'Lucio Fulci Collection' banners on a handful of Anchor Bay DVDs, earnest fans have long sought out specific Italian horror directors by name on earlier video formats such as VHS. Nor is it necessarily true that DVD releases have played down references to gore and other low-cultural appeals on their box covers. Heavily accompanied by bonus paratexts, Grindhouse Releasing's 2008 DVD of Lucio Fulci's *Cat in the Brain* (1990), for example, trumpets the film as 'The most VIOLENT movie ever made!' while also describing it as 'a psychological masterpiece in the tradition of such cinematic classics as *Psycho*, *Strait-Jacket*, *Eraserhead*, and Fellini's *8½*'. Likewise, Anchor Bay's 2001 release of Fulci's *The House by the Cemetery* (1981) sports a tasteful 'Lucio Fulci Collection' banner on the front cover, but the back cover features images of mutilated victims, the tagline 'The Ultimate Gorehound House Party', and the following description:

> *The House by the Cemetery* features a mind-blowing onslaught of throat-ripping, skull-knifing, maggot-spewing and more from Lucio Fulci, 'The Godfather of Gore'. Considered to be one of the master's last great films, this outrageous Italian shocker is now presented uncut, uncensored and – for the first time ever – digitally transferred from the original camera negative!

Reverential nods to Fulci as a 'master' and 'godfather' commingle with promises of excessively gory details that have been digitally restored to an audiovisual state befitting a 'great film'. In this sense, closer inspection finds high- and low-cultural references blending on DVD box covers, bespeaking the texts' inseparability from a cultural history linked as much to a fannish appreciation of gore as to non-ironic auteurism and other high-cultural reading strategies.

Similarly, digital video technologies have not unequivocally restored even the work of a more artistically redeemable Italian horror director such as Argento to the status of art objects, as seen by the heavily cut and poorly framed version of *Deep Red* (1975), included under its alternative American title *The Hatchet Murders* within St. Clair Vision's déclassé *Fright Night Classics* (2004) DVD box set, or *Tenebre* (1982) under its alternative title *Unsane* on Mill Creek's *Drive In Movie Classics* set. Yet, one might ask whether a self-respecting fan would intentionally opt for a degraded VHS or battered 35 mm transfer over a more uncut and restored Blu-ray – but even here, we can find fans whose memories are attached to the more 'authentic', haptic pleasures of historical decay (see Chapters 2 and 3) nostalgised by different generations of consumers. As fan-scholar Howard Hughes writes of the Italian western *Django* (1966), for example, 'Forget about pristine DVD releases – *Django* is best viewed in the grimiest, most scratched print possible, preferably on battered VHS (Inter-Ocean Video released it in Britain), which accentuates Enzo Barboni's gritty Eastmancolor cinematography.'[90] While the majority of fans may not necessarily prefer the déclassé or residual video object over the remastered or remedial version, such unconventionally retrospective preferences suggest an important dimension tied to memories of one's own viewing history with the text.

Overall, then, these examples demonstrate that the format transition from VHS to DVD to Blu-ray has not necessarily resulted in a teleological path of cultural upmarketing for exploitation films – particularly as DVD has shifted from an emergent video technology to widespread market penetration, including users of many different class and taste backgrounds. In this respect, the coexistence of formats and editions which have become desired by fans, for reasons other than audiovisual quality or curatorial extras, complicates what Barbara Klinger calls a 'hardware aesthetic' associated with DVD's former prestige as a new video technology (since bequeathed to Blu-ray). Furthermore, the release of so many once-obscure exploitation titles on upmarket, remastered DVDs signals that purchases of higher-end video technologies need not correlate with the consumption of culturally 'higher' films, because a fan's class position cannot necessarily be determined from his/her choice of fan object.[91] Indeed, if aspirations towards class progress are often marked by the conspicuous consumption of newfangled material goods, then my final section in this chapter builds on how the revaluing of past films allows fans to imagine themselves historically distanced from one-way demands for upward class mobility and the bourgeois taste cultures frequently associated with such demands.

All these modes of remediation sediment the importance of certain mythic narratives and symbols – including the historical place of the drive-in theatre itself – while nevertheless offering multiple possible paths toward a supposedly 'authentic' sense of historical pastness. Yet, this very multiplicity undermines stable claims of subcultural authenticity or coherence by validating many different ways in which fans can use mediated memory objects in the pursuit of subcultural capital. Indeed, as my use of scare quotes should imply, the very notion of 'authenticity' is itself little more than a myth, an asymptotic assertion of more 'auratic' cultural preferences over others – but a myth that, like nostalgia's own mystifications of the past, carries real-world effects when figured as a constitutive part of one's desired identity as a consumer. If particular cultural memories are not the exclusive domain of any one group with select levels of economic, cultural or subcultural capital, then the accessibility of multiple registers of pastness allows historical class inequalities to haunt (but not rigidly structure) the ways in which consumers can contingently make use of *lieux de mémoire* such as the drive-in theatre.

Exploitation, Apocalypse and Re-enchanted Commodities

As Klinger observes, home video's ability to allow the endless replaying of a text at different times in a person's life may confirm individual identities but it can also play upon nostalgia's dialectical nature by juxtaposing past and present experiences in potentially volatile ways.[92] Formative memories of viewing a certain film on a visually degraded VHS bootleg, for instance, can clash with seeing the audiovisually remastered film on an emergent technology such as Blu-ray because the latter experience may threaten to rewrite memories attached to the former technology, especially when a younger generation of fans affixes its own memories to a newer format and declaims that format's superior delivery of textual 'authenticity'. Many fans (myself included) might also resist the ongoing shift towards streaming formats, because it seemingly jeopardises the physical accumulation of objects that serve collectors as triggers for more intangible accumulated memories. Technological shifts thus create a tension between resistance to change and methods of compensation as the spatio-temporal memories attached to one means of film consumption are unsettled or displaced by another. Think also of the generational factions arising around major-studio remakes of independently produced exploitation films first encountered by older fans in niche theatres or on VHS; such remakes seemingly cast the original version's auratic value into question when the property is targeted to more diverse demographics. As the rest of this book will elaborate, these generational shifts in audiences and delivery technologies suggest a history of planned obsolescence that can serve as both a wound and a balm for long-term fans' nostalgias about their *personal histories* of media consumption within a capitalist economy that may no longer explicitly need them.

Paul Watson argues that the concept of 'paracinema' attempts to recuperate exploitation cinema as a marginal and oppositional practice, rather than viewing 'exploitation' as a practice that has motivated (and even pre-dated) the history of film from its earliest days, reaching its current apotheosis with 'the production and marketing strategies of the most mainstream manifestation of cinema – Hollywood'.[93] Yet, even if unhelpful in limiting our analysis to the historical texts labelled by fans as *exploitation films*, Watson's equating of exploitation with the economic demands of mainstream commercial cinema nonetheless retains a certain degree of accuracy; the term 'exploitation' originated, after all, as a common trade term in studio-era publications such as *Motion Picture Herald*, to describe exhibitors' use of distinctive publicity (often including stunts, contests and cross-promotional tie-ins with local businesses) in the advertising of major Hollywood releases, not just lurid independent productions. Fan-made fake posters that digitally manipulate and recode images from well-known Hollywood releases in faux-exploitation style play up this tension between mainstream Hollywood cinema and exploitation cinema. With lurid fonts, decontextualised imagery and screaming taglines – such as *Barry Lyndon* (1975) being 'Shot with a lens aperture so wide they said it could never be filmed!' or *Back to the Future* (1985) featuring 'Science!! Incest!! Rape gangs!! Jazz!!' – these fake posters participate in a nostalgic blend of sincere appreciation and ironic distance towards their historical referents, which can also be found in retro-styled pastiches like *Grindhouse* (2007) and other 'retrosploitation' films (see Chapters 3 and 4).[94] Much as fan-made trailers often generically recode footage from Hollywood films for quasi-parodic purposes, these retro-primitive paratexts humorously imagine a world in which mainstream or middlebrow Hollywood films were marketed in the most distastefully sensationalised ways. Yet, part of this humour implicitly derives from the cynical suggestion that, taste politics aside, it would not be terribly surprising to see major Hollywood studios making such desperately populist appeals to attract film-goers. As incongruous as it would be to see Oscar bait such as *Schindler's List* (1993) marketed like a 1970s Nazisploitation movie (an ominous image of Ralph Fiennes's sadistic SS officer and the tagline 'See what really happened inside the Nazi torture camps!!!'), for example, these fake posters lay bare the shared economic impetus behind the mainstream and exploitation film industries alike. At the same time, however, they point towards the idea that Hollywood films can also provide nostalgically memorable thrills and attractions despite their lower place of subcultural value among fan cultures that privilege independence, authenticity and nonconformity as desirable traits.

Appending questions of affect and memory to his earlier arguments about paracinema, Jeffrey Sconce himself has more recently suggested that paracinematic irony may indeed coexist with earnest evaluations of exploitation films. Like Watson, Sconce notes that exploitation films and Hollywood films both routinely promise more than they can possibly deliver, though 'exploitation by its very name implies a gap between promise and practice, ambition and execution'. One might laugh at the technical deficiencies of exploitation films through an affectionate camp lens, while nevertheless identifying with the romanticised low-budget auteur's struggle to create something – anything – under impoverished working conditions.[95] For Sconce, then, the exploitation fan fosters a strong nostalgia for past periods of film history, like past periods of one's own life, when one could be 'exploited' by these films. As he explains,

> Film history becomes a mirror to our own mortality, bringing with it the bittersweet recognition that one can never again sit among the screaming yokels below. By reveling in this disjunction between expectations and disappointment, the trashophile is constantly reliving a sadomasochistic fantasy organised around binaries of child and adult, desire and disillusionment, naiveté and cynicism. Like a true sadomasochist, the trashophile enjoys both points of identification – transported one moment to a magical world of skeletons, dinosaurs, vampires, and spaceships, and in the next, laughing at the cheap chicanery that long ago, both culturally and personally, held the power to captivate.[96]

Still, by only self-identifying as part of the 'exploited' audience in the past, Sconce differentiates himself from the youth audiences to which more current high-concept genre cinema caters, because there is not enough apparent pastness for contemporary Hollywood films to become nostalgised in like manner as historically dated texts.[97] Consequently, contemporary Hollywood cinema is more likely to be seen, in Matt Hills's words, as '[t]oo obviously a commercial success at the time of its initial release to be feted as underground trash, too historically recent to be recuperated as archival exploitation cinema, too standardised or proficient in its direction to be "bad"'.[98]

As Hills notes, this is a familiar strategy in fan discourse, safely associating with the childhood past both the origins of one's fandom and the 'feminised' ability to be excessively affected by a film, so that the adult self can reassert its more rational, masculine connoisseurship. This lost childhood self is both discursively absented and nostalgically valued, given lingering hopes that a contemporary film could thrill one the way films did when one was younger.[99] As I suggested earlier, imaginatively placing oneself in the shoes of past exploitation patrons like drive-in attendees thereby allows more sincere reactions to commingle uneasily with exploitation cinema's populist appeal to the implicitly 'naive' audiences (Sconce's 'screaming yokels') from which the more mature fan as seasoned connoisseur must distinguish him/herself.

These tensions are especially marked during processes of intertextual adaptation, such as remakes or pastiches of beloved older films, because intertextuality 'can work as sedimentary layers'. That is, 'an "underground" layer may prove to be considerably more important to any given audience member, serving as bedrock to any new layer of silt, text to an adaptation's paratext'.[100] Indeed, as my later chapters show, many fans view the remaking or pastiching of cherished texts as a threat to subcultural capital rather than as an opportunity for younger fans to develop a sincere investment in earlier textual iterations via the cultural visibility of a more recent iteration. Subcultural ideologies of exclusivity and connoisseurship tend to play down how the increased accessibility of exploitation films on home video can provide fan cultures with new blood in the form of younger viewers who gradually develop deep commitments, not just dilettantish fancies, towards these films. Similarly, remediation processes and intergenerational participation do not simply represent a threatening surrender of subcultural capital to outsiders but can provide even long-term fans with fodder for their own ongoing textual discoveries as once-obscure films are located and re-released on video.

Echoing sentiments held by many of his fellow exploitation fans, Sconce's self-described 'elitist populist' stance hopes that current audiences 'might be liberated from the venal stupidity of those who hold the culture industries hostage'. His stance may itself be a nostalgic throwback to older conceptions of fan cultures as adversarial towards the culture industries, yet I believe such nostalgic self-images of subcultural 'resistance' retain their affectivity as desires to defer a subculture's own redundant obsolescence in a mediascape brimming with texts that easily circulate far beyond subcultural boundaries. Adding nostalgia's affective pull to his arguments about economistic struggles over subcultural capital allows Sconce to couch his political critique as jealous revenge over how 'the object of one's affection is constantly threatening to "move on" and start over, sleeping with younger and more brutish audiences'.[101] Yet, his scorn is ultimately directed less at younger, less sophisticated viewers than at a promiscuously fickle film industry that seems guilty of personal betrayal by defying its long-term relationship with genre fans.

As one grows older over the course of a fan career, aging out of the youth-oriented demographic targeted by so many media industries, one may gradually find that a nostalgic longing for the past is infused with a class-based recognition of *one's own exploitation* over time. That is, we can find exploitation cinema's status as a once-timely and highly marketable commodity kept unexpectedly alive in the marketplace echoed in a self-reflexive awareness about one's own labour as extracted, bought and sold over the years – as seen, for example, in Sconce's cynicism about the crass economic motives of the culture industries that no longer target him as a prime film-goer. Hence, if these texts are often sold as retro-coded products when they variously resurface as commodities in the contemporary marketplace, this is significant because *retro* offers a particular species of nostalgia that invokes ironic distance as well as earnest sentiment towards the past. As Elizabeth Guffey argues, 'Like the retro rockets that introduced the term into popular speech in the early 1960s, retro provides a form of deceleration or opposite thrust, forcing us to take stock of our perpetual drive to move forwards in space and time. [. . .] Rather than emphasising continuity, retro implicitly ruptures us from what came before' by exposing 'past futures' to the supposedly 'less naive' perspective of present scrutiny.[102] These retro items may not only transport the fan to imagined earlier moments of personal/cultural history but also provoke the collector towards 'reject[ing] the continual abandonment of objects [and, by extension, the people whose identities those objects help to construct] in commodity culture'.[103]

Inspired by cultural memories that can also evoke the disparate class connotations of *lieux de mémoire* such as drive-in theatres (or, in the next chapter, grind houses), self-reflexivity about one's changing relationship to consumerism over a lifetime helps explain 'the mix of desire and acceptance of its impossibility that is embodied in the . . . idea of yearning' for a youthful time of greater (future) class possibility.[104] It is precisely because 'success in a heteronormative, capitalist society equates too easily to specific forms of reproductive maturity combined with wealth accumulation'[105] that the fan's retreat into memories of earlier lived/cultural times is often denigrated by non-fans as a failure to move beyond juvenile pursuits. As such, fans' nostalgia may play into contemporary consumer economies through the consumption of remediated films but it need not fully endorse capitalism's temporal instrumentality towards a future associated with maturation and material success – particularly among collectors of residual video objects such as outdated/degraded VHS and DVD editions. Indeed, it is precisely the outdated/degraded edition's temporal distance from present market demands that allows collectors to fetishise even fragmented and mutilated iterations of a film (including the aforementioned déclassé DVD transfers). As Kate Egan suggests, residual video collecting can even become a way for aging fans to imaginatively maintain a nostalgically youthful area of their lives, as a sort of mnemonic refuge against the demands of adult responsibility and conformity.[106] Nostalgia for the retro video object might thereby inspire reflection on imagined futures that never came to be, spurring desires to reformulate the cultural past as vital raw material for changing the present – an impulse arguably shared with many of the retrosploitation films discussed in subsequent chapters.

Christian Thorne proposes that the multifarious forms of American retro culture are united by a 'desire, delusional and utopian in equal proportion, for a relationship to objects *as something other than commodities*'. Utopian thought and apocalyptic thought share a preoccupation with the re-enchantment of objects, although the overabundant plenty of classical Utopias now seems, 'under late capital, little more than hideous afterimages of the marketplace itself, spilling over with redundant and misdistributed goods, stripped of their revolutionary energy'. In images of apocalypse, however, commodities 'will crawl out from under the patina of mediocrity that the exchange relationship ordinarily imposes on them. If faced with shortage, each object will come to seem unique again, fully deserving of our attention'.[107]

The almost child-like re-enchantment of (re)discovering 'new' things can thereby reveal what Walter Benjamin considered the 'forgotten futures' which commodities tend to disavow as they settle into routine modes of consumption. These nostalgic traces of other, non-teleological ways in which history could have unfolded represent 'the index of a *temporality* that he considered key to capitalist modernity: the return of archaic, cyclical, mythical time in the accelerated succession of the new (fashion, technology), the mingling of the recently obsolescent "with what has been forgotten of the prehistoric world"'.[108] On one hand, then, I have suggested in this chapter that the historicity encoded into remediated filmic texts may represent an attempt by media distributors to profitably re-enchant these commodities by associating them with more 'conservative' periods of greater textual scarcity. But, on the other hand, these varied attempts do not necessarily obey a clear teleology of mnemonic value among fans. They can thus result in ambivalent reactions among those, like Sconce, who value the historically obscure text's 'rebelliously' deferred obsolescence as a signifier of their own identities but who still scorn the very culture industries that revive retro-coded texts for profit.

Beneath nostalgic images such as the weather-beaten drive-in screen lying dormant on the American landscape lurks this retro-apocalyptic longing for greater textual scarcity, as if projecting on to the past a powerful desire for capitalism's collapse and the attendant cherishing of filmic commodities circulated for mass consumption. Collecting outdated cultural artefacts and images that have been re-appropriated as camp or kitsch, for example, 'constitutes a discourse on the constant re-creation of novelty within the exchange economy'. Accordingly, in their 'collapsing of the narrow time and deep space of the popular into the deep time and narrow space of the antique, they serve an ideology which would jumble class relations, an ideology which substitutes a labor of perpetual consumption for a labor of production'.[109] That is, collecting once-obscure texts becomes not only a means of remembering the wild iterations of past film cycles but also, paradoxically, a means of 'forgetting – starting again in such a way that a finite number of elements create, by virtue of their combination, an infinite reverie'[110] that might nourish one's ongoing personal history as a fan.

The fact that once-timely exploitation films persist indefinitely, despite their relative neglect in official film histories, seemingly separates them from the remediation of more mainstream Hollywood texts with wider cultural currency – but their 'rebellious' refusal to vanish into the cultural past remains largely contingent on consumer culture's own industrial imperatives to preserve cultural memory's raw material as delivery platforms become obsolete. As such, the home video marketplace offers multiple intersections along exploitation cinema's historical road from the drive-in to the living room, with each potential point of access pointing back towards a nostalgic past that helps ground the fan's identity but can ultimately remain as ambivalently regarded as the present and future. Consuming the surviving exploitation text, then, even when remediated to accentuate its retro qualities, need not entail a wholesale capitulation to the socio-economic status quo but can also inspire an awareness of capitalism's unfulfilled promises in the present. As the next chapter elaborates, for instance, implanted nostalgias for niche exhibition contexts associated with social and material decay, such as the urban grind house, draw upon the legacy of long-standing class and gender inequalities for their appeals to subcultural 'authenticity', even as these same appeals are both undergirded and undercut by neo-liberal market forces which measure social value by the freedom to spend.

Notes

1. Michel Maffesoli, *The Time of the Tribes: The Decline of Individualism in Mass Society*, trans. Don Smith (London: Sage, 1996), pp. 136–7.
2. Joe Bob Briggs, *Joe Bob Goes to the Drive-In* (New York: Delacorte Press, 1986), p. 314.
3. The VHS release *Drive-In Madness!* (1987), for example, intersperses exploitation film trailers, footage of classic cars entering a modern-day drive-in, and interviews with exploitation film-makers about their drive-in memories.
4. Stephen Thrower, *Nightmare USA: The Untold Story of the Exploitation Independents* (Godalming: FAB Press, 2007), p. 13.
5. Janelle L. Wilson, *Nostalgia: Sanctuary of Meaning* (Lewisburg, PA: Bucknell University Press, 2005), p. 86.
6. Sarah Thornton, *Club Cultures: Music, Media, and Subcultural Capital* (Middletown, CT: Wesleyan University Press, 1996), pp. 68, 118.
7. Mary Morley Cohen, 'Forgotten Audiences in the Passion Pits: Drive-in Theatres and Changing Spectator Practices in Post-War America', *Film History* 6, no. 4 (1994): 475.
8. Robert C. Allen, 'Relocating American Film History: The "Problem" of the Empirical', *Cultural Studies* 20, no. 1 (2006): 62.

9. American Society of Planning Officials, *Planning Advisory Service: Drive-in Theaters*, Information Report no. 9 (Chicago: American Society of Planning Officials, 1949), p. 11.
10. Morley Cohen, 'Forgotten Audiences in the Passion Pits', pp. 477–9.
11. Kerry Segrave, *Drive-In Theaters: A History from Their Inception in 1933* (Jefferson, NC: McFarland, 1992), p. 147. Drive-ins specifically targeted family audiences by building playgrounds and other child-friendly attractions within easy view of the screen.
12. Morley Cohen, 'Forgotten Audiences in the Passion Pits', pp. 481, 483.
13. Blair Davis, *The Battle for the Bs: 1950s Hollywood and the Rebirth of Low-Budget Cinema* (New Brunswick, NJ: Rutgers University Press, 2012), p. 79.
14. Anthony Downs, 'Where the Drive-in Fits into the Movie Industry', in *Exhibition: The Film Reader*, ed. Ina Rae Hark (London: Routledge, 2002), pp. 123–4.
15. Ibid.
16. Segrave, *Drive-In Theaters*, pp. 30, 54, 59, 142. On the 'animosity of neighborhood and first-run theaters' toward drive-ins, see Rodney Luther, 'Marketing Aspects of Drive-in Theaters', *The Journal of Marketing* 15, no. 1 (1950): 43–5.
17. Bruce A. Austin, 'The Development and Decline of the Drive-In Movie Theater', in *Current Research in Film: Audiences, Economics, and Law*, vol. 1, ed. Bruce A. Austin (Norwood, NJ: Ablex, 1985), p. 67.
18. Downs, 'Where the Drive-in Fits into the Movie Industry', p. 124.
19. Thomas Doherty, *Teenagers and Teenpics: The Juvenilization of American Movies in the 1950s* (Philadelphia: Temple University Press, 2002), p. 91.
20. Rodney Luther, 'Drive-in Theaters: Rags to Riches in Five Years', *Hollywood Quarterly* 5, no. 4 (1951): 403, 410.
21. Kevin Heffernan, *Ghouls, Gimmicks, and Gold: Horror Films and the American Movie Business, 1953–1968* (Durham, NC: Duke University Press, 2004), pp. 65–72.
22. Roger Corman, personal communication, 18 April 2014.
23. Roger Corman, interviewed in Steven Kurutz, 'Why Did B-Movies Vanish From Theaters?', *Wall Street Journal*, 18 September 2010, http://blogs.wsj.com/speakeasy/2010/09/18/film-school-roger-corman-explains-why-b-movies-vanished-from-theaters (accessed 10 January 2011).
24. Segrave, *Drive-In Theaters*, p. 59. Los Angeles drive-ins also experimented in the early 1950s with 'opening a first-run picture simultaneously at several strategically-located drive-ins in one metropolitan area, rather than at one downtown theater' (Downs, 'Where the Drive-in Fits into the Movie Industry', p. 124).
25. Austin, 'The Development and Decline of the Drive-In Movie Theater', p. 64.
26. Justin Wyatt, 'Selling "Atrocious Sexual Behavior": Revising Sexualities in the Marketplace for Adult Film of the 1960s', in *Swinging Single: Representing Sexuality in the 1960s*, eds Hilary Radner and Moya Luckett

(Minneapolis: University of Minnesota Press, 1999), pp. 116–17. Sexual content appearing on drive-in screens visible to curious youths or distractible drivers on nearby roads was a recurrent concern.
27. Jon Lewis, *Hollywood v. Hard Core: How the Struggle over Censorship Saved the Modern Film Industry* (New York: New York University Press, 2000), p. 128.
28. Segrave, *Drive-In Theaters*, pp. 155, 162, 189–99 (quoted).
29. Andrew Horton, 'Turning On and Tuning Out at the Drive-In: An American Phenomenon Survives and Thrives', *Journal of Popular Film* 5, no. 3/4 (1976): 240. In his survey of drive-in patrons in 1981–82, Bruce Austin found that roughly half of respondents planned ahead to go to the theatre – and these respondents were more likely to be drawn by a specific film – whereas some were primarily interested in the drive-in experience itself, regardless of the films being shown ('The Development and Decline of the Drive-In Movie Theater', p. 83).
30. See Gregory A. Waller's articles 'An Annotated Filmography of R-Rated Sexploitation Films Released During the 1970s', *Journal of Popular Film and Television* 9, no. 2 (1981): 98–112; and 'Auto-Erotica: Some Notes on Comic Softcore Films for the Drive-In Circuit', *Journal of Popular Culture* 17, no. 2 (1983): 135-41.
31. Robert Osborne, 'Movie Review: *Hollywood High*', *The Hollywood Reporter*, 26 September 1977, p. 8.
32. Will Tusher, 'Corman Films Hide Nudity, Woo TV's $$', *The Hollywood Reporter*, 24 December 1975, pp. 1, 19; and Sharon Lee Dobuler, 'IIC to Produce Programs for Television, Also Movies', *The Hollywood Reporter*, 29 April 1980, p. 2.
33. Jim Hillier and Aaron Lipstadt, 'The Economics of Independence: Roger Corman and New World Pictures, 1970–1980', *Movie*, no. 31/32 (1986): 49. There were, however, interesting exceptions to this pattern, such as when New World distributed Ingmar Bergman's *Cries and Whispers* (1972) to drive-ins – a choice that allegedly delighted the Swedish auteur, according to Roger Corman with Jim Jerome, *How I Made a Hundred Movies in Hollywood and Never Lost a Dime* (New York: Random House, 1990), p. 190.
34. Derek Nystrom, *Hard Hats, Rednecks, and Macho Men: Class in 1970s American Cinema* (New York: Oxford University Press, 2009), pp. 47, 96–100. Quote at p. 47.
35. Hillier and Lipstadt, 'The Economics of Independence', 52–3; Ed Lowry, 'Dimension Pictures: Portrait of a 70's Independent', *The Velvet Light Trap*, no. 22 (1986): 73–4; and Frank Barron, 'New World Puts B.O. During 1970–78 Span at $392 Mil', *The Hollywood Reporter*, 15 June 1977, pp. 1, 19.
36. Segrave, *Drive-In Theaters*, pp. 179–81.
37. Christine Sprengler, *Screening Nostalgia: Populuxe Props and Technicolor Aesthetics in Contemporary American Film* (New York: Berghahn Books, 2009), pp. 48, 58–9.

38. See Heffernan, *Ghouls, Gimmicks, and Gold*, pp. 154–79; Davis, *Battle for the Bs*, pp. 132–43; and Chris Poggiali, '*Drive-In Movie* on WNEW Metromedia Channel 5, 1981–1988', DVD Drive-In, http://www.dvddrive-in.com/TV%20Guide/driveinmovie5.htm (accessed 23 January 2012).
39. Dan Doperalski, 'Drive-Ins in Digital Bind', *Variety*, 8 February 2012, http://www.variety.com/article/VR1118049857?refCatId=13 (accessed 8 February 2012).
40. Mark Jancovich, 'Cult Fictions: Cult Movies, Subcultural Capital, and the Production of Cultural Distinctions', *Cultural Studies* 16, no. 2 (2002): 315–17.
41. Nystrom, *Hard Hats, Rednecks, and Macho Men*, p. 10.
42. William Ian Miller, *The Anatomy of Disgust* (Cambridge, MA: Harvard University Press, 1997), pp. 241–2.
43. Lawrence W. Levine, *Highbrow/Lowbrow: The Emergence of Cultural Hierarchy in America* (Cambridge, MA: Harvard University Press, 1988), pp. 230–1.
44. Jeffrey Sconce, '"Trashing" the Academy: Taste, Excess, and an Emerging Politics of Cinematic Style', *Screen* 36, no. 4 (1995): 377–8, 379. Quote at p. 379.
45. Nystrom, *Hard Hats, Rednecks, and Macho Men*, p. 41.
46. Pierre Bourdieu, *Distinction: A Social Critique of the Judgement of Taste*, trans. Richard Nice (Cambridge, MA: Harvard University Press, 1984), p. 62.
47. Jancovich, 'Cult Fictions', pp. 311–12.
48. Sconce, '"Trashing" the Academy', p. 373.
49. Matt Hills, *Fan Cultures* (New York: Routledge, 2002), pp. 16–17.
50. Sconce, '"Trashing" the Academy', p. 383.
51. Paul McDonald, *Video and DVD Industries* (London: British Film Institute, 2007), pp. 70, 151.
52. Barbara Klinger, *Beyond the Multiplex: Cinema, New Technologies, and the Home* (Berkeley: University of California Press, 2006), pp. 63–4, 75, 87.
53. McDonald, *Video and DVD Industries*, p. 93.
54. Jeffrey Sconce, in Joe Bob Briggs, et al., 'Cult Cinema: A Critical Symposium', *Cineaste* 34, no. 1 (2008): 49.
55. W. James Booth, *Communities of Memory: On Witness, Identity, and Justice* (Ithaca, NY: Cornell University Press, 2006), pp. 30–1, 35.
56. Andreas Huyssen, 'Present Pasts: Media, Politics, Amnesia', *Public Culture* 12, no. 1 (2000): 24–5.
57. Klinger, *Beyond the Multiplex*, p. 2.
58. Paul Willemen, 'Through the Glass Darkly: Cinephilia Reconsidered', in *Looks and Frictions: Essays in Cultural Studies and Film Theory* (Bloomington: Indiana University Press, 1994), p. 250.
59. Frederick Wasser, *Veni, Vidi, Video: The Hollywood Empire and the VCR* (Austin: University of Texas Press, 2001), p. 198.

60. Morley Cohen, 'Forgotten Audiences in the Passion Pits', p. 479.
61. Joshua M. Greenberg, *From Betamax to Blockbuster: Video Stores and the Invention of Movies on Video* (Cambridge, MA: MIT Press, 2008), pp. 93, 99.
62. See Joan Hawkins, *Cutting Edge: Art-Horror and the Horrific Avant-Garde* (Minneapolis: University of Minnesota Press, 2000), pp. 38–41. Much as one may focus intensely on a specific television programme at home, drive-in spectatorship is not an *inherently* distracted experience, as personal and anecdotal experiences attest.
63. David F. Friedman with Don de Nevi, *A Youth in Babylon: Confessions of a Trash-Film King* (Buffalo, NY: Prometheus Books, 1990), p. 100.
64. Austin, 'The Development and Decline of the Drive-In Movie Theater', pp. 75, 79–80.
65. Thornton, *Club Cultures*, p. 25.
66. Nystrom, *Hard Hats, Rednecks, and Macho Men*, p. 14.
67. Ibid., pp. 90–2, 94.
68. Miller, *The Anatomy of Disgust*, p. 253. On the gendered ambivalence of working-class strength, also see Bourdieu, *Distinction*, p. 479.
69. See, for example, Scott Herring, '"Hixploitation" Cinema, Regional Drive-Ins, and the Cultural Emergence of a New Queer Right', *GLQ* 20, no. 1–2 (2014): 108–10.
70. Vera Dika, *Recycled Culture in Contemporary Art and Film: The Uses of Nostalgia* (Cambridge: Cambridge University Press, 2003), p. 125.
71. Steve Chibnall, 'Double Exposures: Observations on *The Flesh and Blood Show*', in *Trash Aesthetics: Popular Culture and its Audience*, eds Deborah Cartmell, I. Q. Hunter, Heidi Kaye, and Imelda Whelehan (London: Pluto Press, 1997), p. 85.
72. Morley Cohen, 'Forgotten Audiences in the Passion Pits', p. 482.
73. Sconce, '"Trashing" the Academy', p. 384.
74. Linda Ruth Williams, *The Erotic Thriller in Contemporary Cinema* (Bloomington: Indiana University Press, 2005), p. 289.
75. See, for example, The Jaded Viewer, '*Nun of That* (review)', The Jaded Viewer, last modified 19 February 2010, http://jadedviewer.blogspot.com/2010/02/nun-of-that-review.html (accessed 26 January 2012); and Zev Toledano, 'Herschell Gordon Lewis', The Last Exit, http://thelastexit.net/cinema/lewis.html (accessed 26 January 2012).
76. See Jacinda Read, 'The Cult of Masculinity: From Fan-boys to Academic Bad-boys', in *Defining Cult Movies: The Cultural Politics of Oppositional Taste*, eds Mark Jancovich, Antonio Lázaro Reboll, Julian Stringer and Andy Willis (Manchester: Manchester University Press, 2003), pp. 54–70.
77. Richard Terdiman, *Present Past: Modernity and the Memory Crisis* (Ithaca, NY: Cornell University Press, 1993), p. 48.
78. Elizabeth E. Guffey, *Retro: The Culture of Revival* (London: Reaktion Books, 2006), p. 112.

79. Briggs, *Joe Bob Goes to the Drive-In*, p. 210. Testifying to his influence on a younger generation of film-makers, Briggs has a cameo in the retro-styled slasher homage *The Sleeper* (2012) (see Chapter 3) and announces that film's own 'drive-in total' in a DVD special feature.
80. Calvin Trillin, 'The Life and Times of Joe Bob Briggs, So Far', *American Stories* (New York: Ticknor & Fields, 1991), pp. 42, 44, 56. Quote at p. 44.
81. Ibid., pp. 50, 53, 55.
82. David Andrews, *Soft in the Middle: The Contemporary Softcore Feature in Its Contexts* (Columbus: Ohio State University Press, 2006), pp. 199–200.
83. The Primal Root, 'Review: *Black Devil Doll*', From Dusk Till Con, http://www.fromdusktillcon.com/content/27-reviews/744-review-black-devil-doll (accessed 26 January 2012).
84. Linda Badley, 'Bringing It All Back Home: Horror Cinema and Video Culture', in *Horror Zone: The Cultural Experience of Contemporary Horror Cinema*, ed. Ian Conrich (London: I. B. Tauris, 2010), pp. 49–50.
85. Kate Egan, *Trash or Treasure? Censorship and the Changing Meanings of the Video Nasties* (Manchester: Manchester University Press, 2007), pp. 212, 218.
86. Will Straw, '"100 Action Classics": Dilapidation from the Big Screen to the Budget DVD Corpus' (paper presented to the 2010 Society for Cinema and Media Studies Conference, Los Angeles, CA, 17–21 March 2010).
87. On the aesthetic appreciation of age and decay, also see David Lowenthal, *The Past is a Foreign Country* (Cambridge: Cambridge University Press, 1985), ch. 4.
88. Vinzenz Hediger, 'The Original is Always Lost: Film History, Copyright Industries, and the Problem of Reconstruction', in *Cinephilia: Movies, Love, and Memory*, eds Marijke de Valck and Malte Hagener (Amsterdam: Amsterdam University Press, 2005), pp. 136, 140, 142, 147.
89. Raiford Guins, 'Blood and Black Gloves on Shiny Discs: New Media, Old Tastes, and the Remediation of Italian Horror Films in the United States', in *Horror International*, eds Steven Jay Schneider and Tony Williams (Detroit: Wayne State University Press, 2005), pp. 21, 26–9.
90. Howard Hughes, *Cinema Italiano: The Complete Guide from Classics to Cult* (London: I. B. Tauris, 2011), p. 154. Also see Lucas Hilderbrand, *Inherent Vice: Bootleg Histories of Videotape and Copyright* (Durham, NC: Duke University Press, 2009), ch. 4.
91. Klinger, *Beyond the Multiplex*, pp. 62–3, 75.
92. Ibid., pp. 139, 159.
93. Paul Watson, 'There's No Accounting for Taste: Exploitation Cinema and the Limits of Film Theory', in *Trash Aesthetics*, p. 80.
94. The invitation for fans to make their own ersatz posters on the website Something Awful indeed coincided with the 2007 theatrical release of *Grindhouse*. See Josh 'Livestock' Boruff, 'Photoshop Phriday: Grindhouse Movies', Something Awful, last modified 4 May 2007, http://www.some

thingawful.com/d/photoshop-phriday/grindhouse-movies.php (accessed 30 January 2011). A more recent example is available from Cracked Readers, 'B-Movie Posters for Classic Films', Cracked.com, last modified 3 August 2011, http://www.cracked.com/photoplasty_235_b-movie-posters-classic-films/ (accessed 5 August 2011).
95. Jeffrey Sconce, 'Movies: A Century of Failure', in *Sleaze Artists: Cinema at the Margins of Taste, Style, and Politics*, ed. Jeffrey Sconce (Durham, NC: Duke University Press, 2007), pp. 288, 292, 294.
96. Ibid., pp. 290–1.
97. Ibid., p. 278.
98. Matt Hills, 'Para-Paracinema: The *Friday the 13th* Film Series as Other to Trash and Legitimate Film Cultures', in *Sleaze Artists*, p. 232.
99. Matt Hills, *The Pleasures of Horror* (London: Continuum, 2005), pp. 77, 80.
100. Jonathan Gray, *Show Sold Separately: Promos, Spoilers, and Other Media Paratexts* (New York: New York University Press, 2010), p. 125.
101. Sconce, 'Movies', pp. 283, 302.
102. Guffey, *Retro*, pp. 27–8.
103. Mary Desjardins, 'Ephemeral Culture/eBay Culture: Film Collectibles and Fan Investments', in *Everyday eBay: Culture, Collecting, and Desire*, eds Ken Hillis, Michael Petit and Nathan Scott Epley (New York: Routledge, 2006), pp. 37–40. Quote at p. 38.
104. Annette Kuhn, *Dreaming of Fred and Ginger: Cinema and Cultural Memory* (New York: New York University Press, 2002), p. 232.
105. Judith Halberstam, *The Queer Art of Failure* (Durham, NC: Duke University Press, 2011), p. 2.
106. Egan, *Trash or Treasure?*, pp. 121, 156, 163–4, 170, 175.
107. Christian Thorne, 'The Revolutionary Energy of the Outmoded', *October*, no. 104 (2003): 107, 113. Original italics.
108. Miriam Bratu Hansen, 'Benjamin and Cinema: Not a One-Way Street', *Critical Inquiry* 25, no. 2 (1999): 331. Original italics. Also see Guffey, *Retro*, p. 24.
109. Susan Stewart, *On Longing: Narratives of the Miniature, the Gigantic, the Souvenir, the Collection* (Baltimore: Johns Hopkins University Press, 1984), pp. 167–8.
110. Ibid., p. 152.

CHAPTER 2

42nd Street Forever? Constructing 'Grindhouse Cinema' from Exhibition to Genre to Transmedia Concept

> Like everything else in the Square, the spirits are sites of struggle while functioning as a marketing tool. And each shift in the district's history reflects competing fantasies and desires [. . .] The tour guide echoes an official fantasy, but critics of the New Times Square are equally nostalgic and limited in the ghosts that they choose to foreground.
>
> Daniel Makagon, *Where the Ball Drops*[1]

Even more so than the drive-in theatres explored in the previous chapter, *grindhouse* has become both a contemporary signifier for interpreting exploitation cinema's wildly diverse past and a cinephiliac cue for remembering such films within the realm of a specific historical exhibition context. Most commonly associated with the 1960s and 1970s, grind houses are today regarded as independently operated theatres located in downtown or inner-city areas, showing double and triple features of exploitation films at all hours for a low admission price. For exploitation fans, they are also associated with violence, sexual deviance, dirtiness and cheapness – qualities reputedly shared by many of the films shown in such venues. In examining this phenomenon as an extended case study in the implantation of nostalgias, I shall briefly sketch the discursive history of these theatres to determine how and why the label 'grindhouse' gradually expanded from a theatre type to a generic term applied to a range of exploitation films in the post-studio era. My goal is not merely to complicate the present uses of the term but also to suggest how non-normative exhibition sites are more likely to be coded generically, with the effect of normalising Hollywood films and exhibition. Such 'genrification' has arguably made it more possible for present-day fans to use implanted nostalgias as a means of imaginative 'time travel' to past spatio-temporal sites (as discussed in Chapter 1). Here, and in the chapters that follow, however, I also discuss the roots of a so-called 'grindhouse aesthetic' (as numerous critics and fans have dubbed it) linked to a nostalgia for *celluloid decay* – a nostalgia indexing perceived sources of *social decay* that have become classed and gendered markers of 'authenticity' among contemporary fans who imagine themselves linked across time to past grind house patrons.

Though I already cautioned in my previous chapter against over-privileging urban exhibition spaces, it is impossible to deny the centrality that the grind house has achieved in fan-cultural memory, especially in conjunction with the 2007 omnibus film of the same name. Consequently, I would argue that the urban grind house has surpassed the suburban or rural drive-in as a prominent *lieu de mémoire* in fans' consumption of exploitation films. This is especially notable if far fewer grind houses survive today than even drive-ins, initially encouraging a cultural forgetting that has paradoxically allowed the lost site's most recent reappraisal to take on a wider range of contemporary meanings in the absence of prevailing counter-evidence. If nostalgia can both promise and imperil fan-culturally valued notions of 'authenticity', then exploring how the concept of the grind house not only originally formed, but also recently expanded, lays the groundwork for understanding how it has come to serve as a fashionable word for appraising the nostalgic resurrections of exploitation cinema discussed in the following chapters.

In examining the grind house as a symbolic site of memory, we should bear in mind Edward Casey's observation that '[r]ather than thinking of remembering as a form of re-experiencing the past *per se*, we might conceive of it as an activity of *re-implacing*: re-experiencing past places. By the same token, if it is true that all memory has a bodily component or dimension, the memory-bearing body can be considered as a *body moving back in(to) place*.'[2] Yet, I propose that the memory-bearing body need not have actually attended those places, owing to the nostalgias conferred by *cultural* memories instead of by merely personal memories. As previously suggested with the example of 'drive-in movies', the spatio-temporal aspects of genre can also be linked to particular exhibition sites whose commemoration extends well beyond their former patrons. The latter-day exploitation fan who imagines him/herself as a grind house patron participates in the construction and continued circulation of cultural memories about a downmarket, largely lawless urban exhibition site where the viewer's lived experiences as a theatre-goer might seem sensuously to mirror the sleazy spectacles seen on-screen. Indeed, while perusing photos of theatre marquees as research for this chapter, it was difficult not to imagine myself walking seedy, nocturnal streets bathed in electric signage for countless sensationalised films shown in what seems, from today's retrospective viewpoint, like fittingly sordid environs. The classed and gendered distinctions, however, that fans might draw upon in privileging such exhibition sites are difficult to maintain when the films that supposedly occupied grind houses are now open to diverse audiences on home video. Accordingly, the generic uses of 'grindhouse' may largely be the product of a video-era intelligibility with which fans must labour to make sense of exploitation cinema's varied cycles; its roots, however, have earlier origins that I shall trace through a specific urban locale which has taken on mythic proportions in the fan-cultural imagination.

My argument proceeds from the assumption that genre is a categorising tool emerging from historically shifting accretions of discourses; while texts may contain qualities which are associated with certain genres, a film's reception through culturally situated discourse primarily determines its generic status. Steve Neale claims that '[c]inemas, cinema programming, and cinema specialisation' are components in the 'inter-textual relay' that institutions circulate to build and promote a generic framework.[3] Building upon this, I argue that, as a specialised theatre type, 'grindhouse' was constructed as a generic term through industrial-critical discourses originally meant to contain the disruption of economic and cultural capital wrought by these non-normative exhibition venues. While some grind houses were part of mid-size theatre chains, they were generally operated independently of the major studios' theatres and did not enjoy the benefits of major-affiliated circuits. Though their negative connotations primarily materialised during the Great Depression, the genrification of grind houses did not solidify until the 1950s and 1960s as theatre owners, critics and patrons increasingly positioned them as sites of non-mainstream consumption. Though grind houses typically showed genre films, the historical deployment of 'grindhouse' as an overarching generic term linked to 'low' culture reflects conflicts over the economic positioning of exhibition sites both during and after the studio era, especially as genre-derived cycles proliferated with the rise of independent distributors.

Such conflicts have allowed grind houses to become ghettoised in the past yet treated with ironic-cum-earnest nostalgia in recent decades. With their degraded look, hyperbolically exploitative appeals and sleazy compilations of lurid imagery, the revival of trailers for so-called 'grindhouse movies' exemplifies this mode of appreciation, standing as the primary paratextual embodiment of what has developed into a burgeoning grindhouse aesthetic extending across a variety of media platforms. As a locus for nostalgia, then, *grindhouse* has become both a symbolic space and a transmedia concept that can contain a wide variety of films championed by fans who seek (however questionably) to distinguish themselves from 'mainstream' viewers. In this sense, the use of 'grindhouse' as a generic signifier illustrates that the term itself has become spatio-temporally mobile with the spread of video technologies promulgated by the same (neo-liberal) economic forces that have since renewed the very urban areas where such theatres were once located. During the home video era, *gentrification* and *genrification* have ironically gone hand in hand when the grind house as transmedia concept has been repackaged for high-concept marketing and domestic consumption alike – as demonstrated by the recent proliferation of grindhouse trailer compilation DVDs.

Because New York City's 42nd Street at Times Square – or 'the Deuce', as it was affectionately dubbed – has long served as the *actual* historical place that subsequently inspired the grind house as a *generic place*, I shall look at trends in how its theatres were described in the trade and popular press since the 1920s. These shifting discourses help illuminate how 42nd Street's urban entertainment district became increasingly ghettoised – but also, paralleling the exploitation films shown there, how the area itself became subject to a restorative remediation in more recent decades. Yet, as expansive as the generic shorthand 'grindhouse' can be as a mnemonic category for exploitation films of many different periods, genres, cycles and national contexts, the selectivity of fans' cultural memories also tends to limit the category's elasticity by oversimplifying the sheer range of films that appeared in actual grind houses. This selectivity can be examined by looking at how grindhouse film trailers have been compiled and remediated for a plethora of uses, effectively setting the stage for the cycle of retro-coded, 'grindhouse-style' pastiches analysed in the next two chapters.

By exploring how and why discourses about 42nd Street's grind houses have become mnemonically important to fans, we can understand better not only the nostalgias that have powerfully charged the remediation of older texts and paratexts but also contemporary revisionings of exploitation cinema's past. Furthermore, the process of excavating and tracking the cultural history of these influential grind houses reveals anxieties that contemporary fans may experience when their nostalgias for these exhibition sites are complicated by economic forces simultaneously producing the *actual* grind house's physical erasure and the *symbolic* grind house's cultural visibility. Accordingly, this chapter begins with the history of 42nd Street's grind houses during the pre-video era before returning to how cultural memories about grind houses have been mobilised during the very period in which these distinctive exhibition spaces were finally supplanted by home video consumption.

Early Class Connotations of Grind Houses

The *Oxford English Dictionary* defines a 'grind house' as a 'cinema showing a variety of films in continuous succession, usually with low admission fees and freq. concentrating on material regarded as of poor quality or little merit. Also: a burlesque theatre; a strip club.' This definition suggests that the term has long connoted not only a specific site of exhibition but also films of dubious social worth. The *OED* cites the earliest extant mention of 'grind house' as a December 1923 issue of *Variety*.[4] While *Variety* may have originated the term as part of its house slang for various kinds of theatres, the adjectival use of 'grind' was probably adopted from existing slang. The *OED*, for example, suggests that it may have derived from 'grinder', meaning 'a barker who works continuously in front of a single show'. This connotation refers to the coercion of viewers into attending a performance through ballyhoo, as in 'working the grind' or 'grinding in front of the theatre'. Indeed, grind houses often used garish ballyhoo, as Rialto impresario Arthur Mayer testified when describing his 42nd Street lobby advertising displays and lurid retitling of films.[5] Anthony Bianco also notes that in 1953–54, 'all fourteen grind movie theaters on or near 42nd Street ... risked being closed down under the state's so-called decency statute unless they toned down their advertising displays'.[6] With its connotations of sensationalised promotion and gimmickry, this definition of grind as coercion through ballyhoo most closely resembles the meaning of 'grind policy', a common trade term that, judging from its undefined use in the 1923 *Variety* article, probably dates from some years earlier.

Grind policy refers to the screening of films continuously throughout the day and evening for cut-rate admission prices – a 'grind scale' that often increased over the course of the day and peaked below the standard ticket prices of non-grind houses. On 42nd Street during World War II, for example, tickets started at 25 cents in the morning, eventually increasing to 85 or 98 cents in the evening; pre-war ticket prices at these houses averaged 11 to 25 cents. By the 1970s, a typical grind scale was '8 am to noon, $1.25, noon to five, $2.50, five 'til closing, $5.00'.[7] Most 42nd Street grind houses offered midnight shows daily by the 1930s; common operating hours by the 1960s were 8 a.m. to 4 a.m. These long hours also implied an all-day 'grinding' of the projector and film prints, causing significant wear and tear to these physical elements.

During the 1920s, the grind business model assumed that higher audience turnover at cheaper ticket rates would be more profitable than the dominant, non-grind practice of offering less than half a dozen shows per day, and was especially different from the staggering of selected seating prices at first-run picture palaces. The original 1923 *Variety* article differentiates 'legitimate houses' from 'grind houses', reporting that box-office returns dwindled in a Toronto grind house that tried reverting to two shows per day at higher ticket prices after audiences used to paying grind scale for tickets did not adjust their buying habits accordingly. Furthermore, the article reports that, in American theatres, where 'the two-a-day policy has been tried with pictures at $1.50 top in houses that have been playing a grind policy at a popular admission scale[,] the same story seems to be indicated', but 'the pictures can go from a run in a legitimate house or a picture house that has a definitively established scale of $1.50 or $2 top, to a grind house and break records'.[8] A 1929 *Washington Post* article also notes that twelve extended-run houses grossed $3,281,285 over a six-month period, while only eight 'so-called "grind" houses' took in $9,326,673 in comparison.[9] Even from these early mentions, it is clear that grind houses could pose potential economic threats to normative exhibition practices, and this would become more apparent when theatres were forced to change tactics for survival during the Depression. Because of their potential profitability, grind policies were also not exclusive to movie theatres but increasingly used (to the consternation of overworked performers) in vaudeville and burlesque theatres beginning in the late 1920s and early 1930s.[10]

The initial maligning of grind houses was partly linked to the 'low' or 'mass' cultural associations of cinema as an entertainment form in general. This was especially the case when legitimate theatres facing economic peril during the Depression were converted into grind houses for movies and other 'low' entertainments, marking the supposed illegitimacy of these latter tenants. A 1931 *New York Times* article, for example, laments how

> the carnival spirit reigns high with burlesque shows at the Republic and the Eltinge, vaudeville at the Lyric, and a 'grind' policy of films at Wallack's ... What it all comes down to, if you ask for figures, is this: that of the seventy-six New York theatres recognized as being capable of playing legitimate productions, fourteen have been diverted to other uses.[11]

More blatant in these low-class connotations is an 'Elegy on Forty-second Street's Last Legitimate Theatre' that reads, 'The announcement that the New Amsterdam Theatre has been sold for a "grind" house is another indication that the old order has indeed changed. For the New Amsterdam was once the citadel of show business, aloof, aristocratic and rich'.[12]

Much like the drive-in theatres discussed in Chapter 1, the economically undifferentiated seating in grind houses, allowing a greater intermingling of classes, may have also contributed to their eventual disrepute, as retrospectively suggested by a 1963 *Boxoffice* article on young suburbanites trekking back to the city for movies: 'the roadshow picture, the film that calls for reserved seats . . . like a legit stage show, gives the theatregoer a feeling of importance or status, unlike the grind show, where anybody can buy a ticket whenever he's willing to stand in line'.[13] The sheer increase in patronage under grind policies arguably encouraged grind house operators to view their patrons in terms of quantity over socio-economic 'quality', at least compared to exhibitors who prided themselves on running culturally higher establishments. Discussing the continuing success of his 'all-day-grind policy', one theatre manager remarked in 1943, 'If we sold by the seats instead of general admission, we could give only a couple of shows a day and would have to charge more'.[14]

Cut-rate ticket prices, however, were seen as heralding cut-rate products fit only for culturally lower venues. As Suzanne Mary Donahue observes,

> Exhibitors rarely used cuts in admission prices to compete with other exhibitors, because the reduction in rates would lower the standard of their theaters. If third-run theater operators lowered admission prices to increase attendance, their theaters might then become fifth- or sixth-run theaters in the eyes of distributors.[15]

Yet, this was often how grind houses lured patronage away from first-run theatres, though not without critical backlash. For example, a *New York Times* critic praised a handful of 1934 films for falling outside 'the ordinary run of "grind"-house mediocrity, the feeble-minded pap which the studio hacks manufacture like hamburger to fill exhibitor contracts'.[16] Because of the theatres' associations with 'cheapness and deterioration', the programming of 'quality' pictures in grind houses was consequently seen as having an 'undesired effect by mere association'. According to one theatre chain owner, 'If it is a good feature, there is no good reason why it should at any time be contaminated by low-type policies which in effect imply that the pictures or the theatre or both are just postponing the last pangs of death.'[17] Grind house operators, however, may have thought otherwise as they tallied their profit margins. As Rialto owner Arthur Mayer observed, 'cheap pictures and poor ones have in the past been no more invariably synonymous than expensive pictures and good'.[18] Mayer had purchased the failing Rialto from Sam Katz's Paramount Publix chain in 1936, remodelling it in a more minimalist style and adorning its entrance with outlandish ballyhoo for his horror and action double features. His deliberately downmarket changes to the Rialto distinguished him from the Balaban and Katz model of high-class theatre ownership that had gained mainstream acceptance by this period.[19]

During the studio era, the major studios could limit the flow of their product that reached independent theatres by instituting long first runs and clearance periods. This meant that theatres unaffiliated with the majors had to find additional sources of pictures to remain solvent, which pushed them towards cheap genre and exploitation films. Though grind houses primarily played the Hollywood films that eventually trickled down to them, they became increasingly associated with 'low' genre films as concerns about class became more prominent during the Depression. The Brandt family's cluster of 42nd Street theatres even became loosely promoted by genre specialisation: according to a 1954 flyer for Brandt's 42nd Street Theatres, the Times Square promised 'Always 2 top thrillers! Action hits plus Westerns'; the Lyric and Selwyn played the 'Finest first-run pictures direct from Broadway'; the Liberty was 'Where the greatest pictures return by popular demand'; the Apollo was 'Famous as the home of distinguished foreign films'; and the Victory was 'Where you can always see two unusual films'.[20]

Theatre marquee photos from the mid-1930s to late 1950s generally confirm this pattern, though exceptions flourished as films migrated from one house to another. The *New York Times* reported in 1939 on a grind house playing double features of 'worthwhile foreign films' and another playing 'those volatile Western "quickies" that seldom reach New York'. The films 'continually being revived' along 42nd Street belonged to violent, male-oriented genres like gangster, adventure, action, thriller, horror and western films.[21] Yet, many of these films were at least moderately budgeted major-studio fare, not just cheap exploitation and B pictures. James Naremore, for example, points out that film noirs like the Ernest Hemingway adaptation *The Killers* (1946) played in 42nd Street's grind houses but critics often saw such films as 'inferior or disreputable' because their exhibition context was itself seen as sleazy, cheap and potentially dangerous – indicating a conflation of film and theatre that has continued to haunt grind houses ever since.[22] This was partly due to the violent and provocative 'advertising campaigns, posters, stills, and marquee displays' used by grind house owners, which Steve Neale identifies as elements of the intertextual relay that circulates generic terms.[23] For example, licence commissioner Edward T. McCaffrey's 1954 crackdown on 42nd Street film displays followed public complaints about advertising for 'immoral, crime, and gangster pictures'.[24]

Meanwhile, independent distributors, such as Astor Pictures, Realart Pictures and Dominant Pictures, not only dealt in B films and foreign imports but also purchased exhibition rights to (and sometimes recut and retitled) older A pictures for indefinite grind house play via the states' rights market. Major studios sold national distribution rights to Astor on a percentage basis, with president Bob Savini netting 'from 10 per cent upward' by selling his 'approximately sixty features and ten short subjects' in twenty-eight exchanges throughout the country. *Scarface* (1932), for example, which 'bobbed up every month or less . . . at one of the grind houses on Forty-second Street', was shown under new titles such as *The Black Spider of Gangland* and *Wolves of the Underworld* for at least a decade after its initial release.[25] Titles exclusive to, or revived by, independent distributors increasingly set the tone for the genre types that would become broadly known as 'grindhouse films'.

Early Gender Connotations of Grind Houses

Though terms such as 'grinding house' and 'grind joint' are historical slang for brothels, of which Times Square had its fair share during the early twentieth century,[26] it is unlikely that prostitution considerably influenced the term 'grind house'. Further, the widespread perception that the term derives from the phrase 'bump and grind' (referring to the burlesque 'grind' dance) is also largely incorrect, ignoring how theatres were commonly identified in the trade and popular press by their use of a grind policy. By 1932, the Rialto had become the model that other 42nd Street grind houses followed after it began offering discount tickets to double features of subsequent-run films on an all-day schedule in 1929, two years before the first burlesque theatres even opened in the area.[27] Even if burlesque theatres sometimes survived on grind policies during the Depression, the grind dance bears little claim upon but has, nevertheless, erroneously informed the concept of grind houses.

Correct or not, this linguistic slippage became significant because, by the 1930s, cinemas and burlesque theatres were often in close proximity to one another. By 1933, many 42nd Street movie, vaudeville and burlesque theatres had adopted grind policies while many legitimate theatres had gone out of business and been converted to film or burlesque houses.[28] The Brandt family would, for instance, own ten movie grind houses on 42nd Street by the early 1940s, acquisitions made all the more possible after mayor Fiorello La Guardia's series of municipal efforts to stamp out burlesque between 1932 and 1942.[29] This conversion process arguably reinforced the confusion between movie grind houses and 'bump-and-grind houses' – a connotation solidified in the popular imagination by 42nd Street's reputation since at least the 1930s as a place of sexual licentiousness.[30] In other cities, where burlesque was not under such intense attack, movie and burlesque grind houses continued to coexist in the same urban spaces until the 1950s and 1960s when burlesque was replaced by more explicit forms of striptease.

Of course, the films shown in grind houses sometimes reinforced these gendered connotations as well. Pre-1960s classical exploitation films, for example, which were barred from playing studio-run theatres, found exhibitors in independent grind houses. Trade magazines played up the sexual associations of grind houses as well, as when a 1938 issue of *Boxoffice* described its suggested 'selling angles' for the exploitation film *It's All in Your Mind* (1937): 'In the grind houses with mainly masculine patronage – which are the feature's natural outlet – the sex angle should be stressed, with semi-nude art studies featuring lobby displays and advertising.'[31] Unlike mainstream cinema, these films were screened for adults-only audiences during the studio era, even in gender-segregated screenings if the films contained extensive sexual content – helping create the impression that grind houses were places of sexual ill-repute less suitable for women.

But even if exploitation films were not the predominant pictures shown in grind houses, the theatres still became regarded as sites of gendered tastes through their programming of male-oriented Hollywood fare – especially during the 1930s and 1940s, a period when women constituted the majority of general film-goers. As the *New York Times* reported, in 42nd Street's grind houses, '[a]ny opus with the Marx Brothers, Jimmy Cagney, Gary Cooper, George Raft, Spencer Tracy and the Dead End Kids is a practically infallible attraction, while Garbo, Rainer and the other languid ladies of the screen are greeted with profound apathy. Shirley Temple doesn't even cause a ripple at the box office.'[32] Tim Snelson and Mark Jancovich argue that the Rialto's horror-heavy programming, for example, positioned the theatre 'in direct opposition to a middlebrow leisure culture that is feminized through metaphors of consumption and domesticity'. The theatre's declared penchant for films about 'mystery, mayhem, and murder' was linked to its rough-and-tumble ambience as a 'dirty, ill-ventilated, uncomfortable' house – in other words, 'a male paradise'.[33] Such cultural distinctions would inform later conceptions of grind houses, particularly as 42nd Street theatres sought differentiation from other theatres on grind policies (and vice versa).

Increasing Ambivalence about Grind Houses

The denigration of grind houses in the trade press, subsequently picked up by critics in the popular press, was a way of distinguishing them from studio-owned theatres and independent theatres operating at higher admission prices – but this scorn was not always one-sided, suggesting a growing ambivalence within the film industry about the role of grind houses. Film reviewers in trade publications such as *Variety* often estimated the length of a film's run, with the least marketable films consigned to perhaps 'only a single day in what was called a "grind" house'.[34] Grind house runs were typically between one day and one week (though popular films could be held over for far longer) and thus seen as indiscriminately 'grinding' through different pictures with little regard for aesthetic value. Because well-worn, subsequent-run prints were cheaper to rent than first-run prints, grind house exhibitors could increase their own profitability and pay less to the studios; this would also allow them to compensate for the lower daily audience turnover rate caused by the eventual institution of double features.[35] While seemingly unviable films sometimes premiered in grind houses in an attempt to recoup production costs quickly over a few days, more successful and respected films also gradually migrated to grind houses at the end of their theatrical runs, allowing Hollywood studios to mop up residual profits there. This practice continued throughout the history of grind houses, giving them a subordinate – but still important – function in the distribution chain.

According to Douglas Gomery, double features were still uncommon during the 1920s but economic hard times during the 1930s caused audience expectations about affordable entertainment to change, leading to double bills filled out with subsequent-run A films, B films from the majors and Poverty Row, and films from independent distributors.[36] Double features did not always dominate at grind houses, because single films sometimes played all day under a grind policy, but grind houses increasingly showed double features as they became the standard exhibition practice for most theatres by the late 1930s.[37] As one theatre owner noted in 1938, 'Subsequent-run houses ... find double bills almost necessary to their success once the policy has been inaugurated.'[38] The marginalisation of grind houses was thus complicated by the fact that more and more theatres (including chain members) were reluctantly forced to adopt grind policies and double features to stay financially afloat during the Depression years.

How, then, did grind houses garner increasing disrepute if grind policies and double features became increasingly normalised in studio-owned theatres during the 1930s and 1940s? The growing ambivalence about exhibition traits most often associated with grind houses was accompanied by an intensifying industrial and critical scorn for independent downtown grind houses which had to be posited as 'bad objects' from which 'better' theatres could be differentiated. The 42nd Street grind houses themselves also aimed at differentiation from studio-owned theatres, whether by reviving violent, male-oriented films, by treating their creeping decrepitude as a positive mark of cultural distinction, or by playing exploitative films largely unavailable elsewhere. Consequently, grind houses were increasingly seen in the trade and popular press as theatres 'where programs must be sanguinary above all else'.[39]

The popular press also singled out downtown grind houses for their moral laxity, focusing on the culturally lowest pictures screened, and thereby negatively colouring more reputable films that did play there. For example, the *New York Times* observed in 1939 that the 'general loosening of moral standards which always accompanies war was being discounted in advance by a grindhouse in West Forty-second Street, which was advertising the Balinese [*sic*] film, "Isle of Paradise", with the following blistering legend on the marquee: "Hell Breaks Loose on an Island of Virgins"'.[40] According to Eric Schaefer, such exploitation films 'often gave the impression of resistant or alternative positions to mainstream films', becoming 'constructed as "renegade" movies by the mainstream picture industry and, to some extent, by the exploiteers themselves'.[41] In 1947, Ruth Inglis described the so-called 'sex circuit' as 'cheap theaters in the downtown areas of large cities featuring horror pictures and sex thrillers for transients', estimating their number at 125 theatres nationwide.[42] In collapsing several genres together as typical fare for 'transients', the notoriety of grind house content was thus linked to lower class connotations – not just attacking the alleged cheapness of the films shown but also the character of the people who frequented the theatres. These connotations became more prominent with the ghettoisation of inner-city areas during the post-studio era. Indeed, an estimated three or four hundred inner-city grind houses would exist across the nation by the late 1960s, many of them attempting to balance the decline of their urban environs with the profitable post-1950s rise of sexploitation films.[43]

Deviant Places and Deviant Audiences in the Post-studio Era

If the preceding sections sketched the origins of the 42nd Street grind house's cultural meanings, its present-day reputation has largely descended from shifts in the wider film landscape following the end of vertical integration and the subsequent expansion of the exploitation film market. The post-studio period saw these theatres' classed and gendered associations intensifying around the different audiences and programming choices that made the grind house seem a disreputable and even dangerous generic place. The lurid leisure choices associated with grind houses and their immediate environs also tended to promise a wide range of (unfulfilled) fantasies that complicated traditional urban economics, cueing (but not always resolving) their denizens' desires in ways that might not necessarily benefit the entertainment district as a whole. Like burlesque theatres before them, grind houses were seen as not just objects of moral condemnation but as a major impediment to Times Square's economic recovery and the return of legitimate theatre during the post-war era.[44]

Forty-second Street's economy diminished in part due to the growth of television but primarily because white flight moved many people to the suburbs while minorities increasingly moved to inner-city areas as industries relocated elsewhere. As Ed Guerrero says, 'a system of de facto *apartheid* was stabilized and rigidly maintained'. By the late 1960s, 'after years of urban riots and rebellions, shifting demographics accelerated as racial boundaries eroded, and most American cities found whites heading for the suburbs, abandoning city centers and their movie houses to inner-city blacks'.[45] Subsequent efforts at urban renewal were often veiled attempts to gentrify these areas by forcing out minorities such as the African American audiences who later made 1970s blaxploitation and kung-fu films so successful in grind houses.

As noted in the previous chapter, the immediate post-studio era of the 1950s saw production shortages that imperilled small independent theatres.[46] Stepping into the breach, independent producers and distributors could now operate in a much larger percentage of the marketplace, often targeting select audiences with films once impermissible under the now-faltering Production Code. With this increased permissibility, classical exploitation films ceased to be marketable but more explicit genres, such as sexploitation, took their place in grind houses over the next two decades. Such films were seen as financially bolstering the 'wrong' theatres and creating the 'wrong' audiences; as one theatre chain executive explained in 1970, 'I believe we have been creating a new and specific audience which will continue to demand the stag [*sic*] films. I say, let them get their prurient kicks in the kind of grind mills which are springing up all over.'[47] Meanwhile, to make themselves seem a more economical choice than other theatres, grind houses retained double and triple features as the larger industry moved away from them (owing to rising production costs), inadvertently enhancing the apparent cheapness of their product. Bosley Crowther complained that with 'so much blather about the only films made these days being "big ones" or very sophisticated items', people had overlooked the growing threat 'pouring into the cheap grind houses and some of the better-class neighborhood theatres': violent films with 'the qualifications to give vicarious kicks to creeps and kids, despite the cheapness of their production and the inferiority of their quality'.[48]

Indeed, Schaefer argues that 'with advertising appeals based on excitement, adventure, curiosity, and experimentation, the profile of the sexploitation consumer was constructed as someone who was abnormal', linking sexploitation to anxieties about the negative effects of 'urbanism' and the supposed 'collapse of neighborhoods into cesspools of prostitution, crime, and decay' – despite sexploitation patrons actually being '"average" in almost every respect'.[49] *Variety* noted in 1962 that 'Most of 'em appear to be post-adolescents, most are the bald head type who used to frequent the pre-La Guardia burleys, and there are always some servicemen and assorted stragglers. Single femme patrons, of course, are scarce, although mixed couples occasionally are seen.'[50] Even with later hard-core films, many theatre patrons were 'married, college-educated, upwardly mobile white-collar workers with an average income of $12,000 a year'.[51] Yet, because supposedly catering to lurid tastes, the grind house became stereotyped as 'a semi-pornographic theater not considered worthy of a critic's attention, at least not a critic on duty'.[52]

In addition to fears about sexually deviant audiences, fears over urbanism carried a racially charged component, as young African American audiences were often a vital demographic in the 1970s 'action houses' that had once been picture palaces now located in increasingly racialised areas.[53] Indeed, it is difficult not to detect an echo of racial anxiety in fears that the 'wrong' films and 'wrong' audiences would spread to higher-class and less inner-city parts of the New York area beyond 42nd Street.[54] Echoing common stereotypes about race and criminality, 42nd Street's urban decay was often figured in racial terms; as noted in one account of the Victory's patrons during the early 1980s, 'Only difference between now and fifty years ago is that most are Negroes. Ask any theater manager his take on the customers and he'll shrug: "This is 42nd Street".'[55] The negative associations of class mixing that arose decades earlier thus continued but were increasingly correlated with the supposed perils of racial mixing at grind houses as well, where white patrons seemed increasingly 'outnumbered'. It should be little surprise, then, that blaxploitation films were sometimes dismissed under racially tinged reviews such as 'boneheaded black chop-socky pic for grind houses'.[56] If blaxploitation and kung-fu films briefly overlapped in grind houses during the early 1970s, before the latter replaced the former as the decade continued, these seemingly 'lowbrow' films were not only distributed by the same companies (including even major studios such as Warner Bros.) but commonly shared the same audiences through their similar preoccupations with non-white, often working-class heroes engaging in anti-imperialistic struggles through the use of exceptional physicality as 'self-defense or retaliatory violence against racial oppression'.[57]

These morally and politically charged differentiations furthered the stigmatising discourses about grind houses that had appeared since the early years, leading to the increased use of 'grindhouse' as a generic adjective. As Rick Altman observes, 'Only when compared to the exhibition system that sustains it does a particular generic configuration reveal its debt to exhibition institutions.' Because 'exhibition circumstances may destabilise generic identification',[58] the adjectival deployment of grindhouse complicated earlier generic labels by offering an alternative means of categorising films according to standards of quality, tone, and taste that were supposedly different from Hollywood product and its now-threatened dominance over mainstream exhibition.

In a 1960 'Study of Decay', the *New York Times* alleged that the 1930s conversion from legitimate theatres to films had led to 42nd Street's decline within less than five years: 'Much criticism is directed at the ten motion picture theatres . . . known as "grind joints"', says the article.

> Some of these theatres emphasize sex and violence in their street displays, and it is suggested that these displays tend to attract undesirables, especially in the late hours. Many contend that a woman alone is not safe in such a movie; that male perverts use them as places to meet and to misbehave, and that the general atmosphere of the theatres breed[s] crime.[59]

Such discourses about danger and criminality accentuated the gendered appeal of the male-oriented films shown in these 'masculine' places. Indeed, Joanne Hollows argues that the cult fandom accruing around exploitation films in later years partly stemmed from their original exhibition in spaces considered unsafe and uncomfortable for women. Not only were the grind houses themselves coded as masculine spaces but the theatres shared close proximity with the supposedly perilous inner city and the porn-exclusive theatres that sprang up in the 1970s. Some years later, the male cultist could imagine himself a 'manly adventurer' into a semi-licit, anti-domestic world of sleaze – even if access to exploitation films came via a VCR safely positioned in his living room.[60]

While 42nd Street's photographic record dates from its earliest years as an entertainment centre, nocturnal images of grind house entrances feature prominently by the early 1950s, increasing over the next three decades. Men are often pictured crowding around the colourful posters and lobby displays while women are scarce. Myriad film titles, advertising displays, and adult-oriented businesses decorate images of the Times Square scene. These preserved-yet-fleeting details can today conjure desirous yearnings among fans for 'lost' historical times and places of cinematic fantasy, thus allowing nostalgia's insatiable longings to stand in for the unfulfillable pleasures once promised by exploitation cinema's publicity and its privileged exhibition sites. Rows of glowing signage figure prominently in how grind houses have been remembered (Figure 2.1), with theatre after theatre of lurid titles representing a liminal space that 'conjoin[s] the mundanity and materiality of bricks and mortar with the worlds of fantasy and imagination' in a heterotopian milieu of sleazy possibility, with the continuous programming of double features that could be entered at any point offering a flexible, expansive experience of time.[61] As Giuliana Bruno notes, 'The landscape of the city ends up interacting closely with filmic representations, and to this extent, the streetscape is as much a filmic "construction" as it is an architectural one'.[62] Especially in later years, 42nd Street marquees became markers of crime and deviance in films such as *Chained Girls* (1965), *Prostitutes Protective Society* (1966), *The Lusting Hours* (1967), *The Ultimate Degenerate* (1969), *Midnight Cowboy* (1969), *Shaft* (1971), *Fleshpot on 42nd Street* (1973), *Taxi Driver* (1976), and *Basket Case* (1982). Furthermore, Elena Gorfinkel argues that the *vérité*-style footage in 1960s sexploitation films shot in the Times Square area serves a double function as cultural ruins: that is, it documents a time before the influx of hard-core adult films not only squeezed out the sexploitation film as a mode of production during the early 1970s but also transformed the landscape of 42nd Street towards the increasingly degraded condition that would eventually be cleaned up by city and state forces.[63]

Some exploitation films shot in the 42nd Street area, such as *Massage Parlor Murders* (1972), *Maniac* (1980), and *The New York Ripper* (1982), played into feminists' worst fears about supposed media effects because it 'became typical for a screen killer to be shown prowling the 42nd Street drag, as if there was some inexorable link between the screaming billboards and the actions of the patrons'.[64] The eventual proliferation of hard-core adult programming (Figure 2.2) also made 42nd Street emblematic of the evils of pornography for some feminist protest groups, as exemplified by Women Against Pornography's October 1979 march on Times Square. The group conducted tours of 42nd Street's sex shops, although 'this opportunity to demystify a territory that had been off-limits' to women could also inadvertently evoke more 'complex reactions, including envy, fear, and sexual arousal'.[65]

Bette Gordon's film *Variety* (1983), for example, offers a more complicated (albeit fictional) depiction of a woman who works in the ticket booth of Variety Photoplays, a real-life grind house visually associated in the film with the Times Square area. As Christine (Sandy McLeod) reluctantly develops a perverse fascination with the theatre's pornographic program-

Figure 2.1 42nd Street by night, c. October 1970, featuring a sexploitation double bill at the Victory. Photo © by Nick DeWolf. (Source: Nick DeWolf Photo Archive/ www.flickr.com/photos/dboo)

Figure 2.2 The hard-core feature film *Sometime Sweet Susan* (1975) and quasi-hardcore 'white coater' documentary *Swedish Marriage Manual* (1969) are billed together at the Lyric, as seen in *Taxi Driver*'s (1976) portrait of urban decay. (Source: DVD.)

Figure 2.3 In Bette Gordon's *Variety* (1983), Christine (Sandy McLeod) flips through a magazine in a Times Square adult bookstore as a middle-aged male patron nervously looks on, her presence disrupting his privileged space of masculine fantasy. (Source: DVD.)

ming, she begins to fantasise about seeing herself up on the screen, acting alongside a mysterious man (Richard Davidson) whom she suspects is a mobster. Inspired by Gordon's own forays into Times Square adult businesses, Christine is occasionally subject to unwanted advances from men when she enters porn-specific locales but her presence more often causes male patrons to shamefully give her a wide berth, as if she is intruding on a predominantly male fantasy milieu (Figure 2.3). As Gordon notes, the ability to create this reaction may not be *actual* power, yet at least suggests how a lone woman's presence in and around grind houses need not evoke potential victimisation but rather a disruptive complication to the lived and symbolic spaces of masculine fantasy.[66]

I would similarly suggest that the potential disruption that women can create in the imagined spaces of masculine fantasy complicates the gendered connotations of latter-day subcultural belonging within masculine-oriented fan cultures when the old 42nd Street no longer exists and 'grindhouse movies' are largely consumed on home video within lived places associated more with the 'feminine' connotations of domesticity than 'masculine' urban mobility. Discussing women-in-prison films, Judith Mayne observes that

> the very notion of a film 'made for the male spectator' becomes increasingly quaint as many of the factors enforcing such distinctions – particularly having to do with

movie theater attendance – break down. With the advent of video rental/purchase and the attendant availability of films that might otherwise have been forbidden for a variety of reasons, the female spectator (and the male spectator, too) sees films differently and sees different films.[67]

In this respect, contemporary fan nostalgia for grind houses as masculine spaces is not only an extension of long-standing historical anxieties that accreted around such theatres but also an anachronistic defence of the gender-limited access to downmarket urban pleasures that home video has since subverted.

Consequently, it is notable that so many retrospective accounts of 42nd Street imply that the chaos and vice shown in exploitation films were mirrored by the undisciplined conduct of (male) theatre patrons. As Jimmy McDonough recalls,

> Misfits from all walks of life and all manner of race (but largely male) . . . frequently provided a better show than the feature in progress. People talked back to the screen. They fought with each other, and I mean hand-to-hand combat. They had sex in the men's room and in the balconies. A communal experience, 42nd Street, and it all spun around movies.[68]

Though we should not surmise that crime was a causal effect of the films being shown or the presence of the theatres themselves, we can assume that at least some of the misbehaviour occurring in and around grind houses was a symptom of many Times Square residents' economic poverty.

If grind houses encouraged something like a déclassé film-going subculture during their heyday, it was a nebulous and loosely imagined subculture frequently built upon a sense of anonymity, fleeting encounters, and contact only indirectly related to the films themselves. Grind house attendance, especially by heterosexual men, probably less resembled traditionally subcultural conceptions of visible and mutual fan community than the pursuit of *intrapersonal* pleasures over *interpersonal* ones. Because exploitation cinema's hyperbolic promises encouraged viewing desires that were endlessly deferred, '[e]scape into the cinema from the ennui of the streets outside does not represent a mirroring of social realities but a mirroring of the confinement of the city's streets and strangers' ill-met glances'.[69] Complicating adventurous nostalgias about a bleeding over of cinematic space into lived space, then, the screen's inability to satisfy desire indicates just how much disjuncture may have actually existed between 42nd Street's on-screen and off-screen spaces for many men – particularly in the sexual difference between exploitation cinema's preoccupation with heterosexual erotic spectacle and the anonymous queer activities engaged in by some male patrons in these largely homosocial sites.[70] In this respect, solitary heterosexual patrons were *less likely* than queerly engaged patrons to experience a fulfilled sense of both desire and community during their visits, despite the largely heteronormative discourses in straight male fans' remembrance of these theatres today. Indeed, queer sexuality is almost always mentioned (at least, fleetingly) in retrospective accounts of film-going in 42nd Street grind houses, either figured as an understandable by-product of sex work's prevalence in the area or as a potential source of gay panic over the supposed threat of stumbling into the wrong shadowy corner or lavatory cubicle. As one representative account suggests, 'the movies were heterosexual, but the quick and dirty sex action was of the other variety, and the theater was soon everyone's worst AIDS nightmare come to life'.[71]

Cultural memories of 42nd Street often regard it as a lawless area where laissez-faire economics permitted such sexual and moral transgressions that retained their allure precisely because they were taboo, rather than because they represented actual personal freedoms. Like the longing for periods of greater textual scarcity described in the previous chapter, a 'rebellious' longing for once-forbidden pleasures thus infuses contemporary fans' nostalgia – particularly when the dirty old Times Square is figured like a spatio-temporal island of vice amid a less overtly corporatised past. Whether purchasing a ticket to an exploitation double bill, buying into a shell game on the street corner, or paying for public sex, 42nd Street promised exploitation of many kinds, all premised on desires that fell short of normative ideals. Like the insatiability of fandom itself, then, 42nd Street's grind houses figure as *lieux de mémoire* that can seem all the more unruly as economically 'unofficial' loci for unsatisfied desires of multiple valences. Yet, as I will elaborate below, it is ironic that the old 42nd Street as a former site of unsanctioned, laissez-faire economics has since been transformed into a site of officially sanctioned, neo-liberal economics during the home video era, offering the illusion of consumer freedoms within the constraints of copyright law and a commodification of nostalgia.

Grind Houses and Blurred Cultural Distinctions

Complicating the culturally suspect connotations of grind houses, their patrons and their films is the fact that grind houses had, since the mid-1940s, increasingly played foreign films that sometimes overlapped with films shown in art theatres. Art houses were another alternative exhibition context that became genrified in the post-war era through their supposed difference from mainstream Hollywood exhibition. As Barbara Wilinsky observes,

> Grind houses, predominantly run by independent operators, searched, like art houses, for inexpensive films to fill their screen time. Foreign films offered these theaters, like art houses, a practical alternative. Not surprisingly, these theaters tended to promote the sensational attractions of art films.[72]

According to Mark Betz, 1950s–60s European art cinema and American sexploitation were often similarly advertised, 'condens[ing] high and low codes of visibility and identification' by making artsy imports seem more lurid than they might actually be.[73]

As the influx of foreign films continued, attempted concessions to cultural distinction continued on the part of some grind house owners, even if using sex to sell tickets was still the bottom line. In the mid-1960s, the Rialto began programming 'class sex' films – stylish imports such as *I, a Woman* (1965) and *Therese and Isabelle* (1968) – while the cheaper American sexploitation that it previously showed moved to the Globe.[74] Accordingly, Bosley Crowther described 42nd Street as theatres 'where one may find anything from a revival of a distinguished and esoteric French film to a "nudie" or "striptease" whatnot'.[75] Still, critics typically understood the films playing in grind houses as culturally low because of the alleged cheapness and sleaziness of the venues, even if potentially 'art-worthy' films may have occupied those spaces, albeit reframed as sleaze. These connotations were aided by the early-1970s transition from soft-core sexploitation to hard-core adult films in and near some grind houses.

Meanwhile, some Hollywood films continued to play grind houses at the end of their theatrical runs throughout the post-studio era, especially if those films fell into male-oriented genres. As United Artists' publicity director said in 1952, the average movie played first-run theatres for one week, moved to neighbourhood circuits for approximately another week, and then 'goes into the cheap "grind" houses and in six months it's dead'.[76] Consequently, actual grind house programming was considerably more diverse than was often supposed but critics still focused on the cheapness, luridness and inferiority of films (Hollywood-produced or not) that were more likely to call grind houses their native home by spending the majority of their theatrical run on the skids. According to Rick Altman, 'perhaps the most important tactic in the genre world consists in naturalizing one's own discursive claims . . . by attributing to the text itself goals and functions proper to producer, exhibitor, spectator, or critic'.[77] If so, then the genrification of 'grindhouse films' rests on such reductive interpretations of typical grind house programming, marking films and theatres alike as somehow different from more acceptable, mainstream consumption.

As in the studio era, male-oriented genres continued to be popular in grind houses but now coexisted with other genres and cycles introduced through the increased importation of foreign pictures which were not necessarily art films (including Italian westerns, kung fu, and *chambara* films) and through loosened censorship restrictions that allowed films to enter the American marketplace with seemingly no greater aim than making money by appealing to the basest instincts (such as imported sexploitation and mondo films). Many of these films could be inexpensively acquired, dubbed into English, and sometimes recut and retitled by American distributors with smaller capital expenditure than producing their own films. Hollywood films ending up in grind houses were not automatically deemed 'grindhouse films', though films relegated to grind houses for their violent, cheap or lurid content probably were.

With these connotations of aesthetic, moral and economic poverty, the term *grindhouse film* became synonymous with the post-classical exploitation film in both fan and popular discourse, increasingly operating as a generic adjective by the late 1960s.[78] While exploitation films in the post-studio era of increased permissibility and distribution were not as formally distinctive as classical exploitation cinema had been, excess and low production values often remained discernable textual qualities that genrified the films as 'exploitation' through their promotion, exhibition and reception. As I suggested in Chapter 1, this conflation of theatre type and exploitation product was also shared by drive-in theatres, another alternative exhibition context often disparagingly used as a generic signifier ('drive-in movies') in the post-war era, arguably in reaction to the rise of drive-ins as a lucrative, non-mainstream market from the 1950s to 1970s. In fact, one of the early background images on the promotional website for the film *Grindhouse* was an artist's rendition of a decrepit drive-in theatre, suggesting the subculturally held associations between these two generic exhibition sites.

Though not marketing exclusively to grind houses, independent distributors largely fuelled grind house programming during the post-war explosion of independent production and international imports, dominating more of the grind house market than similar companies had in the studio era. After fronting money to distributors for test marketing, subdistributors purchased prints of successful films for the states' rights market; these subdistributors could earn up to 25 per cent of a successfully distributed film's gross, or even more if they owned their own theatres.[79] Independent distributors supplied the majority of titles which are today generically labelled grindhouse films, operating primarily during the supposed 1960s–80s heyday of these theatres, when 'grindhouse film' solidified as an overarching epithet for various exploitation cycles. Major distribution companies included American Film Distributing, Aquarius Releasing, Audubon Films, Bryanston Distributing, Cambist Films, Cannon Films, Continental Distributing, Dimension Pictures, Distribpix and Embassy Pictures.

Other distributors were also prolific production companies in their own right, marketing their own and others' product into grind house circuits; these companies included American International Pictures, Boxoffice International Pictures, Crown International Pictures, Entertainment Ventures Inc., Independent-International Pictures, and New World Pictures. Moving into low-budget exploitation production was seen as easier than sifting through films that other distributors had already rejected, and it offered a means of competing with the spectacular genre pictures increasingly made by the major studios – though Suzanne Mary Donahue notes that these producer-distributors often initially 'ask[ed] for a large acquisition price from a major by using self-distribution as the threatened alternative' if an independent film seemed potentially profitable.[80]

During this period, theatre marquees and newspaper ads indicate that westerns still dominated at the Times Square, the Apollo maintained artsy imports, and the Victory mostly played sexploitation – but most theatres' programming blurred into a mishmash of westerns, horror, action, martial arts, sexploitation, hard-core pornography, and subsequent-run Hollywood product. While focusing on exploitation films oversimplifies the range of films shown at these theatres, it suggests the public visibility of certain cycles and subgenres that have gained prominence in the fan imagination, thus reflecting the popular parameters of subcultural appreciation for grindhouse cinema that intensified in the home video age. Many exploitation fans may celebrate the soft-core antics of sexploitation, for example, but acknowledge and play down the hard-core porn that increasingly occupied grind houses during the 1970s 'porno chic' era. While detractors often conflated porn-exclusive theatres and other grind houses,[81] some fans distinguish between 'grindhouse films' and hard-core porn films, the latter typically distributed by different companies such as Leisure Time Booking and New York Releasing. Though these distinctions may speak to the relative legal availability (and thus wider remembrance) of some films over others today, I would suggest that the prevalent present-day (online) access to hard-core porn within the domestic sphere has paradoxically made all the more desirable those (non-hardcore) sexploitation films mnemonically linked to the nicheness of past theatrical sites like the grind house. With the grind house marketplace increasingly dominated by porn, exploitation producers and distributors were further wounded by competing in an atmosphere of growing industry-wide advertising costs, while audience tastes shifted towards the major studios' high-concept genre films. As Roger Corman said upon selling New World Pictures in 1983, 'It's very difficult to persuade an audience to pay money to see a $1,000,000 film when they can pay the same amount of money to see a $20,000,000 to $30,000,000 film.'[82]

Writing on behalf of the Brandts during the rise of home video, sociologist Herbert Gans reported that the 42nd Street Development Project's urban renewal plans aimed 'to move out lower-income citizens and taxpayers and to replace them with more affluent ones',[83] to say nothing of the conspicuously non-white and queer populations to be displaced. The Brandts and other local business tenants took legal action against joint city–state efforts to condemn many of 42nd Street's theatres, halting redevelopment plans with litigation throughout the 1980s. In addition to having 'more felony and crime complaints than any other [neighbourhood], despite, or perhaps because of, being targeted again and again by law enforcement',[84] the decade's crack cocaine epidemic provoked police raids on many grind houses, providing another excuse for theatres to be closed. Meanwhile, the AIDS crisis provided the excuse for a 1985 city health ordinance criminalising public sex – though specifically targeted at homosexuality – which led to more closures.[85] Criminality, depicted not only in the press but also in the films set in Times Square, had seemingly spawned a conservative vision of 'redemptive and necessary violence' against the undesirable denizens of the area (including the many homeless who used the theatres as places to shelter and rest) and, by extension, the ghettoised environs that had apparently spawned such criminality.[86] By 1992, only three theatres continued to operate in the area, now primarily showing Hollywood action films, perhaps as a concession to cleaning up the area through more 'legitimate' entertainment options.

More importantly, grind houses ceased to be viable during the 1980s because the growth of home video offered a more lucrative market than the theatrical distribution of exploitation and adult films. Influential fanzines, such as Michael J. Weldon's *Psychotronic Video* and Bill Landis's *Sleazoid Express*, sprang up as the exploitation titles formerly played by grind houses were quickly released by video distributors struggling to fill their release schedules. Indeed, the different time periods and cultural contexts created by the revival and import of diverse films at grind houses effectively prefigured the rise of home video by allowing viewers a more democratic range of viewing choices. As *Variety*'s Larry Cohn lamented, 'On 42nd Street, they just showed any old thing and let *us* decide what to see. [. . .] We need some salt-of-the-earth theaters where you can see just about any old thing without a programmer necessarily deciding what's good for you'.[87]

Because video rental stores began taking up this role, nostalgia for grind houses has since bridged into nostalgia for early video technology itself. 'This fresh new world more or less replaced the second-run [*sic*] theatrical grindhouse market dominated by Roger Corman and other filmmakers and producers like him', declares one retrospective article on the rise of direct-to-video releases (see Chapter 3) effectively turning genre fans' homes into their own private grind houses.[88] For example, the book *Portable Grindhouse: The Lost Art of the VHS Box* reprints colourful box covers from exploitation films on VHS, accompanied by wistful memoirs of the author's 1980s video discoveries; the book itself even comes in a package resembling a VHS slipcase.[89] Similarly, Bill Landis and Michelle Clifford's touristic memoir of 42nd Street film-going ends with a listing of video companies where one might track down the films discussed therein, emphasising that these films are not completely lost, even if their original exhibition venues are long gone.[90] Yet, if VHS let a new mode of exploitation film consumption echo the solitary patron's individuated and anonymous excursions into grind houses, video collector cultures still fostered some degree of interpersonal contact – a sort of symbolic stand-in for the nebulous sense of sociality lost in the shift from public to private viewing.

If 42nd Street's decaying environs had begun to resemble the cycle of post-apocalyptic films that appeared on its screens in the early to mid-1980s, this tendency was accompanied by the condemnation and destruction of many decrepit buildings in the area, and the closing of adult-oriented businesses through new zoning laws. As one writer remarked in 1988, 'Moving a few blocks north of the New Amsterdam, the upper reaches of Times Square these days look like London after the Blitz.'[91] For contemporary fans, the romanticisation of 42nd Street and its grind houses may relate to the cinephiliac *nostalgie de la boue* of traversing a sleazy wonderland where one's cinematic fantasies might bleed out into lived urban spaces, but prospective redevelopers had cultural memories of their own. Like the overlapping and conflicting nostalgias over drive-in theatres discussed in my previous chapter, many conservative members of the 42nd Street Development Project and the New York State Urban Development Corporation had memories of a safer and more prestigious 42nd Street associated with the 1920s–50s period before exploitation and adult films became endemic. As one urban developer recalled, 'the regret we felt over the passing of this glamorous world gave the project a powerful emotional boost'.[92] As Marshall Berman argues, however, if Times Square symbolised America's industrial and economic potential until the mid-twentieth century, the area's post-war years of decline and stigmatisation also saw New York City's apparent disconnection from an increasingly decentralised America where zoned suburbs minimised contact with the social others associated with downtown urban areas. The post-1970s redevelopment of Times Square by global business interests and franchises subsequently made 'mobs of American tourists happily at home in the Square every day, and many New Yorkers nostalgic for the days of alienation' from the surrounding world.[93] It is precisely this sense of imagined alienation from 'safe' and 'boring' suburban America that contemporary fans value when selectively recalling the old 42nd Street's downmarket environs as a nostalgic time and place through which to locate and justify their 'different' tastes.

'Grindhouse Films' as Coming Attractions in the Post-theatrical Period

With not even pornography able to keep them afloat in the home video age, most grind houses on 42nd Street and elsewhere closed by the late 1980s, spurring fan-cultural nostalgia for this lost site. Director Frank Henenlotter, who ironically went on to curate films for Something Weird Video, exemplifies this view:

> I'd much rather see films in a movie theater with a group of people, especially in the kind of run-down fleabags that played them – somehow the more peeling paint, the more smell of urine, the more exciting it seemed to be! [. . .] It's a strange concept: all these obscure films that I would have risked injury and death to see (literally, in some of these theaters) are now available at your local clean video store! [. . .] I'm still not used to the fact that these films that I spent my whole life trying to see are now *consumer items*.[94]

Though Vincent Canby remarked in 1975 that '[p]romoters of such films are well aware that they aren't dealing in things that will be hailed as gems by even the maddest movie nuts', he admitted that titles such as *Ilsa, She-Wolf of the SS* (1975) 'represent a subculture that people who do their movie-going on Third Avenue are seldom aware of'.[95] Then, as now, grindhouse fare was increasingly adopted by an alternative taste culture oppositionally prizing the cheap and exploitative as an anti-mainstream aesthetic, marking an early instance of 'paracinematic' reading strategies. Still, it should be remembered that grind houses like the Rialto encouraged such cultural slumming as early as the 1930s and 1940s while also providing sites of bohemian fascination for avant-garde film-makers and critics in subsequent decades.[96] Similarly, while casual film-goers might attend the closest theatre, more dedicated movie buffs sought out the best films on the basis of word of mouth or sensational trailers. Even with 1970s hard-core films, these buffs 'discussed innovations and variations of conventions, noted mistakes in production, and even speculated about the circumstances surrounding the making of the films from internal evidence'.[97] In this sense, fan-cultural memories of so-called grindhouse cinema cannot simply be reduced to paracinematic irony but exist in tension with more sincere appreciation for the endlessly deferred thrills promised by exploitation films. Grindhouse nostalgia grew in cult film communities during the 1990s and 2000s, marketed by companies such as Something Weird Video, Grindhouse Releasing and other video distributors keen on repackaging not only filmic texts but also their outlandish and excessive paratexts.

While once-obscure exploitation films are increasingly returned to more pristine audiovisual quality and greater cultural availability via digital technologies, trailers and other original advertising paratexts typically retain their degraded and archaic quality, full of scratches, grain and other celluloid artefacting – hence the centrality of the trailer and other paratexts to the blend of irony and sincerity intentionally encoded into the 'retrosploitation' pastiches discussed in the following chapters. Whether encoding paratextual cues for nostalgia into more recent formats or casting residual formats into a nostalgic light, home video's propagation of such temporal juxtapositions has only increased with the market-driven shifts towards digital technologies. (Think, for instance, of cinephiles' complaints over the amount of 'noise reduction' digitally removing 35 mm celluloid grain from some Blu-ray restorations of older films, replacing the original image's 'filminess' with an unnaturally contemporary veneer.) Such nostalgia was also encouraged by grindhouse film festivals held in a handful of large cities, effectively transplanting exploitation films back into their 'proper' theatrical settings, including at several of the few remaining theatres priding themselves on being former grind houses (such as The New Beverly in Los Angeles). Yet, it is ironic that the urban theatrical exhibition of exploitation films has been so nostalgised today as a potential source of subcultural capital because, unlike many urban film-goers, patrons outside large cities may have attended exploitation films owing to the sheer dearth of available films in their area, not out of any overt rejection of 'mainstream' cinema. Sixties sexploitation icon Marsha Jordan, for example, recalled promoting one of her films in a small Iowa town where, unlike the typical urban clientele, '90 per cent of the people who came in were couples, married couples and single couples. We said, "Gee, this is weird", and they said, "Oh no, on the weekend people here don't have anyplace to go, so all the married people come to the sex theatres"'.[98]

From the encoding of trailers as DVD paratexts to the attempted recreation of grindhouse-themed theatrical experiences, the contemporary revival of *grindhouse* as a transmedia concept has thereby allowed room for overlapping nostalgias which are symptomatic of a broader video-era taste formation undergirding both the remediation of older exploitation films and the recent rise of retrosploitation. To provide an extended example, I will now explore how the revival of grindhouse film trailers as DVD compilations and bonus features exemplifies this tension between nostalgia's commingling of sincere and ironic valences, spawning a sort of 'grindhouse aesthetic' that fetishises filmic decay. As Lisa Kernan argues, trailers possess a unique temporal status as nostalgic for a film not yet seen, yet also providing a gallery of attractions wrested free from narrative coherence in the creation of intensified anticipation towards future filmgoing. Pieced together through a sort of 'discontinuity editing' that subsumes the use value of any given film's narrative to the exchange value of exploiting the prospective appeal of cinematic attraction in general, these paratexts cue audiences to the most exploitable elements of films that might otherwise disappoint if viewed as a whole, while creating almost surreally incongruous mixes of sex, violence and sensationalism.[99] By foregrounding an exploitation film's 'high points' (often accompanied by ominous/lascivious male narration of the basic plot premise and frequent repetition of the film's title), these trailers are especially useful in offering quick overviews of the most distinctive moments in generically formulaic films – which, for viewers low in subcultural capital but faced with such a nebulous variety of cycles and subgenres, may even work against the desire to bother seeing the individual films being advertised. As one review of a compilation DVD notes,

> Free of the eighty minutes of bad expository [*sic*], lame jokes, and boring buildup found in the feature film, the trailers were pure excitement. [. . .] Though many of these films will be familiar to genre fans, I've never seen any of them. [. . .] And, I honestly have little desire to see any of them now. Yet, the trailers were thoroughly enjoyable in their own right, and they're something that will likely hold up to repeated viewings.[100]

When compiled together on DVD, exploitation film trailers thus represent an effective commercial and subcultural entry point to the exploitation corpus for those willing to invest in it further, temporally compressing a rapid-fire array of thrilling moments from selected titles that one might purchase in remediated form. Functioning like a primer in subcultural competencies, the hyperbole and apparent incoherence of the trailers may encourage ironic reading strategies while their chaotic cataloguing of sleazy thrills points towards their surviving potential to sincerely excite viewers by offering visceral appeals transcending their dated historical contexts. Like scanning a street lined with marquees of enticing titles, traversing multiple DVD menus of trailers offers a domesticated fantasy of traversing nostalgically recalled urban spaces, thus shaping the retrospective contours of the grind house as an exhibition site. In fact, uncommonly long clusters of trailers were common features in actual grind houses, with Vincent Canby noting in 1968 that 'a Manhattan sex–violence house devoted no fewer than 20 minutes to its trailers for future films, including "Shameless Desire" and "Sex is the Game People Play." It was, in effect, a montage, if not an anthology, of various kinds of sex activities and violence'.[101] Similarly, street-side video monitors endlessly looped trailers to lure in passers-by on 42nd Street in the early 1980s, around the same time that some grind houses were converting to video projection for hard-core adult films.[102] Trailer reels could, in theory, better hold the attention of unruly or distracted audiences, and perhaps temporarily offer a greater sense of shared viewing community than the actual double features themselves – foreshadowing how trailer compilation DVDs have been explicitly promoted in product descriptions and reviews as good for party entertainment at home. The VHS box of a 1992 trailer compilation, for example, notes that '[t]he grindhouses of NYC's Times Square have all been torn down, but their memory lives on in *Grindhouse Horrors*'.

The proliferation of trailer compilation videos is a relatively recent phenomenon, with the random access allowed by digital technologies permitting most compilations to be either played through in their entirety or by individual trailer, thus improving upon the democratic appeal of VHS. Though several trailer compilations date from the early 1980s, most have appeared since the rise of DVD.[103] With the growth of DVD and the increased conventionality of including trailers as DVD bonus features, trailer compilations proliferated in the marketplace – including DVD reissues of many of the older VHS ones – sometimes arranging a mix of genres (Montreal Film Studio's multivolume *Fantastic Movie Trailers* series, Drafthouse Films' *Trailer War* [2012]); or sometimes arranged specifically by genre (*Best of Kung Fu Movies* [2005], *A Fistful of Trailers* [2003], and *Cumming Soon!* [2002]); or production company (*Nikkatsu Roman Porno Trailer Compilation* [2010], Distribpix's *35mm Grindhouse Trailers* [2009], and Camp Motion Pictures' *Trailer Trash!* [2008]).

While these trailer compilations may be sold as stand-alone units at retail prices equivalent to other videos and DVDs, several compilations are also offered at budget prices, effectively serving as video sales catalogues for specialist companies. Something Weird's *Extra Weird Sampler*

(2003), for example, contains nearly four hours of exploitation trailers and clips, primarily from films also released on special-edition DVDs in conjunction with Image Entertainment. The inclusion of original theatrical trailers as advertising strategies on the websites of Something Weird and Blue Underground suggests that the thrills promised by these trailers still serve their original purposes of selling the feature text itself to prospective buyers, not merely serving as objects of ironic appreciation. This more straight-faced presentation of original trailers as informative paratexts is further suggested by their occasional inclusion, like evidentiary exhibits, as DVD supplements for documentaries about the history of exploitation cinema, including *Not Quite Hollywood: The Wild, Untold Story of Ozploitation!* (2008), *American Grindhouse* (2010), *Video Nasties: Moral Panic, Censorship, and Videotape* (2010), and *Machete Maidens Unleashed!* (2010).

When looking at the trailers appearing most often across multiple compilations, the repetition of more outlandish, violent, hyperbolic or lurid ones has helped solidify a privileged exploitation film corpus; yet, arguably, this tendency has more to do with the increased video availability of some trailers over others than textual traits of the full films being advertised. In this sense, the loosened copyright status of trailers, initially intended to spread far and wide, has allowed them to be repurposed by whichever competing companies are able to acquire transfers from 35 mm prints. This is not to say that trailers are free from copyright restrictions but that they are more likely to exist in a legal grey area than the films they are advertising (as I also discuss in this book's Conclusion). Yet, whereas these trailers may once have circulated with more legal freedom, their remediation on compilation DVDs is a means by which companies can stake greater copyright claims over the transfers, thereby helping to lock down specific uses of these revived paratextual afterlives. Small wonder, then, that most of the trailers reappearing across multiple compilations are for films whose DVD distribution rights belong to smaller, independent companies, not to exploitation films whose rights may have been bought up by major Hollywood studios, such as MGM's eventual acquisition of rights to the American International Pictures back catalogue (by way of the defunct Orion Pictures).

Perhaps the most popular line of exploitation trailer compilations in the United States, and thus the one most responsible for helping shape the contemporary genrification of so-called grindhouse cinema, is Synapse Films' *42nd Street Forever* series, which began in 2005 and has spawned six DVD volumes and several Blu-ray volumes at the time of writing. As the name implies, these compilations play into fans' cinephiliac desires to travel back as cinematic tourists to the notorious street during its sleazy heyday. Trailers are often generically clustered throughout the running time of each volume, with the prominence of particular genres and cycles reflecting the same sorts of films privileged by Landis and Clifford's account of 42nd Street grind houses. When later volumes seem to veer further away from the mnemonic realm of grindhouse cinema, fan-reviewers often complain that the trailers are either 'too mainstream' or do not fit their romantic ideals of what exploitation cinema supposedly should look like (regardless of which company actually produced or distributed the titles in question). Such complaints are exemplified by this review of the fourth volume:

> [T]here are too many trailers here that seem out of place in a collection devoted to grindhouse exploitation films. There is a legitimate difference between lower budget 'B' films from big studios and the more schlocky, more exploitive type of low budget films which usually appeal more to fans. It is not that there is no place for trailers from larger 'B' movies like *March or Die* or *In God We Trust*, it's just that for me they are given too many seats at the table compared with the real exploitation films. The same can be said for less exploitive fare from indie companies specializing in schlocky films, like AIP (*Our Winning Season*) and Crown International (*Coach*).[104]

Yet, this selective vision denies not only the variety of films that historically played at actual grind houses but also the role of many independent exploitation producers who deliberately drew inspiration from successful major-studio films in an attempt to gain distribution deals with the more reputable member companies of the Motion Picture Association of America.[105]

Compounding the selective nature of the included trailers, the more interpersonally social uses of such compilations also help to colour the shape of grindhouse cinema by segregating certain types of content from others. *42nd Street Forever: XXX-treme Special Edition* (2007), for example, compiles several hours of trailers for 35 mm hard-core porn films. Released between the series's second and third volumes, this DVD's 'adults-only' status positions it outside the rest of the series's sequentially numbered volumes, speaking to the legal separation of soft-core from hard-core content. While the series's nostalgic title acknowledges porn's historical place in 42nd Street's grind houses, this release also segregates porn into a legally permissible archive for those whose tastes cross into hard-core territory. If the trailer segment of the theatrical experience regularly engenders a more carnivalesque atmosphere than the atmosphere of the unfolding feature film itself,[106] then the carnivalesque overlap between on-screen and off-screen action implied in many nostalgias for the supposed 42nd Street grindhouse experience makes sense if intended as ambient viewing at parties that may cinephilically aspire to reminiscent levels of debauchery, alcohol/drug use and general unruliness. The screening of trailer compilations for hard-core films, however, may uncomfortably echo the homosocial or homoerotic dynamics of adult theatre attendance mentioned earlier, and hence be considered less appropriate for certain social events. In addition, the party atmosphere potentially opens these trailers to fans and non-fans alike, necessitating the situational performance of fandom in relation to other viewers with widely varying degrees of subcultural capital – and thus widely differing blends of earnestness and irony in the reception of such objects. The varied uses of trailer compilations therefore have as much potential to foster fans' ideas about 42nd Street as to complicate these implanted nostalgias when the exploitation film corpus is so readily constructed and presented to wider audiences in digest form.

Negotiations for subcultural capital during the domestication of the grind house as a contested *lieu de mémoire* arguably reached their zenith in the wider cultural landscape with the 2007 release of the omnibus film *Grindhouse*. Composed of two feature-length exploitation pastiches directed by Robert Rodriguez and Quentin Tarantino (*Planet Terror* and *Death Proof*), fake trailers (Rodriguez's *Machete*, Rob Zombie's *Werewolf Women of the SS*, Edgar Wright's *Don't*, and Eli Roth's *Thanksgiving*), advertisements, and archival theatre announcements for 'our feature presentation', the entire ersatz double-bill experience is drenched with the digitally simulated appearance of celluloid print damage (scratches and blotches, poorly spliced edits, jumping frames, 'missing reels', bleeding colour emulsion and so on) evoking a particular vision of 'grindhouseness'. As Rodriguez notes, this aesthetic choice was directly intended as a reaction against the remediation of exploitation movies on 'cleaned-up' and remastered DVDs that had lost the haptic quality of pastness associated with damaged celluloid – though he joked that there were early plans to release a later DVD edition of *Grindhouse* that would remove its digitally created decay and be marketed as 'Newly found original negatives. Completely scratch free and remastered' – a gimmick that eventually appeared as a bonus feature on the Blu-ray release.[107] Likewise, Tarantino claims that he began collecting 16 mm and 35 mm film prints because the sheer availability of home video 'devalues films at the same time'.[108]

Yet, with so much historical (and cultural) distance from existing grind houses, contemporary audiences had to be educated in the generic meaning of 'grindhouse'. Condensing exhibition context and exploitative content, the film's trailer began with a definition subsequently adopted by many reviewers: 'GRIND HOUSE *(n)*: A theater playing back-to-back films exploiting sex, violence, and other extreme subject matter'. Since archival exploitation films often used trailers to advertise high-concept thrills on low budgets, the trailer's temporal status as a film remembered in advance works especially well for advertising larger-budgeted, high-concept pastiches like *Grindhouse*, because these privileged moments become 'a form close to the image's total dissolution in a pure flow of audiovisual information to be randomly modulated'.[109] Furthermore, Lisa Kernan argues that trailers are crucial in creating 'generic spaces' that generate anticipation in viewers – although, in this case, such generic spaces have also found an imagined physical space in the grind house as a symbolic site for sleazy genre films.[110] The fact that many exploitation film trailers are too violent and sexually explicit to have been shown beyond specialised houses upon their initial release also emphasises the grind house as a non-normative generic space that implants selective memories of an unruly corpus.

In aligning their own work with earlier exploitation films, Tarantino and Rodriguez attempt to differentiate themselves and their collaborators from the cultural 'mainstream'. Furthermore, as Joanne Hollows argues, cult film fans' anti-mainstream stance opposes the supposedly feminising, 'politically correct' effects of mainstream culture. In this sense, the directors' celebration of grindhouse cinema as a generic synonym for exploitation cinema apparently protests against the replacement of potentially dangerous, male-oriented, inner-city theatres with safe, suburban multiplexes and video stores.[111] Since most contemporary films earn the vast majority of their overall revenues from the home video market, this gendered cultural distinction is rather disingenuous but it nevertheless suggests a partial distrust of the domestic sphere as a 'feminised' consumption space providing access to viewers (such as *Variety*'s female protagonist) well beyond the historical grind house's appeals to men. Furthermore, Caetlin Benson-Allott calls *Grindhouse* a 'digital homage to both a bygone platform (celluloid) and a bygone genre [*sic*] (the exploitation film)'. Because it was initially released to DVD as the separate films *Planet Terror* and *Death Proof*, sans trailers and ads, she argues that one cannot recreate the *Grindhouse* experience at home using standard DVDs, indicating a mourned loss of theatrical exhibition in general, especially during a time when the theatrical projection of non-decaying Digital Cinema Package files was on the rise.[112] Indeed, some critics found *Grindhouse*'s fake trailers to be its most successful feature, encapsulating the project's overall tone and concept without overstaying their welcome.[113] These fake trailers proved successful enough to spin off into two subsequent films, Robert Rodriguez and Ethan Maniquis's

Machete (2010) and Jason Eisener's *Hobo with a Shotgun* (2011). Eli Roth was even rumoured to be following up his faux slasher trailer *Thanksgiving* with *Trailer Trash*, a feature-length compilation of fake trailers.[114] Yet, as I elaborate in the following chapter, the complete theatrical version of *Grindhouse* has since been released in the United States exclusively on Blu-ray, ultimately suggesting less of a resistance to technological change than complicity with its attendant market demands.

Jockeying for subcultural capital, exploitation fans debated the authenticity of *Grindhouse* in comparison to 'real' grindhouse films, suggesting anxieties over the high-concept film's co-opting of the generic label for mainstream consumption. As *Grindhouse* special make-up effects designer Greg Nicotero noted, 'The grindhouse concept aside, you could cut this movie together and release it and it would be just as equally satisfying as a mainstream horror film.'[115] Online fan discourse attempted to define and describe grindhouse films as synonymous with the post-classical exploitation film, accompanied by fan-generated lists of titles demonstrating one's subcultural cachet. Because the exploitation film is less a distinct genre than an aesthetic style or sensibility infused with pastness, Wiki-based websites such as The Deuce: Grindhouse Cinema Database sprang up around *Grindhouse*'s release, trying to navigate the video-era intelligibility of the diverse grindhouse cinema corpus by organising titles by year, cycle, or subgenre – though, like many trailer compilations, largely focusing on either the most well-known or most notorious titles. These displays of ownership and control accompanying the grindhouse concept's increased visibility arguably spring from 'a sense of insecurity and anxiety' that 'the fan can only ever aspire to becoming, at most, a post facto addition to the cultural meaning' of his/her chosen objects.[116] As I expand in the next chapter, this ambivalence or even outright anxiety is particularly acute when digital technologies allow signs of age to be intentionally removed from, or added to, older recordings, potentially creating 'a dialogue between generations of users'.[117]

As the preceding discussion suggests, the repackaging of older texts and the retro-stylisation of newer ones are distinct but interrelated phenomena but they temporally intertwined and accelerated during *Grindhouse*'s pre- and post-release hype as independent companies and major studios capitalised on the nostalgic blend of irony and earnestness discursively crystallising around the generic term 'grindhouse'. In this sense, the relationship between *Grindhouse* and its imitators echoes the reciprocal flow of timely, sensational, or profitable influences that had long occurred between major Hollywood releases and independent exploitation product. Capitalising on *Grindhouse*'s release, independent companies, such as

After Hours Cinema, Code Red, VideoAsia, and BCI, released DVDs containing 'grindhouse' double features and trailer compilations, largely assembled from public-domain works or films with indeterminate copyright status; the Independent Film Channel began a weekly 'Grindhouse' programming slot devoted to cult films; and the documentaries *American Grindhouse* and *42nd Street Memories: The Rise and Fall of America's Most Notorious Street* (2014) featured interviews with notable exploitation actors, film-makers, and critics. BCI's 'Welcome to the Grindhouse' series (begun in 2007), for example, features a DVD menu with film titles superimposed over a photograph of a 42nd Street marquee; the menu allows viewers to select each half of the double bill individually or to 'Start the Grindhouse Experience' which screens both features back to back, interspersed with generically related trailers and theatrical announcements – again pointing to the trailer's centrality as a key marker of the 'grindhouse experience' (Figure 2.4). Similarly, the four-film set *42nd Street Pete's Sleazy Grindhouse Picture Show* (2009) features a 'grindhouse function' allowing continuous play of each disc's double feature of 1970s adult films. As the back cover explains,

> This DVD represents the way these grindhouse gems were shown – non stop! No intermissions, just film after film with the occasional short or trailer. Each film has been branded with burn spots, streaks, and breaks, all of it due to old projectors and the careless handling of projectionists. [. . .] After Hours Cinema realizes how important these films are and we have restored them to the best possible condition with all the defects intact!

In other words, to distinguish itself as more 'authentic' than *Grindhouse*'s digitally simulated celluloid decay, this DVD offers the paradoxical claim of allegedly 'restoring' the films while also preserving their 'careless', unsimulated wear and tear. Avoiding the time- and cost-intensive process of substantially remastering or restoring prints that occupy a legal grey area thus allows small independent distributors like After Hours Cinema to profit from the déclassé grindhouse aesthetic while making the otherwise obscure films themselves more widely available on digital video formats.

These uses of grindhouse as an overarching generic label – or better still, as a synecdoche for containing many different exploitation genres, periods and cycles – indicate its flexibility in becoming a highly sellable commodity, especially in a post-theatrical era in which the grind house as historical referent has vanished from the physical landscape, an absence glossed over by the so-called 'Disneyfication' of Times Square. If the environs of 42nd Street once seemed to mirror the violence, crime and

Figure 2.4 BCI's 'Welcome to the Grindhouse' DVD menus allow each film to be watched separately, while the option to 'Start the Grindhouse Experience' plays both films as a double feature interspersed with trailers and other theatrical paratexts. (Source: DVD.)

sexuality shown on-screen, the 'New 42nd Street' is itself a product of remediation, with a shopping-mall or theme-park aesthetic remediating the long-standing entertainment centre. Indeed, the Empire theatre has even been physically uprooted, moved down the block, and converted into a chain multiplex of the very sort where *Grindhouse* would have played, the cavernous auditorium now transformed into a lobby from which separate screens branch. As one blogger astutely analogised, '*Grindhouse* is to grindhouse movies as the AMC 25 Empire is to the Empire: a gussied-up homage that can't compare to the real thing.'[118]

As this disparaging quote implies, some fans criticised how the economic impetus behind the revival of 'grindhouse' by a Hollywood 'mini-major' studio such as The Weinstein Company shared common ground with the same corporate economics that have revived the 42nd Street entertainment district as an easily accessible, family-friendly bastion of mass-cultural consumerism. Indeed, The Walt Disney Company had owned Dimension Films (not to be confused with the 1970s company Dimension Pictures), the genre label that released *Grindhouse*, until as late as 2005. Consequently, despite the threats to subcultural capital that the 'mainstreaming' of grindhouse films ostensibly represents, distinctions between mainstream and niche cultures are difficult to validate in fans' selective celebration of the old 42nd Street, given the underlying economic imperatives of historical grind houses themselves and their diverse mix of home-grown/imported programming from major and independent producers alike. 'If one looked beyond the paper-thin "do-gooder" veneer redevelopers were peddling, one could grimly appreciate that it was all in the huckster spirit of 42nd Street', remarks Jimmy McDonough. 'The Deuce was all about greed, and one con had replaced another on the Street of Dreams. Out with Bingo Brandt, in with Mickey Mouse.'[119] Meanwhile, the gendered connotations of the area's 'feminising' mainstream makeover have been figured as a 'castration' of a lost 42nd Street that 'will return to a futuristic squalor for our descendents to enjoy. Some apocalyptic, Disneyfied world of sleaze and pornography and blight and ruin . . . [is] genetically encoded into the urban ecosystem called Times Square'.[120] As suggested in the previous chapter, such apocalyptic fantasies about lost or declining exhibition sites are rooted in a certain longing for capitalism's decay, even as these same fantasies may also be unevenly marshalled by media distributors for consumerist ends.

Though 42nd Street's prospective redevelopers allegedly sought to 'protect the area's economic potential from the deleterious effects of the lawless environment',[121] we should recall that 'Times Square was the apotheosis of free-market economics, answering the demand for cheap and easy access to drugs, porn, and prostitution'.[122] In this sense, the old 42nd Street exemplified the very unregulated markets that find socially legitimated contemporaries in the neo-liberal economic practices of The Walt Disney Company and the other large corporations that have 'cleaned up' Times Square for their own uses – including catering for the individual consumers who make up fan cultures. The return of 'legitimate' corporate businesses was, after all, driven by city–state joint intervention into urban redevelopment, despite free-market proponents' diatribes against the same government intervention that has allowed elite corporate power to expand unchecked, at the expense of all those unwilling or unable to purchase happiness via commodities.

In the final analysis, if 42nd Street nostalgically occupies an imagined space of anarchic possibility at the intersection of exploitation fans' cultural memories and cinephiliac fantasies, then the physical and symbolic remediation of 42nd Street has actually replaced a realm of subaltern economics with far more dominant forms of economic exploitation that also threaten to erode visions of subcultural belonging and self-sufficiency (such as the once-thriving bootleg trading networks made increasingly obsolete by official DVD releases). The video-era sales of repackaged archival texts and retro-styled simulations of exploitation cinema are each inextricable from the very market forces that together fuelled the historical grind house's actual demise and symbolic remembrance. Furthermore, as advertisements that can be easily repurposed for both niche and mainstream markets, and shared across multiple formats owing to their indefinite copyright status, grindhouse trailers fit well into this neo-liberal regime of flexible accumulation. Small wonder, then, that contemporary fans' nostalgia for the grind house as a *lieu de mémoire* contains so much ambivalence, fostering both ironic distance and sincere longing towards the past and present advertising of these material sites.

Because most of today's consumers had no experience in actual grind houses, the genrification of 'grindhouse' increasingly works these films back into the bourgeois social fabric with which grind houses historically had such a tenuous relationship. Grind houses and Hollywood were never mutually exclusive, despite the discourses that often promoted them as such. Therefore, in positing these theatres' apparent difference from the 'mainstream', such discourses have largely reinforced Hollywood as American cinema's economic and cultural standard-bearer – not only enabling a niche market for exploitation films but also enhancing the profits made by both Hollywood and grind houses from subsequent-run major-studio films. While the marginalisation of grind houses as alternative exhibition sites may have been both sought by, and imposed on, these theatres from their earliest years, perhaps it is fitting that the struggle for (sub)cultural capital surrounding their genrified films now exposes itself as the struggle for economic capital that it always was. Consuming niche- and mass-marketed signifiers of the grind house to support their ostensibly oppositional stance, these cultural distinctions adopted by predominantly middle-class fans would seem to do little to question the normalisation of mainstream Hollywood as the 'good object' with which the grind house has finally been economically reconciled.

Yet, however implanted these nostalgias may be, their present uses cannot be simply reduced to duplicity or false consciousness. After all, as I posited in the previous chapter, fandom need not merely engender a wholesale reinforcement of the capitalist status quo; nostalgia's dialectic between past and present can also encourage self-reflexive contestations of the past's uses in present consumer economies, particularly because not all appeals to nostalgia will be successful with all fans. Heeding Andreas Huyssen's warning that, in a media landscape overflowing with appeals to memory, we must 'distinguish usable pasts from disposable pasts',[123] the following chapter expands on how *grindhouse* has become significantly productive as a retrospective aesthetic style used across a range of contemporary media texts circulated by official and unofficial producers alike. The non-normative connotations of social decay may remain a central fascination about grind houses as a lost, more 'authentic' site of exploitation film consumption, but decades of social and economic change have also helped deromanticise the cultural memories held by more self-reflexive fans – especially, as my final two chapters will show, for fans whose connoisseurship of archaic popular culture is inextricable from knowledge about recent industrial/technological shifts and ongoing historical inequalities that affect far more than subcultural denizens.

Notes

1. Daniel Makagon, *Where the Ball Drops: Days and Nights in Times Square* (Minneapolis: University of Minnesota Press, 2004), p. 50.
2. Edward S. Casey, *Remembering: A Phenomenological Study*, 2nd ed. (Bloomington: Indiana University Press, 2000), pp. 201–2. Original italics.
3. Steve Neale, *Genre and Hollywood* (New York: Routledge, 2000), p. 40.
4. 'Two-a-Day Policy Failure in Canadian Grind Houses', *Variety*, 6 December 1923, p. 19.
5. Arthur Mayer, *Merely Colossal: The Story of the Movies from the Long Chase to the Chaise Longue* (New York: Simon and Schuster, 1953), pp. 174–7.
6. Anthony Bianco, *Ghosts of 42nd Street: A History of America's Most Infamous Block* (New York: William Morrow, 2004), p. 133; and '42nd Street Movies Bow to Good Taste', *New York Times*, 23 October 1954.
7. 'Grinds on 42nd Street Keep Wartime Prices', *Boxoffice*, 18 June 1949, p. 50-C; and Jimmy McDonough, *The Ghastly One: The Sex–Gore Netherworld of Filmmaker Andy Milligan* (Chicago: A Cappella Books, 2001), pp. 116–17 (quoted).
8. 'Two-a-Day Policy Failure', p. 19.
9. Nelson B. Bell, 'Behind the Screens', *The Washington Post*, 16 July 1929. I lack figures for the comparative number of seats between these two classes of theatres.
10. Bianco, *Ghosts of 42nd Street*, pp. 97, 109.
11. 'The Truant Playhouses', *New York Times*, 22 November 1931.
12. Bernard Sobel, 'New Amsterdam Lament: Being an Elegy on Forty-second Street's Last Legitimate Theatre', *New York Times*, 4 July 1937.
13. 'Downtown Boston Theatres Regaining Patrons as Suburbanites Return', *Boxoffice*, 21 January 1963, p. NE-1.
14. Quoted in Emily Towe, 'So That's the Movies' Trouble – There Just Aren't Enough Seats!' *The Washington Post*, 28 November 1943.

15. Suzanne Mary Donahue, *American Film Distribution: The Changing Marketplace* (Ann Arbor, MI: UMI Research Press, 1987), p. 13.
16. Andre Sennwald, 'Salute for a Brave Beginning', *New York Times*, 21 October 1934.
17. Quoted in 'Ex-Michigan Allied Head Urges Change in Thinking about First Run Theatres', *Boxoffice*, 17 November 1956, p. 24.
18. Mayer, *Merely Colossal*, p. 246.
19. Douglas Gomery, *Shared Pleasures: A History of Movie Presentation in the United States* (Madison: University of Wisconsin Press, 1992), pp. 137–8; and Tim Snelson and Mark Jancovich, '"No Hits, No Runs, Just Terrors": Exhibition, Cultural Distinctions, and Cult Audiences at the Rialto Cinema in the 1930s and 1940s', in *Explorations in New Cinema History: Approaches and Case Studies*, eds Daniel Biltereyst, Richard Maltby and Philippe Meers (Malden, MA: Wiley-Blackwell, 2011), pp. 199–204.
20. Flyer from the private collection of Jerry Kovar.
21. Ezra Goodman, 'Naughty, Bawdy, Gaudy', *New York Times*, 23 July 1939.
22. James Naremore, *More Than Night: Film Noir in its Contexts* (Berkeley: University of California Press, 2008), pp. 138–40. According to theatre owner Charles P. Skouras, 'the grind house, a small theater along a busy downtown street catering to transients, does its biggest business with action melodramas such as "The Killers"'. See Skouras, 'The Exhibitor', *The Annals of the American Academy of Political and Social Science*, no. 254 (1947): 29.
23. Neale, *Genre and Hollywood*, p. 39.
24. 'Hearing is Slated on Film Displays', *New York Times*, 7 October 1954.
25. A. H. Weiler, 'Life in the Old Ones Yet', *New York Times*, 24 August 1941.
26. See Laurence Senelick, 'Private Parts in Public Places', in *Inventing Times Square: Commerce and Culture at the Crossroads of the World*, ed. William R. Taylor (New York: Russell Sage Foundation, 1991), pp. 330–1.
27. Bianco, *Ghosts of 42nd Street*, p. 96.
28. James Traub, *The Devil's Playground: A Century of Pleasure and Profit in Times Square* (New York: Random House, 2004), p. 83.
29. Bianco, *Ghosts of 42nd Street*, pp. 97, 99, 119. See also Robert C. Allen, *Horrible Prettiness: Burlesque and American Culture* (Chapel Hill: University of North Carolina Press, 1991), pp. 253–5; Traub, *The Devil's Playground*, p. 91; Senelick, 'Private Parts in Public Places', p. 338; and Andrea Friedman, *Prurient Interests: Gender, Democracy, and Obscenity in New York City, 1909–1945* (New York: Columbia University Press, 2000), ch. 2.
30. On Times Square as 'a sexual paradise' during the 1930s and 1940s, see Mark Jancovich and Tim Snelson, 'Horror at the Crossroads: Class, Gender, and Taste at the Rialto', in *From the Arthouse to the Grindhouse: Highbrow and Lowbrow Transgression in Cinema's First Century*, eds John Cline and Robert G. Weiner (Lanham, MD: Scarecrow Press, 2010), pp.

111–19. On the area's place in the gay male subculture of later decades, see Samuel R. Delany, *Times Square Red, Times Square Blue* (New York: New York University Press, 1999).
31. 'Exploitips: *It's All in Your Mind*', *Boxoffice*, 2 April 1938, p. 72.
32. Goodman, 'Naughty, Bawdy, Gaudy'.
33. Tim Snelson and Mark Jancovich, '"No Hits, No Runs, Just Terrors"', pp. 204–5. Mayer also promoted his theatre this way in columns written for the *New York Times*, though I lack figures for how many women may have still attended 42nd Street grind houses during this period.
34. Lea Jacobs, *The Decline of Sentiment: American Film in the 1920s* (Berkeley: University of California Press, 2008), p. 19. *Variety*, for example, described the B western *Ridin' for Justice* (1932) as 'best suited for the double bills or lesser grinds' (*'Ridin' for Justice'* [review], *Variety*, 5 January 1932).
35. Bianco, *Ghosts of 42nd Street*, p. 101.
36. Gomery, *Shared Pleasures*, pp. 77–9.
37. 42nd Street's 'famous theaters have been converted into movie "grind" houses devoted to continuous double feature programs', according to the WPA Federal Writers' Project, *New York City Guide* (New York: Random House, 1939), p. 175.
38. Frank H. Ricketson Jr, *The Management of Motion Picture Theatres* (New York: McGraw-Hill, 1938), p. 82. Also see Gary D. Rhodes, '"The Double Feature Evil": Efforts to Eliminate the American Dual Bill', *Film History* 23, no. 1 (2011): 57–74.
39. 'Exploitips: *Black Dragons*', *Boxoffice*, 7 March 1942, p. 275.
40. B. R. Crisler, 'Bulletins and Comment', *New York Times*, 17 September 1939. *Isle of Paradise* (1932) was actually an American film exploiting Bali's supposed exoticism through the sexual objectification of its female 'natives'.
41. Eric Schaefer, *'Bold! Daring! Shocking! True!' A History of Exploitation Films, 1919–1959* (Durham, NC: Duke University Press, 1999), pp. 39, 119, 340.
42. Ruth A. Inglis, *Freedom of the Movies* (Chicago: University of Chicago Press, 1947), pp. 42–4.
43. Vincent Canby, 'Films Exploiting Interest in Sex and Violence Find Growing Audience Here', *New York Times*, 24 January 1968; and Kenneth Turan and Stephen F. Zito, *Sinema: American Pornographic Films and the People Who Make Them* (New York: Praeger, 1974), p. 18.
44. Herman Wouk, 'Proposal for Renewal', *New York Times*, 10 September 1961; Arnold H. Lubasch, 'Broadway Finds Builders Scarce', *New York Times*, 30 September 1962; and Allen, *Horrible Prettiness*, pp. 252–3.
45. Ed Guerrero, *Framing Blackness: The African American Image in Film* (Philadelphia: Temple University Press, 1993), pp. 83–4 (original italics). Also see Robert A. Beauregard, *Voices of Decline: The Postwar Fate of US Cities*, 2nd ed. (New York: Routledge, 2003), pp. 127–78.

46. Heffernan, *Ghouls, Gimmicks, and Gold*, pp. 64–72.
47. 'Exhibitors Urged to Combat Steady Flow of Sexploitation Releases', *Boxoffice*, 23 November 1970, p. K-2.
48. Bosley Crowther, 'Lesser Evils: Considering the Cheap and Violent Films', *New York Times*, 7 February 1960.
49. Eric Schaefer, 'Pandering to the "Goon Trade": Framing the Sexploitation Audience through Advertising', in *Sleaze Artists: Cinema at the Margins of Taste, Style, and Politics*, ed. Jeffrey Sconce (Durham, NC: Duke University Press, 2007), pp. 34–5.
50. George Gilbert, '"Better Show in Lobby" of Most "Burlesk" Pixers', *Variety*, 12 September 1962, p. 11.
51. Turan and Zito, *Sinema*, p. 244. Also see Joseph W. Slade, 'Pornographic Theaters Off Times Square', in *The Pornography Controversy: Changing Moral Standards in American Life*, ed. Ray C. Rist (New Brunswick, NJ: Transaction Books, 1975), pp. 119–39.
52. Clive Barnes, quoted in 'Arts in the 60's: Coming to Terms with Society and Its Woes', *New York Times*, 30 December 1969.
53. Gomery, *Shared Pleasures*, pp. 169–70. Also see Demetrius Cope, 'Anatomy of a Blaxploitation Theater', *Jump Cut*, no. 9 (1975): 22–3.
54. See, for example, Canby, 'Films Exploiting Interest in Sex and Violence'. Yet, as the same article notes, independent theatre owners may have only reluctantly turned towards potentially objectionable material because it was less expensive to acquire the prints for exploitation films.
55. Josh Alan Friedman, *Tales of Times Square* (Los Angeles: Feral House, 2007), p. 145.
56. '*TNT Jackson*' (review), *Variety*, 19 February 1975.
57. Sundiata Keita Cha-Jua, 'Black Audiences, Blaxploitation and Kung Fu Films, and Challenges to White Celluloid Masculinity', in *China Forever: The Shaw Brothers and Diasporic Cinema*, ed. Poshek Fu (Champaign: University of Illinois Press, 2008), pp. 214–17. Also see Amy Abugo Ongiri, '"He Wanted to Be Just Like Bruce Lee": African Americans, Kung Fu Theater, and Cultural Exchange at the Margins', *Journal of Asian American Studies* 5, no. 1 (2002): 31–40. For a retro-styled example of African American exploitation fandom turned film-making, see RZA's *The Man with the Iron Fists* (2012).
58. Rick Altman, *Film/Genre* (London: British Film Institute, 1999), p. 91.
59. Milton Bracker, 'Life on W. 42d St.: A Study in Decay', *New York Times*, 14 March 1960.
60. Joanne Hollows, 'The Masculinity of Cult', in *Defining Cult Movies: The Cultural Politics of Oppositional Taste*, eds Mark Jancovich, Antonio Lázaro Reboll, Julian Stringer and Andy Willis (Manchester: Manchester University Press, 2003), p. 41.
61. Annette Kuhn, *Dreaming of Fred and Ginger: Cinema and Cultural Memory* (New York: New York University Press, 2002), pp. 141, 226.

62. Giuliana Bruno, *Atlas of Emotion: Journeys in Art, Architecture, and Film* (New York: Verso, 2002), p. 27.
63. Elena Gorfinkel, 'Tales of Times Square: Sexploitation's Secret History of Place', in *Taking Place: Location and the Moving Image*, eds John David Rhodes and Elena Gorfinkel (Minneapolis: University of Minnesota Press, 2011), pp. 60, 66. Gorfinkel, however, plays down how later, hard-core adult films filmed in the Times Square area can still garner nostalgia among fans as well. See, for example, hard-core trailer compilations like *As Seen on 42nd Street* (2012) and After Hours Cinema's series of *42nd Street Pete* DVDs.
64. Stephen Thrower, *Nightmare USA: The Untold Story of the Exploitation Independents* (Godalming: FAB Press, 2007), p. 21.
65. Paula Webster, 'Pornography and Pleasure', in *Caught Looking: Feminism, Pornography, and Censorship*, eds F.A.C.T. Book Committee (New York: Caught Looking, Inc., 1986), pp. 30, 33.
66. Bette Gordon and Karyn Kay, 'Look Back/Talk Back', in *Dirty Looks: Women, Pornography, Power*, eds Pamela Church Gibson and Roma Gibson (London: British Film Institute, 1993), p. 93. On the history of Variety Photoplays itself, see Jack Stevenson, 'Grindhouse and Beyond', in *From the Arthouse to the Grindhouse*, pp. 135–9.
67. Judith Mayne, *Framed: Lesbians, Feminists, and Media Culture* (Minneapolis: University of Minnesota Press, 2000), p. 143.
68. McDonough, *The Ghastly One*, p. 98.
69. Peter Stanfield, 'Walking the Streets: Black Gangsters and the "Abandoned City" in the 1970s Blaxploitation Cycle', in *Mob Culture: Hidden Histories of the American Gangster Film*, eds Lee Grieveson, Esther Sonnet, and Peter Stanfield (New Brunswick, NJ: Rutgers University Press, 2005), p. 288.
70. Delany, *Times Square Red, Times Square Blue*, p. 79.
71. Stevenson, 'Grindhouse and Beyond', p. 140.
72. Barbara Wilinsky, *Sure Seaters: The Emergence of Art House Cinema* (Minneapolis: University of Minnesota Press, 2001), p. 124.
73. Mark Betz, 'Art, Exploitation, Underground', in *Defining Cult Movies*, p. 210.
74. Bianco, *Ghosts of 42nd Street*, p. 148. See also 'Bingo Brandt's "Class Sex" Cellar as Mate for His One-Theme Rialto', *Variety*, 10 April 1968, p. 14; and 'Lurid but Profitable 42d Street Hopes to Survive New Cleanup', *New York Times*, 26 March 1966.
75. Bosley Crowther, 'Movies – A Never-Ending Flow', *New York Times Magazine*, 19 April 1964, p. 38.
76. Max Youngstein, quoted in Stanley Frank, 'Sure-Seaters Discover an Audience (1952)', in *Moviegoing in America: A Sourcebook in the History of Film Exhibition*, ed. Gregory A. Waller (Malden, MA: Blackwell, 2002), p. 257.
77. Altman, *Film/Genre*, p. 101.

78. Noteworthy books that treat 'grindhouse' and 'exploitation' cinema as synonymous include Bill Landis and Michelle Clifford, *Sleazoid Express: A Mind-Twisting Tour through the Grindhouse Cinema of Times Square* (New York: Fireside, 2002); and Eddie Muller and Daniel Faris, *Grindhouse: The Forbidden World of 'Adults Only' Cinema* (New York: St Martin's Griffin, 1996).
79. Landis and Clifford, *Sleazoid Express*, p. 66; Donahue, *American Film Distribution*, p. 216; and McDonough, *The Ghastly One*, p. 103.
80. Donahue, *American Film Distribution*, pp. 214, 216-17.
81. For example, see Alan M. Kriegsman, 'Tarnished Palaces: Downtown Theaters Hold on By the Skin of Their Flicks', *The Washington Post*, 14 February 1971.
82. Roger Corman, quoted in Donahue, *American Film Distribution*, p. 228.
83. Herbert Gans, quoted in Lynne B. Sagalyn, *Times Square Roulette: Remaking the City Icon* (Cambridge, MA: MIT Press, 2001), p. 87. Also see Alexander J. Reichl, *Reconstructing Times Square: Politics and Culture in Urban Development* (Lawrence: University Press of Kansas, 1999).
84. Jonathan Soffer, *Ed Koch and the Rebuilding of New York City* (New York: Columbia University Press, 2010), p. 271.
85. Delany, *Times Square Red, Times Square Blue*, pp. 15, 91. On grind houses as historical 'ruins' and (homosexual) spaces of public sexuality, primed for eventual neo-liberal gentrification and (heterosexual) privatisation by the forces of transnational capital, see Rich Cante and Angelo Restivo, 'The Cultural-Aesthetic Specificities of All-male Moving-Image Pornography', in *Porn Studies*, ed. Linda Williams (Durham, NC: Duke University Press, 2004), pp. 162–3.
86. Stanley Corkin, *Starring New York: Filming the Grime and the Glamour of the Long 1970s* (New York: Oxford University Press, 2011), pp. 155, 160–1.
87. Larry Cohn, quoted in Elliott Stein, 'Wither 42nd Street?' *The Village Voice*, 28 June 1988.
88. R. L. Shaffer, 'The 25 Best Movies You Didn't See in Theaters', IGN.com, last updated 14 April 2011, http://dvd.ign.com/articles/116/1161784p1.html (accessed 28 April 2011).
89. Jacques Boyreau, *Portable Grindhouse: The Lost Art of the VHS Box* (Seattle: Fantagraphics Books, 2009).
90. Landis and Clifford, *Sleazoid Express*, pp. 299–300.
91. Stein, 'Wither 42nd Street?'
92. William J. Stern, *The Truth About Times Square*, Perspectives on Eminent Domain Abuse (Arlington, VA: Institute for Justice, 2009), pp. 4–5. Meanwhile, the adult video industry declared such crusading clean-up attempts to be a distraction from local politicians' inability to solve the city's larger problems ('Exile on 42nd Street', *Adult Video News*, November 1994, p. 156).
93. Marshall Berman, 'Too Much is Not Enough: Metamorphoses of Times

Square', in *Impossible Presence: Surface and Screen in the Photogenic Era*, ed. Terry Smith (Chicago: University of Chicago Press, 2001), pp. 67–8.
94. Andrea Juno, 'Interview: Frank Henenlotter', in *Re/Search #10: Incredibly Strange Films*, eds Andrea Juno and V. Vale (San Francisco: V/Search Publications, 1986), p. 8.
95. Vincent Canby, 'Now For a Look at Some Really Bad Movies', *New York Times*, 30 November 1975.
96. Snelson and Jancovich, '"No Hits, No Runs, Just Terrors"', pp. 208–9; and Peter Stanfield, 'Going Underground with Manny Farber and Jonas Mekas: New York's Subterranean Film Culture in the 1950s and 1960s', in *Explorations in New Cinema History*, pp. 212–25. This intersection of traditions is particularly ironic if we consider that some avant-garde film-makers intentionally degraded their celluloid prints with scratches and solvents, whereas more recent propagators of an ersatz 'grindhouse aesthetic' intentionally degrade their filmic images for less overtly experimental purposes.
97. Turan and Zito, *Sinema*, p. 245.
98. Ibid., p. 107.
99. Lisa Kernan, *Coming Attractions: Reading American Movie Trailers* (Austin: University of Texas Press, 2004), pp. 10, 15–17, 208.
100. Chris Nielson, '*42nd Street Forever, Volume 4: Cooled by Refrigeration*' (review), DVD Talk, last modified 27 January 2009, http://www.dvdtalk.com/reviews/35599/42nd-street-forever-volume-4-chilled-by-refrigeration/ (accessed 9 September 2011).
101. Canby, 'Films Exploiting Interest in Sex and Violence'.
102. McDonough, *The Ghastly One*, p. 109.
103. On early VHS compilation releases, see Stephen Jones, 'The Good, the Bad, and the Worthless: A Compendium of Compilations', in *Shock Xpress 2: The Essential Guide to Exploitation Cinema*, ed. Stefan Jaworzyn (London: Titan Books, 1994), pp. 87–90.
104. Jeremy, '*42nd Street Forever, Vol. 4* DVD Review', HorrorDigital.com, last modified 13 January 2011, http://www.horrordvds.com/viewarticle.php?articleid=800 (accessed 9 September 2011).
105. See Richard Nowell, *Blood Money: A History of the First Teen Slasher Film Cycle* (New York: Continuum, 2011), pp. 29–41.
106. Kernan, *Coming Attractions*, p. 6.
107. Eric Moro, 'SXSW 07: *Grindhouse* Revealed!' IGN.com, last modified 11 March 2007, http://movies.ign.com/articles/772/772092p1.html (accessed 14 September 2011).
108. Lance Lawson, 'My Evening with Q', in *Quentin Tarantino: Interviews*, ed. Gerald Peary (Jackson: University Press of Mississippi, 1998), p. 186.
109. Drehli Robnik, 'Mass Memories of Movies: Cinephilia as Norm and Narrative in Blockbuster Culture', in *Cinephilia: Movies, Love, and Memory*, eds Marijke de Valck and Malte Hagener (Amsterdam: Amsterdam University Press, 2005), p. 59.

110. Kernan, *Coming Attractions*, p. 45.
111. Hollows, 'The Masculinity of Cult', p. 37.
112. Caetlin Benson-Allott, '*Grindhouse*: An Experiment in the Death of Cinema', *Film Quarterly* 62, no. 1 (2008): 23–4. Also see Chuck Tryon, *Reinventing Cinema: Movies in the Age of Media Convergence* (New Brunswick, NJ: Rutgers University Press, 2009), pp. 62–3.
113. For example, see William Arnold, '"Grindhouse": Vile, Disgusting, Gory – and Yet, You Have to Laugh', *Seattle Post-Intelligencer*, 5 April 2007; and Tricia Olszewski, '*Grindhouse*' (review), *Washington City Paper*, 13 April 2007.
114. MrDisgusting, 'Eli Roth Confirms "Trailer Trash" Date, New Details!' *Bloody-Disgusting*, last modified 12 October 2007, http://www.bloody-disgusting.com/news/10135 (accessed 26 September 2011).
115. Greg Nicotero, quoted in Quentin Tarantino and Robert Rodriguez, *Grindhouse: The Sleaze-Filled Saga of an Exploitation Double Feature*, ed. Kurt Volk (New York: Weinstein Books, 2007), p. 105.
116. Julian Hoxter, 'Taking Possession: Cult Learning in *The Exorcist*', in *Unruly Pleasures: The Cult Film and its Critics*, eds Xavier Mendik and Graeme Harper (Guildford: FAB Press, 2000), p. 178.
117. José van Dijck, *Mediated Memories in the Digital Age* (Stanford, CA: Stanford University Press, 2007), p. 89.
118. Lawrence Levi, 'Color Me Blood Red', Looker, last modified 13 April 2007, http://looker.typepad.com/looker/2007/04/color_me_blood_.html (accessed 26 September 2011).
119. McDonough, *The Ghastly One*, p. 296.
120. Friedman, *Tales of Times Square*, pp. 285, 288–9.
121. Stern, *The Truth About Times Square*, p. 8.
122. Soffer, *Ed Koch*, p. 271.
123. Andreas Huyssen, 'Present Pasts: Media, Politics, Amnesia', *Public Culture* 12, no. 1 (2000): 38.

CHAPTER 3

Paratexts, Pastiche and the Direct-to-video Aesthetic: Towards a Retrosploitation Mediascape

A cinematic image of nostalgia is a double exposure, or a superimposition of two images – of home and abroad, past and present, dream and everyday life. The moment we try to force it into a single image, it breaks the frame or burns the surface.

Svetlana Boym, *The Future of Nostalgia*[1]

I know we all need another retrosploitation movie like we need a hole in the head.

Cortez the Killer, *Planet of Terror* blog[2]

A red plastic VHS cassette titled *The Sleeper* slides from an oversized slipcase dotted with creases, scuffs and hastily taped corners. A rainbow-striped banner rings the outside of the slipcase's top edge, while a 'Hi-Fi Stereo' logo sits in one corner and a circular sticker with the generic label 'Horror' adorns the other (Figure 3.1). Several still images from the film (a bloodied victim, a brandished knife, a worried young woman on a telephone) appear on the back of the box, just above the prominent warning 'This film contains violence and gore which may be considered shocking. Must be 17 or older to rent'. The cassette itself bears a smiley-faced sticker warning of a '50¢ charge if tape isn't rewound'. Yet, despite its emulation of an early-1980s ex-rental tape, my copy of *The Sleeper* arrived brand new when it premiered on video in January 2012, available as a DVD/VHS combo pack – a strange anomaly more than three years after final shipments of pre-recorded VHS tapes had left American warehouses.[3] A contemporary-styled DVD case featuring completely different cover art, a listing of special features, and other standard information lurks within the same oversized VHS-styled slipcase – a notable subordination of the newer format to the overall shape of the residual one.

Set on a college campus circa 1981, Justin Russell's independent film faithfully captures the look and feel of slasher films such as *Final Exam* (1981), *The Dorm That Dripped Blood* (1982), and *The House on Sorority*

120   GRINDHOUSE NOSTALGIA

Figure 3.1 DVD/VHS combo pack for Justin Russell's retro-styled slasher film *The Sleeper* (2012), with faux-aged packaging emulating a well-worn, 1980s-era ex-rental cassette. (Source: author's collection.)

Row (1983), not only in its packaging but also in its overall filmic design. As Russell explains,

> I grew up going to the video store on the weekends, looking at all the old boxes and artwork. I was too young to rent the movies I saw, but my older brother always

collected these films, which gave me access to a few of the classics [. . .] [B]ecause I love 80's slashers, I knew I couldn't do a modern movie and that the nostalgia aspect of *The Sleeper* was going to be a huge part of making the story work, and so I shopped everywhere I could for vintage stuff.[4]

For Russell, then, the production of his film was largely fuelled by nostalgia, suggesting an area of overlap between the consumption of actual vintage goods from second-hand shops and the fabrication of simulated vintage texts. This nostalgia has even translated into the format specificity of its video playback, recalling the residual VHS tapes today found primarily at second-hand outlets. Unlike the audiovisual 'cleanness' of the DVD transfer, playback of *The Sleeper*'s VHS cassette intentionally bears format-specific artefacting, such as fine white blemishes in the transfer and colours that gently bleed over sharp edges because of the lower image resolution. Indeed, this keen attention to ambient details that would not have been present in a theatrical release on celluloid is particularly telling as a signifier of format-specific nostalgias for exploitation films best known through their video afterlives. Released at a time when home video revenues have thoroughly supplanted theatrical box-office returns and encouraged direct-to-video (DTV) genre films to gradually become less distinguishable from major-studio fare, *The Sleeper*'s nostalgia for dated (para)texts and specifically *non-theatrical* residual technologies adds a notable complication to what previous chapters have described as exploitation fans' longing for the spatio-temporal pleasures of theatrical exhibition.

As *The Sleeper* makes clear, the release of *Grindhouse* (2007) may have represented a high-water mark of popular visibility in the cultural revival of 'grindhouse' as a transmedia concept but we should not neglect that it has been far from alone in offering retro-styled works drawn heavily from the aesthetic sensibilities of 1960s–80s exploitation cinema. Much as I suggested in Chapter 1 that nostalgia for residual video technologies can throw teleological valuations (that is, assumptions that newer forms are always better) into question, the 'rebellious' embrace of outdated theatrical exhibition contexts can also be undercut by some fans' nostalgic embrace of exploitative genre films that would have premiered on home video during and since the VHS era.[5] This chapter thus explores the roots of a retrosploitation cycle that predated the Robert Rodriguez/Quentin Tarantino film, stretching back into a number of 1980s DTV releases – but which has also extended forward into the wider mediascape in recent years, appearing in books, music videos, commercials, video games and so on.

Like the fetishisation of cinematic decay noted in the previous chapter, these works have become more desirable for their simulated wear and tear precisely at a time when so many archival exploitation films are being audiovisually restored and repackaged for widespread consumption. Consequently, though fans have used such terms as 'neo-grindhouse', 'neo-exploitation', 'pseudotronic' and 'fauxsploitation' to describe the recent cycle of anachronistic exploitation throwbacks, I prefer the neologism *retrosploitation* because it also recalls the retro-coded remediation of archival exploitation texts as a related tendency to blend ironic distance and nostalgic sincerity within home video's contemporary appeals.

Retrosploitation represents a particularly salient case of how cinema self-consciously 'turns to the register of the past' as an ostensible defence against the threat of post-cinematic technologies. Contemporary cinema embraces a certain degree of imagined marginalisation through a 'textualisation of film technology's relationship to the past, to human and collective memory, in contrast and competition with the same relationships as mediated by different technologies'.[6] As I shall explain, the role of nostalgic pastness looms large in the taste valuations that fans apply to many exploitation-style films, since some texts seemingly lack the historical datedness to be considered 'exploitation' by many contemporary fans but nevertheless continue to embody the economic and textual characteristics of an earlier period of exploitation cinema. Other titles may evince a retro style in their paratextual marketing materials alone but be otherwise indistinguishable from the average DTV or made-for-cable television movie.

As my previous chapters argued, the increased domestic accessibility of exploitation cinema can seemingly threaten subcultural ideologies of exclusivity, nonconformity, and connoisseurship – regardless of how questionable such gendered and classed claims may be in actual practice. Meanwhile, the spatio-temporal nostalgia that fans attach to niche theatrical contexts is further thrown into question by the increasingly privileged place that exploitation cinema's stylistic and industrial inheritors have secured in the non-theatrical market. *Grindhouse*'s lacklustre theatrical box-office returns, for example, did not staunch the subsequent cycle of works following in its stylistic footsteps, largely because of the overall film industry's reliance on home video profits that substantially exceed box-office receipts. Home video profits have outpaced theatrical returns since 1987–88 but this state of affairs has only become more acute with the rapid market penetration of DVD and its associated sell-through market. By 2004, video retail and rental together 'accounted for over half of all expenditure on filmed entertainment', compared to 24 per cent on theatrical ticket sales.[7] The accompanying rise of a DTV market for genre films, albeit garnering less cultural value than theatrically released titles, has increasingly blurred the distinctions between theatrically released exploitation films from the height of the post-classical era; video-era independent films attempting earnestly to imitate the sensibilities of those earlier works; and films engaging in self-parody to intentionally garner paracinematic responses. By exploring the retro-styled appeal (and lack of appeal) of films such as *Grindhouse* and its kin against the backdrop of these industrial shifts, I argue that the lucrative rise of DTV cinema has allowed generically self-conscious, film-historically referential texts such as retrosploitation to gain greater spatio-temporal mobility in the contemporary marketplace, including extending well beyond niche fan cultures.

With exploitative genre releases now often going straight to video, or even being made by convergence-era 'prosumer' fan film-makers who potentially lack the 'outsider' mystique of old-school, low-budget auteurs, the home has become an especially fraught space for the production and circulation of exploitation film nostalgia. These final two chapters, then, shift more squarely towards how the domesticity of home video has tainted contemporary retro-styled productions of pastness. Focusing on films and other media which fans have identified as belonging to the retrosploitation trend, this chapter examines the various stylistic, aesthetic and tonal strategies that recur throughout the cycle, whereas the following chapter analyses the political implications of its engagement with history. In focusing on the historicity simulated by these retro-styled texts, we can see that retrosploitation relies less on signifiers drained of historical meaning than on evaluatively toned colourings of pastness which fans may engage with considerably mixed feelings as exploitation cinema's past and present increasingly coexist in the home. As arguably the cycle's *ne plus ultra*, *Grindhouse* serves as a centrepiece for this discussion in relation to the larger phenomenon of DVD/Blu-ray packaging, fan-made trailers and posters, and other non-theatrical entertainments during a video-saturated era in which the very lure of theatrical exhibition can itself be recoded as a novel gimmick.

Retrosploitation may promote certain unreliable or misleading cultural memories which distort the past (such as the 'missing reels' that abbreviate *Grindhouse*'s theatrical running time but were exceptional occurrences in actual grind houses), yet forgetting the past can also permit creative uses of pastness for future-oriented goals. Memory and imagination are tightly linked, mutually enabling processes capable of creatively offering 'subversion or parody, alternative or unconventional enunciations', not just constraining the mind into conventional patterns.[8] In this sense, I argue that the uses of cultural memory in these recently created exploitation throwbacks are no more inherently conservative or derivative than nostalgia itself. Awareness of the historical gap between our contemporary moment and the hallowed period of exploitation film history that they reference may lead these media towards the realm of parody – yet most of them are not simply genre parodies but rather mix parody and homage in complex ways closer to the imitative tone of pastiche – especially through a semi-ironic use of deliberate archaism that has come to stand as an ersatz 'grindhouse aesthetic'. Since memory involves a repurposing of the past for the present, these films and other media – much like the concurrent DVD and Blu-ray re-releases of their historical intertexts – participate in marketable forms of memory work that have made exploitation cinema more visible and widely available today than at perhaps any other historical period.

Beginning with a brief overview of retrosploitation's selective uses of archaism as interpretive cues to an intended blend of ironic distance and earnest appreciation, I use Richard Dyer's theories on pastiche to explore the general contours of an aesthetic indebted as much to the early years of home video as to the glory days of grindhouse theatres. Next, I look at the changing reputation of DTV cinema within the American film industry to determine how it complicates the taste valuations and reading strategies that fans have long linked with nostalgia for theatrical exhibition. Finally, I consider how these industrial factors have allowed *Grindhouse* and its imitators to be definitively associated with neither theatrical nor non-theatrical consumption, creating marked ambivalence over the potential subcultural value of their anachronistic retro-stylisation. Echoing my earlier arguments, I will explain how these (para)texts confer some sense of what it might feel like to occupy past times and places of consumption, even at the expense of potentially rewriting perceptions of exploitation film history by opening its once-niche celebration to a broader, more populist viewership. Accordingly, much as the VHS-era roots of retrosploitation arguably grew as a response to the massive sedimentation of texts from different times within video stores and catalogues, its recent cyclical eruption in the late-DVD era perhaps speaks less to accumulated anxieties over impending post-cinematic format transitions than to fans' and film-makers' grudging complicity with the opening market for emergent digital content.

Deliberate Archaism and Interpretive Cues in Retrosploitation

The films and other media forms described in these final two chapters (see Appendix) provide a range of interpretive cues which, though potentially complicated by the inevitably rocky terrain of fan reception, attempt to evoke pastness in different ways, compensating for their historical newness and cultural visibility by drawing mnemonic value from a longer tradition of marginalised film history. Owing to the multivalent mixture of irony and earnestness arising from nostalgia's requisite historical distance from its longed-for times and places, it can become quite difficult to differentiate clearly the tonal qualities evoked in these works, precisely because they tend to blur the lines between the imitative aesthetic categories of pastiche, homage and parody (even at different points within the same text). In my estimation, for example, retro-styled films such as *Pervert!* (2005), *Bitch Slap* (2009) and *Black Dynamite* (2009) open like homages to their historical referents but all three move towards a more parodic tone as their plots gradually become more outrageous. In contrast, films such as *Run! Bitch Run!* (2009), *The House of the Devil* (2009) and *The Sleeper* seem more closely to maintain a straight-faced tone of imitative homage throughout, as if seeking (however much in vain) to seamlessly disguise themselves among their historical referents.

Richard Dyer argues that pastiche relies on historically embedded frameworks of interpretation, including taste distinctions shaped by home video technologies. Pastiche 'may emphasise or downplay the differences between its sources, organise them more or less evidently and emphatically', but its ambivalent position between the negative tone of parody and the positive tone of homage necessarily cues viewers not to read it with a completely straight face; after all, pastiche is formally close to its source material but often marked by temporal or stylistic discrepancies.[9] Furthermore, Christine Sprengler describes *deliberate archaism* as 'a form of pastiche that involves self-conscious simulations as well as reinterpretations of past visual styles', wherein film-makers move beyond the 'surface realism' typically found in period-set films and, instead, invest in recreating 'not only the look and feel of the period in question but also the appearance of art from that distant time' on a formal level.[10] Whereas some retrosploitation films are set in the present day but draw upon visual signifiers of retro pastness (such as *Grindhouse*), others are set during the 1950s–80s height of post-classical exploitation cinema. Within, however, the important distinction that we might draw between present-set and period-set retrosploitation films (especially given the political implications of each, as discussed in the next chapter), there are no consistent uses of surface realism over deliberate archaism. For instance, some retrosploitation media have followed *Grindhouse*'s lead in simulating the look of degraded 35 mm film stock or other forms of material dilapidation but this particularly marked use of deliberate archaism has been applied unevenly to parodies, pastiches and homages alike.

At the same time, however, because a parody's success requires that parodists and viewers are conversant in intertextual knowledge, parody does not solely mock its referents but can also, beneath its negative tone, implicitly acknowledge the pleasures they originally offered. We cannot therefore assume that films or other texts using an aesthetic of simulated damage are necessarily verging towards either parody or homage because the tonal difference between those two imitative styles need not correspond with the creative choice to use that aesthetic. Importantly, the deliberate archaism used by retrosploitation practitioners including, but not limited to, simulated material degradation, represents an imagined mix of *historical use* (as signs of affection through repeated screenings or handling) and *historical neglect* (as artefacts treated as undeserving of cultural longevity and thereby relegated to remembrance by niche taste groups) – without automatically marking the evaluative reasons for that use or neglect. In other words, an ersatz grindhouse aesthetic created through the simulation of filmic dilapidation can very differently signify a retro-styled text's apparent value, depending on both the film-maker's and viewer's perceived degree of nostalgic reverence towards the text's historical referents – hence the ambivalence that fans may consequently feel towards the text's stylistic posturing.

Though shot on high-definition digital video, for example, three different post-production artists on Robert Rodriguez's *Planet Terror* 'experimented with [Adobe] After Effects plug-ins and scanned images of damaged film stock footage' to simulate three different imagined exhibition histories that could be selectively combined in different scenes of the illusory 'celluloid' master print. As Caetlin Benson-Allott observes, this illusion of celluloid history as one of the film's many exploitable elements is foregrounded in its opening credits, wherein the celluloid seems to distort and melt in direct response to the 'hotness' of protagonist Cherry Darling (Rose McGowan) as she go-go dances at a strip club.[11] While these selective effects self-reflexively call attention to the film-maker's hand in constructing the pastiche, they also simulate imagined links to countless past distributors, exhibitors, projectionists and other people through whose hands the degraded 'print' could supposedly have passed. In this sense, retrosploitation texts which use simulated print damage are simultaneously personalised through the fan's recognition of the author as an interpretive lens for attributing the illusion of pastness, yet also depersonalised through the fantasy of the print's own contingent history. As such, if identifying the personalised authorship of ersatz pastness ostensibly supports the individual fan's ego-boosting sense of aesthetic discernment, then the more depersonalised vision of the film as a nebulously circulating object of cultural memory complicates such egotism by implying a wide range of imagined past (and present) viewers well beyond the self – viewers who may not share one's personal or fan-cultural interpretations of the work.

As further examples, we might compare three different contemporary films that use the women-in-prison (WIP) film as referents. Whereas *Prison-A-Go-Go!* (2003) is an outright parody playing the genre's excesses for broad laughs (for example, a countdown clock inset in the corner of the screen throughout indicates how long until the next gratuitous nude shower scene), it also contains cameos by exploitation veterans Lloyd Kaufman and Mary Woronov. Such cameos are a common cue used by retrosploitation films in signalling their indebtedness to past texts – as is the use of soundtrack music borrowed from their historical referents, as when *Viva* (2007) and *Amer* (2009) use tracks from composers Piero Piccioni and Stelvio Cipriani, respectively. Meanwhile, the pastiche *Sugar Boxx* (2009) contains cameos by sexploitation icons Kitten Natividad, Tura Satana, and frequent WIP director Jack Hill – but the film avoids the blatantly parodic tone of *Prison-A-Go-Go!* by instead mixing over-the-top excesses played for deliberate humour and far more serious scenes played with a straight face. Finally, the black-and-white film *Stuck!* (2009) more recognisably occupies the territory of pastiche or even homage, veering further towards the earnestly melodramatic than the retro-sleazy in its story of hardened women trying to make do behind bars. Though the paratexts (lurid trailer narration, retro title fonts, and titillating taglines) accompanying *Sugar Boxx* clearly recall the 1970s, those for *Stuck!* operate similarly but recall an earlier, more social problem-oriented period of WIP films such as *Caged* (1950) and *House of Women* (1962), helping justify its relatively tamer and less outrageous mock-historical tone. All three films draw inspiration from the stock character types and plot devices of earlier WIP cycles but each makes different tonal uses of such signifiers of pastness. The faux-aged poster for *Sugar Boxx*, for example, is the only one from the three films whose promotional paratexts evince simulated material degradation. Indeed, it is not uncommon for simulated artefacting to appear in retrosploitation's paratexts alone, while the main text appears far more pristine – not unlike the restorative tendencies seen in the remediation of older exploitation films on DVD and Blu-ray.

In general, then, some retro-styled texts use deliberate archaism in a sustained way throughout, whereas others mark their appeals to retro pastness in a more limited way through paratexts such as trailers, posters, and opening credit sequences. Though not all parodies, homages or pastiches appeal to pastness in similar ways, paratexts have frequently become a means of evoking the sense of 'grindhouse-ness' discussed in the previous chapter, at least since the Rodriguez/Tarantino film popularised an imagined grindhouse aesthetic pairing material dilapidation with textual excess and sleaze. When, for example, the Southern Gothic melodrama *Black Snake Moan* (2006) went into general release a month before *Grindhouse*'s premiere, critics were divided on the film's tone, with negative reviews citing its 'blaxploitation-style poster' (featuring Samuel L. Jackson standing over a chained and submissive Christina Ricci and the tagline 'Everything is Hotter Down South') and other 'misogynistic' publicity materials as sexually objectifying Ricci – a charge with which a dismayed Ricci later concurred, arguing that the publicity glorified the exploitation of women in order to draw a college-age male audience.[12] The simulated crease lines and frayed edges of the poster (Figure 3.2), meant to resemble a battered and degraded pulp paperback cover, merely seemed to reinforce the image of an ostensibly battered and degraded female protagonist. While these criticisms are not unjustified, *Grindhouse* more blatantly foregrounded its indebtedness to exploitation cinema *beyond* the paratextual level, thereby providing critics and audiences with a more easily recognisable interpretive frame than *Black Snake Moan*. Though *Black Snake Moan*'s paratexts evoke a long-standing tradition of advertising pulpy movies about southern racism in sensationalised ways more closely resembling the marketing for sexploitation films,[13] *Grindhouse* did not share the same sense of incongruence between its publicity materials and the resulting film, especially by weaving paratexts such as (fake) trailers into its actual form. In other words, *Grindhouse* helped 'mainstream' a popular reception context for lurid paratexts by using the name of a historical exhibition context as a frame of reference for recalling a history of exploitation cinema to which *Black Snake Moan* was less overtly indebted on a textual level. Indeed, in the years since the release of *Grindhouse*, the reductive descriptor 'grindhouse-style' has appeared in countless popular press sources as widespread cultural shorthand for the particular look and feel associated with archaic exploitation trailers.

As Jonathan Gray argues, a text's ultimate success often depends upon the success of its paratexts in prospectively cuing viewers into the text's 'preferred' meaning. Consequently, the editor or graphic designer of paratexts such as trailers and posters may have more creative power over a text's eventual interpretation than even the producer or director – especially in cases where 'there is less countervailing textuality on offer from the film or television program itself to challenge the paratextual frames'.[14] With *Black Snake Moan*, the luridness of its exploitation-styled paratexts was not outweighed by enough countervailing textuality to avoid

PARATEXTS, PASTICHE AND DIRECT-TO-VIDEO 129

Figure 3.2 The evocation of a battered and degraded pulp paperback cover in the poster design for *Black Snake Moan* (2006) pre-shaped critics' negative reactions to the film's depiction of a battered and degraded female protagonist.
(Source: Paramount Vantage.)

charges of misogyny, whereas retro-styled text and paratexts worked in tandem for more understanding (though not necessarily more appreciative) critical interpretations of *Grindhouse*. In fact, it is notable that the concept for *Grindhouse* even originated from an archival paratext, with Rodriguez and Tarantino allegedly inspired by a poster for an exploitation double feature of *Dragstrip Girl* (1957) and *Rock All Night* (1957).[15]

As I suggested in the previous chapter, the use of aged paratexts such as trailers, posters, and title cards as cues to a retrosploitation sensibility is linked to the wider collectability of paratextual artefacts as a reaction to remastered editions of exploitation films whose restoration has reduced the surface qualities of historicity associated with mainstream cultural neglect. Yet, the VHS cover art, posters and other paratexts for exploitation films were often more lurid and violent than the films themselves, so this tendency suggests another reason why paratexts offer such a tantalising lure for viewers today, even when (or precisely because) promising more than they can deliver.[16] As I elaborate below, the creation of fan-made trailers and posters for imagined grindhouse films that never existed may even evince a creative desire to rewrite exploitation film history. Though the non-existence of the films being advertised may undermine the 'authenticity' of these fan-cultural fantasies in some ways, the fact that such ideas for hypothetical exploitation films exist only in paratextual form means these fantasies are not complicated by the countervailing existence of actual, corresponding films that fall short of the lurid publicity materials. Much like touristically browsing through the DVD menus of a grindhouse trailer compilation in place of watching, and potentially being disappointed by, the feature films themselves, unfulfilled fantasies of what might have been retain a certain allure among fans who value the marginal and obscure. At a time when bricks-and-mortar video stores are quickly vanishing from the landscape, when theatrical exhibition is becoming an obsolete convention, and when media industries continue discussing a future without physical video formats, it is perhaps little surprise that paratexts associated with past forms of marketing and consumption have become objects of a nostalgia for what *feels* historically lost, even if those referents never truly existed. Because nostalgia can invest certain objects and icons of the past with greater affective importance than actual historical importance, the success of such cues remains open to contestation by fans with varying degrees of subcultural capital – especially when disseminated to wider audiences than members of niche fan groups.

Though there are many ways in which retrosploitation films can evoke an apparent grindhouse aesthetic, there are some recurring cues beyond cameos, simulated material damage and exploitation-style publicity mate-

Figure 3.3 Like simulated celluloid degradation, a title card featuring a small-print copyright date, often combined with a freeze-frame, is a recurrent cue in retrosploitation films, as seen in Robert Rodriguez's original *Machete* trailer that opened *Grindhouse* (2007). (Source: DVD.)

rials. For example, the frequent use of an opening title card (sometimes emphasised by a freeze-frame) with a bold font and a small-print copyright date underneath is a familiar retro cue (Figure 3.3), as seen in Muse's 'Knights of Cydonia' music video (2006), *The Signal* (2007), *The Machine Girl* (2008), *House of the Devil*, *Machete* (2010), *Hobo with a Shotgun* (2011), and countless fan-made trailers. This particular cue recalls the historical need to copyright specific titles that might be selectively used as a film travelled through different regions and markets – a practice that Tarantino humorously references at the beginning of his contribution to *Grindhouse* by showing the title card 'Quentin Tarantino's *Thunder Bolt*' for a split second before it is replaced by a plain, undated intertitle simply reading '*Death Proof*', as if his film had been sloppily retitled by an unscrupulous distributor.

Of course, this self-positioning of 'minorness' is ironic if we consider that so many retrosploitation films are derivative of Tarantino's easily identifiable means of playing taste-maker. Like Rodriguez, Tarantino has graduated from one-time 'indie' cachet to his current status as a major player in the Hollywood studio system. Along the way, he has become an exemplar of the intermedial homage, especially in films such as *Pulp Fiction* (1994), *Jackie Brown* (1997), and *Kill Bill*, Vol. 1 (2003), providing a sort of popular template for how to 'properly' pastiche the past. Indeed, many of the loud title fonts, recurrent musical genres (surf rock, funk, Italian western scores), thematic and stylistic motifs (dynamic camera movements, slick gunplay, self-indulgent dialogue, gore-happy avengers), nostalgic cameos, and decades-old pop-culture signifiers seen in retrosploitation films might lead us to suggest that 'grindhouse-ness' is often seen by other film-makers as synonymous with 'Tarantino-ness'. An example of this potentially derivative quality is the present-set WIP pastiche in Lady Gaga's 'Telephone' music video (2010), which is styled more closely after Tarantino's own pastiches than actual WIP titles. Likewise, *Blood Moon Rising* (2009), *Hora* (2009), the video game *House of the Dead: Overkill* (2009), *Ticked-Off Trannies With Knives* (2010), and *Casa de mi Padre* (2012) blatantly recycle the 'missing reel' gag from *Grindhouse* with little rhyme or reason, as if an arbitrary gesture towards a gimmick that some fans and critics alike had begun believing was a conventional part of the grindhouse experience.[17] In this respect, Tarantino's curatorial marshalling of retro pastness has allowed him to become 'a brand and hence an inter- or paratextual framing device, a matrix of other (inter)texts that serve[s] a paratextual role in directing interpretation'.[18] Yet, if Tarantino has played an influential, even monopolistic, role in informing an emerging retrosploitation corpus, we should remember that fans' evaluative interpretations of his own films and his imitators are far from uniform.

Pastiche and Historicity in the Retrosploitation Aesthetic

Thus far, I have discussed the importance of paratexts in framing the intended nostalgic interpretation of a retrosploitation cycle that largely (though not exclusively) uses anachronistic detail in the service of pastiche. Further exploring the actual uses of the retrosploitation aesthetic requires that I now turn to the nature of its referential relationship to exploitation film history – including the creative rewriting of that history, a tendency which has garnered very mixed reactions from fans. James Morrison describes Tarantino, for example, as 'the quintessential director of a debased cinephilia . . . designed for audiences wanting to be flattered for their knowingness', to the extent that they need not even recognise and understand the intertextual references but simply know that the references are there.[19] While there may be a degree of truth to this lack of (sub)cultural capital for some viewers, because high levels of capital are not required to enjoy exploitation films or their latter-day descendants, we might also speculate to what extent high-minded cinephiles such as Morrison actually recognise and understand the intertextuality deployed by Tarantino in particular, or if such scepticism about the director derives from anxieties over their own vague familiarity with exploitation cycles they have only fleetingly engaged with ironic bemusement. In this sense, Tarantino contrasts significantly with other prominent retro-stylists, such as Guy Maddin, whose low-budget film-making career has consistently used deliberate archaism in simulating the visual look and melodramatic tropes of silent-era cinema while often drawing inspiration from minor corners of film history carrying more 'legitimate' cultural capital than 1970s exploitation cinema.[20]

Indeed, cinephilia may be intentionally recycled within a film itself, creating a bond of complicity between certain films and sympathetic cinephiles, especially when retro styles are used as a means of signalling imagined belonging in affinity groups who may or may not exist on the margins of official power.[21] As Michael Z. Newman observes, Tarantino is often criticised for playing with cinematic intertextuality like a game that lacks deeper meaning, especially if viewers who choose to 'play along' can feel themselves united by an 'anti-Hollywood' ethos – regardless of Tarantino's own position as a major Hollywood player.[22] Yet, Ava Preacher Collins notes that pop-culture texts are not passive victims waiting to be rescued from obscurity or misrepresentation through the good graces of those with high levels of cultural capital, such as scholars and other elite critics. Rather, popular texts actively participate in their own canonisation by intertextually conferring value upon earlier texts that have influenced them, as the work of Tarantino, Rodriguez and other so-called 'meta-cult' film-makers is apt to do in cases where cultural value is not regularly conferred upon exploitation films.[23]

The aforementioned criticisms of Tarantino also recall the hoary anti-postmodernist chestnut that the past is drained of historical meaning or significance when reduced to commodified signifiers – that is, a dissolution of historical or cultural taste value by economic value. An air of 'pomophobia', for example, lurks behind the oft-cited criticism that *Grindhouse* uses a fleet of digital film-making techniques and post-production effects in a paradoxical attempt to create an ersatz Benjaminian 'aura' of authentic celluloid pastness through a simulated veneer of film damage that (unlike, say, *The Sleeper*'s format-specific artefacting) appears uniformly identical across every print and home video edition. After all, it would seem particularly disingenuous for thousands of prints saturation-booked into theatres in 2007 to evoke the wear and tear historically caused not only by the continuous running hours of grindhouse theatres but also by the very shortage of exploitation film prints in circulation at any one time. As Jay McRoy aptly puts it, this is 'a big-budget exploitation film *about* low-budget exploitation films that deploys high-end digital technologies to (re)create a low-tech analogue experience to which only a fraction of their audience may be able to relate first-hand'.[24] Well noted by film critics and fans alike, this paradox fed complaints that the film's budgetary size and mass-distribution scale had misunderstood the supposedly naive and stripped-down appeal of its low-budget inspirations.[25] In a review of the biker retrosploitation film *Dear God No!* (2011), for example, one fan accuses Rodriguez and Tarantino of 'set[ting] the gold standard' for the 'modern grindhouse film' but doing so through modern film-making elements (digital special effects, highly trained actors and so on) that look too professionally polished beneath the simulated film damage – whereas *Dear God No!* was filmed with a 1970s-era Arriflex 16 mm camera, features non-professional actors such as actual bikers and strippers, and ultimately seems less like a contemporary pastiche than a lost 1970s film that is 'genuine and the total real-deal, something not so easy to come by in the age of faux-exploitation'.[26]

While I agree with these critics that *Grindhouse*'s anachronistically degraded style presents a fascinating paradox, I am not so quick to dismiss the project as unfaithful to exploitation film history or little more than a postmodernist sham, particularly given *Grindhouse*'s productive potential in inspiring so many subsequent imitators and variants that use historical referents in different ways. Indeed, if the film attempts to simulate an aesthetic aura associated with unreliable and implanted cultural memories of the grind house, then we should attend to what its uses of historicity *enable*, rather than simply what they foreclose, for fans.

Given this attempt to simulate an auratic 'authenticity', part of the ambivalence that fans might feel towards the contemporaneity of retrosploitation films can be attributed to the uneasy relationship between pastiche and kitsch. Even though kitsch has often been dismissed as the populist revaluing of cheap, mass-cultural goods that encourage easy emotional escapism into myths of past innocence, Marita Sturken argues that 'contemporary kitsch cultures defy simple hierarchies of high and low culture or class-distinct cultures' because they 'move in and out of concepts of authenticity'. Ironic readings of kitsch objects may make 'the edginess and tensions of history . . . more palatable and less present' by recoding tasteless and obsolete objects as valuable but these valuations can also overlap with the more earnest tone of pastiche. For Sturken, kitsch can thus engender a multivalent response that blends '(1) a prepackaged and unreflective sentimental response; (2) a playful irony; and (3) a serious engagement with history, simultaneously both innocence and irony'.[27] Yet, ironic readings of kitsch take time to develop, much as I argued in earlier chapters that the historical distance and subcultural capital accruing over time allow both irony and sincerity to be activated in the nostalgic experience of viewing archival exploitation films today. The question here, then, is whether contemporary retrosploitation films can encourage such reactions by simulating historical distance through a self-conscious use of pastiche that does not aim to wholly fool viewers into simply thinking that they are seeing an archival exploitation text. As one fan notes, many retrosploitation films 'veer dangerously to the edge of kitsch while continually hammering the message that audiences have somehow missed a unique period in the annals of American cinema, and [that] since this time has passed, we should accept their derivative offerings as placebo[s] for the real thing'.[28]

In Susan Stewart's words, kitsch can

> institute a nostalgia of the populace which in fact makes the populace itself a kind of subject. Kitsch objects are not apprehended as the souvenir proper is apprehended, that is, on the level of the individual autobiography; rather, they are apprehended on the level of collective identity. They are souvenirs of an era and not of a self.[29]

Rather than simply selling the sentimental illusion of innocence or ironically blunting the edges of historical conflict, kitsch's proximity to pastiche can potentially open the individual fan to a greater awareness of larger imagined communities, thus raising the spectre of historical tensions that remain in dialogue across past and present eras. As the next chapter elaborates, for instance, cultural memory can also open the fan's consciousness to unresolved political inequalities broached through anachronistic stylisation.

Unlike some of the period-set films that also exist within the realm of retrosploitation, *Grindhouse* foregrounds its particular project as a rewriting of cultural memory from a present perspective, in that it blends retro-1970s signifiers with settings containing George W. Bush-era mobile phones, cars, weapons and references to the 'war on terror'. Benson-Allott argues that the anachronistic mixing of retro and contemporary temporal signifiers 'dismantles nostalgic readings' of *Grindhouse* as an imitation of exploitation cinema's past, yet she also allows that there is a dialectical 'past-present temporality that reveals both its awareness of cinematic nostalgia and its desire to transcend it'.[30] This last comment is much more in line with what I am describing as a general retrosploitation aesthetic, because nostalgia may allow past and present temporal points to become loosened but not divorced from historical fixity, with nostalgia's multivalent temporalities and affectivity thereby preventing the political dimensions of historicity from being completely flattened out. As I argue in the next chapter, the violence in films such as *Grindhouse* may seem excessively hyperbolised or tonally updated for contemporary audiences but it is *not* 'reimagined, reengineered, and exaggerated until it exceeds any referents in the real world and becomes only about itself'.[31] Rather, the anachronistic stylisation of *Grindhouse* and its kin bespeaks a self-aware nostalgia that recognises temporal distance and playfully engages with cultural memories without emptying them of their functional qualities as indexes of historical anxieties and inequalities. As Vera Dika explains of nostalgia films,

> the replication of old images and texts, and the subsequent layering of references . . . has calcified the surface of the image, giving it a material density and rendering it a thing in itself. [. . .] Used as codes, these elements have engendered an internal friction between past and present, between old images and new narratives, and between representation and the real.[32]

For Benson-Allott, *Grindhouse* invokes a *simulacral* (as opposed to *simulated*) relationship to a historical exploitation cinema and exhibition context that never existed in the way they are portrayed here – but her argument is framed as evidence that the film is *not* nostalgic, as a result of ostensibly 'celebrat[ing] film fantasy, not film history'.[33] According to this logic, nostalgia requires original historical referents, which Rodriguez and Tarantino's cavalier imaginations seemingly have little investment in accurately replicating.

Alternatively, while I would certainly agree that the film distorts and oversimplifies the historical complexity of grindhouse programming, I would still argue that the film's ambivalent tone locates it more securely in the realm of pastiche in which fantasy and remembered history are not opposed but imaginatively linked. According to Dyer, pastiche does not simply imitate an original but, rather, 'imitates its idea of that which it imitates (its idea being anything from an individual memory through a group's shared and constructed remembering to a perception current at a given cultural–historical moment)'. Pastiche clearly signals to the viewer its imitative reliance on, and formal closeness to, past texts – taking an ambivalent position between homage and parody that may even make it difficult to recognise a text as unambiguously pastiche in form and tone – but still relying on a certain degree of audience recognition of its historical referents. Unlike the defensively angry or mocking tone of parody, pastiche does not mind being confused with its referents, even if it typically distorts them through accentuating, exaggerating and concentrating selected stylistic traits.[34]

The crucial point here is that, because 'pastiche always involves hearing and producing a version of the referent informed by the expectations and frameworks of understanding available, it involves producing what you want to, or at any rate can, hear in the referent and, usually, what you presume others hear in it also'.[35] As predominantly closer to a pastiche than a spoof, I posit that retrosploitation's tonal wavering between homage and parody is emphatically *not* a free play of postmodern signifiers divorced from history and simply sliding into the realm of fantasy. Rather, its potential for success relies on the historically and culturally specific frameworks of interpretation offered by cultural memory, which include the creators' shared perceptions of what exploitation cinema supposedly is, does and feels like (regardless of how historically accurate such ideas may be). Like other retrosploitation creators, Rodriguez and Tarantino textually acknowledge – through various stylistic, geographical or historical anachronisms – that they are not simply trying to plagiarise, fake or completely emulate actual 1970s exploitation films but are more interested in 'the possibility of inhabiting [the] feelings' associated with a past film-making style, combined with 'a simultaneous awareness of their historical constructedness'. Whether framed in terms of nostalgic loss or self-congratulatory improvement over the past, pastiche 'makes it possible to feel the historicity of our feelings', even while also helping to identify and crystallise cultural perceptions of 'grindhouse-ness' in a particular historical moment.[36]

As I have been arguing throughout this book as a whole, this general desire to inhabit past audiences' feelings is a sort of imagined spatiotemporal transport that can both unite and divide fellow travellers from one another in reference to memories of particular consumption sites. Retrosploitation media, however, also represent a cinephiliac desire to contribute by *creating* an alternative history of exploitation cinema, because pastiche does not require total emulation of its historical referents. Yet, the creation of these 'fake' texts is not a wholesale descent into fantasy but, rather, an affective echo resonating between the presumed experiences of past and present viewers alike. Fake exploitation trailers have become the most common representative examples of creating an alternative film history – even occasionally spawning feature-length films. Examples of the last include *Machete*, *Hobo With a Shotgun*, *Nun of That* (2009), and *Father's Day* (2011); similarly, *Nude Nuns with Big Guns* (2010) originated as a film-within-the-film in director Joseph Guzman's earlier rape-revenge film *Run! Bitch Run!* and was subsequently expanded into a free-standing feature after viewers began contacting Guzman for more information about what they had mistaken for an obscure pre-existing film.[37] This potential transformation of hypothetical trailers into actual feature films even recalls the exploitation industry's tradition of securing early production funding by creating and test-marketing posters, trailers and other alluring paratexts prior to the development of scripts or story treatments. Notably, the above examples all exhibit a degraded celluloid aesthetic in their paratextual origins but are far more pristine in their later feature-length forms, as if re-enacting (in a temporally condensed interval) the aforementioned audiovisual upmarketing that can occur as archival exploitation texts are remediated in the contemporary video market. Nevertheless, because they offer short, concentrated blasts of parody, homage, or pastiche that are accessible for participation by film-makers at virtually all budgetary levels, fake trailers remain perhaps the most creatively productive area of the retrosploitation corpus.

One of the most elaborate examples of this desire to create an alternative exploitation history is graphic artist Stephen Romano's 2008 book *Shock Festival*, a work of fiction that bills itself as 'One hundred and one of the strangest, sleaziest, most outrageous movies YOU'VE NEVER SEEN'. Released by comics publishers RAW Entertainment and IDW Publishing, the book is densely illustrated by countless fake paratexts exhibiting simulated wear and tear (for example, domestic and international posters, lobby cards, production stills, newspaper ads, magazine features, novelisations, soundtrack albums, make-up kits, and candid photos), representing an invented archive of exploitation films and personnel that never existed. The overarching story is not unlike *Boogie Nights* (1997) in depicting a quasi-familial relationship between eccentric and troubled individuals who repeatedly collaborate in the exploitation industry over the 1970s and 1980s, all brought together under the influence of actor/director Roc Benson. Most of the main characters are actors as well as producer/directors, conveniently allowing Romano to routinely conflate on-screen and off-screen chaos and vice – much like the paracinephile's focus on revelatory profilmic moments that may inadvertently end up in the finished picture. As one of Romano's characters reflects, new media may be able to restore these obscure films for a DVD release but no amount of cleaning up the pictures will clean up the depraved low-budget auteurs behind the camera.[38] Apart from the major players, some secondary characters also boast names that are barely veiled references to actual exploitation industry veterans. Romano's characters thus do not occupy a wholly invented parallel universe of exploitation film history but are, instead, figured (with tongue in cheek) as rediscovered additions to the real exploitation corpus – as exemplified by an introductory photo spread, purportedly of Romano's own living room, the walls littered with posters for actual and invented films alike.

In addition to creating posters for retrosploitation films, such as *Black Devil Doll* (2007) and *Beyond the Dunwich Horror* (2008), Romano has also designed retro-styled poster art for Grindhouse Releasing's theatrical reissues of actual exploitation films, including *An American Hippie in Israel* (1972), *Maniac* (1980), *The Evil Dead* (1981), and *Gone with the Pope*

(2010) – the last of which was originally filmed in 1976 but not completed until rediscovered three decades later.[39] The retro-inspired marketing of vintage and contemporary exploitation films blurs together here, much as it does on the three-disc *Shock Festival* companion DVD (2009) which features a plethora of theatrical trailers for real exploitation films, commingled with more than a dozen fake trailers (replete with simulated print damage) for invented films from Romano's book.

By creating an alternative history of texts that cannot be viewed beyond their titillating paratextual promises, *Shock Festival* represents the fan-cultural fantasy of competitively accruing a huge chunk of knowledge about films that other fans have never seen. As Romano fictionally self-aggrandises in his profile of one non-existent film,

> On the legendary 'Deuce' strip of 42nd Street, the film was a staple item, in constant rotation for nearly three years until the print was practically shredded. That same print which knocked 'em dead at The Rialto and The Cameo, pockmarked by age and chopped asunder by hungry projectors and trophy-seeking projectionists, was purchased by this author for one thousand dollars from a collector, and was shown just once to an enraptured audience of friends, after-hours at the Alamo Drafthouse Cinema in the summer of 2000.[40]

Yet, the very notion of most fans never being able to see such films also plays into the possibility that, rather than just egotistically building up his sense of self through the acquisition of subcultural capital, Romano's fictional fantasies are not too far divorced from the reality that rediscoveries of exploitation cinema's actual 'lost' texts – constantly unearthed in dusty storage facilities by enterprising independent video distributors – can actually defy a fan's feelings of historical-cum-personal mastery over the continually unfolding corpus.

Though fans may not evenly celebrate his appeals to nostalgia, the potential success of Romano's use of invented paratexts relies on creating a longing for lost objects that never actually came to pass, much as the misleadingly lurid paratexts for archival exploitation films frequently inspire a longing for textual satisfactions that are indefinitely deferred. Retrosploitation paratexts in general, then, share a common fantasy of providing contemporary viewers with affective access to past experiences of film consumption, even as the very recognition of these paratexts as simulations defers such promises of access as well. Despite the allure of cinephiliac desires for films that never existed, the nostalgic gap between past and present cannot ever be truly bridged, thus preventing fan cultures from coalescing around hegemonic interpretations about the (non-existent) films in question. Similarly, in those exceptional cases where a retrosploitation trailer is expanded into an actual feature film, the disjunction between paratextual promises and textual execution can be seen in the mixed reception that such films have generally received. By offering paratextual cues about films that may only ever exist in the viewer's imagination, retrosploitation's attempts to invent an alternate film history thereby reveal the openness of history and the contingency of fandom in general. Yet, as I elaborate below, such deferred satisfactions are a boon in a video marketplace where 'grindhouse' itself has become a lucrative transmedia concept that curious fans can follow across a path initially carved out by pioneers in the DTV industry. As the cultural reputation of DTV films has shifted over the years, so have the reading strategies that fans might use when such films encompass more diverse market positions and generic appeals than in the past.

Exploitation Films and the Rise of Direct-to-video Movies

Though the theatrical venues they once called home were in sharp decline, the early 1980s saw marginal genres, such as action, erotic thriller and horror films, given a remarkable boost of profitability through the presale of global video rights.[41] A number of prominent pioneers in DTV genre films were veterans of the 1970s theatrical exploitation market, helping flesh out the shelves of video stores in the early 1980s. As Linda Ruth Williams notes, DTV and made-for-television films have been similarly denigrated as 'cheap and formulaic filler products' that 'either never expect a theatrical release or gain only a very limited one to showcase a product whose real market is video'. Differing degrees of potentially offensive subject matter are included or excluded in such releases, depending on the targeted non-theatrical distribution channel (home video, basic cable, premium cable and so on).[42] Then and now, these films were usually produced inexpensively, with budgets ranging from $250,000 (or less) to $2 million, and costs kept down by the limited promotional costs needed. Apart from selected advertisements in genre magazines such as *Fangoria*, many DTV titles initially achieved public visibility with brash cover art, titles, and taglines for snaring prospective viewers passing down video store aisles – in other words, the same sort of paratexts that have long served the production and exhibition ends of the exploitation film market.[43]

Apart from the crossover of producer–distributors from theatrical to DTV exploitation films, the then-newness of VHS as a significant platform shift not only threatened the survival of the theatrical exploitation market but also increasingly associated theatrical exploitation cycles with the realm of pastness. That is, the very technological newness represented by the accumulation of pre-video texts on VHS allowed the historical weight of exploitation film history increasingly to inform the video-era inheritors of that tradition. In this regard, it is not surprising that many DTV genre titles deliberately recall earlier exploitation cycles and subgenres in more marked ways than simply carrying on cyclical or generic momentum but, rather, increasingly internalise a self-reflexive awareness of the ever-yawning historical gap between their present day and a past associated with the height of grindhouse cinema. Titles such as *Hollywood Chainsaw Hookers* (1987), *Chopper Chicks in Zombietown* (1989), *A Nymphoid Barbarian in Dinosaur Hell* (1990), *Bikini Drive-In* (1995), and *Attack of the 60 Foot Centerfolds* (1995) suggest something of the tongue-in-cheek humour that easily veers towards self-parody in films partially catering to the video-centric paracinema fandoms also developing during the same period. Troma Entertainment, for example, established itself as a distinctive brand name for low-to-no-budget cinema, deliberately cultivating an 'outsider' ethos of 'bad taste' and 'reel independence'.[44] The 1980s DTV entrepreneurs could thus nostalgically uphold the image of the heroic and romanticised exploitation producer working at the cultural margins while simultaneously participating in bad-faith strategies that used humour as a means of defensively acknowledging and playing down their engagement with the same older exploitation subject matter that they drew upon for inspiration.[45]

Though certainly not specific to the home video era, this increased turn towards parody, homage and pastiche for mnemonically refiguring exploitation cinema seems a recognisably video-era phenomenon. Indeed, as Dyer argues, pastiche's formal qualities cannot be divorced from the larger cultural and economic modes within which they operate; they are thus most productively generated in historical periods when multiple traditions are brought together, when new media make a huge range of previously inaccessible works available for reworking, and when the conditions of industrial capitalist production encourage the reproduction of genres, cycles and other recognisable templates.[46]

The diversity of these uses of exploitation film history, much like the diversity of video editions discussed in earlier chapters, is thus partly rooted in the class diversity existing in the taste appeals made by DTV films over made-for-cable television films. David Andrews observes that 'home video has supported a generic range loosely approximating the whole of the classical sexploitation circuit, while cable has subsidized tame variants on arthouse and drive-in fare, eschewing the more visceral, masculinized forms of the grindhouse' in an attempt to target a more middlebrow viewing demographic.[47] James Naremore also suggests that the critical tendency to uphold 'ostensibly disreputable, formulaic thrillers by appealing to their moral ambiguity and their lack of bourgeois sentimentality or "high-mindedness"' has proven highly advantageous for the film industry as a whole, because even low-budget DTV films might therefore have 'crossover potential, allowing them to play at the higher end of the [video] market'.[48] The taste/class-based mobility of DTV genre films thereby helps account for the various tonal/evaluative uses of pastness in video-era films, especially if an aesthetic form such as pastiche is 'not the preserve of the powerful or of accredited arbiters of sophistication any more than of the marginalised or oppressed; it is found at all brows, in all social groupings'.[49] In this sense, we should heed how subcultural capital informs the changing taste valuations attending a home video marketplace that rapidly consolidated during and after the late 1980s.

While companies such as Troma were toiling in the low-budget end of the DTV market, home video revenues in the 1980s allowed a number of 'mini-majors' to compete with the major studios by leveraging expected home video, cable television, and international theatrical revenues towards mid-level production budgets. As Justin Wyatt outlines, companies such as Carolco Pictures, Cannon Film Group, and Vestron Pictures banked on pre-sales and the lack of financial overhead spent on studio space. They used a combination of negative pick-ups and their own independently financed productions to release annual schedules of films that would numerically rival the output of the major studios, despite still relying on the majors' distribution networks. The income made from their home video releases could be reinvested in big-budget 'tent-pole' releases, often featuring major Hollywood action stars. As budgets ballooned to cover these annual tent-pole pictures, a number of the mini-majors failed to recoup adequate proceeds from their exploitation and arthouse releases after spreading themselves too thinly with pre-sale distribution deals that returned too little money to the original producers. Consequently, many of the mini-majors went bankrupt by the late 1980s and early 1990s while others, such as New Line Cinema and Miramax, were absorbed into conglomerates such as TimeWarner and The Walt Disney Company.[50] During this period, numerous independent films handled by the floundering mini-majors were released straight to video instead of parlayed into theatres, reinforcing cultural suspicions that the DTV release was a desperate cash grab associated with inferior films. Even on the lowest end of the budgetary scale, these changes affected independents by forcing them to upscale their product in a rapidly consolidating market. As exploitation filmmaker Fred Olen Ray noted in 1991, 'We have extended our shooting schedules from five or six days to seven. Our budgets have risen from $60,000 to $80,000 to $125,000 to $150,000. We are using more expensive stars in our shows (all costing $10,000 a day and up) and adding a second star of lesser value. We have started paying more attention to our storylines, while in the past we had let the genre, concept, and title carry the picture.'[51]

In many ways, middlebrow taste aspirations were the kiss of death for the 1980s mini-majors, much as they had been for theatrical exploitation companies such as New World Pictures and Dimension Pictures in the late 1970s. Though the DTV market may have still retained more diversity in its taste and class appeals than the made-for-television film, the negative reputation garnered by many DTV films echoes the suggestion that exploitation fans may denigrate cinema which seems (again) 'too historically recent to be recuperated as archival exploitation cinema, too standardized or proficient in its direction to be "bad", and yet possessing its own cult fan following'.[52] As Ramon Lobato says, they are 'mediocre' films in both industrial form and generic content, often characterised as 'interchangeable and disposable'. With the DTV market's annual output easily dwarfing the small number of theatrically released films, 'one is awed by its scope, but one also despairs at the thought of having to care too much about these ephemeral texts'.[53] Even as these films may draw upon cultural memories of earlier exploitation cycles for inspiration, they cannot as easily make claims to their predecessors' fan-cultural reputations because of their relative dearth of distance from the taint of contemporary populist entertainment. This lack of historical distance is especially acute when market forces have driven the format transitions allowing the DTV film's older historical referents to circulate more easily as remediated memory objects, serving as reminders of the newer films' apparent inferiority.

In more recent years, this comparative historical weight of the past has arguably been increased by the lower production, replication and distribution costs offered by DVD over VHS, which have accelerated growth in the market for new DTV films. Glyn Davis suggests that this flexibility has allowed film-makers to produce 'genre-messy movies, reliant on the possibility that, with the size of the DTV arena, any one title will always find some audience'. The class diversity of the market for recent DTV films is thus potentially reflected in a generic or cyclical openness that fans may find difficult to square with selective memories of earlier exploitation cycles. As Davis continues,

> Rather than being inept or catastrophically bad (although some may be), the 'undecidable' direct-to-DVD film is likely to be passable, workmanlike, possibly quickly

made and attempting to conceal the limitations of its budget. Flying slightly below the cultural radar of critical respectability, these titles may provide multivalent pleasures and can be riven by contradictory impulses,[54]

especially since a film's budgetary level is no reliable indicator of its appeals to taste. The DTV action film *Bitch Slap*, for example, bills itself as 'a post-modern, thinking man's throwback to the B movie/exploitation films of the 1950s through 1970s, as well as a loving, sly parody of them'. Yet, as a representative fan review complains,

> The movie attempts to be grindehouse [sic], uses elements commonly used in Grindhouse films, but relies entirely on modern film techniques: green screens, modern fight choreography with the film being sped up and slowed down at just the right places. The picture is crystal clear with no scratches, lines, over-saturation, or other comment [sic] elements that you would find in the film quality of a true grindhouse film.[55]

Another negative review notes,

> The true failure of *Bitch Slap* is its full-on mediocrity. To succeed in the low-budget realm, a film has to be surprisingly good or shockingly bad; this is neither. [. . .] These movies need to shine in ways that no other movies have, or they need to fall so flatly on their face that they'd be unrecognizable to their own parents. There's no room for B-movie exploitation that is simply 'okay'.[56]

Despite the film's brash mix of girls, guns and explosions, some fans thus found its retro nods to films such as *Faster, Pussycat! Kill! Kill!* (1965) outweighed by obvious attempts to deliver a slick-looking, present-set DTV feature.

Importantly, this polysemic quality means that DTV films may defy fans' ability to read to what extent a film seems intentionally tongue-in-cheek or self-parodic (as in Troma, American Independent Pictures, or Camp Video releases), or naive and unintentionally humorous (as in many pre-video era examples of exploitation cinema). With nostalgia unevenly inflecting the viewing experience for DTV films that employ a range of budgetary levels and generic conventions to draw upon cultural memories of earlier exploitation cycles, it becomes more difficult for fans to make connoisseurial distinctions between filmic traits which could potentially garner subcultural cachet. Much as fans may reject more recent films that lack the perceived pastness for ready reclamation as 'exploitation' texts, they may also reject films that deliberately simulate the 'badness' reductively associated with paracinema. That is, fans may be put off when the discerning labour of ironic interpretation is already internalised by DTV films that verge on self-parody, presenting irony for easy consumption in lieu of the sincerely appreciative nostalgia attending an older film that tries and fails to deliver straight-faced thrills.[57]

The retrosploitation cycle has increasingly come to occupy this contested ground of multivalent reception, since the emergent corpus coalesced through various blends of homage and parody, with inspiration drawn from the aesthetics and taste appeals of 1980s DTV films and their theatrical exploitation predecessors. Yet, as I shall now explain, this cycle – which ranges in scale from the fake trailers created by no-budget amateur film-makers to big-budget, major-studio releases like *Grindhouse* – also occupies a more flexible market position than its forerunners, since the mediascape has itself changed with the ongoing expansion of a DTV market whose returns are ever more claimed by major Hollywood studios as vital sources of revenue.

As exploitation fan cultures developed more cultural visibility while the home video marketplace evolved from VHS to DVD over the 1990s, a strange web of influences increasingly linked major-studio releases, independent productions and various DTV products. Tim Burton's heavily sanitised biopic *Ed Wood* (1994), for example, helped generate newfound interest in its eponymous director by portraying him as a quirky idealist aspiring to be the next Orson Welles. This interest in the real lives of exploitation film-makers, especially when on-screen and off-screen excesses and eccentricities appear to mirror each other, is also reflected in a burst of documentaries (see Appendix) whose predominantly DTV release during and since the 2000s coincided with the remediation of far more exploitation titles on DVD than previously available on VHS. Since the trailers and clips heavily illustrating these documentaries were now more easily available – often in better transfers – than ever before, the quantity and quality of this raw archival material helped increase the potential audience for both the documentaries themselves and the films they covered.

Another strand related to the retrosploitation aesthetic is the release of late-period films by notable exploitation film-makers, several of whom came out of retirement in the late 1990s – probably in response to the surge of paracinematic interest accompanying *Ed Wood*. Most of these titles went straight to video, and often veer towards self-parodically positioning themselves as intentional paracinema. In fact, I would argue that many of these late-period films are tonally difficult to distinguish from not only blatant parodies of earlier exploitation cycles but also from the films of Troma and other DTV producers.[58] A notable example of these late-period films is *I Woke Up Early the Day I Died* (1998), an independent comedy adapted from an unproduced Ed Wood script but played for intentional camp value by featuring ludicrously exaggerated acting, inserts from 1950s stock footage and educational films, and numerous cameos by notable Hollywood actors whose appearances add to the film's none-too-subtle winking at the audience. Other late-period titles include Herschell Gordon Lewis's gore comedies *Blood Feast 2: All U Can Eat* (2002) and *The Uh-Oh Show* (2009); Ted V. Mikels's *The Corpse Grinders 2* (2000) and *Mark of the Astro-Zombies* (2002); Doris Wishman's *Dildo Heaven* (2002) and *Each Time I Kill* (2007); and Russ Meyer's *Pandora Peaks* (2001).

Some of these films are clearly sequels trading on the cult reputation of their predecessors, while others more earnestly attempt to extend their film-makers' original reputations into the present without demonstrating retro-coded distinctions from more recent forms of DTV exploitation cinema. Set in the present day, Wishman's *Satan Was a Lady* (2001) and Joe Sarno's *Suburban Secrets* (2004), for example, are not played for laughs but ultimately bear a far stronger resemblance to the soft-core films that had exploded in the 1980s–90s DTV and made-for-cable television markets than the film-makers' famed 1960s sexploitation work. Unlike their peers' late-period films, which intentionally encourage paracinematic readings, these latter-day Wishman and Sarno titles do not necessarily encourage nostalgic or ironic reading strategies through temporal discrepancies or retro elements of *mise en scène* meant to invoke pastness.

Conversely, many exploitation parodies internalise the overly simplistic assumption that ironic mockery is the primary mode of exploitation film consumption. Examples of such parodies include *I'm Gonna Git You Sucka* (1988), *The Lost Skeleton of Cadavra* (2001), the television series *Garth Marenghi's Darkplace* (2004), *Frog-g-g!* (2004), *Reefer Madness: The Movie Musical* (2005), *Stupid Teenagers Must Die!* (2006), *Sex Galaxy* (2008), *The Disco Exorcist* (2011), and *Casa de mi Padre* (2012). This is not to say, of course, that these parodies necessarily fail to evoke the dated look and feel of exploitation cinema, or that they fail to deconstruct genre conventions in politically interesting ways, but that their overall tone generally evinces marked negativity towards their historical referents.

All in all, then, a key reception cue in some of the more recent titles which attempt to revive 1960s–70s exploitation film history is an inclination towards parody's hostile distance from the more earnest valences of nostalgia – but, intentionally or not, these films tend to overlap tonally with the low-budget end of DTV genre production. On the other hand, late-period films from exploitation film-makers who attempt to play it straight without drawing upon signifiers of retro pastness are more likely to be mistaken for other types of DTV productions. The use of retro signifiers thus becomes a crucial reception cue in the retrosploitation pastiches that, like *Grindhouse* and its kin, attempt to skirt between parody and homage, signalling their semi-ironic appreciation of nostalgically outdated referents while still trying to deliver affective thrills that are not continually undercut by humour. By deliberately recalling older theatrical exploitation texts, such strategies allow retrosploitation films superficially (if unsuccessfully) to distinguish themselves from the still-stigmatised DTV genre films of the VHS and DVD years – a task made all the more difficult as DTV films have spread into many different levels of the film industry without ever completely losing their reputation as too mediocre to be collectible and too recent to be retro-cool.

Notable examples of the low-budget exploitation tradition's survival in the DTV and made-for-television markets, for example, are the action, horror, sci-fi, and disaster films produced by companies such as The Asylum. With budgets ranging from $100,000 to $1 million, a raft of cheaply produced CGI (computer-generated imagery) special effects, and exploitable appearances by minor actors and celebrities, The Asylum (founded in 1996) specialises in 'mockbusters' made to premiere on video store shelves at the same time as the theatrical or home video release of a high-concept Hollywood tent-pole film, with a typical Asylum picture going from concept to finished product in an average of four months. The Asylum often draws inspiration from public-domain source material (*H.G. Wells' War of the Worlds* [2005], *Almighty Thor* [2011]), the title of an impending Hollywood blockbuster (*The Da Vinci Treasure* [2006], *Snakes on a Train* [2006], *Transmorphers* [2007], *Age of the Hobbits* [2012]), or an outlandishly incongruous concept (*Titanic II* [2010], *Sharknado* [2013]). The company claims that it does not intend to fool hapless customers with misleading titles or concepts but rather to provoke laughter from prospective viewers who recognise the titles' outrageous degree of derivation, not unlike porn parodies of successful Hollywood films.[59] In this sense, The Asylum and its kin recall the exploitation industry's tradition of producing low-budget/high-concept films exploiting the popularity of a major-studio release – yet they seem fully aware of the self-parodic appeals generating their intentionally paracinematic potential. There may be occasional nods to retro nostalgia – as when New Horizons' *Sharktopus* (2010), the story of a shark/octopus hybrid terrorising a beach community, features a peppy surf-rock theme song and a cameo by its famed producer, Roger Corman. Yet, I would argue that, for contemporary viewers with little historical distance from these films, their apparent and even deliberate badness tends to far outweigh the more earnest appreciation that can attend older exploitation texts, doing little to challenge the stigmatisation of DTV or made-for-television films.[60] Nonetheless, even *Sharknado* earned a midnight theatrical screening, simulcast into over two hundred theatres for one night only, after the jokey online buzz garnered by its 2013 Syfy Channel premiere, suggesting not only this DTV content's flexibility for different distribution venues but also an attempt to build its cult value through harking back to the theatrical exhibition of midnight movies.

Meanwhile, a plethora of small, independent producer–distributors have continued to survive in the DTV market (along with several mini-majors such as Lionsgate Entertainment and The Weinstein Company), largely because they do not pose a significant challenge to the major studios which have increasingly capitalised on the non-theatrical market for DTV films.[61] Earlier forays into major-studio DTV sequels were not unprecedented, especially in long-proven non-theatrical staples such as children's films, with Universal Pictures' animated franchise *The Land Before Time* (1988) – which has spawned twelve DTV sequels and over $1 billion worldwide to date – offering an influentially profitable example.[62] During the 2000s, however, most of the major studios created divisions devoted to producing DTV films – or 'DVD premieres', as such titles were euphemistically rebranded. Yet, this shift does not mean that major studios ceased distributing low-budget DTV exploitation titles acquired through negative pick-ups and other deals that have traditionally been useful for lining their coffers.

The recuperation of value associated with DVD premieres was partly rooted in the formerly higher cultural value of DVD compared to VHS's long-time status as synonymous with 'video', along with the major studios' reliance on branded titles, such as sequels and prequels to films that already carried the cachet of having begun as major theatrical releases. 'Franchise extension' became the name of the game for Hollywood DTV divisions, and not only in consistently profitable areas such as children's films or exploitation-ready genres such as horror and action films; particularly profitable extended franchises also included sequels to *Carlito's Way* (1993), *American Pie* (1999), and *Bring It On* (2000). Apart from catching the prospective viewer's eye from store shelves, television ads became one of the most effective means for raising consumer awareness about newly released DVD premieres. This marketing strategy, combined with studio executives' stated desire to make well-polished DTV films that would be indistinguishable from (and as profitable as) theatrical films, testifies to the contemporary truism that a theatrical release merely serves as an expensive advertisement for a film's considerably larger profitability on home video – a profitability that DVD premieres might better capture by eschewing altogether the expense of a theatrical release.[63]

DVD premieres from the major studios often involved an upmarketing of the films themselves, including better-known stars and budgets averaging up to $10 million – but still considerably less than most theatrical releases. As *Variety* reported, 'Usually producers bring back at least one actor from the original [for sequels], but barring that, they can turn the movie into a prequel to get around continuity issues'. As was true with the pioneering DTV distributors of the 1980s, action and horror films remained highly profitable DTV releases, as spectacular box art could still draw in genre aficionados. Similarly, former 1980s marquee-level action stars, such as Sylvester Stallone, Steven Seagal, and Jean-Claude Van Damme, continued profitable careers in DTV films that proved successful enough worldwide to justify $10 million salaries, bringing overall budgets to approximately $20 million – perhaps the highest end of the budgetary scale for DTV films.[64] Sell-through retailers became increasingly willing to stock DTV films on their shelves to generate sales in the months between the DVD releases of big theatrical hits. Especially attractive were franchise extension titles that could sometimes even rival DVD sales of their original theatrical predecessors.[65] Even as the overall DVD market began to plateau in the late 2000s, when the format achieved widespread market penetration, DTV films remained a growing sector of the home video business, with sales of over $1 billion in total revenue in 2008, up 20 per cent from the previous year; during that same year, non-theatrical releases accounted for over 32 per cent of all DVD sales.[66]

Yet, despite this potential profitability and increased targeting of general audiences, ambivalence remained about the stigmas long attached to DTV films, despite their euphemistic rebranding as 'DVD premieres'. Many articles in the trade press attempted to differentiate this newer generation of DTV films from their predecessors but this distinction was belied by the major studios' own practice of releasing a qualitatively diverse range of DTV films. As Marcy Magiera notes in a 2008 *Video Business* article, studio executives were excited to discuss their new DVD premiere divisions but declined to be interviewed about the other, more exploitative DTV titles from culturally denigrated genres ('[t]he word "schlock" may have been used') that they still released. 'Never mind that most of the studios that release the franchise DVD premieres also release the genre direct-to-video-stuff. But they don't want to talk about that,' Magiera observes, suggesting that the major studios' embrace of the DTV market in mainstream-targeted franchise extensions had merely served to further marginalise the sort of DTV genre product that had existed since the 1980s.[67] Dimension Films, the genre arm of Miramax (and later, The Weinstein Company), has also attempted similar differentiations by touting Tarantino/Rodriguez collaborations such as *From Dusk Till Dawn* (1996) and *Grindhouse* – which have garnered larger audiences on video than in theatres – as hip, superior genre releases, while playing down the company's 'continuing dependence' on 'B-grade straight-to-video product'.[68] Much as I argued in the previous chapter that major studios continued to profit from urban grind houses while designating them as culturally disreputable sites, the contemporary distribution of DTV exploitation films has allowed those films to remain posited as 'bad objects' in comparison with the proliferation of mainstream DTV franchise extensions. Many film-makers and stars, meanwhile, still desire the cultural cachet associated with a theatrical release because going straight to video has not entirely lost its early stigma.[69]

Overall, then, DTV productions have gradually moved into more central positions in the home video marketplace in conjunction with the format transitions to DVD and Blu-ray in the late 1990s and 2000s. Though the major studios intended their DVD premieres to become increasingly indistinguishable from theatrical features, they have continued to disavow or marginalise the DTV exploitation films that pioneered their distribution channels and continue to boost their financial bottom lines. As the market for DTV films increasingly extends beyond genre aficionados, such films have become an outlet where distinctions blur between not only the different nostalgic reading strategies that fans might employ but also different appeals to cultural taste. Consequently, the debated place of nostalgia has become far more intense among fan cultures as such films gain a wider potential viewership, calling subcultural valuations of 'authenticity' all the more into question.

Grindhouse, Fan Films and the Ancillary Aftermarket

In my estimation, this blurring of tastes and reading strategies paved the way for mini-majors such as The Weinstein Company to invest in a project like *Grindhouse*, whose middle position between parody and homage might have once made it prime DTV material (its famous directors notwithstanding), as demonstrated not only by the film's afterlife on home viewing formats but also the many DTV films that its retro-styled aesthetic inspired. Bob and Harvey Weinstein had learned a valuable lesson from the fate of other 1980s mini-majors, and therefore allowed The Walt Disney Company to purchase Miramax in 1993, gaining distribution power without openly competing with the major studios.[70]

Though initially successful in applying major-studio distribution strategies (such as heavily marketed nationwide openings) to art film releases, Miramax had faced bankruptcy before this acquisition. The Disney deal, however, allowed them to move into increased original productions, with trendy young genre film-makers such as Tarantino and Rodriguez proving early bankable talent.[71] As Alisa Perren notes, Dimension began significantly out-grossing Miramax following the unexpected success of *Scream* (1996), so the Weinsteins began promoting their genre label as a sophisticated cut above the competition while simultaneously seeking to prevent Dimension's generally low-cultural output from contaminating Miramax's middlebrow reputation for handling artier films.[72] Seeking less studio interference in the wake of Disney's threats to cut severely Miramax's overspent production funds and its refusal to release contentious films such as *Fahrenheit 9/11* (2004), the Weinsteins split from their parent company in 2005, leaving behind the Miramax brand name and forming The Weinstein Company. Shortly thereafter, Dimension Films (a label to which the Weinsteins retained post-split ownership) embraced an annual schedule of DTV releases under the 'Dimension Extreme' brand, such as franchise extension sequels and more original acquisitions, several of which would also receive nominal theatrical releases – including the retrosploitation films *Welcome to the Jungle* (2007) and *Hell Ride* (2008), throwbacks to the cannibal and biker cycles, respectively.[73]

With their extended experience running a mini-major, the Weinsteins were thus well positioned when the larger film industry gradually turned towards the attempted recuperation of DTV films in the 2000s. In 1999 and 2000, Dimension had released two DTV titles extending the *From Dusk Till Dawn* franchise, a film quite comparable to *Grindhouse* in tone.[74] Apart from being similarly named after an outdated exhibition context for exploitation films (the dusk-till-dawn drive-in screening), *From Dusk Till Dawn* opens like a gritty crime thriller as the Gecko Brothers (George Clooney and Quentin Tarantino) flee to Mexico with hostages following a bloody robbery – but halfway through the film, it suddenly takes an abrupt tonal/generic shift into madcap, gore-drenched horror–comedy as they discover their strip-club hideaway is run by ancient Aztec vampires who feast on wayward outlaws. This tonal/generic shift from dark crime thriller to tongue-in-cheek gore–comedy plays like *Grindhouse*'s double-feature format in reverse, prefiguring the shift from Rodriguez's gory, over-the-top zombie/action film, *Planet Terror*, to Tarantino's more measured hot car/action thriller, *Death Proof*. Both halves of these two Rodriguez/Tarantino collaborations contain (albeit in different proportions) humorous moments mixed with highly affective genre thrills but I would argue that neither descends into outright parody of the exploitation cycles to which they are indebted, instead preserving a tone that pays homage while playfully acknowledging their historical distance from exploitation cinema's heyday. In this sense, it remains difficult to draw marked cultural distinctions between *From Dusk Till Dawn*, its DTV progeny, and the *Grindhouse* double feature that appeared amid an industry-wide shift towards modestly budgeted DVD premieres. Furthermore, Michael Parks's Texas Ranger character, Earl McGraw, consistently reappears in not only *From Dusk Till Dawn* and one of its DTV sequels but also in *Kill Bill*, Vol. 1 and both halves of *Grindhouse* – thus roughly situating all these films in the same narrative universe.

Consequently, as DTV films became more 'mainstream' with the industry's moves to make them seem indistinguishable from theatrically screened films, exploitation content which once might have gone straight to video could effectively move into more prominent distribution channels such as a theatrical release (as with *Grindhouse*) – especially if the theatrical release ultimately remained an expensive advertisement for the later DVD and Blu-ray release. While the major studios might have continued to play down their own profitable involvement with the still-stigmatised, low-budget exploitation end of DTV production, the cultural upmarketing conferred by a theatrical release of such content helped potentially disavow just how blurred the lines between the theatrical and DTV markets had become by the late 2000s.

On a textual level, we can see this overlap inadvertently reflected in the selective use of digitally simulated film damage in *Grindhouse* (and especially *Planet Terror*), because this damage becomes most prominent in very violent or action-oriented moments. This technique makes viscerally powerful scenes seem particularly affective on a haptic level by implying that the diegetic violence has somehow exceeded its textual constraints and done actual violence to the film print itself, exciting the viewing body during those disjunctive moments when the film's own 'body' seems to be revealing the viscera of its apparatus.[75] Yet, if this were an actual degraded 35 mm film print, there would be no reason why violent or sensational moments would suffer more wear and tear than others, because the gradual degeneration of even a franchise print shown at grind houses should hypothetically show a relatively uniform degree of dilapidation throughout (apart from the well-worn heads and tails of each reel). Though *Grindhouse* may simulate the specific artefacting of damaged celluloid, I would argue that its selective use at such moments more closely resembles the degradation of VHS, a different analogue format whose image quality can be quickly ruined by viewers' multiple rewindings and replayings of

Figure 3.4 The frame abruptly jumps and a horizontal splice appears for a split second as a zombie smashes a cop's head open in *Planet Terror* (2007). This stylistic choice implies violence done both to the characters and the celluloid object itself, amplifying the moment's visceral assault upon the viewer's senses while actually obscuring the extent of the on-screen gore. (Source: DVD.)

the sexy or violent 'good parts'. In this sense, as much as *Grindhouse* draws much of its nostalgic power from the increasingly outdated cultural status of celluloid film stock and 35 mm theatrical projection, it also remains stylistically indebted to the pastness of another residual technology that has permitted exploitation cinema's afterlife in the age of DTV releases. Further complicating the subcultural capital which might adhere to the nostalgic imitation of distressed celluloid is Rodriguez's admission that its selective use at especially violent moments was a way around cuts initially demanded by the Motion Picture Association of America ratings board (Figure 3.4).[76] That is, while fans typically denounce the censorship of their chosen films as the work of conservative mainstream functionaries, the abrupt splices and flickers that might contribute to a more 'authentic' grindhouse aesthetic were actually attempts to please Hollywood's de facto censorship organisation rather than oppose it. As Matt Hills observes, fans often 'convert the very preconditions for their subcultural distinctions (consuming horror that is too distasteful/obscene for the "mainstream") into a force to be opposed and done away with'. Censorship thereby 'operates, culturally and discursively, as *the enemy and the engine of horror fandom*', helping spawn a lucrative market for remedial video editions that restore previously unseen sex or violence.[77]

In this sense, the lacklustre box-office returns of a film like *Grindhouse* were already a moot point if the project could recoup more than its production and advertising budgets via home video, regardless of the rampant speculation that arose concerning supposed reasons for the low theatrical attendance. As David Lerner summarises,

> Many cultural commentators blamed either the inflated running time or a generalized public misunderstanding regarding the unusual structure and experimental formal elements, arguments that assume both an audience too 'square' to accept the transgressions of the film, and simultaneously an audience not savvy enough to interpret the film's calculated aesthetic and methodology.[78]

In other words, critics suggested that a shortage of (sub)cultural capital seemed to prevent the film from appealing to wider audiences than fans of the individual directors or exploitation cinema in general. Fans also shared such speculations, with one noting that the grindhouse revival might seem too 'depraved' (that is, 'politically incorrect') for mainstream audiences but that it effectively delivered thrills to a jaded younger generation of film-goers while also delivering 'a great wakeup kick to the balls of [studio] executives who only want to play it safe'.[79]

More to the point, however, is Benson-Allott's deft explanation that *Grindhouse*'s double-feature gimmick was initially marketed as a distinctly theatrical event (Figure 3.5) meant to recall a lost downmarket exhibition context, since the Weinsteins had already decided in advance that *Planet Terror* and *Death Proof* would be separated and re-released as two separate, extended films for DVD (including, for example, the footage edited out as 'missing reels'). The $67 million film's opening weekend returns totalled a mediocre $12 million – a sum notably disproportionate to the online fan buzz the film had generated during its pre-release period. The Weinstein Company began publicly promoting the idea that each of the separate films was an authored 'original' whose integrity had been sacrificed in the assembling of the *Grindhouse* double-feature concept. Taken together, then, DVD sales of the disjoined films could ideally double the profits from a single DVD release of the complete *Grindhouse* experience and thereby draw in

> four to five times their initial box-office revenue (that is, $100 to 125 million). In short, *Grindhouse* was not just a loss leader but a stunt, an exploitation movie that exploited the press and the cinema's new *ancillary* role in the real business of the movies, the business of home video.[80]

It was also akin to the Weinsteins' earlier lucrative decision to split Tarantino's four-hour original cut of *Kill Bill* into two 'volumes' separately released to theatres and DVD.

Yet, many fans did not respond favourably to the consequences of the *Grindhouse* 'stunt'. While some were pleased to receive longer and more elaborate films from their cherished directors (or, in some cases, happy that one half of *Grindhouse* would be excised, given the tonal difference

PARATEXTS, PASTICHE AND DIRECT-TO-VIDEO 155

Figure 3.5 Poster for the American double-feature theatrical release of *Grindhouse* in April 2007 as an omnibus text and special exhibition event.
(Source: The Weinstein Company.)

between the two features), others accused The Weinstein Company of meddling with the original theatrical cut for crass economic ends. As one fan remarked at length, several years after its release:

> Those who did venture to the theaters were treated to a fairly unique experience; I can say without a doubt that it was the best cinematic experience I ever had with a crowd. [. . .] Unfortunately, the complete *Grindhouse* experience has remained but a memory – the film's poor reception resulted in each half being split up and distributed separately overseas, and that's how the films eventually made it to home video as well, which is a shame. Sure, *Planet Terror* and *Death Proof* work very well alone, but, when removed from their *Grindhouse* context, a layer of the overall experience is lost. It might not seem like much, but the grab-bag of trailers and ads are [*sic*] vital to the experience. [. . .] In the future, I suspect the amount of people who will claim to have seen the film in theaters will far outnumber the amount of people who actually did. It's already become the stuff of mythic proportions.[81]

As these comments imply, the theatrical experience itself became imbued with mnemonic value, with fans privileging its 'eventness' as a potential source of subcultural capital. Yet, we should question whether this simply resembles the old-school cinephilia that privileged theatrical exhibition over home video, or whether this eventness more closely resembles the fan-dominated midnight screenings that multiplexes have increasingly presented on the eve of opening day for much-hyped major-studio releases. Over the past decade, theatre chains have increasingly compensated for multiplex saturation booking by providing such time-sensitive screenings for fans to inhabit as an interpersonal show of subcultural capital. It is little coincidence, then, that the original theatrical cut of *Grindhouse* has continued to circulate as a midnight movie in the years since its initial release, offering fans the nostalgic pleasures of a cultish viewing context that the film's afterlife on home video cannot so easily confer.

At the same time, rather than the traditional view of the director's cut as a remedial release that 'corrects' the results of a studio's interference with an authorial vision, it is ironic that some fans criticised the splitting of *Grindhouse* into separate, extended films as an economically motivated violation of a sacrosanct original experience, because this decision had actually *restored* an authorial aura to each individual feature by effectively creating two new 'director's cuts'. After the extended cuts of each film were separately released in Europe and the rest of the world, these versions were eventually released on DVD in the United States in late 2007 (sans most of the ads and trailers). Because these longer and supposedly more 'authentic' versions of each film had not yet received a US theatrical release under their own titles, *Planet Terror* and *Death Proof* had

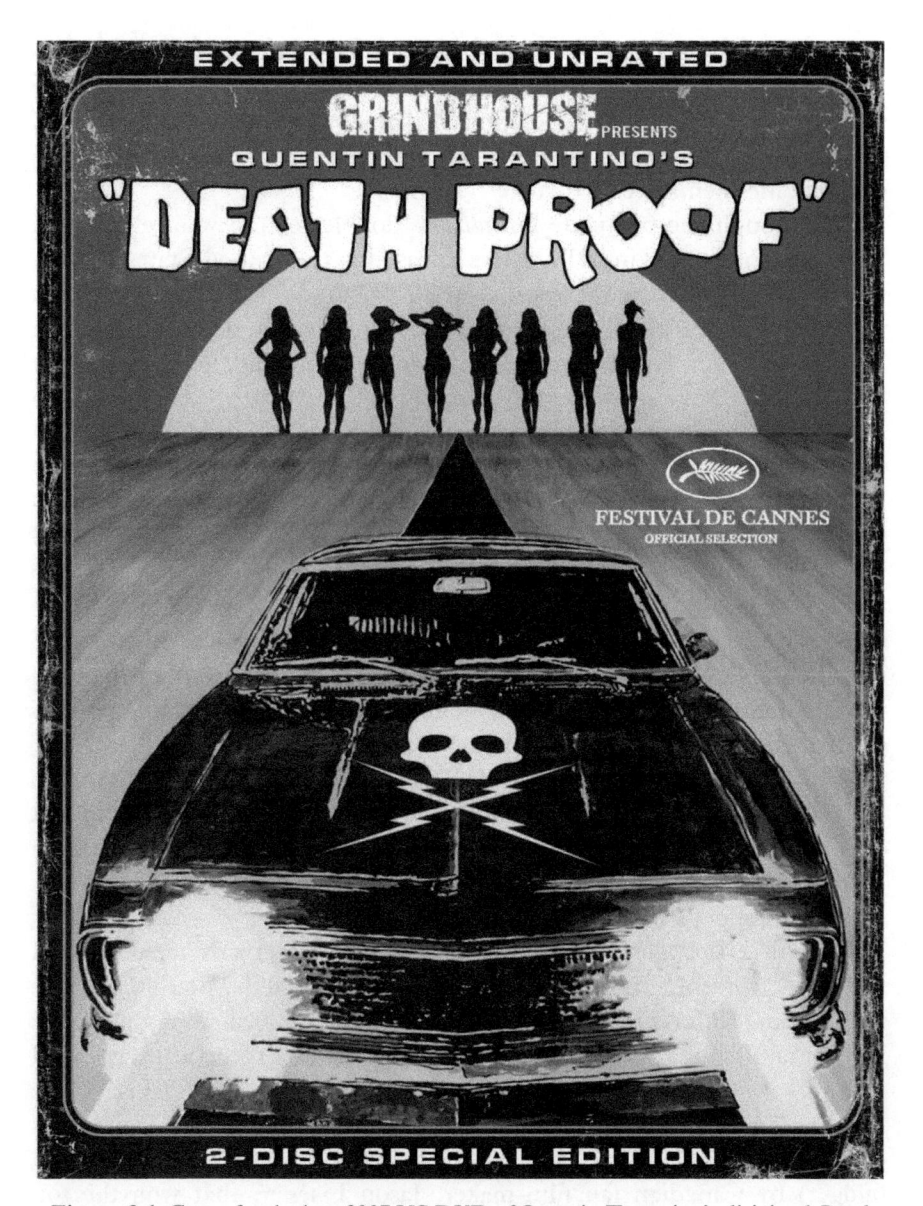

Figure 3.6 Cover for the late-2007 US DVD of Quentin Tarantino's disjoined *Death Proof*, now 'extended and unrated' as an authorial original, complete with the imprimatur of a Cannes Film Festival official selection. (Source: The Weinstein Company.)

effectively become separate 'DVD premieres' (Figure 3.6), which was also Rodriguez's initial plan for distributing the feature-length spin-off of his *Machete* trailer.[82] In this sense, the cachet of *both* an anticipatory theatrical release on one platform (the 2007 US theatrical version) *and* a restored authorial aura on another platform (the extended home video cuts) doubly allowed these two simulated exploitation films to receive a higher degree of cultural legitimacy than the still-marginalised DTV exploitation products from which they might disingenuously attempt to differentiate themselves.

Yet, though the complete *Grindhouse* double feature was released on DVD internationally in 2010, it was released in the United States only on Blu-ray, representing an ironically future-oriented format shift for such a technologically nostalgic film. Released to American audiences with little fanfare, the complete *Grindhouse* experience's visibility on home video has remained largely within the purview not only of those viewers who are attuned to exploitation fan cultures but also those with enough capital to be early adopters of Blu-ray or importers of a non-Region 1 DVD from overseas. With the separate *Planet Terror* and *Death Proof* DVDs released in the United States as 'extended and uncut', they also played into the higher marketability of unrated versions of violent or sexy genre films which, according to *Variety*, account for 80 to 90 per cent of DVD sales compared to a rated edition.[83] In addition, these extended cuts play into the long-standing history of the unstable exploitation text subject to manipulation across regional or national borders, with international cuts often prized by American fans because they contain more footage. Yet, the Blu-ray release of the complete *Grindhouse* does not make these earlier DVD versions of the separate films obsolete (especially as the extended cuts of *Planet Terror* and *Death Proof* were also separately released on Blu-ray) because completists would probably collect the multiple versions when each offers substantial textual differences.

Though *Grindhouse*'s disappointing box-office returns meant it did not spawn a franchise of further 'Grindhouse Presents' double features highlighting different directors and genres, as Tarantino and Rodriguez had initially hoped,[84] it did meanwhile result in the theatrically released spin-offs *Machete*, *Hobo with a Shotgun*, and *Machete Kills* (2013). While *Machete* was the feature-length expansion of Rodriguez's fake trailer that opened *Grindhouse*, *Hobo* originated as a fake trailer (made on a $125 budget) by Canadian fan film-maker, Jason Eisener, that won the top prize (as chosen by Rodriguez himself) in a grindhouse trailer competition held at the 2007 South by Southwest (SXSW) festival in conjunction with *Grindhouse*'s impending release. Canadian distributor Alliance Films subsequently made over 180 prints of the *Hobo* trailer and appended them to select *Grindhouse* prints during its Canadian theatrical run, eventually spawning enough online interest to become expanded into Eisener's debut feature film.[85] The original *Hobo* trailer, however, was omitted from all home video editions of *Grindhouse*, included only on the DVD/Blu-ray of its spin-off feature.

Lerner argues that *Grindhouse* 'defines itself as an anti-convergence text' by nostalgically privileging the theatrical experience and not allowing fans to reproduce it at home on DVD, since the ads, trailers, and abbreviated versions of each feature would be missing.[86] I would argue, however, that regardless of how the film might nostalgically *define itself*, the proliferation of different transmedia texts associated with *Grindhouse* precisely encourages the convergence process by which fans actively migrate across different media formats to follow the spread of desired content, because no single platform can deliver the spin-offs and paratexts that have allowed '*Grindhouse*' to develop into a sort of brand name. As Henry Jenkins notes, the spread of digitisation has allowed everyday consumers to appropriate and manipulate media content in increasingly flexible ways while it has also, paradoxically, allowed media conglomerates to concentrate their power over the production and distribution of said content. This has resulted in '[a] widening of the discursive environment [that] coexists with a narrowing of the range of information being transmitted by the most readily available media channels'.[87] In this sense, as much as *Grindhouse*'s proliferating iterations ultimately serve The Weinstein Company's profit margins and offer a very selective vision of grindhouse history, we can also see venues such as the SXSW grindhouse trailer contest encouraging an eruption of fan creativity that has exceeded the contest's initial role as a short-term marketing tool.[88] Still, as Sara Gwenllian Jones argues, *non*-Hollywood fan-textual production is not the same as *anti*-Hollywood production, because fan film-makers like Eisener may deliberately use their own works as a springboard for professional careers, with access to the traditional means of production/distribution still controlled by the same corporate interests that solicited such fake grindhouse trailers in the first place.[89]

Such dynamics belie Lerner's assertions that *Grindhouse*'s nostalgia for the past is 'unavoidably conservative' by treating 1970s exploitation texts as 'static and unchanging' referents upheld in a hermetically sealed realm of pastness that discourages active engagement with film history and engenders a 'forced passivity' in viewers.[90] After all, as Svetlana Boym suggests, there is a marked difference between a *restorative nostalgia*, which attempts to conquer time by reconstructing past referents in a state of unchanging glory, and a *reflective nostalgia* which recognises the past as in ruins or (perhaps more to the point with Tarantino's films) as 'gentrified beyond recognition'. Indeed, this latter species of nostalgia spurs 'ironic, inconclusive, and fragmentary' responses, 'open[ing] up a multitude of potentialities, nonteleological possibilities of historical development'.[91] Contra Lerner, then, the fact that past exploitation cycles have become stylistic fodder for a high-concept Hollywood film matters little if we recall that those same exploitation films were, in effect, made and marketed like high-concept films (albeit on far smaller budgets) in the years before New Hollywood's own embrace of high-concept cinema. Much as independent producer–distributors developed exploitation cycles by building from cultural memories of earlier films, I see nostalgia's dialectic between past and present as a means of allowing a wide range of users – from Hollywood power players down to no-budget fan film-makers – to use past films as raw material for a range of different purposes. Of course, this is not to suggest that convergence culture has erased the vast differentials in power or influence held by media industries over fan uses of media content but, rather, that making claims for the supposed 'authenticity' of independent producers (whether past or present) over large corporations too easily falls into the realm of romantic myth. Blanket claims about nostalgia's corporate co-opting are easy to make but are no more accurate than outdated notions that fan cultures are overwhelmingly 'resistant' to the culture industries.

Furthermore, as more and more fans with limited resources pick up prosumer-grade cameras and draw inspiration from a socially constructed sense of 'grindhouse-ness', it becomes increasingly unclear how much subcultural capital a given fan film-maker may possess, especially if he/she might rely more on mocking the perceived badness of exploitation cinema than offering sincere homage. In other words, much as retrosploitation's focus on simulating pre-video era films often figures the domestic sphere as a less 'authentic' site for exploitation film consumption than grind houses, retrosploitation production is similarly tainted by its accessibility to home-grown amateurs. Fan film-making typically involves a high degree of familiarity with historical referents recognisable within a given fan culture, thus representing a bid for subcultural capital, but non-professional origins can also cause fan films to be dismissed as the work of wannabes. (What better example of competition for subcultural capital than the SXSW fake trailer contest, with the winning fan crowned by Rodriguez himself?) A parodic tone intended to be read as a loving send-up, for example, may also be interpreted by other fans as a sign that the fan film-maker knows enough about his/her film's historical referents to condense their most salient traits into the butt of humour but ultimately lacks the 'proper' affection for culturally devalued films that non-fans may still see as largely fit for mockery. In this sense, receptional questions about authorial intent can question the apparent 'authenticity' of retrosploitation films made at many different budgetary levels, from films developed in Hollywood boardrooms to films made in fans' bedrooms.

If most fan films rely on timely references to films with popular cultural currency or longevity,[92] a film like *Grindhouse* may certainly have helped inspire a burst of fan film-making, but fan-made retrosploitation texts also draw inspiration from more distant and obscure corners of film history whose very minorness in the contemporary pop-culture landscape would seemingly demand more defensive reverence than, say, parodies of a recent Hollywood blockbuster. As one fan says in criticising the spoof *Nun of That*,

> While I'm sure everyone's heart was in the right place, this film is a disaster and is a disgrace to the Rape/Revenge and Nunsploitation genres. Just because a film is a wink to the 'Grindhouse' style of filmmaking, it shouldn't be given a free pass for a laughable script, horrid acting, and the lack of mammory [*sic*] glands and holy derrière. It's safe to say that Abel Ferrara's *Ms. 45* was the template for this lukewarm exercise in lameness, so I encourage all fans to give that one a look.[93]

Textual traits like laughably 'bad' special effects, dialogue, or acting can be seen as part of the naive charm of archival exploitation films but may provoke greater fan ambivalence in recently made low-budget releases that intentionally make badness a calculated decision during a period when outdated techniques may be interpreted less as anachronistic homage than as self-parodic snark. For independent film-makers without the resources to carefully construct a detailed *mise en scène* evoking past decades, anachronisms can even signal a presumed lack of dedication to exploitation film history, rather than a symptom of budgetary constraints. Take, for example, this mixed review of *Sugar Boxx*:

> Before watching the special features, my biggest complaint was that [director Cody] Jarrett attempted to set this exploitation film in a modern-day setting, which doesn't work the same way it did in the 1970s. In the Making Of, though, Jarrett explains that the film is set in 1975, not present day. [. . .] If Jarrett did more to place the movie where the script says it is – 1975 – the story of the movie may have worked better. There is no doubt this film is exploitative, but that isn't enough.[94]

Similarly, if the veneer of scratched and distressed celluloid is a filter effect that can be easily applied to even the most amateurish films using consumer-grade video-editing software, then the very accessibility of this creative choice undercuts the ersatz 'authenticity' of the grindhouse aesthetic all the more. As one fan complains, 'With these [*Grindhouse*] imitators, when you take away the grindhouse look, you are left with a terrible movie that if it wasn't for the market scheme, would probably have never been picked up by a distributor.'[95]

Nevertheless, if perceived amateurism may complicate the reception of fan-made retrosploitation works, budgetary and other practical limitations may prove a mixed blessing in other ways. The constraints of short forms such as fake trailers, for example, provide a better platform for maintaining the evaluative tone they seek to present. That is, fake trailers may be more effective as one-note jokes than as extended exercises in pastiche, even if their brevity potentially limits detailed engagement with past and present cultural ideologies. Alternatively, the short form can also allow fan film-makers to maintain the straight-faced earnestness of homage over a brief period, without gradually lapsing into self-parody over a feature-length running time. Though not all fake grindhouse trailers are played for parody over pastiche, they typically imitate the already exaggerated promises of exploitation marketing, and can thus crystallise the diverse tonal possibilities of retrosploitation in general. In doing so, however, it can become difficult to tell whether they take comedic aim at the conventions of overwrought exploitation publicity or at exploitation films themselves, raising the nagging question of how appreciative and knowledgeable these home-based fan film-makers really are about an exploitation film corpus predominantly (though, as *The Sleeper* indicates, not exclusively) recalled by fans in reference to theatrical exhibition.

Barbara Klinger notes that 'parodies may in part pay homage, but they create their alternative textual universes through less earnest means than those of' straight homage. Nevertheless, 'even the most irreverent work [of parody] displays a core affection, fascination, or grudging admiration for the original'.[96] For my purposes, I would clarify that parody's paradoxical function of implicitly supporting what it explicitly savages allows it to exist on the fuzzy border with pastiche's middle position between parody and homage. If the potential for retrosploitation texts to slide into parody continues to generate ambivalence among fans, it is because the parodist's negative tone is often more legible in a text than the neutral or positive tone held by the practitioners of pastiche or homage respectively. Unlike parody's distanced and superior tone, pastiche's imitative closeness to its historical referents allows it to be neither inherently critical nor celebratory but can evince a gentle blending of both stances in its very closeness to what it imitates – a closeness that, for Dyer, reveals the performativity of all cultural forms.[97]

Because this performativity undercuts the apparent self-evidence of cultural taste distinctions, it can recode formerly niche cultural forms as more readily sellable as contemporary populist entertainment, much to the vexation of fans still invested in subcultural ideologies of exclusivity. In this respect, the reading strategies used by fans are a recurrent issue at play in the consumption of a potentially franchisable concept like *Grindhouse*, since Lerner claims that *Grindhouse* internalises the ironic readings of paracinema by turning the inadvertent flaws, over-the-top excesses, and damaged artefactual nature of archival exploitation cinema into deliberate marks of authorial intent. Not unlike its self-parodic DTV predecessors from companies such as Troma, *Grindhouse* seemingly robs paracinephiles of their active participation and 'constructs a cinema of stasis, creating a spectatorial relationship that places palpable limitations on the cinemagoer's imaginary possibilities'.[98] Though the range of fan production spurred by *Grindhouse*'s release leads me to disagree with the supposed limitations ('forced passivity') placed upon its viewers, I am certainly sympathetic to the argument that media producers attempting to target fans often try to mirror a fan culture's own values. This is especially the case when texts circulate intertextual subcultural capital that spreads beyond existing fan cultures and reaches wider audiences, thus challenging the very sorts of cultural distinctions that the text may outwardly seek to promote.[99]

Hence the self-reflexive moment in Tarantino's *Death Proof* when an increasingly obsolete below-the-line professional, Stuntman Mike (Kurt Russell), drives his 1969 Dodge Charger through a roadside marquee for *Wolf Creek* (2005) and *Scary Movie 4* (2006) – both of which serve as present-set points of filmic distinction from *Grindhouse*'s own project. While *Wolf Creek* draws its inspiration from 1970s rural survival horror without explicitly signalling its indebtedness through a flurry of retro signifiers, the *Scary Movie* series parodies the already quasi-parodic *Scream* films – a franchise that 'mainstreamed' the supposed 'rules' of the 1980s slasher cycle by internalising cyclical conventions as fodder for mockery. For Tarantino, it seems these two contemporary films struck the wrong tone in their attempts to reach wider audiences, because the former film failed to offer the self-conscious cues associated with pastiche while the latter failed to show proper reverence to its pre-*Scream* referents. The fact that Dimension Films also released *Scream*, *Wolf Creek* and the *Scary Movie* series, however, further suggests the profitable blurring of taste cultures which has occurred as studios confuse the boundaries between theatrical and DTV releases, especially because some of *Grindhouse*'s viewers may also have been appreciative ticket-buyers for Dimension's other horror-related releases.

Nevertheless, if some fans' claims to subcultural exclusivity were seemingly threatened by the wide release of a Hollywood take on 1970s exploitation tropes, we can see the vagaries of reception as a countervailing tendency, because *Grindhouse*'s appeals to nostalgia were not successful with all fans. Some critics argued that such nostalgia was misplaced because actual grind houses were awful places showing boring and grotesque films; whereas some long-term exploitation fans derided *Grindhouse* as a grossly oversimplified, audience-friendly reinterpretation of films that deserved better than being distorted and sold to younger viewers with less subcultural capital.[100] Other fans noted that the film worked better in concept than in practice: 'I applaud the *idea* of it, but in practice the hip, knowing crappiness becomes depressing. [. . .] For all its movie-geek fervor, *Grindhouse* remains a private party, an event that was probably more fun to make (and to market) than it is to watch.'[101] The amount of subcultural capital actualised in the film's critical reception thus plays a considerable role in these responses as performances of connoisseurship and accumulated experience. As one fan appropriately noted, for example, 'Quite a few reviewers griped about Tarantino's half of *Grindhouse*'s double feature, saying that real grindhouse movies were never *this* boring, but anyone who'd say something like that clearly hasn't sat down with all that many exploitation flicks.'[102] Some independent film-makers were also displeased with the retrosploitation trend for similar reasons. As Fred Andrews, director of the notorious box-office flop *Creature* (2011), complained:

> I hated what happened in the last couple of years in the horror genre, where you've had this fake resurgence of grindhouse. The real story of the grindhouse is the guy who's making the best picture he can, carrying five cans of film, going week to week to week from Kansas City to Missouri to Arkansas, playing it for a week and then getting back in his station wagon. I wasn't about treating the film to make it all grainy. The film looks great.[103]

In this respect (and sour grapes aside), the gimmickry of retrosploitation films might not only trouble the degree of interpretive labour used by seasoned viewers of historical exploitation films but also challenge the types of productive labour traditionally performed by low-budget film-makers pursuing careers through the outdated practice of theatrical roadshowing in an era dominated by home video revenues.

Despite such criticisms, I would argue that fans can still view *Grindhouse*'s mediocre box-office returns as testimony to the resilience of subcultural capital, because cult films often originate from texts that notably failed upon their initial release. A 2011 survey to determine the next 'cult classic', for example, found that many online respondents thought *Grindhouse* 'tried too hard to be cult' but that a cult following nevertheless resulted from the very excessiveness of its self-conscious attempts at replicating a sense of 'authenticity'. As one respondent negatively remarked, 'It's trying to be a cult film, it's from a mainstream director, it's too well circulated. Cult film lovers tend to covet underground films and pride themselves on being part of its [sic] secret following. It's very elitist.' Another respondent observed, 'You can't manufacture a cult film. This is exploitation filmmaking for those that would leave halfway through a real exploitation film out of boredom.'[104] Though these disparaging responses suggest that the film's high-concept calculatedness confirms a lack of subcultural capital on the part of its would-be audience, *Grindhouse*'s appreciative fans could alternatively point towards its box-office underperformance as proof that it found loyal admirers only among a niche fan contingent with enough subcultural capital to appreciate the film's historical referentiality.

If blockbusters are often culturally devalued as being cinematic events which are greatly hyped in the short term but leave few lasting cultural traces, then *Grindhouse*'s failure to become an enduring *theatrical* 'cult blockbuster' (such as *Star Wars* [1977] or *Titanic* [1997])[105] means that the nostalgic eventness associated with its theatrical run has been supplanted by a much longer afterlife via video-mediated iterations and paratexts – not unlike the long video afterlives of the otherwise obsolete exploitation films to which it pays tribute. In this sense, it is no coincidence that the home video releases for *Planet Terror* include an 'audience reaction track' recorded live at the Alamo Drafthouse Cinema in Austin, Texas – a domestic viewing option that, as Caetlin Benson-Allott says, perhaps inadvertently reminds the spectator of his/her exclusion from an idealised screening experience at a theatre chain that has taken up the mantle of grindhouse history through its highly publicised screenings of archival exploitation prints.[106] Yet, as the above responses to the film's uses of nostalgia suggest, even this 'idealised' viewing experience located in the not-too-distant past of 2007 can present a variety of reasons why, beyond the inability to recreate the potentially fan-populated theatrical experience at home, other exploitation fans may feel excluded from its raucously celebratory tone.

Of course, fans' potential feelings of exclusion are quite relative when we consider that so many retrosploitation films use a contemporary sense of 'political incorrectness' to cater primarily (but not exclusively) to the tastes and pleasures of straight white men, a demographic far removed from *actual exclusion* in American society. Yet, as I argue in the next chapter, the very ambivalence and even anxiety created by the multivalent appeals to nostalgia in such films can resonate with unresolved cultural tensions beyond this privileged demographic – particularly if, as noted in Chapter 2, home video has opened exploitation films to a wider viewership than their theatrical exhibition once encouraged. Though retrosploitation texts typically signal their contemporary constructedness in distinction from archival exploitation texts, the commingling of both in the home video marketplace highlights how much affect can be generated by the raised edges between archival texts and their descendants. Indeed, these raised edges can even evoke the pains of historical conflict, because the historicity of retrosploitation texts allows them to remain haunted by past and present cultural representations and inequalities. Because retrosploitation texts occupy a pop-culture landscape where industrial shifts such as the rise of DTV films have altered taste distinctions and enmeshed once-marginal cinematic forms within dominant cultural avenues, it is important to ask what ideological premises are served by these retro-styled texts and their fans. That is, if the historicity, tonal/taste appeals, and industrial position of these films inspire considerable ambivalence, then we should question what larger social and political uses said ambivalence allows.

Notes

1. Svetlana Boym, *The Future of Nostalgia* (New York: Basic Books, 2001), pp. xiii–xiv.
2. Cortez the Killer, '*Ticked Off Trannies With Knives* (2010)', Planet of Terror, last modified 28 February 2011, http://www.planetofterror.com/2011/02/ticked-off-trannies-with-knives-2010.html (accessed 12 January 2012). This blog entry was one of the earliest recorded uses of the term 'retrosploitation'.
3. Geoff Boucher, 'Long, Winding Road Hits a Dead End at Last for VHS', *Chicago Tribune*, 28 December 2008, http://articles.chicagotribune.com/2008-12-28/news/0812270237_1_kugler-estimates-vhs-tape-distribution-video-audio (accessed 24 January 2012). Like *The Sleeper*, limited-edition copies of the retrosploitation films *The House of the Devil* (2009) and *Bloody Bloody Bible Camp* (2012) were distributed on VHS to genre publications and film festivals as a nostalgic gimmick. Similarly, small independent labels, such as Intervision Picture Corp. and Massacre Video, have sold limited-edition VHS copies of contemporary horror films that had previously been released only on DVD, as discussed in Daniel Herbert, 'Nostalgia Merchants: VHS Distributors in the Era of Intangible Media' (paper presented to the 2014 Society for Cinema and Media Studies Conference, Seattle, WA, 19–23 March 2014).
4. Thehorrorchick, 'Indie Horror Month: Justin Russell Talks *The Sleeper*, Eighties Slashers, and More', Dread Central, last modified 2 March 2012, http://www.dreadcentral.com/news/53253/indie-horror-month-justin-russell-talks-sleeper-eighties-slashers-and-more (accessed 5 March 2012).
5. As another example, the short films, fake trailers, and features by Winnipeg-

based film collective Astron-6 (founded in 2007) blatantly emulate VHS-era DTV genre films, even opening with a retro-styled 'Astron-6 Video' logo recalling the 1980s Astra Video and Vestron Video logos.
6. Jeffrey Pence, 'Postcinema/Postmemory', in *Memory and Popular Film*, ed. Paul Grainge (Manchester: Manchester University Press, 2003), p. 239.
7. Frederick Wasser, *Veni, Vidi, Video: The Hollywood Empire and the VCR* (Austin: University of Texas Press, 2001), p. 131; Stephen Prince, *A New Pot of Gold: Hollywood Under the Electronic Rainbow, 1980–1989* (New York: Charles Scribner's Sons, 2000), p. 97; and Paul McDonald, *Video and DVD Industries* (London: British Film Institute, 2007), pp. 151–2 (quoted).
8. José van Dijck, *Mediated Memories in the Digital Age* (Stanford, CA: Stanford University Press, 2007), pp. 7, 34, 175. Quote at p. 7.
9. Richard Dyer, *Pastiche* (London: Routledge, 2007), pp. 21, 24, 47, 58–60. Quote at p. 21.
10. Christine Sprengler, *Screening Nostalgia: Populuxe Props and Technicolor Aesthetics in Contemporary American Film* (New York: Berghahn Books, 2009), pp. 85–6, 140. Quotes at p. 140.
11. Caetlin Benson-Allott, *Killer Tapes and Shattered Screens: Video Spectatorship from VHS to File Sharing* (Berkeley: University of California Press, 2013), pp. 139–40, 153 (quote at p. 153). This particular effect, however, is not without precedent in exploitation films. In *The Big Bird Cage* (1972), for example, a climactic fire destroys the titular prison-camp machine, simultaneously seeming to ignite the celluloid of the very film named after that machine.
12. For example, see Dana Stevens, 'It's Hard Out There for a Ho', *Slate*, 1 March 2007, http://www.slate.com/articles/arts/movies/2007/03/its_hard_out_there_for_a_ho.html (accessed 2 February 2012); and 'Christina Ricci Upset by "Black Snake Moan" Marketing', Starpulse.com, posted 20 April 2008, http://www.starpulse.com/news/index.php/2008/04/20/christina_ricci_upset_by_black_snake_moa (accessed 2 February 2012). Also see James A. Crank, 'An Aesthetic of Play: A Contemporary Cinema of South-Sploitation', in *Southerners on Film: Essays on Hollywood Portrayals Since the 1970s*, ed. Andrew B. Leiter (Jefferson, NC: McFarland, 2011), pp. 204–16.
13. See Sharon Monteith, 'Exploitation Movies and the Freedom Struggle of the 1960s', in *American Cinema and the Southern Imaginary*, eds Deborah E. Barker and Kathryn McKee (Athens: University of Georgia Press, 2011), pp. 194–216; and Kevin Heffernan, *Ghouls, Gimmicks, and Gold: Horror Films and the American Movie Business, 1953–1968* (Durham, NC: Duke University Press, 2004), pp. 205–8.
14. Jonathan Gray, *Show Sold Separately: Promos, Spoilers, and Other Media Paratexts* (New York: New York University Press, 2010), pp. 39, 52, 72, 79. Quote at p. 79.
15. Ryan Rotten, 'Rodriguez and Tarantino on *Grindhouse*', Comingsoon.

net, last modified 3 April 2007, http://www.comingsoon.net/news/movie news.php?id=19716 (accessed 8 February 2012).
16. Kate Egan, *Trash or Treasure? Censorship and the Changing Meanings of the Video Nasties* (Manchester: Manchester University Press, 2007), p. 59.
17. For an example of this misperception, see Whitney Joiner, 'Directors Who Go Together, Like Blood and Guts', *New York Times*, 28 January 2007, http://www.nytimes.com/2007/01/28/movies/28join.html (accessed 9 February 2012).
18. Gray, *Show Sold Separately*, p. 127. A notable example of Tarantino-as-brand was his short-lived Rolling Thunder Pictures label, distributed by Miramax from 1995 to 1998, which remediated exploitation films on home video, each with a recorded introduction by Tarantino.
19. James Morrison, 'After the Revolution: On the Fate of Cinephilia', *Michigan Quarterly Review* 44, no. 3 (2005): 413. Morrison's complaint is belied by the active fan-cultural hunt to identify Tarantino's intertextual references, with the editable Wiki-based 'Movie References' section of the Quentin Tarantino Archives fansite as a case in point. See 'Movie References', The Quentin Tarantino Archives, http://www.tarantino.info/wiki/index.php/Movie_References (accessed 24 February 2012).
20. Will Straw, 'Reinhabiting Lost Languages: Guy Maddin's *Careful*', in *Playing with Memories: Essays on Guy Maddin*, ed. David Church (Winnipeg: University of Manitoba Press, 2009), p. 65.
21. Paul Willemen, 'Through the Glass Darkly: Cinephilia Reconsidered', in *Looks and Frictions: Essays in Cultural Studies and Film Theory* (Bloomington: Indiana University Press, 1994), p. 241; and Michel Maffesoli, *The Time of the Tribes: The Decline of Individualism in Mass Society*, trans. Don Smith (London: Sage, 1996), pp. 91, 95.
22. Michael Z. Newman, *Indie: An American Film Culture* (New York: Columbia University Press, 2011), pp. 43, 145, 185.
23. Ava Preacher Collins, 'Loose Canons: Constructing Cultural Traditions Inside and Outside the Academy', in *Film Theory Goes to the Movies*, eds Jim Collins, Hilary Radner and Ava Preacher Collins (London: Routledge, 1992), pp. 90, 94–5. On 'meta-cult' films, see Ernest Mathijs and Jamie Sexton, *Cult Cinema: An Introduction* (Malden, MA: Wiley-Blackwell, 2011), p. 236.
24. Jay McRoy, '"The Kids of Today Should Defend Themselves Against the '70s": Simulating Auras and Marketing Nostalgia in Robert Rodriguez and Quentin Tarantino's *Grindhouse*', in *American Horror Film: The Genre at the Turn of the Millennium*, ed. Steffen Hantke (Jackson: University Press of Mississippi, 2010), p. 226 (original italics). Also see David Lerner, 'Cinema of Regression: *Grindhouse* and the Limits of the Spectatorial Imaginary', in *Cinema Inferno: Celluloid Explosions from the Cultural Margins*, eds Robert G. Weiner and John Cline (Lanham, MD: Scarecrow Press, 2010), pp. 360–1, 363; and Benson-Allott, *Killer Tapes and Shattered Screens*, ch. 4.

25. See Lerner, 'Cinema of Regression', p. 370. Paracinephiles levelled similar criticism at Tim Burton's biopic *Ed Wood* (1994), although that film's faithful recreation of several scenes from Wood's work does not share *Grindhouse*'s detailed veneer of celluloid dilapidation. Consequently, *Ed Wood* may have introduced broader audiences to a cult film-maker and thus seemed to threaten some fans' subcultural capital but the film's primary focus on the behind-the-scenes story of Wood's career does not go as far as *Grindhouse* in self-consciously evoking the *feel* of watching Wood's films in the degraded state first encountered by many fans through shoddy prints and video transfers.
26. Marc Patterson, 'Film Review: *Dear God No!*', Brutal as Hell, posted 13 November 2011, http://www.brutalashell.com/2011/11/film-review-dear-god-no/ (accessed 4 March 2012).
27. Marita Sturken, 'Tourists of History: Souvenirs, Architecture, and the Kitschification of Memory', in *Technologies of Memory in the Arts*, eds Liedeke Plate and Anneke Smelik (New York: Palgrave Macmillan, 2009), pp. 25–7.
28. David Briggs, 'Welcome to the Grindhouse: Philip Carrer Churns Out the Terror', Tri-City Film, last modified 9 August 2011, http://tricityfilm.com/2011/08/09/welcome-to-the-grindhouse-philip-carrer-churns-out-the-terror/ (accessed 4 April 2012).
29. Susan Stewart, *On Longing: Narratives of the Miniature, the Gigantic, the Souvenir, the Collection* (Baltimore: Johns Hopkins University Press, 1984), p. 167.
30. Benson-Allott, *Killer Tapes and Shattered Screens*, pp. 138–9.
31. Ibid., p. 155.
32. Vera Dika, *Recycled Culture in Contemporary Art and Film: The Uses of Nostalgia* (Cambridge: Cambridge University Press, 2003), p. 224.
33. Benson-Allott, *Killer Tapes and Shattered Screens*, p. 146. Following Jean Baudrillard and Gilles Deleuze, she defines a 'simulacrum' as a copy without an original, as opposed to the 'simulation' of an original that clearly did exist at one point in history.
34. Dyer, *Pastiche*, pp. 23, 47, 55–7, 59–60. Quote at p. 55.
35. Ibid., p. 172.
36. Ibid., pp. 23, 30, 59, 128, 130, 133. Quote at p. 130.
37. Jason Coleman, 'Interview: "Nude Nuns with Big Guns" Director Joseph Guzman on Sex, Violence, and Unhallowed Havoc', Starpulse.com, last modified 13 February 2012, http://www.starpulse.com/news/Jason_Coleman/2012/02/13/interview_nude_nuns_with_big_guns_dire (accessed 17 February 2012).
38. Stephen Romano, *Shock Festival* (San Diego: IDW Publishing/RAW Entertainment, 2008), pp. 44, 332, 350.
39. Tom Hodge's similar design work for *Dear God No!* simulates an international distribution history, including numerous lobby cards; separate

posters for the film's release in drive-ins and on 42nd Street; a 1980s theatrical re-release poster; a German VHS cover; and posters for Mexican, Italian and French releases.
40. Romano, *Shock Festival*, p. 157.
41. Wasser, *Veni, Vidi, Video*, pp. 129, 195.
42. Linda Ruth Williams, *The Erotic Thriller in Contemporary Cinema* (Bloomington: Indiana University Press, 2005), pp. 285–6.
43. Ibid., pp. 9, 291; James Naremore, *More Than Night: Film Noir in Its Contexts* (Berkeley: University of California Press, 2008), p. 161; and Glyn Davis, 'A Taste for *Leeches!* DVDs, Audience Configurations, and Generic Hybridity', in *Film and Television After DVD*, eds James Bennett and Tom Brown (New York: Routledge, 2008), pp. 52, 55.
44. Ian Conrich, 'Communitarianism, Film Entrepreneurism, and the Crusade of Troma Entertainment', in *Contemporary American Independent Film: From the Margins to the Mainstream*, eds Chris Holmlund and Justin Wyatt (New York: Routledge, 2005), pp. 109, 114.
45. On 'bad faith' in devalued genres, see David Andrews, *Soft in the Middle: The Contemporary Softcore Feature in Its Contexts* (Columbus: Ohio State University Press, 2006), pp. 184–9.
46. Dyer, *Pastiche*, pp. 128, 131–2.
47. Andrews, *Soft in the Middle*, p. 87.
48. Naremore, *More Than Night*, p. 163.
49. Dyer, *Pastiche*, p. 3.
50. Justin Wyatt, 'Independents, Packaging, and Inflationary Pressure in 1980s Hollywood', in Stephen Prince, *A New Pot of Gold*, pp. 142–59.
51. Fred Olen Ray, *The New Poverty Row: Independent Filmmakers as Distributors* (Jefferson, NC: McFarland, 1991), p. 197.
52. Matt Hills, 'Para-Paracinema: The *Friday the 13th* Film Series as Other to Trash and Legitimate Film Cultures', in *Sleaze Artists*, p. 232.
53. Ramon Lobato, *Shadow Economies of Cinema: Mapping Informal Film Distribution* (London: British Film Institute, 2012), p. 34.
54. Davis, 'A Taste for *Leeches!*', p. 57.
55. NickPeron, 'Exploitation Double Bill: *Bitch Slap!* & *Lesbian Vampire Killers*' (review), Micro-Shock.com, last modified 14 June 2010, http://www.dorkswithoutfaces.com/newmicroshock/?p=242 (accessed 14 July 2012).
56. Will LeBlanc, 'DVD Review: *Bitch Slap*', CinemaBlend.com, http://www.cinemablend.com/dvds/Bitch-Slap-4525.html (accessed 14 July 2012).
57. Lerner, 'Cinema of Regression', p. 372.
58. It is no coincidence that Troma mastermind Lloyd Kaufman has cameos in retrosploitation films including *Prison-A-Go-Go!*, *Caged Lesbos A-Go-Go* (2009), and *Nun of That*; and that his company has distributed Astron-6's self-parodic *Father's Day* (2011) and a 2011 *Astron-6* short-film compilation DVD.

59. Dana Harris and Erin Maxwell, 'Mockbusters: Flattery or Rip-off?' *Variety*, 17 August 2009, pp. 4–5; and Dan Solomon, 'How to Make a Mockbuster (in Five Easy Steps)', AdultSwim.com, last modified 22 August 2011, http://www.adultswim.com/blog/interviews/how-to-make-a-mockbuster.html (accessed 24 August 2011). Notably, *Grindhouse* itself has inspired several DTV porn parodies, including *Grindhouse XXX: A Double Feature* (2011) and *Double Feature XXX* (2012). See 'Grindhouse Parody XXX Streets First Feature, "Machete XXX"', *Adult Video News*, 23 September 2011, http://business.avn.com/company-news/Grindhouse-XXX-Parody-Streets-First-Feature-Machete-XXX-448587.html (accessed 9 April 2012).

60. For examples of viewers' focus on badness, see TK, 'Excuse Me Baby, I Can't Control Myself in the Octopus Mode', Pajiba, http://www.pajiba.com/film_reviews/sharktopus-review-excuse-me-baby-i-cant-control-myself-in-the-octopus-mode.php (accessed 19 February 2012); John Patterson, 'How to Make Mega Piranha Camper Than Mega Shark vs. Giant Octopus? Just Add Tiffany', *The Guardian*, 9 July 2010, http://www.guardian.co.uk/film/2010/jul/10/mega-piranha-tiffany-john-patterson (accessed 19 February 2012); and Devin Faraci, 'SHARKNADO: The Hyper-Ironic Face of Modern Exploitation', Badass Digest, posted 12 July 2013, http://badassdigest.com/2013/07/12/sharknado-the-hyper-ironic-face-of-modern-exploitation/ (accessed 14 July 2013).

61. Laurence Lerman, 'Independents' "Bread and Butter"', *Video Business*, 17 September 2001, p. 22.

62. Chad Greene, 'Aiming for "Direct" Hits', *Boxoffice*, May 2007, p. 37.

63. Scott Hettrick, 'Homevid Franchise Coin a Gold Mine for Sequels', *Variety*, 23 June 2000, p. 1; Diane Garrett, 'U's Cheering as "Bring" Vid Nets $12 Mil', *Variety*, 17 August 2006, p. 9; Jennifer Netherby, 'DVD Premieres Bring on Cash', *Video Business*, 21 August 2006, p. 6; 'Home is Where the Franchise Is', *Variety*, 10 October 2006, p. A3; Susanne Ault, 'DVD Premiere Movies Multiply', *Video Business*, 11 August 2008, p. 1; and Thomas J. McLean, 'Family Fare Does Well in Race for Shelf Space', *Variety*, 8 January 2009, p. A2.

64. Eliza Gallo, 'Horror Genre Surges in DVD', *Video Business*, 29 November 2004, p. 6; Diane Garrett, 'Studios Dizzy Over Disc Divisions', *Variety*, 26 June 2006, p. 8 (quoted); Wendy Wilson and Laurence Lerman, 'DVD Premiere Heroes Still Pack Punch', *Video Business*, 18 February 2008, p. 8; and Laurence Lerman and Scott Hettrick, 'Stars, Money Migrate to DVD Premieres', *DVD Exclusive*, July 2005, p. 6. Like many retrosploitation films, *The Expendables* (2010) franchise has re-elevated aged action stars, like Stallone et al., from the DTV ghetto to big-budget theatrical releases through a similarly nostalgic mix of earnest appreciation (their action sequences are no less thrilling today) and ironic playfulness (joking asides about the stars' aging bodies) towards their 1980s heyday, with the ensemble casting providing much of the pastiche.

65. Marc Graser, 'H'wood's Direct Hits', *Variety*, 13 September 2004, pp. 1, 60; Marcy Magiera, 'Long Live Video', *Video Business*, 5 June 2006, p. 28; Jennifer Netherby, 'Made-for-DVD Divisions Rival Theatrical', *Video Business*, 12 June 2006, p. 29; Netherby, 'DVD Premieres Bring On Cash', p. 6; Susanne Ault, 'Premieres Potential Pops', *Video Business*, 19 February 2007, p. 1; Jennifer Netherby, 'Home Grown Hits', *Video Business*, 4 June 2007, p. 19; and Peter Caranicas, 'Biz Hasn't Lost Disc Drive', *Variety*, 17 August 2009, pp. 4–5.
66. Jennifer Netherby, 'Warner Sees Life in Nontheatrical', *Video Business*, 25 August 2008, p. 4; and 'By the Numbers: Made-for Growth', *Variety*, 8 January 2009, p. A2.
67. Marcy Magiera, 'Where Stars Still Dwell', *Video Business*, 18 February 2008, p. 38.
68. Alisa Perren, *Indie, Inc.: Miramax and the Transformation of Hollywood in the 1990s* (Austin: University of Texas Press, 2012), p. 137.
69. Magiera, 'Where Stars Still Dwell', p. 38; and Ed Grant, 'DVD Premiere: Stigma or Boon?' *DVD Exclusive*, January 2005, p. 13.
70. Wasser, *Veni, Vidi, Video*, p. 182.
71. Alison Machor, *Chainsaws, Slackers, and Spy Kids: 30 Years of Filmmaking in Austin, Texas* (Austin: University of Texas Press, 2010), pp. 146–8.
72. Perren, *Indie, Inc.*, pp. 115, 126, 129, 132.
73. Ibid., pp. 225–9; Eliza Gallo, 'Weinsteins Working Out DVD Details', *DVD Exclusive*, July 2005, pp. 1, 20; Mary Ann Cooper, 'At Home with Bob and Harvey', *Boxoffice*, July 2007, p. 46; and Dade Hayes, 'Dimension Adds Vidpix', *Variety*, 22 October 2008, p. 1.
74. Another precursor for *Grindhouse* was Stanley Donen's *Movie Movie* (1978), a simulated 1930s double feature made by the 'Warren Brothers' studio, including the boxing movie '*Dynamite Hands*' and the backstage musical '*Baxter's Beauties of 1933*', with a fake trailer for the World War I aviation film '*Zero Hour*' sandwiched between. Like *Grindhouse*, these films imitate the visual style and populist sensibility of cycles from roughly three or four decades earlier, with several actors reappearing across both features.
75. Jennifer M. Barker, *The Tactile Eye: Touch and the Cinematic Experience* (Berkeley: University of California Press, 2009), pp. 10, 127–9.
76. Jette Kernion, 'SXSW Gets Grindhouse Fever', Moviefone, last modified 14 March 2007, http://blog.moviefone.com/2007/03/14/sxsw-gets-grindhouse-fever/ (accessed 24 July 2011). A similar use of digitally simulated film damage to obscure censorable material appears in the 2011 director's cut of the found-footage horror film *Cannibal Holocaust* (1980), released in Britain by Shameless Films, in which director Ruggero Deodato added simulated decay and lens flares to mask selectively the unsimulated animal deaths that have long been a sticking point for the British Board of Film Classification.
77. Matt Hills, *The Pleasures of Horror* (London: Continuum, 2005), p. 105.

Original italics. *Samurai Avenger: The Blind Wolf* (2009) offers an interesting variation, opening with a disclaimer from a supposed 'restoration committee' explaining that this 'original theatrical version' of the film has been assembled from multiple print elements. Some restored shots, originally censored because of 'violence and mayhem', now exhibit (simulated) discoloration or damage due to the loss of the original negatives and the restoration's reliance on the best existing positive prints. In constructing a fake censorship history for an ersatz exploitation film which never really existed, this conceit recalls similar disclaimers about patchy print sources that sometimes preface restored DVD and Blu-ray editions of historical exploitation films.

78. Lerner, 'Cinema of Regression', p. 358. Also see the responses of *Variety* subscribers listed in 'Why Did "Grindhouse" Misfire at the Box Office?' *Variety*, 10 April 2007, http://www.variety.com/article/VR1117962824 (accessed 26 July 2011).
79. Keven Skinner, 'All We Need is a Hobo With a Machete to Change Mainstream Cinema's Attitude', The Daily Blam, last modified 11 April 2011, http://dailyblam.com/news/2011/04/11/editorial-grindhouse-cinema-machete-hobo (accessed 26 July 2011).
80. Benson-Allott, *Killer Tapes and Shattered Screens*, pp. 134–7. Quote at pp. 136–7.
81. Brett Gallman, '*Grindhouse* (2007)' (review), Oh the Horror!, http://www.oh-the-horror.com/page.php?id=642 (accessed 18 February 2012). Also see discussion board threads like the January 2010 entry 'Post here if you saw it in a cinema', IMDb Board: *Grindhouse* (2007), http://www.imdb.com/title/tt0462322/board/thread/155427792 (accessed 20 February 2012).
82. 'SXSW 07: *Machete* Movie Coming', IGN.com, last modified 11 March 2007, http://movies.ign.com/articles/772/772081p1.html (accessed 22 February 2012).
83. Marc Graser and Claude Brodesser, 'In Pic-to-DVD Shift, "Unrated" Rates High', *Variety*, 13 September 2004, p. 61.
84. Rotten, 'Rodriguez and Tarantino on *Grindhouse*'.
85. Jason Coleman, 'Interview/Review: "Hobo with a Shotgun" Helmer Jason Eisener Talks Exploitation', Starpulse.com, last modified 20 May 2011, http://www.starpulse.com/news/Jason_Coleman/2011/05/20/interview review_hobo_with_a_shogun_hel (accessed 2 March 2012).
86. Lerner, 'Cinema of Regression', p. 373. To his credit, the Blu-ray release of the compete theatrical version was not yet available when Lerner's essay was written.
87. Henry Jenkins, *Convergence Culture: Where Old and New Media Collide* (New York: New York University Press, 2006), pp. 17–18, 222. Quote at p. 222.
88. Studios have increasingly turned to fan film-makers for generating cheap publicity through contests to make fake trailers and video mash-ups, according to Chuck Tryon, *Reinventing Cinema: Movies in the Age of Media Convergence* (New Brunswick, NJ: Rutgers University Press, 2009), p. 171.

A similar grindhouse trailer contest helped promote the release of *Hobo with a Shotgun*'s feature-length incarnation, with the winning entry, *Daddy Cross*, similarly appended to certain prints of *Hobo*'s theatrical release (and later spun off as a web series in its own right).

89. Sara Gwenllian Jones, 'Phantom Menace: Killer Fans, Consumer Activism, and Digital Filmmakers', in *Underground USA: Filmmaking Beyond the Hollywood Canon*, eds Xavier Mendik and Steven Jay Schneider (London: Wallflower Press, 2002), pp. 170, 175–8.
90. Lerner, 'Cinema of Regression', pp. 362–4, 371–3. Quotes at pp. 364, 373.
91. Boym, *The Future of Nostalgia*, pp. 49–50.
92. Barbara Klinger, *Beyond the Multiplex: Cinema, New Technologies, and the Home* (Berkeley: University of California Press, 2006), p. 228.
93. Jason Bene, '*Nun of That* – DVD Review', Killer Film, last modified 2 February 2010, http://www.killerfilm.com/film_reviews/read/nun-of-that-dvd-review-24742 (accessed 4 March 2012).
94. Branden Chowen, '*Sugar Boxx* – DVD Review', Inside Pulse, last modified 10 March 2011, http://insidepulse.com/2011/03/10/sugar-boxx-dvd-review/ (accessed 6 March 2012).
95. 'The New Grindhouse Era', Horror-Movies.ca, http://www.horror-movies.ca/horror_18041.html (accessed 21 February 2012). The lack of 'authenticity' behind this simulated dilapidation is especially apparent when it appears in a platform that has no logical connection to celluloid materiality whatsoever, such as the 2009 video game *House of the Dead: Overkill*.
96. Klinger, *Beyond the Multiplex*, pp. 212, 225.
97. Dyer, *Pastiche*, p. 157.
98. Lerner, 'Cinema of Regression', pp. 359, 366–7, 372. Quotes at pp. 359, 366 (italics mine). Also see Kevin Esch, '"The Lesser of the Attractions": Grindhouse and Theatrical Nostalgia', *Jump Cut*, no. 54 (2012): http://www.ejumpcut.org/currentissue/EschGrindhouse/index.html (accessed 4 November 2012).
99. Matt Hills, *Fan Cultures* (London: Routledge, 2002), pp. 37–8; and Hills, *The Pleasures of Horror*, pp. 115, 170, 193–4.
100. Grady Hendrix, 'This Old Grindhouse', *Slate*, 6 April 2007, http://www.slate.com/articles/arts/culturebox/2007/04/this_old_grindhouse.html (accessed 4 March 2012).
101. Rob Gonsalves, '*Grindhouse*' (review), Rob's Movie Vault, last modified 6 April 2007, http://robsmovievault.wordpress.com/2007/04/06/grindhouse/ (accessed 4 March 2012). Original italics.
102. Adam Tyner, '*Grindhouse* (Blu-Ray)' (review), DVD Talk, last modified 27 September 2010, http://www.dvdtalk.com/reviews/44706/grindhouse/ (accessed 4 March 2012). Original italics.
103. Stuart Heritage, 'Meet *Creature*: The Biggest Box-Office Flop of All Time', *The Guardian*, 9 December 2011, www.guardian.co.uk/film/2011/dec/09/creature-biggest-box-office-flop (accessed 6 March 2012).

104. This online survey was jointly designed and administered by the University of British Columbia, Brunel University, and the British Film Institute. Summary results about *Grindhouse* were written by Dana Keller and Rovin Onas, 'Stats and Surprises', BFI 100 Cult Films Survey, http://www.cult-survey.org/stats_and_surprises.shtml (accessed 3 April 2012).
105. Matt Hills, '*Star Wars* in Fandom, Film Theory, and the Museum: The Cultural Status of the Cult Blockbuster', in *Movie Blockbusters*, ed. Julian Stringer (London: Routledge, 2003), pp. 181–4.
106. Benson-Allott, *Killer Tapes and Shattered Screens*, p. 165. Also see Donna de Ville, 'Cultivating the Cult Experience at the Alamo Drafthouse Cinema', *Scope*, no. 20 (2011): http://www.scope.nottingham.ac.uk/article.php?issue=20&id=1306 (accessed 24 November 2011).

CHAPTER 4

Dressed to Regress? The Retributive Politics of the Retrosploitation Pastiche

Taste politics clearly remain one of the key dimensions behind the emerging retrosploitation cycle's engagement with history, treating the cinematic past as a 'politically incorrect' wellspring of inspiration and distinction for more recent productions that are largely (but not wholly) targeted at the white, heterosexual male viewer who has long consumed exploitation films as cult objects. Yet because, as I suggested in Chapter 1, archival exploitation films can continue to partially uphold retrograde political ideologies by offering visceral pleasures in sexist, racist or homophobic representations that remain earnestly viewed and not simply ironically laughed away, one of the dangers in retrosploitation films which imitate these historical referents is that, '[a]s entire periods of the recent past are introduced into the popular historical consciousness through retro's accelerated chronological blur, we risk incorporating its values as well'.[1]

I would argue that this warning is especially prescient in the case of retro-styled exploitation pastiches that, by definition, take a middle position between the positive and negative evaluative tones respectively associated with homage and parody. As noted in the previous chapter, pastiche is the retrosploitation cycle's dominant tenor, precisely because it permits such an ambiguous mix of ironic distance and earnest affectivity that viewers may have difficulty tonally distinguishing it from either homage or parody in any clear-cut way. Nevertheless, for films that self-consciously signal their use of pastiche through temporal, cultural, geographical, ideological or gendered distance or dislocation, Richard Dyer argues that pastiche may operate as a sort of 'default mode' that can spin off into various registers of humour, violence, perversity and even serious political commentary – the last of which is of primary interest in this final chapter.[2]

Using a handful of representative films, I shall examine how cultural memory inspires the multivalent political dynamics at work in a number of retrosploitation texts which engage with nostalgia's dialectical tension between the socio-political past and present, both informing and informed by the blurred borderlines between homage, parody and pastiche. In particular, I shall argue that the *ideological ambivalence* fans and critics may discern in these films' anachronistic representations reflects the very *temporal and aesthetic ambivalence* evoked by the retro-styled pastiche, with the mash-up of different tones and periods complicating any clear sense of both political unity and fan-cultural appreciation for these texts. This is because the relative pastness or presentness discernable in each retrosploitation text can weigh more heavily upon the political opportunities or limitations on offer when the politics of one temporal period are upheld over another. Still, this is not to say that pastness corresponds with a reactionary political position any more than presentness corresponds with progressive potential. Indeed, as the following examples will demonstrate, the degree to which temporal frames of reference inflect the political potentiality of a given retrosploitation pastiche largely depends on the particular text in question; though texts cannot fully dictate their reception, they still provide interpretive cues to which viewers may respond in varied ways for more or less ideological reasons. Furthermore, I shall argue that the viewer's horizon of interpretation can also include multivalent desires raised by these films' overlapping historical reference points, suggesting a 'queering' of time itself among traditionally marginalised audiences. The fact that disparate viewers can experience such disparate political and affective reactions is therefore another major case of how, as I have been arguing throughout this book, the impulse to nostalgically repurpose past texts can both unite and fragment viewing communities as the remembered times and places of exploitation film consumption have changed since the rise of home video.

According to Pam Cook, 'nostalgia is predicated on a dialectic between longing for something idealised that has been lost, and an acknowledgment that this idealised something can never be retrieved in actuality, and can only be accessed through images'. Consequently, 'Nostalgia plays on the gap between representations of the past and actual past events', thereby permitting that '[a]udiences can consciously enjoy a playful or affecting engagement with history at the same time as exercising their aesthetic judgement'.[3] If, however, reviews by critics and fans sometimes claim that retrosploitation pastiches are not to be taken seriously and instead 'best enjoyed with your brain switched off',[4] then this advice implies that one must suspend one's contemporary notions of aesthetic quality and political correctness to better enjoy these texts' 'distastefully' déclassé emulation of exploitable elements such as sex, violence and various forms of social prejudice that reared their heads in exploitation films of the past. In the light of such receptional recommendations, it is important to consider the political ramifications of nostalgia's retrospective structure of feeling, because pastiche's imitative closeness to its historical referents can also 'convey most forcefully why that [set of referents] needs to be critiqued, namely, because it [still] works' upon viewers.[5]

In other words, some viewers treat the simulated nature of the retro-styled text as an excuse temporarily to escape the forms of aesthetic and intellectual discernment which include not only political judgements but can also include fan-cultural appeals to connoisseurship, knowledge and other sources of subcultural capital. As I shall elaborate below, this is why other fans may not find it quite so easy to disengage voluntarily from the nagging issue of politically reprehensible representations that extend beyond the politics of taste alone. The potential for ambivalence and outright anxiety among fans over the unresolved taste distinctions raised by retrosploitation's diverse appeals to nostalgia can thus help productively trigger *increased political sensitivity* to how past representations are mnemonically refigured in the present. If, '[d]espite all their claims to authenticity, nostalgic fictions depend upon a slippage between current styles and period fashion in order to draw audiences in to the experience',[6] then consciously engaging these films with brains still 'switched on' allows historical, political, and aesthetic judgement to intertwine when past and present inequalities haunt the retrosploitation pastiche. Accordingly, this chapter's focus on the political ambivalence of retrosploitation pastiches explores both the reactionary and progressive potential that these texts may offer contemporary fans, without presuming that all viewers ideologically respond to their ironic-cum-earnest tenor en masse.

I shall begin, however, by illustrating the different political implications of period-set and present-set retrosploitation films, contrasting several films that use outdated racial stereotypes as authorial mouthpieces and sources of horror alike. Next, I shall look at how authorial intent can be an interpretive lens in retrosploitation films that use raced and classed minorities as (anti-)heroes. In the second half of the chapter, I shift from race and class to the politics of gender and sexuality. As a cycle, retrosploitation tends self-consciously (but not exclusively) to pursue masculinist cultural distinctions from other contemporary genre products, especially when the descendants of historically prominent varieties of exploitation cinema like horror, sexploitation and rape-revenge films have seemingly become more 'feminised' through the increased opening of access to gender-diverse audiences in a post-feminist era coinciding with the rise of home video. Finally, I turn to issues of queerness in terms not just of representation but also how films can 'queer' historicity through the overlapping temporalities that retrospectively broach the impact of past films upon the inner fantasy lives of diverse viewers. If, as I have argued across this book, the retrosploitation phenomenon is informed by a nostalgia for times and places which seem no longer to exist, then the following readings suggest the political implications of films whose representational form and content by definition seem out of time and place, yet still overwhelmingly speak to present-day desires for the retribution of perceived injustices.

Period Settings and the Horrific Performance of Race

It would generally be safe to say that no feature-length retrosploitation film is mistaken wholesale for an archival exploitation picture, even when using deliberate archaism, since retrosploitation's dominant use of pastiche always suggests at least some degree of self-conscious awareness of the past as a lost object of longing. Nevertheless, owing to pastiche's imitative closeness to its historical referents, retrosploitation film-makers and their characters mutually participate in *performances of pastness*, the political connotations of which are particularly foregrounded when dealing with social attitudes that have markedly changed since the time of their referents. In this regard, race is a privileged example for discussing the contemporary sensitivity to social attitudes that have shifted dramatically since the height of post-classical exploitation cinema in the 1960s and 1970s. Representations and rhetorics of race arguably remain more acute sources of heightened sensitivity to issues of 'political correctness' in American society than perhaps any other identity factor; the post-1960s backlash against racial civil rights, for example, has not gained a visible foothold in mainstream popular culture comparable to the post-feminist backlash against second-wave feminism. Thus, when retrosploitation pastiches attempt stylistically and affectively to evoke a 1970s-style exploitation story without being confused with an actual 1970s film, the historical disjuncture that fuels nostalgia also begs the question of how we should respond to the regressive political attitudes lingering in cultural memories of that period, including the cultural memories which these retro-styled films intentionally resurrect and inflect.

As Dyer argues in a discussion of Todd Haynes's 1950s-set melodrama *Far From Heaven* (2002), the structure of feeling evoked by a retro-styled pastiche may ask us to identify with the feelings of the imagined audiences who could have seen the pastiche's historical referents – yet the recognition of a pastiche as *not quite like* its referents 'ought also to alert us to the limitations of this historical imagining', thereby 'remind[ing] us experientially of what we have lost even while confirming that it is lost'. Because we can never truly confirm our own longing to know that past people had similar affective responses as us, we can discern such potential responses only from the cultural artefacts left behind from those earlier times. Hence, we must rely on cultural frameworks of interpretation, which have been passed down to us through mediated memory objects that can encourage us to reflect upon the very historicity of past and present responses to such films.[7]

Yet, when such interpretive frameworks include regressive political attitudes, we can be reminded of the troubling continuities between past and present racism and other social prejudices passed down to more recent generations of viewers. Unlike parody's mocking disdain or paracinema's deeply ironic reappraisal – both of which can easily slide into a historical chauvinism that impedes transhistorical empathy with imagined past audiences – pastiche's more earnest affectivity can allow us to better encounter imagined responses to racist representations on something closer to their own grounds, rather than merely laughing away such representations/responses as products of unenlightened beliefs that have since been resolved by present-day people who 'know better'. As such, fans' aforementioned anxieties over the opening of historical texts to wider potential audiences can find an affective corollary in acknowledging the threats to coherent and stable social identity posed by racism, (hetero)sexism, classism and other prejudices that would deny full and active personhood/citizenship. Hence the ideological tensions raised by nostalgic throwbacks to a period of exploitation cinema that once catered to a more socially dominant audience than the latter-day retrosploitation film's nebulous viewership.

The question of anachronism as an underlying marker of pastiche is crucial here, because I argued in the previous chapter that the relative 'authenticity' simulated by retrosploitation films is inevitably beset by anachronisms (purposeful or not) signalling a film's contemporaneity through its very asymptotic closeness to its historical referents. An important distinction, however, lies between retro-styled films which are deliberately set in the 1950s–80s post-classical exploitation era, and those set in the present but drawing considerably upon retro signifiers. When portrayals of racism and other prejudices, which seem particularly retrograde from our contemporary political perspective, are diegetically framed as unfolding within a past time, our capacity to imaginatively identify with the feelings of past audiences may be quite different from when those prejudices appear as retro signifiers in a present-set film. Yet, in both cases, we retain a lingering awareness that this pastiched prejudice has been included by film-makers who themselves share a sense of historical distance from outdated (but not obsolete) social attitudes and who, therefore, intend said prejudices to serve a highly visible function through their flagrant defiance of contemporary political sensibilities. This is not to say, however, that mnemonically refiguring past prejudices from the perspective of the present day necessarily leads to a politically progressive awareness of those beliefs' unresolved presence in contemporary society. This is an especially notable limitation when retrosploitation films directly evoke the outdated ideologies of earlier exploitation cycles as a 'rebellious' reaction against a 'mainstream' culture whose perceived climate of 'political correctness' may be read by straight white men as increasingly hostile to their traditional political interests.[8]

Several salient examples of retrosploitation films using racially inflammatory imagery as a means of resisting political correctness include *Black Devil Doll* (2007) and *The Minstrel Killer* (2009) but, whereas both films depict such imagery as a generic source of horror, each uses different means to suggest whether the root of that horror lies in the presence of non-white races themselves or in prejudiced reactions to race's socially constructed meanings. Inspired by the direct-to-video (DTV) film *Black Devil Doll from Hell* (1984), *Black Devil Doll* is a present-set film in which the soul of an African American convict – identified as a former Black Power radical who raped and murdered fifteen white teenage girls – is supernaturally transferred into an African American-styled ventriloquist puppet at the moment of his execution. Sporting an Afro hairdo and a T-shirt with a Black Power insignia, the puppet then proceeds to commit all manner of violent, misogynistic and scatological mayhem while he also develops a crude sexual relationship with his female owner (Natasha Talonz), remembering the civil rights era every time he achieves orgasm. As this brief description suggests, the film seems to reproduce stridently anti-black ideologies as it deliberately strives to offend all potential viewers. In my estimation, it is difficult to imagine the eponymous doll as a racially marked anti-hero such as the more sympathetic monsters in blaxploitation horror films like *Blacula* (1972) or *Dr. Black, Mr. Hyde* (1976) but rather a crystallisation of any number of racist stereotypes that seem all the more egregious due to the film's contemporary setting, aiming to inspire off-colour laughs more than fear or sympathy.

For co-creators Jonathan and Shawn Lewis, the racism in their film is allegedly intended as a homage to the racial stereotypes openly exploited in 1970s exploitation films which, they claim, knowledgeable fans would be able to recognise and thereby excuse as historically justifiable.[9] Of course, this defence takes for granted both a hypothetical white audience and the racial privilege of whites as film-makers and viewers because it would be difficult to imagine many members of an African American audience finding much humour in a portrayal of the souls of black folk that is so unsympathetically ugly. Even when white film producers advanced a controversially reductive stereotype of hypersexualised, violent black masculinity in 1970s blaxploitation films targeted at African American audiences, it was rarely framed through *Black Devil Doll*'s unveiled racial contempt. It is particularly telling that Shawn Lewis, a white film-maker, provides the uncredited voice for the doll, electronically modified to sound 'blacker' in a sort of aural blackface, while his biracial half-brother Jonathan does not. In this regard, it is disingenuous that a white rapper named White-T (Martin Boone) appears in the film as a comic foil to Black Devil Doll, portrayed as a ridiculous buffoon who ends up sodomised and killed for appropriating and performing a stereotyped vision of black culture – despite the film-makers' own performance of black stereotypes. As Richard Dyer notes, blackface's historical status as stereotype 'is only seen as a stereotype if that is what you think it is, otherwise you think it is an accurate representation; thus, if you think all blacks look the same (and like this), you think that a stereotypical representation of them (that is, all the same and like this) is a correct one'.[10] Though I explain below that *The Minstrel Killer* depicts blackface itself as a literally dangerous form of grotesquely inaccurate racial pastiche, the film-makers of *Black Devil Doll* consciously exaggerate offensive racial stereotypes despite still recognising them as such – yet it is far less clear how accurate they believe such stereotypes to be. Not unlike the hyperbolic rhetoric found in the marketing of interracial pornography, 'markedly anachronistic taboos and racial discourses that are parts of a different historical era' are recycled to provide *Black Devil Doll* with an air of the forbidden, revealing that such 'historical taboos have been reenacted out of context and yet still resonate'.[11]

Sean Tierney describes how white privilege often masks its own unmarked racial status through 'a distinct assignment of attributes or roles to culture or ethnicity specifically of non-whites often based in the perception that other cultures somehow have a clearer or richer definition and/or sense of culture'. This privilege consequently 'allows one to carry out an impersonation that goes unmarked or unnamed as tasteless, offensive, racist, or insulting publicly'.[12] When Quentin Tarantino, for example, claims that he understands and identifies with African American culture because of his working-class upbringing, and thereby possesses artistic licence to casually use racial slurs in blaxploitation-inspired films such as *Pulp Fiction* (1994), *Jackie Brown* (1997), and *Django Unchained*

(2012), without those words being intended as a reflection of personal racist beliefs, this is itself a defence made possible by the white privilege to disavow charges of personal racism, dismissing critical voices as being ignorant of the superior 'truth' about race supposedly known by the white film-maker. Meanwhile, Tierney continues,

> The audience venerates Tarantino's willingness to cross, and capability of crossing, cultural lines as well as his refusal to be prohibited from doing so. [. . .] Tarantino's dialogue and his defense of it seem to ring with a gleeful, willfully adolescent revelry in negative behavior for nothing more than the sake of shocking others, self-amusement, and a vain display of the privilege of engaging in such behavior.[13]

This critique rings even more clearly with a film like *Black Devil Doll* that blatantly announces the 'tasteless, offensive, racist, or insulting' intent of its regressively stereotypical performances of blackness.

As *Black Devil Doll* aptly literalises, white retrosploitation creators can easily ventriloquise through non-white characters as a means of 'safely' making statements that may grossly misrepresent the culture and politics of racially marked groups, while also denying the unequal histories of racial power that allow such misrepresentations to persist in the present day. This tendency is particularly true when those characters are either located in, or depicted as having lived through, the racism that historical distance allows us better to recognise as more visible in past decades than in its more naturalised forms in our own contemporary moment. Yet, because of past and present socio-cultural inequalities, it is far more problematic for white, hegemonic cultures to pastiche material from non-white, subordinated ones than the other way around. As Dyer explains, pastiches can become offensive when historical distance renders problematic the interpretive framework for a given pastiche – especially when a pastiche foregrounds its own historical moment, 'precisely because of its role in shoring up an unquestioned hegemonic cultural position'.[14]

At the same time, these performances of pastness are instrumentally deployed to mark presumed distinctions in a contemporary media landscape in which race is not the *only* marker of cultural privilege. Indeed, it is interesting that many of these appropriations of cultural otherness are textually or extratextually defended as rising from the experience of both race *and class*. The apparent authorial intent behind the choice to use politically reactionary stereotypes in period settings versus contemporary settings may thus be a crucial factor in fans' responses to the anachronism of retrosploitation but this intent may also be informed by a conscious desire to shock through culturally 'lower' taste/class appeals.[15] These film-makers clearly (and correctly) recognise a number of racial representations from

1970s exploitation films *as racist* but their retro-styled replication of these stereotypes may also speak to their own reluctance to look down upon past independent film-makers through a morally superior lens of historical chauvinism that would denigrate those film-makers for not 'knowing better'. After all, these contemporary low-budget film-makers do not necessarily enjoy a position of hegemonic privilege in terms of economic or cultural capital because high culture tends to naturalise its own pastiching of 'other' cultures (for example, orientalist tropes in the high white tradition of classical music) whereas low culture already remains culturally suspect in its use of diverse influences.[16] This particular film, for example, recalls how the tradition of minstrelsy originated among young, working-class whites, appropriating the cultural power of black masculinity under the culturally 'safe' guise of ridicule. Yet, not only were African Americans subject to ridicule via blackface but also 'moralizing women and white men with aristocratic pretensions' came under fire, because performing as the supposedly unruly black body historically 'challenged the traditional culture of deference and the class hierarchy and self-discipline of the emerging bourgeoisie'.[17] It is no surprise, then, that *Black Devil Doll* defensively internalises the foregone conclusions of its deliberate appeals to bad taste, with its DVD cover offering the prominent 'Warning: This Film Offends Everyone!'

Though the film may be sincerely imitative of its historical predecessors in some ways, such warnings still fall back on a degree of ironic distance that undergirds much of the political ambivalence at play in retrosploitation pastiches more broadly: a celebration of political incorrectness as a 'hip' and 'rebellious' mark of subcultural capital. The viewer is often expected to acknowledge, but ironically disavow, the contemporary norms of political correctness that would render problematic the enjoyment of such pastiches. As Jacinda Read argues, 'irony functions not only to deflect accusations of sexism [and racism, homophobia, and so on] and prevent serious engagement with the issues, but to exclude anyone who is unable or unwilling to read texts in this way'. Coexisting with, and attempting to excuse, more earnest pleasures in a film's sense of bad taste, such interpretive strategies can potentially resist contemporary political challenges to the dominance of straight white masculinity while also assuaging such demographics of the suggestion that their traditional cultural privilege is somehow threatened by the connotations of the 'feminised' or 'desexualised' fanboy.[18] Appreciative reviews of *Black Devil Doll* evidence this ironic disavowal of political anachronisms as just nasty, trashy fun, while also being used as a way of dismissing accusations of racism and other prejudices. As one fan writes, '*Black Devil Doll* (2007) is exploitation writ large[;] it is sleaze unrepentant[;] it is sexist, racist, iconoclastic, depraved, disgusting, and perhaps even apocalyptic. In short, *BDD* is a helluva fun movie.'[19]

For viewers and film-makers who may not have high levels of economic or cultural capital, the celebration of anachronistic political incorrectness can be seen as a potential source of subcultural capital by offering the fantasy that wider imagined audiences will be alienated from such material. Fans who reject these films on political grounds, however, can make their own claims to subcultural capital, rooted more in ideals of connoisseurship than exclusivity. One horror fan (and a self-described black man), for example, finds *Black Devil Doll*'s reliance on 'old-fashioned stereotypes' reprehensible, while asserting that

> [e]xploitation cinema, and more importantly Blaxploitation cinema, is not about simply pandering to a majority white, male, heterosexual audience. Nor is it solely about exploiting the characters, so we can all have a good old laugh at the silly, little foreigner, the midget, or the large-breasted woman. It's about utilizing scenarios, characters, and material to make a social statement. [. . .] This pitiful excuse of a movie simply gives the horror and exploitation genres a very bad name. Something fans have been fighting to remove, and [will] continue to do so.[20]

These comments imply that archival exploitation films can and should be redeemed through the connoisseurship of fans with enough subcultural capital to understand the historical context of representations that may seem outdated today but which nevertheless originally intended to provoke more than shock value and bad-taste humour.

In other words, fans who disavow their awareness of contemporary politics to partake in the pleasures of 'political incorrectness' do so at the risk of also disavowing or playing down the critical awareness of history and aesthetics inextricably entangled therein, therefore undercutting the fan-cultural appeals to knowledgeable discernment upon which so much subcultural capital is rooted. When fans acknowledge and respond (whether through disavowal or outright criticism) to the fact that not all other viewers will laugh away these contemporary depictions of retrograde and horrific racism, they implicitly admit that even retrosploitation pastiches intending to veer towards humour still continue to evoke earnest reactions (not just ironic distance alone) wherein fan-cultural taste distinctions and political sensitivities are intertwined in ambivalent ways. If one of the major political limitations of retrosploitation films is an anachronistic style that can lull and flatter contemporary viewers with the implication that substantial social progress has occurred since the historical periods these films evoke – thereby disavowing the need for further progress in the present – then at least films such as *Black Devil Doll* serve as a potent reminder that much work remains to be done.

In contrast, a more revisionist, less shock-oriented evocation of minstrelsy appears in Michael Fredianelli's film *The Minstrel Killer*, a retro-styled slasher film set in Texas circa 1978, featuring simulated film damage to further evoke its period setting. The film concerns a serial killer, disguised as a blackfaced minstrel, who is stalking and killing the female descendants of a local slave-owning family using the same barbaric methods that had been used to torture and kill slaves (whippings, lynchings and so on). Despite this provocative premise, the film is rarely played directly for laughs, instead maintaining a dramatic earnestness that exists in distinct tension with each ridiculously anachronistic appearance of the titular character. Tex Holland (Fredianelli), a white, college-educated cop, jumps to the conclusion that a black man must have been responsible for murders apparently committed out of historical grievance, but this suspicion is spurred by his own racism and his resentment towards his wife Carol (Vanessa Celso) for having had an affair with a black man. Throughout the film, racism is figured as a threat to Tex's masculinity, as though prejudice has made him impotent. For example, after being saved from a family of cannibalistic rednecks by his new African American partner, Tyrell Jones (Anthony Spears), Tex begins tempering his overtly racist comments and resumes sleeping with his wife. When Carol later accuses him of being a 'full-blown racist', Tex becomes indignant at the accusation and subsequently hires an African American prostitute as a test of whether his threatened masculinity can outweigh his racial prejudice. He is deeply afraid of his own racism, even later admitting to Carol that he felt some guilty satisfaction after accidentally killing Tyrell during a failed confrontation with the murderer.

The film's late-1970s setting partly explains not only the rampant use of racial slurs and prejudices by various characters in the film but also the growing awareness on Tex's part that such beliefs, arising from his roots in a working-class rural culture where casual racism is depicted as an everyday part of life, are inappropriate in a post-civil rights era, especially in distinction from how Carol asserts her racial liberalism as a sign of her own self-empowerment as a woman. Yet, if Tex's masculinity is alternatively called into question by his socially 'backward' beliefs about race, gender and sexuality, we are not encouraged to celebrate his bigotry as a desirable reassertion of straight white masculinity but, rather, to recognise it retrospectively as quickly becoming as anachronistic as the figure of the minstrel himself.

As a monstrous figure, the minstrel killer – archetypically dressed in full blackface with a black suit, top hat and white gloves – evokes both uncomfortable laughter and perverse threat in his very historical incongruity. The offensiveness of blackface from a present-day perspective makes it difficult for viewers to unproblematically identify with him as an avenging figure of historical retribution, especially in the light of the fact that minstrels were largely (but not always) played by white performers. In this respect, it is all the more difficult to find his use of slavery-era torture techniques justified within the logic of the horror genre's more sympathetic monsters since, contra Tex's initial racist assumptions, these acts are presumably not being committed by an African American man beneath the make-up. (In fact, the blackfaced killer is played by Michael Nosé, an Asian American actor, which complicates minstrelsy's history as a genre dominated by white performers. Since contemporary Asian Americans are frequently stereotyped as a 'whiter-than-white' so-called 'model minority', it seems all the more ironic that Nosé's own ethnic features disappear beneath blackface's racial masquerade.)

The minstrel's obvious signification as a grotesque performance of race begs the question of whether his violent actions are more monstrous than the monstrousness of dominant white culture's perceptions of racial others which engendered minstrelsy in the first place; indeed, the fact that the killer is effectively recreating acts of cruelty historically perpetrated by whites adds to our awareness of his deeds as a performance. In an unexpectedly self-reflexive moment midway through the film, for example, we see the minstrel killer approach a working-class white boy along the road. The boy plays 'Dixie' on his banjo as the minstrel dances (Figure 4.1), accompanied by the sudden non-diegetic sound of canned laughter and applause, recalling minstrelsy's history as a popular entertainment for working-class white audiences while also implicating the film's viewer in the act of spectatorship. Yet, the minstrel abruptly kills the boy, picks up the banjo and leaves. This sudden and violent moment of 'breaking character' provokes canned gasps, jeers and nervous chuckles from the non-diegetic 'crowd', as if asking us whether we share such a culturally conditioned response to the minstrel's actions or occupy a far more ambivalent relation to the 'traditional' audience of minstrelsy aurally recalled here.

These reactions are further tested by the film's conclusion, in which the killer captures Tex in a barn and ties him up. We see close-ups of a blackface make-up kit, reinforcing the fact that the killer's appearance is a deliberate performance and not an inherent racial trait, and then the killer saws off Tex's foot in a recreation of a punishment used on runaway slaves. The film ends with a freeze-framed close-up of Tex repeatedly

Figure 4.1 In *The Minstrel Killer* (2009), the titular minstrel dances along to a country boy playing 'Dixie' on the banjo, just before killing him. Meanwhile, the killer's grossly anachronistic blackface performance is accompanied by non-diegetic applause on the soundtrack, self-reflexively implicating the (implicitly white) viewer in a long history of racist caricature as popular entertainment. (Source: DVD.)

screaming 'Nigger!' as the sawing continues, as if falling back on his misrecognition of racial stereotype as essential trait. The hysterical shouts continue over the freeze-frame, suggesting that Tex's unresolved racism has fatally rendered him impotent to save himself from destruction at the killer's hands, the powerful racial epithet ultimately useless as either protest or solution to the threat.

We also never learn the true identity of the killer beneath the blackface, thus preventing us from personalising the individual killer's motives in a way that might play down the larger historical legacy of racism – a legacy evoked by archival images of slavery, minstrelsy and lynchings that appear over the closing credits. With our troubled 'hero' apparently killed and the perpetrator still on the loose, this unresolved ending suggests that the horrors of racism are still out there, as also noted in the film's reception. One fan review, for example, argues that viewers will probably be divided over the frequent use of racial slurs in the film and the difficulty in identifying with Tex:

> On one hand he's easy enough to root for as [a] knock-heads-and-take-names-later kind of fuzz in the Bronson mold (add on [a] Southern drawl); but on the other, he's a derogatory asswipe with a Klu Klux Klan [*sic*] belief system. [. . .] While the thick-skinned will tolerate it, some may be put off by the fact that Fredianelli shows us just precisely how many uneducated towns in the South viewed black people. The way they're spoken about in the dialogue will no doubt strike a nerve with a few. In some ways, The Minstrel Killer himself should be sided with in this regard.[21]

Meanwhile, another review calls attention to how the dialogue sometimes slides into easy, comical stereotypes of rural white people as ignorant and backward, portraying their racist attitudes as laughably repugnant, yet at the risk of reproducing the demonised figure of the 'redneck'.[22]

As Carol Clover argues, the redneck has become a contemporary signifier of 'anxieties no longer expressible in ethnic or racial terms' while 'projected onto a safe target – safe not only because it is (nominally) white, but because it is infinitely displaceable onto someone from the deeper South or the higher mountains or the further desert (one man's redneck is another man's neighbor, and so on)'.[23] Indeed, the sheer length of the subplot featuring Tex's captivity by cannibalistic hillbillies indicates how white, working-class rurality is another key source of horror in the film, even beyond the monstrosity of the racist attitudes espoused by rural white people. In this sense, various stereotypes of whiteness become marked *via class* as an implicitly horrific part of a film that is explicitly about threatening performances of blackness, potentially reproducing problematic beliefs about the conjunction of race and class, despite the film's critique of racial ignorance towards African Americans.

Whereas some fans might celebrate films like *Black Devil Doll* for nostalgically invoking a 'pre-ideological' moment that never really existed, more critical fans may demand that retrosploitation films internally perform the sort of historical contextualisation that *The Minstrel Killer* undertakes. Yet, accounting for the classed taste appeals of these films reveals a thornier picture of how racial prejudices are so often fuelled by class inequalities that become especially visible through performances of whiteness as well as blackness. Indeed, my own privileging of one film as more politically 'sophisticated' than another admittedly plays into a denigration of *Black Devil Doll*'s 'lower' taste/class appeals on anti-racist grounds but at the risk of reproducing a long-standing rejection of certain films and their fans on classist grounds as well. It thus remains crucial to heed the relative taste/class appeals of each retrosploitation text, remaining wary of too easily criticising one core social inequality while remaining complicit with another, because such criticism can replicate the very structural oppositions that allow racism's formative ties to the scarcity of (economic/cultural) capital to be too often overlooked in the popular imaginary. As the preceding chapters have suggested, such classed appeals indicate how fans selectively marshal nostalgia to situationally claim or disclaim allegiance to downmarket consumption experiences, even if not all fans openly admit the legacy of class inequalities as a constitutive part of their identities.

Race and Class in Retro-styled (Anti-)Heroics

The films discussed above recall how minstrelsy was historically seen as a form of vulgar fun associated with the supposed bodily excesses of non-white entertainment forms, licensing 'preposterously sexual, violent, or otherwise prohibited theatrical material' that objectified blackness as an ambivalent source of anxiety and identification alike. In privileging performances of dynamic, animalistic blackness as a source of spectacle over narrative, minstrelsy's misconstrued black body even became a source of pleasure by offering the fantasy of cross-racial remasculinisation.[24] Yet, as I shall now elaborate, this degree of identificatory fantasy, mixed with anxiety over *cultural difference*, extends even to contemporary viewers confronted with *temporal difference*. This is because retrosploitation's raced and classed protagonists occupy an uneasy position between heroes and anti-heroes via the stereotypical shades that mark them as so anachronistically out of place and time in the present-day mediascape.

As the previous section suggested, the historical disjuncture between retro-coded settings/signifiers and contemporary political sensibilities is undergirded by an awareness of unresolved social inequalities that can become diegetically figured in not only monstrous villains but also in flawed heroes. That is, the anachronistic (re)appearance of racist and classist ideologies can cause the lines between heroes and anti-heroes to become blurred (for example, Tex versus the minstrel killer) when retrosploitation pastiches nostalgically treat the past as fodder for both ironic distance and sincere thrills, making outdated stereotypes into simultaneous objects of attraction and repulsion for exploitation fans. The very sense of temporal disjuncture that highlights these performances of pastness clashes with the viewer's awareness of contemporary political sensibilities, creating a tension that can be receptionally inflected towards progressive or regressive identifications with these protagonists. Much as otherwise reprehensible images of violence and prejudice might be framed beneath a veneer of retro 'coolness' in some retrosploitation films (as elaborated in my later discussion of rape-revenge films), other films ally viewers with protagonists whose cultural/temporal difference marks them as not merely bringers of 'bad taste' but as bearers of outdated social attitudes that elicit more politically engaged affinities. In other words, even when treading the lines of political correctness, these films can draw inspiration from historical exploitation cycles in order to create dynamic characters who offer signs of (if not clear directions for) political progressivism through their heroically framed 'resistance' to inequalities that remain resonant today.

In the previous chapter, I argued that retro-stylisation can make the author's hand especially apparent, even as the evaluatively neutral tone struck by pastiche can simultaneously render more ambiguous the film-maker's particular attitude towards his/her film's historical referents and contemporary market demands. Here, however, I posit that, even if ascriptions of authorial intent may not be able to stabilise *completely* the fan's reception of a retrosploitation film, they can at least provide some interpretive framework for political judgements about the extent to which these anachronistic protagonists are primed for identification by contemporary viewers. This is particularly the case when it is not simply white film-makers ventriloquising through non-white characters but when a greater degree of perceived affinity may exist between film-maker and raced/classed protagonist. Indeed, R. L. Rutsky warns that, because exploitation films frequently employ vividly sensationalised imagery, it is easy to condemn them for exoticising racial, cultural or sexual otherness, rather than asking the more complicated question of whether the appeal of their oft-stereotypical representations of cultural difference bespeaks 'a desire for something other than ideological conformity'. For Rutsky, critics and scholars too often use such blanket condemnation to disavow their own potential pleasures in watching exploitation films that may, indeed, be politically problematic in many ways but nevertheless speak to more sincere desires for difference from the status quo – including empathetic longings for cultural difference that cannot be merely reduced to exoticism or co-optation.[25]

As an example of African American film-making practice that draws upon blaxploitation tropes in a comedic way, but with a markedly different political tenor than *Black Devil Doll*, we can turn to *Black Dynamite* (2009). Unlike the blaxploitation spoofs *I'm Gonna Git You Sucka* (1988) and *Undercover Brother* (2002), both of which are set in their contemporary moments and feature African American protagonists whose actions are diegetically inspired by a longer tradition of blaxploitation heroes, *Black Dynamite* is set in the 1970s and uses deliberate archaism to evoke the look and feel of a 1970s film. With a plot inspired by films such as *Three the Hard Way* (1974), *Black Dynamite*'s titular character (Michael Jai White) is a former CIA agent and Vietnam veteran avenging his brother's death while stopping the influx of a dangerous new drug that threatens to emasculate black men by shrinking their genitals. Working for the good of the black community, he allies with a group of Black Panthers to infiltrate the island of Fiendish Dr. Wu (Roger Yuan), a Fu Manchu-esque supervillain, and eventually traces the conspiracy back to the White House. The film concludes with Black Dynamite beating Richard Nixon into submission (with the help of Abraham Lincoln's ghost) and taking charge of the Oval Office, a telling ending for a film released one year after Barack Obama's election.[26]

As this brief synopsis suggests, the narrative becomes increasingly outrageous as its eponymous protagonist moves out of an urban setting and into other arenas, all the while upholding the stereotypically violent, macho and hypersexualised blaxploitation hero – albeit exaggerated for comedic effect. Yet, rather than simply parodying the cycle, the film adequately delivers plenty of genre thrills that achieve their nostalgically convincing effect through the film's archaic aesthetic. Shot on Super 16 film stock, the film's footage has a period-appropriate graininess throughout, plus poorly framed shots, visible boom microphones, abrupt zooms, continuity errors, stilted dialogue and other signifiers of the impoverished film-making seen in historical blaxploitation films such as *TNT Jackson* (1974) and *The Human Tornado* (1976). Though these self-conscious signifiers of 'badness' allow director Scott Sanders to frame the film through an air of intentional paracinema, I would argue that his use of deliberate archaism permits a more measured tone than the negativity that often attends a disproportionate focus on ironic distance. That is, despite its generic framing as a comedy, the film better occupies the fuzzy borderline between parody and pastiche than the aforementioned spoofs. This tone is attributable to *Black Dynamite* adequately imitating how the original blaxploitation cycle had itself quickly started to verge on self-parody – partly through cultural appropriation by white Hollywood producers but largely because of cyclical exhaustion – in films ranging from *Cleopatra Jones* (1973) to *Welcome Home, Brother Charles* (1975) to *Black Shampoo* (1976) to one of *Black Dynamite*'s most central inspirations, the starring vehicles of comedian Rudy Ray ('Dolemite') Moore. Though the outcry among 1970s civil rights groups over the reductive stereotypes in blaxploitation films has been well documented, we might also ask to what extent the very *excessiveness* of such stereotypical roles became a source of (semi-)ironic pleasure for some African American viewers at the time.

Reviving such sources of pleasure, an outright parody such as *I'm Gonna Git You Sucka* clearly signals its indebtedness to the past through its in-jokes about the blaxploitation cycle and supporting roles by cycle veterans Bernie Casey, Jim Brown and Isaac Hayes but I would suggest that it generally veers closer to parody's negative evaluation of its historical referents than *Black Dynamite*. *Sucka* depicts returning veteran Jack Spade (Keenen Ivory Wayans) enlisting the help of his blaxploitation-era childhood heroes to similarly avenge his brother's death and take down a local crime boss, despite the community's view of such heroes as ineffectually over-the-hill relics. Indeed, much of the parodic humour derives from the temporal incongruity of seeing blaxploitation heroics and supporting characters transplanted to the late 1980s, as exemplified by a scene where old-school pimp Flyguy (Antonio Fargas) is released from prison dressed in flamboyant 1970s-era pimp attire and is promptly mocked by all passers-by (on-screen surrogates for the film's audience) for his outdated sartorial excess.

Conversely, *Black Dynamite*'s tone more closely resembles a 'pseudo-parody' that 'establish[es] a level of goodwill with an audience to create the sense of opposition' to its referents, 'even as the text works to reassert the norms of the parodied genre' by effectively playing it straight to some degree.[27] *Black Dynamite*'s more earnestly pastiched elements are further enhanced by the film's allegiance to the power of the black community, a power that may be nostalgically framed but is nevertheless championed – whereas the parodic *I'm Gonna Git You Sucka* 'openly mocks the idea that community and community-oriented spirit can resolve problems in favor of individual solutions'.[28] Black Dynamite may be an action-hero superman but his heroics are bolstered by a team of black revolutionaries (Figure 4.2) with open support from the wider community – in part because the film's early-1970s setting depicts an era in which the blaxploitation cycle resonated with certain threads of black nationalism, rather than

Figure 4.2 Black Dynamite (Michael Jai White) teams with a group of black revolutionaries to stop a governmental plan to emasculate the African American community. While spoofing blaxploitation tropes, *Black Dynamite* (2009) also nostalgically recalls that cycle's initial resonance with the Black Power movement. (Source: DVD.)

being mocked as ludicrously outdated by the time of *Sucka*'s late-1980s milieu.

I'm Gonna Git You Sucka, Undercover Brother, and *Black Dynamite* all fit Harriet Margolis's argument that African American film-makers can use self-directed stereotypes to defensively combat the images ordinarily imposed upon a stereotyped community from outside, thereby 'invok[ing] an ironic response in the spectator, based on an ability to identify with or at least recognize the Other, as well as an inability to stand naively and comfortably in the place of the One relative to the Other'. The political potential of this strategy is especially activated when their films cross over to white audiences – as *Black Dynamite* certainly has. Rather than replacing 'negative' representations with 'positive' ones whose claims to greater authenticity may go unquestioned, films that irreverently make all characters *and the diegesis itself* subject to self-deprecating play undercut the ontological ground from which one might make the political declamations of representational accuracy typically associated with verisimilar depictions of racial difference. As Margolis cautions, 'a misreading of a stereotype, however, may lead to its confirmation, increasing racist (or other prejudiced) perceptions of those being stereotyped'.[29] I would argue that this caveat is all the more relevant for pastiche than parody, owing to pastiche's neutrally evaluative relation to its historical referents – even if its retro-styled period settings and film-making practices may still heighten a sense of ironic distance from the diegesis. Consequently, as much as *Black Dynamite* celebrates racial community, its uses of pastiche can also spur politically ambivalent reactions, because viewers may charge it with reproducing racial stereotypes that are not solely subject to ironic/parodic dismantling.[30]

As a retrosploitation film like *Black Dynamite* extends beyond cult audiences, for example, the possibility remains that viewers with little subcultural capital may read the film's excesses as playing into racist stereotypes instead of self-consciously hyperbolising those historical representations to the point of comedic deconstruction. Yet, by avoiding some of parody's ironic sense of superiority and grounding its retro take on blaxploitation in how past audiences could have earnestly experienced its generic thrills in similar ways as present-day multiracial audiences, the film better invokes the potential power of 'community' writ large, recalling how any community of viewers will inevitably contain receptional differences in opinion that might generate the sort of socially productive dialogue about race and racism that films like *Black Devil Doll* intentionally foreclose.

Besides *Black Dynamite*, a notable number of other films which aesthetically evoke culturally devalued and economically impoverished exploitation pictures also narratively resonate with class anxieties. From the 'white trash' anti-heroes of *House of 1000 Corpses* (2003) and *The Devil's Rejects* (2005) to the undocumented Mexican labourers in *Machete* (2010) to the dystopian slums of *Hobo with a Shotgun* (2011), these films emerged during a period when income inequality reached historic levels in the United States.[31] Though it is arguably a coincidence that many of these retrosploitation films appeared after the worldwide financial crisis precipitated in 2008 (especially since the cycle-accelerating *Grindhouse* had premiered the previous year), it is difficult not to interpret their emergence during that historical context as particularly apropos. Without reducing them to symptomatic reflections of social anxieties or deliberately calculated attempts to capitalise on interest in timely economic issues, the expression of long-standing class issues in these films gained greater poignancy in the light of the economic collapse that concurrently dominated much public discourse.

It seems significant, then, that so many of these films use the form of a *cinematic underclass* to represent revenge narratives undertaken by their respective *economic underclasses*. When Stuntman Mike (Kurt Russell), for example, gains sadistic sexual satisfaction from killing young women with his 'death-proof' car in Quentin Tarantino's half of *Grindhouse*, this violence may conservatively shore up a sense of straight white masculinity threatened less by sexual rejection than by his own obsolescence as a below-the-line worker whose labour is less necessary in an age of computer-generated action spectacle – his prior identity having been effectively replaced by the high-tech artistry of software specialists whose toil seems far divorced from dangerous (masculine) physical labour.[32] Still, Stuntman Mike ultimately fails to kill, and is eventually killed by, a trio of hard-hitting women – including real-life stunt performer Zoë Bell (playing herself) – who quickly supplant Mike as our primary objects of identification. This suggests that his gendered/classed retributive violence can be thwarted by a female team including a woman who survives precisely by putting her old-fashioned, highly physical stunt training to good use in both saving herself and in thrilling *Death Proof*'s viewers as she dangles atop the hood of a speeding hot rod chased by Mike. Bell has worked out how to survive, both within and outside the industry, by transcending her below-the-line occupation and achieving above-the-line stardom here, whereas Mike has descended into homicidal behaviour and self-destruction – all while the film industry (including *Death Proof* itself) continues to capitalise on the non-digitised spectacle of these skilled performers' bodies in action.

As seen with *The Minstrel Killer* or *Death Proof*, a political ambivalence thus exists within this common retrosploitation thread of retributive violence perpetrated by members of socio-economic classes that have been demonised, disempowered or otherwise neglected. This ambivalence resonates with the apparent 'resistance' to cultural obsolescence that I discussed in Chapter 1, because emergent technologies and audiences alike can generate animosity among those whose (past) cultural investments seem different from the dominant (present) socio-economic status quo. Still, even though the resulting denouements of bloody destruction suggest the continuance of unresolved inequalities in the present, these films may offer few political solutions that exceed the brutally retro-styled logic of exploitative sensationalism. Though often figured in correlation with race, class remains a marker of social inequality about which there is far less political sensitivity in contemporary American society. Unlike race, then, classed (anti-)heroes can provoke receptional ambivalence through *greater* closeness to present-day stereotypes than historical distance from them, especially when the economic impetus of these films conflicts with what their economically downtrodden protagonists already recognise as the failed promises of dominant capitalist interests.

Rob Zombie's films *House of 1000 Corpses* and its sequel *The Devil's Rejects* are prominent examples of retrosploitation pastiches taking a demonised economic underclass to great extremes in their portrayal of the murderous Firefly family. While clearly indebted to a long line of backwoods horror films, Zombie's films take a different tone than, say, *The Minstrel Killer*'s portrayal of cannibalistic hillbillies (despite being set in the same historical milieu) by, instead, preserving their horrific eccentricities but elevating his rural 'white trash' characters to the level of macabre anti-heroes. Set in Texas circa 1977, *House of 1000 Corpses* features two young city couples waylaid by a monstrous family while searching for strange and morbid local ephemera that they might profit from by writing a book on roadside attractions. Lured in by a local legend about a serial killer named Dr. Satan, the young men are eager to take ironic pleasure in the 'backwardness' of the local people – at least until members of the Firefly family begin violently expressing their opposition to such patronising attitudes. As family patriarch Otis (Bill Moseley) screams while torturing one of the captive women: 'Listen, you Malibu middle-class Barbie piece of shit . . . I'm trying to work here! Work? You ever work? Yeah, I'll bet you have. Scooping ice cream to your shit-heel friends on summer break!' As this colourful dialogue implies, 'One of the obvious things at stake in the city/country split of horror films, in short, is social class – the confrontation between haves and have-nots, or even more directly, between exploiters and their victims' when economic guilt inspires fears of retribution against city people by the indigenous country residents marginalised from relative (sub)urban prosperity.[33]

Like his characters, Zombie seems to enjoy doing 'the devil's work' as a film-maker but he also shares his characters' hostility towards bourgeois society's ironic disparagement of white, rural, working-class culture – hence his drive to push brutality to uncomfortable extremes. He also intercuts the film with disorienting clips from old exploitation movies, theatrical announcement materials, and 16 mm footage of the Firefly clan offering deranged rants and threats that act as a running commentary. Much like similar 'home movie' footage in *The Manson Family* (2003), this last material is distressed to look like old celluloid and VHS imagery, helping enhance the film's overall retro feel while also evoking a music video aesthetic. Like the accumulated array of detritus decorating the Firefly house, these cutaways cast Zombie himself as a collector of cinematic ephemera that may look like useless junk to 'sophisticated city-folk' but which perhaps better evoke pastiche as a form of 'cultural cannibalism' upon the garbage cast off from dominant capitalist consumption.

While *House of 1000 Corpses* may literalise a sort of 'trash aesthetics', *The Devil's Rejects* is a more stylistically restrained affair, lacking its predecessor's wild intercuts and delirious editing but compensating with even greater brutality. Without 'normal', economically stable (sub)urbanites to serve as audience surrogates, the film plunges immediately into the Firefly clan's escape from a police raid on their home, and their subsequent cross-country flight from a sheriff (William Forsythe) whose penchant for violent retribution is as cruel as their own. Eschewing the horror genre for the outlaw movie, we are positioned throughout as expected to identify with the surviving Firefly trio (Figure 4.3), even as Zombie makes this particularly difficult following a gruelling series of rape/murder scenes at a motel en route to their final demise. Falling in a hail of bullets while driving headlong at a police roadblock to the classic tune of Lynyrd Skynyrd's 'Free Bird', the Fireflys are ultimately depicted as folk (anti-) heroes, even if the preceding rampage has effectively shown us the ghastly truth leading up to this bloody denouement. Likewise, the film's last moments alternate between 'happy' home movie footage of the Fireflys as a family and images of these same characters repeatedly struck by police gunfire. In so self-consciously evoking a long cinematic tradition of outlaw folk heroes, such as Jesse James, Bonnie and Clyde, and, in a much darker vein, the Manson family, I still find it hard not to read this ending with some lingering degree of ironic (though not ironically humorous) distance from the graveness with which Zombie presents his sympathy for the devil

Figure 4.3 Original promotional poster for Rob Zombie's *The Devil's Rejects* (2005), illustrating the surviving Firefly family's visual coding as white, working-class anti-heroes through their battered attire, unkempt hair and backwoodsman weaponry.
(Source: Lionsgate Entertainment.)

– especially when this sympathy is tonally at odds with how monstrous their prior actions have been depicted.

Zombie uses rural working-class signifiers in an earnest way throughout his *oeuvre*, from the casting of professional wrestlers to the use of country and southern rock as soundtrack music. Even beyond the potentially unsympathetic qualities of his 'hellbilly' protagonists, it is this earnest embrace of 'redneck' culture that inspires unveiled classist disgust toward Zombie's work from more bourgeois observers.[34] Yet, Laura Wiebe Taylor also notes that Zombie's pairing of popular music with brutal violence helps prevent the Fireflys from being completely othered. Their violence, like their musical tastes, belongs to American pop culture more generally – so, for all the family's horrific eccentricities, there is also something strikingly and even uncomfortably mundane about them.[35] Furthermore, Linnie Blake argues that the redneck or hillbilly figure in Zombie's work recalls a much longer tradition of the American backwoodsman who resists cultural assimilation into either neo-conservative or liberal models of national belonging and territorial expansionism, often rejecting laws in favour of a very different sense of freedom. The hillbilly is 'tied firmly to a sense of place and an extended kinship structure', resulting in 'a distinct cultural milieu with its own sense of history, tradition, and class', as evoked through the desaturated and sepia-toned palette that connotes *The Devil's Rejects*' artefactual quality.[36] It is this sense of cultural-cum-temporal difference, embodied in outsider identities markedly 'out of step' with contemporary bourgeois politics and morality, that allows the Fireflys to potentially serve as both attractive and repulsive figures for viewers from different class backgrounds, as seen in the cult reputation that Zombie's films have earned among a socio-economic variety of horror fans.

Though I do not wish to overstate the recuperative potential of Zombie's often unrepentantly misogynistic films, we can draw a rough connection between the class-based retributive violence of his protagonists and the film-maker's own class-inflected appropriation of low-cultural exploitation cinema to *épater la bourgeoisie*. Indeed, both films prominently incorporate home movie footage supposedly shot by the Firefly family themselves, with its intercutting into their final death scene suggesting a parallel between Zombie and the Fireflys as rural working-class film-makers emerging from non-traditional backgrounds (rock music stardom and serial killing, respectively). Though many viewers' identification with the Fireflys (mine included) may be more ambivalent than Zombie's own, his films can still be seen as an attempt at resisting assimilation and asserting his own cinematic freedom by exaggerating enduring stereotypes of the monstrous redneck to such shocking heights that he creates a perverse nostalgia for an indigenous American culture whose turns towards violence and depravity are symptomatic of competition for scarce resources – not unlike the industrial and representational strategies of exploitation film-makers in general.

Much like my discussion of Joe Bob Briggs in Chapter 1, then, Rob Zombie does not challenge or deconstruct outright the redneck stereotype so much as present it as an ambivalent figure of pleasure and peril alike, played for crude shock value on some level but potentially left open for cross-class identification with the 'brutish' working-class body. Unlike the offence caused by blackface's outdated performance of race, Zombie's performances of classed rurality are perhaps less likely to be seen as artificial or archaic, and more likely to be mistaken as derived from some degree of reality that continues to this day – in part because political sensitivities to stereotypical representations of class remain far less prevalent than to race. Like exploitation cinema's capacity to encourage a strain of populism that sits uneasily with some contemporary fans' claims to subcultural capital, Zombie's retro evocation of 1970s pastness also recalls a time when working-class whites flocked to rural drive-ins. Consequently, though he may layer his films with a dark vision of working-class populist Americana, some contemporary viewers may feel uneasy about celebrating his pastiches if said viewers also chauvinistically dismiss the 'country folk' who probably would have consumed Zombie's film-historical referents.

In this respect, Zombie's films, like many of the aforementioned retrosploitation pastiches that use raced and classed protagonists as anti-heroes, may position themselves as 'rebelliously' shocking and violent as a sign of class/taste retribution. As I suggested in the previous chapter, however, their appeals to 'bad taste' continue to operate within an economic system in which the drive to capitalise financially on easily exploitable elements can nevertheless undercut the perceived success of their nostalgic longing for (sub)cultural 'authenticity'. That is, general viewers with at least modest amounts of cultural capital may reject these films out of bourgeois distaste; whereas fans with high levels of subcultural capital may also reject these films as convergence-era pabulum for genre-hungry 'fanboys' who might eagerly consume populist thrills when retrofitted in textual forms too recent to be unquestionably recuperated as 'cult'. Though retrosploitation pastiches may allow raced and classed protagonists to become conflicted objects of pleasure and identification (especially during a coincident period of economic crisis) in ways that receptional turns towards authorial intent may help clarify, these examples also illustrate that the taste/class resonances of dominant economic interests still persistently threaten to contaminate what other fans may see as the films' desired affront to 'mainstream' cultural norms.

In Praise of Splat: Remasculinising Contemporary Genre Aesthetics

As the preceding examples suggest, most retrosploitation films follow in the footsteps of their historical referents by occupying genres or cycles that have traditionally been targeted to heterosexual male audiences. Like their predecessors, they typically feature plenty of masculine violence, the objectification or degradation of women, and sometimes the denigration of gay and lesbian characters. At the same time, however, the acceleration of a retrosploitation cycle during the 2000s did not just involve a simple imitation of the highly gendered tropes found in historical exploitation cinema but can also be seen as a response to perceived changes in the gender address of traditionally 'masculine' genres such as horror and sexploitation – regardless of the mixed-gender demographics who may have actually consumed such films.

For many critics, film-makers and fans alike, the 1990s marked a period of sharp thematic and aesthetic decline for the horror genre, even as this supposed 'decline' actually corresponded with a renewed burst of interest in horror cinema. The genre allegedly became more 'mainstream' with the rise of hits like *Scream* (1996) and a long line of remakes of older and international horror films, leading to a particular rhetoric of crisis among critics and fans whose (sub)cultural capital seemed threatened by the genre's turn towards wider audiences – including the increasingly visible courting of younger and female viewers.[37] Since horror is one of the most prominent genres pastiched within the retrosploitation cycle, it provides a noteworthy example of how exploitation cinema's taint of populism can seemingly take on a 'feminine' air when the audiences for traditionally gendered genres seem to open up. Indeed, femininity has long been culturally coded as more physically/emotionally 'open' than masculinity, so it should be no surprise that a perceived *opening up* of 'masculine' genres to other viewers would carry patriarchally reviled connotations of vulnerability, weakness and ignorance.

As Constantine Verevis notes of film remakes, 'Audiences come to the new versions with varying degrees of knowledge and expectation: those who have never heard of the original, those who have heard of it but not seen it, those who have seen it but don't remember it, and those who have a detailed knowledge of it.' For example, 'the producers of *The Texas Chainsaw Massacre* [2003] say that the idea of remaking the seminal slasher movie was in part motivated by research showing that 90 per cent of the film's anticipated core audience (eighteen to twenty-four year old males) knew the title of Tobe Hooper's original but had never seen it'.[38] In addition to seemingly targeting large numbers of young viewers presumed to be without detailed knowledge of genre history, the genre's 1990s 'decline' was widely blamed on its supposed 'feminisation', falling back on long-standing beliefs linking mass culture, femininity and passivity.[39] Partly influenced by television teen soap operas of the same era, greater emotional realism and a focus on teenage melodrama represented appeals to female viewers who might have been underserved by the genre's traditionally (but not exclusively) masculine orientation. This shift made Hollywood's horror output seem 'softer' and, in the eyes of some fans, more readily dismissible in retrospective comparison with older texts – ultimately leading to a critical nostalgia for the 1970s, a period heralded as a creatively and politically progressive boom for the horror genre.[40] Moreover, the early-2000s transnational popularity of East Asian horror films, including prominent American remakes such as *The Ring* (2002) and *The Grudge* (2004), saw the horror genre's main currents returning to a more understated aesthetic of largely gore-free spookery.

It is no surprise, then, that around the turn of the 2000s, some film-makers began looking towards the past for signs of 'politically incorrect' distinction rooted in the aggressively masculinist products of the post-classical exploitation industry. In interviews and publicity materials, fan-favourite directors, such as Tarantino and Robert Rodriguez, began endorsing recent films that not only seemed 'harder' and more brutal in tone but were frequently made by exploitation fans-turned-filmmakers specialising in a heavily allusive style, such as Eli Roth, Rob Zombie, Darren Lynn Bousman, Alexandre Aja and Greg McLean. Unofficially dubbed 'The Splat Pack', these film-makers often influenced and assisted with each other's work; several of them, for example, including Zombie and Roth, contributed fake trailers to *Grindhouse*.[41] Rather than the laughably over-the-top, offensive excesses of Troma films or Peter Jackson's early movies, this emerging generation of retrospectively inspired films generally tempered playful historical allusion with a degree of seriousness that would make their violence seem less palatable to wider/female audiences (despite several of these films, in fact, capturing both sizeable and mixed-gender demographics).[42] These claims to greater exclusivity and potential subcultural capital are reflected by the fact that, unlike the largest Hollywood studios, (off-)Hollywood mini-majors and their associated genre labels, such as Dimension Films and Lionsgate Entertainment, released most of these films[43] – including many that became associated with the controversial label 'torture porn', such as *High Tension* (2003), *Saw* (2004), *Hostel* (2005), *The Devil's Rejects*, *Wolf Creek* (2005), and *Captivity* (2007).[44] (Of course, as I mentioned in the previous chapter, Dimension also released *Scream* and several other films associated with the teen feminisation of 1990s horror, allowing the company to profitably play different generic preferences off each other in mutual acts of distinction.)

Remakes of post-classical exploitation films from various cycles and genres proliferated during this same decade, often seen by fans and other critics as betrayals of their supposedly more 'original' and 'authentic' predecessors. In this sense, the more violent, masculinist sensibility associated with the Splat Pack's retributive reaction against teen horror and horror remakes overlapped with the gendered dynamics of the retrosploitation films emerging during the same period. Yet, these distinctions were certainly not set in stone, because several members of the Splat Pack also contributed to the string of 1970s exploitation remakes – such as Aja's *The Hills Have Eyes* (2006) and *Piranha* (2010) and Zombie's *Halloween* (2007) and *Halloween II* (2009). Likewise, several retrosploitation films are so imitatively close to their historical referents that they are perhaps better considered uncredited remakes of earlier films; the rape-revenge films *Chaos* (2005) and *Hora* (2009), for example, border on outright plagiarism of *The Last House on the Left* (1972) and *I Spit on Your Grave* (1978), respectively. Furthermore, Verevis observes that original versions and their remakes regularly possess a symbiotic relationship, because theatrical remakes typically offer an opportunity for the original version to be re-released on home video in an attempt to cash in on its revived cultural visibility. Consequently, if existing fans feel their subcultural capital can be threatened by such remakes, this reaction neglects how prospective fans might also take this opportunity to discover the remediated original version and claim its superior value over the remake – especially after having heard existing fans justifying their affection for the original.[45]

Yet, exploitation remakes are not simply the work of major studios but also exist at the low-budget end of the market – though this does not mean the latter more faithfully refigure the past in ways that fans would prefer. As David Andrews notes, for example, ei Independent Cinema's Retro-Seduction DVD label has released remediated editions of 1960s–70s sexploitation films by Joe Sarno and Nick Phillips, often including short and feature-length remakes of the originals as bonus features; examples include *Roxanna* (2002), *Pleasures of a Woman* (2002), *Lustful Addiction* (2003), *The Seduction of Misty Mundae* (2004), *New York Wildcats* (2005), and *Chantal* (2007). Yet, these remakes tend to be micro-budget films shot on digital video, usually with even less narrative pretence for long scenes of inter-female sex (featuring recurrent ei Independent Cinema stars like Misty Mundae) than their historical referents. Frequently updating the originals by setting them against elements of the urban crime movie, these remakes contain relatively few retro signifiers and instead claim their fealty to sexploitation history through their intratextual proximity to the originals on the same discs. Ei Independent Cinema (more recently renamed Pop Cinema) thus uses remediation to confer reciprocal legitimacy upon both itself and the historical sexploitation films that it releases – as illustrated when it pictures and gives top billing to Mundae on the DVD cover of *Roxanna* while only mentioning the 1970 Phillips film in small text at the bottom, or when Retro-Seduction released *Inga* (1968), *Female Animal* (1970) and *I Like the Girls Who Do* (1973) with Mundae occupying the DVD covers.[46]

In this sense, the past is not always clearly privileged over the present, much as Retro-Seduction's remakes of historical sexploitation films may not heavily invoke the pastness of their predecessors. Because the existing soundtrack for Phillips's *Roxanna* was heavily damaged, for example, the original narration was re-recorded by actor Chelsea Mundae and an original psychedelic rock score contributed by a present-day band. Though this music is reused in the 2002 *Roxanna* remake, playing over opening credits modelled after the first few shots of the original film, the contemporaneity of the soundtracks across both parts of the same DVD blurs the temporalities at work between the original 1970 film and its 2002 descendant, without unambiguously celebrating one temporal period over another.

Appreciative fan reviews tend to frame the remakes primarily as vehicles for cult actors like Misty Mundae, while excusing or overlooking the factors that more negative reviewers might criticise, such as low production values, the aesthetic flatness of digital video, and the rather tentative engagement with historical referents. As one disappointed reviewer noted of the *Roxanna* remake,

> I was hoping for a revitalization of the independent exploitation scene. Lofty hopes, but there you have it. I was disappointed to find that these movies don't even shoot as high as the low-hanging fruit on Cinemax. [. . .] There may be hope yet for the softcore sex romp, but I'm looking elsewhere. For now, 1970s Italian films will have to do.[47]

Much as I noted about pastiches in the previous chapter, remakes at all levels of the film industry require a pronounced retro-styled evocation of exploitation cinema's production values and overall feel to be seen by fans as earnest engagements with film history, with fans' suspicions about 'authenticity' ratcheting up when moving towards *both* ends of the budgetary scale – the shoddily amateurish and the glossily polished alike.

By pastiching retro signifiers of pastness, from the paratextual strategies associated with historical exploitation films to the simulation of celluloid degradation, the retrosploitation cycle developing during the 2000s could effectively blend the winking knowingness borne of historical distance with the more sincere affectivity signalled by the films' ostensible 'resistance' to the high-gloss appearance of Hollywood remakes and teen-oriented fare. When a 1970s-styled trailer is used to promote *Hell Ride* (2008), *The Minstrel Killer, Sugar Boxx* (2009), *Run! Bitch Run!* (2009), or *Machete*, for example, the advertised film is linked to notions of somehow being temporally 'outside' contemporary Hollywood, regardless of whether independently produced or not. Likewise, the use of digitally simulated film damage to 'rough up' the films' outer veneer evokes their retributive difference from slick-and-clean contemporary Hollywood films ostensibly made for easy, 'feminised' consumption.

In this regard, we can see David Fincher's *Fight Club* (1999) as an influential precursor to this use of simulated dilapidation and artefacting, because it self-reflexively ties a 'rebellious' contemporary masculinity to moments when the filmic apparatus becomes visible. As part-time projectionist Tyler Durden (Brad Pitt) is at work surreptitiously splicing frames of hard-core pornography into family films (and, eventually, into the last few frames of *Fight Club* itself), he literally points out the intermittent appearance of the emulsion punches or scrapes (aka 'cigarette burns', accompanied by a loud beep) appearing in the corner of the filmic frame to signal the reel's approaching end (Figure 4.4). Likewise, when Tyler later delivers a speech to the camera in tight close-up, addressing the (implicitly) male viewer as far more than the illusory identity parlayed by the 'feminising' forces of consumption ('You're not the car you drive . . . you're not the contents of your wallet . . . you're not your fucking khakis'), the cinematic image violently shakes with excitement, the sprocket holes on either side of the frame becoming visible. It is appropriate that Tyler himself occupies the increasingly outdated position of theatre projectionist, linking such eruptions of repressed masculinity to moments when celluloid's own degradation and impending pastness appear as momentary 'transgressions' of verisimilitude. After all, it is not a huge step between, on one hand, Tyler inserting bits of dirty movies (images of 'a nice big cock') into mainstream Hollywood entertainments as a signifier of masculinity's violent and 'politically incorrect' prerogative, and, on the other hand, retrosploitation film-makers similarly linking celluloid damage to an anti-'mainstream' aesthetic ethos. *Hora*, for example, not

Figure 4.4 Part-time projectionist Tyler Durden (Brad Pitt) self-reflexively points out the emulsion scrapes signalling *Fight Club*'s (1999) approaching reel change in a moment linking a violently eruptive masculinity to exposed signifiers of celluloid degradation. (Source: DVD.)

only apes the 'missing reel' gimmick from *Grindhouse* but also repeatedly uses *Fight Club*'s beeping 'cigarette burns' as a homage to Fincher's film. Nevertheless, much like the Splat Pack's penchant for brutal violence and film-historical allusion, these efforts to conjure an anti-mainstream ethos still target fans as a viable market, with particular appeals to male fans doing less to counter or resist dominant or mainstream social values than to reassert the power of traditional gender privilege.

Retro Sexploitation and the 'Feminine' Middlebrow

Among retrosploitation pastiches, then, we tend to see serving as historical referents those exploitation cycles that are markedly masculine, violent or hard to watch, or distinctively outrageous and outdated by today's media standards. This tendency has meant that other prolific exploitation cycles have been disproportionately *underrepresented* in the retrosploitation corpus, signalling certain changes in their historical perception as potential objects of contemporary pastiche. The sexploitation film, to cite an obvious example, was one of the most numerically plentiful forms of exploitation cinema during the 1960s and early 1970s, spawning an estimated one thousand titles during those years, but has nevertheless received relatively little direct imitation by retrosploitation producers (with several exceptions noted below), arguably due to more recent changes in its gender address. For Frankie Latina, director of the retrosploitation spy thriller *Modus Operandi* (2009), 'Any director who shoots a [contemporary] grindhouse film without exquisite, triumphant, dangerous, and naked women is doing a disservice to the genre and should move into a different field'.[48] Yet, much like the post-1970s perspectives on race that have made outdated racial stereotypes seem all the more flagrant when they appear in retrosploitation films, the 'classical' sexploitation film of the 1960s has become irreversibly coloured by a contemporary post-feminist era that promises women's ability to 'have it all' and 'be anything' – albeit through the pursuit of consumerist pleasures that seemingly minimise the need for direct political action against continuing gender inequalities.

As David Andrews explains, post-1980 sexploitation increasingly imitated mainstream theatrical successes, albeit through non-theatrical distribution channels. Seeking middlebrow status through its predominant status as a DTV or cable television genre, it has embraced a certain degree of feminisation by eschewing the often violent and misogynistic excesses of pre-1980s sexploitation (for example, the eroticisation of rape scenes) and, instead, targeted female viewers by pairing post-feminist ideals with the rampant nudity and simulated sex offered largely (but not exclusively) to male viewers. In (mis)characterising second-wave feminism as sex-negative while depicting the sexuality of its upmarket female protagonists (often sexually awakened by a working-class man whose class signifiers she finds mildly disgusting) as tantalising spectacle for any viewer, it embraces links between female desire, traditional forms of beauty, and slick, aspirational consumerism. 'The implicit industrial assumption', says Andrews, 'is that women will tolerate a sexist brand of spectacle if it is complemented by a diegesis that exudes an opposite inequity.' In this sense, contemporary soft-core sexploitation defensively develops a mild misandry that 'adopts a permissive stance *vis-à-vis* female adultery, same-sex contact, masturbation, and rape fantasy' while placing 'anticonsumerist restrictions on male adultery, same-sex contact, masturbation, and rape fantasy'.[49] Classical sexploitation's frequent narrative turns towards ultimately punishing women for their tentative forays into the burgeoning 1960s zeitgeist of sexual liberation would thus seem particularly out of place in a post-feminist era which not only routinely promises that women can 'have it all' but also coincides with the rise of home video markets that have relegated theatrical sexploitation texts to greater obscurity. Elena Gorfinkel succinctly notes that, 'As a dystopian cultural form culled from a period of largely utopian discursive promise, sexploitation's sexual skepticism and wariness regarding the pleasures of free love and sexual liberation refuse easy incorporation into the trajectory of retro-appropriation.'[50]

Importantly, contemporary sexploitation's middlebrow appeals are reinforced through a 'soft' style exemplified by soft-focus cinematography which, through the pioneering work of 1960s–70s directors such as Just Jaeckin, Joe Sarno and Radley Metzger, 'became a fully conventional cultural signifier of feminized sensuality that retained its upper-middlebrow hint of "serious" aesthetic interest', unlike the gritty, blemished, and even *vérité*-style cinematography of many low-budget sexploitation films of the same era.[51] If the latter films' cinematography retrospectively seems to exhibit how rough, blemished and imperfect '[f]lesh fuses with the degradation of the film stock, marking the "objectness" of sexploitation as an obsolete form',[52] then the slick surfaces of contemporary middlebrow soft core and the flat, texture-free veneer of cheap, shot-on-digital-video productions would seem equally insufficient for capturing classical sexploitation's sleazy look and feel. With higher production values than, say, the Retro-Seduction Cinema remakes mentioned above, middlebrow soft-core forms have effectively colonised multiple non-theatrical formats in the contemporary media landscape while engendering even greater demand among predominantly male cult audiences for the more 'masculinised' classical sexploitation of the 1960s.

As sexploitation's industrial descendants have evinced a greater degree of feminisation, I would argue that it has become easier for (male) fans to displace on to the audiences of contemporary soft-core cinema the lingering hints of déclassé populist appeals (such as female nudity) that could otherwise undercut fans' claims to connoisseurship of historical exploitation cinema. That is, in a variation of the conflicting fan-cultural memories about drive-in audiences discussed in Chapter 1, the male fan who nostalgically upholds the value of outdated 1960s sexploitation can better do so by chauvinistically looking down upon today's more feminised soft-core forms *and their viewers* – thus distancing himself from potential associations with historical sexploitation audiences who may not be remembered as highly discerning viewers but rather as relative nobodies duped into promises of a casual leer. As the reviewer of the Retro-Seduction remakes quoted above suggests, the retro-styled return of classical sexploitation with a 'rougher', more masculine look and feel would require a conscious effort to distinguish itself from soft core's post-1980 'mainstreaming' but the sheer multitude of remediated, rediscoverable classical sexploitation texts from around the world might also assuage the very demand for this return. The example of sexploitation thus presents us with a particularly telling shortage in a retrosploitation corpus that has partly emerged in reaction to a perceived crisis of masculinity in several popular genres. Yet, this is not to say that there is a complete dearth of retro-styled sexploitation titles, even if coloured by more recent gendered shifts in soft-core cinema. Exceptions include *Pervert!* (2005)

and *Viva* (2007), both illustrative of gendered limitations upon the retro-historical possibilities for exploitation pastiches.

Framed throughout like a comic book come to life, *Pervert!* is a present-set pastiche of Russ Meyer's late-period sexploitation comedies such as *Supervixens* (1975) and *Up!* (1976) – its comic-book style recalling the characteristically hyperbolic physical traits of Meyer's 'superwomen'. College student James (Sean Andrews) returns to his father's home in the deserts of the American southwest to learn how to 'become a man' but finds himself lusting after Cheryl (Mary Carey), the buxom young woman who has recently married his grizzled redneck father, Hezekiah (Darrell Sandeen). As his appropriately Old Testament name implies, Hezekiah holds myriad misogynistic views on women, fancying himself a misunderstood artist who sculpts the female form from pieces of rotting meat. Meanwhile, Cheryl and several other young women end up literally fucked to death by James's penis (a cartoonish stop-motion creation) – which has, unknown to him, become sentient, periodically detaching itself from his body as the side effect of a witch doctor's spell to make him irresistible to women as a would-be cure for his compulsive masturbation.

Sporting a variety of traits that would be familiar to Meyer fans – such as wilderness settings, blue-collar character types, punning wordplay, gratuitous breast close-ups, exaggerated sound effects and 1960s-style music – *Pervert!* effectively captures the contradictions of its historical referents. In Meyer's films, women's huge breasts connote their 'natural' power, strength and voraciously liberated sexual appetites, whereas men are frequently depicted as burly, working-class brutes whose muscular physicality often masks a 'natural inclination to impotence and irresponsibility'.[53] Traditional masculine authority figures alternately become sources of mockery and/or villainy, unable to satisfy the sexually frustrated superwomen (and sometimes becoming misogynistically violent as a result), suggesting an ambivalent 'dissatisfaction with existing social structures combined with anxiety over the loss of a stable social order'.[54] *Pervert!* modifies these character types by focusing on an introverted college student whose masculinity is already called into question by his autoerotic obsession, and who later seeks to reconcile himself with an out-of-control phallic sexuality that has become destructive. Evoking the cultural rehabilitation of female masturbation over male masturbation (and, of course, the display of female nudity over male), the rogue penis's female victims are initially shown writhing alone in pleasure before the organ goes too far, as if punishing them for attempting to satisfy themselves without men. Though the rampaging penis and Cheryl's former lesbian lover eventually confront and destroy each other, the monster re-emerges six months later to kill James's fiancée in the film's epilogue.

As this synopsis should suggest, *Pervert!* recalls a period of sexploitation film-making on the cusp of second-wave feminism, when 'female subjectivity was . . . simultaneously rendered in greater detail *and* subject to greater violence'.[55] Like Meyer's films, its déclassé depictions of shocking violence against unleashed female desire may differentiate it from the more contemporarily influential, 'feminised' sexploitation films of Sarno, Metzger and Jaeckin but its comic-book style and historical distance from its referents also inspire an ironic, mock-moralistic ending (recalling the epilogue delivered by a backwoods preacher in Meyer's *Lorna* [1964]) in which we are told that the 'sin' of desire must be reigned in by the force of 'true love'. Though the bawdy humour of its first half effectively imitates Meyer's work, the revelation of the murderous, cursed penis in its second half veers broadly into the realm of self-parody.[56] In this respect, the film's nods toward the more misogynistic elements of Meyer's comedies may become parodied but, in the process, the film also mocks James's own struggle to control the male desires that threaten to destroy every woman who arouses him. That is, by not depicting his attempts at libidinal self-control as a wholly serious endeavour, his bumbling but well-intentioned efforts to contain the monster portray the misogynistic murders and their attempted prevention through similarly goofy appeals to 'lowbrow' humour, thus potentially undercutting the film's more progressive commentary about phallic sexuality becoming inadvertently destructive. As in *Black Dynamite*, the entire diegesis becomes subject to a measure of ironic distance which, by winkingly recognising the charm of (simulated) historical datedness, does not wholly undercut exploitation fans' more sincere, non-ironic investments in retro texts – but, even if all the characters in *Pervert!* operate at a similarly stereotypical level, we are less clearly invited throughout to occupy the position of the cultural Other than the heteronormative hegemon. If Meyer's films are themselves ambivalent about male desire, *Pervert!*'s revisioning of the Meyer comedies represents an additional layer of ambivalence about the survival of sexploitation's more lowbrow, masculinised variants in a post-feminist era when the mode has since become far more aspirational, middlebrow, and potentially appealing to female audiences.

In comparison, Anna Biller's *Viva* uses the simulated pastness of its 1972 period setting to expand its gendered appeals while advancing a more coherent political critique of the era's unfulfilled promises of sexual freedom – even if similarly upholding the original gender politics of its historical referents to some extent. Bored suburban housewife Barbi

(Biller) becomes emotionally and sexually frustrated with her globetrotting husband Rick (Chad England) so she and her neighbour Sheila (Bridget Brno) leave their husbands to seek adventure amid a burgeoning sexual revolution that, as they soon discover, is more often than not conducted on men's terms. Indeed, in one of the film's more direct moments, Sheila's swinger husband Mark (Jared Sanford) turns to the camera with a nude woman on his lap and explains to the viewer,

> There's never been a better time to be a man. The willing women, the dandy clothes, the frills, the big rings and jewelry, the open shirts, the sense of entitlement. Take it from me: savour this time, for it will soon be gone, never to return.

Barbi adopts the pseudonym 'Viva' for her sexually liberated persona as a model, call girl and underground sexual icon, swinging from one archetypal sexploitation setting and narrative conceit to another. Conflicts continually arise between Viva/Barbi's own sexual agency and the sleazy men attempting to take advantage of changing social mores, including Mark himself as their paths cross at a climactic orgy. As one of my female students astutely remarked during a classroom discussion of the film, there seem to be no reasonably admirable male characters in the entire picture.

As the sexual excesses grow more and more decadent, Barbi finally returns home, reconciles with Rick, and learns that even suburban swinger Sheila's own sexual adventures were far more chaste than her own ('You don't think I actually slept with any of those guys at the agency, do you?'). Still, Barbi does not wholly repudiate her former actions, feeling them to be a source of sexual empowerment, but admits that she must realistically reign in her wilder impulses in favour of personal stability. Yet, even as the denouement finds the two married couples settling down again to domestic stasis, Barbi's forays into the sexual wilderness have also provided enough fruitful contacts for her to be offered fulfilling opportunities as a stage actor even after she returns to suburbia. Traditional gender roles and sexual decorum may be upheld in the end but not without encouraging us to read them as ultimately insufficient and limiting, drenched in camp pathos. Barbi may not have been able to 'have it all' as a single persona (whether Barbi or Viva) but her sexual experimentation has at least resulted in personal growth and a fuller life outside the traditional strictures of the domestic sphere.

Inspired far more by the visually dense, aesthetically aspirational sexploitation of Radley Metzger than Meyer's blue-collar films, *Viva* shows a non-ironic willingness to nostalgically embrace the historical roots of sexploitation's more recent turns towards middlebrow respectability and female viewership. As Gorfinkel explains in an exemplary reading worth paraphrasing at length, Biller casts herself as the film's primary subject and object of desire, allowing a present-day woman to inhabit and find pleasure in a film-making mode that has historically been seen as hetero-male territory. Like the propensity to watch 1960s sexploitation films today as 'time capsules' of a bygone era's sexual ideologies and material culture, Biller fetishises the profilmic details of her reconstructed *mise en scènes* as a means of associating the obsolescence of once-new consumer goods with the obsolescence of once-new sexual liberationist discourses that proved misleadingly limiting for women. Occupying even more of Biller's attention than moments of sexual spectacle, it is precisely the profilmic details of late-1960s clothing, decor and even bodies which can become potential sources of pleasure for both male and female viewers. Focusing on these materially and politically residual qualities, a female viewer's roving gaze allows her to retrospectively colonise sexploitation spectatorship through the nostalgic lens of historical distance. Similarly, the film's 1972 setting marks it as not only a key period in second-wave feminism but also the year that so-called 'porno chic' exploded, pushing sexploitation out of the marketplace and thereby lending *Viva*'s narrative an additional layer of impending obsolescence. For Gorfinkel, then, the film's remarkably faithful pastiche of period-appropriate *mise en scènes*, stilted acting styles, and clichéd character types may certainly be played for camp value in their historical datedness but Biller's use of camp is more nostalgically affectionate than ironically superior and patronising. Biller 'addresses an audience that is both cognizant of the codes of the sexploitation film and also wary of the easy pleasures of condescension they may often provoke', creating ambivalence in viewers who would want merely to read it ironically.[57] Beth Johnson even argues that the 'continuous, obnoxious laughter of the diegetic characters' may be a pre-emptively deflating response to viewers who might too readily approach *Viva* through a 'one-dimensional' mockery of badness.[58]

Yet, I would argue that Biller's highly selective indebtedness to so-called 'class-sex' film-makers such as Metzger or the pages of early-1970s lifestyle magazines as referents for the look and feel of the era's material culture offers a particularly gendered and classed inflection to its sexploitation pastiche. It is especially telling in this regard that Barbi adopts her pseudonym from the title of *Viva* magazine (a short-lived sex/fashion/lifestyle magazine for women, created by *Penthouse* publisher Bob Guccione as a glossy, high-class competitor to *Playgirl*) which we see her reading during the opening credits (Figure 4.5). If, for example, we compare the stark, monochromatic interiors of mid-1960s sexploitation 'roughies' with the cheery Eastmancolor cinematography of early-1960s 'nudie cuties' or especially Metzger's often lavish and intricate late-1960s

Figure 4.5 In *Viva* (2007), writer/director/actor Anna Biller's starring credit appears while her protagonist reads middlebrow *Viva* magazine, a 1970s publication inspiring not only Biller's art direction but also Barbi's transformation from suburban housewife to eponymous sex icon. (Source: DVD.)

mise en scènes, we quickly see that some of the most common sexploitation variants are not represented in Biller's film. Unlike the roughies' visually spare, low-key style and accompanying pre-feminist narratives of punished female desire, Metzger's films instead exemplify the 'soft', feminised style that has since become a defining trait of latter-day softcore cinema's non-theatrical forms. As Biller herself notes, Metzger's *The Alley Cats* (1966) initially inspired *Viva*, since 'I had never quite seen a film that focused so exclusively on a woman's pleasure and that sexualized the protagonist so completely for both genders. She was equally a sex object to be gazed at, and a narcissistic object of identification.'[59] With Metzger's films representing the potential crossover between art house and grind house, his narratives' middlebrow aspirations about female sexual awakening required severely tempering the misogynistic combinations of sexual violence and violent sexuality found in the cheaply made, hard-edged roughies.[60]

In effect, *Viva* may want to make the retrospective consumption of classical sexploitation 'safe' for women but it does so through a particularly selective focus on aspirational sexploitation films that have already had a lasting effect on post-feminist media culture. This is not, of course, to criticise Biller's film for its understandable hesitance to attempt recuperating the roughies' misogyny but rather to point out how retro-styled pastiches of sexploitation find it difficult to weave between, on the one hand, the pre-feminist politics of misogynistic and masculinised sexploitation variants that historically relied on shocking violence against women, and, on the other, the more feminised variants whose lingering influence has complicated male fans' gendered claims to cultural distinction. Whereas *Pervert!* seemingly cannot maintain a straight face about its deliberately lowbrow appeals to male viewers in a post-feminist era, gradually lapsing into Troma-style self-parody, *Viva* maintains its nostalgic but campy tone throughout, precisely because it offers affective appeals to viewers of different genders in a manner not inconsistent with the soft style and mild misandry of contemporary soft-core cinema. Indeed, as the next section suggests, retrosploitation's representational relation between violence committed *by* women and violence committed *against* them remains a key factor that complicates the nostalgic privileging of heteronormativity in a contemporary moment when the gender and sexual power relations during exploitation cinema's heyday have since significantly shifted but equality still remains elusive.

Gendered Violence and Rape-revenge Tropes

Since retrosploitation films tend to presume a predominantly (but not exclusively) masculine reappropriation of the cinematic past, when female protagonists are featured from cycles other than sexploitation, they are commonly depicted as violent but sexually seductive ass-kickers, provoking a blend of desire and identification that cannot simply be reduced to heterosexual male titillation. For Yvonne Tasker, 'images of women seem to need to compensate for the figure of the active heroine by emphasising her sexuality, her availability within traditional feminine terms'.[61] The threat of physical violence which these protagonists represent allows them to seem as suitable for leading role material as 'one of the boys', even while their amply displayed bodies serve as both a literal and a figurative source of 'feminine' power over men within the films – and a clear reminder that they are not simply symbolically 'male' characters. Several notable examples from the retrosploitation corpus include *Planet Terror* (2007), *Death Proof*, *The Machine Girl* (2008), *Bitch Slap* (2009), *Dead Hooker in a Trunk* (2009), *El Monstro del Mar!* (2010), *Sushi Girl* (2012), and *Bring Me the Head of the Machine Gun Woman* (2012).

Men and women alike might identify with these female protagonists, especially because they are often coded as criminals or nonconformists whose narrative drives involve evading capture by either male authorities or male gangsters. For male fans, who might otherwise be put off by identifying with sexualised women, these female protagonists' 'rebellious' characteristics render more acceptable a particular combination of violence and seductiveness that comfortingly plays into exploitation fandom's ethos of masculine resistance to the 'feminising' forces of conformity. The women also rarely exhibit the 'musculinity' which Tasker deems to be signifiers of a physical strength that need not correspond with biological maleness. Instead, the female retrosploitation protagonist generally bears more resemblance to the retro-feminine pin-up image that has been appropriated by both third-wave feminism and post-feminism through a blend of irony and longing.[62]

Sexually objectified but still active and strong characters, these female protagonists inherit the long tradition of femmes fatales as filtered through the exploitation sensibilities of films such as *Faster, Pussycat! Kill! Kill!* (1965), *She-Devils on Wheels* (1968), the *Stray Cat Rock* series (1970–71), *The Big Doll House* (1971), *Coffy* (1973), and so on. Rikke Schubart posits that female heroes (as played by Pam Grier, Dyanne Thorne and Kaji Meiko) had a longer and more potent tradition in such exploitation films before becoming developed in more mainstream, major-studio productions, even if the former may have also played into anti-feminist pleasures for male viewers. Schubart argues that

> the dual nature of the female hero [is] composed from stereotypical feminine traits (beauty, a sexy appearance, empathy) and masculine traits (aggression, stamina, violence). Rather than unite two genders she is in-between, a position that may only last as long as the plot but which creates *fascination and unease*, ambivalent responses and conflicted interpretations. From a feminist perspective, she is a victim of patriarchy. From a postfeminist perspective, she represents female agency.[63]

Apart from action movie tropes, retrosploitation films featuring women in strong roles tend to draw inspiration most heavily from the slasher, rape-revenge, nunsploitation, and women-in-prison cycles, because those exploitation cycles have long featured women in roles that alternate between an initial position of sexually objectified victimisation and a later position of active vengeance. Though playing out differently in each cycle, scholars have often described this broad pattern of narrative progression as largely targeted at male viewers by allowing the spectacular female body to shoulder the representational burden in scenes of excessive sex and violence, even if female viewers might also find sources of ostensibly 'empowering' representation therein.[64]

While it would be overly binaristic to assume that a female character actively pursuing retributive violence is necessarily 'masculinised' by performing the forms of violence traditionally the prerogative of male characters, Lisa Coulthard offers the caveat that 'the violent action heroine is not phallicized or masculinized through her actions (a common concern in much scholarly and popular writing on action heroines) as much as she is postfeminized' by the more apolitical justification of her violence as avenging a violation done to her (female) body, family, lover or career. The *Kill Bill* films (2003–04), in Coulthard's estimation, exemplify how the representation of violent women can be a post-feminist throwback to earlier, more traditional feminine ideals. That is, female violence is often motivated by traditionally 'feminine' sources of victimisation that are narratively expunged through eroticised scenes of violent revenge, leaving the woman finally able to settle into post-revenge domesticity, motherhood and so on. In this sense, female violence is treated as an 'unnatural' or aberrant act (unlike violence performed by men), committed for private, personal (post-feminist) satisfactions instead of more public, political (feminist) aims that might target the structural foundations of violence against women.[65] For retrosploitation films, then, there can be a marked complication between anachronistic stylisation's ability to, on the one hand, foster fantasies of retributive violence inspired by the context of 1970s cinema/feminism, and, on the other, play into a latter-day post-feminist logic in which the female avenger's temporary threat to representatives of patriarchy is reassuringly dispelled through the narrative closure achieved by her narrowly construed success.

Following Coulthard's argument, we should heed that 'if women on the screen are excessively sexualised then so is the violence to which they are subject', especially when figured as rape – a form of violence that women not only disproportionately suffer but which disproportionately justifies their violent narratives.[66] Because it crystallised during the 1970s heyday of exploitation cinema as a response to the political exigencies of second-wave feminism (including the feminist redefinition of rape as a crime on a par with murder) and has been subsequently revived in the retrosploitation cycle, I shall address the rape-revenge film as a problematically privileged node for retro representations of female protagonists during the post-feminist era. The following examples illustrate that, in addition to the presentness which can complicate retrospective film-historical searches for feminist inspiration, the very retro qualities which would mark these performances of pastness *as artifice* may also reinforce, instead of challenge, the violent subordination of women by figuring the retro-appropriation of rape imagery as a form of non-threatening masculinist spectacle for male viewers.

Though I concur with Carol Clover that viewers of any gender are likely to find the woman's vengeance readily justified in rape-revenge films which do not depict the female rape victim (our prime figure of identification) as somehow complicit in her victimisation (*Straw Dogs* [1971] is a notorious example of such complicity), I still find that one of the greatest political limitations to the rape-revenge cycle's 'explicitly articulate[d] feminist politics' is the implication that a woman must suffer great trauma (and a trauma often figured in terms of the female body's 'openness') before she can find empowerment in/as revenge.[67] Despite the fact that men can similarly occupy the raped victim–hero position in films such as *Deliverance* (1972), the corporeal confirmation of femaleness as the bodies most commonly subject to rape illustrates how second-wave feminism's successful re-articulation of sexual violence as a political act logically proceeds from the larger feminist premise that women in particular have long endured, and must now seek redress against, the forms of patriarchal violence once depicted as titillating pre-feminist spectacle in films such as sexploitation roughies.

Indeed, Peter Lehman and Jacinda Read have complicated Clover's argument about the female avenger's eventual masculinisation via revenge, arguing that Clover plays down the extent to which the female avenger is actually *eroticised* in traditionally feminine ways, using her sexuality as a retributive snare for her male prey.[68] In Abel Ferarra's influential *Ms. 45* (1981), for example, female avenger Thana (Zoë Tamerlis) dresses in increasingly seductive attire following her traumatic rape, finally donning a sexy nun's costume for a climactic massacre of men at a Halloween party. Lehman posits that, even if these films' rape scenes are not themselves eroticised, heterosexual male viewers still share with the diegetic male rapists some degree of desire for the conventionally attractive female protagonist, but feminism's recoding of rape as atrocity means that this similar desire cannot be openly acknowledged. Consequently, this disavowed desire must be projected on to the repulsiveness of the rapists whose deaths the male viewer can (masochistically) enjoy as justified, especially because their comeuppance is often framed as containing the alluring eroticism of the attractive avenging woman.[69]

As noted by Virginie Despentes, author and co-director of the film *Baise-moi* (2000) – itself a partial throwback to the 1970s rape-revenge film – rape culture has been allowed to proliferate because women and men both use euphemisms to avoid discussing such acts *as rape*; women resist discussing the experience to avoid suspicions that their survival was premised on somehow inviting or enjoying rape, whereas men generally 'condemn rape and despise rapists' and thus avoid the term to distance their own actions from common perceptions of rapists as psychopathic monsters.[70] In this sense, even if rape-revenge films may offer a feminist fantasy of retributive violence which could, as Judith Halberstam suggests, produce hesitation in real-world perpetrators of sexual assault by raising the threat of imagined violence in the popular consciousness,[71] this fantasy is partially compromised by an attendant sexualisation of the female victim–hero, despite (or precisely because of) the force of a vengeance framed largely as an alluring *woman's* cross to bear. Though Despentes agrees that rape would be far less prevalent if men were more fearful of violent retribution by their female victims, she argues that a large part of rape's violence includes women's internalisation of the belief that their bodies are open and accessible in ways that men's bodies are not, because women are acculturated into avoiding violence against men. Even though she notes that rape is a potential danger for any woman who refuses the cultural imperative to submit to domesticity, this destructive internalisation of gender inferiority means that rape-revenge films made by men (specifically, *I Spit on Your Grave*, *Ms. 45*, and *Last House on the Left*) are more reflective of 'how men, if they were women, would react to rape'. Thus, these film-makers neglect the extent to which women are culturally taught that 'nothing worse could happen to us, and yet that we must neither defend or revenge ourselves'.[72]

For my purposes, it is important to ask why retrosploitation pastiches contain so many conspicuous nods to the 1970s rape-revenge film, not the later, more 'mainstream' forms that have inherited this narrative structure. That is, what does this nostalgically reworked period of exploitation film history potentially offer present-day viewers, above and beyond retrosploitation's generalised longing for fan-culturally privileged cycles and decades? Read notes that Clover's own privileging of 1970s rape-revenge films such as *I Spit on Your Grave* over more mainstream (but perhaps less progressive) films such as *The Accused* (1988) 'impli[es] that there was a moment of authenticity that has now passed', with 'the low-budget horror film as the site of the "true" rape-revenge film from which mainstream and other generic examples are excluded'. In doing so, Clover inadvertently figures more mainstream iterations of the rape-revenge narrative (for example, 'feminised' middlebrow genres like the DTV erotic thriller and neo-noir) as 'too feminine to be feminist'.[73] Ironically, then, even as Clover underplays the female avenger's feminisation, she overemphasises the more 'masculine' sense of authenticity supposedly associated with past exploitation cycles.

Not unlike my earlier argument about the Splat Pack's ethos of brutality, I would posit that, much as rape-revenge films often depict rape as a male backlash against advances in women's social power, the aggressive return of 1970s-style rape-revenge tropes in retro pastiches such as *Kill Bill*, *Hora*, *Cherry Bomb* (2011), *Girls Against Boys* (2012), *Crack Whore* (2012), and *Cry for Revenge* (2013) similarly speaks to a masculinist backlash against the more mainstream, middlebrow varieties of rape-revenge cinema that have proliferated since the 1970s. Part of this backlash may be rooted in what Clover deems a

> way of shifting responsibility from the perpetrator to the victim: if a woman fails to get tough, fails to buy a gun or take karate, she is, in an updated sense of the cliché, asking for it. Moreover, if women are as capable as men of acts of humiliating violence, men are off the guilt hook that modern feminism has put them on.[74]

Furthermore, as an exercise in retro appropriation, I would argue that the excessive sleaziness of the rapists is not always framed as *wholly* repulsive in these pastiches but also coded as perversely attractive *at a meta-textual level* through its very quality as an anachronistic throwback to the heyday of the 1970s rape-revenge cycle. In other words, the very temporal incongruity of the self-consciously 1970s-styled rape-revenge throwback can effectively reopen the retro rape-revenge film to a displaced misogyny that has as much to do with masculinist taste distinctions as with disavowed hetero-male desire for the eroticised female victim–hero – especially if these films are centrally concerned with male film-makers imagining how *they* would violently react to rape.

As a prime example, Joseph Guzman's 1970s-set *Run! Bitch Run!* opens with two young women isolated on a missionary trip selling Bibles and other religious paraphernalia door to door in rural America. Holier-than-thou Catherine (Cheryl Lyone) wants to spread God's love whereas her more rebellious counterpart Rebecca (Christina DeRosa) just wants to be relieved of their merchandise soon enough to enjoy the brief respite from school. Though Catherine is initially depicted as mousy and asexual, particularly in contrast to Rebecca's first appearance emerging from a motel shower fully nude, the camera continually fetishises their archetypal Roman Catholic schoolgirl attire for the presumed heterosexual male viewer. The women are taken captive after visiting a vicious gang's headquarters just as one of the gang's female connections is killed in a botched drug deal. While cruel leader Lobo (Peter Tahoe) and stuttering sidekick Clint (Johnny Winscher) are out disposing of their former associate's body, bisexual prostitute Marla (Ivet Corvea) forces Rebecca at gunpoint to perform oral sex on her, and then kills her in a game of Russian roulette. The trio next takes Catherine into the woods where the men repeatedly rape her but Clint hesitates when finally ordered to kill their victim who is left for dead. Later leaving the hospital dressed in nurse's attire, Catherine silently tracks down and kills each of her victimisers, finally shooting herself once her vengeance is complete.

Echoing Coulthard's discussion of *Kill Bill*, Catherine's transformation and vengeance is, indeed, depicted as an aberrant shift for such a pious character, 'resolved' with an abrupt suicide that marks her vendetta as having satisfied a personal, post-feminist mission instead of a larger, feminist retaliation against patriarchal power. Though the film does not overtly eroticise Catherine's acts of revenge as seductive, instead depicting them as matter-of-factly accomplished, her literal and symbolic gender is never thrown into question; for example, she is never shown without being either nude or dressed in a stereotypically feminine uniform that would not be out of place in heterosexual pornography. While the young women's initial capture derives from being in the wrong place at the wrong time, Rebecca's rape and murder quickly follow her decision to dress more provocatively to sell more goods, narratively suggesting that she was 'asking for it' in a way that Catherine was not. Meanwhile, apart from Catherine and Rebecca, nearly all the women in the film are sex workers shown plying their trade, and the film's trailer trumpets the many varieties of attractive 'bitches' on display.

Marla's role as a rapacious woman within the gang (while not without precedent in films such as *Last House on the Left*) also complicates the film's would-be indictment of patriarchal power, because her fluid sexuality does not figure her as symbolically 'male' but as a monstrously perverse woman and a source of misogynistic disgust. In the film's opening scenes, for example, she is introduced fucking and stabbing an obese male client to death, and later shown using the wooden end of a toilet plunger for masturbating on the lavatory. In Marla, the film's overarching misogyny neatly shades into the homophobia associated with gender inversion, as also seen when Lobo and Marla repeatedly taunt Clint as a 'faggot' for not immediately wanting to rape Catherine, and when Catherine eventually kills Lobo by repeatedly sodomising him with a machete – a tellingly homophobic instance of a heterosexual film-maker imagining his own means of vengeance through the figure of the female victim–hero. Whereas films such as *I Spit on Your Grave* indict male homophobia as an impetus for homosocial acts of gang rape intended to shore up a male group member's questioned masculinity,[75] similar scenes of rape-as-male-gamesmanship in *Run! Bitch Run!* are far more ambivalent in the light of the film's overall retro-masculinist tone and associated disgust towards queerness.

In this sense, even if the female victim–hero may ostensibly challenge traditional notions of who performs violence and why, the masculinist project of producing retrograde sleaze as a form of shock value that would seemingly differentiate retrosploitation from 'softer', 'feminised', contemporary rape-revenge narratives undercuts much of the feminist potential found in the 1970s rape-revenge cycle. The rape scenes in Guzman's follow-up *Nude Nuns with Big Guns* (2010), for example, are accompanied by a hard-rocking tune aping *Planet Terror*'s opening credit music but, whereas the recurrence of that theme music in *Planet Terror* glorifies Cherry's powerful potential as an action protagonist, by contrast, the similar tune's recurrence in *Nude Nuns* seemingly glorifies women's brutal victimisation. In these films, rape is, indeed, depicted as a weapon of violence against women but the films' nostalgic tenor for rape as a retro- 'cool' exploitation trope, disproportionately associated with a celebrated film-historical past, means that the patriarchal power which licenses rape is not as clearly condemned as in their second-wave feminist-era referents.

Nevertheless, far more controversy attended the retro-styled rape- revenge film *Ticked-Off Trannies With Knives* (2010) which was condemned by numerous members of the transgender community and the Gay & Lesbian Alliance Against Defamation (GLAAD) when it played at the relatively prestigious 2010 Tribeca Film Festival. Allegedly inspired by openly gay director Israel Luna's viewing of *I Spit on Your Grave* and news reports of gay bashing, the film features a group of drag queens who must take revenge upon a trio of men after one of their own, Bubbles (Krystal Summers), is drugged, raped and beaten by Boner (Tom Zembrod), a 'white trash' character recalling the urban/victim versus rural/rapist divide in so many 1970s rape-revenge films. Feeling that Bubbles lied to him about being a 'real woman', Boner and his two friends lure the women from a nightclub to a nearby warehouse, aiming to silence Bubbles permanently. In the ensuing brawl, two of the women are killed and Bubbles is beaten into a coma. Upon emerging from the coma, Bubbles and her friends Rachel (Willam Belli) and Pinky (Kelexis Davenport) train themselves in fighting skills for seeking revenge. When Boner stalks and captures Bubbles to settle his unfinished business, the women spring their trap, finally torturing and killing their assailants (again, with the anal insertion of weapons, as in *Run! Bitch Run!*).

For Luna, the film was allegedly intended as an entertainingly cathartic revenge story that might also encourage queer people to fight gay-bashing violence with retributive violence of their own, instead of responding with a more passive 'fight hate with love' response.[76] Yet, the fact that his film specifically features drag queens instead of more accurate representations of either gay men or trans women is a telling choice for a film in which revenge is depicted as a more actively 'masculine' political response to hate crimes – though the campy tagline 'It takes balls to get revenge' is a notable giveaway that Luna privileges the (literally) underlying correlation between maleness and retributive violence that Despentes describes.

Most arguments arose over how well intentioned Luna's anti-hate crime message truly is, because the film's uneven tone – alternating between depictions of brutal hate crimes and scenes of camp humour – ambiguously signals neither a parody nor a serious social-problem film. In the film's campily self-deflating final moments, for instance, Pinky asks the other avengers, 'Do you know what the difference is between us and them?' But rather than attempting to clarify *Ticked-Off Trannies*' indebtedness to the notoriously complicated politics of the rape-revenge victim–hero, she off-handedly admits 'Me either' and asks where they want to go eat.

Though their position is certainly understandable, I would disagree with critics (many of whom denounced the film based on the trailer alone) who argue that the hate crimes are played for laughs or entertainment simply because of their narrative proximity to such campy scenes. If anything, this proximity creates a jarring tonal disjuncture in which transphobic violence is made all the more shocking because it erupts with such sudden fury. The campy dialogue that dominates the film's opening scenes immediately ceases, for example, when the women entering the warehouse ascertain the threat confronting them. When Bubbles subsequently calls Pinky on her mobile phone before losing consciousness, Pinky is shown continuing her catty conversations when the film cross-cuts back to her answering her phone at the nightclub – but only until realising that something is very wrong. GLAAD may see images of a baseball bat covered with clumps of women's hair as 'played for cheap laughs' and 'serv[ing] only as horror movie-like gore' but I would argue that Luna accurately portrays such violence *as horrific*, not as a source of comedy. Boner's later stalking of Bubbles feels as though it was lifted from a horror movie, for instance, even if it comes following a martial arts training scene filled with distastefully orientalist camp humour. Unlike the overwhelming turn towards self-parody in the second half of *Pervert!*, the later threats of transphobic violence in *Ticked-Off Trannies* remain charged with a genuine sense of menace that is not entirely undercut by the surrounding scenes. When violence is present, humour is far more often found in the violent retribution scenes – particularly when the three bigots are disarmed and at their least threatening – than in the initial attacks upon the women, thus using humour better to encourage identification with the avengers. As GLAAD's publicised call to action continues, 'Anti-LGBT hate crimes are serious issues that do not translate into an exploitation film. The very nature of exploitation films is to shock and titillate audiences with extreme, sensationalized violence.'[77] Yet, the 1970s rape-revenge cycle adequately proved decades ago that not only have hate crimes against women successfully translated into exploitation films but that sensationalised violence and serious social issues are not mutually exclusive.

Major criticisms of *Ticked-Off Trannies* also focused on the use of drag queens instead of actual trans women – hence one of the major reasons that critics considered the titular slur 'trannies' as a gross misappropriation by a cisgender gay man insensitive to the trans community. Furthermore, some of these critics feared that the film would incite transphobic viewers to commit hate crimes after feeling similarly 'deceived' by a trans woman – much as the initial critics of 1970s rape-revenge films often erroneously presumed that films like *I Spit on Your Grave* were incitements to rape and/or demonising depictions of women as monstrous killers. Similarly, some critics of *Ticked-Off Trannies* argued that the film presented female drag as a misogynistic parody of womanhood instead of a deconstruction of gender norms; whereas others suggested that, despite the excessiveness of the drag performances, the film merely played into the stereotype that trans women must trick men into promiscuous sexual situations (as attested to by 'gay panic' murder defences that attempt to blame the victims of homophobic violence as supposed 'victimisers' of heterosexual privilege).[78]

Though many of these criticisms are well deserved, the film does display *Grindhouse*-style artefacting associated with the cultural past, suggesting that its anachronistic vision includes a 1970s-era film-historical view of transgender people more closely attuned to, say, the drag performances in John Waters's early films than to the modern-day trans community. Aside from the revenge plot, for example, it shares much in common with the DTV camp comedy *Killer Drag Queens on Dope* (2003) which features cameos by exploitation director Don Edmonds and veteran Russ Meyer star Haji. Beneath the simulated layer of distressed celluloid, however, *Ticked-Off Trannies* is unmistakably set in the present day, so its emphasis on hate crimes presents a contemporary political resonance that many viewers could not laugh away. Indeed, the trans community was justifiably outraged over the initial trailer's use of allusions to the recent real-life murders of Angie Zapata and Jorge Mercado as a timely but tasteless exploitation hook.

For critics, then, the film's political intent was compromised on the grounds of bad taste by, on the one hand, the pastness associated with 1970s exploitation films and the outdated image of drag queens as synonymous with transgenderism, and, on the other, the presentness of the film's opportunistic references to real-life tragedies. Whereas *Run! Bitch Run!* spoils its political potential by disproportionately romanticising the pastness of sexual violence, the disproportionate presentness associated with the sexual violence in *Ticked-Off Trannies* undercuts the success of its retributive stance against hate crimes. Though Waters's 1970s camp exercises in drag-related bad taste (a common comparison made by many of *Ticked-Off Trannies*' critics) could be excused as dated, funny or simply the reflection of an earlier, less 'enlightened' political climate, Luna's film seemed too recent and exploitative for easy reclamation – a reaction not unlike some heterosexual male fans' generalised distrust of the retrosploitation cycle's contemporaneity and calculatedness.

Much as these last fans may lament retrosploitation's opening of 'inauthentic' visions of exploitation film history to wider audiences through films such as *Grindhouse*, the *Ticked-Off Trannies* uproar was chiefly inspired by the film's planned appearance at a high-profile cultural venue like the Tribeca Film Festival, instead of the more marginal, fan-populated genre film festivals that screened the uncontroversial *Killer Drag Queens on Dope*. Despite the fact that *Ticked-Off Trannies* and *Killer Drag Queens* both effectively went straight to video after their festival play, it remains remarkable that the political reception of retrosploitation pastiches centrally relies on not only the evaluative tone of their stylised pastness but also on a question of cultural access to exploitation tropes that garner different connotations of 'authenticity' as they move from one differently classed and demographically specialised site of consumption to another.

Queering Time in the Performance of Historicity

As I have suggested throughout this book, then, the material sites of film consumption cannot be reduced to selective (sub)cultural and political connotations without also attending to the temporal connotations that cultural memory confers upon such sites. Yet, beyond the dominant heteronormative tenor of exploitation cinema's remembrance, these temporal connotations do not merely derive from sexually hegemonic experiences of past films. Rather than simply reinforcing heterosexual male desire – though, as preceding parts of this chapter have shown, that is always a distinct possibility – I am also interested in the productive potential offered by films and spectatorial relations that might play upon a *queering of time itself*. That is, retro-styled films can allow the juxtaposition of *different temporalities* to encourage *different desires* on the part of viewers, including viewers whose ironic-cum-earnest consumption may speak to more diverse pleasures than the privileges of male heteronormativity. As such, the very *undecidability* of the retrosploitation pastiche can open space for imagined feelings of transport into past viewing experiences, highlighting unconventional pleasures and painful longings that queerly operate across multiple temporal registers.

Patricia White coins the term 'retrospectatorship' to describe a type of retrospective film reception that accounts for the structuring impact of cultural texts upon the viewer's identity and inner fantasy life but always by 'revis[ing] memory traces and experiences, some of which are memories and experiences of other movies', thereby allowing past texts to open 'new ways of seeing' in the present. Furthermore, these retrospectively inflected ways of revisiting past texts in new contexts allow the historically marginalised viewer (such as lesbian viewers of classical Hollywood cinema) to recognise her own desires and experiences reflected even within a text that ostensibly participates in her marginalisation. For White, fandom is a privileged means of fostering such reception because it encourages repeated viewings and close identifications between viewer and text over time.[79]

In my estimation, exploitation cinema's predominant address to a heterosexual male audience can offer female and queer viewers similar opportunities for retrospectatorship's structure of feeling because the intentionally anachronistic pastness of the retrosploitation pastiche performs a nostalgic sense of loss that can resonate with the loss of other personal and cultural pasts while also spurring rich fantasies rooted in memories of one's past cinematic experiences. Retrospectatorship's potential in aiding and constructing personal and cultural identity through the powerful recognition of oneself in one's chosen fan object can thereby allow the fan not merely to search the past for 'positive' sources of celebratory reclamation but also to recover what Heather Love calls 'negative or ambivalent identifications with the past [that] can serve to disrupt the present. Making connections with historical losses or with images of ruined or spoiled identity in the past can set in motion a gutting "play of recognitions"' in which past representational limitations (such as stereotypes) serve as affective reminders of the unresolved pains and prejudices suffered in one's personal/cultural present.[80]

Indeed, it is often difficult to claim in any uncomplicated way that retrosploitation films are politically *progressive*, owing to their very anachronistic form and content which call into question the teleological logic upon which claims to social progress are typically based. As Elizabeth Freeman observes, the social progressive's characteristic emphasis on the forward march of history necessitates that 'whatever looks newer or more-radical-than-thou has more purchase over prior signs, that parodically "signifying" on a sign is more powerful than taking it up earnestly, and that whatever seems to generate continuity seems better left behind'.[81] Sincerely repurposing the past often seems more ideologically suspect to the bourgeois social progressive than using ironic distance to chauvinistically flatter his/

her own knowing political sophistication – hence the question of how to deal with the ideological impurity raised by retro-styled texts that blend ironic and sincere appreciation of past films. In contrast to a smugly teleological emphasis on forward progress, I would suggest that the dialectical relationship to history offered by nostalgia looks backwards and forwards alike, assuaging melancholic loss with ironic distance while still earnestly recalling the past as a means of remembering social movements' earlier histories and representations – such as past sources of pleasure and identification for gay, lesbian and queer audiences. After all, nostalgia can enable a longing for certain privileged aspects of the past without uncritically embracing all the dominant ideological implications of a given historical period.

The performativity of film history in retrosploitation pastiches can enact what Freeman terms 'temporal drag' which represents 'the power of anachronism to unsituate viewers from the present tense they think they know, and to illuminate or even prophetically ignite possible futures in light of powerful historical moments' – ultimately offering 'a *productive* obstacle to progress, a usefully distorting pull backward, and a necessary pressure on the present tense'. This is a form of drag based less in bodily performing and deconstructing the reiterated tropes of *another gender* than in bodily performing and deconstructing the lost potentiality of *another time*, with multiple temporalities playing out upon the same bodies in disorienting ways.[82] Elena Gorfinkel, for example, specifically cites Anna Biller's performance in/of 1960s sexploitation tropes in *Viva* as a case of temporal drag because the film's evaluative tone faithfully performs a pre-Stonewall camp sensibility without merely approaching the outmoded sexploitation film with an ironically mocking air of condescension which would gloss over the more problematic viewing pleasures on offer both then and today.[83]

By refuting the notion that contemporary viewers have somehow progressed beyond politically problematic histories of representation, temporal drag may outwardly appear ideologically regressive in its self-conscious evocation of pastness but it retains an underlying concern with 'forgotten futures', or the former opportunities for artistic and political change that have since been relegated to cultural obsolescence (as broached at the end of Chapter 1). Altogether then, White, Love and Freeman share a common concern with looking backwards at past cultural productions that might offer present-day viewers affectively charged memories that cannot be wholly reclaimed through politically celebratory appeals. If nostalgia offers a degree of felt continuity between past and present, then its role in informing the temporal multivalence of concepts such as retrospectatorship and temporal drag also serves as a lingering reminder of historical inequalities which continue to this day.

In a discussion of the retrosploitation action film *Bitch Slap* (2009), for example, Katrin Horn argues that its allusions to sexploitation, nunsploitation and women-in-prison (WIP) films allow it to achieve greater political potential as a lesbian text than as a post-feminist one. These exploitation cycles have been historically targeted to hetero-male viewers but have also offered pleasures to lesbian viewers – as illustrated by their prominent inclusion in Michelle Johnson's compilation documentary *Triple X Selects: The Best of Lezsploitation* (2007) which toured major LGBTQ film festivals. As pastiched elements from older exploitation cycles, 'lesploitation' may still be depicted in retro-styled films as an 'exotic' source of spectacle playing upon heterosexual male fantasies about inter-female sexuality, but Horn concludes that this is due to exploitation cinema's willingness to exploit images of lesbianism that more mainstream forms of cinema seldom offered. In this respect, pastiches such as *Bitch Slap* can still evoke an earnestly queer nostalgia for an earlier historical period when gay or lesbian sexual difference was still seen as 'dangerous' and 'transgressive', instead of increasingly catered to today as an 'acceptable' form of lifestyle consumerism.[84] That is, these films invoke what Clare Whatling calls a generative nostalgia which, by recalling a more homophobic past when lesbians could be cinematically stereotyped only as threats to the heterosexual order, 'operates as an antithesis to what often seems like the Laura-Ashleyisation of contemporary lesbian culture'. Retrospectively viewing the limitations of these past cinematic lesbians today gains a powerful political resonance in the light of the fact that the former social taboo of lesbian desire has been increasingly surmounted in a homonormative age of greater sexual acceptance – yet, a nostalgic longing remains for a time when the taboo itself gave lesbianism a profoundly erotic and rebellious charge.[85] These films thus represent another case of how exploitation pastiches internalise a blend of irony and sincerity that has already been circulating in the home video reception of historical exploitation films with lesbian content – as when, for example, leading LGBTQ video distributor Wolfe Video distributes the lesbian-themed sexploitation films *That Tender Touch* (1969) and *Just the Two of Us* (1975) as part of its 'Vintage Collection' DVDs accompanied by mini-reproductions of the films' original press books, contextualising the films' original address to hetero-male viewers and the connotations of pastness that foster their recuperation as camp objects for lesbian viewers today.[86]

I want to explore this noteworthy 'lesploitation' potential in the WIP pastiche *Sugar Boxx* which is indebted to 1970s films such as *The Big*

Doll House and *Black Mama, White Mama* (1973) for depicting lesbians as main characters in ways that pre-1970s WIP incarnations did not. Set in 1975, investigative reporter Valerie March (Geneviere Anderson), a white lesbian in a committed partnership, poses as a prostitute to infiltrate Florida's Sugar State Women's Correctional Facility, a notoriously brutal work camp, where she befriends Loretta Sims (Thela Brown), a straight black woman who has also been locked up for prostitution. Valerie discovers that a disproportionate number of young women have been jailed by the corrupt local sheriff (Nick Eldredge) on the same prostitution and narcotics charges. It is revealed that warden Beverly Buckner (Linda Dona) uses the prison as a brothel staffed by her most attractive inmates and frequented by crooked politicians and businessmen. After escaping and assembling a team of vigilantes, Valerie and Loretta sneak back into Sugar State, massacring the male guards and brothel patrons while taking Buckner captive during the ensuing riot. In an epilogue, Buckner is now behind bars, corruption is punished and Valerie has become Sugar State's new and better warden.

Featuring a cruel lesbian warden working on behalf of the patriarchal order and sexually abusive male guards as major and minor villains, respectively, the film faithfully pastiches the plot and character dynamics of the 1970s WIP formula. As such, it uses images of 'a kind of feminist rebellion against patriarchy and in the process holds up a mirror to 1970s feminism insofar as "sisterhood" is concerned – between black and white women, between lesbians and straight women, between women who have committed different kinds of crime against patriarchy'.[87] Valerie's earlier journalistic exposure of a corrupt male businessman after going undercover as his receptionist suggests her transgression against unchecked patriarchal power, whereas the sheriff incarcerated Loretta after her boyfriend attacked him for directing racial slurs at her. In this sense, *Sugar Boxx* reproduces the intertwined 'discourses of race and lesbianism' that mark its historical referents. Beyond some mild innuendo, there may not be an overt eroticism in the interracial friendship between Valerie and Loretta but they similarly suffer beneath dominant social prejudices, both jailed on related charges and effectively forced into carceral sex work.[88] Female prisoners are instructed that 'sexual encounters – solo or duo' are punishable offences, yet they are still subject to coercion into prostitution by the warden and rape by the male guards – thus suggesting the prison's underlying function as the oppressive tool of a male heterosexual order that would be threatened by unchecked lesbian desire. This is not to say, however, that *Sugar Boxx* is free from homophobic or racist caricatures of some characters (a Latina prison lesbian, an excessively sassy black woman, a closeted gay sheriff) but that such characteristics do coexist with an unconventional emphasis on lesbianism which I find to be the film's key progressive opportunity for retrospective genre revisionism.

Though blatant displays of nudity and inter-female sexuality are common beacons to the WIP cycle's intended hetero-male audience, Ann Ciasullo observes that WIP narratives typically feature a straight female protagonist who must perform as a 'pseudo' lesbian to survive prison life and eventually escape to heterosexual normalcy, whereas the 'true' lesbian is literally and figuratively contained within prison walls as an irredeemable criminal who threatens to contaminate other women with her aberrant desires.[89] In *Sugar Boxx*, however, historical connotations between lesbianism and criminality are, beyond Buckner and several minor inmate characters, largely played down in favour of Valerie's committed relationship with her partner/co-worker Lori Sutton (Ariadne Shaffer). A binary division between pseudo/innocent/free and true/guilty/incarcerated lesbians is not upheld because Valerie is depicted as both a 'true' lesbian and a crusader for justice from the start, eventually remaining at Sugar State as a free woman, not a prisoner. Though Valerie must seduce Buckner to gain entry into the brothel programme, and later excludes Lori from her vigilante plans, causing a serious rift in their relationship, the film's denouement finds Lori and Valerie happily reunited. Valerie may have had to temporarily 'play lesbian' in prison but the fact that she is never shown having sex with men in the brothel, and also begins and ends the film in the same loving relationship, shows that she never has to renounce her true sexuality. If the aforementioned binaries in traditional WIP films allow male viewers to safely objectify inter-female sexuality and female viewers temporarily to identify with the 'pseudo' lesbian, all under the presumption that the protagonist will recover her heterosexuality once she leaves prison, *Sugar Boxx* suggests how '[w]ithout such demarcations and order . . . the boundaries between heterosexuality and homosexuality begin to look remarkably fragile'.[90]

Though *Sugar Boxx* is no exception to convention in portraying the ultimate defeat and humiliation of the 'lesbian, repressive boss-woman – a popular stereotype in the women's prison and convent genres', by ending with a role reversal between Valerie and the now-incarcerated Buckner, the film does break with tradition because it is not an androgynous, heterosexualised or asexual female character who turns the tables.[91] Rather, Valerie has already been established early in the film as a strong, intelligent and confidently sexualised lesbian who, like Lori, is more often than not depicted in femme attire – and, even though she eventually assumes control of Sugar State as the new warden, she does so with Lori and Loretta at her side, suggesting that her power will not wholly operate under the order of male heterosexuality. Consequently, associating these central lesbian characters with a veneer of film-historical pastness can spur fantasies mnemonically linked to the retrospectatorial queer pleasures found in 1970s WIP films – even if such desires are still depicted in those past texts as 'exotic' or 'threatening' sources of personal/cultural distinction that queer viewers may nostalgically long for, in spite of present-day political correctness.

Despite *Sugar Boxx*'s intended hetero-male viewership, its more progressive retro-styled revisions to the 1970s WIP film did not go unnoticed by lesbian media critics. As one critic suggests,

> Is *Sugar Boxx* an important movie? Probably not. [. . .] This isn't a lesbian movie. *Sugar Boxx* fits squarely in the women-in-prison category, without question. But what this movie shows – that we've never seen before – is that actual lesbians in prison face a different set of problems than LURDs (Lesbian Until Release Date).

Reader reactions to this mixed review include rejections of the film as 'nothing else than a jerk-off movie for guys', while other readers suggest that, regardless of the intended audience, queer pleasure can be found in exploitation films precisely because they break from contemporary social-realist representations: 'If there were no OTT [over-the-top] movies written by men, then there would be no . . . lesbolicious classics that wouldn't be either lesbolicious or classic if they weren't fantastically trashy.'[92] The film thereby inspires such conflicting responses because of how it overlays 'fantastically trashy' retro-styled excess (Figure 4.6) with representations of a lesbian partnership which is more earnestly recuperable by present-day queer attitudes (especially if, as I noted in the previous chapter, the film may not clearly signal its 1970s period setting). Even if *Sugar Boxx* may not be 'a lesbian movie' in some respects, the simultaneous political pastness/presentness offered by a protagonist in temporal drag like Valerie still offers lesbian viewers some privileged access to queer identification and pleasure. Like Valerie herself, lesbian viewers of the film may be ostensibly trapped within a patriarchal disciplinary structure (a historically male-oriented cycle) but, remaining true to their sexuality can offer (film-historical) avenues for escape.

Perhaps unsurprisingly, however, given its largely masculine ethos, undercurrents of homophobia and gay (male) panic are far more common in retrosploitation films than favourable depictions of male homosexuality – though several partial exceptions include the 1960s beach party parodies *Psycho Beach Party* (2000) and the 'I Was a Teenage Werebear' segment of *Chillerama* (2011), the latter of which also played LGBTQ film festivals as a short film extracted from its framing within a larger anthology film.

Figure 4.6 'Lesbolicious', 'a jerk-off movie for guys', or both? Valerie (Geneviere Anderson) is sprayed down by a female prison guard (played by Russ Meyer favourite Kitten Natividad in a choice cameo) in *Sugar Boxx* (2009). (Source: DVD.)

With their light, comedic tone, these films admittedly veer somewhat closer to the negative evaluative tone of parody than pastiche, as a means of violating the morally 'clean' and 'wholesome' connotations of their historical referents by playing up the homoeroticism of the biker and surfer gangs found therein. Yet, as R. L. Rutsky notes, American International Pictures' beach party cycle would seem a particularly easy target for parody, largely because the original films were themselves already parodic of youth-subcultural figures and trends, such as beatniks and motorcycle gangs.[93] Consequently, the comedic tone of these retro takes on beach movies imitatively blurs the lines between camp's ironic disdain and earnest affection for their already silly 1960s referents (as in the anachronistic use of rear-projection screens to film the 'surfing' scenes, which looks as patently fake as the same technique did in the original cycle).

Chillerama's anthology segments are framed as exploitation films playing on the closing night of the last drive-in theatre in America, thus reinforcing the sense of nostalgic loss lurking behind these campy shorts. Written and directed by Tim Sullivan (who also directed the DTV exploitation remake *2001 Maniacs* [2005] and its sequel), the 'I Was a Teenage Werebear' segment also shares *Psycho Beach Party*'s 1962 Malibu setting for its rock 'n' roll musical story of Ricky (Sean Paul Lockhart), a James Dean-styled angst-ridden teenager who leaves his girlfriend for Talon (Anton Troy), the rebellious leader of a gay biker gang who transforms into leather-bound 'werebears' when sexually aroused. In its obvious nods to *I Was a Teenage Werewolf* (1957) within the dominant referential framework of the beach party musical, the potential monstrosity of repressed teenage sexuality finds Ricky unsuccessfully struggling to prevent his queer desire from coming out in scenes of homoerotic beach wrestling and other high jinks similarly depicted in *Psycho Beach Party*. 'Did the bite put the beast in you or let it out?' Talon asks Ricky, trying to convince his new lover/protégé to join the gang in infiltrating the upcoming luau and taking revenge on the straight 'haters' who have shunned them. Not unlike some critics of *Ticked-Off Trannies*' fantasy of queer retribution, Ricky argues that revenge is not the best way to gain acceptance, and he finally kills Talon (by sodomising him with a silver baseball bat) to prevent the gang from massacring the straight teens. With his dying breath, Talon asks newly out-and-proud Ricky to tell the world that werebears are not monsters but deserve love and acceptance. Playing upon gay subcultural imagery, Ricky and the gang's lycanthropic transformation from 'twinks' to 'bears' suggests a certain fluidity, and even political solidarity, between two gay subcultural niches that have sometimes opposed each other in gendered terms.[94]

Yet, the violent werebears also represent a gay subcultural niche that seems potentially 'monstrous' because the image of the bear has not been easily recuperated into widespread contemporary images of queer lifestyle commodification. Like the 'lesploitation' potential of *Bitch Slap* and *Sugar Boxx*, the (were)bear's aggressive queer masculinity offers a different gender inflection from that typically found in the safely mainstreamed, homonormative media images of gay men as trendy accessories for post-feminist women. In this respect, 'I Was a Teenage Werebear' may conclude on a note of liberal integrationism, with the radically retaliatory Talon destroyed and the werebear 'curse' lifted, but beneath the plea for social understanding and acceptance is a lingering, nostalgic desire for a past, less accepting era when queer identity seemed a more rebellious threat to social conformity. This ambivalence led some reviewers to suspect that, in the light of the adolescent male humour about sex and bodily functions in many of *Chillerama*'s other segments, 'Werebear' could be seen as upholding anachronistically homophobic imagery about leather-clad gay men as infectious monsters – an implication that Talon's death by forced sodomy does not allay, given the recurrent images of violent sodomy as a humiliating means of killing men in several other retrosploitation films.[95]

Testifying to the apparent threat that 'Werebear' (despite its modestly liberal plea for social inclusion) poses to dominant ideological constructs, it is the *Chillerama* segment that has garnered the most mixed fan reviews – generally earning praise when screened in the context of queer cinema but often receiving less acclaim within the predominantly hetero-male auspices of horror fandom. While some homophobic reviews by horror fans openly blast the segment's queer imagery, others couch their criticism in declaring that 'Werebear' either makes the overall anthology too long (an ironic complaint if we compare *Chillerama*'s 119-minute duration to the similarly segmented *Grindhouse*'s 191-minute running time), contains too many musical numbers and/or political grandstanding, or differs too markedly in generic tone from the more obviously hetero-masculine exploitation cycles spoofed in the other segments (the werebears' hyper-masculinity apparently notwithstanding). Though these complaints speak to how the relative 'cleanness' of 1950s rock 'n' roll teenpics and 1960s beach party movies has tended to marginalise these once-prominent cycles from the selectively retrospective construction of the exploitation cinema corpus as 'rebelliously' masculine territory, it is hard not to read some of these criticisms as coloured by veiled homophobia or a sexist rejection of the musical as a 'feminine' genre. For one fan reviewer, for instance, 'Werebear' ruined his first viewing experience of *Chillerama*, comparing it to a 'gangrenous leg' that would kill 'an entire man' if not removed, whereas a subsequent screening that omitted 'Werebear'

> just feels and flows better. Without the additional segment, I was no longer too worn out and exhausted to enjoy the merits of the film. [. . .] [T]he cheap gory thrills that [the remaining film] has to offer can be taken more in stride and it's something that you and your buddies can crack open a few beers and watch without feeling like an endurance challenge.[96]

Whereas hetero-male fans might safely identify with the homosociality of the hetero-male fans-turned-filmmakers who comprise the Splat Pack which made *Grindhouse*, Sullivan's openly queer 'Werebear' allows the homosociality of *Chillerama*'s own 'boys club' of film-makers to shade over into something perhaps more sexually 'threatening' to some straight viewers.

As the above examples suggest, the interjection of queer content into retro-styled films can cause conflicted responses within strongly gendered fan cultures if these images uncomfortably impinge upon the actual or imagined homosociality of such fandoms. Excavating such content and placing it more fully on-screen in retro-styled pastiches may be a nostalgic process but, as I have suggested in these final chapters, it is also inspired (for better or for worse) by the technological capacity to open remembered sources of past pleasure to wider, more diverse audiences in the modern mediascape. The process of touring *Chillerama* to actual surviving drive-in theatres, for instance, was important for Sullivan because, rather than viewing the contemporary accessibility of filmic texts as a means of keeping them alive in cultural memory, he also sees the possibility for films to become quickly forgettable when viewers are bombarded by so much content: 'And that's what's so sad to me, to see film – whether it's classic films or new films – just so disposable. And the importance of them just doesn't seem to be there like it used to be when you had to seek it out at a drive-in, or a VHS tape, or a 42nd Street grindhouse.'[97]

In this sense, reconfigurations of historical exploitation tropes may seem to threaten some fans' heteronormative subcultural ethos by distinctly remembering the queer potentiality which has always lurked within 'politically incorrect' films that might otherwise seem targeted at a hetero-male audience. Yet, by self-consciously overlaying multiple historico-political sensibilities (such as pre- and post-Stonewall queer consciousness) in an anxious blending of ironic distance and earnest appreciation akin to temporal drag, these pastiches instructively perform a range of limitations and possibilities – effectively teaching contemporary viewers that, despite the massive proliferation of available media texts today, there is value in taking time to seek out the queer pleasures to be found in exploitation cinema's own past.

Though Sullivan is openly gay, other films, such as *Bitch Slap* or *Sugar Boxx*, demonstrate that the deployment of retrospectatorship need not depend on knowledge of the creators' sexual orientation as an interpretive cue. On the one hand, there is certainly merit behind arguments that the post-Stonewall mainstreaming of a camp sensibility for straight audiences has eroded the political charge that once attended pre-Stonewall camp as a subterranean sexual vernacular. On the other hand, however, I would posit that queerly attuned film-makers and audiences will continue not only to find meaningful sources of fantasy and identification within historical exploitation texts such as WIP, sexploitation and beach party films but also in latter-day films that imaginatively and (semi-)earnestly refigure the cinematic past as 'a horizon of experience shaping film reception for some spectators'.[98] Finding progressive potential in retrosploitation cinema might seem to some observers like a naive objective – and I have tried in this chapter to outline a number of the pitfalls involved – but it is no more naive than the strategies for cultural survival long used by film history's marginalised audiences.

Overall, then, retrosploitation films bespeak a multivalent nostalgia for cinematic forms whose mnemonic reclamation resonates, in both form and content, with a sometimes-violent preoccupation with historical retribution against obsolescence. In this sense, they share a common concern with the residual and déclassé video collecting practices discussed in earlier chapters as a desired turn against contemporary consumerism – even if ultimately inextricable from such economic forces. The regressive elements of political backlash within this tendency do not mean that this desired retribution is always progressive, nor that the fan-cultural demographics who experience feelings of cultural marginalisation are necessarily as disempowered as they might think. Yet, there is still hope for progressive potential when pastiche's very ambivalence in tone, aesthetics and politics can destabilise ostensibly reactionary interpretations. A retro-styled film's perceived pastness or presentness can weigh too heavily for comfort on diverse viewers for diverse reasons so, even if the simulated pastness of these films may seem to contain their political implications (again, for better or worse) in a historically 'backward' context, the viewer's awareness of these films as present-day productions also grounds their potential relevance as retrospective interpretations informed (implicitly or not) by contemporary political values. Indeed, regardless of the sense of 'authenticity' that these films may aim to emulate, they remain shot through with a streak of pathos as texts which nostalgically long to be, but cannot ever truly become, the mythicised films that once appeared 'at a drive-in, or a VHS tape, or a 42nd Street grindhouse', or whatever other *lieux de mémoire* that fans may celebrate. It is ultimately this pathos – this sense of unrequited longing for something spatio-temporally lost, something stubbornly lingering from the past, something continuing to infect and inflect one's identity – that, if nothing else, unites retrosploitation fans of all stripes.

Notes

1. Elizabeth E. Guffey, *Retro: The Culture of Revival* (London: Reaktion Books, 2006), p. 163.
2. Richard Dyer, *Pastiche* (London: Routledge, 2007), pp. 105, 117.
3. Pam Cook, *Screening the Past: Memory and Nostalgia in Cinema* (London: Routledge, 2005), p. 4.
4. See, for example, Preston Jones, 'Violent, Gory, Mindless Fun in "Machete"', *The Olympian*, 3 September 2010, http://www.theolympian.com/2010/09/03/1357027/violent-gory-mindless-fun-in-machete.html (quoted; accessed 8 July 2012); Rob Kidman, 'Geek Beat: Modern Grindhouse Movies You Need to See', Geek Life, last modified 19 July 2011, http://geek-life.com/2011/07/19/geek-beat-modern-grindhouse-movies-you-need-to-see/ (accessed 8 July 2012); and The Primal Root, 'Review: *Black Devil Doll*', From Dusk Till Con, http://www.fromdusktillcon.com/content/27-reviews/744-review-black-devil-doll (accessed 26 January 2012).

5. Dyer, *Pastiche*, p. 163.
6. Cook, *Screening the Past*, p. 11.
7. Dyer, *Pastiche*, pp. 177–8.
8. Jacinda Read, 'The Cult of Masculinity: From Fan-Boys to Academic Bad-Boys', in *Defining Cult Movies: The Cultural Politics of Oppositional Taste*, eds Mark Jancovich, Antonio Lázaro Reboll, Julian Stringer and Andy Willis (Manchester: Manchester University Press, 2003), pp. 61–3, 67.
9. B. Alan Orange, 'EXCLUSIVE: *The Black Devil Doll* is On the Loose!' Movieweb, posted 16 June 2008, http://www.movieweb.com/news/exclusive-the-black-devil-doll-is-on-the-loose (accessed 26 January 2012).
10. Dyer, *Pastiche*, p. 148.
11. Susanna Paasonen, *Carnal Resonance: Affect and Online Pornography* (Cambridge, MA: MIT Press, 2011), p. 128.
12. Sean Tierney, 'Quentin Tarantino in Black and White', in *Critical Rhetorics of Race*, eds Michael G. Lacy and Kent A. Ono (New York: New York University Press, 2011), pp. 83–4.
13. Ibid., pp. 89–91.
14. Dyer, *Pastiche*, p. 156. As an example of a non-white culture pastiching from more hegemonic cultures, Miike Takashi's *Sukiyaki Western Django* (2007) mixes Japanese *chambara* films with Italian westerns, a cultural re-appropriation recalling how Sergio Leone's cycle-defining *A Fistful of Dollars* (1964) was itself inspired by Kurosawa Akira's *Yojimbo* (1961).
15. On a comparable use of culturally 'lower' taste/class distinctions, see Laura Kipnis, *Bound and Gagged: Pornography and the Politics of Fantasy in America* (New York: Grove Press, 1996), pp. 122–60.
16. Dyer, *Pastiche*, p. 156.
17. Michael Rogin, *Blackface, White Noise: Jewish Immigrants in the Hollywood Melting Pot* (Berkeley: University of California Press, 1996), pp. 36–7 (quoted); Eric Lott, *Love and Theft: Blackface Minstrelsy and the American Working Class* (New York: Oxford University Press, 1993), pp. 52–3; and W. T. Lhamon Jr, *Raising Cain: Blackface Performance from Jim Crow to Hip Hop* (Cambridge, MA: Harvard University Press, 1998), pp. 22, 117.
18. Read, 'The Cult of Masculinity', pp. 62–7. Quote at p. 63.
19. John Bem, 'Like Two Hams in Your Pants: *Black Devil Doll*', I Will Devour Your Content, posted 30 January 2011, http://iwdyc.blogspot.com/2011/01/like-two-hams-in-your-pants-black-devil.html (accessed 28 February 2012).
20. Pooch, '*Black Devil Doll*' (review), Sex Gore Mutants, http://www.sexgoremutants.co.uk/reviews/bldevdollus.html (accessed 28 February 2012).
21. Devin Kelly, '*The Minstrel Killer*' (review), Cinema Nocturna, http://www.cinema-nocturna.com/index.php?ind=reviews&op=entry_view&iden=156 (accessed 5 March 2012).
22. Josh Miller, '*The Minstrel Killer*' (review), *MovieZone Magazine*, December 2011, p. 59.

23. Carol J. Clover, *Men, Women, and Chainsaws: Gender in the Modern Horror Film* (Princeton, NJ: Princeton University Press, 1992), p. 135.
24. Lott, *Love and Theft*, pp. 140–1, 152–3. Quote at p. 141.
25. R. L. Rutsky, 'Surfing the Other: Ideology on the Beach', *Film Quarterly* 52, no. 4 (1999): 21–2.
26. Indeed, several viral videos hyped the film's release, including a deleted scene inspired by *The Mack* (1973), in which Black Dynamite reprimands a young boy named Barry for wanting to emulate him, instead inspiring the boy to grow up to become the Democratic nominee for president of the United States. See Chuck Tryon, *Reinventing Cinema: Movies in the Age of Media Convergence* (New Brunswick, NJ: Rutgers University Press, 2009), pp. 141–2.
27. Jason Mittell, *Genre and Television: From Cop Shows to Cartoons in American Culture* (New York: Routledge, 2004), p. 193.
28. Harriet Margolis, 'Stereotypical Strategies: Black Film Aesthetics, Spectator Positioning, and Self-Directed Stereotypes in *Hollywood Shuffle* and *I'm Gonna Git You Sucka*', *Cinema Journal* 38, no. 3 (1999): 63.
29. Ibid., pp. 54–5, 60, 62. Quotes at pp. 54, 60.
30. See, for example, David Cox, 'Blaxploitation Spoof *Black Dynamite* May be Witty, But Is It Racist?' *The Guardian*, 16 August 2010, http://www.guardian.co.uk/film/filmblog/2010/aug/16/blaxploitation-spoof-black-dynamite (accessed 4 April 2012).
31. Congressional Budget Office, *Trends in the Distribution of Household Income Between 1979 and 2007* (Washington, DC: Congressional Budget Office, 2011).
32. Tarantino's own reluctance to use computer-generated imagery in *Death Proof* suggests that he shares Stuntman Mike's concerns about a loss of physicality in contemporary genre film-making. See Jay McRoy, '"The Kids of Today Should Defend Themselves Against the '70s": Simulating Auras and Marketing Nostalgia in Robert Rodriguez and Quentin Tarantino's *Grindhouse*', in *American Horror Film: The Genre at the Turn of the Millennium*, ed. Steffen Hantke (Jackson: University Press of Mississippi, 2010), pp. 228–9; and Caetlin Benson-Allott, *Killer Tapes and Shattered Screens: Video Spectatorship from VHS to File Sharing* (Berkeley: University of California Press, 2013), pp. 144–5.
33. Clover, *Men, Women, and Chainsaws*, pp. 126, 134. Quote at p. 126. Similar confrontations occur in retrosploitation pastiches with bikers as rural anti-heroes, such as *Hell Ride* (2008) and *Dear God No!* (2011).
34. For a representative example, see Tony Lazlo, 'Redneck Pride: Why Rob Zombie Sucks', CC2K: The Nexus of Pop-Culture Fandom, last modified 22 March 2009, http://www.cc2konline.com/component/content/647?task=view (accessed 8 August 2012).
35. Laura Wiebe Taylor, 'Popular Songs and Ordinary Violence: Exposing Basic Human Brutality in the Films of Rob Zombie', in *Terror Tracks: Music, Sound, and Horror Cinema*, ed. Philip Hayward (London: Equinox, 2009), pp. 231, 233–6.

36. Linnie Blake, '"I Am the Devil and I'm Here to Do the Devil's Work": Rob Zombie, George W. Bush, and the Limits of American Freedom', in *Horror After 9/11: World of Fear, Cinema of Terror*, eds Aviva Briefel and Sam J. Miller (Austin: University of Texas Press, 2011), pp. 188, 191–2, 195–6. Quote at p. 196.
37. Steffen Hantke, 'Introduction: They Don't Make 'Em Like They Used To: On the Rhetoric of Crisis and the Current State of American Horror Cinema', in *American Horror Film*, pp. vii–xxiv.
38. Constantine Verevis, *Film Remakes* (Edinburgh: Edinburgh University Press, 2006), pp. 145–6.
39. See Andreas Huyssen, *After the Great Divide: Modernism, Mass Culture, Postmodernism* (Bloomington: Indiana University Press, 1986), pp. 44–62; and Sally Robinson, 'Feminized Men and Inauthentic Women', *Genders*, no. 53 (2011): http://www.genders.org/g53/g53_robinson.html (accessed 12 August 2012).
40. Pamela Craig and Martin Fradley, 'Teenage Traumata: Youth, Affective Politics, and the Contemporary American Horror Film', in *American Horror Film*, pp. 80–3, 87.
41. Rebecca Winters Keegan, 'The Splat Pack', *Time*, 22 October 2006, http://www.time.com/time/magazine/article/0,9171,1549299,00.html (accessed 8 August 2012).
42. Indeed, revisionist scholarship has importantly noted how horror films have long been marketed to female audiences as well as to the genre's long-presumed male viewership. See, for example, Rhona J. Berenstein, *Attack of the Leading Ladies: Gender, Sexuality, and Spectatorship in Classical Horror Cinema* (New York: Columbia University Press, 1996); and Richard Nowell, *Blood Money: A History of the First Teen Slasher Film Cycle* (New York: Continuum, 2011).
43. Sarah Wharton, 'Welcome to the (Neo)Grindhouse! Sex, Violence, and the Indie Film', in *American Independent Cinema: Indie, Indiewood, and Beyond*, eds Geoff King, Claire Molloy, and Yannis Tzioumakis (London: Routledge, 2013), pp. 198–209.
44. This term was coined in David Edelstein, 'Now Playing at Your Local Multiplex: Torture Porn', *New York Magazine*, 28 January 2006, http://nymag.com/movies/features/15622/ (accessed 10 August 2012). Needless to say, horror fans who have seen 'underground' faux-snuff films such as *Niku daruma* (1998) are not as likely as Edelstein to lazily toss around such moralistically overloaded terms.
45. Verevis, *Film Remakes*, p. 138. For an astute fan-cultural assessment, see 'Hate Horror Remakes? Studios are Glad!' Horror-Movies.ca, http://www.horror-movies.ca/horror_15000.html (accessed 10 March 2012).
46. David Andrews, *Soft in the Middle: The Contemporary Softcore Feature in Its Contexts* (Columbus: Ohio State University Press, 2006), pp. 243–6.
47. Rob Lineberger, '*Misty Mundae Euro Vixen Collection*' (review), DVD

Verdict, http://www.dvdverdict.com/reviews/mistymundae.php (accessed 11 March 2012).
48. Matthew Sorrento, 'Loving the Bad: An Interview with Frankie Latina and Sasha Grey on *Modus Operandi*', *Bright Lights Film Journal*, no. 71 (2011): http://www.brightlightsfilm.com/71/71livmodusoperandi_sorrento.php (accessed 14 December 2011).
49. Andrews, *Soft in the Middle*, pp. 4, 7–8, 10–16. Quotes at pp. 11, 14.
50. Elena Gorfinkel, '"Dated Sexuality": Anna Biller's *Viva* and the Retrospective Life of Sexploitation Cinema', *Camera Obscura* 26, no. 3 (2011): 104.
51. Andrews, *Soft in the Middle*, pp. 37–44. Quote at p. 42.
52. Gorfinkel, '"Dated Sexuality"', p. 107.
53. Jonathan L. Crane, 'A Lust for Life: The Cult Films of Russ Meyer', in *Unruly Pleasures: The Cult Film and its Critics*, eds Xavier Mendik and Graeme Harper (Guildford: FAB Press, 2000), pp. 91–7. Quote at p. 97.
54. Kristen Hatch, 'The Sweeter the Kitten, the Sharper the Claws: Russ Meyer's Bad Girls', in *Bad: Infamy, Darkness, Evil, and Slime on Screen*, ed. Murray Pomerance (Albany: State University of New York Press, 2004), p. 148.
55. Andrews, *Soft in the Middle*, pp. 53–4, 164–5. Quote at p. 54.
56. As Meyer himself noted, his films 'can be taken on two levels: as parodies or as being completely straight. I guess they're both'. Quoted in Jimmy McDonough, *Big Bosoms and Square Jaws: The Biography of Russ Meyer, King of the Sex Film* (London: Jonathan Cape, 2005), p. 150. The cursed penis subplot shares distinct similarities with 'Wadzilla', a 1950s monster movie spoof within the parodic exploitation anthology film *Chillerama* (2011) which features a man whose experimental attempts to raise his sperm count and thereby enhance his normative manhood result in a giant, mutated spermatozoon attacking New York.
57. Gorfinkel, '"Dated Sexuality"', pp. 97, 101, 110, 112, 114, 116–17, 121, 123, 125. Quote at p. 112.
58. Beth Johnson, 'Semblance and the Sexual Revolution: A Critical Review of *Viva*', in *Peep Shows: Cult Film and the Cine-Erotic*, ed. Xavier Mendik (New York: Wallflower Press, 2012), p. 266.
59. Biller, quoted in Elena Gorfinkel, 'Unlikely Genres: An Interview with Anna Biller', *Camera Obscura* 26, no. 3 (2011): 137.
60. Andrews, *Soft in the Middle*, pp. 34–8.
61. Yvonne Tasker, *Spectacular Bodies: Gender, Genre, and the Action Cinema* (London: Routledge, 1993), p. 19.
62. Ibid., p. 149; and Maria Elena Buszek, *Pin-Up Grrrls: Feminism, Sexuality, Popular Culture* (Durham, NC: Duke University Press, 2006), pp. 345, 347–8.
63. Rikke Schubart, *Super Bitches and Action Babes: The Female Hero in Popular Cinema, 1970–2006* (Jefferson, NC: McFarland, 2007), p. 2. Italics mine.

64. For examples concerned with exploitation films in particular, see Clover, *Men, Women, and Chainsaws*; Peter Lehman, '"Don't Blame This on a Girl": Female Rape-Revenge Films', in *Screening the Male: Exploring Masculinities in Hollywood Cinema*, eds Steven Cohan and Ina Rae Hark (London: Routledge, 1993), pp. 103–17; Jacinda Read, *The New Avengers: Feminism, Femininity, and the Rape-Revenge Cycle* (Manchester: Manchester University Press, 2000); and Suzanna Danuta Walters, 'Caged Heat: The (R)evolution of Women-in-Prison Films', in *Reel Knockouts: Violent Women in the Movies*, eds Martha McCaughey and Neal King (Austin: University of Texas Press, 2001), pp. 106–23.
65. Lisa Coulthard, 'Killing Bill: Rethinking Feminism and Film Violence', in *Interrogating Postfeminism: Gender and the Politics of Popular Culture*, eds Yvonne Tasker and Diane Negra (Durham, NC: Duke University Press, 2007), pp. 161–3, 166–8, 173. Quote at p. 173.
66. Tasker, *Spectacular Bodies*, p. 152.
67. Clover, *Men, Women, and Chainsaws*, pp. 151–4. Quote at p. 151. Clover herself parenthetically admits, 'Paradoxically, it is the experience of being brutally raped that makes a "man" of a woman' but Clover does not treat the impetus for this transformation as a major obstacle to a feminist politics if the victim's literal biological sex is secondary to the 'social gendering of the acts it undergoes or undertakes' (p. 159).
68. Lehman, '"Don't Blame This on a Girl"', pp. 107, 113; and Read, *The New Avengers*, pp. 35–6, 40, 50–1.
69. Lehman, '"Don't Blame This on a Girl"', pp. 112, 115–16.
70. Virginie Despentes, *King Kong Theory*, trans. Stéphanie Benson (New York: The Feminist Press, 2010), pp. 33–7.
71. Judith Halberstam, 'Imagined Violence/Queer Violence: Representation, Rage, and Resistance', *Social Text*, no. 37 (1993): 196, 198–9.
72. Despentes, *King Kong Theory*, pp. 39–45. Quotes at pp. 42–3.
73. Read, *The New Avengers*, pp. 9, 28, 39, 45, 48–50. Quotes at pp. 9, 28.
74. Clover, *Men, Women, and Chainsaws*, pp. 143, 145. Quote at p. 143.
75. Ibid., pp. 121–3.
76. Daniel Villarreal, 'Gay Director Israel Luna is Sick of Bashing Victims Sucking It Up. So He Made a Movie Where They Stab Their Attackers to Death', Queerty, last modified 22 January 2010, http://www.queerty.com/gay-director-israel-luna-is-sick-of-bashing-victims-sucking-it-up-so-he-made-a-movie-where-they-stab-their-attackers-to-death-20100122/ (accessed 18 August 2012).
77. 'Demand That *Ticked-Off Trannies With Knives* Be Pulled From Tribeca Film Festival Line-up', GLAAD, last modified 26 March 2010, http://www.glaad.org/calltoaction/032510 (accessed 18 August 2012).
78. For examples, see Gina, 'The Tranny Day of Remembrance', Skip the Makeup, last modified 18 March 2010, http://skipthemakeup.blogspot.com/2010/03/tranny-day-of-remembrance.html (accessed 20 August 2012);

and Rebecca Juro, '"Ticked-Off Trannies With Knives" Fails, as a Movie and as a Concept', The Bilerico Project, last modified 6 April 2010, http://www.bilerico.com/2010/04/like_horsradish_and_hot_fudge_ticked-off_trannies.php (accessed 20 August 2012).
79. Patricia White, *Uninvited: Classical Hollywood Cinema & Lesbian Representability* (Bloomington: Indiana University Press, 1999), pp. 196–7, 204, 207, 214. Quote at p. 197.
80. Heather Love, *Feeling Backward: Loss and the Politics of Queer History* (Cambridge, MA: Harvard University Press, 2009), p. 45.
81. Elizabeth Freeman, *Time Binds: Queer Temporalities, Queer Histories* (Durham, NC: Duke University Press, 2010), p. 63.
82. Ibid., pp. 59–65. Quotes at pp. 61, 64 (original italics). Also see Lucas Hilderbrand, 'Retroactivism', *GLQ* 12, no. 2 (2006): 303–17.
83. Gorfinkel, '"Dated Sexuality"', p. 124.
84. Katrin Horn, 'The Return of the B-Movie: *Bitch Slap!* and Lesploitation' (paper presented to the 2012 Society for Cinema and Media Studies Conference, Boston, MA, 21–5 March 2012).
85. Clare Whatling, *Screen Dreams: Fantasizing Lesbians in Film* (Manchester: Manchester University Press, 1997), pp. 80–2. Quote at p. 82.
86. Claire Hines, '"How Far Will a Girl Go to Satisfy Her Needs?": From Dykesploitation to Lesbian Hard-core', in *Peep Shows*, pp. 212–13.
87. Judith Mayne, *Framed: Lesbians, Feminists, and Media Culture* (Minneapolis: University of Minnesota Press, 2000), pp. 136–7.
88. Ibid., pp. 133–9. Quote at p. 138.
89. Ann Ciasullo, 'Containing "Deviant" Desire: Lesbianism, Heterosexuality, and the Women-in-Prison Narrative', *Journal of Popular Culture* 41, no. 2 (2008): 199, 201–6.
90. Ibid., pp. 211–12, 217–18. Quote at p. 218.
91. Paula Graham, 'Girl's Camp? The Politics of Parody', in *Immortal, Invisible: Lesbians and the Moving Image*, ed. Tamsin Wilton (London: Routledge, 1995), pp. 168, 170. Quote at p. 168.
92. The linster, '"Sugar Boxx" Introduces the LBI: Lesbian Before Incarceration', AfterEllen.com, last modified 24 March 2011, http://www.afterellen.com/movies/2011/03/sugar-boxx-introduces-the-lbi-lesbian-before-incarceration (accessed 22 October 2012).
93. Rutsky, 'Surfing the Other', p. 15–16.
94. Ricky's portrayal by Sean Paul Lockhart is especially notable in this regard, because he began his acting career as a famed performer within the 'twink' niche of all-male pornography.
95. For a representative example, see Angelo B, '*Chillerama*' (review), Bloody Good Horror, last modified 6 October 2011, http://www.bloodygoodhorror.com/bgh/reviews/10/06/2011/chillerama (accessed 15 October 2012).
96. EvanDickson, 'Who Woulda Thunk? "Chillerama" Plays Better Without "Werebear"!' Bloody-Disgusting.com, last modified 2 December 2011, http://

bloody-disgusting.com/news/27435/who-woulda-thunk-chillerama-plays-better-without-werebear/ (accessed 15 October 2012).
97. Charles Webb, 'A Chat with CHILLERAMA Director Tim Sullivan', Twitch, last modified 29 November 2011, http://twitchfilm.com/interviews/2011/11/a-chat-with-chillerama-director-tim-sullivan.php (accessed 17 October 2012).
98. White, *Uninvited*, p. 15.

Conclusion

In his essayistic meditation on 'film's end', Stephen Barber details the decaying string of old theatres concentrated on Broadway avenue in central Los Angeles, which he deems physical fragments of cinema's living end in the digital age. Once glamorous picture palaces whose audiences have since migrated to other, newer theatres elsewhere in the vicinity, these cavernous spaces fell into disrepair during the second half of the twentieth century, eventually becoming grind houses for Spanish-language films, exploitation cinema and hard-core adult movies. When I coincidentally ventured down this same street in 2010, during the period of my research about 42nd Street, I quickly recognised the lingering traces of former grind houses in these ignored, repurposed theatre facades nestled amid the surrounding inner-city bustle. The pavements below, primarily peopled with Latino faces, remained vibrantly alive with activity but the ornate theatre frontages seemingly aroused little attention. In discussing the memories attached to these spaces, Barber's elegiac tone (not uncommon to such treatises on the 'death' of cinema) is worth quoting at length:

> The impact of haunting carried by the disintegrated or re-used spaces of cinema results from a simultaneity of vision in which the entire temporal history of a cinema, with its contrary phases of glory and destitution, is compressed into the present moment, since the integrity of its filmic history has disintegrated along with its architectural infrastructure ... with the result that any moment in a cinema's existence can abruptly resurge at will into the present, like a ghost-presence in a horror film, sonically underscored by the cacophony of memory. In that oblivious levelling of a cinema's history, each of its distinctive phases becomes equivalent to every other, and its temporal hierarchy is erased: the moment at which it served as a riotous all-night site for cult-film mania or pornography becomes inseparable from that of its prestigious moment of ascendancy as the venue for searchlight-illuminated star-premieres. Time blurs, stops dead, and transmits itself intensively and multiply in the abandoned cinema, like a celluloid film-image trapped in the projector-gate, heated to incandescence before it finally burns up and vanishes.[1]

Though I am taken by this description of cinematic spaces infused by the non-linear vagaries of memory, I am not so quick to subscribe to the suggestion that, when confronted by its apparent demise, cinema's history flattens out and renders equivalent all those periods which came before.

Rather, I have suggested throughout this study that exploitation cinema, as taken up by appreciative fans, paradoxically seems acutely aware of its own *passing* (which is not the same as *death*) in proportion with its renewed rediscoverability on home video in recent decades – hence the particular attention to those moments of 'trapped' and 'burning' celluloid images evoked by the remediation of battered archival exploitation trailers or the retrosploitation text's simulated degradation. Unlike the products of the glamorous Hollywood premiere, the very clash between exploitation cinema's sheer textual proliferation over the decades and its continuing historical marginality on taste-related grounds allows the grindhouse era to be upheld by fans with a fervour that belies Barber's assertion that all film-historical periods become graspable in simultaneity. In distinction from some other species of fandom, exploitation films' textual afterlives are markedly infused with the fraught taste politics deriving from these texts' long-standing cultural marginalisation which, in turn, informs the sense of pastness that has become a crucial factor in defining and valuing 'exploitation' as such. In the eyes of the dominant historical record, not all films that played in entertainment districts such as Broadway or 42nd Street were created equal, which is why mediated cultural memories paradoxically attempt to redress such inequalities through a selective revaluation of the cinematic past while still ostensibly preserving the conditions of cultural difference that are so important to fans' identities.

If a temporal simultaneity exists, it exists on home video where films from different periods and cultural contexts commingle on store shelves and website search results – but, even there, we have seen how different technological frameworks can allow specific films to serve as objects of textual nostalgia and vehicles for contextual nostalgia associated with uneven historical terrain, not a level field of cultural preferences. Furthermore, the various nostalgias endemic to fans' celebration of exploitation films also provide instructive examples for reconsidering the importance of cultural memory to other video-mediated objects of film fandom as well. For Barber and many other premature eulogists of cinema-as-we-know-it, 'the industry of film gives the illusion of continuation, as though nothing had happened' in the shift from celluloid to digital imagery, not unlike the 'seamless' transitions engrained in the economic motives of Hollywood continuity editing.[2] Yet, as Caetlin Benson-Allott observes, the discipline of film studies too often speaks of a monumental shift from the analogue/

theatrical to the digital/non-theatrical, without adequately considering the not-yet-lost technological intermediaries that have already altered our understanding of cinema.[3] As much as digital technologies dominate our current means of media consumption, certain means of accessing the personal/cultural past stubbornly stick out as rough edges complicating any seamless teleology. Indeed, we might reasonably ask whether there is anything more perplexing or absurd about present-day fans who fetishise residual technologies such as magnetic videotape than those hip, young technology users entranced by the semi-annual buzz over the latest Apple iFetish® – particularly when this year's emergent dingus will quickly become as obsolete and subject to mnemonic revaluation as, say, 1980's Sony Betamax SL-5400 VCR. With such questions in mind, scholars attending to the historical reception of technologies which inflect our representations of the past can thereby also discover the very ability for niche groups to consider such representations *ours*, particularly when different kinds of value intersect. In this respect, I situate my work among a younger generation of scholars raised on VHS – many of them cited in this book – who have recently turned towards analysing the history and cultures of home video formats since the mid-1970s. If their work can be read as symptoms of nostalgia for temporal and technological passages across the video era, then so too are my own preceding arguments about home video and fandom inextricable from what will perhaps one day be seen as a generational desire for physical-cum-textual traces that have since been supplanted by digital data clouds.

On perhaps the most basic level, 'just as *everything* is representation, *everything* is memory'. That is, all sensory stimuli which our brains receive must be mnemonically stored long enough to be cognitively processed, so a slight temporal delay always exists between intake and comprehension. Consequently, we may practically experience daily life as a continually unfolding present but all we can ever truly have access to is the past.[4] And for some people, myriad shades of pastness may be all the more alluring than the patently present, less out of a sense of retreatism than a search for more expansive sources of identity. For my purposes, then, it has been important to ask why some cinematic experiences register with more pastness than others when technologically mediated, and why some people may gravitate towards these media experiences more than towards others (whether on the basis of affect, politics, taste and so on) – which will doubtless remain an open question for future scholarship on cultural memory.

As I have suggested, the shape of exploitation fandom has shifted alongside technologies of cultural memory, with nostalgic turns towards remembered times and places both threatening and assuaging the subcultural value placed upon authenticity, exclusivity and nonconformity. This multivalent affect derives from persistent anxieties surrounding both media and nostalgia, particularly in moments of format transition that call past modes of personal remembrance into question. In José van Dijck's words, 'On the one hand, media are considered aids to human memory, but on the other hand, they are conceived as a threat to the purity of remembrance. As an artificial prosthesis, they can free the brain of unnecessary burdens and allow more space for creative activity; as a replacement, they can corrupt memory.'[5] In its specific role as a retrospective longing for an (at least partly) idealised past, nostalgia also appears as a double-edged sword, capable of marshalling both critical and conventional ideologies – or, in the case of exploitation fandom, both the supposed rebellion of cultism and the implied conformity of populism, each of which is coloured by politically problematic taste distinctions.

In creatively repurposing the past for present uses, the retrosploitation phenomena explored in this book thus slide between 'nostalgia's darkest impulse (*the past will be what we say it was*) and the most utopic nostalgic liberation (*we can reject tradition, to which we are not bound forever*)'.[6] Whether coalescing across the remediated exploitation DVD or internalised in the retro-styled pastiche, the past is selectively consumed with a complex blend of sincere desire and ironic distance, spurring ongoing debate over how to properly perform one's adherence to chosen fan objects. Yet, with fan identities so contingent upon nostalgia for bygone films, consumption sites and technologies alike, it is little surprise that this fandom remains haunted by fears not only of exploitation cinema's cultural obsolescence but also its own. As the hallowed cinematic past increasingly recedes into the historical distance, and as home video becomes the sole means for younger fans ever to have accessed these films, changing video technologies will become all the more important as *lieux de mémoire* marking the mourned passage of exploitation cinema and its fandom alike – in spite of video's actual continuing role as a key preserver and purveyor of that retrospectively constructed history. As I hope this study has shown, foregrounding the role of cultural memory within studies of fan practices can reveal a more diverse picture of media fandom, including those fan cultures deeply sceptical of (but still partially inflected by) the convergence-era technologies and socialities that currently occupy so much of the field's attention. Indeed, in its drive to counter long-standing stereotypes about fans as passive consumers and antisocial misfits, the area of fan studies has arguably swung so far in the opposite direction that it has reinforced its own stereotypes of convergence-era fans as perpetually engaged, technologically vanguard social-media connoisseurs for whom cultural presentism carries far more weight than imagined territories of pastness. The increasing scholarly conflation of fandom and whatever are presently considered 'new media' thus not only does a disservice to the diversity of meaningful practices attending older media forms such as cinema but can also threaten to shade into a thinly veiled corporate boosterism.

Technologies of film distribution may have reciprocally influential effects upon perceptions of audiences and texts alike but these effects cannot always be neatly predicted. After all, the perceived pastness of the remediated text – reproduced in all its well-worn, physically deteriorated glory, as opposed to pristinely restored – can be a large part of its allure for some viewers, as well as the impetus for a historically chauvinistic attitude towards past films, film-makers and audiences. This latter approach bespeaks an especially egregious case of presentism when the apparent flaws in a surviving archival film (such as jump cuts inadvertently caused by missing frames) are less attributable to sloppy film-making or callously undiscerning patrons than the unforeseen results of a given print's unpredictable or marginal distribution history. Where films like *Grindhouse* (2007) imitate such flaws as an in-joke to today's knowing audiences, older exploitation films may not have the same luxury in reception – hence the fact that some fans push back against disproportionately favouring ironic mockery as a default reading mode. Whereas retrosploitation films may aspire to a non-ironic sense of historical pathos which they can grasp only at a temporal remove, some fans' heartfelt appreciation of the temporally/culturally dilapidated text is mirrored by the pathos of their own protracted hunt for an ever-elusive sense of personal 'authenticity' that can never be guaranteed through ongoing struggles over the subcultural capital accruing to these textual afterlives.

To offer a particularly rich example of the larger implications for further research raised by this book's underlying focus on the politics of taste and tone, I want to return briefly to the image of the Broadway grind houses – those theatres whose fall from grace Barber implicitly figures in terms of a turn towards not only Spanish-language and exploitation films but also the local Latino audiences who frequent the area. This overlap of historically and nationally marginalised theatres localised in an older neighbourhood, spatially and temporally distanced from the newer multiplexes built elsewhere in the American film capital, invites the question of who is left out of traditional cinema histories, and how the interrelation of imagination and cultural memory can productively address such inequalities. Indeed, the diverse connotations that fans and non-fans hold about historically *worthless* and historically *priceless* texts/experiences open up when we start to consider memory as an ongoing labour performed by media producers, users and industries whose motives for nostalgically revaluing the past seldom neatly overlap. In this respect, the former fare of those Broadway grind houses recalls a larger history of disparities – crisscrossed by capital, technology and niche audiences – raised by Robert Rodriguez's fake *Machete* trailer which originated as part of *Grindhouse* and later became reworked to publicise the 2010 feature film of the same name.

As noted in the preceding chapters, the trailer has become one of the quintessential elements of film marketing in the convergence era, offering viewers a means of accessing and 'pre-reading' a film's content across multiple platforms and technologies. Their fragmentary nature allows trailers to flow across borders with relatively little effort on the part of media producers, as they are often picked up and dispersed by eager fans through blogs and social networking sites, potentially reaching far larger numbers of global viewers than television spots or theatrically released promos. At the same time, however, many 'official' trailers remain products of multinational media conglomerates operated from media capitals, such as Hollywood or Hong Kong, whose reach extends far beyond a single nation's borders.[7] Since the deregulation period of the 1980s, the major Hollywood studios have all become holdings of such conglomerates, potentially undercutting notions of 'American cinema' as necessarily tied to national/cultural sovereignty. As Andrew Higson argues, all cinema is inherently transnational, since 'the degree of cultural crossbreeding and interpenetration, not only across borders but also within them, suggests that modern cultural formations are invariably hybrid and impure'.[8] Given their fragmentary, highly mobile nature, and the fact that they become a prospective part of a film's consumption even before the main text itself is available for purchase, trailers represent a popularly circulating media form that can blur the traditional understandings of shared spatiality and temporality upon which a concept like 'the nation' is built.

While trailers would seemingly be quite ephemeral (with several different versions often appearing over the course of a publicity campaign), they persist indefinitely via digital technologies, whether archived on to DVDs and Blu-rays or easily locatable through a web search. Forming an archive of marketing strategies (and, for some fans, an archive of emotions connected to memories of past trailer viewings), the persistence of trailers capitalises on the value of historicity itself. Typically requiring considerable financial investment by film producers and distributors, and provoking varying levels of emotional investment by fans, trailers provide lingering traces of capital's historical attempts to solicit consumers. Similarly, much as trailers offer an intensified compression of a film's narrative (in terms of events and of duration), they also offer intensified and compressed signifiers of the nation from which the advertised film apparently originated. As vehicles for promoting new products as part of a nation's longer history of film production, trailers play a crucial role in announcing how nations imagine themselves on-screen and how they position their creative industries on the global stage. Since national narratives are implicitly encoded into the fictional narratives of commercial films, both are promoted in tandem through the abbreviated and hyperactive pleasures offered by the trailer form. Yet, like national ideologies, trailers typically promise more than the featured film can possibly deliver.

The product of a Mexican American film-maker who began his professional career with *El Mariachi* (1992), a low-budget, border-set action film originally intended for the Spanish-language DTV exploitation market, Rodriguez's original *Machete* trailer may have begun as part of a major (off-)Hollywood film but it draws inspiration from action cinema's 'minor' mode, which is typically more 'transnational in industrial composition and highly variable in mode of address' by appearing on home video and in a handful of Spanish-language theatres.[9] On the level of its present-set plot, the *Machete* trailer also depicts a violent (if tongue-in-cheek) story about the potential implications of unforeseen border crossings, particularly around the controversially porous United States–Mexico border. 'Machete' (Danny Trejo), a former member of the Mexican Federal Police, illegally in the United States as a day labourer, is hired by a mysterious Anglo-American businessman (Jeff Fahey) to assassinate a senator; after being double-crossed and almost killed, Machete turns action hero and hunts down his former employers who 'fucked with the wrong Mexican' (as the narrator growls). The film most clearly recalls the ethnically marked (anti-)heroes of blaxploitation films, including the magnification of potentially stereotypical traits involved in framing race as a retributive motivator of violent action, while also filtered through a distinctly Mexican sensibility that has remained a minor presence in the larger exploitation film corpus.

Though the trailer is clearly intended as a humorous commentary on ongoing American debates about 'illegal' immigration, its retro style recalls an earlier period of film-making; the 'Rated X' logo that marks the trailer's end, for example, recalls the years between 1968 and 1990, when the Motion Picture Association of America (MPAA) still used the 'X' rating. The trailer is thus particularly interesting because of its conscious self-stylisation as an object already loaded with a number of existing histories – from past histories of the exploitation film as a mode of production and exhibition, to histories of nationalism and racial exploitation across the contact zones between the United States and Mexico. In other words, the trailer's simulated signs of prior use recall the very longevity of the political tensions embedded within its narrative cues, though its nostalgic ode to the brazen political incorrectness of the outmoded exploitation film is perhaps unsuccessful in distancing the trailer from its present imbrication in a capitalist commodity culture premised upon actual exploitation. Indeed, the American exploitation industry's own use of international co-productions and negative pick-ups has long allowed American producers and distributors to inexpensively acquire films made cheaply outside the United States under the sort of exploitative, non-unionised working conditions that have been endemic to the unequal relationship between so-called First and Third World nations.[10] Even if this trailer is 'fake' (or at least *was*, until *Machete* became a feature film in its own right), it still served as a promotional tool for the heavily marketed (off-)Hollywood production *Grindhouse*, even following Rodriguez's film-within-a-film *Planet Terror* to DVD and Blu-ray before being partially repurposed to promote the standalone *Machete* feature.

National history, film history and mythic visions of the cinematic past merge uneasily in Rodriguez's trailer but, because these histories are heavily mediated, it can become difficult to cleanly separate any sense of historical 'authenticity' from cinematic flights of fancy. The trailer raises the very real issue of racially charged nationalism along the United States–Mexico border: as the businessman tells Machete, 'illegal aliens such as yourself are being forced out of our country [the United States] at an alarming rate', so the senator's death is supposedly 'for the good of both our people'. Coming from a proudly Mexican American film-maker, Machete's eventual vengeance against the businessman is thus figured as not simply personal but as a defiant assertion of Mexican nationalism in the face of the capitalist exploitation of underclass labourers lacking legal recourse to challenge their subordination – as suggested by the trailer's image of an army of Latinos wielding machetes (Figure C.1), a tool potentially used in underpaid garden work for the aesthetic benefit of affluent white Americans. In the American national imagination, Mexico represents a sort of repressed otherness 'as an uncanny figure for the United States because the continental proximity of the two countries and their shared revolutionary histories make them estranged national neighbors'.[11] With its images of bloody uprisings and assassinations set against state capitol buildings, the *Machete* trailer thereby explicitly recalls a sort

Figure C.1 The image of machete-wielding Latino immigrants – led into retributive action by Danny Trejo's eponymous character in the original *Machete* trailer – raised white supremacist paranoia about a coming 'race war' and led to mild controversy over the use of Texas state film subsidies. (Source: DVD.)

of revolutionary violence as justice for the conditions faced by undocumented workers.

Esteban del Río argues that these appeals to sensational spectacle satirise the recurrent xenophobia of 'Brown Peril' discourses, because '[t]he ridiculousness of *Machete* fits in rather well with the far-fetched claims of reverse racism toward whites that characterize the current discourse of difference on the right'.[12] I would also suggest that retrosploitation's uneasy mix of earnestness and ironic self-awareness are addressed to a racially indeterminate viewer ideally well aware of the tongue-in-cheek tone that itself straddles borders between the not-so-mutually exclusive bounds of sincerity and irony, making difficult any blanket claims about the political valence of its reception. Yet, even though the trailer implicitly mocks how social conservatives often portray illegal immigration as a threat to US economic resources and national sovereignty, the issue is ironically raised here within a form simulating a pre-1990s period of film history when Hollywood's *own* position as a media capital was seemingly less threatened by potential competitors lurking beyond the United States's national borders.

Though the *Machete* trailer is modelled after other exploitation film trailers that primarily promote American capitalist interests on a basic level in trying to sell a cheaply made product to the broadest possible audience, it still speaks to serious concerns felt by many within the Latino American community today. It is notable that once *Machete* broke free from its positioning as a fake trailer situated within the larger *Grindhouse* omnibus film, its trailer for a stand-alone film was first leaked online with a filmed preface featuring Machete ominously implying that the following violence was 'a special Cinco de Mayo message . . . to Arizona!' This allusion to Arizona Senate Bill 1070, the harsh anti-immigration bill passed into state law less than two weeks earlier in April 2010, created free publicity for the film, as far-right conservatives decried the trailer for supposedly inciting a coming 'race war' while being produced with Texas state film subsidies.[13] Because this new trailer was now promoting a feature-length film that could narratively elaborate upon the politics of the original (fake) trailer in far greater detail than was initially allowable by the constraints of the short form, Rodriguez could thus expand the stakes of his political engagement. While taking this explicitly political turn became one more exploitable element for drawing in potential viewers (including Latino audiences typically underserved by Hollywood films), it also brings exploitative national histories to bear in ways not often seen in commercial genre cinema.

In addition to travelling quickly and easily across borders, albeit promoting national ideologies and industries along the way, the trailer as a paratextual form does not lay out a linear plot summary or a strictly self-contained overview; instead, the non-linear and fragmentary qualities of trailers offer multiple points of access, cuing viewers' imaginations to prospectively fill in the gaps between such intriguing images. The trailer, like the nation itself, can be entered at many different points, despite its creators' inevitably partial efforts to control how people gain access to it. The *Machete* trailer thus potentially reflects issues of illicit border crossings in both form and content which is especially ironic at a time when trailers are allowed to circulate online and elsewhere more freely, whereas legal copyright control over intellectual property remains more rigorously policed than ever. The logic of media convergence is internally conflicted between media producers encouraging viewers to actively participate by appropriating and reworking legally protected properties, yet setting unclear limits on how viewers can make use of such material without violating copyright law.[14] The original, *fake Machete* trailer, for example, is embedded (and legally expected to remain) within a larger copyrighted work, so it is more strongly protected than the *real* trailer for the later feature film, despite the latter trailer's greater economic importance in promoting the realised *Machete* feature around the world. Nevertheless, both trailers have circulated widely, whether in bootleg or officially sanctioned forms, owing to the desires of globally dispersed fans taking advantage of the same high-speed information networks that allow for the functioning of transnational capital.

By inevitably crossing borders with varying degrees of legality, these two trailers point towards the arbitrary limits placed upon national boundaries, industrial practices and legal restrictions upheld by the state. Like loudly voiced concerns about bodies illegally crossing borders (such as long-standing fears about drug and arms trafficking between the United States and Mexico), media corporations and trade organisations routinely voice concerns about media products illegally travelling across borders, especially through piracy. Yet, as Barbara Klinger argues, piracy is not necessarily antithetical to the work of media producers because it 'helps to maintain a visibility and desire for Hollywood cinema in corners of the world that might lack access to viable film outlets or be more strongly defined than they already are by indigenous films or other popular national cinemas on the global stage'.[15] We might similarly argue that labouring bodies crossing national borders are not substantial threats to American capitalism, since 'illegal' immigrants, such as those who head north to evade US-run *maquiladoras* in the Mexican borderlands, still contribute to the United States economy through taxes and support of local businesses in their adopted homes. While industry groups like the MPAA may rhetorically equate piracy with anti-American violence and organised crime, the multiple histories and rhetorics of violence raised by seemingly disposable paratexts like the *Machete* trailers suggest how violence (both actual and mediated) *always* struggles to contain cultural entities (people, texts, industries and so on) that invariably elude control. This is particularly ironic, however, because, in styling themselves after the look and feel of a pre-1990 exploitation film, *Machete*'s trailers recall a period before the 1989 signing of the North American Free Trade Agreement (NAFTA) which 'signaled the arrival of an era in which open borders would be essential to the region's prosperity' as goods and services could flow more easily between the United States, Mexico, and Canada.[16] In loosening trade restrictions, largely according to American wishes, NAFTA may have allowed transnational media corporations to exert greater economic influence throughout the continent but the agreement ultimately complicated their degree of control over the possible *uses* of their increasingly mobile products. As I have noted in this study, however, the very marginality of exploitation films, in particular, has allowed them sometimes to enter an indistinct copyright domain not strictly policed by conglomerates – especially by moving across national territories and video formats – thus exemplifying how historically contingent such textual afterlives can truly be.

If trailers position national ideologies and self-images upon the global stage, the *Machete* trailers present the United States as remembering cinematic and racial histories of exploitation that cannot be solely consigned to the past. These trailers figure the borderlands as not only a contested space between Mexico and the United States but also between past and present, with nationalism playing out in conflicting ways therein. Much like the simulated scratches and discoloration that seem to have done significant damage to the film print itself, the reciprocally supporting concepts of 'nation' and 'history' show their cracks in *Machete*'s vision of retribution undertaken by those who still suffer from the imposition of national borders upon an imagined region (*Aztlán*) that was their originary claim. If these trailers – like all trailers – nevertheless implicitly promote an ostensibly 'national' cinema, then perhaps their overt emphasis on violence and spectacle reflects the threat of subordination lurking at the heart of American exceptionalism and US-based capitalist interests. Those who refuse to accept the 'sovereign' rights of state and capital become the marginalised and the 'fucked with' (to use the trailer's apt phrasing).

Yet, as a tool of transnational capital, *Machete*'s trailers can perhaps go only so far, limiting this playful revenge fantasy to the realm of the adolescent imagination. That is, the trailers' anachronistic look can also suggest that this violent fantasy is ultimately insufficient as a viable answer to the political exigencies faced by Latinos today, except as nostalgically remembered traces of Mexico and the United States' revolutionary pasts. Importantly, then, as I have argued in these final chapters, the possible perception of simulated pastness as a marker of cultural fantasies too outdated to be taken seriously is one of the major obstacles facing the progressive potential in any retrosploitation film. Consequently, the streak of pathos recalled in the deliberately archaic retro film receives part of its affective resonance from the sympathetic viewer's recognition that such politicised fantasies may be unlikely ever to bleed over from the film-historical imaginary into real-world efficacy – although whether this sensed disparity between actual and imagined action is an impediment or an incentive towards productive political participation by fans remains a tantalising question.

Unlike undocumented workers, such as Machete himself, trailers are openly encouraged by transnational media conglomerates to do their work wherever they can, facing few detriments for travelling across borders. Placed in the service of capital's global reach, the *Machete* trailers may point towards contradictions in the American national project but their paratextual uses as promotional tools may offer less of a coherent challenge to the nation than yet more commodifiable fragments which can be subsumed into a nationalistic sense of archived history. In this sense, their simulated pastness seemingly signals a speedy relegation into the realm of older cinematic material being repurposed on to newer digital video formats as marketable containers of nostalgia for the United States' ever-growing cinematic heritage. Nevertheless, reducing the *Machete* trailers' evocation of so many unresolved historical and political tensions to a simple case of ideological co-optation would merely reproduce the common belief that nostalgia is necessarily conservative – an idea that I have repeatedly tried to dispel in this book. Instead, accounting for the multivalent uses of nostalgia – even when anxiously coexisting within the same text, consumption site or fan culture – remains a valuable task for any scholar scanning a media object's possible horizon of reception.

As I have demonstrated, the taste valuations linked to pastness raise the political stakes of interpretation and circulation in contemporary film and video culture, providing lessons for media study beyond simply revising our understanding of exploitation cinema's ongoing appeal. This book has been, in one sense, an archaeology of recent mnemonic uses of exploitation cinema's past. In another sense, however, these case studies have evoked the social implications of intrapersonal and interpersonal desires existing among niche consumer cultures that are both linked together and separated from each other on the basis of contested memories. Likewise, as much as these chapters have focused on the remembered sites of media consumption, they have also broached the shifting role of materiality in digital culture, which will no doubt remain a topic of concern for future studies of emergent and residual media.

Yet, when it comes to the specific texts under consideration in this study, one of the largest open questions is how their reception will change with the accumulation of more historical distance (and attendant claims to subcultural capital) from their period of (re)entering the marketplace. That is, when *Grindhouse* or *Machete* are no longer retro-styled products of the quite recent past but, rather, come to occupy the more nebulous gulf of time currently shared by their historical referents, how will future audiences respond to their self-conscious interplay of pastness and presentness? These films may never be wholly mistaken for their cinematic predecessors (nor has that ever really been their goal) but, whether viewed on a new technology which we cannot yet foresee or on the residual technology that Blu-ray will one day become, they may indeed help us acutely recognise 'the historicity of our feelings' at a particular moment in time.[17] Will these films and video objects be understood as symptomatic of our society's former fears about the impending demise of cinema/celluloid/tape/physicality altogether, or just another in a long series of historical spasms over shifts in our technologies of memory? At the risk of upholding a conveniently linear thread of historical rationalisation, I would cautiously veer towards the latter explanation, even as I still cherish my carefully arranged DVD collection, my obscure VHS tapes, and the battered shipping label that sits framed above my desk as I write these words – a surviving piece of ephemera reminding me that a 35 mm print of *Kung Fu: The Punch of Death* (1974) played at the Empire theatre on 42nd Street in December 1982, two weeks before I was born.

Notes

1. Stephen Barber, *Abandoned Images: Film and Film's End* (London: Reaktion Books, 2010), pp. 34–6.
2. Ibid., p. 60.
3. Caetlin Benson-Allott, *Killer Tapes and Shattered Screens: Video Spectatorship from VHS to File Sharing* (Berkeley: University of California Press, 2013), pp. 10–12.
4. Richard Terdiman, *Present Past: Modernity and the Memory Crisis* (Ithaca, NY: Cornell University Press, 1993), p. 8. Original italics.
5. José van Dijck, *Mediated Memories in the Digital Age* (Stanford, CA: Stanford University Press, 2007), p. 16.
6. Jason Sperb, 'Be Kind . . . Rewind/Or, The A–Zs of an American *Off-Modern Cinephilia*', in *Cinephilia in the Age of Digital Reproduction*, Vol. 2, eds Scott Balcerzak and Jason Sperb (London: Wallflower Press, 2012), p. 93. Original italics.
7. Michael Curtin, 'Media Capital: Towards the Study of Spatial Flows', *International Journal of Cultural Studies* 6, no. 2 (2003): 202–28.
8. Andrew Higson, 'The Limiting Imagination of National Cinema', in *Transnational Cinema: The Film Reader*, eds Elizabeth Ezra and Terry Rowden (London: Routledge, 2006), p. 19.
9. Meaghan Morris, 'Transnational Imagination in Action Cinema: Hong Kong and the Making of a Global Popular Culture', *Inter-Asia Cultural Studies* 5, no. 2 (2004): 189.
10. For example, see Tamara L. Falicov, 'US–Argentine Co-productions, 1982–1990: Roger Corman, Aries Productions, "Schlockbuster" Movies, and the International Market', *Film & History* 34, no. 1 (2004): 36.
11. Jesse Alemán, 'The Other Country: Mexico, the United States, and the Gothic History of Conquest', in *Hemispheric American Studies*, eds Caroline F. Levander and Robert S. Levine (New Brunswick, NJ: Rutgers University Press, 2008), p. 77.
12. Esteban del Río, '¡VIVA LA BROWN PERIL! The Political and Temporal Landscape of *Machete*', *Flow* 12, no. 8 (September 2010): http://flowtv.org/2010/09/viva-la-brown-peril/ (accessed 15 October 2010).
13. Jay A. Fernandez and Borys Kit, 'How "Machete" Inflames Immigration Debate', *The Hollywood Reporter*, 27 August 2010, http://www.hollywoodreporter.com/news/how-machete-inflames-immigration-debate-27149 (accessed 27 August 2010); Alex Jones and Aaron Dykes, 'New Film "Machete" Evokes Race War', Prison Planet, last modified 9 May 2010, http://www.prisonplanet.com/new-film-%E2%80%98machete%E2%80%99-evokes-

race-war.html (accessed 4 April 2012); and Kurt Nimmo, 'Confirmed: "Machete" is a Race War Epic', Prison Planet, last modified 4 September 2010, http://www.prisonplanet.com/machete-race-war-propaganda-under-the-cover-of-a-mexploitation-film.html (accessed 4 April 2012). For a more comprehensive discussion of the finished feature film itself, see Marina Wood, '"Machete Improvises": Racial Rhetoric in Digital Reception of Robert Rodriguez's *Machete*', *Jump Cut*, no. 54 (2012): http://www.ejumpcut.org/currentissue/MWoodMachete/index.html (accessed 15 November 2012).

14. Henry Jenkins, *Convergence Culture: Where Old and New Media Collide* (New York: New York University Press, 2006), pp. 142, 173.
15. Barbara Klinger, 'Contraband Cinema: Piracy, *Titanic*, and Central Asia', *Cinema Journal* 49, no. 2 (2010): 108.
16. Rachel Adams, *Continental Divides: Remapping the Cultures of North America* (Chicago: University of Chicago Press, 2009), p. 190.
17. Richard Dyer, *Pastiche* (London: Routledge, 2007), p. 130.

APPENDIX

Selected Filmography and Videography of Retrosploitation Media

Feature Films
Back to the Beach (Lyndall Hobbs, 1987)
I'm Gonna Git You Sucka (Keenan Ivory Wayans, 1988)
Matinee (Joe Dante, 1993)
Ed Wood (Tim Burton, 1994)
Pulp Fiction (Quentin Tarantino, 1994)
Teenage Tupelo (John Michael McCarthy, 1995)
From Dusk Till Dawn (Robert Rodriguez, 1996)
5 Dead on the Crimson Canvas (Joseph F. Parda, 1996)
Original Gangstas (Larry Cohen, 1996)
Mystery Science Theater 3000: The Movie (Jim Mallon, 1996)
Boogie Nights (Paul Thomas Anderson, 1997)
The Bloody Ape (Keith J. Crocker, 1997)
Jackie Brown (Quentin Tarantino, 1997)
I Woke Up Early the Day I Died (Aris Iliopulos, 1998)
Psycho Beach Party (Robert Lee King, 2000)
The Corpse Grinders 2 (Ted V. Mikels, 2000)
The Double-D Avenger (William Winkler, 2001)
Satan Was a Lady (Doris Wishman, 2001)
Pandora Peaks (Russ Meyer, 2001)
The Lost Skeleton of Cadavra (Larry Blamire, 2001)
CQ (Roman Coppola, 2001)
Blood Feast 2: All U Can Eat (Herschell Gordon Lewis, 2002)
Mark of the Astro-Zombies (Ted V. Mikels, 2002)
Dildo Heaven (Doris Wishman, 2002)
Baadasssss! (Mario Van Peebles, 2003)
House of 1000 Corpses (Rob Zombie, 2003)
The Manson Family (Jim Van Bebber, 2003)
Killer Drag Queens on Dope (Lazar Saric, 2003)
Lustful Addiction (Erin Brown, 2003)
Kill Bill, Vol. 1 (Quentin Tarantino, 2003)
Kill Bill, Vol. 2 (Quentin Tarantino, 2004)

Bettie Page: Dark Angel (Nico B., 2004)
Frog-g-g! (Cody Jarrett, 2004)
The Seduction of Misty Mundae (Michael Raso, 2004)
Suburban Secrets (Joe Sarno, 2004)
Pervert! (Jonathan Yudis, 2005)
The Notorious Bettie Page (Mary Harron, 2005)
Reefer Madness: The Movie Musical (Andy Fickman, 2005)
The Devil's Rejects (Rob Zombie, 2005)
Chaos (David DeFalco, 2005)
Black Snake Moan (Craig Brewer, 2006)
Grindhouse (Robert Rodriguez, Eli Roth, Quentin Tarantino, Edgar Wright, Rob Zombie, 2007)
Planet Terror (Robert Rodriguez, 2007)
Death Proof (Quentin Tarantino, 2007)
Sukiyaki Western Django (Miike Takashi, 2007)
Viva (Anna Biller, 2007)
Welcome to the Jungle (Jonathan Hensleigh, 2007)
Finishing the Game: The Search for a New Bruce Lee (Justin Lin, 2007)
Black Devil Doll (Jonathan Lewis, 2007)
Chantal (Tony Marsiglia, 2007)
Each Time I Kill (Doris Wishman, 2007)
Hell Ride (Larry Bishop, 2008)
Beyond the Dunwich Horror (Richard Griffin, 2008)
Blitzkrieg: Escape from Stalag 69 (Keith J. Crocker, 2008)
Endless Orgy for the Goddess of Perversion (Trace Burroughs, 2008)
The Machine Girl (Iguchi Noboru, 2008)
Sex Galaxy (Mike Davis, 2008)
Sugar Boxx (Cody Jarrett, 2009)
Smash Cut (Lee Demarbre, 2009)
Dead Hooker in a Trunk (Jen and Sylvia Soska, 2009)
The House of the Devil (Ti West, 2009)
Stuck! (Steve Balderson, 2009)
Blood Moon Rising (Brian Skiba, 2009)
The Minstrel Killer (Michael Fredianelli, 2009)
The Lost Skeleton Returns Again (Larry Blamire, 2009)
Death Stop Holocaust (Justin Russell, 2009)
Amer (Hélène Cattet and Bruno Forzani, 2009)
Modus Operandi (Frankie Latina, 2009)
Mutilation Mile (Ron Atkins, 2009)
Bitch Slap (Rick Jacobson, 2009)
Black Dynamite (Scott Sanders, 2009)
Nun of That (Richard Griffin, 2009)
Run! Bitch Run! (Joseph Guzman, 2009)
Hora (Reinert Kiil, 2009)

The Uh-Oh Show (Herschell Gordon Lewis, 2009)
Dead Snow (Tommy Wirkola, 2009)
Samurai Avenger: The Blind Wolf (Mitsutake Kurando, 2009)
Machete (Robert Rodriguez and Ethan Maniquis, 2010)
Ticked-Off Trannies With Knives (Israel Luna, 2010)
Sharktopus (Declan O'Brien, 2010)
Nude Nuns with Big Guns (Joseph Guzman, 2010)
Beyond the Black Rainbow (Panos Cosmatos, 2010)
El Monstro del Mar! (Stuart Simpson, 2010)
Hobo with a Shotgun (Jason Eisener, 2011)
Cherry Bomb (Kyle Day, 2011)
Shriek of the Sasquatch! (Steve Sessions, 2011)
Manborg (Steven Kostanski, 2011)
Rat Scratch Fever (Jeff Leroy, 2011)
Chillerama (Adam Green, Joe Lynch, Bear McCreary, Adam Rifkin, Tim Sullivan, 2011)
Father's Day (Adam Brooks, Jeremy Gillespie, Matt Kennedy, Steven Kostanski, Conor Sweeney, 2011)
Dear God No! (James Bickert, 2011)
The Disco Exorcist (Richard Griffin, 2011)
Climb It, Tarzan! (Jared Masters, 2011)
A Cadaver Christmas (Joe Zerull, 2011)
The Victim (Michael Biehn, 2011)
The Sleeper (Justin Russell, 2012)
Casa de mi Padre (Matt Piedmont, 2012)
The Ghastly Love of Johnny X (Paul Bunnell, 2012)
Bloody Bloody Bible Camp (Vito Trabucco, 2012)
The Man with the Iron Fists (RZA, 2012)
Iron Sky (Timo Vuorensola, 2012)
Berberian Sound Studio (Peter Strickland, 2012)
The Lords of Salem (Rob Zombie, 2012)
Bring Me the Head of the Machine Gun Woman (Ernesto Díaz Espinoza, 2012)
Girls Against Boys (Austin Chick, 2012)
8 Reels of Sewage (Jared Masters, 2012)
Crack Whore (Lance Polland, 2012)
Sushi Girl (Kern Saxton, 2012)
Lovelace (Rob Epstein and Jeffrey Friedman, 2013)
Machete Kills (Robert Rodriguez, 2013)
Big Hair, Long Lashes (Jared Masters, 2013)
The Green Inferno (Eli Roth, 2013)
The Strange Colour of Your Body's Tears (Hélène Cattet and Bruno Forzani, 2013)
Snap Shot (Frankie Latina, 2014)

Feature-length Documentaries

Drive-In Madness! (Tim Ferrante, 1987)
Sex and Buttered Popcorn (Sam Harrison, 1989)
On the Trail of Ed Wood (Michael Copner, 1990)
The Legend of Dolemite (Foster V. Corder, 1994)
Ed Wood: Look Back in Angora (Ted Newsom, 1994)
Schlock! The Secret History of American Movies (Ray Greene, 2001)
Mau Mau Sex Sex (Ted Bonnitt, 2001)
Drive-in Movie Memories (Kurt Kuenne, 2001)
Coffin Joe: The Strange World of José Mojica Marins (André Barcinski and Ivan Finotti, 2001)
Baadasssss Cinema (Isaac Julien, 2002)
Inside Deep Throat (Fenton Bailey and Randy Barbato, 2005)
American Stag (Benjamin Meade, 2006)
Going to Pieces: The Rise and Fall of the Slasher Film (J. Albert Bell, Rachel Belofsky, Michael Derek Bohusz, 2006)
Spine Tingler! The William Castle Story (Jeffery Schwarz, 2007)
Triple X Selects: The Best of Lezsploitation (Michelle Johnson, 2007)
Not Quite Hollywood: The Wild, Untold Story of Ozploitation! (Mark Hartley, 2008)
The Wild World of Ted V. Mikels (Kevin Sean Michaels, 2008)
Best Worst Movie (Michael Stephenson, 2009)
Popatopolis (Clay Westervelt, 2009)
American Grindhouse (Elijah Drenner, 2010)
Video Nasties: Moral Panic, Censorship, and Videotape (Jake West, 2010)
Machete Maidens Unleashed! (Mark Hartley, 2010)
Herschell Gordon Lewis: The Godfather of Gore (Frank Henenlotter and Jimmy Maslon, 2010)
Corman's World: Exploits of a Hollywood Rebel (Alex Stapleton, 2011)
Dad Made Dirty Movies (Jordan Todorov, 2011)
Films of Fury: The Kung Fu Movie Movie (Andrew Corvey and Andrew W. Robinson, 2011)
Screaming in High Heels: The Rise and Fall of the Scream Queen Era (Jason Paul Collum, 2011)
I Am Bruce Lee (Pete McCormack, 2012)
Bettie Page Reveals All! (Mark Mori, 2012)
Eurocrime! The Italian Cop and Gangster Films That Ruled the '70s (Mike Malloy, 2012)
Slice and Dice: The Slasher Film Forever (Calum Waddell, 2012)
The Sarnos: A Life in Dirty Movies (Wiktor Ericsson, 2013)
Going Attractions: The Definitive Story of the American Drive-In Movie (April Wright, 2013)
Adjust Your Tracking: The Untold Story of the VHS Collector (Dan M. Kinem and Levi Peretic, 2013)

Rewind This! (Josh Johnson, 2013)
That's Sexploitation! (Frank Henenlotter, 2013)
That Guy Dick Miller (Elijah Drenner, 2014)
The Creep Behind the Camera (Pete Schuermann, 2014)
Plastic Movies Rewound: The Story of the '80s Home Video Boom (Mike Malloy, 2014)
Electric Boogaloo: The Wild, Untold Story of Cannon Films (Mark Hartley, 2014)
42nd Street Memories: The Rise and Fall of America's Most Notorious Street (Calum Waddell, 2014)

Short Films, Web Series and Music Videos
RZA – 'Tragedy' (RZA, 1997)
Beastie Boys – 'Body Movin'' (MCA, 1998)
Black XXX-Mas (Pieter Van Hees, 1999)
Roxanna (Ted W. Crestview, 2002)
Pleasures of a Woman (Ted W. Crestview, 2002)
New York Wildcats (Johnny Crash, 2005)
Muse – 'Knights of Cydonia' (Joseph Kahn, 2006)
Tales of Times Square (Paul Stone, 2006)
Trailers from Hell (Joe Dante, et al., 2007–present)
Foxxy Madonna vs the Black Death (Jakob Bilinski, 2007)
Treevenge (Jason Eisener, 2008)
Stephen Romano's Shock Festival (Stephen Romano, Victor Bonacore, Michael Gingold, Richard Griffin, compilation, 2009)
'ABSOLUT Lemon Drop' (Traktor, 2010)
Lady Gaga – 'Telephone' (Jonas Akerlund, 2010)
Mother Superior: Let There Be Lead (Matthew Scott Johnston, 2010)
Thy Kill Be Done (Greg Hanson and Casey Regan, 2010)
Missing Reel (Kurt Loyd and David Walker, 2010)
Lost Trailer Park: Never Coming Attractions (Chris LaMartina, 2010–11)
Wu-Tang vs the Golden Phoenix (RZA, 2011)
Mike Pecci's Grindhouse Shorts (Mike Pecci, compilation, 2011)
I Was a Teenage Werebear (Tim Sullivan, 2011)
Sisters of No Mercy (Joseph R. Lewis and Lew Ojeda, 2011)
Astron-6 (Adam Brooks, Jeremy Gillespie, Matt Kennedy, Steven Kostanski, Conor Sweeney, compilation, 2011)
The Mercury Men (Christopher Preska, 2011)
Daddy Cross (Evrim Ersoy, James Pearcey, Russell Would, 2012)

Television Series
Joe Bob Briggs's Drive-In Theater (The Movie Channel, 1987–96)
Mystery Science Theater 3000 (KTMA/Comedy Central/Sci-Fi Channel, 1988–99)
Rebel Highway (Showtime, 1994)

MonsterVision (TNT, 1996–2000)
Creature Features (Cinemax, 2001)
Look Around You (BBC2, 2002–05)
Garth Marenghi's Darkplace (Channel 4, 2004)
Black Dynamite (Adult Swim, 2012–)

Video Games
House of the Dead: Overkill (Headstrong Games, 2009)
Call of Duty: Black Ops ('Call of the Dead' episode) (Treyarch, 2011)
Lollipop Chainsaw (Grasshopper Manufacture, 2012)

Selected Bibliography

Adams, Rachel. *Continental Divides: Remapping the Cultures of North America*. Chicago: University of Chicago Press, 2009.

Alemán, Jesse. 'The Other Country: Mexico, the United States, and the Gothic History of Conquest'. In *Hemispheric American Studies*, edited by Caroline F. Levander and Robert S. Levine, pp. 75–95. New Brunswick, NJ: Rutgers University Press, 2008.

Allen, Robert C. *Horrible Prettiness: Burlesque and American Culture*. Chapel Hill: University of North Carolina Press, 1991.

—'Relocating American Film History: The "Problem" of the Empirical'. *Cultural Studies* 20, no. 1 (2006): 48–88.

Altman, Rick. *Film/Genre*. London: British Film Institute, 1999.

American Society of Planning Officials. *Planning Advisory Service: Drive-in Theaters*. Information Report no. 9. Chicago: American Society of Planning Officials, 1949.

Andrews, David. *Soft in the Middle: The Contemporary Softcore Feature in Its Contexts*. Columbus: Ohio State University Press, 2006.

Austin, Bruce A. 'The Development and Decline of the Drive-In Movie Theater'. In *Current Research in Film: Audiences, Economics, and Law*, vol. 1, edited by Bruce A. Austin, pp. 59–91. Norwood, NJ: Ablex, 1985.

Badley, Linda. 'Bringing It All Back Home: Horror Cinema and Video Culture'. In *Horror Zone: The Cultural Experience of Contemporary Horror Cinema*, edited by Ian Conrich, pp. 45–63. London: I. B. Tauris, 2010.

Barber, Stephen. *Abandoned Images: Film and Film's End*. London: Reaktion Books, 2010.

Barker, Jennifer M. *The Tactile Eye: Touch and the Cinematic Experience*. Berkeley: University of California Press, 2009.

Beauregard, Robert A. *Voices of Decline: The Postwar Fate of U.S. Cities*. 2nd ed. New York: Routledge, 2003.

Benson-Allott, Caetlin. '*Grindhouse*: An Experiment in the Death of Cinema'. *Film Quarterly* 62, no. 1 (2008): 20–4.

—*Killer Tapes and Shattered Screens: Video Spectatorship from VHS to File Sharing*. Berkeley: University of California Press, 2013.

Berenstein, Rhona J. *Attack of the Leading Ladies: Gender, Sexuality, and Spectatorship in Classical Horror Cinema*. New York: Columbia University Press, 1996.

Berman, Marshall. 'Too Much is Not Enough: Metamorphoses of Times Square'. In *Impossible Presence: Surface and Screen in the Photogenic Era*, edited by Terry Smith, pp. 39–70. Chicago: University of Chicago Press, 2001.

Betz, Mark. 'Art, Exploitation, Underground'. In *Defining Cult Movies: The Cultural Politics of Oppositional Taste*, edited by Mark Jancovich, Antonio Lázaro Reboll, Julian Stringer and Andy Willis, pp. 202–22. Manchester: Manchester University Press, 2003.

Bianco, Anthony. *Ghosts of 42nd Street: A History of America's Most Infamous Block*. New York: William Morrow, 2004.

Blake, Linnie. '"I Am the Devil and I'm Here to Do the Devil's Work": Rob Zombie, George W. Bush, and the Limits of American Freedom'. In *Horror After 9/11: World of Fear, Cinema of Terror*, edited by Aviva Briefel and Sam J. Miller, pp. 186–99. Austin: University of Texas Press, 2011.

Bolter, Jay David and Richard Grusin. *Remediation: Understanding New Media*. Cambridge, MA: MIT Press, 2000.

Booth, W. James. *Communities of Memory: On Witness, Identity, and Justice*. Ithaca, NY: Cornell University Press, 2006.

Bourdieu, Pierre. *Distinction: A Social Critique of the Judgment of Taste*. Translated by Richard Nice. Cambridge, MA: Harvard University Press, 1984.

Boym, Svetlana. *The Future of Nostalgia*. New York: Basic Books, 2001.

Boyreau, Jacques. *Portable Grindhouse: The Lost Art of the VHS Box*. Seattle: Fantagraphics Books, 2009.

Briggs, Joe Bob. *Joe Bob Goes to the Drive-In*. New York: Delacorte Press, 1986.

Briggs, Joe Bob, J. Hoberman, Damien Love, Tim Lucas, Danny Peary, Jeffrey Sconce and Peter Stanfield. 'Cult Cinema: A Critical Symposium'. *Cineaste* 34, no. 1 (2008): 43–50.

Brooker, Will. 'A Sort of Homecoming: Fan Viewing and Symbolic Pilgrimage'. In *Fandom: Identities and Communities in a Mediated World*, edited by Jonathan Gray, Cornel Sandvoss, and C. Lee Harrington, pp. 149–64. New York: New York University Press, 2007.

Bruno, Giuliana. *Atlas of Emotion: Journeys in Art, Architecture, and Film*. New York: Verso, 2002.

Buszek, Maria Elena. *Pin-Up Grrrls: Feminism, Sexuality, Popular Culture*. Durham, NC: Duke University Press, 2006.

Cante, Rich and Angelo Restivo. 'The Cultural-Aesthetic Specificities of All-male Moving-Image Pornography'. In *Porn Studies*, edited by Linda Williams, pp. 142–66. Durham, NC: Duke University Press, 2004.

Casey, Edward S. *Remembering: A Phenomenological Study*. 2nd ed. Bloomington: Indiana University Press, 2000.

Cha-Jua, Sundiata Keita. 'Black Audiences, Blaxploitation and Kung Fu Films, and Challenges to White Celluloid Masculinity'. In *China Forever: The Shaw Brothers and Diasporic Cinema*, edited by Poshek Fu, pp. 199–223. Champaign: University of Illinois Press, 2008.

Chibnall, Steve. 'Double Exposures: Observations on *The Flesh and Blood Show*'. In *Trash Aesthetics: Popular Culture and its Audience*, edited by Deborah Cartmell, I. Q. Hunter, Heidi Kaye, and Imelda Whelehan, pp. 84–102. London: Pluto Press, 1997.

Church, David. 'One on Top of the Other: Lucio Fulci, Transnational Film Industries, and the Retrospective Construction of the Italian Horror Canon'. *Quarterly Review of Film and Video* 32, no. 4 (2015), forthcoming.

Ciasullo, Ann. 'Containing "Deviant" Desire: Lesbianism, Heterosexuality, and the Women-in-Prison Narrative'. *Journal of Popular Culture* 41, no. 2 (2008): 195–223.

Clover, Carol J. *Men, Women, and Chainsaws: Gender in the Modern Horror Film*. Princeton, NJ: Princeton University Press, 1992.

Congressional Budget Office. *Trends in the Distribution of Household Income Between 1979 and 2007*. Washington, DC: Congressional Budget Office, 2011.

Conrich, Ian. 'Communitarianism, Film Entrepreneurism, and the Crusade of Troma Entertainment'. In *Contemporary American Independent Film: From the Margins to the Mainstream*, edited by Chris Holmlund and Justin Wyatt, pp. 107–22. New York: Routledge, 2005.

Cook, Pam. *Screening the Past: Memory and Nostalgia in Cinema*. London: Routledge, 2005.

Cope, Demetrius. 'Anatomy of a Blaxploitation Theater'. *Jump Cut*, no. 9 (1975): 22–3.

Corkin, Stanley. *Starring New York: Filming the Grime and the Glamour of the Long 1970s*. New York: Oxford University Press, 2011.

Corman, Roger with Jim Jerome. *How I Made a Hundred Movies in Hollywood and Never Lost a Dime*. New York: Random House, 1990.

Coulthard, Lisa. 'Killing Bill: Rethinking Feminism and Film Violence'. In *Interrogating Postfeminism: Gender and the Politics of Popular Culture*, edited by Yvonne Tasker and Diane Negra, pp. 153–75. Durham, NC: Duke University Press, 2007.

Craig, Pamela and Martin Fradley. 'Teenage Traumata: Youth, Affective Politics, and the Contemporary American Horror Film'. In *American Horror Film: The Genre at the Turn of the Millennium*, edited by Steffen Hantke, pp. 77–102. Jackson: University Press of Mississippi, 2010.

Crane, Jonathan L. 'A Lust for Life: The Cult Films of Russ Meyer'. In *Unruly Pleasures: The Cult Film and its Critics*, pp. 88–101. Guildford: FAB Press, 2000.

Crank, James A. 'An Aesthetic of Play: A Contemporary Cinema of South-Sploitation'. In *Southerners on Film: Essays on Hollywood Portrayals Since the 1970s*, edited by Andrew B. Leiter, pp. 204–16. Jefferson, NC: McFarland, 2011.

Cubitt, Sean. *Timeshift: On Video Culture*. London: Routledge, 1991.

Curtin, Michael. 'Media Capital: Towards the Study of Spatial Flows'. *International Journal of Cultural Studies* 6, no. 2 (2003): 202–28.

Davis, Blair. *The Battle for the Bs: 1950s Hollywood and the Rebirth of Low-Budget Cinema*. New Brunswick, NJ: Rutgers University Press, 2012.
Davis, Fred. *Yearning for Yesterday: A Sociology of Nostalgia*. New York: The Free Press, 1979.
Davis, Glyn. 'A Taste for *Leeches!* DVDs, Audience Configurations, and Generic Hybridity'. In *Film and Television After DVD*, edited by James Bennett and Tom Brown, pp. 45–62. New York: Routledge, 2008.
Delany, Samuel R. *Times Square Red, Times Square Blue*. New York: New York University Press, 1999.
Del Río, Esteban. '¡VIVA LA BROWN PERIL! The Political and Temporal Landscape of *Machete*'. *Flow* 12, no. 8 (September 2010): http://flowtv.org/2010/09/viva-la-brown-peril/ (accessed 15 October 2010).
Desjardins, Mary. 'Ephemeral Culture/eBay Culture: Film Collectibles and Fan Investments'. In *Everyday eBay: Culture, Collecting, and Desire*, edited by Ken Hillis, Michael Petit, and Nathan Scott Epley, pp. 31–43. New York: Routledge, 2006.
Despentes, Virginie. *King Kong Theory*. Translated by Stéphanie Benson. New York: The Feminist Press, 2010.
De Ville, Donna. 'Cultivating the Cult Experience at the Alamo Drafthouse Cinema'. *Scope*, no. 20 (2011): http://www.scope.nottingham.ac.uk/article.php?issue=20&id=1306 (accessed 24 November 2011).
Dika, Vera. *Recycled Culture in Contemporary Art and Film: The Uses of Nostalgia*. Cambridge: Cambridge University Press, 2003.
Doherty, Thomas. *Teenagers and Teenpics: The Juvenilization of American Movies in the 1950s*. Philadelphia: Temple University Press, 2002.
Donahue, Suzanne Mary. *American Film Distribution: The Changing Marketplace*. Ann Arbor, MI: UMI Research Press, 1987.
Downs, Anthony. 'Where the Drive-in Fits into the Movie Industry'. In *Exhibition: The Film Reader*, edited by Ina Rae Hark, pp. 123–6. London: Routledge, 2002.
Dyer, Richard. *Pastiche*. London: Routledge, 2007.
Egan, Kate. *Trash or Treasure? Censorship and the Changing Meanings of the Video Nasties*. Manchester: Manchester University Press, 2007.
Elsaesser, Thomas. 'Cinephilia or the Uses of Disenchantment'. In *Cinephilia: Movies, Love, and Memory*, edited by Marijke de Valck and Malte Hagener, pp. 27–43. Amsterdam: Amsterdam University Press, 2005.
Esch, Kevin. '"The Lesser of the Attractions": *Grindhouse* and Theatrical Nostalgia'. *Jump Cut*, no. 54 (2012): http://www.ejumpcut.org/currentissue/EschGrindhouse/index.html (accessed 4 November 2012).
Falicov, Tamara L. 'US–Argentine Co-productions, 1982–1990: Roger Corman, Aries Productions, "Schlockbuster" Movies, and the International Market'. *Film & History* 34, no. 1 (2004): 31–9.
Frank, Stanley. 'Sure-Seaters Discover an Audience (1952)'. In *Moviegoing in America: A Sourcebook in the History of Film Exhibition*, edited by Gregory A. Waller, pp. 255–8. Malden, MA: Blackwell, 2002.

Frank, Thomas. *The Conquest of Cool: Business Culture, Counterculture, and the Rise of Hip Consumerism*. Chicago: University of Chicago Press, 1997.
Freeman, Elizabeth. *Time Binds: Queer Temporalities, Queer Histories*. Durham, NC: Duke University Press, 2010.
Friedman, Andrea. *Prurient Interests: Gender, Democracy, and Obscenity in New York City, 1909–1945*. New York: Columbia University Press, 2000.
Friedman, David F. with Don de Nevi. *A Youth in Babylon: Confessions of a Trash-Film King*. Buffalo, NY: Prometheus Books, 1990.
Friedman, Josh Alan. *Tales of Times Square*. Los Angeles: Feral House, 2007.
Gomery, Douglas. *Shared Pleasures: A History of Movie Presentation in the United States*. Madison: University of Wisconsin Press, 1992.
Gordon, Bette and Karyn Kay. 'Look Back/Talk Back'. In *Dirty Looks: Women, Pornography, Power*, edited by Pamela Church Gibson and Roma Gibson, pp. 90–100. London: British Film Institute, 1993.
Gorfinkel, Elena. 'Cult Film, or Cinephilia by Any Other Name'. *Cineaste* 34, no. 1 (2008): 33–8.
— '"Dated Sexuality": Anna Biller's *Viva* and the Retrospective Life of Sexploitation Cinema'. *Camera Obscura* 26, no. 3 (2011): 94–135.
—'Tales of Times Square: Sexploitation's Secret History of Place'. In *Taking Place: Location and the Moving Image*, edited by John David Rhodes and Elena Gorfinkel, pp. 55–76. Minneapolis: University of Minnesota Press, 2011.
—'Unlikely Genres: An Interview with Anna Biller'. *Camera Obscura* 26, no. 3 (2011): 136–45.
Graham, Paula. 'Girl's Camp? The Politics of Parody'. In *Immortal, Invisible: Lesbians and the Moving Image*, edited by Tamsin Wilton, pp. 163–81. London: Routledge, 1995.
Gray, Jonathan. *Show Sold Separately: Promos, Spoilers, and Other Media Paratexts*. New York: New York University Press, 2010.
Greenberg, Joshua M. *From Betamax to Blockbuster: Video Stores and the Invention of Movies on Video*. Cambridge, MA: MIT Press, 2008.
Guerrero, Ed. *Framing Blackness: The African American Image in Film*. Philadelphia: Temple University Press, 1993.
Guffey, Elizabeth E. *Retro: The Culture of Revival*. London: Reaktion Books, 2006.
Guins, Raiford. 'Blood and Black Gloves on Shiny Discs: New Media, Old Tastes, and the Remediation of Italian Horror Films in the United States'. In *Horror International*, edited by Steven Jay Schneider and Tony Williams, pp. 15–32. Detroit: Wayne State University Press, 2005.
Gwenllian Jones, Sara. 'Phantom Menace: Killer Fans, Consumer Activism, and Digital Filmmakers'. In *Underground USA: Filmmaking Beyond the Hollywood Canon*, edited by Xavier Mendik and Steven Jay Schneider, pp. 169–79. London: Wallflower Press, 2002.

Halberstam, Judith. 'Imagined Violence/Queer Violence: Representation, Rage, and Resistance'. *Social Text*, no. 37 (1993): 187–201.
—*The Queer Art of Failure*. Durham, NC: Duke University Press, 2011.
Hansen, Miriam Bratu. 'Benjamin and Cinema: Not a One-Way Street'. *Critical Inquiry* 25, no. 2 (1999): 306–43.
Hantke, Steffen. 'Introduction: They Don't Make 'Em Like They Used To: On the Rhetoric of Crisis and the Current State of American Horror Cinema'. In *American Horror Film: The Genre at the Turn of the Millennium*, edited by Steffen Hantke, pp. vii–xxxii. Jackson: University Press of Mississippi, 2010.
Hatch, Kristen. 'The Sweeter the Kitten, the Sharper the Claws: Russ Meyer's Bad Girls'. In *Bad: Infamy, Darkness, Evil, and Slime on Screen*, edited by Murray Pomerance, pp. 142–55. Albany: State University of New York Press, 2004.
Hawkins, Joan. *Cutting Edge: Art–Horror and the Horrific Avant-Garde*. Minneapolis: University of Minnesota Press, 2000.
Hediger, Vinzenz. 'The Original is Always Lost: Film History, Copyright Industries, and the Problem of Reconstruction'. In *Cinephilia: Movies, Love, and Memory*, edited by Marijke de Valck and Malte Hagener, pp. 135–49. Amsterdam: Amsterdam University Press, 2005.
Heffernan, Kevin. *Ghouls, Gimmicks, and Gold: Horror Films and the American Movie Business, 1953–1968*. Durham, NC: Duke University Press, 2004.
Herring, Scott. '"Hixploitation" Cinema, Regional Drive-Ins, and the Cultural Emergence of a New Queer Right', *GLQ* 20, no. 1–2 (2014): 95–113.
Higson, Andrew. 'The Limiting Imagination of National Cinema'. In *Transnational Cinema: The Film Reader*, edited by Elizabeth Ezra and Terry Rowden, pp. 15–26. London: Routledge, 2006.
Hilderbrand, Lucas. 'Retroactivism'. *GLQ* 12, no. 2 (2006): 303–17.
—*Inherent Vice: Bootleg Histories of Videotape and Copyright*. Durham, NC: Duke University Press, 2009.
Hillier, Jim and Aaron Lipstadt. 'The Economics of Independence: Roger Corman and New World Pictures, 1970–1980'. *Movie*, no. 31/32 (1986): 43–53.
Hills, Matt. *Fan Cultures*. London: Routledge, 2002.
—'*Star Wars* in Fandom, Film Theory, and the Museum: The Cultural Status of the Cult Blockbuster'. In *Movie Blockbusters*, edited by Julian Stringer, pp. 178–89. London: Routledge, 2003.
—*The Pleasures of Horror*. London: Continuum, 2005.
—'Para-Paracinema: The *Friday the 13th* Film Series as Other to Trash and Legitimate Film Cultures'. In *Sleaze Artists: Cinema at the Margins of Taste, Style, and Politics*, edited by Jeffrey Sconce, pp. 219–39. Durham, NC: Duke University Press, 2007.
—'Attending Horror Film Festivals and Conventions: Liveness, Subcultural Capital, and "Flesh-and-Blood Genre Communities"'. In *Horror Zone: The*

Cultural Experience of Contemporary Horror Cinema, edited by Ian Conrich, pp. 87–101. London: I. B. Tauris, 2010.

Hines, Claire. '"How Far Will a Girl Go to Satisfy Her Needs?": From Dykesploitation to Lesbian Hard-core'. In *Peep Shows: Cult Film and the Cine-Erotic*, edited by Xavier Mendik, pp. 206–18. New York: Wallflower Press, 2012.

Hollows, Joanne. 'The Masculinity of Cult'. In *Defining Cult Movies: The Cultural Politics of Oppositional Taste*, edited by Mark Jancovich, Antonio Lázaro Reboll, Julian Stringer, and Andy Willis, pp. 35–53. Manchester: Manchester University Press, 2003.

Horton, Andrew. 'Turning On and Tuning Out at the Drive-In: An American Phenomenon Survives and Thrives'. *Journal of Popular Film* 5, no. 3/4 (1976): 233–44.

Hoxter, Julian. 'Taking Possession: Cult Learning in *The Exorcist*'. In *Unruly Pleasures: The Cult Film and its Critics*, edited by Xavier Mendik and Graeme Harper, pp. 172–85. Guildford: FAB Press, 2000.

Hughes, Howard. *Cinema Italiano: The Complete Guide from Classics to Cult*. London: I. B. Tauris, 2011.

Huyssen, Andreas. *After the Great Divide: Modernism, Mass Culture, Postmodernism*. Bloomington: Indiana University Press, 1986.

— 'Present Pasts: Media, Politics, Amnesia'. *Public Culture* 12, no. 1 (2000): 21–38.

Inglis, Ruth A. *Freedom of the Movies*. Chicago: University of Chicago Press, 1947.

Jacobs, Lea. *The Decline of Sentiment: American Film in the 1920s*. Berkeley: University of California Press, 2008.

Jancovich, Mark. 'Cult Fictions: Cult Movies, Subcultural Capital, and the Production of Cultural Distinctions'. *Cultural Studies* 16, no. 2 (2002): 306–22.

Jancovich, Mark and Tim Snelson. 'Horror at the Crossroads: Class, Gender, and Taste at the Rialto'. In *From the Arthouse to the Grindhouse: Highbrow and Lowbrow Transgression in Cinema's First Century*, edited by John Cline and Robert G. Weiner, pp. 109–25. Lanham, MD: Scarecrow Press, 2010.

Jenkins, Henry. *Convergence Culture: Where Old and New Media Collide*. New York: New York University Press, 2006.

Johnson, Beth. 'Semblance and the Sexual Revolution: A Critical Review of *Viva*'. In *Peep Shows: Cult Film and the Cine-Erotic*, edited by Xavier Mendik, pp. 264–74. New York: Wallflower Press, 2012.

Johnson, Derek. 'Fan-tagonism: Factions, Institutions, and Constitutive Hegemonies of Fandom'. In *Fandom: Identities and Communities in a Mediated World*, edited by Jonathan Gray, Cornel Sandvoss, and C. Lee Harrington, pp. 285–300. New York: New York University Press, 2007.

Jones, Stephen. 'The Good, the Bad, and the Worthless: A Compendium of Compilations'. In *Shock Xpress 2: The Essential Guide to Exploitation Cinema*, edited by Stefan Jaworzyn, pp. 87–90. London: Titan Books, 1994.

Juno, Andrea. 'Interview: Frank Henenlotter'. In *Re/Search #10: Incredibly Strange Films*, edited by Andrea Juno and V. Vale, pp. 8–17. San Francisco: V/Search Publications, 1986.
Kansteiner, Wulf. 'Finding Meaning in Memory: A Methodological Critique of Collective Memory Studies'. *History and Theory* 41, no. 2 (2002): 179–97.
Kernan, Lisa. *Coming Attractions: Reading American Movie Trailers*. Austin: University of Texas Press, 2004.
Kipnis, Laura. *Bound and Gagged: Pornography and the Politics of Fantasy in America*. New York: Grove Press, 1996.
Klinger, Barbara. *Beyond the Multiplex: Cinema, New Technologies, and the Home*. Berkeley: University of California Press, 2006.
— 'Contraband Cinema: Piracy, *Titanic*, and Central Asia'. *Cinema Journal* 49, no. 2 (2010): 106–24.
Kuhn, Annette. *Dreaming of Fred and Ginger: Cinema and Cultural Memory*. New York: New York University Press, 2002.
Landis, Bill and Michelle Clifford. *Sleazoid Express: A Mind-Twisting Tour through the Grindhouse Cinema of Times Square*. New York: Fireside, 2002.
Lawson, Lance. 'My Evening with Q'. In *Quentin Tarantino: Interviews*, edited by Gerald Peary, pp. 183–97. Jackson: University Press of Mississippi, 1998.
Lehman, Peter. '"Don't Blame This on a Girl": Female Rape-Revenge Films'. In *Screening the Male: Exploring Masculinities in Hollywood Cinema*, edited by Steven Cohan and Ina Rae Hark, pp. 103–17. London: Routledge, 1993.
Lerner, David. 'Cinema of Regression: *Grindhouse* and the Limits of the Spectatorial Imaginary'. In *Cinema Inferno: Celluloid Explosions from the Cultural Margins*, edited by Robert G. Weiner and John Cline, pp. 358–79. Lanham, MD: Scarecrow Press, 2010.
Levine, Lawrence W. *Highbrow/Lowbrow: The Emergence of Cultural Hierarchy in America*. Cambridge, MA: Harvard University Press, 1988.
Lewis, Jon. *Hollywood v. Hard Core: How the Struggle over Censorship Saved the Modern Film Industry*. New York: New York University Press, 2000.
Lhamon Jr, W. T. *Raising Cain: Blackface Performance from Jim Crow to Hip Hop*. Cambridge, MA: Harvard University Press, 1998.
Lobato, Ramon. *Shadow Economies of Cinema: Mapping Informal Film Distribution*. London: British Film Institute/Palgrave Macmillan, 2012.
Lott, Eric. *Love and Theft: Blackface Minstrelsy and the American Working Class*. New York: Oxford University Press, 1993.
Love, Heather. *Feeling Backward: Loss and the Politics of Queer History*. Cambridge, MA: Harvard University Press, 2007.
Lowenthal, David. *The Past is a Foreign Country*. Cambridge: Cambridge University Press, 1985.
Lowry, Ed. 'Dimension Pictures: Portrait of a 70's Independent'. *The Velvet Light Trap*, no. 22 (1986): 65–74.

Luther, Rodney. 'Marketing Aspects of Drive-in Theaters'. *The Journal of Marketing* 15, no. 1 (1950): 41–7.
—'Drive-in Theaters: Rags to Riches in Five Years'. *Hollywood Quarterly* 5, no. 4 (1951): 401–11.
McCarthy, Anna. *Ambient Television: Visual Culture and Public Space*. Durham, NC: Duke University Press, 2001.
McDonald, Paul. *Video and DVD Industries*. London: British Film Institute, 2007.
McDonough, Jimmy. *The Ghastly One: The Sex–Gore Netherworld of Filmmaker Andy Milligan*. Chicago: A Cappella Books, 2001.
—*Big Bosoms and Square Jaws: The Biography of Russ Meyer, King of the Sex Film*. London: Jonathan Cape, 2005.
Machor, Alison. *Chainsaws, Slackers, and Spy Kids: 30 Years of Filmmaking in Austin, Texas*. Austin: University of Texas Press, 2010.
McRoy, Jay. '"The Kids of Today Should Defend Themselves Against the '70s": Simulating Auras and Marketing Nostalgia in Robert Rodriguez and Quentin Tarantino's *Grindhouse*'. In *American Horror Film: The Genre at the Turn of the Millennium*, edited by Steffen Hantke, pp. 221–33. Jackson: University Press of Mississippi, 2010.
Maffesoli, Michel. *The Time of the Tribes: The Decline of Individualism in Mass Society*. Translated by Don Smith. London: Sage, 1996.
Makagon, Daniel. *Where the Ball Drops: Days and Nights in Times Square*. Minneapolis: University of Minnesota Press, 2004.
Margolis, Harriet. 'Stereotypical Strategies: Black Film Aesthetics, Spectator Positioning, and Self-Directed Stereotypes in *Hollywood Shuffle* and *I'm Gonna Git You Sucka*'. *Cinema Journal* 38, no. 3 (1999): 50–66.
Mathijs, Ernest and Jamie Sexton. *Cult Cinema: An Introduction*. Malden, MA: Wiley-Blackwell, 2011.
Mayer, Arthur. *Merely Colossal: The Story of the Movies from the Long Chase to the Chaise Longue*. New York: Simon and Schuster, 1953.
Mayne, Judith. *Framed: Lesbians, Feminists, and Media Culture*. Minneapolis: University of Minnesota Press, 2000.
Miller, William Ian. *The Anatomy of Disgust*. Cambridge, MA: Harvard University Press, 1997.
Mittell, Jason. *Genre and Television: From Cop Shows to Cartoons in American Culture*. New York: Routledge, 2004.
Monteith, Sharon. 'Exploitation Movies and the Freedom Struggle of the 1960s'. In *American Cinema and the Southern Imaginary*, edited by Deborah E. Barker and Kathryn McKee, pp. 194–216. Athens: University of Georgia Press, 2011.
Morley Cohen, Mary. 'Forgotten Audiences in the Passion Pits: Drive-in Theatres and Changing Spectator Practices in Post-War America'. *Film History* 6, no. 4 (1994): 470–86.
Morris, Meaghan. 'Transnational Imagination in Action Cinema: Hong Kong

and the Making of a Global Popular Culture'. *Inter-Asia Cultural Studies* 5, no. 2 (2004): 181–99.

Morrison, James. 'After the Revolution: On the Fate of Cinephilia'. *Michigan Quarterly Review* 44, no. 3 (2005): 393–413.

Muller, Eddie and Daniel Faris. *Grindhouse: The Forbidden World of 'Adults Only' Cinema*. New York: St. Martin's Griffin, 1996.

Naremore, James. *More Than Night: Film Noir in its Contexts*. Berkeley: University of California Press, 2008.

Neale, Steve. *Genre and Hollywood*. London: Routledge, 2000.

Newman, Michael Z. *Indie: An American Film Culture*. New York: Columbia University Press, 2011.

Nora, Pierre. 'Between Memory and History: *Les Lieux de Mémoire*'. *Representations*, no. 26 (1989): 7–24.

Nowell, Richard. *Blood Money: A History of the First Teen Slasher Film Cycle*. New York: Continuum, 2011.

Nystrom, Derek. *Hard Hats, Rednecks, and Macho Men: Class in 1970s American Cinema*. New York: Oxford University Press, 2009.

Olney, Ian. *Euro Horror: Classic European Horror Cinema in Contemporary American Culture*. Bloomington: Indiana University Press, 2013.

Ongiri, Amy Abugo. '"He Wanted to Be Just Like Bruce Lee": African Americans, Kung Fu Theater, and Cultural Exchange at the Margins'. *Journal of Asian American Studies* 5, no. 1 (2002): 31–40.

Paasonen, Susanna. *Carnal Resonance: Affect and Online Pornography*. Cambridge, MA: MIT Press, 2011.

Pence, Jeffrey. 'Postcinema/Postmemory'. In *Memory and Popular Film*, edited by Paul Grainge, pp. 237–56. Manchester: Manchester University Press, 2003.

Perren, Alisa. *Indie, Inc.: Miramax and the Transformation of Hollywood in the 1990s*. Austin: University of Texas Press, 2012.

Poole, Ross. 'Memory, History, and the Claims of the Past'. *Memory Studies* 1, no. 2 (2008): 149–66.

Preacher Collins, Ava. 'Loose Canons: Constructing Cultural Traditions Inside and Outside the Academy'. In *Film Theory Goes to the Movies*, edited by Jim Collins, Hilary Radner, and Ava Preacher Collins, pp. 86–102. London: Routledge, 1992.

Prince, Stephen. *A New Pot of Gold: Hollywood Under the Electronic Rainbow, 1980–1989*. New York: Charles Scribner's Sons, 2000.

Ray, Fred Olen. *The New Poverty Row: Independent Filmmakers as Distributors*. Jefferson, NC: McFarland, 1991.

Read, Jacinda. *The New Avengers: Feminism, Femininity, and the Rape-Revenge Cycle*. Manchester: Manchester University Press, 2000.

—'The Cult of Masculinity: From Fan-boys to Academic Bad-boys'. In *Defining Cult Movies: The Cultural Politics of Oppositional Taste*, edited by Mark Jancovich, Antonio Lázaro Reboll, Julian Stringer, and Andy Willis, pp. 54–70. Manchester: Manchester University Press, 2003.

Reichl, Alexander J. *Reconstructing Times Square: Politics and Culture in Urban Development*. Lawrence: University Press of Kansas, 1999.

Rhodes, Gary D. '"The Double Feature Evil": Efforts to Eliminate the American Dual Bill'. *Film History* 23, no. 1 (2011): 57–74.

Ricketson Jr, Frank H. *The Management of Motion Picture Theatres*. New York: McGraw-Hill, 1938.

Robinson, Sally. 'Feminized Men and Inauthentic Women'. *Genders*, no. 53 (2011): http://www.genders.org/g53/g53_robinson.html (accessed 12 August 2012).

Robnik, Drehli. 'Mass Memories of Movies: Cinephilia as Norm and Narrative in Blockbuster Culture'. In *Cinephilia: Movies, Love, and Memory*, edited by Marijke de Valck and Malte Hagener, pp. 55–64. Amsterdam: Amsterdam University Press, 2005.

Rogin, Michael. *Blackface, White Noise: Jewish Immigrants in the Hollywood Melting Pot*. Berkeley: University of California Press, 1996.

Romano, Stephen. *Shock Festival*. San Diego: IDW Publishing/RAW Entertainment, 2008.

Rutsky, R. L. 'Surfing the Other: Ideology on the Beach'. *Film Quarterly* 52, no. 4 (1999): 12–23.

Sagalyn, Lynne B. *Times Square Roulette: Remaking the City Icon*. Cambridge, MA: MIT Press, 2001.

Sandvoss, Cornel. *Fans: The Mirror of Consumption*. Cambridge: Polity Press, 2005.

Schaefer, Eric. *'Bold! Daring! Shocking! True!' A History of Exploitation Films, 1919–1959*. Durham, NC: Duke University Press, 1999.

—'Pandering to the "Goon Trade": Framing the Sexploitation Audience through Advertising'. In *Sleaze Artists: Cinema at the Margins of Taste, Style, and Politics*, edited by Jeffrey Sconce, pp. 19–46. Durham, NC: Duke University Press, 2007.

Schubart, Rikke. *Super Bitches and Action Babes: The Female Hero in Popular Cinema, 1970–2006*. Jefferson, NC: McFarland, 2007.

Sconce, Jeffrey. '"Trashing" the Academy: Taste, Excess, and an Emerging Politics of Cinematic Style'. *Screen* 36, no. 4 (1995): 371–93.

—'Movies: A Century of Failure'. In *Sleaze Artists: Cinema at the Margins of Taste, Style, and Politics*, edited by Jeffrey Sconce, pp. 273–309. Durham, NC: Duke University Press, 2007.

Segrave, Kerry. *Drive-In Theaters: A History from Their Inception in 1933*. Jefferson, NC: McFarland, 1992.

Senelick, Laurence. 'Private Parts in Public Places'. In *Inventing Times Square: Commerce and Culture at the Crossroads of the World*, edited by William R. Taylor, pp. 329–53. New York: Russell Sage Foundation, 1991.

Skouras, Charles P. 'The Exhibitor'. *The Annals of the American Academy of Political and Social Science*, no. 254 (1947): 26–30.

Slade, Joseph W. 'Pornographic Theaters Off Times Square'. In *The Pornography*

Controversy: Changing Moral Standards in American Life, edited by Ray C. Rist, pp. 119–39. New Brunswick, NJ: Transaction Books, 1975.

Snelson, Tim and Mark Jancovich. '"No Hits, No Runs, Just Terrors": Exhibition, Cultural Distinctions, and Cult Audiences at the Rialto Cinema in the 1930s and 1940s'. In *Explorations in New Cinema History: Approaches and Case Studies*, edited by Daniel Biltereyst, Richard Maltby, and Philippe Meers, pp. 199–211. Malden, MA: Wiley-Blackwell, 2011.

Soffer, Jonathan. *Ed Koch and the Rebuilding of New York City*. New York: Columbia University Press, 2010.

Sorrento, Matthew. 'Loving the Bad: An Interview with Frankie Latina and Sasha Grey on *Modus Operandi*'. *Bright Lights Film Journal*, no. 71 (2011): http://www.brightlightsfilm.com/71/71ivmodusoperandi_sorrento.php (accessed 14 December 2011).

Sperb, Jason. 'Be Kind . . . Rewind / Or, The A–Zs of an American *Off-Modern Cinephilia*'. In *Cinephilia in the Age of Digital Reproduction*, Vol. 2, edited by Scott Balcerzak and Jason Sperb, pp. 71–107. London: Wallflower Press, 2012.

Sprengler, Christine. *Screening Nostalgia: Populuxe Props and Technicolor Aesthetics in Contemporary American Film*. New York: Berghahn Books, 2009.

Stanfield, Peter. 'Walking the Streets: Black Gangsters and the "Abandoned City" in the 1970s Blaxploitation Cycle'. In *Mob Culture: Hidden Histories of the American Gangster Film*, edited by Lee Grieveson, Esther Sonnet, and Peter Stanfield, pp. 281–300. New Brunswick, NJ: Rutgers University Press, 2005.

—'Going Underground with Manny Farber and Jonas Mekas: New York's Subterranean Film Culture in the 1950s and 1960s'. In *Explorations in New Cinema History: Approaches and Case Studies*, edited by Daniel Biltereyst, Richard Maltby, and Philippe Meers, pp. 212–25. Malden, MA: Wiley-Blackwell, 2011.

Stern, William J. *The Truth About Times Square*. Perspectives on Eminent Domain Abuse. Arlington, VA: Institute for Justice, 2009.

Stevenson, Jack. 'Grindhouse and Beyond'. In *From the Arthouse to the Grindhouse: Highbrow and Lowbrow Transgression in Cinema's First Century*, edited by John Cline and Robert G. Weiner, pp. 129–52. Lanham, MD: Scarecrow Press, 2010.

Stewart, Susan. *On Longing: Narratives of the Miniature, the Gigantic, the Souvenir, the Collection*. Baltimore: Johns Hopkins University Press, 1984.

Straw, Will. 'Embedded Memories'. In *Residual Media*, edited by Charles R. Acland, pp. 3–15. Minneapolis: University of Minnesota Press, 2007.

—'Reinhabiting Lost Languages: Guy Maddin's *Careful*'. In *Playing with Memories: Essays on Guy Maddin*, edited by David Church, pp. 58–69. Winnipeg: University of Manitoba Press, 2009.

Sturken, Marita. *Tangled Memories: The Vietnam War, the AIDS Epidemic, and the Politics of Remembering*. Berkeley: University of California Press, 1997.

—'Tourists of History: Souvenirs, Architecture, and the Kitschification of

Memory'. In *Technologies of Memory in the Arts*, edited by Liedeke Plate and Anneke Smelik, pp. 18–35. New York: Palgrave Macmillan, 2009.

Tannock, Stuart. 'Nostalgia Critique'. *Cultural Studies* 9, no. 3 (1995): 453–64.

Tarantino, Quentin and Robert Rodriguez. *Grindhouse: The Sleaze-Filled Saga of an Exploitation Double Feature*. Edited by Kurt Volk. New York: Weinstein Books, 2007.

Tasker, Yvonne. *Spectacular Bodies: Gender, Genre, and the Action Cinema*. London: Routledge, 1993.

Terdiman, Richard. *Present Past: Modernity and the Memory Crisis*. Ithaca, NY: Cornell University Press, 1993.

Thorne, Christian. 'The Revolutionary Energy of the Outmoded'. *October*, no. 104 (2003): 97–114.

Thornton, Sarah. *Club Cultures: Music, Media, and Subcultural Capital*. Middletown, CT: Wesleyan University Press, 1996.

Thrower, Stephen. *Nightmare USA: The Untold Story of the Exploitation Independents*. Godalming: FAB Press, 2007.

Tierney, Sean. 'Quentin Tarantino in Black and White'. In *Critical Rhetorics of Race*, edited by Michael G. Lacy and Kent A. Ono, pp. 81–97. New York: New York University Press, 2011.

Traub, James. *The Devil's Playground: A Century of Pleasure and Profit in Times Square*. New York: Random House, 2004.

Trillin, Calvin. 'The Life and Times of Joe Bob Briggs, So Far'. *American Stories*. New York: Ticknor & Fields, 1991.

Tryon, Chuck. *Reinventing Cinema: Movies in the Age of Media Convergence*. New Brunswick, NJ: Rutgers University Press, 2009.

Turan, Kenneth and Stephen F. Zito. *Sinema: American Pornographic Films and the People Who Make Them*. New York: Praeger, 1974.

Van Dijck, José. *Mediated Memories in the Digital Age*. Stanford, CA: Stanford University Press, 2007.

Verevis, Constantine. *Film Remakes*. Edinburgh: Edinburgh University Press, 2006.

Waller, Gregory A. 'An Annotated Filmography of R-Rated Sexploitation Films Released During the 1970s'. *Journal of Popular Film and Television* 9, no. 2 (1981): 98–112.

—'Auto-Erotica: Some Notes on Comic Softcore Films for the Drive-In Circuit'. *Journal of Popular Culture* 17, no. 2 (1983): 135–41.

Walters, Suzanna Danuta. 'Caged Heat: The (R)evolution of Women-in-Prison Films'. In *Reel Knockouts: Violent Women in the Movies*, edited by Martha McCaughey and Neal King, pp. 106–23. Austin: University of Texas Press, 2001.

Wasser, Frederick. *Veni, Vidi, Video: The Hollywood Empire and the VCR*. Austin: University of Texas Press, 2001.

Watson, Paul. 'There's No Accounting for Taste: Exploitation Cinema and the Limits of Film Theory'. In *Trash Aesthetics: Popular Culture and its Audience*, edited by Deborah Cartmell, I. Q. Hunter, Heidi Kaye, and Imelda Whelehan, pp. 66–83. London: Pluto Press, 1997.

Webster, Paula. 'Pornography and Pleasure'. In *Caught Looking: Feminism, Pornography, and Censorship*, edited by F.A.C.T. Book Committee. New York: Caught Looking, Inc., 1986.

Wharton, Sarah. 'Welcome to the (Neo)Grindhouse! Sex, Violence, and the Indie Film'. In *American Independent Cinema: Indie, Indiewood, and Beyond*, edited by Geoff King, Claire Molloy, and Yannis Tzioumakis, pp. 198–209. London: Routledge, 2013.

Whatling, Clare. *Screen Desires: Fantasizing Lesbians in Film*. Manchester: Manchester University Press, 1997.

White, Patricia. *Uninvited: Classical Hollywood Cinema & Lesbian Representability*. Bloomington: Indiana University Press, 1999.

Wiebe Taylor, Laura. 'Popular Songs and Ordinary Violence: Exposing Basic Human Brutality in the Films of Rob Zombie'. In *Terror Tracks: Music, Sound, and Horror Cinema*, edited by Philip Hayward, pp. 227–35. London: Equinox, 2009.

Wilinsky, Barbara. *Sure Seaters: The Emergence of Art House Cinema*. Minneapolis: University of Minnesota Press, 2001.

Willemen, Paul. *Looks and Frictions: Essays in Cultural Studies and Film Theory*. Bloomington: Indiana University Press, 1994.

Williams, Linda Ruth. *The Erotic Thriller in Contemporary Cinema*. Bloomington: Indiana University Press, 2005.

Wilson, Janelle L. *Nostalgia: Sanctuary of Meaning*. Lewisburg, PA: Bucknell University Press, 2005.

Wood, Marina. '"Machete Improvises": Racial Rhetoric in Digital Reception of Robert Rodriguez's *Machete*'. *Jump Cut*, no. 54 (2012): http://www.ejumpcut.org/currentissue/MWoodMachete/index.html (accessed 15 November 2012).

WPA Federal Writers' Project. *New York City Guide*. New York: Random House, 1939.

Wyatt, Justin. *High Concept: Movies and Marketing in Hollywood*. Austin: University of Texas Press, 1994.

—'From Roadshowing to Saturation Release: Majors, Independents, and Marketing/Distribution Innovations'. In *The New American Cinema*, edited by Jon Lewis, pp. 64–86. Durham, NC: Duke University Press, 1998.

—'Selling "Atrocious Sexual Behavior": Revising Sexualities in the Marketplace for Adult Film of the 1960s'. In *Swinging Single: Representing Sexuality in the 1960s*, edited by Hilary Radner and Moya Luckett, pp. 104–31. Minneapolis: University of Minnesota Press, 1999.

—'Independents, Packaging, and Inflationary Pressure in 1980s Hollywood'. In Stephen Prince, *A New Pot of Gold: Hollywood Under the Electronic Rainbow, 1980–1989*, pp. 142–59. New York: Charles Scribner's Sons, 2000.

Index

academia, 14–16, 41–3, 48, 50, 132–3, 200, 225, 244–7
access, 3–4, 6, 8–9, 16–19, 22–3, 42, 49–50, 57, 60, 63, 65–6, 75, 87–8, 90–1, 104, 106, 109–10, 122–4, 126–7, 130, 139, 145, 147, 150, 159, 161–2, 165, 178, 180, 194, 201–2, 224, 233–4, 252–3
Accused, The, 218
action films, 34, 79–80, 95, 140, 147–9, 151, 171n, 214–15, 221, 227, 249
Adventures of Lucky Pierre, The, 38
advertising, 11–12, 18, 19–21, 40, 53, 56, 60, 74–7, 80, 82, 85, 87–8, 94–5, 99, 101–2, 104–5, 110, 122, 127–8, 130, 137, 140, 148, 152–3, 156, 159, 162, 197, 205, 227, 248–50, 254
After Hours Cinema, 107, 115n
After Sunset: The Life & Times of the Drive-In Theater, 51
Age of the Hobbits, 147
Aja, Alexandre, 202–3
Alamo Drafthouse Cinema, 139, 165
Allen, Robert C., 33
Alley Cats, The, 213
Alliance Films, 158
Allied Artists, 39
Almighty Thor, 147
Altman, Rick, 87, 93
ambivalence, 9, 20–1, 24, 46–7, 51–3, 59, 76, 82–3, 106, 110–11, 123–6, 132, 134, 136–7, 140, 144–5, 149, 161–2, 164–6, 177–8, 180, 184–5, 187, 190, 194–6, 199–200, 209–10, 212, 214–15, 220, 224–6, 230, 232–5, 246, 255
Amer, 127
American Film Distributing, 95
American Grindhouse, 102, 107
American Hippie in Israel, An, 138
American Independent Pictures, 144
American International Pictures (AIP), 11, 35–6, 39, 95, 102–3, 231
American International Television, 39
American Pie, 148
Anchor Bay Entertainment, 56–8
Andrews, David, 141, 203, 207
Andrews, Fred, 164
Apollo Theatre, 80, 95
Aquarius Releasing, 95

Argento, Dario, 57–8
Arizona Senate Bill 1070, 252
art cinema, 14, 17, 37–8, 43, 57, 80, 92–3, 95, 142, 151
artefacting, 21, 56–7, 99, 104, 107, 117n, 121, 125–7, 130, 133, 137, 139, 144, 152–3, 161, 163, 172–4n, 186, 197, 199, 205, 223, 244, 247, 254
art theatres, 41, 43, 92–3, 141–2, 213
Astor Pictures, 80
Astra Video, 167n
Astron-6, 167n, 170n
Asylum, The, 147
Attack of the 60 Foot Centerfolds, 141
Audubon Films, 95
Austin, Bruce A., 68n
authenticity, 4, 7–8, 17–18, 20, 23, 50, 56–61, 66, 74, 106–7, 111, 130, 133–4, 150, 153, 156, 160, 164, 174n, 178, 180, 194, 200, 203, 205, 218, 224, 235, 246–7, 250
avant-garde film, 14, 41–3, 98, 117n

Back to the Future, 61
Bad Girls Go to Hell, 51
badness, 2–3, 8, 10, 14–15, 44, 48, 52, 141, 144–7, 160–1, 171n, 192, 212
Baise-moi, 217
Balaban and Katz, 79
ballyhoo *see* advertising
Barber, Stephen, 243–4, 247
Barboni, Enzo, 58
Barry Lyndon, 61
Basket Case, 88
Baudrillard, Jean, 169n
BCI, 107
beach party films, 230–4
Because of Eve, 11
Bell, Zoë, 195
Benjamin, Walter, 65, 133
Benson-Allott, Caitlin, 105, 126, 135–6, 154, 165, 244
Bergman, Ingmar, 68n
Berman, Marshall, 97
Betz, Mark, 93
Beyond the Dunwich Horror, 138
Bianco, Anthony, 77
Big Bird Cage, The, 167n
Big Doll House, The, 215, 227–8

INDEX

biker films, 134, 151, 237n
Bikini Drive-In, 141
Biller, Anna, 210–13, 226
Billy Jack, 12
Bitch Slap, 125, 144, 214, 227, 232, 234
Black Devil Doll, 138, 181–6, 189, 191, 194
Black Devil Doll from Hell, 181
Black Dynamite, 125, 191–4, 210
Black Mama, White Mama, 228
Black Shampoo, 192
Black Snake Moan, 128–9
Blacula, 181
Blake, Linnie, 199
blaxploitation films, 85–6, 128, 181–2, 185, 191–4, 249
Blood Feast, 50
Blood Feast 2: All U Can Eat, 146
Blood Moon Rising, 132
Bloody Bloody Bible Camp, 166n
Blue Underground, 56, 102
Blu-ray, 2, 32, 44–5, 50, 56, 58–60, 99, 102, 104, 106, 123–4, 127, 150, 152, 158–9, 173n, 248, 250, 255
B movies, 2, 34–5, 49, 80, 83, 103, 113n, 144, 150
Boogie Nights, 138
Bousman, Darren Lynn, 202
Boxoffice, 82
Boxoffice International Pictures, 95
Boym, Svetlana, 9, 119, 159
Brandt, Bingo, 109
Brandt, Harry, 80–1, 96
Brandt's 42nd Street Theatres, 80–1
Briggs, Joe Bob, 29, 51–2, 200
Bring It On, 148
Bring Me the Head of the Machine Gun Woman, 214
British Board of Film Classification, 172n
Bronson, Charles, 188
Brooker, Will, 6
Brown, Jim, 192
Bruno, Giuliana, 6, 88
Bryanston Distributing, 95
burlesque, 77–8, 81, 85–6
Burton, Tim, 145, 169n
Bush, George W., 135

Caged, 127
Caged Lesbos A-Go-Go!, 170n
Cagney, James, 82
Cambist Films, 95
cameos, 71n, 127, 130–1, 146, 170n, 223, 231
Cameo Theatre, 139
camp, 14, 49, 61, 65, 141, 146, 211–12, 214, 222–4, 226–7, 231, 234
Camp Motion Pictures, 101, 144
Canby, Vincent, 98, 101
cannibal films, 151, 172n
Cannibal Holocaust, 172n
Cannon Films, 95, 142

capital, cultural, 16, 41–3, 49, 59, 75, 92–3, 122, 132–4, 142, 148–50, 154, 158, 161, 184–5, 189, 200; *see also* taste, cultural
capitalism, 20, 41, 60, 64–6, 75, 78, 92, 98, 106, 108–10, 141, 159–60, 196–7, 200, 205, 247–54
capital, subcultural, 5, 13, 15–19, 22–3, 31–2, 45, 50–1, 53, 59, 61–3, 90–1, 99–100, 104, 106, 108–10, 124, 130, 132, 134, 139, 142, 144, 150, 153–4, 156, 160, 163–5, 178, 184–5, 194, 200–3, 246–7, 255; *see also* fandom
Captivity, 203
Carlito's Way, 148
Carolco Pictures, 142
Casa de mi Padre, 132, 146
Casey, Bernie, 192
Casey, Edward S., 74
Cat in the Brain, 58
censorship, 2, 12–13, 30, 35, 37, 50, 56–8, 77, 80, 94–5, 103, 153, 158, 172–3n, 249
Chained Girls, 88
chambara films, 94, 236n
Chantal, 203
Chaos, 203
Cherry Bomb, 218
Chillerama, 230–3, 239n
Chopper Chicks in Zombietown, 141
Ciasullo, Ann, 229
Cinema Shares, 40
cinephilia, 16–17, 24, 44, 56, 87–8, 91, 97, 99, 102–4, 109, 132–3, 137, 139, 156
Cipriani, Stelvio, 127
civil rights movement, 50, 179, 181, 192–3
class, 16, 23, 30–3, 39, 41–8, 50–4, 57, 59, 64, 66, 73–4, 78–80, 84, 86, 91, 96, 122, 134, 141–3, 178, 180, 182–4, 186–7, 189–91, 194–200, 207–9, 211–12, 224, 249–53
Cleopatra Jones, 192
Clifford, Michelle, 96, 103
Clover, Carol, 189, 216–19, 240n
Coach, 103
Code Red DVD, 107
Coffy, 215
Cohn, Larry, 96
collecting, 12–14, 20, 44, 64–5, 97, 104, 121, 147, 234, 255
comedy, 15–16, 38, 151, 184, 187, 191–2, 194, 209–10, 222–3, 231; *see also* parody
connoisseurship, 2, 4, 8, 15–17, 24, 31–2, 52, 62, 111, 122, 144, 158, 164, 177–8, 185, 208
conservatism, 9, 24, 47–50, 65, 123, 153, 159–60, 177–81, 184–6, 190, 195, 199, 210, 218–19, 221, 225–7, 235, 246, 251–2, 255
Continental Distributing, 95
convergence, 4, 24, 46, 75–6, 100, 121, 123–4, 140, 159–60, 163, 200, 235, 246–8, 252–3
Cook, Pam, 7, 177

Cooper, Gary, 82
copyright, 13, 53–7, 60, 92, 102, 107, 109–10, 131, 147, 252–3
Corman, Roger, 12, 15, 35, 51, 54, 96–7, 147
Corpse Grinders 2, The, 146
Coulthard, Lisa, 215–16, 220
Crack Whore, 218
Creature, 164
Cries and Whispers, 68n
Crown International Pictures, 16, 38, 95, 103
Crowther, Bosley, 85, 93
Cry for Revenge, 218
cultism, 8, 13, 16–18, 30, 40–1, 44, 50, 87, 105, 133, 146, 148, 164–5, 176, 194, 200, 208, 243, 246
cultural memory, 4–10, 17–25, 30–2, 44–5, 50, 54, 59, 64, 66, 74, 76, 92, 97, 111, 123, 127, 134–7, 143–4, 160, 176, 179, 208, 224–5, 234, 243–8, 255; *see also* nostalgia

Daddy Cross, 174n
D'Amato, Joe, 2
Da Vinci Treasure, The, 147
Davis, Glyn, 143
Dead End Kids, 82
Dead Hooker in a Trunk, 214
Dean, James, 231
Dear God No!, 134, 169n, 237n
Deathdream, 38
Death Proof, 104–5, 131, 154, 156–8, 163, 195, 214, 237n
Deep Red, 58
Deleuze, Gilles, 169n
deliberate archaism, 49, 124–7, 133, 146–7, 161, 163, 179, 191–2
Deliverance, 217
Del Río, Esteban, 251
Deodato, Ruggero, 172n
Despentes, Virginie, 217–18, 221
Destination Moon, 12
Destroy All Monsters, 36
Deuce: Grindhouse Cinema Database, The, 106
Devil's Rejects, The, 195–9, 203
Digital Cinema Packages (DCP), 40, 105
Dika, Vera, 136
Dildo Heaven, 146
Dimension Films, 108, 150–1, 163, 202–3
Dimension Pictures, 38–9, 95, 108, 143
direct-to-video (DTV) films, 24, 97, 121–4, 140–53, 158, 163, 166, 167n, 171n, 181, 207, 218, 223–4, 231, 249
disability, 33, 185
disaster films, 38, 147
Disco Exorcist, The, 146
Distribpix, 95, 101
Django, 58
Django Unchained, 182
documentaries, 51, 102, 107, 145, 227
Dr. Black, Mr. Hyde, 181
Dominant Pictures, 80

Donahue, Suzanne Mary, 79, 95
Donen, Stanley, 172n
Dorm That Dripped Blood, The, 119
double features, 30, 35, 40, 73, 79, 81, 83, 85, 88–9, 101, 104, 107–8, 130, 151–2, 154–5, 158, 164, 171n
Double Feature XXX, 171n
Downs, Anthony, 34
Dragstrip Girl, 130
Drafthouse Films, 101
Drive-In Madness!, 66n
Drive-In Massacre, 38
Drive-In Movie Memories, 51
drive-in theatres, 1, 5–6, 12, 16, 23, 29–41, 45–8, 50, 53–7, 59, 64–5, 73–4, 78, 94, 141, 151, 170n, 200, 208, 231, 233–5
Duras, Marguerite, 47
dusk-till-dawn shows, 35, 47, 151
DVD, 1–3, 16–17, 19, 21, 32, 40, 43–6, 50–1, 53–4, 56–9, 64, 100–7, 110, 119–24, 127, 130, 138, 143, 145, 147–50, 152, 154, 157–9, 166n, 173n, 203–4, 227, 246, 248, 250, 255
  box sets, 54–8
  director's cut, 56–8, 154, 156–7, 172n
  DVD premieres, 148–52, 157
  trailer compilations, 76, 100–4, 106–7, 115n, 130, 139
DVD Drive-In, 40
Dyer, Richard, 124–5, 136, 141, 162, 176, 179, 182–3

Each Time I Kill, 146
earnestness *see* sincerity
Edmonds, Don, 223
Ed Wood, 145, 169n
Egan, Kate, 64
8½, 58
ei Independent Cinema, 203–4, 208
Eisener, Jason, 106, 158–9
Elite Entertainment, 53
El Mariachi, 249
El Monstro del Mar!, 214
Elsaesser, Thomas, 17
Embassy Pictures, 39, 95
Empire Theatre, 108, 256
Entertainment Ventures Inc., 95
Eraserhead, 58
erotic thrillers *see* thriller films
Escape 2000, 52
Evil Dead, The, 138
Expendables, The, 171n
exploitation cinema
  classical exploitation films, 11, 82, 85, 94
  defined, 3–4, 10–12, 17, 60
  distribution/exhibition of, 1, 3–4, 6, 11–14, 18–20, 23–4, 30–2, 34–5, 37–40, 45–8, 50–1, 53–4, 59–60, 62–3, 73–6, 80–5, 88, 90–1, 93–5, 97, 103, 126, 131, 133, 136, 138, 140–2, 148–50, 158, 164–5, 243, 247, 250

production of, 4, 10–12, 14–15, 24, 35, 39, 60–1, 75–6, 84–5, 94–5, 99, 103, 106, 122–3, 126, 128, 136–7, 140–1, 143, 147, 160, 182, 191–2, 200, 206, 208, 212, 215, 222, 227, 250

Fahrenheit 9/11, 151
fandom, 3–10, 13–18, 22, 30–2, 37, 39, 43, 48–51, 56–9, 62, 65–6, 73–6, 90–2, 95, 97–9, 103–4, 106, 108–10, 121–4, 126, 130, 134–5, 139–40, 143–5, 150, 153–4, 156, 159–6, 177, 181, 184, 200–2, 204, 208, 214–15, 224–5, 233–5, 243–7, 252, 254–5
   fan conventions, 17–18, 44, 224
   fanzines, 13, 18, 96, 140, 166n
   fan films, 123, 130–1, 138–9, 145, 158–62, 173n
   generations of, 2–3, 12, 19, 30–1, 40, 45, 60, 62–4, 106, 164, 180, 196, 201–2, 245–6
Fangoria, 140
Far From Heaven, 179
Faster, Pussycat! Kill! Kill!, 144, 215
Father's Day, 137, 170n
Female Animal, 204
feminism, 50, 88, 179, 207, 210, 212–13, 215–21, 228, 240n; *see also* post-feminism
Ferrara, Abel, 161, 217
Fiennes, Ralph, 61
Fight Club, 205–6
film noir, 3–4, 80, 215, 218
Final Exam, 119
Fincher, David, 205–6
Fistful of Dollars, A, 236n
Fleshpot on 42nd Street, 88
42nd Street (New York City), 24, 76–8, 80–98, 101, 103, 107–9, 139, 170n, 234–5, 243–4, 256
42nd Street Development Project, 96–7
42nd Street Forever (series), 102–4
42nd Street Memories: The Rise and Fall of America's Most Notorious Street, 107
42nd Street Pete (series), 107, 115n
Fragasso, Claudio, 27n
Franco, Jess, 2
Fredianelli, Michael, 186, 188
Freeman, Elizabeth, 225–6
Friedman, David F., 47
Frog-g-g!, 146
From Dusk Till Dawn, 150–2
Fulci, Lucio, 57–8
Futurama International Pictures, 1

gangster films, 80–1
Gans, Herbert, 96
Garbo, Greta, 82
Garth Marenghi's Darkplace, 146
Gay & Lesbian Alliance Against Defamation (GLAAD), 221–2
gender, 13, 23, 44, 48, 52, 62, 66, 70n, 74, 80–2, 84, 86–8, 90–1, 105, 109, 122, 128, 141, 165, 176, 178, 185–6, 195, 201–24, 226–34, 238n, 240n
generic place, 5–6, 23–4, 31, 39–40, 46, 53, 73–6, 94, 105
genrification, 73, 75–6, 92–4, 102, 110
Gestapo's Last Orgy, 49
Ghoulardi, 2
Girls Against Boys, 218
Globe Theatre, 93
Godard, Jean-Luc, 42
Gone with the Pope, 138–9
Gordon, Bette, 88, 90
Gorfinkel, Elena, 17, 88, 115n, 207, 211–12, 226
Gray, Jonathan, 128
Great Depression, 75, 78, 80, 83
Great Texas Dynamite Chase, The, 47
Grier, Pam, 215
Grindhouse, 61, 74, 94, 104–8, 121–3, 125, 128, 130–3, 135–6, 145, 147, 150–2, 154–6, 158–9, 161, 163–5, 169n, 171n, 172n, 195, 202, 206, 223–4, 233, 247–8, 250–1, 255
grindhouse aesthetic, 61, 73, 75, 100, 104, 107, 111, 117n, 122, 124–8, 130–5, 137, 146, 150, 152–3, 161, 164, 169n, 174n, 180, 192, 195, 197, 199, 204–5, 216, 219, 221, 223, 230, 235, 244, 249–50, 254
Grindhouse Releasing, 58, 99, 138
grind houses, 1, 6, 19, 24, 64, 66, 73–111, 123–4, 128, 132–3, 136, 141, 150, 152, 154, 159–60, 164–5, 213, 234–5, 243–4
Grindhouse XXX: A Double Feature, 171n
grind policy, 77–9, 81–3
Grudge, The, 202
Guccione, Bob, 212
Guerrero, Ed, 85
Guffey, Elizabeth, 50, 63
Guins, Raiford, 57
Guzman, Joseph, 137, 219, 221
Gwenllian Jones, Sara, 159

Haji, 223
Halberstam, Judith, 217
Halloween, 203
Halloween II, 203
Hayes, Isaac, 192
Haynes, Todd, 179
Hediger, Vinzenz, 56
Hell Ride, 151, 205, 237n
Hemingway, Ernest, 80
Henenlotter, Frank, 98
H. G. Wells' War of the Worlds, 147
high-concept films, 12, 76, 96, 105–6, 147, 160, 165
High Tension, 203
Higson, Andrew, 248
Hilderbrand, Lucas, 20
Hill, Jack, 127

Hills Have Eyes, The, 203
Hills, Matt, 17, 62, 153
Hitchcock, Alfred, 35
hixploitation, 39, 47
Hobo with a Shotgun, 106, 131, 137, 158–9, 174n, 195
Hodge, Tom, 169n
Hollows, Joanne, 87, 105
Hollywood Boulevard, 38
Hollywood Chainsaw Hookers, 141
Hollywood (industry), 11–12, 16, 24, 34–5, 37–41, 44, 53–4, 60–2, 66, 73, 75, 78–80, 82–3, 87, 92–3, 96, 102–3, 106, 108–10, 124, 131, 133, 142, 145, 147–50, 152, 156, 159–61, 163, 166, 173n, 192, 195, 202–3, 205, 215, 218, 244, 248–53
homage, 108, 124–5, 127, 131, 136, 138, 141, 145, 147, 150, 152, 160–2, 176–7, 181
home video, 1–3, 5–7, 9, 11–14, 17–25, 30, 33, 38, 40, 44–6, 51–60, 64, 66, 75–6, 87, 90–1, 95–110, 119–24, 127, 130, 133, 138–54, 156–60, 164–6, 177–8, 203, 207, 227, 234–5, 244–6, 253–5
homosexuality, 87, 91–2, 96, 104, 113n, 116n, 201, 219–20, 227–34, 244
Hooper, Tobe, 202
Hora, 132, 203, 205, 218
Horn, Katrin, 227
horror films, 1, 15, 20, 22, 38, 57–8, 79–80, 82, 84, 95, 106, 119, 140, 147–9, 153, 163–4, 172n, 178, 181, 185, 187, 189, 196–7, 201–3, 218, 222, 233, 238n, 243
Horton, Andrew, 38
Hostel, 203
hot car films, 38, 151
House by the Cemetery, The, 58
House of 1000 Corpses, 195–7
House of the Dead: Overkill, 132, 174n
House of the Devil, The, 125, 131, 166n
House of Women, 127
House on Sorority Row, The, 119
Hughes, Howard, 58
Human Tornado, The, 192
Huyssen, Andreas, 7, 19, 110

I, a Woman, 93
I Like the Girls Who Do, 204
Ilsa, She-Wolf of the SS, 98
Image Entertainment, 54, 102
I'm Gonna Git You Sucka, 146, 191–4
Independent Film Channel, 107
Independent–International Pictures, 95
Inga, 204
Inglis, Ruth A., 84
In God We Trust, 103
Internet Archive, 56
Internet Movie Database, 2
Inter-Ocean Video, 58
intertextuality, 21, 62, 80, 123–6, 131–3, 136, 160, 163, 168n, 203

Intervision Picture Corp., 166n
irony, 2–3, 8–10, 14–16, 24, 42–4, 48–9, 51, 61, 63, 75, 99–100, 102, 104, 106, 110, 122, 124–5, 132, 134, 144–7, 159–60, 163, 171n, 176, 180, 184–5, 192, 194, 196–7, 210, 212, 215, 224–7, 231, 234, 246–7, 251
Isle of Paradise, 84, 113n
I Spit on Your Grave, 203, 218, 220–1, 223
It's All in Your Mind, 82
'I Was a Teenage Werebear', 230–3
I Was a Teenage Werewolf, 232
I Woke Up Early the Day I Died, 145–6

Jackie Brown, 131, 182
Jackson, Peter, 202
Jackson, Samuel L., 128
Jaeckin, Just, 208, 210
Jancovich, Mark, 42–3, 82
Jarrett, Cody, 161
Jaws, 12
Jenkins, Henry, 159
Joe Bob Briggs's Drive-In Theater, 51
Johnson, Beth, 212
Johnson, Michelle, 227
Jordan, Marsha, 99
Just the Two of Us, 227

Kaji, Meiko, 215
Katz, Sam, 79
Kaufman, Lloyd, 127, 170n
Kernan, Lisa, 100, 105
Kill Bill, 131, 152, 154, 216, 218, 220
Killer Drag Queens on Dope, 223–4
Killers, The, 80
Kiss of the Tarantula, 38
kitsch, 134–5
Klinger, Barbara, 20–1, 44, 59–60, 162, 253
'Knights of Cydonia' (music video), 131
kung-fu films, 85–6, 94–5
Kung Fu Theater, 40
Kung Fu: The Punch of Death, 256
Kurosawa, Akira, 236n

La Guardia, Fiorello, 81, 86
Land Before Time, The, 148
Landis, Bill, 96–7, 103
laserdisc, 44
Last House on the Left, The, 203, 218, 220
Latina, Frankie, 206
Lehman, Peter, 217–18
Leisure Time Booking, 95
Leone, Sergio, 236n
Lerner, David, 153, 159–60, 163
lesploitation, 227–30, 232
Lewis, Herschell Gordon, 50, 54, 146
Lewis, Jonathan and Shawn, 181–2
Liberty Theatre, 80
lieu de mémoire, 5–6, 23, 31–2, 46, 59, 64, 74, 92, 104, 110, 235, 246

INDEX

Lionsgate Entertainment, 148, 202
Lobato, Ramon, 143
lobby displays, 11, 77, 80, 82, 87, 138
Lockhart, Sean Paul, 241n
Lorna, 210
Lost Skeleton of Cadavra, The, 146
Love, Heather, 225
Luna, Israel, 221–4
Lustful Addiction, 203
Lusting Hours, The, 88
Lyric Theatre, 78, 80, 89

McCaffrey, Edward T., 80
McDonough, Jimmy, 91, 109
Machete (feature), 106, 131, 137, 157–8, 195, 205, 248, 250–5
Machete Kills, 158
Machete Maidens Unleashed!, 102
Machete (trailer), 104, 131, 137, 157–8, 248–5
Machine Girl, The, 131, 214
Mack, The, 237n
McLean, Greg, 202
McRoy, Jay, 133
Maddin, Guy, 132
Maffesoli, Michel, 29
Magiera, Marcy, 149
Makagon, Daniel, 73
Malibu High, 16
Maniac, 88, 138
Maniquis, Ethan, 105
Manson Family, The, 197
Man with the Iron Fists, The, 114n
March or Die, 103
Margolis, Harriet, 194
Marihuana, 11
Mark of the Astro-Zombies, 146
Marx Brothers, 82
Massacre Video, 166n
Massage Parlor Murders, 88
Mayer, Arthur, 77, 79, 113n
Mayne, Judith, 90
mediated memories, 7, 9–10, 19–22, 30, 45, 59, 143, 180, 244
Mercado, Jorge, 223
meta-cult films, 133
Metzger, Radley, 208, 210–13
Meyer, Russ, 146, 209–11, 223, 231, 239n
MGM, 102
Midnight Cowboy, 88
midnight movies, 16–17, 41, 77, 148, 156
Miike, Takashi, 236n
Mikels, Ted V., 146
Mill Creek Entertainment, 54–5, 58
Minstrel Killer, The, 181–2, 186–9, 195–6, 205
minstrelsy, 182, 184, 186–90, 200
Miramax, 142, 150–1, 168n
misogyny *see* sexism
mockbusters, 147
Modus Operandi, 206

Mom and Dad, 11
mondo films, 94
MonsterVision, 51
Montreal Film Studio, 101
Moore, Rudy Ray, 192
Morley Cohen, Mary, 33, 46
Morrison, James, 132
Motion Picture Association of America (MPAA), 38, 103, 153, 249, 253
Motion Picture Herald, 60
Movie Movie, 172n
Ms. 45, 161, 217–18
multiplex theatres, 39–40, 53, 105, 108, 156, 247
Mundae, Chelsea, 204
Mundae, Misty, 204
musical films, 231–3
Mystery Science Theater 3000, 1–3, 15, 43, 46

Naremore, James, 3, 80, 142
Natividad, Kitten, 127, 231
Nazisploitation films, 49, 61
Neale, Steve, 75, 80
neo-grindhouse *see* retrosploitation
neo-liberalism, 24, 66, 76, 92, 98, 108–10, 116n, 248, 252
New Amsterdam Theatre, 78, 97
New Beverly Cinema, 99
New Horizons Pictures, 147
New Line Cinema, 142
Newman, Michael Z., 133
New World Pictures, 38–9, 68n, 95–6, 143
New York Releasing, 95
New York Ripper, The, 88
New York State Urban Development Corporation, 97
New York Times, 78–80, 82, 84, 87, 113n
New York Wildcats, 203
Nicotero, Greg, 106
Niku daruma, 238n
nonconformity, 4, 8, 14, 19, 30, 32, 47, 50, 61, 63, 75, 98, 105, 121–2, 141, 160, 180, 184, 191, 199–200, 205–6, 214–15, 227, 231–3, 246
non-theatrical distribution, 1, 23, 121–3, 140, 148–9, 207–8, 213, 245; *see also* home video
Nora, Pierre, 5
North American Free Trade Agreement (NAFTA), 253
nostalgia, 4–9, 16–23, 25, 30–2, 39–41, 43, 45, 48, 52–3, 59–61, 63–4, 73–6, 87, 91–2, 97–9, 109–10, 119, 121, 123, 125–6, 130, 134–7, 139, 144, 150, 156, 159–60, 163–5, 177–9, 189, 202, 211–12, 214, 218, 221, 225–7, 232–5, 244–6, 254–5
implanted, 9, 19–20, 45, 66, 73, 100, 104, 110, 134, 200
reflective, 159
restorative, 159

Not Quite Hollywood: The Wild, Untold Story of Ozploitation!, 102
Novak, Harry, 15
Nude Nuns with Big Guns, 137, 221
Nun of That, 137, 161, 170n
nunsploitation films, 161, 215, 227, 229
Nymphoid Barbarian in Dinosaur Hell, A, 141
Nystrom, Derek, 42, 47

Obama, Barack, 192, 237n
obsolescence, 1, 13, 16, 21, 31, 60, 63, 126, 134, 158, 181, 195–6, 205, 207–8, 212, 226, 234, 245–6
Orion Pictures, 102
Our Winning Season, 103

Pacific Drive-In Theatres, 37
Pandora Peaks, 146
paracinema, 14–15, 27n, 42–4, 48, 60–1, 98, 123, 138, 141, 144–7, 163, 169n, 180, 192
Paramount Publix, 79
paratexts, 11, 19, 44, 53, 56–7, 59, 61, 75–6, 99–102, 121–4, 127–32, 137–9, 159, 165, 205, 252–4
Parks, Michael, 152
parody, 61, 123–7, 136, 138, 144–7, 150, 152, 160–3, 171n, 176–7, 180, 191–4, 210, 214, 222, 225, 231, 239n
pastiche, 24, 61–2, 99, 104–5, 124–7, 131–2, 134–8, 141–2, 147, 162–3, 171n, 176–80, 182–4, 190–4, 196, 200, 206, 212, 213, 218–19, 224–5, 227–8, 233, 235, 246
Penthouse, 212
Perren, Alisa, 151
Pervert!, 125, 208–10, 214, 222
Phillips, Nick, 203–4
Piccioni, Piero, 127
picture palaces, 77, 86, 243
Piranha, 203
Planet Terror, 104–5, 126, 152–4, 156, 158, 165, 214, 221, 250
Playgirl, 212
Pleasures of a Woman, 203
political incorrectness, 14, 24, 49–50, 53, 105, 141, 154, 165, 176, 179, 181, 183–5, 190, 202, 205–6, 210, 220, 230, 234, 250
Polyester, 47
Pom Pom Girls, The, 38
populism, 23, 30–2, 48, 50, 52–4, 56–7, 62, 124, 134–5, 143, 162, 172n, 200–1, 208, 246
pornography, 38, 86–8, 93, 95, 97–9, 101, 103–4, 109, 115n, 116n, 147, 171n, 182, 205, 212, 220, 241n, 243
post-apocalyptic films, 97
posters, 11, 61, 80, 123, 127–30, 137–8, 155, 170n, 198
post-feminism, 207, 210, 214–16, 220, 227, 232
postmodernism, 133–7, 144

Preacher Collins, Ava, 133
Prison-A-Go-Go!, 127, 170n
Production Code, 11, 85
Prostitutes Protective Society, 88
Psycho, 35, 58
Psycho Beach Party, 230–2
Psychotronic Video, 96
publicity *see* advertising
Pulp Fiction, 131, 182

queerness, 92, 177–9, 220–34
Quentin Tarantino Archives, The, 168n

race, 29, 33, 47, 49, 85–6, 91, 96, 165, 176, 179, 181–96, 200, 207, 228, 247, 249–54
racism, 49, 86, 96, 128, 176, 178, 180–91, 194, 207, 228, 249–54
Raft, George, 82
Rainer, Luise, 82
rape-revenge films, 137, 161, 178, 190, 203, 215–23
Ray, Fred Olen, 142
Read, Jacinda, 184, 217–18
Realart Pictures, 80
rebellion *see* nonconformity
redneck (stereotype), 47–8, 51–2, 186–7, 189, 195–200, 221
Reefer Madness: The Movie Musical, 146
remakes, 53, 60, 62, 201–5, 208, 231
remediation, 4–5, 7–8, 19–22, 24–5, 30, 32, 45, 49, 51–9, 63, 65–6, 75–6, 98–104, 106–10, 122–4, 127, 130, 138, 143, 145, 153, 165, 203–4, 208, 244, 246–7, 254
retro culture, 21, 39, 54, 63–6, 122, 131–3, 176
Retro-Seduction Cinema *see* ei Independent Cinema
retrospectatorship, 225–7, 230, 234
retrosploitation, 21, 23–4, 61, 64, 76, 99, 106, 119, 121–7, 130–4, 144–7, 151, 160–6, 176–81, 183–5, 189–91, 194–5, 200–1, 205–6, 208, 214–16, 218, 220, 224–7, 232–5, 244, 246–7, 254–5
Rialto Theatre, 77, 79, 81–2, 93, 98, 139
Ricci, Christina, 128
Ridin' for Justice, 113n
Ring, The, 202
roadshowing, 11, 78, 164
Rock All Night, 130
Rocketship X-M, 12
Rodriguez, Robert, 104–5, 126, 128, 130–1, 133–4, 136–7, 150–3, 157–8, 160, 202, 248–50, 252
Rolling Thunder Pictures, 168n
Romano, Stephen, 138–9
Rosemary's Baby, 1
Roth, Eli, 104, 106, 202
Roxanna, 203–4
Run! Bitch Run!, 125, 137, 205, 219–21, 223
rurality, 30–1, 37, 39, 47–8, 52, 99, 186, 189, 196–7, 200, 221

INDEX

Russell, Justin, 119–21
Rutsky, R. L., 191, 231
RZA, 114n

St. Clair Vision, 58
Samurai Avenger: The Blind Wolf, 173n
Sanders, Scott, 192
Sandvoss, Cornel, 6, 8, 10
Sarno, Joe, 2, 146, 203, 208, 210
Satana, Tura, 127
Satan Was a Lady, 146
saturation booking, 12, 133, 151, 156
Savini, Bob, 80
Saw, 203
Scarface, 81
Scary Movie 4, 163
Schaefer, Eric, 11, 84–5
Schindler's List, 61
Schubart, Rikke, 215
science fiction films, 12, 147
Sconce, Jeffrey, 14–15, 42–3, 61–3, 65
Scream, 151, 163, 201, 203
Seagal, Steven, 149
Seduction of Misty Mundae, The, 203
Segrave, Kerry, 34, 38
Selwyn Theatre, 80
sequels, 146, 148–9, 151–2, 163, 196, 231
Sex Galaxy, 146
sexism, 13, 16, 49, 128–30, 176, 180–1, 184, 199, 207, 209–10, 213–14, 219–20, 223
Sex is the Game People Play, 101
sexploitation films, 15, 37–8, 54, 84–6, 88, 93–5, 99, 127–8, 141, 146, 178, 201, 203–4, 206–14, 217, 226–7, 234
sexuality, 49, 64, 81, 91–2, 96, 104, 108, 116n, 165, 176, 178, 186, 195, 207, 209–10, 213–15, 217, 219–34
Shaft, 88
Shameless Desire, 101
Sharknado, 147–8
Sharktopus, 147
She-Devils on Wheels, 215
Shock Festival, 138–9
Signal, The, 131
simulacra *see* postmodernism
sincerity, 2–3, 8–9, 14–16, 18, 24, 31, 43–4, 49–51, 58, 61–3, 75, 99–102, 104, 106, 110, 122, 124–5, 127, 134, 145–7, 160–2, 171n, 176, 180, 184–6, 191, 193–4, 210, 224–7, 231, 234, 246–7, 251
slasher films, 71n, 119–21, 163, 186, 202, 215
Sleazoid Express, 96
Sleeper, The, 71n, 119–21, 125, 133, 162, 166n
Snakes on a Train, 147
Snelson, Tim, 82
Something Weird Video, 2–3, 98–9, 101–2
Sometime Sweet Susan, 89
South by Southwest, 158–60
Splat Pack, The, 202–3, 206, 218, 233
Sprengler, Christine, 125

SS Experiment Love Camp, 49
Stallone, Sylvester, 149, 171n
Star Wars, 165
states' rights market, 11, 80–1, 94
Stewart, Susan, 135
Strait-Jacket, 58
Straw Dogs, 216–17
Straw, Will, 20–1, 54, 56
Stray Cat Rock, 215
streaming media, 56, 60, 95, 130, 159, 245–6, 252, 255
Stuck!, 127
Stupid Teenagers Must Die!, 146
subcultures, 4–5, 7–8, 12–14, 16–19, 22, 52, 57, 59, 63, 133, 163, 224; *see also* fandom
Suburban Secrets, 146
Sugar Boxx, 127, 161, 205, 227–32, 234
Sullivan, Tim, 231, 233–4
Sunn Classic Pictures, 37
Superchick, 38
Supervixens, 209
Sushi Girl, 214
Swedish Marriage Manual, 89
Synapse Films, 102

Tarantino, Quentin, 104–5, 128, 130–4, 136–7, 150–2, 154, 157–9, 163–4, 168n, 182–3, 195, 202, 237n
Targets, 38
Tasker, Yvonne, 214–15
taste, cultural, 7–11, 13–14, 17–20, 23, 32, 41–4, 49–50, 52–4, 57–9, 61, 75, 77–80, 82–6, 92–3, 110, 122, 124, 132–4, 141–4, 147–51, 160, 162–3, 165, 176–8, 182–4, 189–90, 196–7, 199–203, 207–8, 218–19, 223–4, 244–6, 248, 255
Taxi Driver, 88–9
Teenage Mother, 38
teenpics, 11–12, 35, 38, 233
'Telephone' (music video), 132
television, 1, 3, 34, 38, 40, 43, 44–6, 48, 51, 56, 70n, 85, 107, 122, 140–3, 146–8, 202, 207, 248
Temple, Shirley, 82
temporal drag, 226–7, 230, 234
Tenebre, 58
Texas Chainsaw Massacre, The, 201
That Tender Touch, 227
theatre (legitimate), 77–9, 81, 85, 87
Therese and Isabelle, 93
Thorne, Christian, 64
Thorne, Dyanne, 215
Thornton, Sarah, 13, 31
Three the Hard Way, 191
thriller films, 80, 84, 140, 142, 151, 206, 218
Ticked-Off Trannies with Knives, 132, 221–4, 232
Tierney, Sean, 182
Times Square *see* 42nd Street (New York City)
Times Square Theatre, 80, 95

TimeWarner, 142
Titanic, 165
Titanic II, 147
TNT Jackson, 192
torture porn, 203
Touch of Satan, The, 1–3, 8, 15
Toy Box, The, 38
Tracy, Spencer, 82
trailers, 11, 21, 53, 56, 61, 75–6, 99–107, 110, 127–8, 130–1, 137–40, 145, 156, 158–60, 162, 173–4n, 205, 220, 222–3, 244, 248–55
transgenderism, 221–4
transmedia *see* convergence
Transmorphers, 147
transnationalism, 248–54
Tribeca Film Festival, 221, 224
Triple X Selects: The Best of Lezsploitation, 227
Troll 2, 27n
Troma Entertainment, 141–2, 144–5, 163, 170n, 202, 214
Two Thousand Maniacs!, 51
2001 Maniacs, 231

Uh-Oh Show, The, 146
Ultimate Degenerate, The, 88
Undercover Brother, 191, 194
underground cinema, 41
United Artists, 93
Universal Pictures, 148
Up!, 209
urbanity, 31, 33, 74–6, 81, 84–8, 91, 96–8, 196–7, 243–4, 247

Van Damme, Jean-Claude, 149
Van Dijck, José, 7, 246
Variety (film), 88, 90, 105
Variety Photoplays, 88
Variety (publication), 77, 82, 86, 96, 113n, 149, 158
vaudeville, 78, 81
Verevis, Constantine, 201, 203
Vestron Pictures, 142, 167n
VHS, 1–3, 13, 21–2, 30, 39, 44, 54, 57–60, 64, 97, 101, 119–21, 124, 130, 140–1, 143, 145, 147–8, 152–3, 166n, 170n, 197, 234–5, 245, 255
Victory Theatre, 80, 86, 89, 95
Video Business, 149

Video Nasties: Moral Panic, Censorship, and Videotape, 102
video stores, 19–22, 30, 46, 50, 57, 97–8, 105, 119–20, 122, 124, 130, 140, 147–8, 244
Vinegar Syndrome, 54
Viva (film), 127, 209–14, 226
Viva (magazine), 212–13
Vraney, Mike, 3

Walking Tall, 47
Walt Disney Company, The, 107–9, 142, 150–1
Walter Reade Organization, 37
Warner Bros., 86
Washington Post, The, 78
Waters, John, 47, 223–4
Watson, Paul, 60–1
Weinstein, Bob and Harvey, 150–1, 154
Weinstein Company, The, 108, 148, 150–1, 154, 156, 159
Welcome Home, Brother Charles, 192
Welcome to the Jungle, 151
Weldon, Michael J., 96
Welles, Orson, 145
westerns, 34, 58, 80, 94–5, 113n, 131, 236n
Whatling, Clare, 227
White Line Fever, 47
White, Patricia, 225–6
Wiebe Taylor, Laura, 199
Wilinsky, Barbara, 92
Willemen, Paul, 45
Williams, Linda Ruth, 140
Wishman, Doris, 146
Wolf Creek, 163, 203
Wolfe Video, 227
Women Against Pornography, 88
women-in-prison films, 90–1, 127, 132, 215, 227–30, 234
Wood, Edward D., 42, 145–6, 169n
World Northal, 40
Woronov, Mary, 127
Wright, Edgar, 104
Wyatt, Justin, 142

Yojimbo, 236n
YouTube, 56, 252

Zapata, Angie, 223
Zombie, Rob, 104, 196–200, 202–3
zoning restrictions, 38, 96–7

Sleaze Artists

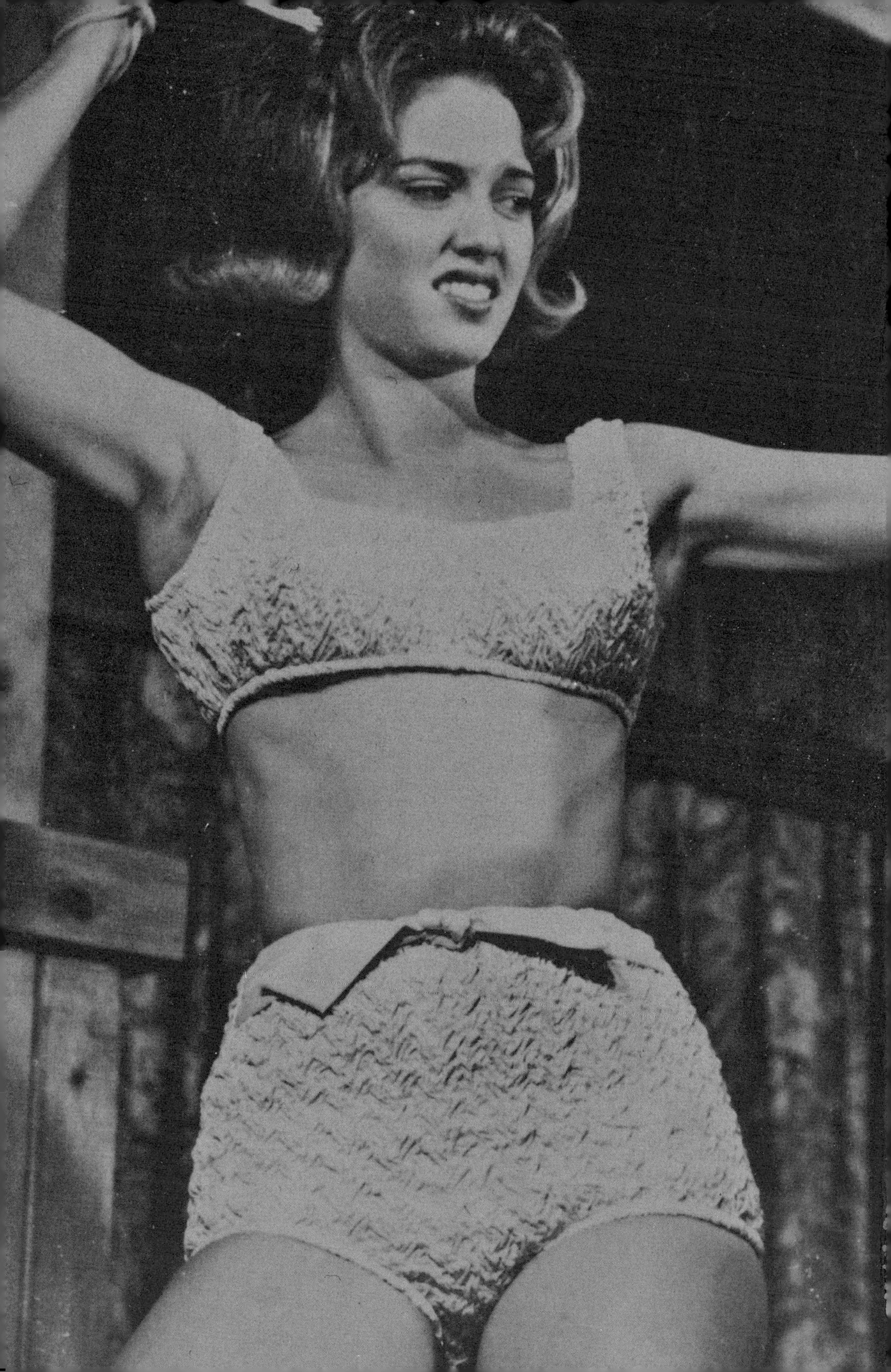

Sleaze Artists

CINEMA AT THE
MARGINS OF
TASTE, STYLE,
AND POLITICS

JEFFREY SCONCE, ED.

DUKE UNIVERSITY PRESS   DURHAM AND LONDON   2007

© 2007 Duke University Press

All rights reserved

Printed in the United States of America
on acid-free paper ∞

Designed by Heather Hensley

Typeset in Minion by Tseng
Information Systems, Inc.

Library of Congress Cataloging-in-
Publication Data appear on the last
printed page of this book.

Title page: Still from *Scum of the Earth*
(dir. H. G. Lewis, 1963)

Frontispiece: Still from *Strait Jacket*
(dir. William Castle, 1964)

Contents

vii Acknowledgments

1 Introduction

PART 1: *Sleazy Histories*

19 Pandering to the "Goon Trade": Framing the Sexploitation Audience through Advertising
Eric Schaefer

47 Women's Cinema as Counterphobic Cinema: Doris Wishman as the Last Auteur
Tania Modleski

71 Representing (Repressed) Homosexuality in the Pre-Stonewall Hollywood Homo-Military Film
Harry M. Benshoff

96 Pornography and Documentary: Narrating the Alibi
Chuck Kleinhans

121 *El signo de la muerte* and the Birth of a Genre: Origins and Anatomy of the Aztec Horror Film
Colin Gunckel

144 Art House or House of Exorcism? The Changing Distribution and Reception Contexts of Mario Bava's *Lisa and the Devil*
Kevin Heffernan

PART 2: *Sleazy Afterlives*

167 Troubling Synthesis: The Horrific Sights and Incompatible Sounds of Video Nasties
Kay Dickinson

189 The Sleazy Pedigree of Todd Haynes
Joan Hawkins

219 Para-Paracinema: The *Friday the 13th* Film Series as Other to Trash and Legitimate Film Cultures
Matt Hills

240 Boredom, *Spasmo*, and the Italian System
Chris Fujiwara

259 Pure *Quidditas* or Geek Chic? Cultism as Discernment
Greg Taylor

273 Movies: A Century of Failure
Jeffrey Sconce

311 Selected Bibliography

321 Contributors

325 Index

Acknowledgments

First and foremost, I would like to thank the contributors for their patience during the long genesis of this project, as well as the readers who reviewed the manuscript and provided many useful suggestions for the authors. In addition to his excellent contribution to the book, Eric Schaefer also graciously made his photo-still and pressbook collection available for illustrative material. I would also like to thank my colleague Scott Curtis and the members of the Chicago Film Seminar for the opportunity to present and debate an early version of my contribution to this volume. A section of "Movies: A Century of Failure" appeared in *Framework* (45:2) as "The (Depressingly) Attainable Text." I would like to thank Brian Price and Meghan Sutherland for their invitation to contribute to that volume.

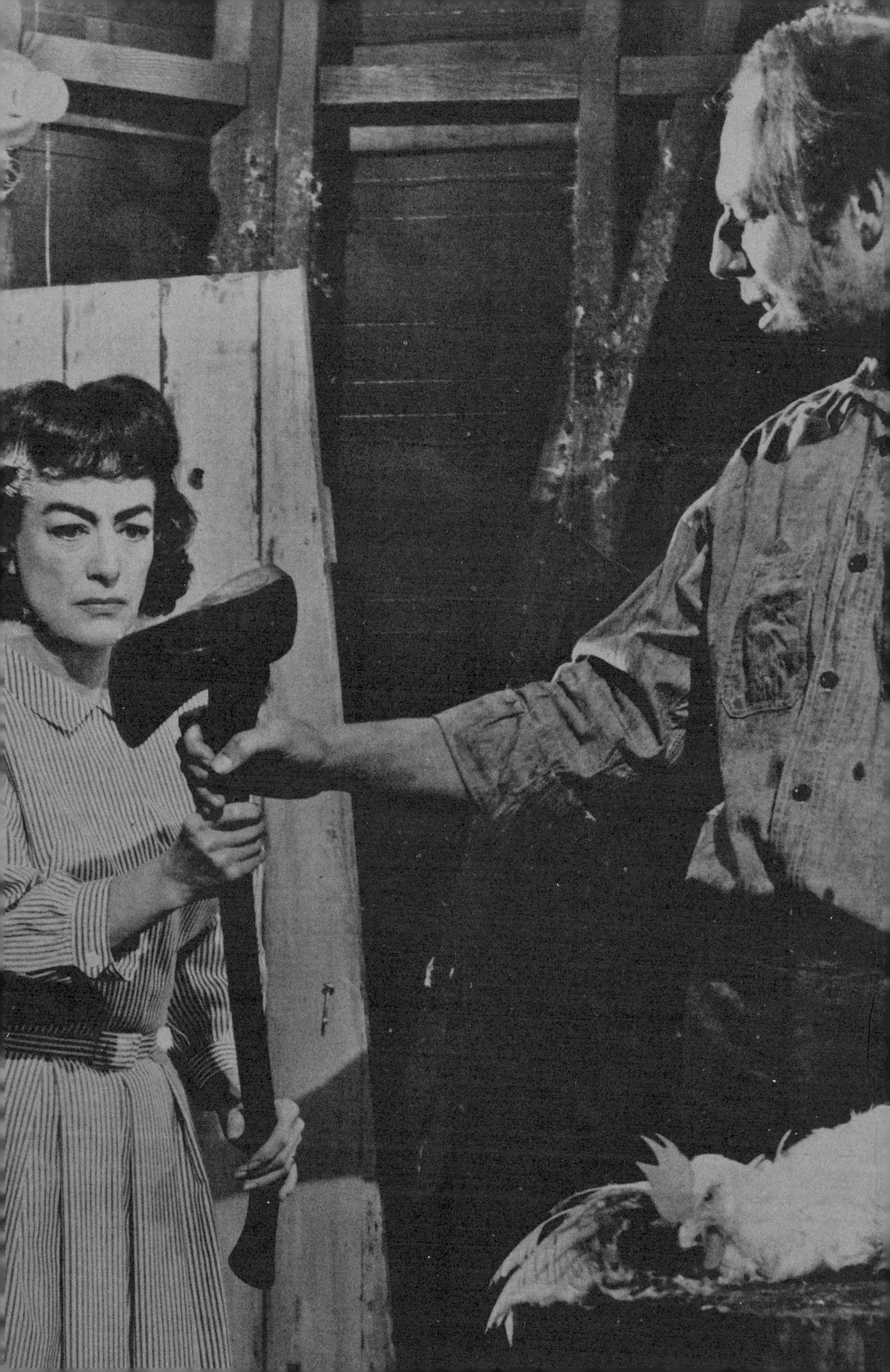

JEFFREY SCONCE

Introduction

In her 1968 essay "Trash, Art, and the Movies," Pauline Kael devotes a great deal of copy to extolling the rather scandalous pleasures of American International Pictures' hippie schlockfest, *Wild in the Streets* (1968), at one point judging it more interesting than that year's achingly important *2001: A Space Odyssey* (1968). No doubt to the calculated shock of her *Harper's* readership, she goes so far as to defend the right of teen audiences to prefer *Wild in the Streets* over the era's allegedly more sophisticated art cinema. At least *Wild in the Streets*, she argues, "connects with their lives in an immediate even if a grossly frivolous way, and if we don't go to movies for excitement, if, even as children, we accept the cultural standards of refined adults, if we have so little drive that we accept 'good taste,' then we will probably never really care about movies at all."[1] The love of cinema, Kael argues provocatively, is in some sense both childish and based in the disreputability of the cinema's origins in popular spectacle. "Movies took their impetus not from the desiccated imitation European high culture," she reasons, "but from the peep show, the Wild West show, the music hall, the comic strip—from what was coarse and common" (103). While there have always been "schoolmarms" determined to transform this coarse and common medium into a more refined art, Kael champions (here at least) another tradition of cinephilia that, like so much cultural

FIGURE 1 In the goofy teen-pic allegory *Wild in the Streets* (1968), teen fascists force the elderly to drop acid at a new government re-education camp.

criticism in the twentieth century, seeks to rescue a once vibrant form from the banal trappings of middlebrow respectability. True cinephiles, she argues, always recognize one another's company at once because "they talk less about good movies than what they love in bad movies" (89).

Today many cinephiles still love to talk about "bad" movies, be they studio-era B-films, low-budget 1950s sci-fi, grindhouse porn and horror, or even wildly excessive contemporary summer blockbusters. "Guilty pleasures" lists remain a staple of popular film writing, allowing otherwise tasteful critics to temporarily escape the crushing responsibility of promoting a more artistically ambitious cinema to champion their own personal love of down-and-dirty genre pictures. On the DVD market, meanwhile, a proliferating number of companies scavenge through abandoned theater attics and drive-in closets for the most obscure, degraded, and unusual films of the past century, responding to an ever growing audience of "trashophiles." For better or worse, the entire oeuvre of Doris Wishman is now available on DVD while John Ford's is not. Elsewhere, the anthropological thrill of finding a jaw-droppingly implausible film on late-night television has been channeled into the prepackaged irony of television's *Mystery Science Theater 3000* and mock 1950s Z-films like *The Lost Skeleton of*

FIGURE 2 America's patron saint of sleaze: John Waters hosting *Art:21*, a PBS documentary series on art in the twenty-first century.

Cadavra (2001). Meanwhile, recent work in film scholarship has made exploitation, sleaze, and other "low" genres increasingly acceptable as objects of academic inquiry. Most shocking of all, the cinema's patron saint of sleaze, John Waters, recently served as the host of *Art:21*, a PBS documentary on (consecrated) art in the twenty-first century. Indeed, Waters's career trajectory—from director of sleazy staples of the midnight movie circuit like *Pink Flamingos* (1972) and *Polyester* (1981) to respected gallery photographer, exhibit curator, and contributor to *Art Forum*—testifies to the growing centrality of "sleaze" on all levels of the cultural imaginary.

All of the above despite Kael's admonition that cinephiles should not "use their education to try to place trash within an acceptable academic tradition" (112). Ignoring Kael's now comfortably distant and increasingly irrelevant warning, *Sleaze Artists* continues cinephilia's ongoing conversation about the low, bad, and sleazy face of cinema by collecting a range of contemporary critical voices with a shared intellectual interest in the many questions posed by disreputable movies and suspect cinema. Writing in 1968, Kael was concerned that academics overly eager in their attempts to elevate popular movies into significant art would use auteurism, cine-structuralism, and good old-fashioned textual explication to over-intellectualize and ultimately dissipate the mindless pleasures of films like *Wild in the Streets* and *The Thomas Crown Affair* (1968). Happily, film studies has now expanded beyond the perpetual inferiority complex of its youth and thus no longer has to ape the interpretive excursions of New Criticism to find complexity and worth in every movie. Increasing intellectual contact with a wide range of historical, theoretical, and critical paradigms in the humanities has greatly expanded the scope of appropriate objects and significant questions that might fall under the broad label of "film studies." No longer as concerned with questions of film's aesthetic legitimacy, film studies has been able to enter into a wider dialogue with other voices in art, culture, and history. So, while *Wild in the Streets* may not be "great art" (by almost anyone's criteria), as a pop parable of hippie fascism rendered in a uniquely AIP melding of go-go teen pic and ersatz New Wave, it is nonetheless a "great artifact," one well worthy of critical attention on any number of fronts. The essays in this volume speak then, not only to the ongoing centrality of low cinema in all strata of film culture, but to the continued vibrancy of film studies itself as a diverse and diversifying discipline within the humanities at large.

As "sleaze" is less a definable historical genre than an ineffable quality—a tone that is a function of attitude as much as content—it by necessity evokes a whole range of textual issues, from the industrial mechanics of low-budget exploitation to the ever shifting terrains of reception and taste. Sleaziness is a presence that must be inscribed into a text by some manner of evaluation and critical labor; that is, sleaze is a feeling one has about a film (or television show, or book for that matter) that requires judging, if only in one's imagination, that there is something "improper" or "untoward" about a given text. Often, sleaziness implies a circuit of inappropriate exchange involving suspect authorial intentions and/or displaced perversities in the audience. One could easily argue, for example, that hard-core pornography is not sleazy in that there is little subterfuge in terms of its production and reception. It is what it is—a textual contract sealed around the unambiguous "money shots" that give the genre its identity. *Mantis in Lace* (1968) or *Wanda, the Sadistic Hypnotist* (1969), on the other hand, are sleazy in the extreme, each attempting to motivate soft-core pornography across a weak narrative field of LSD, witchcraft, and other vaguely titillating horrors of hippiedom. No one would dare call *Psycho*

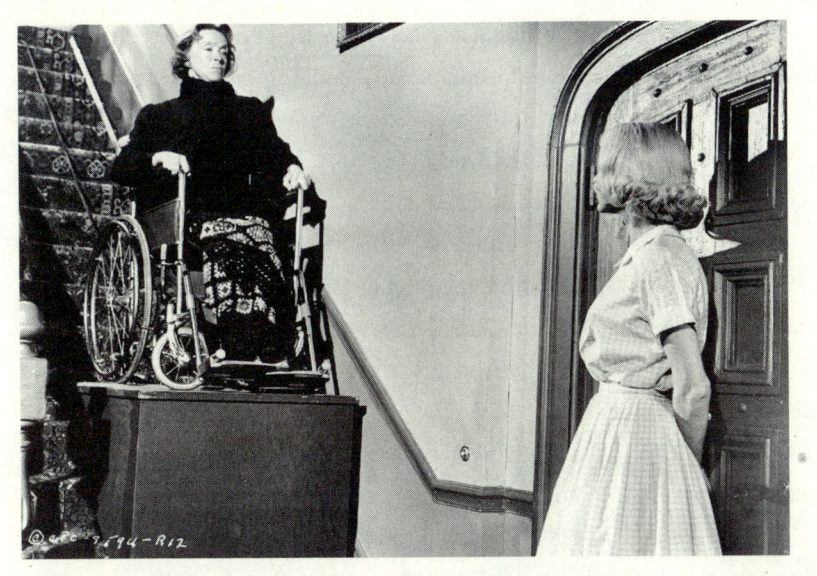

FIGURE 3 Imitation as a form of sleazy flattery: William Castle's *Psycho* knock-off, *Homicidal* (1962).

(1960) sleazy, and yet William Castle's clumsy (yet compelling) rearticulation of *Psycho*'s basic architecture in *Homicidal* (1961) is sleaze at its most brilliant, "unseemly" in both its crude financial opportunism and its ham-handed revisiting of Hitchcock's cross-dressing shock tactics. Herschell Gordon Lewis's oscillation between sexploitation "roughies" and gore-soaked drive-in horror in the 1960s is a sleazeography without peer, a body of work that confronts the entire spectrum of sensationalism with a uniformly leaden visual style. Finally, though the directors associated with Troma films try desperately to achieve sleaziness, their mannered gorefests fail miserably when confronted with the effortless sleaze of a Hollywood studio making a film about a husband worried that a psycho cop will break in to the house and rape his wife, and then titling the film *Unlawful Entry* (1992).

As a necessarily imprecise and subjective concept, sleaze in the cinema has always lurked at the ambiguous boundaries of acceptability in terms of taste, style, and politics. Indeed, as a fundamentally evaluative—indeed judgmental—concept, the very term *sleaze* demonstrates just how crucially intertwined issues of taste, style, and politics are in all film practice. That the "sleazy," "trashy," and just downright "bad" lie outside the borders of normative film practice is not surprising. The fact that cinephiles—as Kael suggests—remain so enthralled by such cinema, on the other hand, remains a fascinating question and suggests that an enduring rift in film culture between encouraging "quality" and venerating "crap" remains wholly unresolved.

As Greg Taylor demonstrates in his elegant history of postwar film criticism, *Artists in the Audience*, the contrarian desire to champion the low over the high, the obscure over the known, the disreputable over the canonized has been a familiar gesture among the film intelligentsia for over fifty years now.[2] Taylor concentrates especially on the "vanguard criticism" of Manny Farber and Parker Tyler, crediting Farber as the most influential figure in the foundation of "cultism" and Tyler as a leading voice of "camp." For many years, Farber's aesthetic focused on finding redeeming details in an otherwise moribund cinema, cultivating the "cultist" impulse that even today allows certain cinephiles to argue that Edgar G. Ulmer is a more interesting auteur than Eliza Kazan, or that an obscure Monogram Noir is inherently more "cinematic" than a more traditionally canonical film. Tyler, on the other hand, used his early film writing as a means of reimagining and rewriting Hollywood cinema as the *Hollywood Hallucination*, taking the predictable mediocrity of Hollywood product and transforming it through "camp," if only in very personal terms, into a more vibrant and playful textual field. Associated with aesthete gay subcultures dating back to the precinematic world of Oscar Wilde, camp found its most public discussion in Susan Sontag's controversial 1964 essay "Notes on Camp," and it continues to resonate as a key strategy for engaging motion pictures.[3]

What is at stake in this ongoing debate over the high or low soul of the cinema? As the work of Pierre Bourdieu should remind us, to champion (but not necessarily enjoy) a particular film or cinema in opposition to another has less to do with any objective criteria for cinematic worth than with the social position and cultural status of the cinephile that chooses to weigh in on this question. Imagine, for example, two cinephiles debating the career of Steven Spielberg. Which is Spielberg's greater achievement—*Schindler's List* (1993) or *Jurassic Park 2: The Lost World* (1997)? Those who still hold hope for the cinema's legitimacy as an important art form *must* by default choose the relentless artistic sobriety of *Schindler*. After all, it aspires to the status of a timeless classic in range, scope, and treatment, and by engaging the Holocaust, invokes per-

FIGURE 4 *Jurassic Park 2: The Lost World* (1997): Steven Spielberg's greatest cinematic achievement?

haps the single most profound subject matter of the twentieth century. Those who embrace the cinema's more accidental forms of commercial poetry, on the other hand, are rooting instead for the T-Rex that runs amok in San Diego at the close of *Lost World*. It is an unexpectedly inspired moment in an otherwise pedestrian film that reminds many of us of the vertiginous surrealism that brought so many to the cinema in the first place. Sure, it's merely a goofy homage to the Godzilla cycle—but in that gesture, Spielberg acknowledges that the entire *Jurassic Park* phenomenon, with all its sheen of quality and state-of-the-art effects, can still only aspire to the childhood joy of seeing men in cheap lizard suits stomping on Tokyo.

On a most superficial level this may seem merely a question of taste, but as so much recent work in cultural theory reminds us, taste is anything but superficial. Those who would champion *The Lost World* over *Schindler's List*, much like Kael praising *Wild in the Streets* over *2001* almost forty years ago, clearly understand they are making a calculatedly disruptive and scandalous choice, one that is explicitly political, whether confined to the arena of cinema poetics or engaging the larger ideological terrain of American popular culture. Similarly, those defending *Schindler's List* as "important" cinema do so from an equally entrenched sociocultural position with equally political implications.

Indeed, as Bourdieu's work would also remind us, if we were shown the living rooms, libraries, and wardrobes of the two people involved in this hypothetical debate, most of us could no doubt quickly match the cinephile with his or her accessories.

Yet jockeying for position in the eternal rat race of symbolic capital can explain only so much. In an earlier article, "'Trashing' the Academy" (1995), I relied heavily on Bourdieu's mapping of taste in *Distinction* to discuss the activities of "badfilm" fans in the 1980s, and in particular, this community's strategic shift from approaching these films with mocking derision to a discourse of outsider appreciation. I used the term *paracinema* to describe this sensibility, a viewpoint epitomized in fanzines like *Zontar*, *Psychotronic*, and *Film Threat*, and whose bible remains the Juno and Vale RE/Search volume *Incredibly Strange Films*.[4] I think this approach is still very useful in considering how various audience factions view themselves on the cultural terrain, and how they enter into often fractious dialogue with one another over issues of cinema, taste, and art. Still, looking back, there is something missing in thinking about a passion for the bad, sleazy, or paracinematic simply in terms of symbolic economies and social trajectories.[5] While providing an excellent template for understanding the positioning of fan discourses and their self presentation in a larger social field—be it the letters column of a zine or flame wars on a Russ Meyer website—Bourdieu's rationalist economies have less to contribute in understanding the issues of pleasure, affect, and even obsession that attend a sincere passion for deviant cinema.

Film culture's seemingly unending fascination with the low and sleazy, and its closely related critical competition among cultists and aesthetes to capture the essence of "true" cinema, suggests that fundamental contradictions attending the definition, practice, and appreciation of "cinematic art" remain wholly unresolved. Here we are probably better served, not by Bourdieu's rather clinical analysis of the cultural field, but by that other extreme in French aesthetic theory—Roland Barthes; especially the Barthes of *S/Z* and *The Pleasure of the Text*. In "Trash, Art, and the Movies," for example, Kael empathizes with the plight of fellow film critics who have simply given up out of boredom. "Many film critics quit," she observes, because "they can no longer bear the many tedious movies for the few good moments and the tiny shocks of recognition"

(93). To put this in Barthesian terms, critics who immerse themselves in any art form are bound to grow tired of the "text of pleasure," the text "linked to the comfortable practice of reading." Once a cinephile has mastered the Hollywood lexicon and has a reasonable grasp on what to expect from the various international schools of art cinema, it becomes increasingly difficult to have these "tiny shocks of recognition," to find any film that truly challenges the stifling boredom of normative film practice and culture or, for that matter, the stifling boredom of normative "avant-garde" film practice and culture. As Kael puts it, "After all the years of stale stupid acted-out stories, with less and less for me in them, I am desperate to know something, desperate for facts, for information, for faces of non-actors and for knowledge of how people live—for revelations, not for the little bits of show-business detail worked up for us by show-business minds who got them from the same movies we're tired of" (128–29). Kael's search for the revelatory here is not unlike the Zontarian notion of the "badtruth"—that moment when the narrative logic and diegetic illusions of cheap exploitation cinema disintegrate into a brutally blissful encounter with profilmic failure.[6] With its low-budgets, frequent incompetence, and explosive subject matter, sleazy exploitation cinema is probably the closest thing to "outsider art" possible in the capital and technology intensive world of cinema. As such, it remains our best hope for Barthes's "text of bliss: the text that imposes a state of loss, the text that discomforts (perhaps to the point of a certain boredom), unsettles the reader's historical, cultural, psychological assumptions, the consistency of his tastes, values, memories, brings to a crisis is relation with language."[7] Kael, Barthes, and Zontar may be writing for different audiences in different languages, but they are united in an increasingly difficult task of avoiding textual boredom. This desire for the shock of recognition, a random moment of poetic perversity, the epiphany of the unexpected, remains a major current in the cinephile's seemingly unquenchable desire to "talk less about good movies than what they love in bad movies."[8]

Very few of the films discussed in *Sleaze Artists* are at the top of conservation lists or are likely to replace canonical titles in the film studies curriculum. The essays themselves, however, present a range of new historical, industrial, political, and aesthetic questions that suggest exciting new avenues in examining the mechanisms of film practice and cultural production. The essays in this volume are divided into two sections. The articles collected in part 1 are the most explicitly historical in nature, although within this shared interest in excavating a cinema previously invisible to close historical analysis, the authors in this section pursue extremely different methodological and critical approaches in placing style, taste, and politics in historical dialogue. Part 2, meanwhile, is more concerned with the "afterlife" of low cinemas as artifacts circulating in various personal, formal, and subcultural imaginations. Here too, however, there is a sustained effort to understand this cinema in the historical context of memory, exhibition, or appropriation.

Part 1 begins with Eric Schaefer's examination of the advertising strategies adopted by sexploitation producers in the early 1960s to promote the increasingly explicit cinema that was in the process of supplanting the era of classic exploitation. Responding to a very specific set of demands and restrictions on the limits of explicit sexual discourse, sexploitation advertising, Schaefer argues, had to employ advertising appeals based on humor, adventure, and experimentation, strategies that in turn increasingly associated the sexploitation patron as deviant and abnormal. As in his foundational study of classic exploitation cinema, Schaefer here combines close historical research with a discussion of these films (and their audiences) as objects presenting a crisis to the era's normative (though changing) codes of respectability. The essay also provides a useful gateway to the other essays of part 1, all of which interrogate the 1960s and early 1970s as a particularly volatile moment in negotiating the appropriate boundaries of film practice and content.

Playing on Pam Cook and Claire Johnson's landmark call for women's "counter-cinema" in the early 1970s, Tania Modleski's "Women's Cinema as Counterphobic Cinema" provides a welcome new perspective on the work of Doris Wishman, the New York housewife turned sexploitation director of the 1960s who has become a major cult figure in bad cinema circles over the past decade. Modleski's piece was actually written a decade ago but never before published due to the author's own uneasiness with Wishman's films, especially the "roughies" Wishman made during the mid-1960s. In a provocative rejoinder to the often unproblematic celebrations of Wishman as an iconoclastic feminist subversive, Modleski challenges the school of feminism that would simply ignore Wishman's often disturbing but frequently fascinating work, as well as the Wishman apologists who embrace the filmmaker and yet ignore the often violent misogyny of the films themselves. In addition to providing a much-needed critical overview of Wishman within the contexts of American feminism, the article also offers a renewed dialogue with key issues in gendered spectatorship.

In "Representing (Repressed) Homosexuality in the Pre-Stonewall Hollywood Homo-Military Film," Harry Benshoff examines a cycle of films in the 1960s exploring homosexual desire in the military. Looking at titles like *The Strange One* (1957), *The Gay Deceivers* (1969), *Billy Budd* (1962), and *Reflections in a Golden Eye* (1967), Benshoff argues these films offer "more complex and theoretically queer ideas about human sexuality" than the supposedly more progressive "post-Stonewall" cinema of the 1970s and 1980s. In narrativizing the ambiguous borders between homosociality and homosexuality in the military, Benshoff argues these films often end up indicting the *repression* of homosexual desire rather than homosexuality itself. Benshoff's article should also remind us that art and "progressive politics" are not necessarily always linked in a teleological march toward liberation and enlightenment; rather, he suggests, the possibilities for representing queerness—like all political struggles of signification—often advance and retreat independently of developments in the terrain of conventional politics.

Building on his extensive work in documentary forms, Chuck Kleinhans's "Pornography and Documentary: Narrating the Alibi" considers the strategies adopted by sexploitation filmmakers of the 1960s and 70s to integrate images and voice-over narration. Specifically, Kleinhans concentrates on the "slippages" between image and narrator in the infamous Mondo (and Mondo-inspired) documentaries of the era, arguing that the sleazy profile of these films stems from a disconnect between traditional documentarian strategies like voice-of-God narration and expert testimony and the wholly prurient and voyeuristic images offered the spectator. In addition to providing welcome close analysis of these important (yet often repressed) examples of documentary film, Kleinhans's article will also be of interest to anyone interested in that alternative "documentary" tradition stretching from the Mondo films to contemporary reality television, a shadow tradition to the more canonized documentarians of the past three decades.

In his study of *El signo de la muerte* (*The Sign of Death*), Colin Gunckel examines the place of the "Aztec horror film" in larger political debates over creating Mexican national identity. Beginning with the cultural policy of *indigenismo*, an attempt in post-revolutionary Mexico to align Mexican identity with the country's pre-Columbian heritage, Gunckel demonstrates how horror films like *El signo de la muerte* (1939) and *The Robot vs. the Aztec Mummy* (1958) provided a counternarrative to the romantic valorizations of Mexico's indigenous populations and cultures found in so much Golden Age Mexican cinema. Employing Robin Wood's work on the Other, "surplus repression," and the horror film, Gunckel examines how the films bracket a period of immense social and cultural transformation in Mexico, replacing the "idyllic landscapes and tragically noble Indians" of the indigenismo tradition with "human sacrifice, decaying corpses, and maniacal scientists." Routinely dismissed as inferior and incoherent copies of Hollywood horror, the Aztec horror cycle is instead for Gunckel a fascinating site for the negotiation of not only indigenous peoples and heritages, but also other period transformations in class and gender.

Kevin Heffernan's "Art House or House of Exorcism?" ends part 1 by detailing the interesting industrial saga of Mario Bava's *Lisa and the Devil* (1973), an ambitious art horror film that debuted to good reviews at Cannes but quickly fell into a distribution void, only to emerge after the international success of *The Exorcist* (1973) in a highly compromised and critically maligned form as *House of Exorcism*. By charting the film's unusual journey through the highs and lows of art cinema, fringe television, grindhouse circuits, and the connoisseur DVD markets, Heffernan provides intriguing insight as to how both the reception and reputation of this troubled film were significantly affected by its various venues of distribution. Based in part on interviews with the film's producer, Alfredo Leone, Heffernan offers a fascinating account of the complicated economics behind the surprisingly intertwined art house, television, and grindhouse circuits of the early 1970s.

Part 2 begins with Kay Dickinson's interrogation of ambivalence and cinema poetics in "Troubling Synthesis," a discussion of how the antiseptic, cold, and seemingly detached synthesizer scoring of Italian horror movies in the 1970s and 1980s contributed to their later vilification in the infamous "video nasties" debates in England. Dickinson explores a double ambivalence at work in these films—the seeming disjunction between sound/music and image, and the conflicting cultural meanings associated with electronic, synthesized music in the 1970s and 1980s. In this way, Dickinson finds an innovative strategy for engaging the frequently formalist question of sound/image relations, arguing finally for maintaining the power of ambiguity, both in art and in academic criticism.

Building on many of the themes in her book *Cutting Edge*, Joan Hawkins's contribution to the volume examines the "sleazy pedigree" of art-house favorite Todd Haynes. By engaging key Haynes films like *Superstar* (1987), *Velvet Goldmine* (1998), and *Far from Heaven* (2002), Hawkins examines the dialectical relationship between art and trash in Hayne's oeuvre. As Hawkins argues, Haynes's work epitomizes the increasing hybridity of high and low taste cultures in contemporary cinema, producing a form of art camp that, while every bit as self-conscious as the shock metacamp of a filmmaker like John Waters, speaks to a very different strategy for integrating camp history and aesthetics into contemporary cultural production. Indeed, filmmakers like Haynes who are increasingly veterans of the cinema's high/low debates over the past twenty years can be seen as fashioning a new cinematic voice that seamlessly integrates the art and exploitation traditions rather than simply pitting them against one another.

Matthew Hills's article on fans of the *Friday the 13th* series (1980–2003) sets out to complicate the idea of oppositionality in the taste wars between "trash" and "legitimate" cinema. As Hills points out, slasher films in general and the *Friday the 13th* series in particular remain a cinematic pariah—clearly beyond the aesthetic/taste boundaries of quality cinema and yet most decidedly not embraced by the aficionados of "paracinema." Dubbing these films "para-paracinema," Hills quite persuasively (and parodically) demonstrates that even a reading protocol devoted to "transgressive bad taste" has its limits and blind spots. Hills goes on to argue that slasher films are most frequently dismissed by critics high and low for their repetitive "formulaic" structure, but then demonstrates that this "formula fallacy" is often based on outright distortions, omissions, and misreadings of the texts themselves. Rarely seen by film critics, but nonetheless frequently commented upon, the *Friday the 13th* films become for

Hills a screen on which a certain critical sensibility projects its worst nightmares about the state of film art.

Expanding on themes encountered in his always intriguing explorations of "bad" cinema in *The Hermanaut*, Chris Fujiwara focuses here on the Italian horror film *Spasmo* (1974) to explore the various implications of boredom in the realm of film aesthetics. After considering a range of theorists on the relationship between boredom, diegetic belief, and cinematic identification, Fujiwara presents a close analysis of boredom as trope, tone, and technique in *Spasmo*. In a reading that incorporates Heidegger, the cinematography of immobility, and the peculiarities of Italian postdubbing practices, Fujiwara's essay suggests that the indeterminacy and disinterest enabled by boring cinema makes it an ideal candidate for the Situationist practices of *detournement* and *dérive*. As the opposite of "entertainment," the boring film suspends us not betwixt and between, but in a perpetual state of waiting, thus providing a useful tool in combating the powers of mass spectacle.

In "Pure *Quidditas* or Geek Chic?" Greg Taylor further explores the critique of Farberesque cultism he proposes in the final chapter of *Artists in the Audience*. Looking at such diverse venues of geek cultdom as D. B. Weiss's *Lucky Wander Boy*, Chuck Klosterman's *Sex, Drugs, and Cocoa Puffs*, and the short-lived Comedy Central series *Beat the Geeks* (2001), Taylor unpacks the contradictions of cultists who pretend to marshal superior forms of aesthetic discernment as an oppositional force yet remain wholly unable (or unwilling) to confront and/or understand the basis of their own aesthetic evaluations. In *Artists in the Audience*, Taylor warns that unexamined cultist and camp approaches to the cinema work as a corrosive force on a still maturing art form. Expanding on that sentiment, Taylor here calls for the actual hard work to be done in understanding the mechanisms and criteria of what Stuart Hall and Paddy Whannel identified forty years ago as "popular discrimination"—the ability of audiences to make informed aesthetic judgments about all manner of popular culture.

Sleaze Artists concludes with my own essay, "Movies: A Century of Failure." This piece considers the recent emergence of what might best be termed "cine-cynicism," an adversarial form of cinephilia searching for a new critical language through which to engage the worst aspects of contemporary Hollywood cinema. Using Kael's "Trash, Art, and the Movies" as a starting point, the essay considers how a range of "bitterly comic" and "comically bitter" film writers have elaborated a now century old fascination in film culture with cinematic failure into a sensibility that *loves* movies and yet *hates* the cinema. Once seen as the most promising and revolutionary art form of the twentieth century, film's early colonization by commercial interests and the accompanying (and ongoing) alienation of creative labor quickly made the medium a disappointing source of frustration and lost opportunity. Over the years, cinephiles have developed endless strategies for reframing the limitations of cinema into new textual games and possibilities. But what is one to do in a world where both art cinema and Hollywood blockbusters seem clichéd and bankrupt and where the A, B, and Z catalogues of Hollywood have been completely exhausted? What can be done when the jaded cinephile faces the depressing realization that no film on earth will ever again be a genuine revelation or even slightly surprising? The cine-cynics, I argue, create a form of pop-textual play where having a position on the movies is ultimately more rewarding than actually seeing them, abandoning the futile hope for cinematic art and replacing it instead with a fascination for a larger field of cinematic practice.

Notes

1. Pauline Kael, "Trash, Art, and the Movies," *Going Steady: Film Writings, 1968–1969* (New York: Marion Boyars, 1994), 105.
2. Greg Taylor, *Artists in the Audience: Cults, Camp, and American Film Criticism* (Princeton, N.J.: Princeton University Press, 1999).
3. Susan Sontag, "Notes on Camp," *Against Interpretation* (New York: Dell, 1966), originally published in the *Partisan Review*, 1964.
4. V. Vale and Andrea Juno, *Incredibly Strange Films* (San Francisco: V/Search, 1985).
5. Most critics of the article have critiqued it for seeming to offer an unproblematic divide between "mainstream Hollywood" and "paracinema," or for portraying this community as too homogenous and thus ignoring the turf battles within this group. That may be true, and it may well be in my own enthusiasm for films like *Robot Monster* and *Brainiac*, the article reads in places more like a manifesto than a sober description of a subcultural phenomenon. Still, I believe the language of the article—if read closely— takes great pains to describe these "boundaries" as self-perception and self-promotion within this community, most loosely defined, and not as an attempt to lay down the law about what is and is not "paracinema" (it is described as an elastic sensibility, after all). Perhaps such critiques are the product of working with Bourdieu's scientific, taxo-

nomic, and spatialized categories in the first place—drawing lines of taste, distinction, and counterdistinction inevitably leads to claims that one has not done so properly.
6. Jeffrey Sconce, "'Trashing' the Academy: Taste, Excess, and an Emerging Politics of Cinematic Style," *Screen* 36 (1995): 371–93.
7. Roland Barthes, *The Pleasure of the Text* (New York: Hill and Wang, 1975), 14.
8. Kael, "Trash, Art, and the Movies," 89.

1

Sleazy Histories

ERIC SCHAEFER

Pandering to the "Goon Trade" Framing the Sexploitation Audience through Advertising

Sexploitation films have always been a disreputable form. As "adult" titles proliferated during the 1960s, even those films that maintained the gloss of European art cinema were seen as little more than streetwalkers, classed up with better carriage and foreign accents. That disreputability also extended to the audiences for the films, the filthy old men in rumpled raincoats who peopled the public imagination. Whether it was journalistic accounts of the growing number of theaters that specialized in "dirty movies," snide asides in film reviews, or cartoons in the popular press, the audience for adult films was characterized as a shady collection of characters at best, deviant and potentially dangerous at worst. They were "the goon trade."[1] I want to examine the way sexploitation films were advertised and consider the ways that advertising contributed to the stigmatization of their audience—despite the fact that in reality the audience was largely comprised of "respectable" citizens. This tacit framing of the audience for sexploitation—and later hard-core pornography—eventually led to bans on newspaper advertising for these movies in many cities across the country, a ban that had serious consequences for the production of adult films in the late 1970s.

Sexploitation films emerged around 1960 in the form of moving cheesecake pictures known as "nudie cuties" (e.g., *The Immoral Mr. Teas*, 1959), a new crop of nudist camp epics (e.g., *Daughter of the Sun*, 1962), and racy foreign entries often goosed up with additional inserts of nudity and sexually suggestive scenes (e.g., *The Twilight Girls*, 1961). Low-budget and unashamedly lurid, the movies initially played in urban theaters and other failing venues, programmed by product-starved exhibitors who wanted to keep their struggling operations alive. By the end of the 1960s, however, sexploitation movies were plentiful enough, and some sufficiently improved in quality, to cross over into the showcase theaters of established chains.

The Art of the Eye Stopper

Advertising for sexploitation films came in two primary categories: trailers and print. Although copy for radio spots was sometimes included in pressbooks and prerecorded spots were occasionally made available, radio seems to have been used only sporadically, and television advertising was almost nonexistent. Trailers were the most important for sexploitation films in the early years because they were seen by the clientele that regularly patronized theaters specializing in sexploitation product. But it was the print ads that appeared in newspapers and the posters slapped up in front of theaters that were seen by the largest numbers of eyes—people who went to the movies, as well as those who would never dream of seeing an adult film. Print ads for sexploitation films were placed on the same newspaper pages with mainstream films and offered sexploitation the most direct opportunity to differentiate itself from Hollywood movies and more conventional foreign films.

As the independent sexploitation films began to appear in the late 1950s and early 1960s, members of the Motion Picture Association of America (MPAA) were still governed by the Advertising Code for Motion Pictures. The Code stated that "good taste shall be the guiding rule of motion picture advertising," that "profanity and vulgarity shall be avoided" and that "nudity with meretricious purpose and salacious postures shall not be used."[2] Yet the confirmation of First Amendment rights on the motion picture by the Supreme Court's 1952 *Burstyn v. Wilson* decision, the gradual erosion of the Production Code and state and municipal censorship during the 1950s, and an increasingly adult slant in Hollywood films led to more provocative ads through the period.[3] Whether it was showing off Jane Russell's most famous assets in posters for films such as *Underwater* (1955) or presenting a thumb-sucking Carroll Baker sprawled on a day bed in posters for *Baby Doll* (1956), Hollywood movie promotion increasingly favored feminine pulchritude and provocative situations. Advertising for teenpics and films from low-rent outfits such as American International Pictures (AIP) often focused on suggestive scenes or revealing costuming that seldom appeared in the films themselves (e.g., *Naked Paradise* [1957], *High School Hell Cats* [1958]). By the time *Lolita* was released in 1962, with the infamous art showing a cherry-red lollipop resting between Sue Lyon's pouting lips, the early sexploitation films were already being given a run for their money by the majors. Thus, the low-budget sexploitation film was faced with a problem: how to convince ticket buyers that their movies were more suggestive, more revealing, and ultimately more "naughty" than the increasingly "adult" pictures coming out of Hollywood—not to mention the growing crop of frank foreign films.

In his classic 1957 exposé of the advertising industry, *The Hidden Persuaders*, Vance Packard wrote of "eye stoppers," those sexy images that can arrest the eye.[4] There was certainly nothing hidden in the persuasive power of the earliest sexploitation advertising, which relied first and foremost on eye stoppers—images of scantily clad women. Ads for nudie cuties display a great deal of similarity to the burlesque films of the "classical exploitation" era that preceded them, and which were on the wane in the early 1960s.[5] Such images could take the form of artwork or photographs. Like burlesque films, but unlike most classical exploitation movies that had preceded them, nudie cuties made no pretense of having any educational motives or material. This was made clear in their humorous taglines and joking titles. Humor can often be found in the titles of the films themselves, which at times relied on wordplay, alliteration, and a general sense of playfulness: *The Immoral Mr. Teas*, *The Ruined Bruin* (1961), *Mr. Peter's Pets* (1962), *The Bare Hunt* (1963), *Bell, Bare and Beautiful* (1963), *Boin-n-g!* (1963), *Goldilocks and the Three Bares* (1963), *My Bare Lady* (1963), and so on. In addition to humorous titles, an accompanying use of cartoons or cartoonish imagery in nudie-cutie advertising was also standard. For instance, all of Russ Meyer's earliest films were advertised with cartoon imagery. Ads for *Eve and the Handyman* (1961) included caricatures of star Anthony-James Ryan

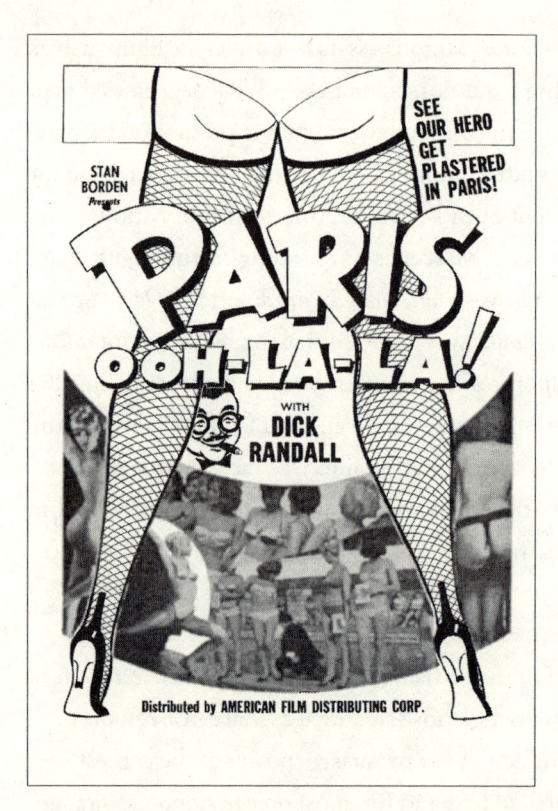

FIGURE 1 Advertising for the "nudie-cutie" *Paris Ooh-La-La* (1963) making use of humor and cartoon imagery in an effort to deflect accusations of appealing to a "prurient interest."

wearing his handyman togs and toting a plunger. In one image he knocks on the glass door of a shower, behind which stands a curvaceous female silhouette. In other art he hauls a claw-foot tub, filled with bubbles and a smiling young woman. In each instance Ryan wears a sly smile. The ads for the film promised "You'll NEVER See This on TV!" as a way of indicating the fare in the film was something not for general viewership. Another tagline was blatant in its dual-meaning, claiming the movie was "A Riot of Voluptuous Laughs & Sex! For the BROAD-minded adults only." *The Adventures of Lucky Pierre* (1961), David F. Friedman and Herschell Gordon Lewis's first foray into nudie cuties, featured a cartoon Frenchman, complete with beret, ogling girls through binoculars. Not only were ticket-buyers offered "Delightful, Delectable, Desirable, Delicious Damsels Devoid of Any and All Inhibitions," the film was served up in "Flesh-tone Color and Skinamascope." Similarly, AFD's *Paris Ooh-La-La!* (1963), with Dick Randall, included a caricature of the grinning Randall along with the line "See Our Hero Get Plastered in Paris!"

The joking, fraternal nature of the advertising linked the films to traditional male smokers where stag films were screened. Just as joking and commentary served to diffuse some of the erotic tension in such homosocial situations, the cartoonish and playful strategy of nudie-cutie advertising served a similar function. To acknowledge sexual desire or the generation of lust in the ads would have been to admit that the films were made to appeal to prurient interest under the Supreme Court's *Roth* decision and thus potentially obscene. In that 1957 case, the Court held that protected expression included anything that contained "ideas" no matter how unconventional or controversial, and that the only expression that might not be accorded protection must be "utterly without redeeming social importance."[6] Sexually oriented material was protected, according to the ruling, if it was not obscene, and obscenity could be determined only if, for "the average person, applying contemporary community standards, the dominant theme of the material taken as a whole appeals to prurient interest."[7] The vast majority of nudie cuties thus attempted in their advertising to displace direct erotic appeal with humor. Effective, perhaps, in avoiding censorship, such a strategy also left the films open to charges that they were juvenile, if not downright infantile, in their approach to both humor and sexuality. Writing about nudie films in 1962, David Moller described the plot of *Hideout in the Sun* as "so ludicrous that had it been intended for a ten-minute short it would have been one of the funniest, wildest ever. Spread over seventy minutes, it was like slow death."[8] A Los Angeles critic sneered that *The Immoral Mr. Teas* "has much the same subtle, urbane wit to be found in any one of our undergraduate humor magazines."[9] A Philadelphia judge who declined to find *Mr. Teas* obscene still said the movie was "vulgar, pointless, and in bad taste."[10] Those who attended the films could also be singled out as being vulgar and having juvenile taste for their willingness to sit through such witless films. When the early nudie movies were reviewed—which was a fairly rare occasion—critics often commented on the childish nature of the films and their audience.

The two other major categories of early sexploitation, nudist movies and pseudo-art films, used other techniques to blunt potential criticism. Nudist films stressed "beauty" and "nature" in their ads. *World without Shame* (1962), for example, was the "fascinating story of young people who left civilization to commune with nature" and promised "Beauty as it was created." Topping things off, the film was "In Beautiful Eastman Color." *Let's Go Native* (ca. 1962) presented "The Untold Mysteries of TRUE NATURE LOVERS!" and claimed to be "Beautiful ... beyond comprehension!" Protected by a string of court decisions from the mid-1950s, the associations with beauty and nature provided a shield against charges that nudist films were salacious. Foreign films with an art slant, meanwhile, coupled suggestive imagery with nods to drama and emotion. Ava Leighton and Radley Metzger's films for Audubon specialized in this strategy. Ads for the French film *The Twilight Girls*, released by Audubon in 1961, hinted at lesbian themes in the art while the taglines served up passion: "No longer children ... not yet women ... caught in the turmoil of their unformed emotions!" Although the ads for nudist and art films were somewhat more sophisticated than those for nudie cuties, the fact that all the films played in the same venues, often on double features, meant that they were aligned in the public's imagination as often indistinguishable dirty movies.

Not surprisingly, most sexploitation ads in the period before the creation of the MPAA ratings system in 1968 stressed that the films were for "Adults Only!" Earlier classical exploitation films may have been pitched as "Adults Only," but those with an educational imprimatur often permitted high-school- and junior-high-school-aged boys and girls to attend. The age of admission for sexploitation films may have varied slightly, depending on community tolerance, but seventeen or eighteen was generally the minimum age for admission. The lure of films made for adult eyes only was sufficient to set them apart from the pack of mainstream films, the bulk of which were still directed at as broad an audience as possible.

Just as sexploitation films ran the gamut from elegant European imports made in exotic locales to shabby black-and-white quickies shot in cold-water flats in New York, the ads also deployed a range of styles. Higher-end films from companies like Audubon, or movies that had crossover potential, tended to feature slick, well-designed art and copy, in many instances the equivalent of those from their major studio counterparts. David Friedman has commented that Harry Novak's Boxoffice International often used the talents of Steve Offers. "His ads looked more like regular ads. I disagreed with that. I thought they should look like adult film ads. The art and the layout looked good, but not the copy."[11] According to Joe Steinman of Boxoffice International, the company used "dif-

FIGURE 2 Sexploitation's appeals to "beauty" and "nature" in ad copy for *Let's Go Native* (1962).

ferent artists depending on the type of campaign that we are working on. The planning and inspiration behind these is always a joint effort. That is why we are able to achieve diversification in our campaigns, but the overall credit must be given to Harry Novak. He gives every campaign his personal attention."[12] Friedman's Entertainment Ventures, Inc. (EVI) and several other producers used the talents of Rudy Escalera, who made most of his money cranking out art for Azteca, a company that distributed Mexican films to Spanish-language theaters in the United States. According to Friedman, "He had great imagination. He worked from stills to create the artwork." Escalera's art is distinctive for its curvy women and use of heavy black line. Low-end companies often relied on staff at poster companies such as Consolidated in New York. Friedman claims, "They probably handled art for over 1,000 pictures."[13]

For promotional campaigns, sexploitation film producers tended to use the services of smaller accessory companies, such as Consolidated, Donald Velde, Louis Scheingarten, and Bartco, rather than National Screen Service. These smaller companies generally offered a more limited range of promotional materials, usually restricted to trailers, one-sheets, stills, and pressbooks. In 1966 EVI joined with producers Bob Cresse and Armand Atamian to create United Theatrical Amusement (UTA), a company that produced one-sheets, pressbooks, and stills. Friedman explains, "The whole idea was to keep as much as possible under one roof." EVI also operated a wholly owned subsidiary called Ultra Volume Photo, a photo processing operation that could crank out thousands of photos per day. "In addition to doing our stuff [EVI]," Friedman said, "they did all Cresse's, Novak's, UTA, Bartco, and some for Velde. They also did [Los Angeles] Dodger fan photos for a year."[14]

Regardless of who produced or distributed the advertising material, as with sexploitation films themselves, the ads for the movies have a large degree of intertextual similarity. This extends from the images to the words used in taglines. Some words turn up over and over in the advertising for sexploitation films. Not surprisingly, "adult" is the most constant signifier, usually to indicate the intended audience either with "adults only" or "strictly adult." Other words that recur repeatedly include "sex," "erotic," "passion," "intimate," "pleasure," "love," and variations on "lust." "Daring," "shocking," "raw," "thrills," "lurid," "orgy," and "sin" also appear often. Finally, descriptors such as "exotic," "abnormal," and "bizarre" turn up with some frequency. Movies weren't just in color, they were inevitably in "revealing" color (*Notorious Big Sin City* [1970]) or "throbbing" color (*Acapulco Uncensored* [1968]).

In 1966, the Supreme Court's *Ginzberg v. United States* decision threw a new wrinkle onto the sheets in its determination that material that dealt with sex or erotica might not be obscene "in the abstract, but [could be considered] obscene when promoted by 'pandering.'"[15] The sexploitation business was on notice that even if a film itself might not be obscene, if its advertising "pandered" it could be *considered* obscene. Dual versions of ads and posters, "hot" ads for the more permissive markets and "cold" ads for the conservative ones, had been around from the earliest days of exploitation. Following *Ginzberg* they became an even greater necessity. Friedman notes, "When newspapers got too sensitive we had two sets of ads. *Thar She Blows* [1969] became *Thar She Goes*. We had ads for *Trader Hornee* [1970] with two *es* and ads with one *e*. *The Big Snatch* [1968] became *The Big Catch*. We just printed extra Cs that the exhibitor could substitute

FIGURE 3 The press book for 1968's *The Big Snatch* included an extra C so that newspapers in more conservative communities could promote the film as *The Big Catch*.

in the ads."[16] Boxoffice International's *Country Hooker* (1968) had ad cuts so exhibitors could substitute the title *Country Playgirls*. The pressbook for *Acapulco Uncensored* included substitute art so the film could be changed to *Acapulco Exposé* or *Acapulco Sex* "according to local tastes." *The Daisy Chain* (1969) became simply *Daisy C.* in some ads, although they retained the image of the flower encircled by a chain to fill in those in the know. One-sheets featured either the flower and chain art at the center or a circular formation of eight nude men and women for less sensitive situations.[17]

Creating Appeals, Framing Patrons

By the mid-1960s ads for sexploitation films operated on two levels. At the most obvious, they were selling a single commodity, one particular film. As such, they had to intrigue potential ticket buyers with words and images, to set that particular film apart from competing sexploitation films as well as other movies in theaters and drive-ins. But beyond this they were also broadly selling the idea of sexuality and the potential ticket buyers' relationship to it. In so doing, sexploitation advertising created an implicit profile of its abstract, but rather diverse audience. This profile, in turn, brought with it larger cultural assumptions about the "typical" patron for sexploitation. As Pierre Bourdieu has indicated, "Taste classifies, and it classifies the classifier. Social subjects, classified by their classifications, distinguish themselves by the distinctions they make, between the beautiful and the ugly, the distinguished and the vulgar."[18] Sexploitation advertising, in other words, worked to classify both the films and their ticket-buying public, constructing an image of the films' patrons based on their taste in movies. A product of one's purchases of goods and services, this "commodity self," as Jib Fowles has defined it, "offers up potential meanings and . . . helps signal identity to oneself as well as to others."[19] In concert with efforts to avoid censorship through appeals to humor, beauty, and art, sexploitation advertising also promised a commodity (and thus produced a commodity self) based on four primary sexual appeals: excitement, adventure, curiosity, and experimentation.[20]

As one might expect of these films, the promise of sexual excitement and stimulation through nudity or erotic situations was standard in sexploitation advertising. Images of women nude, nearly nude, or provocatively clothed were a staple in the ads, designed to appeal to the heterosexual males who initially made up the vast majority of the audience for sexploitation films. Even when nudity or its suggestion was limited, provocative images of women's faces with lips parted or with ecstatic expressions on their faces figured prominently. As sexploitation films developed over the 1960s to include scenes of simulated sex, images of nude or partially clothed men began to appear in ads as well.

Ads often featured sketches or shots of several girls, giving the impression that a smorgasbord of women would be featured. Taglines also alluded to a variety of women: "Prisoner in a Harem—A G.I.'s dream come true" (*A Good Man Is Hard to Find* [1969]); "You will experience, along with Henry, the delights of 26 different wives!" (*Substitution* [1970]). This technique of showing multiple women in posters and ads would become an important strategy for many sexploitation films, particularly low-end movies without recognizable stars. The notion of variety and plenty, of multiple willing women on display, not only recalls the burlesque stage and films as well as nudie cuties, but also the men's magazines that had proliferated since the mid-1950s. Making good on the ads, this fantasy of multiple, willing sex partners structured the narrative form of most sexploitation films.

Excitement could also take the form of shock, and many movies promised to startle viewers or to shake their sensibilities. Ads for *Suburbia Confidential* (1966) stated that "*The Kinsey Report* shocked readers, *Suburbia Confidential* . . . will shock you!" Olympic International's Japanese import, *Hentai* (1965), was "a film that couldn't have been made in this country!" The Cam-Scope production *Mini-Skirt Love* (1967) offered "A Shocking Glimpse into the Warped Morals of the Modern World." By promising shocking images and scenes, the advertisements for such films suggested that they would take the ticket-buyer out of his everyday life. By tying that shock to sexuality, the films suggested a sexual thrill that was beyond the realm of the average individual's experience.

Adventure was another key appeal in sexploitation advertising, a lure grounded in exotic or unusual locales where the average filmgoer was unlikely to find himself. This included countries considered at the time to have more open views on sex, such as France and, by the mid-1960s, the Scandinavian countries. It also included portions of the city that were considered dangerous or forbidden, such as red light zones and skid rows ("Raw Sex begins with a rainy day on skid row!" promised *Take Me Naked* [1966]). Even the countryside could also be a place for sexual adventure, in the form of nudist camps and other backwoods locales where loose morals were thought to be the rule of the day. Adventure could also be had in more seemingly mundane settings that the 1960s had eroticized in some way: photographer's studios, motel rooms, suburban homes, college campuses, hippie pads, and so forth. Such erotic adventuring could also be found in distant historical periods (*The Exotic Dreams of Casanova* [1971]), and fantasy/science-fiction situations (*Hot Erotic Dreams* [1967], *Space Thing* [1968]).

Curiosity was another major appeal of sexploitation ads. Beyond a desire to see multiple, naked bodies, advertising also promised patrons they would see and understand more about various "forbidden" sexual practices. Movies often promised to satisfy sexual curiosity by revealing "intimate secrets" (*Key

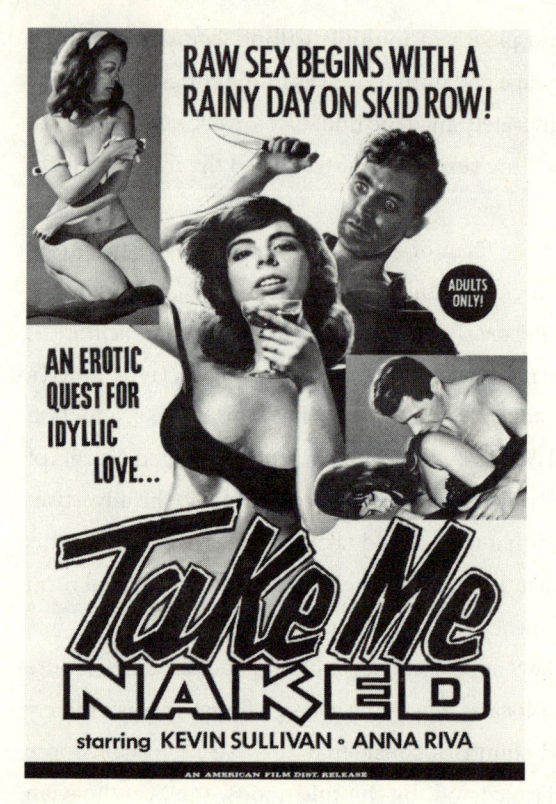

FIGURE 4 Like much other sexploitation advertising, *Take Me Naked* (1966) associated sex with dangerous and forbidden locales, in this case skid row.

Club Wives [1968]). This was particularly the case with movies about lesbianism, which constituted a major theme in the late 1960s, as well as movies that dealt with sadomasochism, bondage and discipline, or other "perversions." Before the advent of hard core, a common theme was the breaking of new sexual ground. For instance, *Massacre of Pleasure* (1966) was billed with the line "Olympic International presents a shattering step forward in the sensual revolution in filmmaking." "Until now the screen did not dare," whispered slicks for *Body of a Female* (1964). And ads for *Naked Fog* (1966) claimed, "For the first time, a film dares . . ." Echoing the puffery of mainstream cinema, these nonspecific references to erotic advances and innovative daring appealed to viewers' curiosity to see new sights, or to see just how much films were capable of showing as obscenity law continued to evolve.

Although the low-end films made by outfits such as Mitam, Distribpix, and AFD were seldom reviewed, those films that did get notices were apt to incorporate them into their ad campaigns. Such ads were capable of appealing to the intellectual curiosity of viewers by creating a tension between a low form and apparent approval (or at least notice) from the critical establishment. *Without a Stitch* (1968), a Danish film initially impounded by U.S. Customs, eventually became a substantial crossover hit. Decontextualized lines from reviews used in the advertising included, "The heroine spends as much time stark naked as any performer since 'Flipper'" (*San Francisco Chronicle*) and "Some of the most explicit sex scenes allowed to be shown publicly" (*Newark News*). Audubon's *Camille 2000* (1969) used lines from the *New York Times* ("Captures beautifully colored, explicit sex") and the *New York Post* ("An eye dazzler ... sex exciter!"). Not only did critical blurbs seem to offer an objective account of what audiences might hope to see in a movie (as opposed to the typical hype from the distributor), they served to provide a seal of approval from the critical establishment.

As Christopher Lasch has observed, "Advertising serves not so much to advertise products as to promote consumption as a way of life. It 'educates' the masses into an unappeasable appetite not only for goods but for new experiences and personal fulfillment."[21] Sexual experimentation was one of the hallmarks of the sexual revolution, and sexploitation advertising catered to the desire for new and different sexual experiences. Whether or not viewers engaged in oral sex, bondage and domination scenarios, extramarital sex, swapping, or other practices, sexploitation film ads invited them to consider the possibility through their images and copy. (More often than not, the films themselves showed the negative implications of unhindered experimentation.) Among the situations alluded to in ads were unusual sex practices: "She sought the normal in sex but found it in the abnormal!" (*Come Play with Me* [1968]); age difference: "Older men driven into the arms of teenage temptresses! (*Red Lips* [1963]); bisexuality: "These girls played both sides of the fence!" (*The Girl with Hungry Eyes* [1967]); lesbianism: "They did it because they had to" (*Donna & Lisa* [1969]); promiscuity: "A casual pick-up shows her the way to escape from the boredom of sexual frigidity!" (*Oona* [1970]); and wife swapping: "Filmed in a swapping center!" (*Love Thy Neighbor and His Wife* [1970]). Other films suggested that to experience them was to engage in a both a sexual and cinematic experiment. *You* (1968), shot with a subjective camera and supposedly in "Feel-A-Vision," claimed "the star of the picture is YOU! YOU will feel every sensuous sensation! YOU will live through every shattering climax! YOU will perform every depraved act in the picture! YOU will participate in every unspeakable performance!"

While the titles of some sexploitation films were similar to their mainstream counterparts, or fairly innocuous, others appeared to serve as descriptions of their imagined audience: *The Animal, The Abductors, The Brutes, The Curious Female, The Debauchers, The Defilers, For Single Swingers Only, The Immoral, Lusty Neighbors, The Marriage Drop-Outs, The Molesters, Moonlighting Wives, Scum of the Earth,* and *The Smut Peddler,* to name just a few. Other titles seemed to describe the attitudes or behaviors of their viewers: *Anything Once, Caught in the Act—Naked, Do Me! Do Me! Do Me!, Excited, Forbidden Pleasure, I Crave Your Body, Let's Play Doctor, Many Ways to Sin, Orgy at Lil's Place, Odd Tastes, Sensual Encounters, The Swappers, She's . . . 17 and Anxious, Some Like It Violent,* and *Too Young, Too Immoral!* Although *The Molesters,* a 1963 Swiss film, played dates in Atlanta, Buffalo, and Columbus, the release ran into trouble in both Pittsburgh, where local newspapers censored the advertising, and Cleveland, where the *Plain Dealer* editorialized about the film's "sick" producer and local booker.[22] The movie itself was a series of fairly sober courtroom sketches dealing with various psychosexual problems. But the advertising caused an uproar. The *Plain Dealer* rejected the ads, and in their editorial suggested "no normal person could find either entertainment or helpful information in *The Molesters.*" The implication, clearly, was that only deviates would see the film.

In defending their product, producers may have inadvertently reinforced the stereotype of the sexploitation customer as a deviate or social outcast. David F. Friedman, who operated theaters in addition to producing and distributing movies, often characterized the sexploitation "regular" as a rather sad, lonely, man:

You are pandering to the most horrible of all human emotions, loneliness. The average guy, why does a guy buy a dirty book, why does a guy buy a girlie magazine? A guy buys a dirty book primarily to take home or wherever he is and masturbate while he reads it, because it creates a fantasy. If you were a lonely guy, let's say you were on the road, you're in a strange town, not one guy out of a thousand knows how to get a date unless he's paying for it, and

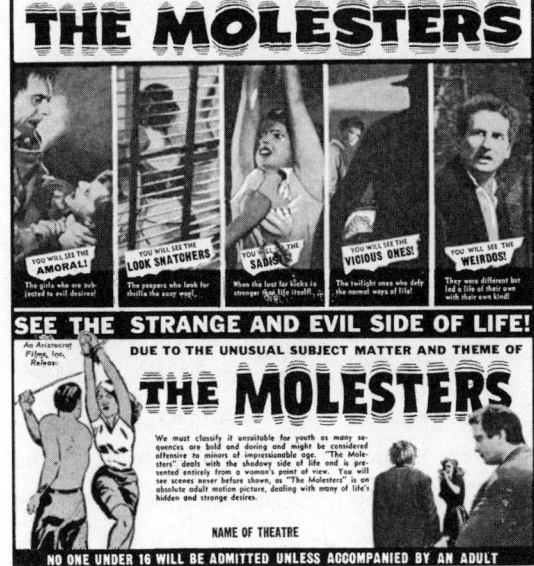

FIGURES 5 & 6 Titles like *Scum of the Earth* and *The Molesters* did much to confuse the psychopathic subjects on the screen with patrons in the theater.

even when he's paying for it, he's too embarrassed to ask. So he goes to a Nudie theater and he fantasizes.[23]

Indeed, until the late 1960s most sexploitation films played in decaying urban theaters, while the earliest sexploitation films, with their copious amounts of female nudity and *Playboy* aesthetic, drew heavily on the single male patron.

Friedman clearly believed that he and his cohorts were providing a service to lonely men. Whether those individuals considered themselves lonely or not is open to question. Observation on the part of theater managers and researchers indicated that people who went to see sexploitation films were "average" in almost every respect. For instance, two owners of a Charlotte, North Carolina, adults-only theater characterized their audience as "mostly businessmen, white-collar types, and sometimes a preacher." One of the owners, Charles Hodges, said that most of his customers were "middle-aged men killing time between business appointments." Hodges told *Variety* that "the general consensus is that you get degenerates, winos, bums . . . it's really quite the contrary."[24] The relatively normal nature of the sexploitation audience was confirmed by studies performed by the Commission on Obscenity and Pornography and published in 1971.[25]

But with advertising appeals based on excitement, adventure, curiosity, and experimentation, the profile of the sexploitation consumer was constructed as someone who was abnormal—like those people who sought out *The Molesters*. Such individuals were insatiably curious, voyeuristic, and sexually adventurous. This profile linked the sexploitation consumers to other urban-centered anxieties at the time. The profile of the sexploitation filmgoer embodied many of the features of "urbanism"—low community social bonding, anonymity, tolerance, alienation, and deviance.[26] Put another way, those living in a state of urbanism were, among other things, "anonymous, isolated, secular, [and] relativistic."[27] Crime was on the rise, and over half the women polled, compared to 20 percent of the men, asserted in a 1972 survey that they were afraid to walk in their neighborhoods at night.[28] Although lacking a sound basis in fact, the advertising for sexploitation movies, and later X-rated films of both the soft-core and hard-core varieties, contributed to the perception that the movies catered to lonely, sexually frustrated perverts. Such a construction made it a fairly easy proposition for opponents to attack the films that seemed to prey on desires that were constructed as deviant. For many, there appeared to be a causal link between the appearance of adult films and theaters and the collapse of neighborhoods into cesspools of prostitution, crime, and decay.[29] Opposition to the films and their patrons also came from the MPAA, concerned that the films were taking screens away from the major distributors, as well as from religious groups and other anti-smut factions. Some newspapers took it upon themselves to begin a cleanup.

Cleanups and Crackdowns

Whether it was through their advertising appeals or because patrons were more willing to resist potentially negative social pressures, by the later part of the 1960s a segment of sexploitation film output was achieving a broader audience, and in particular the coveted couple or date market.[30] Breakout films such as *I, a Woman* (1966) and *Vixen* (1968) paved the way for other movies to mine this lucrative niche. For instance, the pressbook for *Bunny & Clod* (1970), a less-than-subtle stab at sexing up the 1967 Warren Beatty/Faye Dunaway hit, encouraged exhibitors by claiming, "*Bunny & Clod* is a film that has great appeal to ladies and should be sold with couples in mind. Think couples—they are the key to the future of our business." Ads for *Together* (1971), featuring Marilyn Chambers before she went *Behind the Green Door* (1972), breathed a sigh of relief: "Finally, an X rated movie your wife or girlfriend can enjoy!" Such films tended to eschew leering copy and suggestive photographs for humor, topicality, or sensuality. What was clear was that "dirty movies" were reaching a larger audience and moving onto screens that they did not have access to in the past. As sexploitation films succeeded in reaching a bigger, more diverse audience, however, they also faced increasing opposition.

Newspapers had already started to take an increasingly dim view of ads for adult movies. In 1964 *Variety* claimed, "In hundreds of small towns around the United States the voice and muscle of unofficial censorship is the local newspaper advertising manager. He stands as a barrier to the sexy hot imported features and Hollywood underworld bare skin epics. He is the final and highest authority on whether a film can be advertised." The article described the power wielded by ad managers to refuse ads, though "he seldom, if ever, sees the films questioned and invariably bases his judgement on the 'leer' in the proposed

FIGURES 7A & 7B The press book for *Bunny and Clod* (1970) included advice to exhibitors emphasizing the importance of couples to the future of the business.

copy, a certain amount of hearsay about the film, and the example of nearby big city police censors."[31] In one such small-town case, the Michigan State Court of Appeals affirmed the right of the *Battle Creek Enquirer and News* to bar ads on adult films in 1966.[32]

But such cases were not limited to smaller cities and towns. In 1965 the Hearst newspapers in San Francisco established guidelines for amusement ads because of what it called "the excesses of a few." Among the taboo topics were bust measurements, couples in bed, double-entendres, nude figures or silhouettes, perversion, and references to nymphomania. *Variety* detailed that "frowned on words include cuties, flesh-a-scope, girlie, homosexual, immorality, lesbian, lust, naked, nothing on, nudies, nudist camp, nymphs, pervert, professional girls, prostitute, rape, scanty panties, seduce, skin-a-scope, sex . . . sex rituals, sexpot, sexsational, strippers, and third sex."[33] A 1968 survey of forty-four newspaper advertising directors representing sixty-eight metropolitan papers found that most were "concerned that in far too many instances motion picture advertising [was] becoming progressively more distasteful," according to the survey's author, Raymond Wild. Most felt that they had a moral obligation to their readers to censor objectionable movie ads.[34]

A clear example of such censorship at work appeared in a May 1969 issue of *Time* magazine. The article noted that "the New York *Times* recently ran a movie ad for *The Libertine* [1969] showing the back of a girl, bare except for panties. The *Daily News* ran the same ad for one edition—but then sloppily sketched in a bra strap. Apparently, even the notion that the girl might be barechested was too much for the *News* censor."[35] Other newspapers were taking a page from their small-town counterparts by completely refusing to run ads for X-rated and unrated films, and in some instances even refusing ads for R-rated movies.

On August 1, 1969, James S. Copley, the publisher of the *San Diego Union* and *Evening Tribune*, announced that his two newspapers would no longer promote X-rated or unrated movies and would not accept advertising from theaters showing such films. If Copley's action wasn't the first of its kind on the part of a big city newspaper, it was the first to attract serious notice in the trades, and some not-so-serious commentary as well. The *San Diego Door*, an alternative weekly, editorialized against Copley's "moral judgements" made on behalf of San Diegans by poking fun at his policy. "Incidentally, the *Door* has a movie ad censorship policy too, which most people in San Diego are unaware of. We will not accept ads from any movie theater that shows the cervix of the uterus or the male prostate glands. We feel this is going too far."[36] But irony was an insufficient weapon against publishers worried about their images and their readers' sensibilities. In short order the *Detroit Free Press* jumped on the antismut bandwagon,[37] and by the close of 1969 the *Independent Film Journal* calculated that twenty-seven newspapers across the country had banned ads for X- and R-rated films. In addition to small city papers, larger city dailies included the two San Diego papers, the *Phoenix Gazette* and *Phoenix Republic*, the *Indianapolis Star & News*, and the *Dallas Times Herald*.[38]

Within several months, producers were feeling the pinch. Dan Cady, who operated Clover Films, claimed,

Every theater has problems of one sort or another. To deny any paid advertisement is to deny your own company revenue. They should have the discretion or the power to say you're not going to print any obscene words—whatever an obscene word is—and you're not going to have phallic symbols throughout the paper, but I don't think they should discriminate by arbitrarily ruling that the adult motion picture houses cannot be represented as they are in San Diego and Arizona and Chicago and Detroit and Florida.[39]

Just as producers and distributors had to contend with wildly differing "community standards" for what could be put on screen based on the *Roth* test, they increasingly had to contend with differences in what constituted acceptable ads—sometimes within the same city.

In 1970 San Francisco's two major dailies, the *Examiner* and the *Chronicle*, which shared advertising revenues and printing costs, engaged in a war of words when the *Examiner* decided to drop ads for all sex films. The *Examiner* "lamented the city's reputation as 'the smut capital of the world'" and said, "We should have thrown this ugliness out of our advertising columns long ago." The *Chronicle* responded that the ban would "debase the coinage of the American free press."[40] Other dailies picked up on the debate, such as the *Denver Post*, which detailed the Bay Area controversy while explaining to readers that the *Post* kept its house in order "by insisting that the advertising content itself not be offensive to good taste." The article went on to suggest that a refusal to run X ads would "encourage the film industry to give up any attempt at the self-discipline of ratings because those ratings would have been turned into economic weapons against it."[41]

Even if the ratings system was itself not threatened by the newspaper ban on X-rated ads, the ban could not have come at a worse time for sexploitation theaters and the adult film industry as a whole. Such a ban in the early or mid-1960s, when sexploitation films catered to a largely male audience of regulars, would have had little effect. Regulars could rely on posters and trailers to keep themselves abreast of upcoming movies. As both sexploitation and hard-core films, which began to appear in 1969 and 1970, began appealing to a more diverse audience, curious couples and women who sought to have their interest satisfied would have relied on newspaper ads to find out what films were playing, where, and when. While there is no documentation immediately available to back up the contention, we can theorize that theaters unable to advertise X-rated or unrated films would have been forced to turn to mainstream products—and increased competition in buying and booking—in order to remain afloat. On Long Island, the Bethview Amusement Corporation, parent company of the Bethview Theater, resorted to filing a lawsuit in Nassau County against two local newspapers, *Newsday* and the *Long Island Press*, and the Bethpage Civic Association, charging that they had engaged in a conspiracy to destroy the business. According to the defendants, the Bethview, which had a sexploitation policy, was the subject of coercive tactics on the part of the civic group and the newspapers, which refused to run ads for the sexploitation product the theater booked.[42]

The *Des Moines Register* editorialized, "If newspapers attempt to close theaters by stopping advertising, they are assuming the function of the legislators and the courts in determining what is obscene and deciding what the public may see." Yet some individuals were very explicit about their desire "to dry up patronage for [X-rated] movies and to stop their production and exhibition."[43] Efforts to undercut adult films by restricting their advertising increased on several fronts. For instance, in South Dakota a bill was introduced in the state senate to prohibit ads for X-rated movies "in any general advertising medium" in the state. Bills in New Mexico and Massachusetts would have forbid showing trailers for X-rated films with family or G-rated pictures.[44] The Oklahoma Publishing Company, which owned newspapers and radio stations, not only refused to run ads for X-rated films, but also refused to carry ads for R-rated movies unless the movies were first screened and met with the approval of the publishers. A Columbia executive rhetorically asked whether the publishers "sampled every restaurant or used every suppository they advertise?"[45] Some papers refused to use the word *sex* in titles, substituting *love* or other words, or substituting the *ex* with stars in a misguided effort to make the word less lurid.[46] Newspapers in Portland, Oregon, and Boston joined the X ban.

Sexploitation theaters were also under pressure from municipalities and neighborhood groups when they used posters, stills, and lurid come-ons to draw patrons in off the streets. Kevin Thomas reported on a meeting of the Adult Film Association of America (AFAA) in 1971 for the *Los Angeles Times*. Among the concerns addressed at the meeting were continuing censorship and the increasing move to hard core, but Thomas stated that "the one issue that concerns many citizens that was not explored at length was that of lurid advertising, especially outside theaters and store fronts." Thomas claimed that many adults who might defend the right of individuals to see porn films "resent tasteless, graphic stills and posters on public display—especially when they're so easily seen by children." He advised that "the AFAA would be wise to consider that there may be countless people who would defend their right to show anything they want inside their theaters as long as they don't thrust it on an unwilling audience outside them."[47]

The MPAA made noise periodically about the ban on X-rated advertising, especially when it threatened to creep into the R and GP (later PG) categories. For the most part, however, its films had remained untouched. But in 1972 both the MPAA and Warner Bros. were forced to reckon with the ban directly when Stanley Kubrick's *A Clockwork Orange* was rated X by the MPAA. Publishers of the *Detroit News* finally followed the lead of the *Free Press* and banned X advertising, which drew MPAA president Jack Valenti to the Motor City for a meeting with the paper's publishers. During a news conference following "a cordial conversation" with representatives of the *Detroit News*, Valenti stated that "'the X rating does not connote pornography.'" He then went on to urge the newspapers that refused ads for X films to "distinguish between quality pictures that may be rated X and the so-called skinflicks that fall into the X category."[48] In typical fashion, the MPAA could not advance an unequivocal argument against censorship. To do so would have given a potentially strategic advantage to a segment of the motion picture industry not affiliated with the MPAA and at times seen as robbing member companies of time on now increasingly prime urban screens.

Sam Chernoff, owner of adult theaters in Detroit, wrote a letter to the *Detroit News* in which he claimed,

> With the exception of a small group of storefront 16mm theaters that possibly show films without story line or short subjects depicting acts of sexuality that may go beyond the limits of candor, none of the standard 35mm adult theaters in Detroit ever shows pornography or hardcore films. All adult-oriented films shown in this type of theater, projected by union projectionists and staffed by hard working people trying to make a living, are

within the limits set by the U.S. Supreme Court and have a lot of social [sic] redeeming value.

Like Valenti, who spoke for mainstream pictures, Chernoff made distinctions as well, differentiating between the hard-core character of 16mm films and the soft-core nature of sexploitation films. When asked, he pointed to the difficulty in categorizing films: "How can the brass of *The News* make an overall statement that points out that Detroit adult theaters show hardcore and pornographic films? Even the highest court in the country can't determine what constitutes pornography, so how can you?"[49]

The *Los Angeles Times* eventually segregated adult movie ads into their own section in the newspaper, and in 1977 Otis Chandler, publisher of the *Times*, sent a memo to the paper's staff announcing that ads for all hard-core films would be banned. "Given our long and deep commitment to free expression, the decision to drop this advertising was reached reluctantly and after long and careful deliberation," wrote Chandler: "The truth is, we have been dealing with an indefensible product, one with absolutely no redeeming values, and this phenomenon shows no sign of leaving the contemporary social scene. Cutting through the arguments on all sides, we think it is entirely out of character for *The Times*, with its long history of vigorous citizenship in this community, to continue to play a role in the promotion of commercialized pornography. Thus, effective today, we have banned advertising which appeared formerly under the 'Adult Movie' heading."[50] The *Times* replaced the adult movie heading with a "Family Film Guide." Also in 1977 the *New York Times* implemented a policy to severely restrict the size and content of adult film ads.[51] Both the Los Angeles and New York papers assumed the role of determining what constituted redeeming social value or importance.

As much as any other factor, the ban on X advertising served to turn back the clock for the adult film business. Producers either worked to cut their films to a solid R-rating or pushed headlong into the increasingly ghettoized production of hard core. Friedman has said,

> When the LA *Times* stopped the advertising cold that was the beginning of the end for the [California-based] Pussycat and other [adult movie] circuits. That one paper had more than anything else to do with it. In New York it

didn't make that much difference. In New York the trade came from people just walking by, bums stumbling into the theaters. But in LA no one walks, everybody drives. The [LA] *Times* had circulation of a million, the [*Herald-Examiner*] paper only 200,000. Without the ads in the *Times* it really began to hurt things.[52]

He notes that even when the Pussycat Theaters attempted to place an ad in the *Los Angeles Times* that claimed that the chain served the freshest popcorn in town and simply listed locations—with no mention of any film titles—the ads were refused.[53] The *Los Angeles Times*, which depended on the First Amendment to remain a viable institution, refused to accept advertising for another business touting fresh popcorn. The Pussycat Theaters were forced to advertise in the *Herald-Examiner*, local papers, "throwaways," and to even experiment with advertising on independent television stations.[54]

Although other factors were among the determinants in the decline of sexploitation and the theatrical exhibition of adult films (among them the disappearance of the drive-ins and the rise of video), newspaper bans on adult film advertising in key markets served to substantially disable the economic viability of the form. Yet it was the adult film distributors themselves who sowed the seeds for the advertising ban early on. By employing appeals that focused on sexual excitement, adventure, curiosity, and experimentation, they had shaped a negative profile of the sexploitation customer. Despite evidence to the contrary, the sexploitation audience was framed as dangerous and deviant, and their presence in the urban landscape was considered a factor in the decline of those areas. This led to calls for cleanups and urban renewal that ultimately shuttered the grindhouses that had given sexploitation films their earliest venues, established their profitability, and led to the proliferation of the form.

Notes

1. John Hallowell, "Making Movies for the Goon Trade—Sex! Money! Monotony!" *New York World Journal Tribune*, January 8, 1967.
2. "An Advertising Code for Motion Pictures," in *The 1961 Film Daily Yearbook for Motion Pictures* (New York: Film Daily, 1961), 917.
3. Motion pictures had essentially been without First Amendment protection since the *Mutual v. Ohio* decision of 1915. In *Burstyn v. Wilson* the Court affirmed that "motion pictures are a significant medium for the communication of ideas" and thus "protected

by the constitutional freedom of speech and press." See Edward de Grazia and Roger K. Newman, *Banned Films: Movies, Censors and the First Amendment* (New York: R. R. Bowker, 1982), 81.

4. Vance Packard, *The Hidden Persuaders* (New York: David McKay Company, 1957), 84–85.

5. For a full explanation of the parameters of "classical exploitation films," see my book *"Bold! Daring! Shocking! True!": A History of Classical Exploitation Films, 1919–1959* (Durham, N.C.: Duke University Press, 1999).

6. The concept of social importance was reaffirmed in the Supreme Court's decision in the *Jacobellis v. Ohio* case of 1964. In that decision, Justice William J. Brennan wrote that "material dealing with sex in a manner that advocates ideas, or has literary or scientific or artistic value or any other form of social importance, may not be branded as obscenity" and banned. See de Grazia and Newman, *Banned Films*, 264–65.

7. See de Grazia and Newman, *Banned Films*, 95–96.

8. David Moller, "Nuderama," *Vision* 1, no. 2 (1962): 19.

9. Charles Stinson, "'Immoral Mr. Teas' Ends Era in Movies," *Los Angeles Times*, January 26, 1960.

10. "'Vulgar, Pointless, in Bad Taste' but 'Mr. Teas' Not Pornography," *Variety*, November 2, 1960, 7.

11. David F. Friedman, telephone interview with the author, February 26, 2003.

12. "Boxoffice International's Joe Steinman," *The Late Show*, undated 1974 clipping, Boxoffice International File, Academy of Motion Picture Arts and Sciences Library.

13. Friedman interview, February 26, 2003.

14. Entertainment Ventures, Inc., *1969–1970 Annual Report*, 5 (Los Angeles: Entertainment Ventures, Inc., 1970); Friedman interview, February 26, 2003.

15. Richard S. Randall, *Censorship of the Movies: The Social and Political Control of a Mass Medium* (Madison: University of Wisconsin Press, 1970), 60.

16. Friedman interview, February 26, 2003.

17. It is worth noting that the pressbooks for sexploitation films, which were sent to theater managers and buyers, were often far more explicit than the films themselves in the days before hard core. A motion picture that might feature only a flash of pubic hair could appear to be a "beaver" spread when frozen as a series of stills in a pressbook. The degree of explicitness and the attractiveness of the performers, coupled with the elaborateness of the pressbook (color, size, layout), no doubt had an influence on the willingness of a buyer to book a film.

18. Pierre Bourdieu, *Distinction: A Social Critique of the Judgement of Taste*, trans. Richard Nice (Cambridge, Mass.: Harvard University Press, 1984), 6.

19. Jib Fowles, *Advertising and Popular Culture* (Thousand Oaks, Calif.: Sage Publications, 1996), 47–48.

20. Ibid. See also Fowles's "Advertising's Fifteen Basic Appeals," in *American Mass Media: Industries and Issues*, ed. Robert Atwan, Barry Orton, and William Vesterman, 3rd ed. (New York: Random House, 1984), 43–54. In the latter article Fowles discusses "Murray's List," a list of general advertising's appeals based on the work of psychologist Henry A. Murray.
21. Christopher Lasch, *The Culture of Narcissism: American Life in an Age of Diminishing Expectations* (New York: Norton, 1991), 72.
22. "Peek at Trailer Brings Roar from Cleveland Editorialist; Never Seen, Molesters Yanked," *Variety*, June 3, 1964, 11.
23. Quoted in Kenneth Turan and Stephen F. Zito, *Sinema: American Pornographic Films and the People Who Make Them* (New York: Praeger, 1974), 45.
24. "Bums Few in N.C. 'Sex' Audiences," *Variety*, December 10, 1969, 9.
25. See Charles Winick, "Some Observations on Characteristics of Patrons of Adult Theaters and Bookstores," *Technical Report of the Commission on Obscenity and Pornography*, vol. 4 (Washington, D.C.: U.S. Government Printing Office, 1971), 225–44.
26. On "urbanism," see, for example, Charles R. Tittle and Mark C. Stafford, "Urban Theory, Urbanism, and Suburban Residence," *Social Forces* 70 (1992): 725–44.
27. See Herbert J. Gans, "Urbanism and Suburbanism as Ways of Life: A Re-evaluation of Definitions," in *Human Behavior and Social Processes: An Interactionist Approach*, ed. Arnold M. Rose (Boston: Houghton Mifflin Company, 1962), 626.
28. Quoted in Margaret T. Gordon, Stephanie Riger, Robert K. LeBailly, and Linda Heath, "Crime, Women, and the Quality of Urban Life," in *Women and the American City*, ed. Catherine R. Stimpson, Elsa Dixler, Martha J. Nelson, and Kathryn B. Yatrakis (Chicago: University of Chicago Press, 1981), 141.
29. For a full elaboration on the ways these arguments were mobilized, see Eric Schaefer and Eithne Johnson, "Quarantined! A Case Study of Boston's Combat Zone," in *Hop on Pop: The Politics and Pleasure of Popular Culture*, ed. Henry Jenkins, Tara McPherson, and Jane Shattuc (Durham, N.C.: Duke University Press, 2002), 430–53. While I am trying to indicate that perceptions of the adult movie audience as a whole were clearly skewed to the negative, this should not be construed as suggesting that all patrons of adult movies, or all theaters, were squeaky-clean. Some theaters, especially in big cities and particularly after the advent of hard-core, had reputations as cruising spots where men engaged in quick, anonymous sexual encounters. See, for instance, Samuel R. Delany's memoir about cruising Times Square theaters in the 1970s and 1980s, *Times Square Red, Times Square Blue* (New York: New York University Press, 1999).
30. *Deep Throat* (1972) is often considered to be the first adult film to crack the couples market. But like so many of the tales surrounding that film, this is simply incorrect. For more on the sexploitation films and pre–*Deep Throat* hard-core movies that succeeded with the couples market, see Eric Schaefer, "Gauging a Revolution: 16mm Film and the

Rise of the Pornographic Feature," *Cinema Journal* 41, no. 3 (2002): 6. The article also appears in a slightly altered form in *Porn Studies*, ed. Linda Williams (Durham, N.C.: Duke University Press, 2004).

31. "Moral Arbiters of Stixville," *Variety*, March 4, 1964, 1, 78.
32. "Paper May Refuse 'Adult' Film Ads," *Variety*, November 16, 1966, 1.
33. "Throw Rocks at Sexpot Copy: Hears Joins War on Leer," *Variety*, February 24, 1965, 5.
34. Ronald Gold, "Dailies Copy Censors Call Film Ads 'Pornographic to Refined' in Tone," *Variety*, April 3, 1968, 5.
35. "Laundering the Sheets," *Time*, May 30, 1969, 54.
36. "Copley: Morals Dictator," *San Diego Door*, August 14, 1969, 17. See also "'X' Film Ads Dropped," *Independent Film Journal*, August 5, 1969, 6.
37. "Newspaper Ban on 'Smut Ads' Names Theaters," *Independent Film Journal*, September 16, 1969, 8.
38. "27 Newspapers Ban 'X' Ads," *Independent Film Journal*, December 23, 1969, 3.
39. "An Eye for Quality: An Interview with Dan Cady," *Exploiter*, February 8, 1970, 13.
40. Quoted in "N.Y. Arrest Moratorium; Papers Duel in Frisco," *Independent Film Journal*, December 23, 1970, 7.
41. Quoted in "Denver Post Explains Rationale for 'x' Ads," *Independent Film Journal*, February 4, 1971, 5.
42. "Newspaper Bans on 'X' Films Get Contagious," *Independent Film Journal*, December 9, 1969, 4.
43. "Trade Hits Newspaper Ban on X-Rated Films," *Independent Film Journal*, April 13, 1972, 3, 10.
44. "Legislators on Rampage with Plethora of Bills," *Independent Film Journal*, February 18, 1971, 3.
45. "No X or R in Oklahoma Ads," *Variety*, March 21, 1973, 5, 28; see also "Oklahoma Papers KO 'R' Rated Ads; 'PG' Advertising OK Required," *Independent Film Journal*, March 5, 1973, 6.
46. "N.Y. Obscenity Law Upheld by Appeals Court Decision," *Independent Film Journal*, January 7, 1974, 5; Charles Teitel, "No E-X in 'Sex' Chi Press Rules Stay Chintzy," *Variety*, January 8, 1975, 8.
47. Kevin Thomas, "Current Censorship Status in Adult Film Market," *Los Angeles Times Calendar*, February 7, 1971.
48. "Trade Hits Newspaper Ban on X-Rated Films," *Independent Film Journal*, April 13, 1972, 3.
49. Sam Chernoff, "Theater Owner Protests Ban on X-Films," letter to the editor, *Detroit News*, April 15, 1972. Reprinted in AFAA *Bulletin*, June 1972, 2.
50. "Los Angeles Times Management Bulletin," AFAA clipping file, Margaret Herrick Library, Academy of Motion Picture Arts and Sciences, Los Angeles, California.

51. Anna Quindlen, "The Times Will Curb Ads for Pornographic Films," *New York Times*, June 21, 1977, 66.
52. Friedman interview, February 26, 2003.
53. David F. Friedman, telephone interview with the author, January 17, 2003.
54. "Take Hardcore Ads into Homes via TV," *Variety*, January 11, 1978, 1, 82.

TANIA MODLESKI

Women's Cinema as Counterphobic Cinema
Doris Wishman as the Last Auteur

When Lorena Bobbitt was on trial for castrating her husband, who she said had repeatedly abused her, there was one aspect of her story that the media, who were generally on her side, found particularly troubling: Bobbitt's resentment even as a battered wife over the fact that she was not deriving sexual pleasure from her husband. Obviously, the media, like a large majority of Americans, were unable to sustain an image of Lorena Bobbitt as a victim without explaining away the remarks she made to friends about her sexual dissatisfaction. Typically, the media would cite her lack of familiarity with the language: that is, she did not speak English well enough to express what she really meant, and what she meant was that she was purely and simply a battered woman.

Could it not be argued that at least part of Lorena Bobbitt's abuse consisted of being denied the sexual pleasure that her husband repeatedly experienced in relation to her body? Feminists like Carol Clover have celebrated the scenario encountered repeatedly in rape revenge films in which women castrate their violators.[1] What about a scenario in which a woman is cheered on as she seeks revenge both for being battered *and* for being sexually unsatisfied? However much I might have reservations about recommending that women in reality adopt Bobbitt's solution to a complicated but surely not uncommon and only very superficially contradictory social problem, I'd sure like to see the movie.

For feminism, it seems to me, has every reason to affirm women who make female eroticism an issue, even, or perhaps especially, under circumstances where that eroticism is violently suppressed. In the early 1980s, this was something that was vociferously expressed by a number of feminists who participated in the so-called sex wars. For example, the pioneering lesbian writer Joan Nestle wrote of her mother's sexual adventurism: "Oh my mama, the things you liked to do / fuck and suck cock / one customer knocked your teeth out . . . you lay in a pool of blood and teeth until the police broke the door down. . . . 'No wonder you are a Lesbian they will say.' No the wonder is my mother who taught me when to go on my knees / and when not / who kept alive her right to sexuality when sex was killing her."[2]

One of the questions I wish to ask here is whether in analyzing the films of women working in especially violent male genres we can locate moments that both protest sexual violence *and* keep alive woman's "right to sexuality" when sex is killing her. This question bridges the two sides of the sex wars debate—the side taken by the radical feminists, who emphasized women's victimization in patriarchy and claim that women's sexuality is alienated or stolen from them, and the self-proclaimed "sex positive" feminists who affirmed women's sexuality no matter what form it takes or how violently it seems to be expropriated. I cannot emphasize enough the fact that this debate was inaugurated over twenty years ago by second-wave feminists. Revisionary feminists like Katie Rophie would have the mainstream public believe that it is only a third wave of feminists who insist on the importance of women seeking pleasure rather than always and only condemning female victimization.

In looking at the work of Doris Wishman, "the granddame of the grindhouse" cinema circuit, as one catalogue blurb calls her, a woman who in many respects is surely the radical feminist's worst nightmare, I would like to keep in the foreground the sex wars' debates and their aftermath. Is the oeuvre of Wishman, as her very name suggests, the result of a straightforward case of penis envy in a woman who capitulated to the conventions of male pornography and "sexploitation" at its sleaziest? Or is it possible that a woman living in a prefeminist time and trafficking in genres that routinely dealt in violence against women may be said to have kept alive the right of women to sexuality even when it was killing them?

There can be no question of entirely rehabilitating someone working in a genre that as a rule was far more misogynist and brutally violent in its treatment of women than even the standard hard-core pornographic films that were destined to supersede the sexploitation films made by Wishman and others. Indeed, it is no doubt symptomatic that in her relatively upbeat book on pornography, Linda Williams omits from her history of the genre all references to sexploitation except for a brief mention of the most benign and relatively short-lived subgenre of "nudie cuties."[3] These flourished for a brief time in the early 1960s and represented a step beyond 1950s nudist camp films, which had become legal as a result of a Supreme Court ruling that exempted films set in nudist camps from the general ban on filmed nudity, holding that such films were allowable because they were educational! Wishman made a number of nudist camp films—for example, *Nude on the Moon* (1962), a film about two scientists who travel to the moon, which has a rather Floridian landscape, and discover inhabitants who look very much like nude humans sporting antennae that suspiciously resemble pipe cleaners. In cutting between the activities of these aliens (nude volleyball) and the men studiously taking notes as they observe them (thereby demonstrating the "educational value" of what they see), the film from this vantage point in time strikes the viewer as a humorous commentary on the Court's—and by extension America's—naïveté and hypocrisy in matters of sexual representation.

After producers of sexploitation had gained some ground in the courts fighting censorship battles over nudie cuties like Russ Meyer's *The Immoral Mr. Teas* (1959), a film about a man who has the power to see through women's clothes, they decided that if they couldn't include as much sex as they would like they would increase the sensationalist quotient by adding violence. Just as education furnished an alibi for viewers of exploitation films, so too did violence in late 1960s sexploitation films provide viewers with a fetishistic substitute for sexuality, the sight of which was both desired and—in terms of mainstream mores—feared.

The films that supplanted the nudie cuties were usually called "roughies" or "kinkies" (the latter supposedly dealing more with perversions than the former)

FIGURE 1 Poster art for Wishman's *Nude on the Moon* (1962), one of the director's early nudist camp films.

and contain some of the most disturbing depictions of male violence against women ever filmed. Indeed, what is most striking about many of these films is the extent to which they shamelessly traffic in battery. For example, in *The Defilers* (1965), produced by the king of sexploitation David Friedman, the two male protagonists kidnap a young woman and imprison her in a rat-infested basement where they retire periodically to molest her. The sexual abuse they visit on her usually culminates in overwrought beating scenes, in which, for instance, one of the men punches the woman with his fists until her face is a bloody mess. At the very end, after the more evil protagonist assures the less evil one that they are finally going to release their captive, the former loses control and beats her with a belt until she is either unconscious or dead—the film seems not to care which.

As a female viewer of such scenes, I find myself ardently desiring to see the woman begin to experience her torture as sexually pleasurable so that it becomes more tolerable to her (in other words I am placed in the position of one

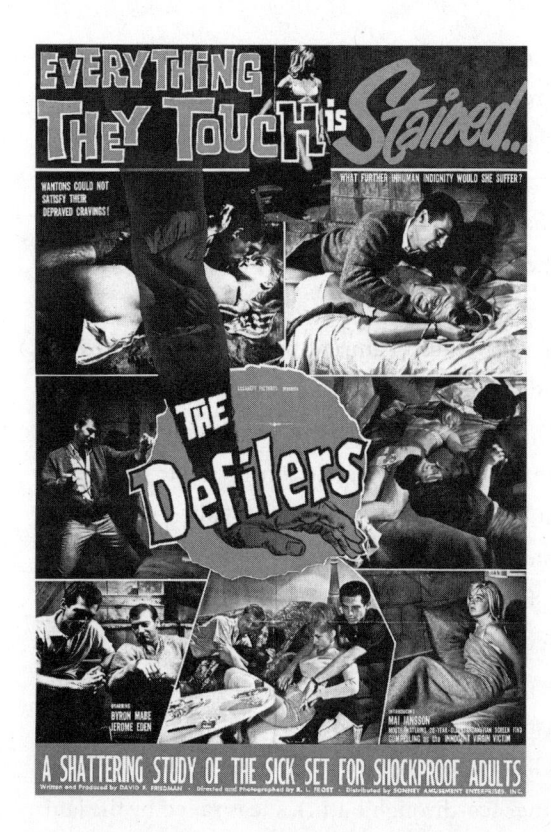

FIGURE 2 Released in 1965, *The Defilers* epitomized a growing "traffic in battery" in the sexploitation "roughie."

who embraces in all seriousness the male joke: if rape is an inevitability, relax and enjoy it). One of the side effects of these films is, then, that they actively instill in women spectators—those hardy enough to sit through them with their eyes open—the desire for women's suffering to be sexualized. But let us make no mistake about it; while a critic like Linda Williams can argue that pornography's stake is female pleasure, so that even scenes of rape must demonstrate to their presumably male audience that women really "want it," in many sexploitation films it is at best a matter of indifference whether or not the woman finds pleasure in her pain and at worst, a desideratum that she experience her pain as simply painful.

Doris Wishman's filmmaking career closely followed the trajectory of sexploitation films through the 1960s and early 1970s. As was the case in the work of many filmmakers, even mainstream ones like Alfred Hitchcock, the level of violence, nastiness, and degradation in Wishman's films increased during the late 1960s—though they never reached the heights of sadism seen in films like *Love Camp 7* (1969) or *The Defilers*. "Sick cinema" really came into its own in 1970, the year Hitchcock's *Frenzy* was released. Wishman directed two of the most bizarre films ever made that year, earning her—if she didn't already possess it—an enduring place in the pantheon of directors of sleazy underground movies. But I anticipate.

Beginning in the early 1960s with nudist camp films, which bore titles like *Nature Camp Confidential* (1961), *The Prince and the Nature Girl* (1965), and *Blaze Star Goes Nudist* (1960), Wishman moved on to directing roughies. After Russ Meyer came out with *Lorna* (1964), widely considered to be the first roughie and considered as well to have inaugurated the so-called noir period of sexploitation, Wishman wrote and directed *Bad Girls Go to Hell* (1965), one of her best-known films. Shot, like other such films at the time, in black and white on an extremely low budget, the film depicts the trials and tribulations of a woman named Meg. At the beginning of the film, it is a Sunday morning and Meg attempts to seduce her husband into staying at home rather than going to work. He rebuffs her, and she is left alone. Taking out the trash (in a skimpy outfit which she "covers" with another see-through outfit), she is raped by the janitor of her apartment building, kills him in self-defense, and runs away to New York City because she fears no one will believe her. There she meets a man who befriends her and lets her stay in his apartment. Meg is at first suspicious of him, but it soon becomes evident that he has no sexual interest in her. Indeed, he exhibits a kind of coldness and controlled anger that seems puzzling. Won over by his kindness, Meg at one point tries to initiate a romantic encounter, but Al angrily pulls away. Later Meg puts out drinks for the two of them, but it turns out that Al is an alcoholic, who proceeds to get very drunk and beat her savagely with his belt, the camera looking on dispassionately the whole time.

Meg next finds herself in the apartment of a woman named Della. One night Della comes to Meg's bed, and Meg at first turns away, but then turns back to embrace Della, again taking some sexual initiative. The next day Meg prepares to quit the apartment and Della protests, saying, "You know that I love you." Meg replies, "I love you, too; that's why I must go." Della gives her money to help her on her way, and Meg finds a room to rent. At her new residence the husband of the landlady tries to rape her, knocks her out when she resists, and finishes molesting her while she lies unconscious. At the end of the film Meg wakes up and discovers that she has been dreaming, but the film goes on to indicate that the dream has foretold the reality.

What are we to think of this film? The title seems unambivalent, and indeed a reading that sticks purely with the narrative and sees the title as a guide to interpretation could plausibly argue that the heroine is punished for acting on her own sexual desire, although questions will linger. She tries to seduce her husband and keep him from going to work. (Yes, but it is her *husband*—this is not *Psycho*, for God's sake, and, what's more, it is a Sunday, as Meg observes. Why *is* he going to work?) She seems to want to get beyond the friendship stage with Al. (Yes, he *has* treated her rather decently; still, he's a nut case whom we mistrust from the beginning.) She has lesbian sex. (Yes, but she immediately departs, taking herself out of temptation's way.)

A French critic maintains in an article written soon after the director's death, that the film is an "unconscious urban remake of *Justine ou les Infortunes de la Vertu*."[4] While it's possible that for this critic the accent falls not on the virtue of the character but rather on her seeming cluelessness, it is nevertheless highly significant that he sees Meg as resembling Justine rather than her sister, the bad girl Juliette. Indeed, it is apparent to me that the film in no way adopts a judgmental attitude toward Meg. Often it adopts her point of view, in fact, and our sympathies lie with her. It might even be argued that at times the film brings together the two poles of feminist theorizing about female sexuality discussed earlier in that while Meg is constantly victimized by men, she does not relinquish her sexual desire, even though in the end it kills her (to paraphrase Nestle). However, let us make no mistake about it. The film in general plays to the male gaze, as the camera lingers on various female body parts of the scantily clad Meg and the soundtrack plays the cheery, chintzy Muzak that is a staple of pornography to this day.

Yet even in this regard the situation is somewhat more complicated than might at first appear. To understand this, we need to look more closely at Wishman's style of directing. Here is how one worshipful commentator describes it.

> Doris Wishman's style is all her own. Only Jean-Luc Godard can match her indifference to composition and framing; if two people are talking and one

FIGURE 3 *Bad Girls Go to Hell* (1965): One of Wishman's best-known films and a prime text in discussions of Wishman's visual style.

is partially obscured by a post, so be it—the camera will not change its angle. Sometimes we are treated to static shots of feet—or torsos or hands—while voices talk off-screen. At other times, Ms. Wishman will trade off shots in such a way that we never see the person who's talking—instead we watch the listener, his head nodding thoughtfully to words from a speaker we can't see. Often her camera imitates a human eye roving restlessly around the room, occasionally allowing insignificant objects to hold its attention. For example, the camera might follow a person to a dresser then stop to dwell on the various items (objects completely irrelevant to the plot) it finds there.[5]

It needs to be noted, however, that this "style" was dictated in part by economic exigencies: Because the films were so low-budget, they were shot without sound, which was dubbed in later. "Silent footage has to be edited to keep the number of times you post sync with lip movement at a minimum," remarks one commentator, who succinctly adds, "It forced a style on her."[6] It is tempting for a feminist critic like me to claim that the style that was "forced on her" performs a deconstruction of the authority of the speaking subject: in no other films I have seen does the camera spend more time looking at people who are listening than at those who are doing the talking.

Economic imperatives, censorship codes, and, it would appear, personal predilection combined in Wishman's films to expand on the fetishistic possibilities of cinema. Thus, especially in Wishman's early films, when people make love the camera will discreetly focus on their intertwined legs; when women are undressing the camera will linger on a shot of the discarded underwear. But the fact that even when it's not required by the exigencies of dubbing, the camera seems so interested both in random objects and in bodily fragments (the legs and feet of people walking in a park or on a city street, for instance) that in general the woman's body comes to be less isolated as a site of fragmentation than it usually is within male-dominated cinema. At the very least, the films seem to suggest that there are more things of interest to look at in the world than women's butts. Perhaps it's possible to go further. Insofar as objects like lamps or clocks or items on a dresser frequently substitute for fetishistic items (e.g., a lamp instead of the underwear which stands in the stead of female genitalia), eroticism is diffused across the text.

While Wishman's plots are often (and with considerable justification) faulted for containing episodes that have implausible (or nonexistent) narrative or psychological motivation, some of the implausibility bespeaks the sexual confusion experienced by women throughout the greater part of the decade, a confusion that has not been entirely dispelled for many to this day. What is a bad girl? Is a victim of sexual assault responsible for that assault? One male commentator, betraying immense but not uncommon naïveté about the way rape victims have been treated and blamed for their assaults, finds the heroine's running away after she has been raped in her apartment to be one of the most baffling aspects of *Bad Girls Go to Hell* (1965).[7] A feminist viewer of *Bad Girls* might indeed find another aspect of the movie to be more mysterious: why does lesbianism automatically disqualify itself in a world riddled with male violence, where men ruthlessly prey on women, while many women—like Della—are kind to other women, love them, and are loved in return?

A film Wishman made somewhat later in the decade, *The Amazing Transplant* (1970), continues to traffic in sexual violence, although if possible in an even queasier way. Shot in color and displaying Wishman's usual tacky, next-to-no budget mise-en-scène, the film deals with a man named Arthur who goes around sexually assaulting women, knocking them out, or even killing them when they resist. His uncle, a police detective, investigates the crimes and interrogates the various women with whom the young man has had contact. Although in this respect the film seems to be classically structured around the male point of view, a series of flashbacks accompanies the women's narration of their encounters with Arthur, thus putting the emphasis much more on women's reactions to sexual violence than is usually the case in the genre. For the most part, the women are devastated by their experience. For example, after relating her story of rape (during which she is knocked out and molested while unconscious), one of the women dissolves into tears, saying she didn't go to the police because she didn't want the publicity. Besides, she asks, "what good would it have done?" She apologizes for being so upset (!), and after the detective leaves, the camera lingers while the woman buries her face in her hands and sobs. During the rape of another woman, the woman struggles, is hit, and vomits as the rape is taking place; after Arthur departs, the camera focuses on her splotchy buttocks as she leans over the toilet to vomit some more.

We might say there's something for everyone here—for any male spectator who might enjoy witnessing the brutalization of women; for the feminist, or more precisely, perhaps, the radical feminist who clearly sees confirmation of women's victimization within male-dominated culture and systems of representation. Yet in the middle of the film occurs an episode that is bound to unsettle the radical feminist reading: one of the women who told the detective when he initially questioned her that she had not seen Arthur for a long time calls to retract her statement and to admit that she and Arthur had been together recently. In the flashback the woman and Arthur chat for a bit and then we see him suddenly push her down on the bed. She resists at first and then, when Arthur says, "Please don't fight me," she relaxes and clearly enjoys the experience. On the one hand, this episode might seem to undermine any possible message about the unacceptability to women of rape. On the other hand, the woman finishes her story by confessing that she had long been attracted to Arthur—thus suggesting that the definition of rape in a given situation might have something to do with women's desire (or lack of it).

Interestingly, *The Amazing Transplant* involves a rather literal case of male

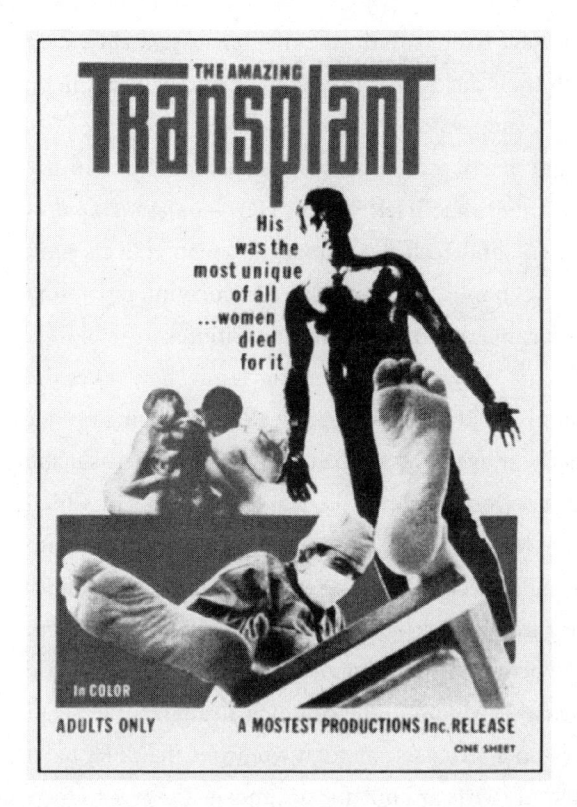

FIGURE 4 Wishman's *The Amazing Transplant* (1970), a confused foray into both the politics of rape and the politics of the phallus.

penis envy, since Arthur's problem, it turns out, is caused by a penis he has had transplanted from his dead friend Felix, whose sexual prowess Arthur had long admired (there is no doubt that Wishman had a genius for thinking up gimmicks). Confusing, as it were, his friend's penis with the phallus, Arthur has the operation only to find that he is in *less* control than before. Arthur has to learn the sad Lacanian lesson (so often disavowed in pornography) that nobody really does possess the phallus: as his uncle, the detective, discovers, Arthur is driven to assault women when he sees them wearing certain kinds of earrings—just as Felix, we learn, used to get very excited by the sight of such jewelry.

In the final image of the film, after Arthur has been apprehended, we see a close-up of a newspaper bearing the headline, "JURY FINDS ARTHUR BAILEN . . . ." But the final word is obscured by an ashtray resting on the paper. In frustrating the desire for closure, the film leaves various questions in the air about the nature of sexuality and of guilt and innocence with respect to sexual violence that would only be fully articulated by feminists in the next decade. Some of these questions have to do with the nature of male sexuality, such as: Do men really "think with their dicks"—or indeed (as theorists of mimetic desire would have it) with someone else's?

Of all the many and usually nasty little films Wishman turned out in the 1960s, at least one other distinguishes itself in my view—*Indecent Desires* (1967), which is about a pathetic and reclusive young man who collects junk and one day finds a doll he brings home. Some time later he encounters a young blonde woman, Ann, and the camera shows a superimposition of the blonde doll onto the body of the woman. When the man returns home, he strokes the doll all over its body, and Ann back at her apartment feels the fondling on her own body, her hands tracing the movements of the unseen hands. It is as if she were subject to some sort of voodoo version of Foucauldian theory in which female autoeroticism—the staple of soft-core pornography—is inscribed onto the body from forces operating outside of it. In this film, then, the possibility of female sexual desire, as regards the heroine, seems entirely foreclosed, and when the woman dies after becoming increasingly panic-stricken, desperate and agoraphobic, she performs a striking mime of being strangled, her head twisting about like a puppet's on a string as the man wrenches the doll's head from its socket. The camera itself twists around and around as it moves in for a final close-up of the lifeless woman.

Before her death, Ann's one attempt to reach out for help is rebuffed when she tries to get in touch with a friend, whom the camera has featured throughout in scenes of autoerotic display in front of a mirror. The friend will not respond to Ann's pleas for help because she is in the middle of making love with her European boyfriend Monty (who wears a fake moustache and dark glasses he keeps on even during sex). The film in this regard reads almost like an anticipatory parable of the divisions between radical feminists, who hold that woman's sexuality is not really their own, and sex-positive feminists who, busy fulfilling what they see as their relatively unconstrained sexuality, refuse the radical feminist message and resist solidarity with the female victim.

The two films for which Doris Wishman is perhaps best known and most loved by her fans are those she directed in the early 1970s starring a woman whose pseudonym was Chesty Morgan, an actress billed as having seventy-three-inch breasts, a measurement that truly seems scarcely an exaggeration. In the first of these, *Deadly Weapons* (1967), the title of which refers to the breasts themselves, a gang of thugs murders the boyfriend of Crystal, played by Morgan, who retaliates by smothering each of them to death with her breasts. Nowhere is lowbrow contestation of highbrow culture (often, of course, without deliberately setting out to do so) more pronounced than in this film. If, as Jean-Louis Baudry once famously suggested, the screen is a stand-in for the breast, then the sight of the huge breasts of Chesty Morgan stifling the screams of the man whose head is held between them until the life is smothered out of him phantasmatically confirms the child's worst fears about the potency of the "bad object" (to adopt Kleinian terminology).

In the second Chesty Morgan film, *Double Agent 73* (1974), a film that draws on the James Bond films so popular at the time, the plot involves Jane (Morgan) as an agent of the government who tracks down and kills members of a Soviet drug ring using a variety of methods, including spreading some sort of poisonous substance on the breasts and then making love with the victim. Because she needs to prove the men's identity, Jane snaps a photograph of each dying man with a camera which has been surgically implanted in one of her pendulous breasts (so large, they hang down to her waist). As she presses on her breast, it bounces up and we hear the sound of a camera going off. The camera (Wishman's, that is) typically cuts back and forth from shots of the man dying to shots revealing his wavering point of view captured in close-ups of the breasts blurring in and out of focus. (The nicest touch in the film involves Jane's paramour accidentally tripping the camera during lovemaking, which leads to the discovery of his identity as the head of the drug ring, and to his death at the hands of Jane herself, who shoots him.)

For those of us feminists who have been steeped in a tradition of leftist theories that stress the political importance of self-reflexive art, the film must strike us as somewhat of a parody of our ideas. Wishman might be said to have created a sort of female version of Michael Powell's *Peeping Tom* (1960, a film much celebrated in feminist film theory).[8] In *Double Agent 73*, the *men* become the constantly photographed subjects, forced to look upon the lethal object—the breast-camera—that has exposed them in their death throes. However, if any-

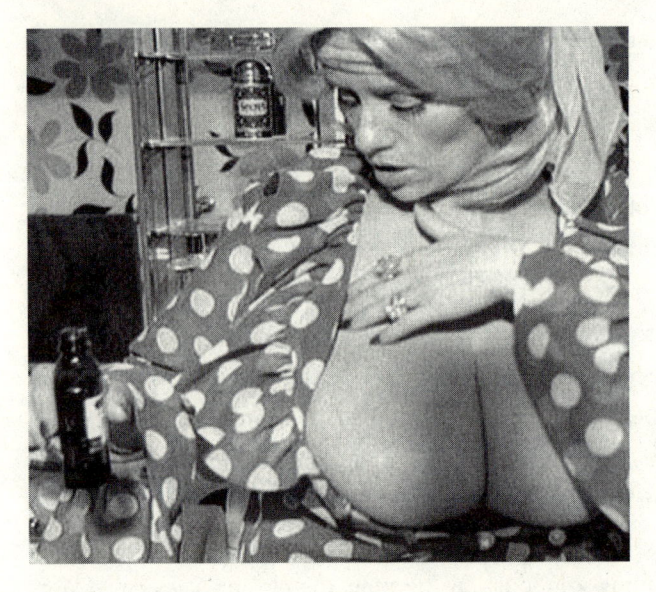

FIGURE 5 Chesty Morgan in *Double Agent 73* (1974), a film that proves doubly alienating by virtue of its self-reflexive plot and a ludicrous obsession with breasts.

thing works to distance and alienate a viewer from the visions upon the screen, it is less the self-reflexive dimension of the plot than the camera's ludicrous obsession with the breasts, which are seen in lengthy close-ups, for example, as Jane talks on the phone, or hanging out of the negligees she wears at home. The heavy breasts are so large that when Jane strokes them in scenes apparently meant to be autoerotic, it is as if she is actually trying to soothe the soreness she must feel from having to carry them around unbound most of the time. Even Joe Bob Briggs, who has put a few of Wishman's films out on his video series, "The Sleaziest Movies in the History of the World," asks at the end, "Don't you just get *sick* of looking at those boobies all the time?" Moving away from the diffuse fetishism of her earlier films and reflecting the trend of that time (and, it must be said, now again in our own) toward extreme fetishization of women's breasts, Wishman quite literally rubs men's faces in it—fetishizing with a vengeance.

It may seem fitting that the last film made by the woman named Wishman was a pseudo-documentary about transsexualism—though the film deals mostly with men wishing to be women. Throughout the early years of sexploitation, the format of the documentary had enabled filmmakers and film producers to get sensationalist movies past the censors. The earliest and most enduring of such movies was a film about birth called *Mom and Dad* (1945). Promoted in the old American spirit of hucksterism (sexploitation films are traceable back to the heyday of carnivals), the film would be introduced with a lecture about birth control, especially the rhythm method. According to David Friedman, the only film his wife ever objected to his showing was *Mom and Dad*: "Carol never objected to the carnivals, to pickled punks, to the nudie cuties or even to hardcore. But to the birth-of-a-baby shows she said, 'That was the worst thing you have ever done. . . . I hate to think of the poor girls who are pregnant today because of Vatican Roulette.' She thought the whole thing was a scam (which it was) and that we were exploiting a very natural medical function."[9] It gives me some pleasure to think that in the very last phase of the genre, which began by trapping some women into reproductive sexuality, a woman would make a film about the ability to change one's sex voluntarily.

"We all know what sex we are," says the male voice-over in the beginning of the movie. "We know deep inside us, we are a man or a woman. But perhaps it's not so simple." Our guide into the world of transsexualism is Dr. Leo Wollman—"doctor, surgeon, psychologist, minister, medical writer." Wollman lectures directly to the film audience, exhibits naked transsexuals, using a pointer to illustrate parts of their anatomies, conducts group therapy sessions with transsexuals and would-be transsexuals, and even displays and discusses dildos. Periodically a Puerto Rican transsexual talks to the camera about her experiences, her views, and her feelings. We also watch several scenes of lovemaking—including one that involves a woman who picks up a man in a park, takes him home, allows herself to be fondled, and, when the man leaves, removes her clothing to reveal a penis. It turns out she has been taking female hormones but has not yet had the operation.

Inserted into the middle of the film is some outrageous surgical footage of a sex-change operation. Wollman's voice-over describes what we see on the screen: "First a circular incision is made around the base of the penis. The incision is then extended in one continuous line along the middle of the penis. The skin is then inverted to form a sheath much as a sock is turned inside out. It is this inverted penile sheath which forms the vagina." If *Mom and Dad* had sexualized "a very natural medical function," titillating audiences by regaling them with the so-called facts of life, *Let Me Die a Woman* (1978) takes the fetishism at the heart of male sexual fantasy, medicalizes it, and materializes the fear behind it: the fear that the penis can be cut off and one will be (like) a woman. In making such a film Wishman, who had spent so much of her career creating the kinds of films women find hard to look at, discovers and exploits images which assault *male* vision: for, as the man who writes the blurb on the video jacket says, this is footage that, years after first seeing the film on Forty-second Street, he "still can't watch."

But of course this unwatchability paradoxically functions precisely as a lure to the male spectator. How to explain such a paradox? Let us above all not leap too hastily to the facile conclusion that we are dealing with the phenomenon of male masochism. In *Men, Women, and Chainsaws*, Carol Clover has famously argued that one can view as masochistic the appeal to men of scary and violent movies such as the rape revenge films that sometimes feature scenes of male castration.[10] If masochism is indeed involved in the male spectator's response to such films, it is surely so in a way entirely consonant with an ideal of the "phallic" tough guy able to withstand the most intense horror and pain. Such a response is probably most accurately understood as a counterphobic mechanism, enabling the spectator to go out to meet, to face down, and to survive his very worst fears.

What interests me here, in considering the implications of the work of a woman whose films often went to extremes in fetishizing female sexuality and in objectifying women and depicting violence against them, is the possibility that such films may also function counterphobically for women filmmakers and their female spectators. To take myself as an example, my own interest in horror films and violent films in general began as a deliberate attempt to conquer the abject terror they inspired in me as a child. In going frequently to see such films, I have been, I think, far from masochistically indulging in assaults on my vision and on my female proxies on the screen; instead I was psychically refusing to succumb to the terror these films inspire in many of us. (I don't mean to claim to have been more resistant than my friends who would not go to see such films at all; I am simply saying that not looking is only one possible form of refusing to be intimidated and terrified.) In the early 1970s, Claire Johnston proposed the term *counter-cinema* to refer to films by women that strained the codes and conventions of patriarchal cinema and male genres.[11] Perhaps a second category could, only partly facetiously, be added to explain the appeal to women of adhering to these codes and taking them to extremes. Thus, in addition to the notion of women's cinema as counter-cinema, we would have woman's cinema as counterphobic cinema—the prefix serving as the token of resistance. Positing a counterphobic notion of filmmaking and filmgoing enables us to consider the psychically contestatory powers of excess without always having to confine ourselves to the useful but limited notion of parody.

Let me explain carefully what I am saying and what I am not saying. Recently I showed some films of Doris Wishman to a graduate seminar on women in exploitation and horror films, and one of the few male students in the course, a truly brilliant student, supported my position by recounting an experience he had had recently of being in an audience watching a film in which a woman was tortured at length before being killed. When men in the audience would holler out "Bitch" to the woman on the screen, a group of women would holler the epithet even louder. My student cited this experience as one that supported my idea of women's counterphobic response to female victimization. I was aghast. Is this what I meant by the term? If so, I was ready to abjure it on the spot.

But no, this is *not* what I meant. I am assuming there may be a kind of split response on the part of some female viewers who recognize their connection to the woman on the screen but are ready to face the most extreme forms of female victimization without blinking, that is, without letting themselves be victimized (terrorized) by a *representation* of that victimization. Such a viewer neither repudiates her identity as a woman nor identifies with the (often) psychotic male on the screen (or in front of the screen, for that matter)—she does not merge her identity with that of the torturer, at least not to the point where she disavows any connection with images of female suffering.

Even though what I am proposing suggests a split response on the part of the female viewer, it does not bring us back, or fully back, to the early positions of feminist film theory (as elaborated by Laura Mulvey and Mary Ann Doane) that descried the split experience of the woman spectator forced to identify with both male and female characters. First, it posits the notion that the female viewer is not merging with the images on the screen but is more aware of their status as images than early film theory sometimes supposed. Second, this notion of a somewhat macho mode of film viewing may be aligned with the more positive aspects of gender performance that have been celebrated in queer studies over the last decade or so (as in the work of Case and Garber). And as the theorists of female masculinity tell us, one can be macho without being misogynist.

I have always thought of sleazy, gross-out films as very male, essentialist as this idea may be. Is there any ultimate value in finding evidence that women can be every bit as raunchy and sleazy as men? What do women have to gain by entering the realm of the grotesque?

The grotesque has of course been a category affirmed in recent years by those who have taken up the work of Mikhail Bakhtin (including feminist scholar Mary Russo, in her book *The Female Grotesque*). According to Bakhtin, the emphasis on the grotesque body "liberates objects from the snares of false seriousness, from illusions and sublimations inspired by fear."[12] Now, it seems to me that Wishman's work, like most sexploitation, touches at the heart of fears of both men and women—in the former case, of course, one of the ensnaring illusions is that of the intact body, an illusion that protects against fears of castration and dismemberment. The illusion of the screen as breast, theorized by Baudry, provides one example of "false seriousness," and Wishman drives right to the heart of this illusion in *Deadly Weapons*. Feminist theories designed to understand and ward off women's fears, which tend to be a bit more rooted in reality, have sometimes had their ludicrous side as well, and the degree to which we have banked upon self-reflexive, experimental cinema to rid us of the snares of patriarchal cinema now often seems excessive. A film like *Double Agent 73* has the potential to make us see the humor in the excess.

Slavoj Žižek, renowned for juxtaposing high theory with low culture, justifies his enterprise by citing the ability of popular culture to illustrate "not only the vague outlines of the Lacanian theoretical edifice but sometimes also the finer details." He goes on to admit, "It is clear that Lacanian theory serves as an excuse for indulging the idiotic enjoyment of popular culture."[13] Presumably, Lacan himself never produced idiocies that popular culture might expose. But feminists, constantly admonished by men to recognize the importance of having a sense of humor, might be able to lead the way, showing not only that popular culture provides an alibi for enjoying idiotic forms of popular entertainment, but that it can help us laugh at our sacred theories as they appear from the perspective of the profane.

Although it has been somewhat updated, I wrote much of the foregoing essay a decade ago and never published it. I never published it because when all is said and done, Wishman's films leave a very nasty aftertaste, and when they are shown to, say, sophisticated feminist students, they are often shocked and repelled at the level of constant violence directed against women in these films. I myself experienced such a shock after first viewing many of them and continue to do so to this day. I had obviously chosen very selectively in trying to make a feminist case for a woman working in a virtually all-male domain, exploitation and sexploitation cinema. Of course, critics always choose selectively, and certainly male critics have wished on Wishman, sometimes with ludicrous and deplorable results.

Take Michael Bowen, who as Wishman's biographer interprets Wishman's films in terms of her own life experiences, especially her so-called bodily experiences. It is always tricky for a biographer to attempt to understand the relationship between a person's life and her art, and this is particularly the case in an era mistrustful of categories like "gender," "biological sex," and even "experience." The more talented critics are nevertheless able to achieve a subtle analysis that carefully negotiates the minefield of essentialisms. Bowen, however, is not one of these critics. Formulating a grotesque argument that focuses in the last segment on the "grotesque" elements in Wishman's later work, Bowen writes:

> At issue in Wishman's work of this period is a body which can no longer be trusted, a body which has acquired the fatal will to go astray. This theme, I would argue, is largely a manifestation of Wishman's own concern about the status of her own body at the time. Aging, having just experienced the failure of a second childless marriage, very likely menopausal, Wishman began to organize her work into an exploration of the body's capacity to betray its operator, to degenerate, and to empty itself through bloody excess.[14]

(Let us disregard Bowen's bizarre understanding of the phenomenon of menopause, which after all is about the cessation of bloody excess, if one must put it that way.) To support his argument Bowen focuses on *The Amazing Transplant*, which is, as we have seen, about a man losing control of his body (with deadly consequences to women), and on *Double Agent 73*. Speaking of the latter film, Bowen cites the fact that the camera implanted in Jane's breast turns out to be a time bomb waiting to go off. Anyone who hasn't seen the film might get the impression that the spectator is on the edge of his seat during most of the movie, thinking that Jane will die if she doesn't accomplish her mission in time. But in fact, we only learn about the time bomb at the very end of the film, and no real suspense is built around it before the problem is eliminated. True to her "style" of working, Wishman must have said at the last minute of filming, "I know—let's make the camera a time bomb," but rather than go back and redo the film—something that would not have been economically feasible—she just threw it in as a gimmick at the last minute. No suspense is built around the time-bomb device, as it would be in, for example, Hitchcock. What fascinates the spectator throughout the film instead is the sight of Jane killing men and coldly filming them when they die, a sight we witness over and over and over. Whose body is out of control in such a scenario?

Not only does Bowen, in his discussion of the grotesque aspects of Wishman's later work, turn male fears back onto the grotesque body of woman—character, actress, and director—but, as evidenced in the above passage, he renders all female bodies grotesque insofar as they are destined to become menopausal, grow old, and die—and insofar as they give or don't give birth. Indeed, throughout the article Bowen makes much of the fact that Wishman never had children, even going so far as to propose that the work may be seen in terms of an "aesthetics of procreation," a sublimation of the desire for children! Interestingly, he doesn't invoke *Deadly Weapons* to suggest that it is the imaginative product of a woman whose mothering instinct has gone awry, although one could sure see how that argument would go. But a feminist weary not only of the mammary madness of our own time but of our culture's harping on the horrors of women's biological clocks running down (at which point the clocks might as well turn into time bombs for all the importance typically accorded childless women), might rather smile at a sensibility that contrived a plot in which gigantic breasts smother rather than nurture life.

Other male critics have been rather more sophisticated in their approach to Wishman's work. Thibaut, it will be recalled, characterizes *Bad Girls Go to Hell* as an "unconscious urban remake of *Justine ou les Infortunes de la Vertu*." The article goes on to note (more than once) Wishman's "total absence of cynicism" and characterizes the work as marked by a "total refusal of received methods" and as revealing "the ingenuousness and naïveté of the novice." One can't help but notice here another projection along the lines of what we have seen operating in Bowman's article. Wishman the director is seen as possessing the same traits as her film's innocent character. Here is the author invoking a comparison to Andy Warhol:

> Far from the movie theaters of Times Square, the sanctuary of exploitation cinema, the New York intelligentsia thrilled to the bold experimentalism of the Warhol family. In the same city, there coexisted two kinds of cinema, both having little to do with the current clichés. The one big difference: Warhol filmed in order to assure his artistic survival; Doris Wishman to assure economic survival. Strangely fascinated by Hollywood, the ascetic fair-haired boy ("l'ascetique blondinet") threw temper tantrums while Doris Wishman unconsciously created the perfect anti-star, the true negative of the Hollywood model, of which the artistic underground could up to then only dream.[15]

For this French critic, the price of Wishman's canonization as auteur whose work served as the "veritable negatif du modele hollywoodien," was consciousness itself. As a female auteur she is praised for her very lack of ambition, her indifference to all aesthetic standards and to Hollywood commercialism.

One can only wonder: if Wishman had appeared to have a little more ambition, had revealed herself to be a pretender to the throne of queen of sleaze, would she have been so eagerly crowned? Pardon my own cynicism—so unlike the alleged naïveté of a Doris Wishman—but it seems to me that this kind of analysis is strictly an affair between men. Wishman is invited to assume the throne in order to eject Warhol. But since (or rather precisely because) she herself is unconscious of the critical and aesthetic stakes and indifferent to fame, the person who becomes the true auteur is the critic, one of the "inside dopesters," as Pauline Kael so memorably called the auteur critics back in the 1960s, who can describe her style, locate her meaning, and assign her place in the pantheon *anti-hollywoodienne*.[16]

I can well believe that Wishman was extremely cynical. She needed money;

there was money to be made in the aptly named exploitation and sexploitation genres, especially when they indulged in hard-core violence against women—so she went for the gold, or at least the gilt. I can believe she might also have been cynical about the viewers of such movies, and I can imagine her satisfaction in the kind of revenge I see operating in the two films with Chesty Morgan. But do I believe that Wishman was conscious of, for example, supporting lesbianism in *Bad Girls Go to Hell*? No, I don't. Does that make me like the authors I have been criticizing, those who project their own meanings and desires and fears onto the director who herself is seen as unconscious of what she has wrought? In a way, yes. But I have at least been consistent throughout my career on this point. In detecting feminist meanings, whether they are located in certain moments of Hitchcock's films or in those of Doris Wishman, I have followed the strand of auteur criticism that emphasizes the unconscious aspects of films and their directors, connecting those meanings to ideology (and I have, moreover, always argued that the critic invariably brings her own set of values to texts). Yet I fear that many critics, and certainly many French critics, betray a double standard, and continue, perhaps in spite of themselves, to grant all sorts of conscious, artistic intent to the male directors of the movies they love, while, at best, patronizing movies made by women.

Both Bowen and Thibault return us to prefeminist days of criticism in which women authors were treated in the most condescending manner imaginable. Before the late 1970s and 1980s, criticism of female authors (such as Charlotte Brontë, Emily Brontë, and Emily Dickinson, to name a few who were routinely subjected to grotesque paternalistic criticism) habitually treated women's works in terms of their biographies (and biology) and attributed felicities of female texts to the operations of the unconscious—in contradistinction to the supposedly artfully crafted, brilliant works of canonized male authors. The same criticism operates now paradoxically in relation to texts that lack felicities, that are often ill-made and even idiotic. Those directors and producers who make it into the canon of sleaze are generally those who care the least about art, ideas, and craft, but the men among them are frequently given credit as admirable old-time hucksters who thumbed their noses at a hypocritical and pretentious Middle America, subverting it from below.

But let us not forget that Middle America's standards of artistic taste and the moral values embedded in, say, Book of the Month Club fare were more often than not upheld by women, and in this respect—and not only in the more obvious ones—it might be said that the sexploitation genre as a whole had a misogynist cast. At the same time, however, given that women of the period wound up being the stuffy purveyors of hackneyed art, good manners, and repressive morals, it means something to me, at least, that one woman emphatically rejected the role and expanded the borders of bad taste. This returns us, in effect, to the argument with which I began: feminists' insistence on their right to politically incorrect fantasy and behavior has to be seen (and I'm of course hardly the first to make this argument) in light of the repression historically imposed upon them.

In many respects Wishman's films are no different from those of the misogynist fraternity of cinematic exploiters. Feminism forgets or disavows this at its peril. But handing Wishman over to the boys, permitting male critics to have their way with her, does not seem to me advisable, especially given the kinds of arguments we have seen them advance. Hence my decision, after all these years, to publish this essay.

I believe I have shown that there are elements in Wishman's work that allow for (I don't say "force" or "impose") a feminist reading. Yet we would do well to recall these many years later the arguments of Pam Cook and Claire Johnston, writing in the early days of feminist film theory. Women directors work with the codes and conventions of patriarchal ideologies and genres. It is impossible for women working within a male-dominated cinema to effect a radical break with it. But there are moments when their texts reveal the tensions and contradictions that are the result of their peculiar and marginal positions. These are the moments—transitory, fleeting, and almost inevitably recuperated—when the impulses of a female flesh peddler and the wishes of at least one feminist critic may converge.

Bad girls, unite.

Notes

1. Carol Clover, *Men, Women, and Chainsaws: Gender in the Modern Horror Film* (Princeton, N.J.: Princeton University Press), 1993.
2. Joan Nestle, *A Restricted Country* (Ann Arbor, Mich.: Firebrand Books, 1987), 86.

3. Linda Williams, *Hardcore: Power, Pleasure and the "Frenzy of the Visible"* (Berkeley: University of California Press, 1999).
4. Professeur Thibaut, "Une affaire de femme," *Cineastes* 8 (2002): 44.
5. Andrea Juno, "Doris Wishman," in *Incredibly Strange Films: A Guide to Deviant Films*, ed. Jim Morton (San Francisco: Re/Search, 1986), 113.
6. Mike Quarles, *Down and Dirty: Hollywood's Exploitation Filmmakers and their Movies* (Jefferson, N.C.: McFarland, 1993), 144.
7. "When she is raped by the janitor, she decides she has to run away, so her husband will not know what happened. This may be a commentary on mid-1960s morality, but it doesn't make a lot of sense," Quarles writes (ibid.). Of course, feminism has shown that this kind of reaction *does* make a lot of sense. Interestingly, Quarles here omits mentioning that Meg has killed the man who rapes her twice.
8. Linda Williams, "When the Woman Looks," in *Revision: Essays in Feminist Film Criticism*, ed. Mary Ann Doane, Patricia Mellencamp, and Linda Williams, American Film Institute Monograph Series (Frederick, Md.: University Publications of America, 1984), 3:90–93.
9. David F. Friedman, "Wages of Sin," interview by David Chute, *Film Comment* 22, no. 4 (1986): 32–39; 42–48.
10. Clover, *Men, Women, and Chainsaws*, 166–230.
11. The term *counter-cinema* had a polemical force but perhaps undermined the subtlety of the argument advanced by Cook and Johnston, since both took care to note that ideology could not be contested from a place outside ideology. A woman filmmaker had to rely on the grammar of Hollywood cinema even as she could be seen to deform it. See Claire Johnston, "Women's Cinema as Counter-Cinema," in *Movies and Methods*, vol. 1, ed. Bill Nichols (Berkeley: University of California Press, 1985).
12. Mikhail Bakhtin, *Rabelais and His World* (Bloomington: Indiana University Press, 1984), 376.
13. Slavoj Žižek, *Enjoy Your Symptom! Jacques Lacan in Hollywood and Out* (New York: Routledge, 1992), viii.
14. Michael Bowen, "Embodiment and Realization: The Many Film-Bodies of Doris Wishman," *Wide Angle* 19, no. 3 (1997): 79.
15. Thibaut, "Une affaire de femme," 44.
16. Pauline Kael, "Circles and Squares," *Film Quarterly* 16, no. 3 (1963): 12–26.

HARRY M. BENSHOFF

Representing (Repressed) Homosexuality in the Pre-Stonewall Hollywood Homo-Military Film

In the late 1960s, gay film critic Jack Babuscio wondered: "Why . . . should some gays choose to join the military? . . . The answer, though muted, is plain: the Forces are a refuge, a military mask that calms the chaos rumbling in the closets of those who repress their gayness. The bureaucratic structure of military life, with its constant surveillance and strict discipline, aims to obliterate the former identity of its members and replace it with a sense of self as Soldier."[1] Military psychiatrists of the era echoed Babuscio's musings, admitting that many men with homosexual tendencies joined the armed forces in the hope that "the army would be a salubrious and perhaps even curative experience for them."[2] However, the "concentration of young men in close association with the intimacy of barracks life [often created] subsequent temptations."[3] When soldiers were caught in homosexual acts, or accused of being homosexual, they were immediately segregated from their units, evaluated by military psychiatrists, and in most cases dismissed from the armed services.[4] Careers were destroyed and lives were ruined by "undesirable" discharges that frequently listed homosexuality as their cause.

The issue of gays in the military became a national debate in the 1990s when President Bill Clinton attempted to integrate the armed services. The hysteria surrounding the debate and the resultant "don't ask, don't tell" policy (which in fact has led to even more homosexuals being discharged from the armed services) indicates that even in the 1990s homosexuality was considered a distasteful subject to many. Yet this essay demonstrates that the issue was alive (if "unwell") in mainstream American popular culture as early as the late 1950s, perhaps most visibly represented through a small cycle of films that I have dubbed the Hollywood homo-military film. These films include lower-budget exploitation films such as *The Strange One* (1957) and *The Gay Deceivers* (1969), as well as more prestigious "A-film" literary adaptations like *Billy Budd* (1962) and *Reflections in a Golden Eye* (1967). Indeed, by 1972 there were so many films that explored or exploited homosexual desire within the military that Parker Tyler could devote an entire chapter of *Screening the Sexes: Homosexuality in the Movies* to what he called "Homeros in Uniform."[5]

Nevertheless, during the pre-Stonewall era, the very idea of homosexuality in the armed services was an inherently sleazy one, an issue—like homosexuality in general—that could barely be spoken about in coherent terms. This essay examines the sociocultural context, production history, and reception of several of these homo-military films, in order to illuminate the diverse and often contradictory ways that the issue was understood in the 1960s. Contrary to what one might assume, many of these films actually feature more complex and theoretically queer ideas about human sexuality than many of those produced during the 1970s and 1980s. The films raise issues of sexual identity and repressed homosexual desire, and explore—however confusedly—the borders between male homosociality and homosexuality. While in many cases these films appear to depict "gays in the military" as a situation either hopelessly comedic or tragic, upon closer examination many of them actually indict the *repression* of homosexual desire and not homosexuality per se, an idea that many film critics of the era slowly began to acknowledge.

Homo-Militarism in Postwar America

Cultural intercourse between queer men and the military has existed for centuries, and such intersections were especially prominent in America during and after World War II. Some historians even point to the military's antihomosexual policies as a major factor in the development of postwar gay communities: as queer people were dishonorably discharged, many settled in urban gay ghettos rather than return home to face further discrimination.[6] As such, homo-military iconography and themes were prevalent in postwar gay male culture. As Michael Bronski has noted, "beautiful, sexy, well-built servicemen are perpetual inhabitants of wartime and postwar gay fiction, surfacing in works as diverse as [Carson] McCullers's *Reflections in a Golden Eye* (1941), John Horne Burns's *The Gallery* (1947), [Gore] Vidal's *The City and the Pillar* (1948), Russell Thacher's *The Captain* (1951), and Lonnie Coleman's *Ship's Company* (1955)."[7] The era's gay physique magazines and avant-garde films—perhaps most famously Kenneth Anger's *Fireworks* (1947)—also explored homosexual desire within military trappings. And, as postwar Hollywood faced an increasingly unstable social, economic, and industrial climate, such "unsavory" themes began to seep into mainstream film practice.

Classical Hollywood war films had always celebrated homosocial bonds between military men. Love scenes and even passionate kisses were shared between (ostensibly heterosexual) men in films such as *Wings* (1927), *Test Pilot* (1938), and *Only Angels Have Wings* (1939). Occasional buddy comedies such as the Dean Martin–Jerry Lewis vehicle *At War with the Army* (1950) based their hijinks on the repeated failures of less-than-masculine men to adapt to macho military worlds. Yet, as the 1950s progressed and the cultural image of the male homosexual shifted from the pansy stereotype to the more menacing "invisible" homosexual—one who could or did pass for straight—intense homosocial buddy relationships (both onscreen and in real life) became more and more suspect. A kiss between men was no longer a sign of fraternal friendship, but now a sign of potential sexual perversity. This cultural anxiety over the border between male homosocial and male homosexual desire—a central concern of the homo-military film—is also prevalent in the era's buddy films (*Midnight Cowboy* [1969]), boarding school films (*If...* [1968]), prison melodramas (*Fortune and Men's Eyes* [1971]), and biker films (*The Leather Boys* [1964]). It was also a central concern of the U.S. armed services themselves.

Official Army policies of the era not only maintained that homosexuality was incompatible with military duty but also divided homosexual offenses into three types, in order to classify more precisely who was and who was not "truly" homosexual. Class I homosexuality consisted of those cases which involved assault or coercion. Class II homosexuality was defined as all cases of homosexual conduct not defined as Class I (i.e., acts committed consensually). Class III homosexuality consisted of cases in which "personnel exhibit, profess, or admit homosexual tendencies [but] wherein there are no specific homosexual acts or offenses."[8] As such, the provisions of Class III sought to remove homosexual persons from the military and not just people convicted of homosexual acts. The provisions of Class III did (and still do) create a widespread culture of paranoia and witch-hunting, as the mere suggestion of being homosexual could warrant an investigation.

Military psychiatrists were routinely called upon to distinguish "between true and confirmed homosexuals and 'those individuals who solely as the result of immaturity, curiosity, or intoxication have been involved in homosexual acts.'"[9] This classification was usually made on very little evidence. "Scientific" tests for patulous rectums and repressed gag reflexes (thought to be indicative of sexually passive or "true" homosexuality) were called for by some specialists, while others based their decisions on a brief verbal interview.[10] In that case, "true" homosexuality was defined in terms of effeminacy, while "shower-room horse-play" among traditionally masculine men tended to be overlooked.[11] Such distinctions were made out of necessity: as one official report put it, "Suppose everyone who has engaged in homosexual play were to report himself as having 'homosexual tendencies' at the induction station! This might affect more than one-third of the candidates for enlistment."[12] Clearly, the military's need for young masculine men overrode its official policies proscribing homosexual behavior among them.

Despite its obsession with psychiatric categorization, this official classificatory schema rarely took into consideration any theorization of repressed homosexuality. Indeed, men accused of homosexuality who consciously denied such desires were more likely to be retained in the services. As such, the system tended to self-select for either consciously lying or repressed homosexuals—individuals in greater or lesser states of psychic conflict—while discharging adequately functioning men at ease with their homosexuality.[13] The idea that a repressed homosexual might be more of a problem to the military than an open one was an idea rarely countenanced within official documents, even as the era's homo-military films seemed to suggest as much.

Dropping Hairpins: **The Strange One** *(1957)* and **Billy Budd** *(1962)*

In pre-Stonewall gay male subcultures, "dropping a hairpin" meant alluding in covert, coded ways to one's own homosexuality. If an individual being so addressed "picked up the hairpin"—responded knowingly to the coded statement or question—then one was safe is assuming they too were gay. Two of the first films of Hollywood's postwar homo-military cycle might be thought of in those terms: they hint at homosexuality in the military in oblique ways, but maintain plausible deniability should they be suspected of actually being "about" homosexuality. (As Chon Noriega has argued, the queer content of such films was also put into discourse by their advertising copy and reviews.)[14] Thus, much like contemporary Madison Avenue's use of "gay window advertising"—a practice that targets gay and lesbian consumers in ways meant to be overlooked by most heterosexual spectators—so did these films allude to homosexual meanings in more-or-less coded ways. From today's perspective, one can view these films as excellent examples of the very discourse of the closet—they employ connotative and symbolic means to signify homosexuality for those "in the know" while ostensibly being about something else altogether.

Such connotative means were the only way homosexuality could be signified under the dictates of the Hollywood Production Code (written in 1930 and officially "enforced" in 1934). Although it was continually challenged throughout the 1950s (by films such as *The Moon Is Blue* [1953] and *Baby Doll* [1956]), the Production Code still exerted a profound effect on the content of Hollywood film, especially in relation to homosexual themes. The Production Code Administration (PCA) edited queer backstories and subtexts out of the film adaptations of Tennessee Williams's plays *A Streetcar Named Desire* (1951) and *Cat on a Hot Tin Roof* (1958). Vincente Minnelli's film of the Broadway hit *Tea and Sympathy* (1956) had to be rewritten in order to emphasize that the young student's problem was not so much male homosexuality as it was heterosexual male effeminacy.[15] However, even though the Production Code Administration tried to delete overt homosexuality from the films it policed, it often failed to eradicate a more diffuse, connotative queerness. *Suddenly Last Summer* (1959), another Tennessee Williams adaptation revolving around a pedophilic homosexual and his horrible cannibalistic fate, is perhaps the most spectacular example of the Production Code's failure to remove queer content from 1950s Hollywood cinema.

The Strange One (1957) is another excellent example of how male homosexuality could be spoken within the censoring discourse of the Hollywood Production Code. The film, based on Calder Willingham's novel and play *End as a Man*, takes place at the fictional Southern Military College and centers on Jocko de Paris (Ben Gazarra), a cunning and manipulative upperclassman who sadistically brutalizes his fellow students. None of the characters are represented as being forthrightly homosexual, but the film wallows in a steamy mixture of homoerotic imagery and verbal innuendo. The mise-en-scène is filled with phallic signifiers such as towers, trumpets, cigars, flashlights, nightsticks, bottles, brooms, swords, and scores of erect young men marching sweatily through the night. The specter of homosexuality also envelops the characters of Cadet Perrin, an effete poet who idol-worships Jocko, and Cadet Simmons, a Peter Lorre look-alike who refuses to date girls or shower with the other cadets. Ultimately, all this queerness is displaced onto Jocko's violent sadism, a linkage not uncommon in the era's medical discourse about homosexuality. Thus, when Jocko calls Cadet Perrin a "three-dollar bill" and repeatedly "towel whips" his ass in the crowded shower room, it is hard not to read the scene as an act of metaphoric sodomy, wherein (Code-sanctioned) homosocial violence displaces (Code-forbidden) homosexual contact.

The story itself is an extended gloss on secrecy in the barracks, centering on a bizarre narrative event that also speaks homosexuality in barely coded ways. At the start of the film, a drunken poker game, organized by Jocko, turns violent and implicitly sodomitic when Cadet Simmons is beaten on the ass with a broom handle. The next morning another cadet is found beaten and drunk on the quad, having been force-fed liquor through an enema bag, an act suggesting both oral and anal rape. A later scene wherein Jocko is grilled about "the gag reflex" extends the analogy even further. ("Cadet De Paris, don't tell me you— *you* don't know what a gag reflex is!") Ultimately, all the cadets find themselves in a double-bind situation similar to that faced by homosexuals in the military (both then and still today): should they admit they lied about these transgressive events (and thus be expelled), or should they stay silent about their behaviors so that they may continue to serve in the corps?

FIGURE 1 In *The Strange One* (1957), Jocko's (Ben Gazarra) violence repeatedly manifests in acts of metaphorical sodomy, creating a confused conflation of homosexuality, homosexual repression, and sadism.

Despite the Production Code Administration's attempt to censor overt homosexuality from the film, many reviews made some comment on the film's homosexual overtones.[16] For example, *Weekly Variety* suggested the film would "need strong selling [since] stories involving military school's haven't been too popular with filmgoers nor do homosexual themes figure to be either."[17] Trying to make some sense of the film, *Time* magazine theorized that Jocko's sadism was the result of his "repressed homosexuality,"[18] but *Motion Picture Daily* complained that that link was not made strongly enough: "The scenes do not add up to a . . . credible portrait of a sadistic man. The motivations for all his hate and hostility are only superficially explored."[19] Thus, while the film may have been an attempt to show "how sexuality is school-disciplined into sadism,"[20] it failed to make a clear distinction between homosexuality, homosexual repression, and sadism, all of which are blurred together rather unthinkingly within the film.

Peter Ustinov's film of Herman Melville's classic novella *Billy Budd* (1962) works in similar ways, hinting at homosexual desire among sailors through its mise-en-scène and suggestive dialogue. Yet, whereas *The Strange One* was produced and sold as borderline exploitation fare (despite its literary pedigree),

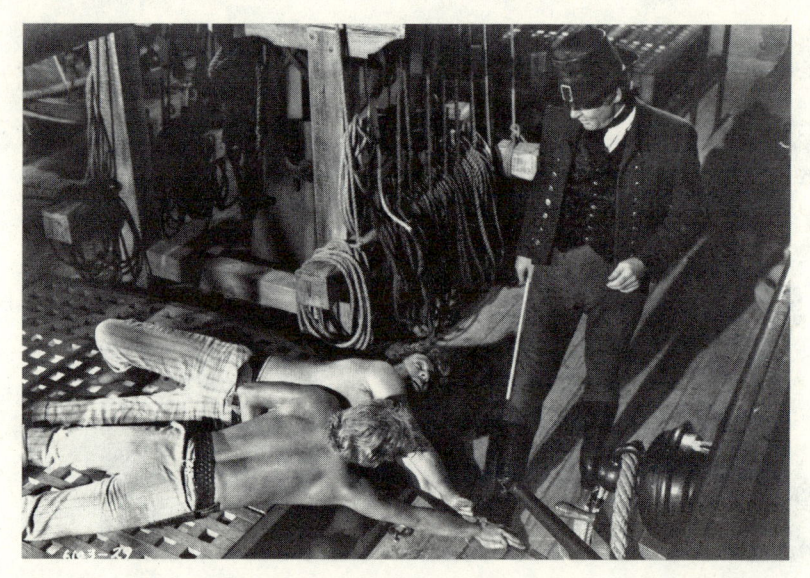

FIGURE 2 *Billy Budd* (1962): Homosexuality made invisible to the Production Code through the power of literary prestige.

Billy Budd was conceived of and marketed as a prestigious literary adaptation. In an interview from the era, Ustinov acknowledged that the novella contained homosexual themes, but that he had decided to mute them out of propriety, or perhaps fear of censorship.[21] Nonetheless, the film lingers on crotch shots, phallic signifiers ("a lovely knife you've got there"), and prolonged, unexplained gazes between Master-at-Arms Claggart (Robert Ryan) and the object of his obsession, the beautiful sailor Billy Budd (Terence Stamp). The film's ad campaign also highlighted homoerotic beefcake, with bare-chested sailors knife-fighting and being lashed on deck, while the print copy breathlessly exhorted: "The Men! ... The Might! ... The Mutiny!"[22] Master-at Arms Claggart can best be understood as a repressed homosexual: he is both attracted to and repulsed by Billy, afraid of "being charmed" by him, and so will not allow himself to be physically or emotionally touched by him. Claggart's speech about the nature of the ocean—calm above but teeming with monsters below—metaphorizes this repression while simultaneously figuring his homosexual desire as monstrous. At one point Billy even comes close to diagnosing Claggart as an ego-dystonic homosexual, asserting that Claggart "hates himself," but the cause of that self-hatred is never made manifest.

The Production Code Administration never objected to homosexual content in *Billy Budd* because it didn't see any.[23] Instead, it was reviewed as part of a cycle of naval stories including *Mutiny on the Bounty* (1962) and *Damn the Defiant* (1962).[24] Upon its release the film was hailed by critics as a faithful adaptation of a literary classic about the eternal struggle between good and evil; it was even screened in high school English classes for years after its initial theatrical run.[25] Most reviewers discussed Claggart not as a repressed homosexual but as a "devil incarnate."[26] However, a few reviews did hint at what was missing from the film. One complained that the "force and fearfulness of [Claggart's] nature and power, and the reasons for his consuming hatred, are insufficiently conveyed."[27] Another critic called Claggart "a strange invert who appears to hate all those who do him a kindness," but despite the pointed use of the term "invert," did not follow up on the possible meanings of that assertion.[28] Only in recent years have reviewers been freer to acknowledge the text's queer dynamics. In 1990, Eve Kosofsky Sedgwick devoted a chapter of her book *Epistemology of the Closet* to it,[29] and in 1993, *Gays and Lesbians in Mainstream Cinema* called the film an "overt study of homosexual frustration leading a man—here the villain—to his doom and, in the process, destroying the naïve hero."[30] Although the cultured British actor and director Peter Ustinov might have acknowledged the novella's homosexual themes, most mainstream American critics—even academic ones—were loath to do so in the early 1960s.

Coming Out: Reflections in a Golden Eye *(1967)* and The Sergeant *(1968)*

Hollywood's homo-military film reached its apex in the late 1960s. Much had changed in a relatively short span of time: what could only be hinted about in *The Strange One* and *Billy Budd* was beginning to emerge from the closet. In the fall of 1961, the Production Code had been amended to allow for the "sensitive treatment" of homosexuality, although what this seemed to mean in practice was that homosexuals could be depicted as long as they were also punished, often via suicide or murder. Perhaps because of that, many of the era's films encode rather complex ideas about homosexuality and its repression. For example, homophobic blackmail is explored as a political weapon in *Advise and Consent* (1962) and *The Best Man* (1964), while *Rachel, Rachel* (1968) implied that lesbian desire is sometimes displaced into religious fervor. Perhaps most forcefully, *The Detective* (1968) suggested that antigay violence is itself linked to conflicted or repressed homosexual desire, an observation that behavioral scientists have only recently demonstrated to be valid.[31]

Both *Reflections in a Golden Eye* (1967) and *The Sergeant* (1968) focus on military men whose repressed homosexual desires lead to violence. Though released a year after *Reflections*, *The Sergeant* had actually been in the production pipeline for many years. In it, Army sergeant Callan (Rod Steiger) becomes obsessed with a young soldier under his command. When the nature of his fascination becomes clear to the sergeant, he commits suicide. Although the words *homosexual* or *gay* are never uttered, the audience is meant to understand that the sergeant is experiencing a homosexual passion that even he does not understand. As revealed by an interoffice production memo, *The Sergeant* was designed to "be the story of a man [who] is not a practicing homosexual, though he *is* a homosexual who cannot express it in the usual fashion, under the circumstances."[32]

Negotiations occurred during the last few months of 1961 between *The Sergeant*'s production team and PCA officials. At first, it seemed as though the film would be permitted to be made under the provisions of the newly liberalized Production Code. Geoffrey Shurlock expressed general discomfort with the film's subject matter but did advise that "this material, dealing with sex aberration, seems generally acceptable under the current interpretation of the Production Code."[33] However, just a few weeks later, that decision was reversed when the Appeals Board of the Motion Picture Association of America upheld the rejection of a Code Seal for the British film *Victim* (1961). As a MPAA memo put it, the Appeals Board denied *Victim* a Code Seal because it "dealt with the subject of sex perversion far beyond their intent." The PCA was told not to "countenance any picture in which the theme dealt wholly, or in major part, with the subject of sex perversion."[34] As such, the planned production of *The Sergeant* was shut down by the PCA in the last days of 1961. In a similar move, despite the newly liberalized Code, "*The Victors* (1963) lost several scenes that would have indicated that American soldiers (George Peppard and George Hamilton) were sleeping with a young French male prostitute (Joel Flateau)."[35]

The Sergeant would eventually be made and released in 1968, but by then its provocative subject matter had been stolen by the flagrantly baroque *Reflections in a Golden Eye*, released one year earlier. *Reflections*, based on the scandalous southern gothic novella by Carson McCullers, focuses on Major Penderton (Marlon Brando) and his obsession with the handsome Private Williams (Robert Forster). Penderton's wife Leonora (Elizabeth Taylor) is having an affair with Colonel Langdon (Brian Keith), whose neurotic wife Alison (Julie Harris) has mutilated her breasts with a pair of garden shears. Alison is tended to by a flamboyantly effeminate Filipino houseboy named Anacleto (played by Zorro David, a former Saks Fifth Avenue hairdresser "discovered" by director John Huston). True to the form of southern gothic melodrama, the film ends with a shocking act of violence as Penderton shoots his object of desire while Leonora looks on in horror—a scene made even more hysterical by John Huston's wildly panning camera.

Reflections in a Golden Eye combines elements of serious literature, psychological melodrama, campy sexploitation, and baroque psychedelia—a hybrid form common to many Hollywood films of the era desperate to connect with younger, more countercultural audiences. The production was designed from its inception to push at the boundaries of Hollywood form and content, and perhaps unsurprisingly, its production history was a long and tortuous affair. In 1964, the PCA tentatively approved the film, but cautioned that "there should be no overt homosexual approaches between the Captain [*sic*] and Private Williams."[36] The need to suggest rather than show such a key element of the story presented a challenge to the many screenwriters who worked on the screenplay (including Francis Ford Coppola, Christopher Isherwood, William Archibald, and Truman Capote).[37] Warner Brothers executive William Fadiman found himself confused by the scripts sent to him: "I'm not at all certain that the writer wishes to indicate any homosexual relationship, inferred or direct, between Penderton and Williams. Or if he does, it is done in such a shadowy manner as to be unclear. If I am right then there is no real relationship between these men, which I would consider a defect since this relationship has enormous dramatic possibilities. But as I said, I may be wrong and can only judge from the rather tentative, groping outline."[38]

While it seems remarkable that even the producers of *Reflections in a Golden Eye* would be in the dark about the homosexual content of their property, only a few years earlier Shirley MacLaine and Audrey Hepburn had starred in *The Children's Hour* (1962) without discussing their characters' lesbianism.[39] Homosexuality was still, quite literally, "the love that dare not speak its name." The silence that surrounded it—as dictated by dominant regimes of taste and politesse—was an effective tool used to circumscribe the very existence of pre-Stonewall queers.

Perhaps as a way to circumvent the PCA should they ultimately deny the film a Seal of Approval, the production of *Reflections in a Golden Eye* was heavily hyped in the press. The various changes in scriptwriters were duly noted by *The Hollywood Reporter* and *Variety*, as was a major cast change: Marlon Brando replaced Montgomery Clift in the role of Penderton after Clift was found dead.[40] By 1966, as the film was being shot in Italy, the trade and fan magazines were awash with stories of trouble on the set, tempestuous stars, and the potential nudity of both Elizabeth Taylor and Robert Forster.[41] And as the film entered postproduction, director Huston decided to tint the film with a sepia/gold wash, a process that desaturated all the colors in the film except red—which instead registered as pink.[42] Eventually the film was released with a PCA Seal of Approval, but under the condition that it be advertised as "Suggested for Mature Audiences."[43] That decision did not appease everyone, however. Mrs. Marjorie Snyder, President of Family Theatres, Inc. of Tulsa, Oklahoma, wrote to the PCA to chastise Geoffrey Shurlock for allowing the film to be released at all.[44]

While the film's depiction of repressed homosexual desire is fairly obvious (with countless shots of the major following and mooning over the private), its press materials were still unable to mention it directly. Thus the film was described as the story of "a complex Army officer battling his own bizarre emotions" while trapped in "a marriage of strange and opposing passions."[45] When the *New York Daily News* panned the film, Warner Brothers' publicity department excerpted the following memorable line for a new round of ad copy: "It's dirty—a combination of lust, impotency, vulgarity, nudity, neurosis, brutality, voyeurism, hatred and insanity that culminates in murder." (Note that homosexuality or repressed homosexuality is still not mentioned in this list of alleged atrocities.)[46] Many other reviews panned the film as well, calling it "a strong candidate for the year's worst,"[47] and at least one commentator objected very strongly to the whole idea of homosexual desire in the military, stating that "such a story makes more sense in a psychiatrist's case book than in a picture dealing with an Army Post murder."[48]

Nonetheless, many reviews did get the point of the film: that the major's mental breakdown and resulting violence was the result of his repressed homosexuality. *Variety* called the film an attempt to be "a literate exposition of latent homosexuality"[49] and *Cue* magazine opined that "the film is a character study that pits those who live by self-repression against those who reach for sensitivity or passion."[50] Charles Champlin similarly praised it: "Its major theme is of a man's anguished realization not only of his latent homosexuality but also of his failing powers or will to repress much longer the furies within himself."[51] By 2001, when the film was revived for contemporary audiences, it was hailed as "a perversely perceptive study of how repression cultivates poisonous emotional fetishes."[52]

One year later, the reception of *The Sergeant* was framed within similar patterns of denial and confusion. As with *Reflections*, its press materials could not (or would not) openly speak about the film's subject matter, euphemistically calling it a "tense drama of the conflicts and frustrations of peacetime army service [that] centers on a veteran sergeant (Steiger) who tries to break up the romance between a private ([John Philip] Law) and a French girl."[53] Rod Steiger went on record saying the film was not about homosexuality but loneliness,[54] and the film critic of *Women's Wear Daily* seemed especially offended that anyone could read the film as being about homosexual desire, repressed or otherwise:

> I cannot warn you strongly enough to ignore the advertising and the advance word that [*The Sergeant*] is a homosexual film. It is an insult to anyone's intelligence to promote it as such; sure, you *can* read it into the film if you want to, but it would be stretching several points way out of recognition. [The sergeant wants the private to] be his confidant, his buddy, his drinking companion, his *friend*. To claim any hint of homosexualism in this is a lot of crap. . . . who has not been jealous when a really close friend takes up with another friend?[55]

The feverish—almost panicked—tone of this review seems to be the result of the reviewer's need to make clear-cut boundaries between male homosocial

FIGURE 3 Though clichéd in its depiction of repressed homosexuality, *The Sergeant* (1968) nevertheless made the more radically queer suggestion that homosexual desire is coterminous with heterosexual identity and homosociality.

and male homosexual desire—a need still endemic in most Western patriarchal cultures.

Much of the moral indignation that the bizarre *Reflections in a Golden Eye* had engendered was missing from the reception of *The Sergeant*. Whereas the National Catholic Organization of Motion Pictures had condemned *Reflections in a Golden Eye* as an "exploitation picture," it passed *The Sergeant* as "A-III."[56] In fact, by the time *The Sergeant* premiered at the San Francisco International Film Festival (in between screenings of *Weekend, Lonesome Cowboys,* and *Yellow Submarine*), its old-fashioned social-problem approach to its topic seemed almost quaint. Stanley Kauffmann quipped that "Rod Steiger takes two hours to find out what the rest of us knew in 15 minutes: he's a repressed homosexual."[57] Vincent Canby complained about the film's obvious symbolism, citing "a beer bottle handled as if it were a phallus, fondled guns, and the like."[58] Whereas those obvious symbols were the chief ways that homosexual desire was spoken in Hollywood films only ten years earlier, by 1968 they had become tired clichés.

Nonetheless, the film's slow, obvious plotting did allow its theme to be understood by many reviewers (the *Women's Wear Daily* critic notwithstanding). The *Los Angeles Times* stated clearly that the film was about "latent homosexuality,"[59] while the *Motion Picture Herald* also reported that the sergeant was afflicted with "homosexual inclinations that are so latent that he does not recognize why he is strongly attracted to a handsome young private under his command."[60] Other reviews connected the sergeant's macho sadism to his repression of his homosexual desires, suggesting he "fears his own weakness so much that he bears down brutally on weakness in others."[61] At least one review found in the film a broad critique of the military mindset: there is "a good deal more to *The Sergeant* than merely the case history of a homosexual. As soon as one poses the question of how he could have concealed his latent tendencies for so long, one realizes (as in *Reflections*) that the Army provides a base of power that not merely gives rein, but tacit approval to sadistic impulses."[62]

Many of the more interesting comments made in reviews of *The Sergeant* focus on the character of Private Swanson, and why, as one reviewer puts it, he "gives up the lovely young girl with whom he is in love to drink and go out on the town with the older man."[63] Several reviews spoke of how the private's character seemed queer—not quite straight, and not quite gay. For example, *Playboy* noted that John Philip Law (as the private) "catches precisely the right nuances of ingenuousness and sexual ambivalence in a small town American golden boy.... Wary at first, he becomes compliant, even subconsciously seductive at times, until the unequivocal eruption of perversity frightens, then enrages him and finally leaves him wondering just a little bit about himself."[64] The film may have used clichéd devices to depict repressed homosexual desire, but its suggestion that homosexual desire is a coterminous and even constitutive aspect of heterosexual identity and homosociality makes it seem radically queer, even by today's standards.

Flaunting It: The Gay Deceivers *(1969)*

The era's homo-military film came to an end with a glossy exploitation film made on the fringes of Hollywood. While *Reflections in a Golden Eye* and *The Sergeant* were cautionary tales about the tragedy of repressed homosexual desire, *The Gay Deceivers* (1969) treated its subject matter as farce. Although the film invites audiences to laugh at homosexual stereotypes, it also contains pro-gay sentiments and raises queer ideas about the social construction and fluidity of male sexual identity. Ultimately, for some reviewers, the sexual and textual ambiguity of *The Gay Deceivers* was effective in deconstructing traditional models of sexuality, blurring the lines between straight and gay, homosocial and homosexual.

The Gay Deceivers focuses on Danny and Elliot, who, at their Army induction hearing, pretend to be gay in order to avoid the draft. Dogged by Lieutenant Colonel Dixon, a military officer who suspects their ruse, Danny and Elliot are forced to keep their heterosexuality closeted and live a gay lifestyle. The general hilarity of these antics turns more serious when Danny and Elliot come to realize that their performance has been too good, and they are forced to confess their deceit to Dixon. However, in a twist ending (what one reviewer called "a nice dirty dig at the military establishment"),[65] it is revealed that Dixon is himself homosexual, that he *does* believe the boys are straight, and that that fact is what disqualifies them from the service. As Dixon coos to his aide in the final moments of the film, "We don't want their kind in the Army, do we Joe?"

Yet, lest the film be considered too radical, it also frames its story in terms of compensating moral values that stress that deceiving the U.S. Draft Board is wrong. (As the film's pressbook synopsis put it, Danny and Elliot's "world of deception crumbles, forcing them to face the consequences of their actions when to their dismay, they discover no one will believe the truth.")[66] Clearly, the film was calculated to have a broad appeal. The *Los Angeles Times* noted that it was "so shrewdly and amiably written that not only homosexuals but also hawks are not likely to be turned off."[67] The *Hollywood Citizen-News* found it palatable,[68] and the *Catholic Newsletter* awarded the X-rated film an "A-IV" and called it "very humorous."[69] Even the *Advocate* (grudgingly) endorsed the film: "All the gay characters are acted as if one straight is telling another a 'Thay thweetie!' joke. Still, Dammit, it's funny."[70]

The Gay Deceivers is something of an oxymoron: it is a polished and comparatively sophisticated exploitation film, seemingly produced by straight white men but also aimed at a gay male audience (most obviously through the repeated objectification of blond lifeguard Elliot's nearly naked body).[71] The film was successful in attracting the newly discovered gay audience: as *Film Daily* snidely noted, the sneak preview "audience was almost entirely male, if considerably less than masculine."[72] In another attempt to make the film more appealing to gay men, the producers hired Michael Greer to play Danny and

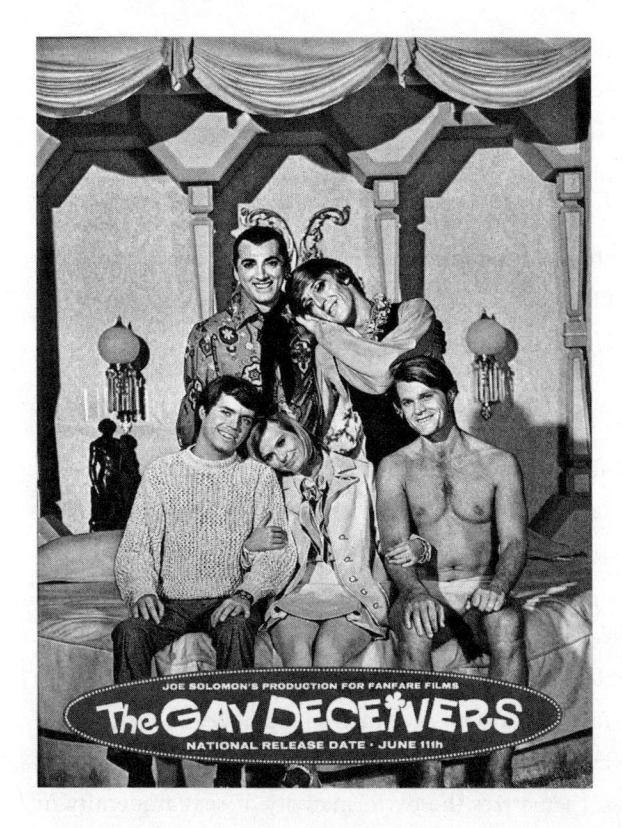

FIGURE 4 *The Gay Deceivers* (1969) in the wake of Stonewall: "sickening prejudice" or "unintentional insight into the plight of the homosexual"?

Elliot's swishy neighbor, Malcolm De John. Greer was a gay cabaret performer who himself had served three years in the Air Force before being discovered by Judy Garland and propelled onto the burgeoning gay nightclub scene. According to Vito Russo, it was Greer who brought a more gay-friendly tone to the film, rewriting some of his and others' dialogue.[73] Greer was so memorably over-the-top in the film that there was even talk about a Best Supporting Actor Oscar nomination for him—surely a first for a sexploitation film.[74]

However, not all homosexuals were happy with the film. When it opened in San Francisco just two weeks after the Stonewall Riots, it was picketed by a dozen members of the Committee for the Freedom of Homosexuals. Far from seeing it as gently satiric, the activists complained that the film "flaunts every sickening prejudice and bigoted misconception that supposes we homosexuals are both lacking in manliness and patriotism."[75] A resultant letter to the editor of the *San Francisco Chronicle* took the opportunity to critique the military's antigay policies: "This film is not only an insult to the proud and 'manly' gay persons of this community but to the millions of homosexuals who conceal their identity to fight bravely and die proudly for their country, which rejects them."[76] Thus, regardless of how the film was decoded by its various audiences, it became a platform for more overt commentary about the military's discriminatory policies.[77]

In fact, the film is much more than a collection of simple-minded fag jokes. *Boxoffice* noted that the film provides "subtle, if unintentional insight into the plight of the homosexual in contemporary society," but many of the points the film makes about discrimination are strongly sounded and seem far from unintentional.[78] Elliot is fired from his lifeguard job because he might be a "bad influence on the kids," and he and Danny lose everything of importance to them when they are perceived by their friends and family as gay. In another example, a character in a gay bar relates how he was fired from his government job for security clearance reasons, and the ending of the film seems to argue that homosexuals are already in the military and doing just fine. The film also presents a loving and stable gay relationship (that of Malcolm and his partner), and perhaps most importantly represents gay men as members of a social minority group and not psychiatric abnormalities.

The Gay Deceivers also thematizes the performativity of sexual identity in multiple ways. From Danny and Elliot "acting" either straight or gay, to a climactic costume ball wherein a drag queen punches out a leather daddy, the film repeatedly constitutes sexual identity as performative. This multiple role playing is present in Michael Greer's performance of Malcolm, what the *Advocate* called "a phony overly exaggerated parody of a parody."[79] Perhaps most interestingly, and recalling actual psychiatric attempts to police the homosocial/homosexual divide, the interrogation scene that opens the film acknowledges the gray area between having a homosexual *experience* ("depends on how you would define an experience") versus *being* homosexual.

Reviews of *The Gay Deceivers* raised these and other questions about sexual fluidity. The critic for the *Baltimore Sun* noted that due to the "ambiguity in Jerome Wish's screenplay . . . compounded by Larry Casey's performance as Elliot . . . one can't help but wonder a bit about old Elliot. . . . He throws himself into his homosexual impersonation with such to-the-manner-born breeziness that the spectator can never be sure that, underneath all those muscles, Elliot may not be the real thing."⁸⁰ Elliot's oft-stated need for frequent heterosexual sex (and his career as a gigolo) were seen by other critics as overcompensation for his repressed homosexuality. Indeed, Elliott tells Danny that he might develop a "complex" if he doesn't have frequent sex with women, echoing another moment in the film when a doctor says that "latent tendencies sometimes don't show themselves until there's a crisis." The *Hollywood Reporter* noted that Elliott "takes to the camping with suspicious ease. . . . [and although] the latent possibilities and stud pose never converge in resolution or insight . . . there are several inexplicable scenes which defy logic. Why, for example, would he casually head to a gay bar to taunt the customers if the whole homosexual scene were supposedly just a recently appropriated act solely for the diversion of the draft investigators?"⁸¹ Other reviewers were also disturbed by these implications, noting that Elliot's potential queerness made "his problem of having to pretend to be something he isn't less amusing than it might have been otherwise."⁸² In other words, for some reviewers the joke stopped being funny when it stopped being just a joke.

Conclusion

As the war in Vietnam trickled to an end, and Hollywood regained its economic footing, homo-military themes retreated from mainstream film. Occasionally a television movie (*Sgt. Matlovich vs. the US Air Force* [1978]) or an independent film (*Streamers* [1983]) would address same-sex desire within the armed services, but it was not until the 1990s that "gays in the military" once again became a subject of national discussion. A few documentaries and social-problem television movies (*Coming Out under Fire* [1994], *Serving in Silence: The Margarethe Cammermeyer Story* [1995]) were made in support of ending the ban against gays in the military, but mainstream media more regularly framed the topic as a nervous joke in countless sitcoms, talk show monologues, and militaristic blockbusters such as *Independence Day* (1996). Male-male desire within the military was strictly dichotomized: in Hollywood it was represented as good clean homosocial bonding, while within gay pornography, such homosociality always gave way to explicit homosexuality. Only rarely would mainstream media dare to link military homosociality and homosexuality. For example, in the independent film *Sleep with Me* (1994), a character played by

Quentin Tarantino explains in minute detail how and why *Top Gun* (1986) is really "a story about a man's struggle with his own homosexuality." However, the ironic way in which the monologue is delivered allows the spectator the chance to laugh it off, effectively repressing the reading and thus maintaining a strict homosocial-homosexual divide.

Hollywood's pre-Stonewall homo-military films raised significant and complex questions about masculinity and sexual identity and suggested that the borders between male homosocial and homosexual desire—between straight and gay—were not always so clear cut. They hinted at why, in Parker Tyler's observation, sexual repression is "so important in the annals of war, where soldiering [is] an aspect of love."[83] And they dramatized how, in Jack Babuscio's formulation, sexual repression "invariably ends in violence, be it psychic or physical."[84] Writing in the 1970s, seminal queer theorist Guy Hocquenghem put it this way: the "latent homosexuality so beloved of psychoanalysts corresponds to the oppression of patent homosexuality; and we find the greatest charge of latent homosexuality in those social machines which are particularly anti-homosexual—the army, the school, the church, sport, etc. At the collective level, this sublimation is a means of transforming desire into the desire to repress."[85] In other words, "sublimated homosexuality provides [Western patriarchal] society with the minimum humanitarian cohesion it needs" to survive—and ultimately, to make war, not love.[86]

Notes

1. Jack Babuscio, "Screen Gays: Military Masks," *Gay News* 86 (circa 1970), exact date and pages number missing. Xeroxed columns compiled and on file at the One Institute, Los Angeles.
2. Richard G. Druss, MD, "Cases of Suspected Homosexuality Seen at an Army Mental Hygiene Consultation Service," *Psychiatric Quarterly* 41 (1967): 65.
3. Ibid., 63.
4. For a psychiatric overview of the situation as it pertained to the late 1950s and early 1960s, see Louis Joylon West, William T. Doidge, and Robert L. Williams, "An Approach to the Problem of Homosexuality in the Military Service," *American Journal of Psychiatry* 115 (1958): 392–401.
5. Parker Tyler, *Screening the Sexes: Homosexuality in the Movies* (1972; New York: Da Capo, 1993), 240–81.
6. For an overview of these issues, see Allan Berube, *Coming Out under Fire: The History*

of Gay Men and Women in World War II (New York: Penguin, 1990) and Lillian Faderman, *Odd Girls and Twilight Lovers: A History of Lesbian Life in Twentieth-Century America* (New York: Penguin, 1991).

7. Michael Bronski, *Pulp Friction: Uncovering the Golden Age of Gay Male Pulps* (New York: St. Martin's Griffin, 2003), 26. Similar points are made by Richard Dyer in *Now You See It: Studies on Lesbian and Gay Film* (New York: Routledge, 1990), 111–13. For more contemporary accounts of how gay male desire infiltrates and circulates within military settings, see Steven Zeeland, *Sailors and Sexual Identity: Crossing the Line between "Straight" and "Gay" in the U.S. Navy* (New York: Harrington Park, 1995) and *Military Trade* (New York: Harrington Park, 1999).

8. West, Doidge, and Williams, "An Approach to the Problem of Homosexuality," 392–93.

9. Druss, "Cases of Suspected Homosexuality," 62.

10. See Berube, *Coming Out under Fire*, 149–74; see also Nicolai Gioscia, "The Gag Reflex and Fellatio," *American Journal of Psychiatry* 107 (1950): 380.

11. As many queer theorists have pointed out, being a passive male homosexual is "feminizing" and therefore considered pathological by much of Western culture. Guy Hocquenghem writes, "Only the phallus dispenses identity; any social use of the anus, apart from its sublimated use, creates the risk of a loss of identity. Seen from behind we are all women" (*Homosexual Desire*, trans. Daniella Dangoor [1978; Durham, N.C.: Duke University Press, 1993], 101).

12. West, Doidge, and Williams, "An Approach to the Problem of Homosexuality," 398. This particular article continues: "Approximately 25% of the picked group of normal controls in our special study gave histories of sexual 'irregularities' during childhood and adolescence, including sexual contacts with parents and siblings (both hetero- and homosexual), with farm animals, and even (in three cases) with watermelons. These were basically well-adjusted 17- and 18-year-old airmen who were doing well in their training and who presented no signs or symptoms of abnormality. Nearly half had at one time or another engaged in homosexual play."

13. Very rarely, the era's popular press did address the issue of homosexuals in the army. See David Sanford, "Boxed In," *New Republic*, May 21, 1966, 8–9. In 1961, *Newsweek* acknowledged the fact that homosexuals "are often exceptionally courageous in battle, and on the job they're frequently intelligent and efficient [but] the Army doesn't want them" ("Homosexuals: One Solider in 25?" *Newsweek*, May 15, 1961, 92).

14. Chon Noriega, "'SOMETHING'S MISSING HERE!': Homosexuality and Film Reviews during the Production Code Era, 1934–1962," *Cinema Journal* 30, no. 1 (1990): 20–41.

15. See Vito Russo, *The Celluloid Closet*, rev. ed. (New York: Harper and Row, Publishers, 1987), 100–123, for an overview of the changes the Production Code mandated to these and other queer films of the 1950s.

16. Specifics on how *The Strange One* was edited by the PCA are detailed in memos from Geoffrey Shurlock. "Today we met with Sam Spiegel and agreed to the following reediting of the above picture: The scene between DeParis and Perrin has been lengthened so that Perrin reads his manuscript up to the point where he says 'NIGHT BOY—that is the name of the book.' At this point we cut to the other student entering. The later scene in the drug store has been reinstated, with the deletion of the underlined words in the line "Leave that girl *and come with me*" (memo dated April 9, 1957, on file in Production Code archives, Margaret Herrick Library, Los Angeles).
17. Review of *The Strange One*, *Weekly Variety*, April 3, 1957. The review also pointed out that "three minutes of these scenes were deleted from the original print following a ukase of the Production Code Administration that this footage violated its rules banning 'sex perversion or any inference of it.'"
18. Review of *The Strange One*, *Time*, April 22, 1957.
19. Richard Gertner, review of *The Strange One*, *Motion Picture Daily*, April 3, 1957.
20. The phrase is Parker Tyler's, though he first used it to describe the German film *Young Torless* (1968). See Tyler, *Screening the Sexes*, 245.
21. "The homosexual theme that sometimes obtrudes in the story has been removed and the sense of hopeless tragedy in the death of Billy Budd has been tackled while still keeping to Melville's ending" (Anthony Gruner, "London Report," *Boxoffice*, July 10, 1961, 17).
22. Other print ads prominently featured Claggart ogling Billy, while a blurb quote from Hazel Flynn of the *Hollywood Citizen News* asserted that "new star Terence Stamp, with the face of an angel, is powerfully virile!" (press book, Margaret Herrick Library, Los Angeles).
23. Instead they objected to the use of the word *bastard* and asked that the filmmakers shorten a lashing scene (PCA files memo, April 26, 1961, Margaret Herrick Library, Los Angeles).
24. Bosley Crowther, "Flogging in Three Sea Films," *New York Times*, November 21, 1962.
25. Hazel Flynn, "Melville Classic Fine for Family," *Hollywood Citizen-News*, November 14, 1962.
26. Harrison Carroll, "*Billy Budd* Rates an Oscar Prospect," *Los Angeles Herald-Examiner*, November 15, 1962.
27. James Powers, "Lubin-Ustinov Pic Strong on Action," *Hollywood Reporter*, August 27, 1962.
28. Flynn, "Melville Classic Fine for Family."
29. Eve Kosofsky Sedgwick, *Epistemology of the Closet* (Los Angeles: University of California Press, 1990), 91–130. I remember having my queer reading of the novella in an undergraduate seminar in the mid-1980s summarily dismissed.

30. James Robert Parish, *Gays and Lesbians in Mainstream Cinema* (Jefferson, N.C.: McFarland, 1993), 42.
31. Henry E. Adams, Lester W. Wright Jr., and Bethany A. Lohr, "Is Homophobia Associated with Homosexual Arousal?" *Journal of Abnormal Psychology* 105 (1996): 440–45.
32. Martin Ritt Collection, folder 515, correspondence—Ray Stark, Margaret Herrick Library, Los Angeles.
33. Memo, November 7, 1961, MPPA files on *The Sergeant*, Margaret Herrick Library, Los Angeles.
34. Jack Vizzard, memo, November 20, 1961, MPPA files on *The Sergeant*, Margaret Herrick Library, Los Angeles.
35. Russo, *The Celluloid Closet*, 136.
36. Geoffrey Shurlock, MPPA memo dated September 15, 1964, collected in the MPPA files on *Reflections in a Golden Eye*, Margaret Herrick Library, Los Angeles.
37. See "Coppola on Screenplay of 7 Arts 'Golden Eye,'" *Hollywood Reporter*, May 10, 1963, and Mike Connolly, "Rambling Reporter," *Hollywood Reporter*, March 10, 1966.
38. William Fadiman, memo dated April 21, 1966, John Huston Collection, Margaret Herrick Library, Los Angeles.
39. MacLaine discusses this anecdote in the film version of *The Celluloid Closet* (1995).
40. There was also brief speculation on whether or not Richard Burton would take over the role. See "Peter Glenville Helms Richard Burton Film," *The Hollywood Reporter*, August 24, 1965.
41. "A Topless Liz 'Promised' by WB," *Weekly Variety*, November 21, 1966.
42. After a brief run, 100 of the tinted prints were pulled from theaters and replaced by 250 full color ones. See "W7 Heeds 'Demand,' Makes 250 Tint Print of 'Reflections' Available," *Variety*, November 13, 1967. The special color process was itself reported on by *American Cinematographer* in December 1967.
43. "'Golden Eye' Gets 'Mature' Code Seal; 'Won't Make Cuts,'" *Variety*, September 6, 1967.
44. MPPA files on *Reflections in a Golden Eye*, Margaret Herrick Library, Los Angeles.
45. Pressbook, Margaret Herrick Library, Los Angeles.
46. The controversy over that ad line was itself covered in the trade press. See "W7 Thinks Better of 'It's Dirty' as Sell Copy for 'Golden Eye,'" *Variety*, October 25, 1967.
47. Allen Eyles, "Reflections in a Golden Eye," *Films and Filming*, May 1968, 24.
48. Reported about a *New York Post* essay in the *Motion Picture Herald*, November 1, 1967.
49. Murf., review of *Reflections in a Golden Eye*, *Variety*, October 11, 1967.
50. Review of *Reflections in a Golden Eye*, *Cue*, October 21, 1967.
51. Charles Champlin, "'Reflections' Tours the Southern Gothic Style," *Los Angeles Times Calendar*, October 8, 1967, 14.

52. Program notes for a screening at the American Cinematheque, February 11, 2001, Margaret Herrick Library, Los Angeles.
53. Press book, Margaret Herrick Library, Los Angeles.
54. P.K., "'Sergeant' Star Says Film Not 'Unnatural,'" *San Francisco Chronicle*, October 19, 1968.
55. Peter Davis Dibble, "Film: *The Sergeant*," *Women's Wear Daily*, October 26, 1968, 29. Bold print in original.
56. Under the National Catholic Organization's rating scheme, A-III designated a film as "suitable for adults only." MPPA files on *The Sergeant*, Margaret Herrick Library, Los Angeles.
57. Stanley Kauffmann, "On Films," *New Republic*, January 25, 1969.
58. Vincent Canby, "Review of *The Sergeant*," *New York Times*, November 21, 1968. Similarly, the *Hollywood Reporter* complained that "there is a dialogue between Law and Steiger during which Steiger taps a rather blatantly symbolic tattoo on a beer bottle as they speak. Even in full shot, the hand business is highlighted and the overstressed sound further draws attention from every other element in the overextended sequence. Afraid we may have missed the only thing in the scene that hasn't been missed, [director] Flynn repeats the action in a hand close-up" (John Mahoney, "W7s 'Sergeant' Artie BO; 'Vixen' for Skin Trenches," *Hollywood Reporter*, October 28, 1968).
59. Kevin Thomas, "'Sergeant' on Screen of Picwood Theater," *Los Angeles Times*, December 24, 1968.
60. Richard Gertner, review of *The Sergeant*, *Motion Picture Herald*, December 4, 1968, 71.
61. "New Films: *The Sergeant*," *Cue*, January 4, 1969.
62. Arthur Knight, "SR Goes to the Movies," *Saturday Review*, January 4, 1969.
63. Elsa, "The Showmen's Trade Reviews: *The Sergeant*," *Motion Picture Exhibitor*, December 25, 1968.
64. Review of *The Sergeant*, *Playboy*, February 1969.
65. John Mahoney, "*The Gay Deceivers* Offers an Alternative to Canada," *Hollywood Reporter*, June 5, 1969.
66. *The Gay Deceivers* press book, Margaret Herrick Library, Los Angeles.
67. Kevin Thomas, "*Gay Deceivers* at Two Southland Sites," *Los Angeles Times*, July 16, 1969.
68. Dean Holzapple, "*Gay Deceivers* Proves Hilarious," *Hollywood Citizen-News*, July 18, 1969.
69. *Catholic Newsletter*, July 1969, MPAA file on *The Gay Deceivers*, Margaret Herrick Library, Los Angeles.
70. J. R., "*Gay Deceivers*: With So Many *Faults*, Why Is It So Funny?" *Advocate*, September 1969, 31.
71. I have been unable to find any evidence—either concrete or circumstantial—that might

suggest that director Bruce Kessler, producer Joe Solomon, or writers Gil Lasky, Abe Polsky, and Jerome Wish were anything but heterosexual. Each of them worked primarily in television or low-budget filmmaking.

72. Francis O. Beermann, "*The Gay Deceivers*," *Film Daily*, June 23, 1969.
73. Russo, *The Celluloid Closet*, 186.
74. Review of *The Gay Deceivers*, *Boxoffice*, June 11, 1969. The press book for another Greer film, *Fortune and Men's Eyes* (1971), alleges that 1960s übercritic Andrew Sarris felt Greer should have been nominated for an Oscar for his role in *The Gay Deceivers*.
75. Reported in "Pansies Picket Opening of Gay Film in Frisco," *Variety*, July 18, 1969.
76. Reported in ibid.
77. Similarly, *Boston After Dark* commented that the film might indicate an important cultural shift in how the gay community was being treated: "If the public is ready to laugh at them they may be ready to stop persecuting them." Tom Ramage, "Gay Deceivers Film: 'Tis Gay to be 'Fey' for Fun and Profit," *Boston After Dark*, September 20, 1969.
78. "Review of *The Gay Deceivers*," *Boxoffice*, June 11, 1969.
79. J. R., "Gay Deceivers," 31.
80. R. H. Gardner, "Satirical Film Cites One Way to Beat the Draft," *Baltimore Sun*, September 26, 1969.
81. John Mahoney, "*The Gay Deceivers*."
82. R. H. Gardner, "Satirical Film."
83. Tyler, *Screening the Sexes*, 249.
84. Jack Babuscio, "Screen Gays: Military Masks."
85. Hocquenghem, *Homosexual Desire*, 72.
86. Ibid., 110.

CHUCK KLEINHANS

Pornography and Documentary Narrating the Alibi

From its beginnings, photography braided documentary form and sexual content, using pin-up and pornographic images of female performers and prostitutes. The introduction of moving images continued this paired development and the interwoven nature of the erotic and the factual. We know that this pairing goes back to the origins of cinema, when Maxim Gorky notes that he first saw the Cinematograph in a brothel, or when Edison's twenty-second film, *The Kiss* (1896), was denounced as obscene. The pattern continues. Today in the United States on the most successful subscription cable channel, Home Box Office (HBO), the most productive programming area is HBO documentary (gaining the greatest viewership for the lowest production costs). The most successful HBO documentary series is *Real Sex*, a one-hour program typically featuring four to six short documentary segments covering such topics as an adult masturbation club or a manufacturer of extremely realistic sex toys or mannequins. Also in the United States, the music video channels MTV and VH-1 regularly produce sex-themed documentaries, including a survey of porn stars who appear in rock videos and a depiction of how young women can audition for hard-core pornography videos in Los Angeles. The broadcast networks have followed suit and presented occasional "investigative" documentaries on aspects of the sex industry. In each

FIGURE 1 Highly rated HBO series like *Real Sex* and *Cathouse* (above) continue a documentary tradition as old as Edison's notorious film of 1896, *The Kiss*—the cinematic documentation of sexual practice.

of these, the content is sex, employing a transgressive voyeurism showing us what is normally censored, but at the same time marking the transgression with digital blurs of nipples and butt cracks. The defense of this forbidden content is the documentary form itself: documentary's "gravity," the "discourse of sobriety," provides the excuse that allows the naughty content to appear in the public sphere with little controversy.

To say this is to restate commonplace observations. First, even when presented as dramatic fictional narrative or as freewheeling fantasy, pornography has a fundamental core of documentation: this is it, this is sex, this is what it looks like. Second, one legal defense of pornography has been precisely its educational possibility; thus pornographers have often tried to evade censorship by explicitly presenting sexual images as factual documentation (or sometimes as art). My interest here is to move beyond these well-marked points and extend recent work. What happens when documentaries move beyond their usual sober realism directed at significant social matters to more bizarre, eccentric, and "low" subject matter? Further, in such sleazy voyeurism, what is the role of the narrator, almost always present in voice, if not in onscreen person? What are the politics of the alibi?

I take it as axiomatic that sleaze, as understood by both makers and audiences, depends on an understanding of existing conventions and also on a sense of those conventions being worn out. The "voice" of sleaze in documentary is always cynical.[1] Therefore, looking at one key element in most sleazy documentaries—the narrator—should help us better understand these works and, not so incidentally, more fully comprehend narration in mainstream documentaries as well. The narrator, whether appearing only in off-screen voice or in person on-screen, is a presence between the screen sound and image and the audience. Understanding the margins, the limit cases, always clarifies the center, the norm, and "normal," and underlines the social construction of both. To advance this analysis, I will examine several particular cases and arrange their discussion chronologically. However, my main interest is in constructing a critical typology of sleazy narrator styles rather than a true history of development and change. This survey (with several detours) should allow a conclusion about the aesthetic politics of sleazy documentary.

An Aside on Sleaze

What do I mean by *sleazy*? I'll offer a working definition here and return to the question of definition in conclusion. *Sleazy* in current usage refers to something disgusting, filthy, nasty; that is, it has the connotation of being "low" culturally and morally. In current British usage the word is often used in discussions of politics to refer to politicians compromised by payoffs, graft, or mercenary actions overriding law, principle, or the common good. And the term is often present in making distinctions about sexual matters: *sleazy* means sexually promiscuous, sexually active without discrimination.

In an earlier essay, I distinguished a tendency in popular commercial art that I called self-aware kitsch.[2] These texts are filled with parodic clichés and depend on exaggerating and underlining, thus setting up a camp response, as in the heightened bedroom-and-boardroom television series *Dynasty*. Following Susan Sontag's discussion of camp and significant gay/queer critical elaborations of the concept, high camp can be seen as a strategy for ironic and comic reading of the highly aestheticized (*The Importance of Being Earnest*, the typical staging of Verdi operas, Cole Porter lyrics, etc.).[3] Low camp, or trash, can be a strategy for celebrating the debased: in the counterculture avant-garde (early

John Waters films, Jack Smith, George Kuchar) and in the commercial cinema (*Dumb and Dumber* [1994], *American Pie* [1999]).

Sleaze, then, is used pejoratively, judgmentally. It depends on making cultural distinctions (understanding distinction as a class and cultural term, as in Pierre Bourdieu's definition).[4] Essentially ironic, it depends on looking down on something. In the case of the work considered here, there is also a strong sense that the "sleazy" work is crass, that it is not sincere but is adopting whatever ethical and moral stance it has simply to exploit its subject. A classic example can be found in the scenes of slave trading in *Mondo Freudo* (1966) and *Mondo Bizarro* (1966). These fake documentaries purport to show the auctioning of (mostly) women in Mexico and Lebanon. The scenes are patently staged ("Lebanon" is a well-known Los Angeles–area location, Bronson Canyon). The "slaves" are disrobed, to display female breasts, but genitals are obscured with scratched-on censor bars, thus implying that the female pubic area (viewed in a distant telephoto image) is more shocking than trading in humans. If we assumed the documentation was genuine, the filmmakers' moral/ethical stance is obviously questionable in that they simply record and do not intervene in the moment of the sale, nor do they provide their cinematography as evidence to the police or other authorities, nor do they publicize what is going on to the press or social and political organizations. *Mondo Bizarro* actually goes so far as to have an extended sequence showing the camera crew's heroic efforts to move their heavy equipment to a hilltop, using a block and tackle and sledge, for secret telephoto filming of slave trading. Clearly the aim of the slavery sections is not justice or human sympathy for (fictional) victims, but simply to show something sensational, titillating (and tits), combining this with a pompous voice-over narration that makes a feeble attempt to justify it as information.[5] With sleaze, the joke, the demeaning part, is on the audience.

1960s exploitation

Mondo Freudo and *Mondo Bizarro* follow after *Mondo Cane*, an internationally successful sensationalist documentary phenomenon from 1962.[6] Cheaply made rip-offs, they belong economically and industrially to the exploitation film market. The exploitation film has roots in the fairground show, the circus sideshow, and the traveling carnival. The carnival pitchman's basic plan is this: (1) gather a crowd; (2) promise them something sensational; (3) get their money; and (4) fool them and get away. At its worst-intentioned, in the classic con job, the "mark" is left at the end so confused, embarrassed, humiliated, or compromised that he does not go to the police or authorities to complain (and this is relatively easy when the content is sexual). But there is also a much milder version of exploitation, closer to P. T. Barnum's celebrated "humbug" effect. Barnum observed and exploited the fact that if the deception was done in a fairly jovial, over-the-top manner, marks would gladly pay to observe the fraudulent and leave amused rather than outraged.[7]

Building on this exploitation tradition, the Mondo films of the 1960s simply adapted this con to new technologies, audiences, and rationales.[8] In *Mondo Freudo*, for example, the filmmakers purportedly explore a world of nude performance, topless-dancing night clubs, and other sexual scenes, using the pretense of a journalistic investigation into unusual social behaviors to present mostly fake scenarios (created and performed only for this film). During this period, the only legitimate legal defense against obscenity in the United States was to claim artistic, social, scientific, or educational value in exhibiting nudity (the juridical constraint on media circulation). It would take tortured logic to claim scientific or educational value for this material, and it would be difficult to claim it was art (at least as art was understood by most people and the judicial system at the time). Therefore it was safest to claim value in social investigation: the social sciences and investigative journalism come to the rescue of sexual looking. (We might note that in 1960s America, after the basic college introductory course, the favorite sociology course for undergraduates on many campuses was Sociology of Deviance, often known by campus slang as "Nuts and Sluts.")[9]

Following the model of *Mondo Cane*, *Mondo Freudo* offers an anthology of "unusual" activities and behaviors, mostly centered around some form or another of sexual display, which in the mid-1960s world of U.S. theatrical cinema meant bare breasts. In an early sequence, *Mondo Freudo* purports to show "night vision" images of heterosexual couples caressing on a beach in Los Angeles. Ordinary young people are thus presented as ethnographic Others.[10] The film then shows teenagers gathering on Hollywood Boulevard and driving around in vehicles (using poorly executed, very cheap location footage shot without sound) followed by footage of various nightclubs, with local variations and restrictions on nudity and dancing. But from the very beginning, an off-screen narrator marks the visuals with an ironic tone:

> Long Shot: ocean beach from palisades above.
> Male Voice-Over:
> It is Saturday afternoon in Southern California. A lazy summer afternoon, and on this day some 25,000 people will come onto this beach for fun and relaxation. Our cameraman has established a vantage point on a hill high above the beach.
> Medium Shot (man removes lens from case):
> This is a 1000-millimeter telescopic lens with a telebar attachment developed by Burns and Sawyer Cine Equipment Rental of Hollywood. The unit is equal to a 1,700-millimeter lens. The lens is being mounted on an Arriflex model 11B 35-millimeter motion picture camera. This camera and lens will provide you with the majority of what you are about to see in the film. They will give you a long close-up look at our society. This lens and this camera will be your eyes to peer into Mondo Freudo—a Freudian world of sex and sex symbols and the strange and unusual laws that govern them. (Surfer sound music up.)
> Credits begin, alternated with daylight telephoto shots of people on the beach.

In addition to a montage of telephoto shots of ordinary people on the beach, medium shots show the removal of the long lens, which is then mounted on the camera. The voice-over's recitation of details such as the length of the lens and the name of the equipment rental company (still in business today) grounds the images with selective fact, giving the film an aura of investigative truth (and most likely also a rental discount for promoting the equipment house).

While the film claims to show Los Angeles, San Francisco, London, Hamburg, and Kyoto (a kind of comparative ethnography of strip clubs), the claims become suspect when you notice that "London" has the same tablecloth patterns as Los Angeles, and that "Hamburg" is identified only by common travel posters on the wall of an inexpensive set. A topless dancer in "Los Angeles" appears to also be (magically) in the audience in "London." Similarly, the film claims that it is showing us a public wall where London prostitutes freely advertise, but the location is the mythological space of "Piccadilly Square."[11]

The title sequence in *Mondo Bizarro*, meanwhile, purports to show a hidden camera view inside a lingerie store; the voice-over narrator tells us it's "the east side of Chicago" (another mythical place, since the east side of Chicago is Lake Michigan).[12] The narrator explains the camera is behind a "two-way mirror" (a disconcertingly weird detail—one would expect a one-way mirror) and that the filmmakers were forced to censor the models' faces. This censorship is accomplished visually by scratches on the film to obliterate the eyes).[13] Here a parade of women remove their clothes and try on different bras to peculiar changes of music, producing a weird musical collage. After this introductory credit sequence with fictitious crew names and acknowledgments to imaginary organizations (apparently to make the production seem more impressive), there follows a shot of a slowly turning and badly rendered handmade globe. A male voice-over intones a nonsensical epistemological statement: "To the worm in the cheese, the cheese is the universe. To the maggot in the cadaver, the cadaver is infinity. And to you, what is your world? How do you know what is beyond the Beyond? Most of us don't even know what is behind the Beyond."

In both films, the unseen Mondo narrator recites his "facts" to us in an uneven rhetorical stance. At times the voice-over seems to give unnecessarily specific factual details (the 1000-mm lens with the telebar attachment) and at other times it simply lies about what is on screen. Thus in *Mondo Freudo*, after the daylight shots of the beach, a camera assistant is shown rigging a pitifully small scoop reflector light while the narrator describes it as an infrared "night vision" apparatus that will allow the surreptitious night filming. At other times, the narrator presents as fact statements that, upon reflection, seem incredible. In *Mondo Bizarro*, for example, over some standard tourist shots of urban areas in the Bahamas, the narrator explains that the former African slaves still practice voodoo on the island and promises that the telephoto lens will reveal a secret nighttime ceremony. The xenophobic narration contrasts the presently "civilized" everyday appearance of Bahamians with their wild and primitive ancestors, claiming that in the past celebrants sacrificed a "white baby" in such ceremonies (but today substitute a white chicken). Yet simple reason would assume that in a slave culture with a small group of white settlers and a large black population, the whites could hardly produce enough babies for the frequent ceremonies. Moreover, even if this incredible event did happen, even just once, the immense power differential between colonialists and slaves would produce swift and severe punishment, making it impossible for any voodoo cultists to maintain the practice. In the end, what we actually see is a distant group dancing around a fire at night, and possibly the beheading of a fowl and the sacrifice of a large snake (though it could easily be a fake—perhaps a length of rope). The real content, however, is a racist fantasy of an African threat concocted from tourist footage, staged dancing, and shaping powers of the offscreen narrator.

Historical Side Trip:
God Interpellates the Audience

The classic off-screen narrator is often called the Voice of God, since the audience hears his pronouncements without seeing the embodied speaker. Usually this is a male voice with deep tones, sure phrasing, and an "educated" accent, which in the United States often means a hint of British intonation or a voice that seems trained for stage delivery. Through wartime and postwar educational materials, audiences in the military, industry, and schools became extremely habituated to such narration, or even a single omnipresent voice talent. In Canada, for example, actor Lorne Greene (later best known as the family patriarch in the popular television western series, *Bonanza*) was the standard stentorian offscreen voice for a generation of National Film Board documentaries.

Having grown up with this convention, it is easy to see why a younger generation of documentary filmmakers, especially in the 1960s, were eager to move away from this kind of authoritative (even authoritarian) voice. They chose to work instead in classic Direct Cinema style, employing a narrational style that seemed to eschew such external authority. This often involved placing the narrator on screen, either on location as an on-the-spot investigator or as a relay for eyewitness accounts. In this respect, the narrator becomes a more embodied character, a teller of the tale who, though perhaps unreliable, allowed the audience to better gauge his veracity.

Both forms of narration, however, demonstrate cinematic strategies for adapting the older form and forum of the public lecture. In the United States in particular, the public lecture blossomed in the nineteenth century with the

Chautauqua and other forms of informational address. In a society that stressed public education, literacy, and democratic citizenship (for white men), the public lecture, like political oratory and religious preaching, served an epistophilic function. The serious voice-over narrator in documentary media began with the nineteenth-century slide-lecture show and continued with the live voice-over narration of film travelogues before the advent of the sync-sound film. Typically, the presenter, posed as an educated gentleman, narrated trips to "civilized" places and adventures in exotic locales. Visiting the Holy Land was a favorite lecture topic in Middle America, and like the rhetoric of *National Geographic*, the presentations usually mixed a quasi-intellectual edification with banal imperial tourism. In a lecture with a slide show or silent film, the voice appeared embodied in the initial setup but then became simply a presence in the dark that explained the visuals. The same model developed as well in broadcast journalism that followed print's "eyewitness" reportage model.[14] The defining moment took place in the mid-1930s with the transformation of the *March of Time* documentary to a voice-over format, abandoning its origins as a silent film short (with intertitles) that followed the editorial lead and style of *Time* magazine. The announcer, Westbrook Van Voorhis, quickly became recognizable delivering "*Time*-speak" voice-overs for the monthly series. A *New Republic* critic made the analogy to a god explicit: "Just such a voice . . . would have been hired to speak the lines of one of Euripides' suave male gods—those gods who appeared so opportunely at the end of a tragedy when everything was going up in flames and agnosticism, and explained matters away. Nobody has ever been quite sure what those gods believed in or whether they even believed in themselves; and this gives them a real affinity with the voice that does the talking for the March of Time."[15] Within the business, Van Voorhis was dubbed "the voice of fate," and by the late 1930s, comedians often imitated his distinctive style. At the same time, U.S. radio drama flourished, often using the announcer as a prime character, voice, and organizing presence in the narration, as in much of Orson Welles's radio work of the period.

By the time the Mondo films adopted this convention in the early 1960s, the voice of God was a well-established and familiar device. The authoritarian voice, delivered in the same implacable tone across a diversity of topics, has over the years led to a perhaps inevitably ironic, even cynical audience response. Indeed,

FIGURE 2 Lobby card for *Time* magazine's famous *March of Time* series, which established Westbrook Van Voorhis as the documentary form's "voice of fate."

even in the 1940s, the mock *March of Time* newsreel at the start of *Citizen Kane* (1941) was as much a parody of these conventions as mere exposition, a satiric aspect usually lost on today's audience.[16] This irony becomes especially salient when the subject turns from the recitation of dry facts to advising on matters of policy and personal behavior. The voice of God in classroom "scare films," for example, is often a target of derision, laughter, and outright hostility as it moralistically lectures teens about reckless driving, drug use, alcohol abuse, or premarital sex.

In the classic voice-of-God vehicle, then, a disembodied voice provides an authoritative interpretation of the images on screen. The Mondo films, on the other hand, frequently revel in contradicting the narrator's discursive sobriety. For example, in a *Mondo Bizarro* segment on Frederick's of Hollywood (the mail-order store of "sexy" women's underwear), we meet designer/owner Mr. Frederick, who demonstrates such items as cutaway-rear girdles that produce round rather than flat buttocks (illustrated with a live model). Many other types of underclothing are exhibited as well, including brassieres incorporating novelties such as cutout tips, cutaway tops, and inflatable cups (shown repeatedly with the wearer blowing into a plastic tube to enlarge the appearance). The sequence ends as the narrator proclaims "an industrial symphony": there follows a poorly executed montage sequence of the shipping room efficiently sending off orders, accompanied by the strains of Beethoven's Fifth Symphony. Thus does *Mondo Bizarro* capture the heroic grandeur of shipping women's underwear!

Is such a narrational inte rjection telling us something we don't know, indulging our epistephilia? In *Mondo Freudo*'s time it was widely known that some cities had topless dancing, and it was simple to obtain a copy of *Playboy* if one wanted to see bare breasts. What exactly does this comic voice of God add to this cinematic parade of (near) nudity? Echoing Barnum's "humbug effect," the narrator's voice and persona is that of a carnival pitchman with a touch of (usually jovial) condescension. I will call this narrative device "reverse disavowal": I know this is fake, but I still want to see it. The audience knows it is seeing not some actuality but an event staged for the camera—which is the basic technique of most U.S. newsreels in celebrity and staged-publicity events.[17] But the audience doesn't necessarily resent this kind of deception, since the film and its narrator are also giving it something else: a pretext for indulging its voyeurism while also leaving room for an ironic response. In other words, the film offers the viewer a desirable spectatorial position of amusement, curiosity, and visual pleasure in a quasi-dramatized cinema. The Mondo films encourage viewers to laugh at, or along with, the "voice of sobriety": the narrator pretends to be serious, but we know his presence merely provides an excuse for the images on screen. We are drawn into the narrator's attitude—"let me show you this strange thing or event." We agree and accept the contract because it gives us the gratification of naughty transgression in the mocking guise of epistophilic discovery.

This strategy of reverse disavowal is a prominent feature of many current reality television programs, especially the Mondo-like forum of *The Jerry Springer Show*. Here a series of people visibly and behaviorally marked as low-class are brought forward to behave badly in front of a jeering audience (who are themselves marked as low-class) and enact various scenarios of abjection in public. Momentary fame overcomes any sense of pain or shame. The basic gesture is flaunting one's attitude. In addition to the show's female guests often

FIGURE 3 Jerry Springer: inheritor of Barnum's "humbug effect" and a central practitioner of "reverse disavowal" in current reality television.

displaying their breasts (digitally blurred), recently Springer has added—in a nod to the incredible popularity of the *Girls Gone Wild* video series—audience participants who spontaneously flash and flaunt in order to get a string of cheap beads from the show's staff. As an onscreen narrator and provocateur, Springer ends each show with his "Final Thoughts," sham moralizing that once again justifies the preceding charade as edifying.

We doubt these narrators—we are skeptical, we know that we may be put on, cheated, taken advantage of. But we want it. We can enjoy the rogue, especially if he is charming. We want the forbidden; at the same time we also see it as somewhat ridiculous or, in the Mondo case, juvenile, especially in its portrait of heterosexual masculinity. As we look at the displays of sexy underwear and the industrial symphony of underwear shipping in *Mondo Bizarro*, our response today can only be camp. In their own time, however, these Mondo films also allowed for a campy pleasure, since the narrator, even in his cynicism, pretends to address an impossibly naive viewer. As in the pitch of the carnival sideshow, they employ the mechanism (detailed by Freud) of being in on the smutty joke.[18] The pleasure, then, is not in knowing or learning, but in sincerely appreciating the spectacle even as we ironically revel in the lowbrow tackiness of the presentation—imagining an absent viewer who would actually fall prey to the narrator's absurd claims. Much like current fascination with supermarket tabloids that promise new and lurid exposés, Mondo viewers, both then and now, enjoy a "smarty-pants" pleasure that presumes a naive viewer who probably never existed.

Ripe Danish Blue

While *Mondo Freudo* and *Mondo Bizarro* clearly, often comically, convey cynicism in their narration, *Sexual Freedom in Denmark* (1970) instead presents an apparently sincere discourse on the public sphere, only occasionally betraying a mercenary voyeurism. The commercially successful film played fairly widely in porn/adult venues in the early 1970s, just as more explicit foreign dramatic fictional films, such as *I Am Curious Yellow* (1969), were achieving wider exhibition as court decisions gradually opened the field of legal content. "Documentarians" could exploit this new environment by arguing that their films didn't show anything more than the fiction films that were being defended as cinematic art.

Sexual Freedom in Denmark uses an off-screen narrator whose voice qualities are similar to those of narrators for standard educational/informative documentary essay films of the time. This quietly stated aura of professionalism smooths the film's style and contextualizes the explicit visual content within the norms of "good taste," a device that, in turn, potentially broadens the audience. Rather than play in the male-only porn venues of the 1960s, the film could thus cross over to the growing and crucially important couples market of the early 1970s.

The film itself presents a pastiche of various types of exploitation documentaries. We hear a lecture about representations of sex within the history of art while we see still images from art books. At times the narrator argues that most of society's ills—including war, overpopulation (and thus starvation), prostitution, venereal disease (with a close-up of a syphilitic penis) and so forth—are due to sexual repression. Various heroes are mentioned: Freud, Kinsey, and Masters and Johnson. Other passages describe with visual support the joys of nudism, the presence of sexualized images in print advertising, and the recent history of image and performance censorship (which provides an opportunity to show topless and bottomless dancing). The film's long conclusion presents an elaborate sex-education segment that includes images of an egg entering the fallopian tubes, microscopic sperm, a zygote dividing, different forms of birth, anatomy lessons, demonstrations of Kegel exercises, and the mechanics of various methods of birth control. In addition, the section contains a fairly complete depiction of heterosexual intercourse using live models shot in negative-space studio settings with soft focus of various sexual positions. This sequence is intercut with drawings giving cutaway views of the penis in the vagina. Combining science, medicine, practical advice, and soft romantic images of young couples in coitus, the film combines older exploitation forms with the new limits of protected content in the 1970s. The narrator is key to unifying these disparate documentary forms, bringing the film in line with the era's liberal agenda in progressive sex education.

The film's title cues its most peculiar aspect. Intercut with the standard exploitation fare are recurring on-the-scene reports from Denmark addressing assorted topics related to the then-recent liberalization of Danish censorship laws. During this period, sexual liberalization advocates in the United States frequently referred to Denmark as a positive example, particularly for a reported decline in sex crimes following legalization of explicit pornography.[19] Reinforcing this image of a progressive, well-adjusted, and sexually active Denmark, the onscreen male reporter interviews a range of subjects discussing an array of sexual controversies (at least in the United States). In one on-the-street interview, for example, a young woman explains in front of a crowd of passersby that she and her unmarried friends are sexually active but have no access to legal abortion and if needed have to go to "the East countries" (apparently Asia) for the procedure. The reporter mentions Poland as another possibility. On the set of a porn film, our interviewer (now hatless, revealing an odd male pattern baldness that underlines his middle-aged nerdiness) talks to the filmmaker and then several nude women during a break. He asks about how much money they make, if they have boyfriends, and the age at which they first had intercourse. One model places her arm over his shoulder, laughing, perhaps smirking, at him. A female fashion model is asked the same questions. A male research psychologist discusses the decrease in sex crimes after legalizing pornography, and a female journalist discusses laws and policies affecting youth. She shows a new sex education book for teens that includes images of masturbation, use of a diaphragm for birth control, and an erect penis and close-up of a clitoris. She argues for future increased liberalization including education in sexual technique to increase female orgasms and produce "more happiness."

Overall, the narrator's tone in *Sexual Freedom in Denmark* strives for dispassionate professionalism. At key moments, however, disparities between this sober narration and images on the screen allow the film to drift into sleaze. As the narrator begins reading the Biblical creation story, for example, the image shows an attractive couple with contemporary hairstyles strolling nude in a forest setting. Discussion of legal changes in Denmark is accompanied by images of (presumed) Danes on a nude beach, and then later revelers frolicking naked on a small sailing ship in what amounts to the basic soft-core sunbathing footage seen in so many other exploitation titles. Later, as the narrator discusses the open sale of pornography in Copenhagen, we see exterior shots of shops before cutting to an interior where a female in a revealing mesh body stocking retails magazines to a male purchaser. Illustrations from porno magazines, nude females being body painted, and topless/bottomless performers illustrate other sequences of factual narration. While not accommodating the cynical hilarity of the Mondo films, *Sexual Freedom in Denmark* nevertheless allows viewers to adopt dual reading strategies, attending to either the sober discourse on sexual policy or the titillation of forbidden spectacle (or both).

The On-screen Expert in Decline

While *Sexual Freedom in Denmark* is staged as an informative, expository documentary, *The Postgraduate Course in Sexual Love* (1970) employs the ruse of a college classroom in which a "Professor Collins" lectures a group of students, mostly about sexual techniques. Here the lecture's exposition provides the alibi for very low budget sex scenes typical of 1970s porno films. His lecture begins with a "review" of previous lectures and a slide show of obscene art through the ages. Then the professor introduces the day's topic: sexual activity. As he discusses his topic, the camera zooms in on the faces of students who are then shown demonstrating whatever behavior the professor's voice-over describes. The film thus faintly borders on the magical, as if simply hearing an abstract medical lecture would stimulate students into fantasizing a detailed scenario.

Alternatively, we could assume that the students are recalling events (and thus indicating that the students know more than the professor, at least in terms of carnal knowledge). The sex scenes are shot without sync sound in medium long shot with occasional zooms, accompanied by postdubbed sounds of groans, moans, and West Coast acid rock. The lecture is mildly progressive in its sexual politics: students are encouraged to experiment before marriage, men are encouraged to use much foreplay with female partners, and variety is endorsed throughout. After a scene featuring two gay men, the professor's Vietnam-era politics come into play as he points out that two men having sex can be jailed while one man killing another in combat will be rewarded. After a final "orgy" with three heterosexual couples awkwardly coupling on one double bed, the bell signaling the end of class sounds. But the professor insists the students stay for a short film on venereal disease. This film-within-a-film describes the need to "Fight Love Pollution" as a pipe-smoking "doctor" advises a young couple about the dangers and prevention of syphilis and gonorrhea, including the required worst-case close-ups and illustrations of advanced stages of disease. With charts he marks a recent rise of syphilis, which he directly links to the Vietnam War.

The Postgraduate Course in Sexual Love thus relies on two narrators, Professor Collins and the anonymous pipe-smoking doctor of the VD film-within-the-film. Each serves as an authority figure, of sorts, although operating in different discursive contexts. Like much sexploitation cinema, the movie uses a standard VD-warning film to pad out its length with more "sexual" content, in the process bringing the onscreen authority of the MD in contact with his more comic embodiment in the character of the professor. With the professor, slight smirks among the students (setting up transitions from lecture material to fantasy, memory, or anticipation) seem possibly to undercut his absolute authority (as do the sex scenes, which demonstrate they have already mastered the material). With the MD, on the other hand, the couple takes every admonition as a strict rule. When the female partner complains her guy was sleeping around with some tramp and brought the disease home to her, the doctor uses his authority to stop this quarrel and focus on preventive medicine and proper treatment. Through this basic juxtaposition of medical and soft-core footage, the film inadvertently demonstrates the eroding authority of the on-screen nar-

FIGURE 4 Ad copy for *The Postgraduate Course in Sexual Love* (1970), a film with two narrators operating in very different discursive contexts.

rator as an absolute arbiter of sexual knowledge. The expert becomes merely a comic pretext for motivating sexual spectacle.

Doris Wishman's infamous transsexual documentary *Let Me Die a Woman* (1977) presents a similar crisis of authority for the onscreen narrator, a conflict once again provoked by the presence of an "MD" within more mercenary exploitation fare. This expert, Dr. Wollman, invokes medical discourse and sexual science to promote a sympathetic understanding of transsexualism. But Wishman, a veteran of such exploitation subgenres as the nudist-camp film and the roughie, constantly undermines the doctor's discourse of tolerance with footage that presents transsexuals as freaks and staged episodes that exploit transsexualism for sensationalistic effect. At one point, *Let Me Die a Woman* features a heartfelt interview with Leslie, a young Puerto Rican woman who tells a story of childhood gender dysphoria, the transformation process, her current postoperative situation, and her optimistic hope for an ovary and uterus transplant. Yet, to increase its exploitative appeal, the film also inserts explicit

FIGURE 5 Ad art for Doris Wishman's infamous *Let Me Die a Woman* (1977). The disjointed film combines a putative call for "tolerance" of transsexuals with exploitative images of sex-change surgery and reenactments of prostitution, self-mutilation, and suicide.

surgical footage of a male-to-female operation. The original version of the film also included a bloody reenactment of a desperate male who began to cut off his own penis and testicles (a procedure finished in a hospital when the fellow collapsed).[20] There is also a staged sequence of a female transsexual picking up a man in Central Park. After their sexual encounter, she "shocks" the viewer by removing her underpants to reveal a small penis.

Dr. Wollman is charged with the responsibility of weaving these disparate segments together. Even with this familiar device, however, the current version of the film is particularly disjointed, and I surmise from internal evidence that reels have been placed in the wrong order, increasing the film's disorientation.[21] Shot over a five-year period, *Let Me Die a Woman* is riddled with continuity errors as Wollman attempts to connect anatomy lectures, personal stories, dramatic reenactments, medical footage, anatomical demonstrations, and footage from Wishman's previous films. Though a "documentary," the film nevertheless exhibits many of the trademark stylistic quirks of Wishman's narrative films, most notably her penchant for awkward postdubbed dialogue and frequent cutaways to seemingly meaningless objects in the mise-en-scène. This clumsy aspect of the film enhances its aura of sleaziness, especially in the inelegant juxtaposition of the MD's "authoritative" call for tolerance and understanding (supported by the affecting testimony of actual transsexuals) with footage of cheap porn, anatomical close-ups, penile surgery, and sensationalistic reenactments of prostitution, self-mutilation, and suicide. The film is striking for its ironic contrast of the on-screen expert's good intentions and the exploitation tactics of shock, cheap sensationalism, freakishness, and prurient voyeurism.

The Sleazy Narrator

As these examples of 1960s documentary exploitation demonstrate, the putative authority and discernable earnestness of a narrator (on- or off-screen) is often unable to withstand the crisis presented by the trashy, suspect, and incongruous images of exploitation cinema. While it would be easy to dismiss these films (and their narrators) as examples of pure, naive camp, the strategies deployed by these stylistically diverse films suggest a more complex relationship between filmmaker, subject, and audience. I argued earlier that sleaze is marked in a way that reveals the maker's cynical nature; therefore it is a matter of nuance and interpretation, most often cued by form. In its documentary form, perceiving sleaze depends on both the narrator's relationship to the material and the audience's perception of the filmmaker's relationship to the narrator. It contrasts with naive camp, which is often inept but sincere (with the gap between intention and ability providing the irony and humor). The classic example here is Ed Wood's *Glen or Glenda* (1953), where the director's obsessive concern to portray male transvestism as normal, socially acceptable, and in no way related to homosexuality collides with clumsy and cheap filmmaking techniques. Nor does sleaze mirror the deliberate trash stance of *Pink Flamingoes* (1972) or *The Devil's Cleavage* (1975), films that invite the audience to play along with the filmmaker's own delight in being bad, violating norms of good taste, and reveling in general outrageousness.

In contrast to the dramatic fictions of Wood, Waters, and Kuchar, the authorial presences of the sleazy documentaries I'm discussing here reveal their cynical and mercenary intent largely though the voice-over or on-screen narrators

FIGURE 6 An impassioned plea for the public acceptance of transvestism, Ed Wood's *Glen or Glenda* (1953) avoids "sleaziness" by virtue of its naïveté and ineptitude.

themselves. The films break down in the narrators' inability to bring a convincing unity or purpose to their disparate elements of actuality footage, awkward reenactments, and endless opportunities for (near) nudity. Whether attempting to play it straight, as in *Sexual Freedom in Denmark* and *Let Me Die a Woman*, or through a winking parodic mode as in the Mondo films and *The Postgraduate Course in Love*, a narrator and film drift toward sleaze when this narrational authority becomes unconvincing in its attempt to perform artistic, educational, or journalistic motivations. Such slippage would seem to contradict the usual critique of the voice-over narrator, particularly that offered by the Direct Cinema documentarians. In arguing that the voice-over narrator is authoritarian as well as authoritative, that the narration dominates the visuals (which become mere illustrations) and forces a reading on the audience, such critics underestimated the audience's ability to perceive and exploit fissures, incongruities, and ironies between voice and image.

No doubt these slippages, ironies, and an overall sense of "sleaziness" increase with historical distance and changing cultural contexts. Considered today in the contemporary U.S. political climate, *Sexual Freedom in Denmark*'s argument that the state education system should include instruction in sexual technique so women could have more orgasms seems truly revolutionary. In the Clinton administration, after all, Surgeon General Jocelyn Elders lost her job for suggesting that masturbation might give teens a sense of personal autonomy and was useful for controlling teen pregnancy and the rapid spread of AIDS and other sexually transmitted diseases. Today, with a conservative president and Congress pushing "family values" by restricting sex education and enforcing abstinence-only instructions, the film's journalist-narrator seems a throwback to Wilhelm Reich's Sex-Pol movement.

The sexploitation documentaries discussed above can be fully understood only within the context of sexual commercialization under late capitalism. The cash nexus around sex means that "everyone knows" you have to pay to get information: for carnal knowledge it's prostitution; for intellectual knowledge, it's pornography. The argument made by pornographers that porn is educational has almost always been dismissed as a lame defense for profiting on voyeurism. But in the 1960s, porn was to some extent informative. In a society with very limited information and education about sex, even showing "this is it, this is what it looks like," carried with it a progressive element. Today sex education in the state sector is heavily restricted by Republicans and Christian fundamentalists, but "for-profit" sex information continues to expand its presence across the media—as long as you pay for it. However, as the ineffable quality of "sleaze" that permeates these early forms of sexploitation suggests, the embedding of sex in consumer culture also carries with it a certain consumer skepticism. In this way, these sleazy documentaries present an inversion of art's aspiration to the sublime and become instead examples of the capitalist grotesque.

Notes

Earlier versions of this paper were given at the Visible Evidence Conference, Marseille, France, December 2002, and the Media, History, and Culture Colloquium, Northwestern University, January 2003. A shorter version was presented at the Society for Cinema and Media studies conference, Atlanta, March 2004. I thank people who gave me helpful comments and answered questions: Michael Booth, Michael Bowen, Gary Fine, Jane Gaines, Jyotsna Kapur, Julia Lesage, Larry Lichty, Josh Malitsky, Derek Paget, Jim Schwoch, Jeffrey Sconce, and Tom Waugh.

1. "The voice of documentary . . . is the means by which this particular point of view or perspective [of the world] becomes known to us," observes Bill Nichols in *Introduction to Documentary* (Bloomington: Indiana University Press, 2001), 43. Nichols established

this concept for documentary in his original article "The Voice of Documentary" (*Film Quarterly* 36.3 [1983]: 17–29), which was elaborated in *Representing Reality: Issues and Concepts in Documentary* (Bloomington: Indiana University Press, 1991). Basing his discussion on rhetorical concepts, Nichols develops a typology of documentary modes that employ different rhetorics. Nichols is not referring primarily to the particular vocal qualities of narrators and characters in sound cinema (a concern of Michel Chion in *The Voice in Cinema*, trans. Claudia Gorbman [New York: Columbia University Press, 1999]), although this is a concern with some works discussed here.

2. Chuck Kleinhans, "Taking Out the Trash: Camp and the Politics of Irony," in *The Politics and Poetics of Camp*, ed. Moe Meyer (New York: Routledge, 1994), 182–201.

3. Susan Sontag, "Notes on Camp," *Partisan Review* 31 (fall 1964): 515–30.

4. Pierre Bourdieu, *Distinction: A Social Critique of the Judgment of Taste*, trans. Richard Nice (Cambridge, Mass.: Harvard University Press, 1984).

5. International human rights organizations have shown that human slavery does exist, particularly in parts of sub-Saharan Africa, and in exploitation of immigrants, often in prostitution and sometimes in the United States and Europe as domestics or sweatshop workers.

6. *Mondo Cane* (dir. Gualtiero Jacopetti, Italy, 1962) documented unusual human activities around the world ranging from cannibalism to nude art. The narration draws parallels between presumed civilization and primitive impulses and behaviors to excuse the voyeurism. An international hit, it spawned Jacopetti's *Mondo Cane 2* and many imitators.

7. As Neil Harris writes, "This delight in learning explains why the experience of deceit was enjoyable even after the hoax had been penetrated, or at least during the period of doubt and suspicion. Experiencing a complicated hoax was pleasurable because of the competition between victim and hoaxer, each seeking to outmaneuver the other, to catch him off-balance and detect the critical weakness. Barnum, Poe, Locke, and other hoaxers didn't fear public suspicion; they invited it. They understood, most particularly Barnum understood, that the opportunity to debate the *issue* of falsity, to discover how deception had been practiced, was even more exciting than the discovery of fraud itself. The manipulation of a prank, after all, was as interesting a technique in its own right as the presentation of genuine curiosities. Therefore when people paid to see frauds, thinking they were true, they paid again to hear how the frauds were committed. Barnum reprinted his own ticket-seller's analysis. 'First he humbugs them, and then they pay to hear him tell how he did it. I believe if he should swindle a man out of twenty dollars, the man would give him a quarter to hear him tell about it'" (*Humbug: The Art of P. T. Barnum* [Boston: Little, Brown and Company, 1973], 77).

8. The definitive scholarly history is Eric Schafer's *"Bold! Daring! Shocking! True!": A History of Exploitation Films, 1919–1959* (Durham, N.C.: Duke University Press, 1999).

9. Sociology of deviance was also a central contributing stream of British cultural studies, as in 1970s studies of youth gangs, soccer hooliganism, and subculture activities.
10. Jane Gaines has written a pioneering article on how the ordinary is made strange in some documentaries. See Gaines, "Everyday Strangeness: Robert Ripley's International Oddities as Documentary Attractions," *New Literary History* 33 (2002): 781–801.
11. Apparently this was a conflation of the real Piccadilly Circus and Leister Square. As anyone who has been to London at the time of the film knows, there were public messages for various forms of sex work including massage, domination, and so on, usually posted in telephone boxes at various heavily trafficked locations such as the Underground. While the voice-over announces we are in this imaginary place, we see stock footage of London at night with neon and advertising signs with a cut to a wall with handmade postings. All the notices are slight variations of the same handwriting.
12. Again, a voice-over tells us where we are while an exterior visual of a modest lingerie store window appears before we cut to the dressing room and its one-way mirror, with the camera looking through the mirror at the models and the various title cards provided by directly painting on the glass.
13. The same scratched-eye technique is used by experimental filmmaker Stan Brakhage in his landmark *Reflections on Black* (1955). "By attacking the surface of the film and by using materials which reflect back on the conditions of film-making, Brakhage begins to formulate an equation between the process of making film and the search for consciousness which will become more clearly established in his later work as he has greater confidence in the truth of the imagination," writes P. Adams Sitney in *Visionary Film: The American Avant Garde* (New York: Oxford University Press, 1974), 177.
14. Of course, much of the time news events do not have professional reporters as eyewitnesses (notable exceptions: unanticipated—the Hindenberg disaster; anticipated—Murrow's rooftop reporting during the German Blitz of London), but rather usually appear as on-the-scene reporters after the news breaks. The subsequent advent of television has simply changed an unseen voice into an authoritative standup presence, a persistent convention taken to idiotic lengths when a network news reader who doesn't know the local language appears in a foreign elsewhere telling us authoritatively what is going on, or the late-night news reporter stands at 11:15 p.m. in an empty location where something significant happened earlier in the day.
15. *New Republic*, August 19, 1936; George Dangerfield quoted in Raymond Fielding, *The March of Time, 1935–1951* (New York: Oxford University Press, 1978), 102–3.
16. Similarly, the surrealist Luis Buñuel's documentary *Las Hurdes* (*Land without Bread*, 1932) employs a narrator to make political points about the poverty depicted, which depends on an audience understanding the offensive voice-over as ironic. Not all audiences (or critics) are able to do so.
17. A classic example was discovered by Dan Streible, in which a fake "Leon Trotsky"

appears in a Fox Movietone newsreel. See Streible, "Tom Mix Meets Leon Trotsky: Newsreel Outtakes as Documentary," www.sc.edu/orphanfilm/orphanage/symposia/scholarship/streible/park-row.html.
18. Sigmund Freud, *Jokes and Their Relation to the Unconscious*, trans. James Strachey (New York: Norton, 1960).
19. The Johnson administration commissioned an extensive academic research–based report on pornography that was received at the beginning of the Nixon administration. Nixon refused the report and its liberal conclusions, but the report was widely distributed and influenced public discussion. A nongovernment reprinting with illustrations including hard-core images of penetration, fellatio, anal sex, and so forth was sold with (depending on how it was read) the official text providing the excuse for the obscene illustrations, or the images providing the visual explanation not included in the Government Printing Office text-only version. See Earl Kemp, ed., *The Illustrated Presidential Report of the Commission on Obscenity and Pornography* (San Diego: Greenleaf Classics, 1970).
20. According to several reports, this footage was removed as too objectionable. The current Something Weird Video version has an MD narrator telling the incident on camera, which then cuts to a different scene; apparently the gory self-mutilation footage was elided in the cut. Michael Bowen has restored a full version, forthcoming on DVD, that shows the preparation with a wood chisel and hammer, the swinging mallet, and (film) cut to a fake bloody aftermath.
21. I initially worked with the video version distributed by Something Weird Video; however Wishman's as-told-to biographer Michael Bowen provided me with a copy of his master copy for DVD (private correspondence, October 2003–February 2004). My initial argument rested on the fact that the film begins in medias res with Dr. Wollman leading a discussion group for transsexuals. The group is discussing whether one should tell people one is dating or an employer that one is transsexual. At about twenty-two minutes into the film, we have what I take to be the dramatically appropriate beginning of the film, with Puerto Rican transsexual Leslie talking to the camera and then in close-up saying, "Last year I was a man!" with a cut to the title "Let Me Die a Woman." This is followed by a male voice-over announcer telling us over images of Adam and Eve what we can expect during the film, then introducing "our guide" Leo Wollman, "MD, PhD, doctor, psychologist, minister." The same voice-over announcer appears at the conclusion of the film and provides a summary of what we have seen. This is, of course, classic bookending technique.

Given this, the most logical explanation is that somewhere along the line, the reels were put together in the wrong order, but that no one ever noticed or straightened the matter out. Bowen's version starts with the pretitle remarks by Leslie and then the titles. However, there's little if any evidence that Wishman was ever attentive to the aesthetic integrity of her films or their prints. No one seems to know who made the decision to excise the self-mutilation fake footage from the film. Tom Waugh reviewed the film in its initial seven-week run in Montreal with the self-castration intact. See Thomas Waugh, "Medical Thrills: *Born a Man . . . Let Me Die a Woman*, 1978–79," in *The Fruit Machine: Twenty Years of Writings on Queer Cinema* (Durham, N.C., Duke University Press, 2000), 72–73. Further, in the abject grindhouse theaters where *Let Me Die a Woman* and other exploitation and porn films played, it was common to witness fairly atrocious projection. In such theaters, personally I have seen films with reels out of order, or sections of different films spliced together, trailers suddenly appearing during a reel change with a subsequent return to the narrative, as well as the results of unattended and inattentive projections such as films breaking, being stuck and burning in the gate, breaks followed by the projector still running for minutes on end, and so forth. This was, after all, the lowest end of the theatrical film world; much of the audience was unable or unwilling to complain (except to shout out, uncomprehending that there is enough noise in the booth that the projectionist cannot hear the audience). Many in the audience were sleeping, drunk, drugged, or engaged in some kind of sexual activity with themselves or others, thus inattentive to the niceties of professional film projection. For an excellent ethnography of the porn theaters in particular, see Samuel R. Delany, *Times Square Red, Times Square Blue* (New York: New York University Press, 1999).

COLIN GUNCKEL

El signo de la muerte *and the Birth of a Genre*
Origins and Anatomy of the Aztec Horror Film

Following the social and political upheaval of the Mexican Revolution, intellectuals and policy makers deployed a series of discourses that interrogated and attempted to reconstruct a national identity in crisis. Among the most visible of these was *indigenismo*, an ideological formation that situated Mexican national character within the country's pre-Columbian heritage, while proposing a variety of strategies for the integration of the indigenous.[1] Perhaps the most celebrated manifestations of this discourse were the murals of artists like Diego Rivera and David Siqueiros, who invoked the indigenous past as both subject matter and formal strategy. Since Mexican cinema also contributed significantly to the dialogue surrounding national identity, *indigenismo* often achieved cinematic form, influencing early productions like *Redes* (dir. Fred Zinnemann, 1934) and *Janitzio* (dir. Carlos Navarro, 1934), and emerging as a principal theme in the films of Emilio Fernández, including *María Candelaria* (1943) and *Río escondido* (1947). While such efforts, in keeping with the prominent strains of this discourse, frequently engage in a simplified, romanticized glorification of an apparently homogenous indigenous culture, another body of work disrupts this reverence through an extreme reversal, situating the Aztec past as horror. In films like *El signo de la muerte* (*The Sign of Death*, dir. Chano Urueta, 1939) and those of the later Aztec

FIGURE 1 Mexico's "Aztec Mummy" cycle: indigenismo gives way to human sacrifice, decaying corpses, and maniacal scientists.

mummy cycle (e.g., *The Robot vs. the Aztec Mummy*, dir. Rafael Portillo, 1957), idyllic landscapes and tragically noble Indians are replaced by human sacrifice, decaying corpses, and maniacal scientists. By examining the specificities and sociohistoric context of both Urueta's film and the later exploitation genres, this paper will attempt to explain how a heritage often characterized as central to national identity can provide the basis for both fear and ridicule. Although to some extent these films constitute a satire of indigenismo's sanctimony, they also engage issues of national identity in a period of social transformation, using cinematic horror to engage the tensions and anxieties of a Mexican culture and nation in transition.

El signo de la muerte:
Present Horrors of an Indigenous Past

El signo de la muerte is comprised of three distinct, yet converging narrative trajectories. First, Dr. Gallardo (Carlos Orellana), a renowned archaeologist, has discovered an ancient codex, using its inscriptions to plot the resurrection of the Aztec race through a series of prescribed sacrifices. At the same time, Carlos (Tomás Perrín Jr.) and Lola (Elena D'Orgaz) are two romantically involved reporters who compete for interviews and clues regarding the rash of mysterious murders that are ultimately linked to the doctor's gruesome rituals. During the course of her investigation, Lola is targeted as the final sacrificial victim, her capture and eventual rescue providing a dramatic climax during which the villains are thwarted. Throughout the course of the film, Cantinflas (Mario Moreno), a guide at the National Museum and assistant to the archaeologist, and Medel (Manuel Medel), portraying an ineffectual house detective, appear in a series of apparently autonomous comedy segments, which often take on a magical or surreal quality. Throughout the film, these two characters also sustain a humorous rivalry for the attentions of Lola's aunt Tía Mati (Matilde Correll). While both men are aware of the events of the principal narrative and interact with the other characters, their bumbling ineptitude and self-absorption prevent them from intervening in a meaningful way.

In his brief analysis of *El signo de la muerte*, Jeffrey M. Pilcher, citing the "avant-garde" tendencies of director Chano Urueta and his collaborators (who included composer Silvestre Revueltas and screenwriter Salvador Novo), situates the film as an intentional parody of the indigenismo championed by Rivera and others.[2] Pilcher claims that by casting Orellana, a fair-skinned actor with somewhat of a "Spanish visage," as an obsessive indigenist scholar, the filmmakers engaged in an obvious critique of "the sham of Indian identity among Mexico's postrevolutionary elite."[3] While approaching this film as satire certainly proves illuminating, it also fails to account for a large portion of the text and its appeal.

Dan Harries defines parody as "the process of recontextualizing a target or source text through the transformation of its textual (and contextual) elements, thus creating a *new* text. This conversion—through the resulting oscillation between similarity and difference from the target—creates a level of ironic incongruity with an inevitable satiric impulse."[4] Although *El signo* engages multiple source texts, the manner in which it does so complicates its classification as parody. While clearly ridiculing indigenismo, for instance, the film also displays the influence of Universal horror features such as *Frankenstein* (dir. James

Whale, 1931). Rather than lampooning these films, however, *El signo* reproduces many of their conventions (lighting, narrative, mise-en-scène) without irony. In this instance, differences between the target texts and the new text are not necessarily a function of parodic distance, but conceivably a result of the genre's translation to a Mexican context. Similarly, the antics of Medel and Cantinflas, while certainly satiric at points, also manage to transcend parody (and even logical explanation). Harries also points out the importance of selecting an appropriate target text upon which the parody is based: "limited genres or unknown prototexts do not usually generate enough of an anchor from which the parody can deviate effectively."[5] While knowledge of the public rivalry between Novo and Rivera informs Pilcher's analysis, this information may not have been universally available to various audiences over time, and, furthermore, enjoyment of the film certainly does not depend on a familiarity with this issue. Dr. Gallardo, for instance, can just as easily (or simultaneously) be interpreted as a variation upon Universal's mad doctor characters. In fact, even Mexican film scholar Emilio García Riera criticizes the film for its servile imitation of Hollywood horror formulas, failing to acknowledge any of its parodic dimensions.[6] My intention here is not to privilege one reading over another, but to suggest that in this case, as in any, numerous readings and interpretations are made available by the text. Following a dialogic approach, then, perhaps the most advantageous way to approach the complex, apparently fragmented *El signo de la muerte* is through a consideration of its multiple intertexts: Cantinflas's persona and career, the politics of the filmmakers, Mexican comedy film, the horror genre, melodrama, parody, indigenismo, and sociohistorical contexts. Taking these various factors into account allows for a more nuanced understanding of the film, offering a number of approaches and readings without fixing the film to a single, definitive interpretation or intention.

Having established this, however, I will to a large extent be treating *El signo* as a horror film, although, as even a brief plot summary suggests, its diverse pleasures certainly cannot be reduced to those of a single genre. My reasons for approaching the film accordingly are multiple. First, since I am primarily interested in examining the horrific manifestations of Aztec culture across a variety of films, this seems in many respects the most obviously logical way to proceed. Appropriately, the film's narrative tension and suspense, its threat of violence, and its graphic depiction of human sacrifice (a dagger plunged into the bare breast of a young woman, blood flowing copiously forth) serve to place it squarely within this genre. Furthermore, its more comic elements do not disqualify it from being classified, at least for our purposes, as a horror film. As Andrew Tudor points out, "the systems of codes and conventions that constitute horror change over time in major as well as minor ways, changing also the terms in which horror appeals to its users."[7] This fluid notion of genre allows for cross-fertilization between genres, and for the translation of the mad scientist subgenre to a Mexican context. In addition, as both Tudor and Rhona Berenstein argue, horror films elicit a variety of often contradictory responses, from laughter to terror and points between, a concept that problematizes any notion of an inimical relationship between comedy and horror.[8] Consequently, the presence of Cantinflas and Medel does not invalidate *El signo*'s status as horror. In fact, the comedy segments, although apparently digressive in narrative terms, are not structurally or thematically autonomous, and, as we shall see, become integral to any consideration of the film as a whole, including its more horrific aspects. Finally, *El signo* conforms to the narrative conventions that Noël Carroll has identified as central to the genre. Specifically, it might be regarded as a combination of what he labels the "Discovery Plot," which emphasizes the discovery, confirmation, and confrontation of a threatening force, with the "Overreacher Plot" (of which the mad-scientist narrative is the most recognizable variant) which "often stresses the short-sightedness of science" and "criticizes science's will to knowledge."[9]

Perhaps the most effective way to begin drawing out the various tensions and anxieties mobilized by the indigenous past in *El signo* is through a close examination of an early scene in which the illustrious Dr. Gallardo delivers a lecture on the prophecy of Quetzalcoatl, and the missing section of the Xilitla codex that contains the necessary instructions for the revival of the Aztec race. As Gallardo explains the Aztec sacrifice ritual, a woman in the audience turns to the reporter Carlos and sighs, "Que admirable civilización, ¿verdad?" (What an admirable civilization, don't you think?). Carlos, obviously somewhat disgusted by the lecture's graphic nature, replies, "¿Le parece usted?" (You really think so?). This immediately establishes the ambivalence toward Aztec culture that will continue throughout the text: a simultaneous admiration and disdain, attraction and repulsion. On the one hand, indigenous culture is recognized as an important aspect of national patrimony and identity. After completing his lecture, for instance, Gallardo is approached by the woman and her friends who, practically swooning, shake his hand and ask for his signature. One woman boasts of having read all his books, while her companion credits Gallardo with imparting important knowledge about "viejas culturas" (ancient cultures) through his "descubrimientos asombrosos" (amazing discoveries). Similarly, Carlos approaches the doctor for an interview, citing the necessity of exposing the public to Gallardo's "meritoria y patriótica" (meritorious and patriotic) body of work.

The terms of this attraction, especially as it emerges in the women characters, is especially intriguing. In her conversation with Carlos during the lecture, the woman explains how noble and romantic it would be to offer one's heart to a deity and virtually trembles in ecstasy as she imagines being stripped naked and held down by four priests. Carlos, apparently speechless, merely responds with an expression bordering on discomfort and disbelief. While this exchange is played largely for humor, the horrific aspects of Aztec culture begin to emerge in this scene not only through Gallardo's eccentric appearance or his suspiciously passionate description of human sacrifice, but through an association with female assertions of (deviant) desire and the masculine response these engender. This manifests itself not only in Carlos's reaction to the woman's fantasy, but also in another conversation between the same woman and another man, presumably a friend. While exiting the lecture hall, she and her female companion continue praising Gallardo and his accomplishments. Eventually, the male acquaintance undermines their unconditional infatuation by repeating rumors that the doctor is "sombroso y maniático" (shadowy and maniacal), that he lives surrounded by indigenous servants, and frequently disappears from the city. This particular scene thus begins sketching rather effectively not only the villainy of Gallardo and the experiment he is devising, but also the dynamic that makes Aztec culture and its intellectual representatives both admirable and excessive, a potential threat to stability and normalcy, and, for Mexican women, an irresistible force both seductive and potentially destructive.

Following Pilcher, this particular scene does indeed betray a critique of indigenismo, casting suspicion upon the motives and sincerity of its promoters, as well as expressing ambivalence regarding their influence over an apparently gullible Mexican public. Consistent with a parodic reversal, the film also exaggerates and fetishizes the bloody and brutal aspects of Aztec culture that seem antithetical to a romanticized discourse. Those drawn to this doctrine, particularly Gallardo's female admirers, are also ridiculed, both for their overtly passionate enthusiasm and for their slavish devotion. Once again, however, this satirical bent is complicated by the murderous threat Gallardo's scheme eventually poses to characters within the film, and *El signo*'s consequent adherence to the conventions of horror. Thus the film is imbued with an atmosphere of anxiety and fear. Through its evocation of indigenismo, Aztec iconography, and issues of gender, it becomes associated with a crisis of national identity in a period of uncertainty and transition.

Robin Wood's ideas regarding repression in the horror genre present an especially useful conceptual framework through which to consider the multiple implications of Aztec horror in this context. Following the work of Gad Horowitz (which in turn builds on Freud and Marcuse), Wood distinguishes between "basic repression," upon which our proper development as human beings depends, and "surplus repression," which he characterizes as "specific to a particular culture . . . the process whereby people are conditioned from earliest infancy to take on predetermined roles within that culture."[10] This form of repression requires, in the U.S. context, the sublimation of sexual energy in general, and that of bisexuality and female sexuality in particular. Inseparable from this is the concept of the Other, an entity that "functions not simply as something external to the culture or to the self, but also what is repressed (though never destroyed) in the self and projected outward in order to be hated and disowned."[11] According to Wood, the monsters of horror film embody this Other, which represents "the struggle for recognition of all that our civilization represses or oppresses, its reemergence dramatized, as in our nightmares, as an object of horror."[12] Consequently, horror cannot justifiably be considered an escapist genre, for its fantasies "represent attempts to resolve those tensions in more radical ways than our conscious can countenance."[13]

While *El signo de la muerte* does not feature a monster in the strictest sense, the specter of an Aztec resurrection sufficiently mobilizes the fear and apprehension Wood associates with the Other. Considered in the light of indigenismo, one might speculate that the film dramatizes the vengeful reemergence of the actual indigenous groups, or a cinematic representation of the Others repressed within this discourse, whose "champions often failed to acknowledge linguistic, historical, and cultural differences or even variations in racial stock among the diverse groups that made up the indigenous populations."[14] While metaphorically such an explanation may be valid, the film is not interested in correcting indigenist representations, nor in creating psychologically complex or more "authentic" indigenous characters. In fact, *El signo* deploys the familiar iconography often associated with muralism and calendar illustrations: muscular Aztec warriors (sporting loin cloths and headdresses), scantily clad sacrificial virgins, and monolithic idols assembled in the performance of a ritual. The difference here is that the picturesque representations have become grotesque and horrific, a reversal that never pretends to engage social reality or cultural specificity. Instead, *El signo* capitalizes upon negative stereotypes of indigenous character, using the notion of a violent and primitive Aztec race to instill fear in the other characters.

A corrective, or more realist approach, in fact, seems antithetical to horror, which depends on the terror and anxiety generated by an unknowable Other to achieve its intended effect. Screenwriter Novo's personal antagonistic relations with Rivera, for instance, represent a more probable explanation for these representations, as does his opposition to the Lázaro Cárdenas administration. Along with support for organized labor and the repatriation of the petroleum industry, Cárdenas, expanding the agrarian reform promised by the Mexican Revolution, redistributed 50 million acres of land to rural peasants and instituted education programs and economic initiatives with an indigenist orientation.[15] If, as Pilcher argues, these policies "inspir[ed] a wave of nostalgia among the urban middle classes that assured the success of *Allá en el Rancho Grande*," could it also, for anti-Cárdenists like Novo, go beyond the level of satiric critique to express an anxiety about the shifts of power and wealth, and the priorities of an administration that appeared to favor the peasant and working classes?[16] In this respect, the bloodthirsty Aztecs, Gallardo's "raza subyugada por los hombres blancos" (race subjugated by white men) may embody or at least coincide with the elite's fear of social and racial upheaval, a return of the oppressed and of the revolution that threatened to upend traditional power structures. This anxiety is perhaps borne out through the progression of sacrifices throughout the film. While the first two rituals involve two priests and four attendants who secure the victim, the final climactic sacrifice includes a veritable army of Indians who chant, bow, and drum in anticipation of the impending resurrection. Appropriately enough, an equally impressive regiment of police, representatives of state authority, arrives at the appropriate moment, and in an extended fight scene, resubjugates the potentially insurgent Indians.

As an extension of the insecurity generated by social transformation, the film may also betray a more general uncertainty about the manner in which these discourses translate to personal identity and national policy. According to Charles Ramírez Berg, Mexico's "'Indian problem' is the governing metaphor for an entire nation," the "hypersensitive national sore," a central dilemma that extends to multiple aspects of Mexican life.[17] For instance, if "*indigenismo* argued that the roots of modern Mexican identity—*lo mexicano*—lay in the cultural legacy of pre-Columbian Indian cultures," how is the mestizo population to internalize or reconcile the negative attributes (embodied in the films as a penchant for human sacrifice) historically invoked to situate the Indian as an inferior race and class?[18] Following the model of repression, the Aztec horror of *El signo* (and other films) may function as a projection on to "Mexico's inescapable Other" of what are perceived as the darker, more undesirable inheritances of an indigenous past that must be repressed within the individual self and the denial of a heritage that occupies the lowest rung of the social hierarchy, whose representatives within the text must consequently be defeated.[19] Thus the indigenous past, in the context of the film, also participates in the dynamic of attraction and repulsion that, according to Carroll, constitutes the central appeal of horror, the genre's attempt to negotiate themes and issues that generate complex, contradictory responses.[20] Considering Ramírez Berg's argument, this dynamic then traverses a number of crucial issues: ambivalence about the consequences of Indian blood for the constitution of Mexican character, about the feasibility of an indigenous-based identity in the context of a modernizing Mexico, uncertainty about how to integrate Indians into mainstream society, and, more broadly, "an interrogation of Mexico's future," the terms of its progress and development.[21] In many respects these dilemmas, the anxieties that circulate throughout the film, strike at the heart of the attitudes that inform official policy and public discourse in Mexico during this period.

This persistent, fundamental ambivalence, rather than being focalized, per

Carroll, upon a central monster, is distributed across the text of *El signo*, extending to any individual or object contaminated by Aztec culture. This is perhaps most directly embodied by the character of Dr. Gallardo, who suffers from an excessive embrace and enactment of indigenous heritage and thus provides a fitting example of what Ramírez Berg refers to as Mexico's divided subjectivity.[22] Simultaneously an elite intellectual and murderous megalomaniac, he periodically exchanges the ascot and tuxedo of his public life for the ornate robes of an Aztec priest, as the codices, artifacts, and statuary of his "meritorious and patriotic" professional endeavors are transformed into sacrificial tools. This double existence is expressed as a murderous, irreconcilable tension that creates narrative havoc, demanding resolution. The apparent contradictions between his indigenist aspirations and his career as a modern scientist are resolved at the film's finale, when, unwilling to sacrifice his own daughter, he is speared by his Indian followers. As a heightened, exaggerated engagement with contemporary concerns, the film uses Gallardo to hint at both the violent, conflictive implications of this heritage for Mexican identity and an uncertainty regarding its place in modern existence.

Not surprisingly the film's lighting and mise-en-scène actively participate in this dynamic of attraction and repulsion, using darkness, shadow, and confined space to signify hidden and dangerous forces lurking beneath the surface of a glorified heritage. The sacrificial chamber, for instance, appears to be lit by nothing more than two small fires on either side of the altar; all the ritual sacrifices thus transpire against a background of nearly complete darkness. Appropriately, this foreboding underground chamber is accessible only by stairs or through a series of damp, claustrophobic tunnels. The site of considerable violence, where on two occasions we witness an obsidian knife plunged into the chest of an unconscious maiden, this room is easily interpreted as a metaphorical space, a recess where repressed, primeval desires and tendencies are given form. The filmmakers do not, however, establish a clean binary between this space and the more publicly accessible museum. In *El signo*, the impressive idols housed in the National Museum, rather than merely standing as signs of a noble national origin, cast imposing multiple shadows upon the walls, their cluttered arrangement and immense proportions combining to overwhelm the humans with whom they share the screen. Thus even the farcical tours periodically guided by Cantinflas convey, at least aesthetically, a foreboding and anxiety regarding this patrimony, an uneasiness regarding the power, fascination, and significance these monuments mobilize, an emotion apparently justified by subsequent narrative events.

As I mentioned previously, the darkness and danger emerging from the Aztec resurrection in *El signo* is also closely associated with female desire, which appropriately enough, Wood cites as a primary target of surplus repression. On one hand, Aztec culture represents a source of irresistible fascination for the women characters. The museum tours led by Cantinflas are attended primarily by curious and attentive women, and it is often to them that he addresses his commentary. As we have seen during Gallardo's lecture, this interest is potentially deviant, involving sexual fantasy infused with violence and masochism. Thus while an indigenous heritage seems to imply for men (i.e., Gallardo) a potential toward violence and bloodshed, for women it seems to entail an unleashing of desire and sensuality. Ultimately, the sacrifices required by the codex make this desire destructive and dangerous, punishing women for their sexual transgression and curiosity. For instance, Tía Mati, reading the same newspaper in which the first sacrifice was reported, discovers and becomes intrigued by an advertisement for an Aztec spiritualist who treats only women. The mysterious energy that draws women to this fortune teller, we soon discover, also endangers them: he is later revealed to be an associate of doctor Gallardo, using his spiritual powers to identify the "doncellas predestinadas" (predestined maidens) prescribed by the codex. The sacrifices themselves, consistent with the first woman's fantasies, are indeed sexually charged, with muscular men in loincloths subduing a young woman draped in nothing more than sheer cloth, a ritual culminating in the penetration of her naked breast. During these moments, violence and sensuality unite in a perverse spectacle that unleashes desires and impulses whose containment promises to restore balance and normality.

The sacrifices, however, become a matter not only of containing female sexual energy, but also of stifling their increasing social ambition and independence, imbuing the film with the heightened moral dilemmas and the personalization of social conflicts associated with melodrama. According to Joanne Hershfield, Mexico during this period was experiencing "an unprecedented economic boom, stepped-up industrialization . . . [that] combined to pressure the women to continue working outside the home."[23] Hershfield argues that "this alteration in women's economic roles threatened existing traditional structures, including the family and patriarchy, which in turn threatened male identity."[24] In *El signo de la muerte*, Lola's prominence as a reporter clearly threatens the ego and career of her boyfriend Carlos, an imbalance of traditional gender roles that is expressed and resolved through the threat of sacrifice. While Lola secures an interview with the reluctant Gallardo, Carlos is demoted by his editor for linking the professor to the series of murders. His new assignment: a section titled "La esposa y la cocina" ("Wife and Kitchen"), where he will be responsible for dispensing home decorating tips and recipes. Carlos is clearly emasculated by his girlfriend's success, and when he finally proposes marriage to her, he mentions her resignation as a condition of their union. Although Lola accepts, she points out that she was such a skillful reporter, that she managed to steal the front page from her boyfriend. Imitating Gallardo's apocalyptic language, he counters: "Pero los dioses la castigaron" (But the gods punished her). As if a projection of Carlos's sublimated aggression, the film indeed proceeds to punish Lola for her ambition. After a comment from Tía Mati begins to suggest a connection between the spiritualist and the murders, Lola decides to investigate further, scheduling a session with the hooded fortune teller. A palm reading reveals that she bears the appropriate mark, and she is thus kidnapped, nearly becoming the final victim. This turn of events is directly linked to her inquisitiveness and professional aspirations, and her femininity is ultimately posited as incongruous with her participation in a potentially dangerous career.

Her eventual rescue at the hands of Carlos not only restores his masculinity but also cements their marital engagement and Lola's domestication. As she quite succinctly intones, this means a movement from the front page to the matrimony section, and a transition from physical sacrifice to a professional one. The defeat of the Aztec revivalists therefore channels excessive and dangerous female sexuality into the confines of marriage, while successfully repressing a more destructive masculine violence (the obliquely expressed desire to punish Lola) in favor of a more constructive and acceptable form of heroism. Thus the multiple anxieties and imbalances released by a horrific Aztec revival are thus effectively contained: the upheaval of social and racial hierarchies, the unseemly character traits lurking in an indigenous heritage, the crossing of gendered boundaries, and the unconditional trust placed in intellectuals with questionable motives.

As is often the case with melodramatic resolutions, however, not all of these tensions are completely recuperated by the end of *El signo*, an excess that can largely be attributed to the performance of Cantinflas. Although on the one hand his star billing may have assuaged suspicions of the film's subversive tendencies by ostensibly placing it within a comedic genre, to a significant extent he actually intensifies its irreverence. While lighting and composition imbue museum exhibits with a menacing aspect, his commentary mocks and threatens to undermine the solemnity of official history. During the film's opening sequences, for instance, he stands beneath the Aztec calendar, or Sun Stone, and pretends to be supporting it on his shoulders. Quite literally, he appears to dislodge the piece, transforming an enshrined monument to national identity into a comic prop. His subsequent explanations of a sacrificial altar and the sculpture of Coatlicue achieve a similar effect through their almost indecipherable, nonsensical quality. This tendency to confound approximates his effect on *El signo*'s narrative, with his segments often derailing the linear trajectory of the principal story lines. Appropriately, he and Medel even problematize the film's resolution by, in a scene mirroring the reunion between Carlos and Lola, both agreeing to marry Tía Mati and each planting a kiss on her cheek.

Cantinflas's irreverent, sacrilegious attitude toward history and the boundaries of propriety persists unabated throughout the film, compounded by his ability to align himself with every other character in the text. While working for Gallardo (unaware of his illicit activities), he engages in friendship and rivalry with Medel, accompanies both Tía Mati and Lola to the spiritualist, and assists Carlos in his attempts to prevent the final sacrifice. In a short montage of the Spanish Conquest that opens the film, both he and Medel appear briefly dressed as Aztecs. This shifting between social, racial, and class affiliations extends to his personal behavior and the ability to absorb the influence of those around him. While on his first trip to the fortune teller, for instance, he acquires magical powers, making a beverage cart, and then Medel, appear and disappear at will. Similarly, during his second visit, he accompanies Lola dressed as a

FIGURE 2 Cantinflas in *El signo de la muerte* (1939), undermining the solemnity of official history.

woman. Thus while a transgression of gendered boundaries and the mysterious powers of Aztec culture terrorize the other characters, for Cantinflas (and to some extent Medel) these become an opportunity for play. This culminates in perhaps the film's most absurdly bizarre scene and its most significant narrative digression, in which Medel and Cantinflas, rather than participating in the climactic rescue of Lola, become inebriated and transform themselves into the Emperor Maximillian (Medel) and Carlotta (Cantinflas). Obviously mutually enraptured, the two spout comic phrases in formal Spanish, climb into a carriage on display in the museum, turn on the radio (!), appear to nearly kiss, and fall asleep in each other's arms. According to Pilcher, homoeroticism and gender reversal had become a part of the interaction between Medel and Moreno in previous films and in stage performances, "forcing the audience to laugh at the breakdown of family values that became increasingly apparent in modern urban life."[25] In the context of *El signo*, this also engages issues of history and identity, with Cantinflas moving effortlessly between representations of indigenous and European heritage, ultimately laying siege to the sanctity of both. Consistent with his personification of the often transgressive, resistant *pelado*, Cantinflas here embodies an archetype of racial mixture (*mestizaje*) and poverty, a figure caught between rural origins and urban existence.[26] Cantinflas's early association with Novo (and others) often placed this character in the service of political and social critique, a tradition that likely informs his performance in this film.[27] Throughout *El signo*, the liminal and contradictory qualities of the pelado replicate and delight in the kind of divided subjectivity mentioned by Ramírez Berg, ultimately refusing to resolve the complexity and tensions pried open by the text, managing to mock propriety, history, and convention in the process.[28]

Aztec Mummies: The Resurrection

Although, as I have already argued, *El signo de la muerte* can hardly be characterized as a progressive treatment of the indigenous, it nonetheless diverges markedly from the more reverent cinematic reproductions of indigenismo. Consider, for instance, the films of Emilio Fernández, perhaps the most celebrated director of the Golden Age, whose indigenist films "elevated the Indians to mythic stature, romanticized their lives, and, following the model of earlier films, linked the meaning of *lo mexicano* visually and narratively to Mexico's indigenous roots."[29] While Laura Podalsky's analysis of his film *María Candelaria* uncovers a more ambiguous attitude toward the representational practices informed by indigenismo, this example nonetheless "plug[s] into an iconic tradition that equates the Indian with the uniqueness of Mexico."[30] Curiously, Fernández's recourse to established stereotypes also resulted in a flirtation with the same representations of indigenous peoples and culture that inform Aztec horror films. In *María Candelaria*, for instance, María's (Dolores del Río) refusal to pose nude for the artist (Alberto Galán) is contrasted with the willingness of a visibly darker Indian woman to disrobe without reservation. The baring of her body, once again positing a more permissive indigenous sensuality, ultimately leads to María's death, when the inhabitants of Xochimilco, believing that she herself posed nude, stone her to death. This collective homicide itself indicates an indigenous constitution impervious to reason, whose violent, destructive instincts are not even blunted by the civilizing influence of the church. Thus

María Candelaria exhibits a conception of the indigenous that is amplified and expanded upon in representations of Aztec horror. By establishing a conflict between the lighter-skinned, virtuous María and the "backward" tendencies of the Indians that threaten her, the film also engages in the ambivalence apparent in *El signo*, a fundamentally contradictory attitude at the center of official discourse on the indigenous.

While during the Golden Age, an industry sustained by state financing generated studio films that, however complex, generally reproduced and often promoted dominant discourses of nationalism, production on the margins of this industry provided opportunity for variations upon or divergences from the official strains of this rhetoric. Susan Dever, for instance, has illustrated the more inclusive nationalism proposed by director Matilde Landeta's independently produced *Lola Cassanova* (1948), which rather than merely situating the indigenous as a symbol of national essence suggests the possibility of their meaningful integration into society.[31] Manuel Barbachano Ponce's independent production of Benito Alazraki's *Raíces* (1953) likewise departed from indigenist convention, offering a glimpse of indigenous life that oscillates between tragedy and satire. *El signo de la muerte*'s parodic, anxiety-ridden distortions of indigenismo might likewise be attributed to its independent status (produced by entrepreneurs Pedro Maus and Felipe Mier), which allowed it to diverge from the more orthodox, state-financed representations of the 1930s, including the images of Indian peasant life in *Redes*. In addition, as Eduardo de la Vega Alfaro points out, because the industry was on the verge of consolidation during this particular decade, filmmakers benefited from an atmosphere of experimentation in which the terms and conventions of Mexican cinema were still a matter of contention.[32] This was itself reflected in the career of Cantinflas, who not yet having secured his stardom with *Ahí está el detalle* (dir. Juan Bustillo Oro, 1940), still retained a somewhat subversive quality that would be dulled by his attempts to negotiate mass appeal and a bourgeois audience.[33] To some extent, these industrial conditions may explain how *El signo*'s outlandish reversal of indigenismo was even permissible or conceivable.

Appropriately enough, when the industry began to disintegrate in the late 1950s, Mexican cinema experienced a resurrection of Aztec horror, emerging this time in the low-budget horror, wrestling, and exploitation genres that proliferated during the industry's collapse. It is not entirely coincidental that Charles Ramírez Berg chooses to situate Ismael Rodríguez' *Tizoc* (1956) as a marker of the golden age's decline.[34] This glamorous prestigious epic deploying narrative conventions and representations entirely consistent with Fernández's tragic indigenist romances was followed by an inundation of cheap films that capitalized upon a similar iconography in the service of both humor and fright. These efforts include *La Llorona* (dir. René Cardona, 1958), *The Robot vs. the Aztec Mummy*, *The Living Head* (dir. Miguel San Fernando and Chano Urueta, 1961), and *Las luchadoras contra la momia* (dir. René Cardona, 1964). As audiences apparently tired of the themes and subject matter of the golden age, and their reiteration was perceived as outmoded, these films seemed to ridicule and defile what in previous decades was often held sacred, while many producers abandoned prestige for quick profits.[35]

Curiously, although they are separated by nearly twenty years, a remarkable continuity emerges between *El signo de la muerte* and the later cycle of Aztec horror films. It is not surprising, therefore, that Jorge Ayala Blanco proposes *El signo* as a precursor of the horror/fantasy films starring masked wrestler El Santo, which emerged as the most successful variation of the low-budget genres.[36] As a matter of fact, Chano Urueta continued his career in this era by directing horror and wrestling films, including *The Living Head* and *La bestia magnífica* (1952). On a visual level, works of the new cycle employ a vocabulary established by the earlier film: shadowy, subterranean tombs and temples dramatically lit by flickering flames and submerged in the smoke of burning copal, mysterious rituals presided over by foreboding idols, and half-naked damsels stretched over sacrificial altars. What proves even more intriguing, as we shall see through a brief consideration of the somewhat representative *The Robot vs. the Aztec Mummy*, is the extent to which horrific manifestations of Aztec culture mobilize a similar set of anxieties.

The Robot vs. the Aztec Mummy takes place as a series of flashbacks, in which Dr. Eduardo Almadan (Ramón Gay) narrates the strange events of the film to his assembled colleagues. In an attempt to prove the possibility of revealing past lives through hypnosis, he has used his wife Flora (Rosa Arenas) as an experimental subject, discovering that in a previous incarnation she died in an Aztec sacrifice. Her lover, Popoca, was later buried with a breastplate and bracelet

FIGURE 3 Poster art for *La momia azteca contra el robot humano* (1961).

that when deciphered reveal the location of the Aztec treasure. Naturally, the couple, along with several friends, set out to locate Popoca's tomb. They succeed in doing so, only to awaken and anger the mummified warrior and to discover that they have acquired a competitor for the Aztec gold: the evil Dr. Krupp (Luis Aceves Castañeda), also known as "The Bat." After a series of multiple reawakenings of Popoca, Dr. Krupp decides that only by devising a "human robot" can he hope to defeat the apparently invincible Aztec. The inevitable, final confrontation results in the defeat of the robot and Dr. Krupp, and the return of Popoca's adornments, which presumably facilitates his peaceful, eternal rest.

Quite obviously, this film constitutes a Mexicanization of the Hollywood horror creatures that had become internationally recognized and imitated by this point in time. The mummy and the robot are thus clearly variations upon the many mummies, zombies, Frankensteinian monsters, and science-fiction monstrosities that populate not only Universal films, but also the countless low-budget B-movies being produced concurrently in the United States. Likewise,

FIGURE 4 The "atomic powered" robot of *The Robot vs. the Aztec Mummy*, Mexico's contribution to the era's iconography of the science-fiction B-film.

the maniacal Dr. Krupp is a rather conventional mad scientist, a character that, as Noël Carroll reminds us, typically betrays a generalized uncertainty about the advances of science.[37] His cyborg creation is even imbued with "atomic" powers, echoing the nuclear anxieties of similar U.S. films of this period. Once again, however, the arrangement of these elements around a heritage often equated with national identity suggests that it at least metaphorically engages contemporary tensions regarding this issue. While many of the same dynamics that inform *El signo* are consequently evident, they are treated with less complexity and ambiguity (nothing even approaches Cantinflas's anarchic transgressions, for instance) and are reduced to a series of heightened battles between good and evil.

Science, as I have already suggested, repeatedly emerges in *The Robot* as a potentially destructive force, the unethical use of which threatens to unleash dire consequences. The respective unearthing capacities of modern psychology and archaeology (even in the virtuous hands of Eduardo), for instance, conspire to awaken the slumbering Aztec, while the nuclear-powered abomination designed by Dr. Krupp becomes a tool for greed and devastation. As in *El signo*, there also seems to be an uncertainty about the role of traditional culture and heritage in a country experiencing the effects of modernization and industrialization. This is embodied rather blatantly by the climactic confrontation between the robot and the mummy. The outcome of this battle naturally reinstates the supremacy of the "good" scientists and the necessary defeat of the villain, whose megalomania ultimately provokes his own demise. This resolution also proposes a compromise: while responsible scientists like Eduardo promise to control the progress of technology, the Aztec warrior is returned to his tomb, a figment of the past revered as history although ultimately irrelevant and dangerously out of place in the present.

As with the other films of this cycle, *The Robot* centers the attraction/repulsion dynamic in a single monstrous character. On one hand, the Aztec mummy is perceived by the various characters as an element of national patrimony, a research opportunity, and a potential source of riches. Simultaneously, however, he is inhumanly powerful, indestructible, ferocious and physically deformed from centuries of decay. As in *El signo*, this may hint at the fundamental ambivalence toward the implications of this heritage for national and personal identity. Extending to mise-en-scène, Eduardo's vastly cavernous and brightly lit bourgeois home finds its antithesis in the subterranean Aztec tomb, a locus of violence and repressed desire that threatens to disturb the stability of modern life. In a structural correlation, as a series of flashbacks related to an audience of fellow scientists assembled in Eduardo's opulent abode, the entire narrative and its threat of graveyards and tombs are located safely in the past, a trauma unearthed yet cleanly resolved and relegated to memory. Once again, this positions the indigenous past as history, a narrative worth reciting but whose protagonists remain at temporal and spatial distance.

The repression that the Aztec past unleashes, not surprisingly, finds its origins in Flora, Eduardo's wife. As he uses psychoanalysis (a discipline traditionally associated with the sexual drives of women) to unravel her past life, he manages to uncover her ancient relationship with a strapping Aztec warrior, and her willing participation in a ceremony that culminated in her penetration by a sacrificial knife. Once again, the indigenous past becomes associated with anxieties about female sexuality, and the hidden desires lurking within the respectable bourgeois wife. Of course, the resolution of the film also entails a reburial of Flora's sexual past, of which the mummy's persistent reawakening served as a constant reminder.

While *The Robot* gives expression to certain anxieties regarding identity, heritage, and issues surrounding gender, its failure to engage more specific social and cultural subject matter make its relevancy rather vague and indefinite. Its only identifiably Mexican quality is the Aztec mummy himself, making the film's tensions and terrors more applicable to a general anxiety about modern life, consequently aligning it with similar U.S. productions. In fact, *The Robot* is among the films of this cycle that was dubbed in English for distribution in this country by AIP, the pyramids of Teotihuacan evidently proving a ready substitute for those of Egypt. Nonetheless, in the context of a cycle of such films, and given the possible influence of *El signo*, it is still possible to perceive traces of persisting doubts and the tumult generated by modernity's social and economic transitions.

Conclusion

Although it is certainly tempting to dismiss the improbable lunacy of Aztec horror as B-movie zaniness, or as an inferior imitation of Hollywood horror film, I hope this essay has suggested additional, even provocative explanations for the existence of this curious subgenre. While any number of horrific configurations could have been fashioned from a creative mining of Mexican history and current issues, this particular approach betrays a fearful confrontation of national identity and the self, uncertainty about modernization and the social transformations this entails, and the appropriate role of tradition in contemporary life. While striking aesthetic and thematic continuities between *El signo de la muerte* and the exploitation films might indicate the former as a foundational text, their similarities also suggest a consistent set of anxieties mobilized by indigenous culture and heritage. Accordingly, these films appear to engage conflicting attitudes regarding the indigenous of Mexico and the ways in which this population and their legacy/influence will be incorporated into national politics and discourse. Just as revealing as the diverse traits and desires ascribed to Aztecs in these films are the dynamics these characters are consequently used to represent: a fear of the darkness lurking beneath a cultivated middle class or bourgeois exterior, and tensions surrounding social transformation and shifts in gender roles.

Notes

1. An outline of indigenismo's basic tenets and variations is available in Alan Knight, "Racism, Revolution, and *Indigenismo*: Mexico, 1910–1940," in *The Idea of Race in Latin America, 1870–1940*, ed. Richard Graham (Austin: University of Texas Press, 1990), 71–113.
2. Jeffrey M. Pilcher, *Cantinflas and the Chaos of Mexican Modernity* (Wilmington, Del.: Scholarly Resources, 2000), 60.
3. Ibid., 60–62.
4. Dan Harries, *Film Parody* (London: BFI, 2000), 6.
5. Ibid., 34.
6. Emilio García Riera, *Historia documental del cine mexicano: 1983–1942* (Guadalajara: Universidad de Guadalajara, 1992), 96.
7. Andrew Tudor, "Why Horror? The Peculiar Pleasures of a Popular Genre," in *Horror: The Film Reader*, ed. Mark Janovich (London: Routledge, 2002), 51.
8. Rhona J. Berenstein, *Attack of the Leading Ladies: Gender, Sexuality, and Spectatorship in Classic Horror Cinema* (New York: Columbia University Press, 1996), 21–22; Tudor, "Why Horror," 53.
9. Noël Carroll, "Nightmare and the Horror Film: The Symbolic Biology of Fantastic Beings," in *Film Quarterly: Forty Years—A Selection*, ed. Brian Henderson and Ann Martin with Lee Amazonas (Berkeley: University of California Press, 1999), 170.
10. Robin Wood, *Hollywood from Vietnam to Reagan* (New York: Columbia University Press, 1986), 71.
11. Ibid., 73.
12. Ibid., 75.
13. Ibid., 78.
14. Joanne Hershfield, "Race and Ethnicity in the Classical Cinema," in *Mexico's Cinema: A Century of Film and Filmmakers*, ed. Joanne Hershfield and David R. Maciel (Wilmington, Del.: Scholarly Resources, Inc., 1999), 85.
15. Jeffrey Pilcher, "Cantinfladas of the PRI: (Mis)Representations of Mexican Society in the Films of Mario Moreno," *Film Historia* 9, no. 2 (1999): 191.
16. Pilcher, *Cantinflas and the Chaos of Mexican Modernity*, 50.
17. Charles Ramírez Berg, *Cinema of Solitude: A Critical Study of Mexican Film, 1967–1983* (Austin: University of Texas Press, 1992), 156, 138.
18. Hershfield, "Race and Ethnicity," 84.
19. Ramírez Berg, *Cinema of Solitude*, 138.
20. Carroll, "Nightmare and the Horror Film," 159–71.
21. Ramírez Berg, *Cinema of Solitude*, 153.
22. Ramírez Berg, *Cinema of Solitude*, 138.

23. Joanne Hershfield, *Mexican Cinema/Mexican Woman, 1940–1950* (Tucson: University of Arizona Press, 1996), 29.
24. Ibid., 29.
25. Pilcher, *Cantinflas and the Myth of Mexican Modernity*, 63.
26. Both Jeffrey Pilcher and Carlos Monsivás provide an analysis of the pelado character and its role in Cantinflas's career and persona. See Pilcher, *Cantinflas and the Myth of Mexican Modernity*, and Carlos Monsiváis, "Cantinflas: That's the Point!" in *Mexican Postcards* (London: Verso, 1997), 88–105.
27. Pilcher details Cantinflas's role in political debates and satire during the Cardenas administration in *Cantinflas and the Myth of Mexican Modernity*, 33–64.
28. Ramírez Berg, *Cinema of Solitude*, 137.
29. Hershfield, "Race and Ethnicity," 87.
30. Laura Podalsky, "Disjointed Frames: Melodrama, Nationalism, and Representation in 1940s Mexico," *Studies in Latin American Popular Culture* 3 (1984): 68.
31. Susan Dever, *Celluloid Nationalism and Other Melodramas: From Post-Revolutionary Mexico to fin de siglo Mexamérica* (Albany: State University of New York Press, 2003), 106–38.
32. Eduardo de la Vega Alfaro, "Origins, Development and Crisis of the Sound Cinema (1929–1964)," in *Mexican Cinema*, ed. Paulo Antonio Paranaguá (London: BFI, 1995), 81–85.
33. Pilcher, *Cantinflas and the Chaos of Mexican Modernity*, 64.
34. Charles Ramírez Berg, "The Cinematic Invention of Mexico: The Poetics and Politics of the Fernández-Figueroa Style," in *The Mexican Cinema Project*, ed. Chon A. Noriega and Steven Ricci (Los Angeles: UCLA Film and Television Archive, 1994).
35. Eduardo de la Vega Alfaro details the factors that contributed to a decline in quality of Mexican film and the consequent rise of cheaply made horror and fantasy films that offered producers promising returns on minimal investment in "The Decline of the Golden Age and the Making of the Crisis," in *Mexico's Cinema: A Century of Film and Filmmakers*, ed. Joanne Hershfield and David R. Maciel (Wilmington, Del.: Scholarly Resources, 1999), 165–86.
36. Jorge Ayala Blanco, *La busqueda del cine mexicano (1968–1972)* (Mexico, D.F.: Editorial Posada, 1986), 285.
37. Carroll, "Nightmare and the Horror Film," 170–71.

KEVIN HEFFERNAN

Art House or House of Exorcism? The Changing Distribution and Reception Contexts of Mario Bava's *Lisa and the Devil*

Here we have, ladies and gentlemen, a unique example of medieval Christian art. TOUR GUIDE IN *LISA AND THE DEVIL* (1972)

BOMB. Incoherent witch's brew of devil worshiping, exorcism, and perfectly awful acting that has [Telly] Savalas as a lollipop-popping M.C. in a house of horrors where one of the wax dummies may or may not be a girl possessed by Satan. LEONARD MALTIN

Between 1971 and 1973, Italian American producer Alfredo Leone and Italian director Mario Bava collaborated on three gothic horror films. The first, *Gli Orrori del Castello di Noremburga* (*Baron Blood*, 1971) starring Elke Sommer and Joseph Cotten, was picked up by American International Pictures and became a worldwide box-office success. Their second collaboration, *Lisa and the Devil* (1972), enjoyed Bava's largest-ever budget of $1 million, the return of star Elke Sommer, and several successful screenings at the Paris Theater during the 1972 Cannes Film Festival. Still, the film was unable to secure a distribution deal. In 1973 Leone and Bava reshot portions of the film and added new scenes featuring Robert Alda as a psychologically tormented priest exorcising the possessed Elke Sommer in a hospital room. This re-edited film, now bearing the title *House of Exorcism*, was eventually released in the United States

FIGURE 1 A "cursed" film? Endlessly recut and repackaged, Mario Bava's *Lisa and the Devil* (1972) has over the years been regarded as a Cannes sensation, a knock-off of *The Exorcist*, fodder for late-night television, and a "lost masterpiece."

by independent distributor Peppercorn-Wormser in 1975 and grossed over $5 million through bookings in American drive-in theaters and inner-city grind houses specializing in lowbrow genre fare. The film also benefited from lucrative foreign sales in Great Britain, Europe, and the Far East.[1]

The two versions of this film and their respective commercial and critical fates offer fascinating insights into the relationship between popular culture, canons of taste, and the financing and distribution of 1970s exploitation cinema. The original cut of *Lisa and the Devil*—with its nonlinear narrative, painterly compositions, wild exaggerations of Italian horror film conventions, and dizzying allusions to religion, mythology, and art history—was considered "bad art" (or at least "bad product") by AIP's Samuel Arkoff and other purveyors of more conventional horror fare. Three years later, critics also tagged *House of Exorcism* with the label of "bad art," but now the film "failed" for being sensationalistic, morbid, pornographic, exploitative, and derivative of *The Exorcist* (1973). Here the film languished, shackled with its reputation as a "cursed film" or dismissed as a bomb by Maltin and other mainstream movie critics. Twenty years later, however, a lucrative and upscale demand for restored auteur cinema on laserdisc, videocassette, and (later) DVD would allow both versions of the film to circulate widely, contributing to a new appreciation for the influential stylistic innovations of director Mario Bava. The film's many incarnations illustrate an often-ignored reciprocal relationship between changing technologies of film distribution and the instability in genre and audience address in a popular cinema seeking to take advantage of those changes.

The Witch's Brew

The entire setting is so right for a tall tale of gloom and perdition. We could make it up as we go along. SOPHIA LEHAR IN *LISA AND THE DEVIL*

Lisa and the Devil is a wild mixture of the starkly original and the brazenly borrowed. The story begins with Lisa Reiner (Elke Sommer), a young tourist in Spain, transfixed in an antique shop by a music box depicting the medieval *danse macabre*. The box's buyer, Leandro (Telly Savalas) reminds her of an image of Satan carrying away the damned that she has just seen on a fresco painting. Leandro is carrying a life-size wax mannequin of a dark man with a mustache, and soon Lisa sees this man, Carlo (Espartaco Santoni) on the street, where he aggressively embraces her and calls her Elena. She knocks him to the ground and flees. As darkness falls, she asks for a ride out of town from an aloof and wealthy married couple, Francis and Sophia Lehar (Eduardo Fajardo and Sylva Koschina) and their chauffeur, George (Gabriele Tinti).

In one of the most shopworn clichés of the horror genre, the automobile breaks down, and the group goes to a secluded villa to use the telephone. Lisa is terrified to find the sinister Leandro welcoming them at the gate, and she discovers that he is the majordomo to a dying aristocratic family with (to put it mildly) a shameful family secret. The blind matriarch (Alida Valli) lords over her neurotic and emotionally arrested son Maximilian (Alessio Orano) in a plot element clearly lifted from *Psycho* (in fact, Bava and Leone had originally wanted Anthony Perkins for the role of Max).[2] Unbeknownst to the other characters, Carlo shows up and begins creeping around the mansion, apparently involved in some type of investigation.

Sophia turns out to be the lover of the much younger chauffeur George. Both the *contessa* and the soft-spoken but wild-eyed Max obsess over Lisa and keep comparing her to an unnamed "she." Lisa begins to lapse into hallucinations (to the strains of Rodrigo's *Concierto de Aranjuez*) in which she is the lover of Max, or Carlo, or both. Meanwhile, the butler Leandro is amassing a collection of wax dummies, each of which resembles a member of the family. Then, about halfway through the film, the characters begin to murder each other: George's throat is slit with a pair of garden shears; Sophia runs over her husband Francis half a dozen times with their car; Max bludgeons Sophia and Carlo to death and chloroforms Lisa, places her in bed next to the skeleton of "Elena," the woman whom she so closely resembles, and attempts to have sex with her unconscious body. It is only in the following scene, some fifteen minutes before the end of the film, that the family's elaborate backstory is revealed: The contessa had been married to Carlo, and Max had been married to Elena. Elena and Carlo fell in love and began an obsessive and forbidden relationship, and, it is implied, the impotent and enraged Maximilian killed his adulterous wife and kept her body in an upstairs bedroom. All of this is revealed in an incredibly long take in the family chapel as the camera arcs distractingly around Max, dressed as a groom, and the contessa, and back again. At the end of their confrontation, Max stabs his mother to death.

Now, the completely unhinged Max runs through the house and finds all of the corpses, including the skeleton of Elena in full bridal gown, arranged at the dinner table in a parody of the Last Supper (or of the danse macabre figures on the music box). Grave worms writhe about in the icing of the wedding cake. He attempts to flee the floating ghost of his mother, approaching him in what is obviously an invitation to join them in death, only to fall out of the window and impale himself on the metal gates below. The gliding ghost is revealed to be the contessa's perfectly dead corpse being carried into the dining room by an exhausted and distracted Leandro. The next morning, Lisa wakes up nude in the exposed ruins of what was once Elena's bedroom. Birds fly across the bed, and vines and branches are everywhere. She walks, mesmerized, through the overgrown chateau grounds and flees quickly to the airport to catch a plane home. Surprised that she is the plane's only passenger, Lisa walks through the cabin and finds the staring corpses of all of the family members seated together and Leandro piloting the plane. Her face takes on a cadaverous pallor, and she collapses dead.

Leonard Maltin and his colleagues could not have been more inaccurate in their description, much less their assessment, of *Lisa and the Devil*. There is no devil worshipping or exorcism anywhere in the film, and there is no wax dummy that resembles Lisa until five minutes before the end of the movie. Narratives of Satanism and devil worshipping proliferated in the horror film after the worldwide success of *Rosemary's Baby* in 1968, certainly, but *Lisa and the Devil* draws upon an entirely different set of generic norms. Specifically, Bava and Leone's script contains many elements of the Italian gothic cinema of the early 1960s—of which Mario Bava was the most accomplished practitioner— exaggerated almost to the point of parody. Like so many other Italian gothics, *Lisa and the Devil* uses female reincarnation as a structuring device. Through her descent into the hellish world of the contessa's family, Lisa discovers that she is the reincarnation of Elena. Bava himself treated this theme in his directorial debut, *La maschera del demonio* (*Black Sunday*) in 1960. In the earlier film, British actress Barbara Steele, the greatest star and central icon of 1960s Italian horror, plays both Asa the witch, burned at the stake during the Inquisition, and her nineteenth-century descendant, the virginal Princess Katya. Steele went on to play similar dual roles in 1960s Italian gothics, including *Amanti d'oltretomba* (*Nightmare Castle*, 1965).[3] A variation on this theme can be found in one of Bava's most distinctive mid-1960s works, *Operazione paura* (*Kill, Baby, Kill*, 1966), a vampire film in which Erika Blanc plays Monica, a young nurse who is initially presented as a damsel character and helper to the film's Van Helsing character, Dr. Eswai (Giacomo Rossi-Stuart). Eventually, all of the male characters recede into the background, and the viewer discovers Monica is the lost daughter of the bitter necromancer Baroness Graps, and sister to the resurrected vampire child responsible for all of the killings.

This theme of reincarnation in Italian horror is one of many elements obsessively focused on what Andrew Mangravite has called "a murderous past that stalks a present—'guilt-free' only by virtue of ignorance or willful omission—to extract payments of blood from it."[4] From this central core extends the Italian horror film's most infamous convention, a preoccupation with incest and necrophilia, usually painted in the hues of a delirious romanticism. The powers of family, Christianity, and heterosexual love, the three markers of a redemptive "normality" in conventional horror films from *Dracula* (1931) to *The Exorcist*, wither and warp under the onslaught of darker forces of the past in the Italian horror film. Riccardo Freda's *L'Orrible Segreto del Dr. Hichcock* (*The Horrible Dr. Hichcock*, 1963), for example, recounts the story of a bourgeois doctor who has sex with female cadavers in the morgue and drugs his wife to simulate death in their bedroom. After one of these sex games seemingly goes too far, the wife is buried and, years later, he returns to his mansion with a young bride (played by Barbara Steele). The original wife, buried alive by mistake, turns up to demand revenge.[5] In *Lisa and the Devil*, this confusion of the forces of Eros and Thanatos approaches the baroque.[6] Bava introduces this theme early in the film when the antique-shop owner tells Leandro that he has outfitted the wax mannequin of Carlo with a black tie because "it would be good for both weddings *and* funerals." By the end of the film, the drugged and nude Lisa shares a bed with the desiccated corpse of Elena and the still-alive but deranged Maximilian who, disrobing, says gently to the unconscious Lisa, "It will be different with you." As he attempts sex with the unconscious woman (once again to the strains of *Aranjuez*), Maximilian hears the haunting sounds of Elena's laughter and is unable to sustain an erection. In *I tre volti della paura* (*Black Sabbath*, 1963), the young Zdenya attempts to escape her undead father with a handsome young count. "Nobody can *love* you as much as we do. You know that," coos her father, the vampire patriarch Gorka (Boris Karloff). Maximilian's exchanges with his mother the contessa in *Lisa and the Devil* are similarly tinged with hints of incest, as she calls him "my love" and reacts with cold jealous fury to his halting expressions of attraction to Lisa after she arrives at the villa.

This bewildering proliferation of aberrant sexualities is also on display in Antonio Margheriti's *Danza Macabra* (*Castle of Blood*) from 1964. In this film, a journalist meets Edgar Allan Poe in a London pub and wagers with Poe's drinking companion that he can spend the night in a remote castle. In his one night in the castle, Alan, the journalist, meets the ghosts of all of the people who have died there, alive for this one night to ensnare Alan and increase their number. He sleeps with the beautiful but melancholic Elisabeth (Barbara Steele again), who is told by the bitter, icy lesbian ghost Julia that it is impossible that she "could ever find happiness with a man." The master of ceremonies in the haunted house is the ghost of metaphysician Dr. Kalmus, who shows an initially skeptical but increasingly terrified Alan the violent deaths of all who have come before him. In one scene, rape, lesbianism, adultery, and murder result in a bedroom strewn with corpses, laid out in various stages of undress in a gruesome and erotic tableau. At the end of the film, the ghost of Elisabeth helps Alan leave the house, but he is impaled on the closing iron gate just before dawn. Poe and his drinking companion arrive soon after and collect the gambling debt from the coat pocket of Alan's corpse. There is much in *Castle of Blood* that anticipates *Lisa and the Devil*—the isolated mansion with the family secrets and sexual taboos that are relived and which draw the visitor into their vortex; the necrophilic moment that Alan and Elisabeth cuddle in postcoital repose and he discovers that her heart is not beating; the narrative resolution of reuniting the heterosexual couple in death; and a climax in which the last living human runs from room to room only to find ghosts everywhere who summon him to the world of the dead. This last motif even carries over into the film's Italian title, "The Dance of Death," which is of course depicted on the music box that first draws Lisa into Leandro's nightmare world of the damned.

The danse macabre was a common motif in murals and European fresco paintings of the fourteenth and fifteenth centuries and is a recurring icon in the Italian horror film.[7] In this tableau, the figure of Death, usually personified as a skeleton, summons a group of humans to their fate in order of their earthly prominence.[8] One of the conventions used by the mural painters to suggest Death's sequential summoning of his victims was to alternate his skeletal form with that of the doomed humans, creating a long line of figures appearing as part of an elaborate dance. Many mural depictions of the *danse macabre*, such as the Cloister of the Innocents in Paris or the Hungerford Chapel in Salisbury Cathedral, also featured a narrative poem recounting each person's agony over attempts to refuse Death's invitation to the dance. In the Hungerford Chapel, for example, a youth attempts to run away, but Death points to the other bodies in the dance and says to the fashionably dressed young man, "Behold them well, consider and see / For such as they are, such shalt thou be"[9] (a couplet that could serve as the epigraph for a book on the Italian horror film). In 1463, in a chapel in Lübeck, Switzerland, a spectacular life-sized Dance of Death was painted on the walls and wrapped all the way around the chapel. In the background of the painting was a landscape panorama of Lübeck, against which the Dance depicts all strata of earthly society, from pope to beggar. The mural was restored in 1701

FIGURE 2 Locandina poster for *Danza Macabra* (1963).

after centuries of deterioration, only to be destroyed during Allied bombing in World War II.[10] A portion of the mural illustrates Death calling a usurer, curate, and a merchant, each identified by his costume and surroundings: the usurer is still carrying his abacus; the curate is dressed in the cassock and black circular-brimmed *capello romano* of the parish priest; and the merchant stands in front of ships ready to carry his goods to market.

Even before *Lisa and the Devil*, the danse macabre was a familiar iconic and narrative device in Italian horror. Bava's own *I tre volti della paura*, for example, features the members of a vampirized family coming to claim their remaining holdout, the virginal Zdenka. She begs with them to let her stay in the world of the living, but they are everywhere she turns and eventually claim her as one of their own; *Sei donne per l'assassino* (*Blood and Black Lace*, 1964) represents a variation of the theme as the female corpses of a serial killer are arranged in grotesque poses that mock the erotic vitality of living women; and *La frusta é il corpo* (*Whip and the Body*, 1963), with its narrative of a sadomasochistic relationship between a woman and her lover that continues beyond the grave, exemplifies the danse macabre's mythological sibling, Death and the Maiden.[11] An Italian/Belgian co-production from 1971, *La plus longue nuit du diable* (*Devil's Nightmare*), features a narrative strongly prescient of *Lisa and the Devil*, with a bald Satanic trickster, a demon succubus, a female lead named Lisa, and, in Phil Hardy's description, "the clichéd situation of the family curse and the travelers stranded in an aristocratic mansion with the folkloric theme of the seven deadly sins,"[12] with each of the seven travelers representing one of the deadly vices. A highlight of the film is a scene of the demon succubus (Erika Blanc) seductively goading the gluttonous coach driver to eat himself to death at an elaborate midnight banquet.

Like most of the narrative and stylistic elements in *Lisa and the Devil*, the film pushes these allegorical depictions of characters to more obvious and almost comical extremes. With its figures of Death, a king and queen, a bride, and a laborer, the music box featured at the film's opening explicitly references the Dance of Death. The parallels between these figures and the guests at the mansion are obvious: Francis and Sophia are the king and queen, Lisa is the bride, and George is the laborer. The bald and sinister Leandro, of course, is the film's compression of Death and Satan into a single character. This imagery of the music box bleeds over into the mise-en-scène throughout the film. As Leandro leads the visitors to the guest cottage, their reflection in the water as they cross the footbridge suggests the music box; Maximilian appears to float off of the music box and into Lisa's arms at the onset of one of her hallucinations; the makeshift funeral procession for the murdered George moves behind a screen in a parody of conventions of fresco painting (compare this also to the poster art for *Danza Macabra*); and the final camera track across the corpses at the dinner table suggests the spinning music box.

The stylized presentation of reincarnation, paraphilia, and mythological allusion helped establish the commercial success of the era's Italian horror films. Why, then, did *Lisa and the Devil* find no takers at the Cannes Film Festival, especially given the unqualified success of Leone and Bava's preceding film? The answer lies, I think, in the film's serious transgressions of audience expectation for horror films—specifically, a lack of narrative clarity and an indifference to dramatic suspense. AIP had produced and distributed horror/comedy hybrids before: *Bucket of Blood* (1960), *Tales of Terror* (1962), and *Comedy of Terrors* (1964) all had strong elements of low comedy and genre satire. The company's biggest star, Vincent Price, would be the lynchpin in AIP's crowning horror camp masterpiece, *The Abominable Dr. Phibes*, just a few months after Arkoff turned down *Lisa and the Devil*. Still, Bava and Leone were a full two or three years ahead of their time in introducing the high levels of camp, black humor, and art cinema leavened with graphic violence and sexual perversion into the horror genre without the commercial safety net of either a major horror star or a GP (later PG) rating. Putting even the hysterical Price to shame, Savalas's extraordinary turn as Leandro/Satan—sucking Tootsie Pops, singing songs to himself, telling jokes, and pretending to serve the needs of the helpless damned souls in the mansion with mock-solicitous seriousness—is an object study of a performance on the edge of self-parody. A line that never fails to rock a movie audience with laughter is his presentation of dessert cake to the contessa and her dinner guests while fussily whispering, "It's with chocolate sprinkles!"

In his landmark 1984 study of Bava's oeuvre, French critic Pascal Martinet refers to *Lisa and the Devil* as "Mario Bava's *Marienbad*."[13] Martinet writes of the film's proliferation of doubles and its subplot of Leandro's growing collection of wax dummies, "The genius of Bava in *La casa dell'esorcismo* [*Lisa and the Devil*] is visible in his consideration of mental illness, seen in every frame of the film, as a perfect understanding of the relationship of the spectator to the false image which is, of course, the basis of the art of the cinema."[14] Here we find a critic who, less than three years after Bava's death and, never having seen the original cut of *Lisa and the Devil*, has found the key to understanding the commercial failure of the film, namely, its general evocation of the conventions of European art cinema and its quite specific reworking of motifs from one of the most celebrated and difficult of the received masterworks of that cinema, Alain Resnais's *L'année dernière à Marienbad* (*Last Year at Marienbad*, 1961).

Last Year at Marienbad begins with a long series of tracking shots through the hallways of a lush French villa-turned-hotel as ominous organ music plays and we hear a male voiceover recount in a hypnotically repeated refrain, "I advanced once again through the corridors, salons, galleries, the structure of this mournful mansion from another age, this huge and luxurious mansion, where corridors without end follow upon corridors." The narrative, such as it is, concerns a stranger, X (Giorgio Albertazzi), who becomes entranced by a woman, A (Delphine Seyrig), married to the gaunt and sinister M, her escort or husband (Sascha Pitoëff), and X's efforts to remember if he and the woman know each other, perhaps from a previous sexual affair, perhaps from last year, perhaps in Marienbad. The character of M, like Leandro in *Lisa and the Devil*, is a sinister trickster figure who is a master of games and illusions, and X is unable to beat him in a number of parlor games over which M has an almost supernatural mastery. The confusion of the characters about their own backstory is doubled in the Fredericksburg garden, where the characters of X and A argue about the story behind the statues there. While the camera moves around its interchangeable human and stone subjects, we hear the voice of the man say, "You asked me their names. I said their names didn't matter. You disagreed and proceeded to name them at random, I think. Then I said they could as well be you and I or anyone." The actors, particularly Delphine Seyrig, exhibit an almost dancelike stylization in their movements through the decor, and Seyrig's distracted, vacant-eyed performance as she is circulated between the two male leads could be a template for Elke Sommer's performance in the last half of *Lisa and the Devil*.[15] *Marienbad*, of course, would have a lasting impact on European and American art cinema. Just a year after its release, American producer Robert Lippert would use a similar pretext of alienated characters in an isolated environment in his nightmarish remake of one of the classics of expressionist fantasy cinema, *Cabinet of Caligari* (1962). Clearly indebted to the commercially viable motifs, themes, and mythology of Italian horror in the previous decade, *Lisa and the Devil*'s ambitious attempt to translate this material into the emerging aesthetics of camp and art cinema doomed the film to failure—at least in the eyes of distributors looking for more sensationalistic genre fare.

From "Cursed Film" to Eurotrash to Lost Masterpiece

The people of this region believe that it is only the power of the Devil himself that has kept this entire fresco from ruin. TOUR GUIDE IN *HOUSE OF EXORCISM*

The curious fate of *Lisa and the Devil*'s unusual art-horror hybridity was as much a result of changing taste in the world film market as it was of Mario

Bava's peculiar artistic sensibilities. As producer, Leone's engagement of this changing marketplace had a major impact on the film's commercial and critical destiny. When the first Bava/Leone collaboration, *Baron Blood*, was completed in 1971, Leone screened the film for buyers at Allied Artists, hoping to secure a distribution deal. Allied Artists had its origins in the Poverty Row studio Monogram, which had been successful in the 1940s supplying supporting titles for the bottom half of double features. After becoming Allied Artists in 1953, company head Steve Broidy attempted several times to enter the production of prestige A-film releases. Even with this change of corporate strategy, however, much of the company's success during this period—and into the 1960s—depended on providing programmers for the genre market.[16] By 1971, the company had finally positioned itself to produce a string of prestige attractions, including *Cabaret* (1972), *Papillon* (1973), *The Man Who Would Be King* (1975), and *Conduct Unbecoming* (1975). For this new corporate philosophy, *Baron Blood* presented a step backward in the company's quest to improve its reputation and status.

Baron Blood eventually did find a home at American International Pictures, the most successful provider of exploitation and genre films to the world market, where it proved to be a sizeable hit for its distributor. Perhaps regretting the earlier decision to pass on such a bankable film (even if it was from a "low" genre), Allied Artists expressed an interest in securing Leone and Bava's next project, *Lisa and the Devil*. Andy Jaeger of AA's television distribution arm was particularly interested in the film and persuaded Leone to shoot network-friendly cover shots for the expected scenes of nudity and graphic violence. Meanwhile, AIP's Sam Arkoff also wanted Leone and Bava's follow-up to the successful *Baron Blood*, offering Leone $250,000 upfront for distribution rights to the as-yet-unseen *Lisa and the Devil*. Hoping to recoup more of his million-dollar investment in the film, however, Leone held out for $300,000. Arkoff had breakfast with Leone at Cannes the morning of the film's premiere at the Paris Theater and again offered Leone the quarter-million-dollar check. "Al, don't be a fool. Take the check," Arkoff said. "You never know what happens with a movie."[17] That night, Arkoff attended *Lisa and the Devil*'s premiere and then promptly withdrew his offer. "The horror film audience doesn't like camp," he told Leone. "You can't toy with that. They're very serious." Ironically, in less than a year, Leone had moved from one potential distributor, Allied Artists, which passed on *Baron Blood* because it was a mere horror film and a troubled fit in their increasingly upscale release schedule, to another, American International, which turned down *Lisa and the Devil* because it was too arty, obscure, and campy. One international buyer offered Leone a pittance for Far East rights to the film, but Leone turned him down as well.

For about a year, *Lisa and the Devil* sat on the shelf while Leone tried to put together other projects. Of course, the film's million dollars of red ink on the ledger was an extraordinary burden for an independent producer to accommodate, and so Leone eventually returned to the problem picture in an attempt to translate this sizeable investment into a more saleable commodity. The most promising solution for Leone was to add new footage that could reframe the story while providing more commercially exploitable story elements for the film's promotion campaign. As both Tim Lucas and Troy Howarth have detailed elsewhere, Bava, Leone, and actress Elke Sommer spent three and a half weeks reshooting a new subplot to the film featuring Lisa's demonic possession at the base of the fresco depicting Satan. This also involved adding Robert Alda as Father Michael, a priest haunted by memories of his lover Anna (Carmen Silva), who had perished in a car accident. Father Michael consults with hospital doctors about Lisa's condition and eventually performs an exorcism in the hospital room.

To this day, Leone is unsparing in his praise for the artistic integrity of director Bava and his willingness to work for free on shooting the new scenes. Still, Bava could not imagine how this new footage, redolent of motifs from *The Exorcist*, could be successfully integrated into the existing version of *Lisa and the Devil* and was afraid that the cobbled-together film would be an embarrassment to all of the filmmakers. He eventually walked off of the set and asked that his name be removed from the credits. Leone, working with editor Carlo Reali, successfully solved the technical and narrative problems through a clever crosscutting between scenes of the exorcism and the backstory at the villa, which now recounted the story of the ghost who was possessing Lisa. Transitions were indicated through an elegant use of sound bridges and rhyming match cuts between the old and new footage.

With an answer print of this newly recut movie in hand, Leone was once again contacted by Andy Jaeger at Allied Artists and offered a television deal for the original cut of *Lisa and the Devil*. Jaeger offered Leone an advance of $150,000 for the television rights on the original *Lisa and the Devil*, which Leone eagerly accepted in order to, in his words, "take the edge off" of the money that he had spent on producing two versions of the film. In addition to the television rights for the original version of *Lisa and the Devil*, the contract also gave Allied Artists a lien on the "new" version, *House of Exorcism*, until *Lisa* was in active television distribution and their debt was paid.

This turned out to be a devil's bargain. Leone began screening *House of Exorcism* for potential distributors in 1974 and 1975, and Universal, which had enjoyed blockbuster success with *Jaws* (1974), was ready to offer Leone a deal for the film. To protect their original investment in *Lisa and the Devil*, Allied Artists began to spread word throughout the industry of their lien on *House of Exorcism*. A skittish Universal withdrew its offer. Word of Allied Artists' potential legal action against other distributors over *House of Exorcism* also destroyed possible deals with both AIP and Paramount. In the midst of this turmoil, Leone received a call from Andy Jaeger at Allied Artists with the welcome news that *Lisa and the Devil* was to be part of a feature-film package for prime-time network broadcast on ABC. Other films in the package included *Cabaret*, *Papillon*, and *The Man Who Would Be King*. This would have cleared Leone's debt to Allied Artists and allowed him to shop *House of Exorcism* to other distributors without further interference. But in the end, the producers of *Papillon* exercised their option for a better deal and took the movie to CBS. Without *Papillon* as the crown jewel of the ABC feature package, the deal collapsed and Leone was out in the cold yet again.

Leone then secured a $300,000 offer for *House of Exorcism* (the identical sum he had demanded from Sam Arkoff three years before) from independent distributor Peppercorn-Wormser. Since 1965, Peppercorn-Wormser had successfully distributed an eclectic mix of art-house entries and exploitation films from Europe and the United Kingdom, including Welles's *Chimes at Midnight* (1965), Wertmuller's *Love and Anarchy* (1973), the Italian-French farce *Le Sex Shop* (1973), and the Hong Kong women-in-prison melodrama *Bamboo House of Dolls* (1974). This skill for tapping high and low markets made them well-suited to handle *House of Exorcism*. Once again, however, Allied Artists stepped in to inform Peppercorn-Wormser that Leone did not own the rights to the film because of his outstanding debt.[18] Eventually, Leone watched from the sidelines as Allied Artists, Peppercorn-Wormser, and independent investor Gus Bern negotiated a deal among themselves for theatrical distribution of *House of Exorcism*. The film finally reached the screen in 1976 and was a significant commercial success. *House of Exorcism* was profitably slotted into what the trade called "underbelly runs," playing as a supporting title in drive-ins and inner-city grind houses alongside kung-fu films, blaxploitation pictures, and midnight horror screenings. *Variety* did not even bother to review the film, nor did any other trade or popular publication take notice of its release. Released in this context, the film was simply another example of "Eurotrash"—inexpensively mounted genre pictures, usually co-productions between two or more European studios featuring down-at-the-heels American players in roles designed to capitalize on hits from Hollywood's major studios.[19]

To add to the confusion, even as *House of Exorcism* finally found theatrical distribution, another version of the original and still unreleased *Lisa and the Devil* began to circulate. Allied Artists struck a number of 16mm television prints of the film, but instead of going to the lab and inserting Leone and Bava's original cover shots for the scenes of nudity and violence, these television prints either cut the material out entirely or substituted "slugs" in the place of the offending images. These slugs were then covered by stills or reaction shots of characters from elsewhere in the film. Allied Artists then placed this "prostituted version" (in Leone's phrase) into syndication for local late-night television, the broadcast equivalent of the grind house and drive-in circuits. Once a highly anticipated property with multiple suitors, *Lisa and the Devil* would remain unseen—at least in its original cut—for the next two decades, Italian horror's contribution to the cinematic lore of the tortured and lost masterpiece.

Conclusion

During the 1970s, Leone's and Bava's artistically ambitious *Lisa and the Devil* mutated from its premiere at Cannes into two highly compromised versions— the reedited *House of Exorcism* and the mangled print syndicated by Allied Artists television. But even this was not to be the end of the film's complicated and seemingly endless engagements with a changing terrain of taste and exhibition. As the growth of videocassette, laserdisc, and DVD formats during the 1980s and 1990s created new and voracious niche markets for home distribution, genres, films, and directors once known only to buffs and cognoscenti found new life. Mario Bava's work, particularly in the Italian gothic, became a focus of renewed critical and popular attention. By the mid-1980s, book-length studies of Bava and other Euro-horror auteurs began to appear in France, Italy, and Benelux. Eventually, a younger group of American critics began to echo the missionary zeal of the 1950s *Cahiers du cinéma*, actively championing the cinematic "art" of such previously invisible and/or disreputable filmmakers as Bava, Jess Franco, Antonio Margheriti, and others.[20] Drawing on the *Cahiers* model of auteurist analysis of styles and themes for a decidedly nonacademic readership, this new generation of criticism appeared in magazines such as *Photon*, *Cinéfantastique*, and, later, *Video Watchdog*. At the same time, cult, camp, ultraviolence, porn, "bad" movies (such as those of Edward D. Wood Jr., whose films achieved major cult status as a result of home video) exploded in popularity and continued to shift canons of taste in the omnivorous video market.[21] By the mid-1990s, the Internet provided an even more extensive resource for buying, selling, discussing, and creating shrines to films and filmmakers on the margins of taste, style, and politics.

This critical reappraisal of the artistry of filmmakers working in lowbrow genre forms is, among other things, an epiphenomenon of changing technologies of film distribution and exhibition. Almost every change in film distribution is followed by a temporary shortage in product, and the attempt to meet the increased demand for movies often results in a confounding of commercial categories. This is apparent in the postwar rise in the art theater, in which exhibitors forced into showcasing imported and other films from small distributors deliberately cross-marketed auteur cinema with exploitation films; the perpetually underserved drive-in theater market of the fifties, which AIP and other companies mined as a market for its preconstituted double features; the rise of television as a lucrative subsequent-run market for movies, in which both local syndication and network runs of feature films led to a similar mix of high and low forms in the same exhibition context; the rise of home video on Betamax and VHS in the 1980s, which resurrected obscure and forgotten films and filmmakers to feed the insatiable maw of a rental-driven retail business; and, finally laserdisc and DVD, which sought to carve out a more "upscale" niche of home video by showcasing a more exacting presentation of films often enhanced by restored or never-before-seen cuts of films long available in other incarnations.[22]

Lisa and the Devil played a part in many of these later changes. It premiered at a film festival as a prestige item, but was unable to straddle the art-cinema and exploitation markets. Then, it was reshot and reconstituted for the drive-in and grind house market, the most desperate and undiscriminating venue of its day, by a distributor of both Lina Wertmuller movies and Asian women-in-prison flicks. Next, it found unlikely sisters such as *Cabaret* and *Papillon* in a network television package during the height of the early 1970s sellers' market for movies before the made-for-television film stabilized the role of feature films in network programming. It turned up on the first home grind house, late-night syndicated television, in the "prostituted" Allied Artists cut. Then, the second home grind house, videotape, rescued from critical dismissal the entire filmmaking tradition from which *Lisa and the Devil* emerged. Responding to this new market and critical environment, the long-lost and long-suffering original cut of *Lisa and the Devil* finally appeared in restored form in 1995 (Leone had kept the extant 35mm prints and original sound/picture elements for some twenty years). Image Entertainment released the film on a two-disc set with *Baron Blood* (after what must have seemed to Leone like an interminable twenty-year distribution deal with AIP finally came to an end). Then, in 2000, Image released a single-disc double feature of *Lisa and the Devil* and *House of Exorcism* with audio commentary by producer Leone and star Elke Sommer. Now, the two films could finally be seen as what they in fact were, a diptych of two separate works of art. Once divided by the demands of art and commerce in the 1970s film market, the two films were reunited on disc in 2000 as a case study available for historical, critical, artistic, and commercial reappraisal by a new generation of gothic cinephiles. The 2003 review of *Lisa and the Devil* in *Leonard Maltin's Movie and Video Guide* provides a final testament to the film's extremely unstable identity over the past thirty years. Dismissed by Maltin's guide only a decade ago as a "BOMB," *Lisa and the Devil* now rates two and one-half stars, its "incoherent witches' brew" now described as a "truly strange, surreal psychological horror tale filled with hallucinatory imagery."[23]

Notes

1. For a detailed history of the production, Cannes premiere, reshooting, release, and restoration of *Lisa and the Devil*, see Tim Lucas's indispensable critical biography, *Mario Bava: All the Colors of the Dark* (Cincinnati: Video Watchdog, 2007). See also Troy Howarth, *The Haunted World of Mario Bava* (London: FAB, 2001), and Alfredo Leone's audio commentary on Image Entertainment's 2000 DVD release of *Lisa and the Devil* and *House of Exorcism*.
2. Leone's audio commentary on the DVD edition of both films provides a wealth of detail about the casting and art design of *Lisa and the Devil*. The filmmakers had also wanted Burt Lancaster for the role of the adulterous Carlo, which would have expanded the film's web of allusions to include Visconti's *Il Gattopardo* (*The Leopard*, 1963).
3. A rhapsodic consideration of Steele's iconic status in Italian horror is Alan Upchurch, *Barbara Steele, an Angel for Satan*, in the Horror Pictures series (Cahors: G. Noël Fanéditions, 1991). A shorter version appears as "The Dark Queen," *Film Comment* 29, no. 1 (1993): 53.
4. Andrew Mangravite, "Once upon a Time in the Crypt," *Film Comment* 29, no. 1 (1993): 51.
5. *L'Orrible Segreto del Dr. Hichcock*, along with many of the other early 1960s horror films discussed in this essay, was written by screenwriter Ernesto Gastaldi. The prolific Gastaldi, whose screen credits are often hidden by a number of pseudonyms, was responsible for over one hundred movies in the peplum, horror, science-fiction, spaghetti western, giallo, and crime genres from the 1960s to the 1990s and was an uncredited contributor to the script of Sergio Leone's *Once upon a Time in America* (1984). His key role in the history of Italian cinema has yet to be fully documented or appreciated, although, in classic Italian fashion, Gastaldi himself attempted this task in his autobiography, *Voglio entrare nel cinema: Storia di uno che ce l'ha fatto* (Milan: A. Mondanori, 1991).
6. A year after *Lisa and the Devil*, producer Andrew Braunsberg unleashed a film that would seize the camp humor, necrophilia, and incest crowns for all time, the Paul Morrissey- and Antonio Margheriti–directed *Flesh for Frankenstein*, which features a protracted and explicit scene of necrophilia between the Baron Frankenstein (Udo Kier) and his eviscerated and completely nude female creation (Dalia di Lazzaro) in widescreen and 3-D, no less. The film was shot by Mario Bava's cinematographer, Ubaldo Terzano.
7. For an introduction to and historical survey of the danse macabre in the visual and literary arts, see James M. Clark, *The Dance of Death in the Middle Ages and Renaissance* (Glasgow: Jackson, Son, and Company, 1950); Sarah Webster Goodwin, *Kitsch and Culture: The Dance of Death in Nineteenth-Century Literature and Graphic Arts* (New York:

Garland and Company, 1988); and Jean Wirth, *La jeune fille et la morte: Recherches sur les thèmes macabres dans l'art germanique de la Renaissance* (Geneva: Librairie Droz, 1979), 20–28.

8. Clark, *The Dance of Death*, 1.
9. Ibid., 11–12.
10. A remarkably detailed Web site about the Lübeck *Totentanz* that recounts its history and provides photographs of the entire mural can be found at www.dodedans.com/Eindex.htm.
11. For a discussion of the relationship between the myths of Death and the Maiden and the danse macabre and their common ancestors in classical mythology, see Wirth, *La jeune fille et la morte*.
12. Phil Hardy, ed., *The Overlook Film Encyclopedia: Horror* (Woodstock, New York: Overlook Press, 1995), 240.
13. Pascal Martinet, *Mario Bava: Filmo n. 6* (Paris: Edilig, 1984), 35.
14. Ibid., 36. This and other translations from French and Italian are my own.
15. Although *Last Year at Marienbad*, along with Fellini's *8 1/2*, became a sort of watershed film for intellectuals with a passion for film who never went to "the movies," the film bristles with references to pop culture and genre cinema, from Seyrig's Theda Bara–like costumes in some of the fantasy flashbacks to a matted-in cameo by Alfred Hitchcock ten and a half minutes into the film. This aspect of Resnais's film has never received the attention that it warrants.
16. A discussion of Allied Artists' role in 1950s genre cinema against the background of its attempt to enter A-film production can be found in Kevin Heffernan, *Ghouls, Gimmicks, and Gold: Horror Films and the American Movie Business, 1952–1968* (Durham, N.C.: Duke University Press, 2004).
17. This following detailed recounting of the distribution problems of *Lisa and the Devil* and *House of Exorcism* was provided by Alfredo Leone in a September 2003 interview with the author.
18. Later, Leone discovered that Allied Artists had sold *Lisa and the Devil* for a tax shelter for $90,000. Throughout all of his attempts to pay his debt and secure distribution for *House of Exorcism*, Leone was never told that his debt had therefore been reduced to only $60,000 plus interest.
19. Two of the most infamous of these Eurotrash knockoffs, the *Exorcist* clone *Beyond the Door* (1974) and the *Jaws*-inspired pastiche *Great White* (1980), were actually successfully enjoined by the Hollywood studios whose properties they slavishly imitated. A year later, Woody Allen's 1977 Academy Award–winning comedy *Annie Hall* featured a middle third that is a nonstop assault on the witlessness, cultural sterility, banality, and insanity of Los Angeles. Featured prominently in one of Allen's travelogue sequences of this cultural wasteland is a movie marquee advertising a double feature of *Messiah of Evil* and *House of Exorcism*.

20. An extensive bibliography of this writing can be found in Stefano Poselli and Riccardo Morrocchi, eds., *Horror all'italiana, 1957–1979* (Florence: Glittering Images, 1996), 168–71.
21. Two of the most well-considered historical and cultural accounts of this phenomenon can be found in Jeffrey Sconce, "'Trashing' the Academy: Taste, Excess, and an Emerging Politics of Cinematic Style," *Screen* 36 (1995): 371–93, and Joan Hawkins, *Cutting Edge: Art-Horror and the Horrific Avant-Garde* (Minneapolis: University of Minnesota Press, 2000).
22. See Heffernan, *Ghouls, Gimmicks, and Gold*, for a detailed account of many of these changes.
23. Leonard Maltin, ed. *Leonard Maltin's 2003 Movie and Video Guide* (New York: Plume, 2003), 806.

2
Sleazy Afterlives

KAY DICKINSON

Troubling Synthesis The Horrific Sights and Incompatible Sounds of Video Nasties

> False clarity is only another name for myth; and myth has always been obscure and enlightening at one and the same time: always using the devices of familiarity and straightforward dismissal to avoid the labour of conceptualization. THEODOR ADORNO AND MAX HORKHEIMER

> I approve of any form of scepticism to which I can reply, "Let's try it!" But I want to hear nothing more about all the things and questions that don't admit of experiment. This is the limit of my "sense of truth"; for there, courage has lost its right. FRIEDRICH NIETZSCHE

Italian horror, particularly the schlocky, confusing, unrelenting, bizarre, and graphic strain that spans the late 1970s and the early 1980s, has had its fair share of academic attention. However, almost all of these writers have huddled around what they understand to be a preoccupation with imagery in these movies. Leon Hunt, for example, informs us that the 1987 Dario Argento movie "*Terror at the Opera* presents an entire film devoted almost exclusively to issues of visibility, spectatorship and horror."[1] Geoffrey Nowell-Smith makes a similar claim about that director's work: "The imaginary breaks free from narrative and Argento allows vision to take priority, in a kaleidoscope of glowing images which reflect an original poetry of the horrific."[2]

However, these films are more than elaborate spectacles; the

FIGURE 1 Cover art for the U.K. video release of *Cannibal Holocaust* before its ban under the 1984 Video Recordings Act.

bewilderment and shock they engender are partially generated by their equally startling soundtracks. The specimens splayed on this essay's dissection table—*Cannibal Holocaust* (dir. Ruggero Deodato, 1979), *Inferno* (dir. Dario Argento, 1980), *Cannibal Ferox* (dir. Umberto Lenzi, 1981), *The Beyond* (dir. Lucio Fulci, 1981) and *Tenebrae* (dir. Argento, 1982)—all share two things. They overlay a barrage of unflinchingly violent imagery with often smooth, mellifluous synthesizer scoring. And, perhaps partially as a consequence, they were all banned in the United Kingdom under the 1984 Video Recordings Act, making them, in colloquial terms, "video nasties."[3] What marks these movies—what may in fact have contributed to their illegal status within the United Kingdom—is their soundtracks' refusal to condemn or morally justify the images and ideas they are accompanying.

Yet we—as scholars—are historically lacking a framework within which to scrutinize this disjunction between soundtrack and its cinematic carrier. Film music analysts have seemed drawn, for the most part, to interactions where the soundtrack and the moving image appear somehow to move to compatible rhythms. Whether these writers find their niche in the realms of industrial synergy or "suitable" orchestral scoring, their theoretical touchstones have usually been hewn out of a belief in the superiority of moments of uncomplicated union between music, visual imagery, and narrative agenda. Surprisingly, considering these researchers' love of the aural, there is a certain tendency to cast music as a mere support system for supposedly more central diegetic priorities, perhaps because, in the classical Hollywood Fordist-Taylorist model, the score is created in postproduction (although this is by no means an all-encompassing way of building up a movie).[4] The specially written score that refuses to reiterate a closely empathetic message about the film's action is still wildly under-researched.[5]

What often gets left by the wayside in traditional soundtrack analysis is the fact that music and film are communication systems obeying grammars, syntaxes, and vocabularies that are often completely alien to one another. Many of the compositional traditions of music predate the arrival of cinema, and music's physical makeup (which is primarily sonic, while most movies create an audiovisual balance) occludes nearly all suppositions that music qua music and film share a substantial amount of core properties. There are parallels to be drawn between musical expression and how, for example, cinematographic information is delivered, or emotion is achieved through narrative—*aims* may be shared—but the languages themselves are different, and less reconcilable than most writers admit. Following this line of thinking, there arises a sense of distance, of things perhaps being untranslatable, and of both music and film constantly making declarations that the other could never entirely comprehend. This opens up the potential for understanding music as more than a slave to the narrative; indeed, its very divergence from filmic enunciation makes such an arrangement difficult to shunt into place. So, with two (at the very least) articulate and educated voices speaking at once, it is entirely possible that the semantics of the composite object might be jumbled and clashing, might tell us contradictory stories, might provoke a strange form of ambivalence.

The political potential of such a state—which will assume a central structural position in this chapter—is thoroughly acknowledged in Zygmunt Bauman's book *Modernity and Ambivalence*. Bauman argues that ambivalence creates fault lines in the smooth and ordered domain of language. These, in turn, produce a type of instability and cultural anxiety aroused by a lack of taxonomic control—a condition anathema to the post-Enlightenment world, where we struggle to rid ourselves of such confusion. For Bauman, "Though born of the naming/classifying urge, ambivalence may be fought only with a naming that is yet more exact, and classes that are yet more precisely defined."[6] What ambivalence apparently compels us to do is either systematically expand the language system or, more worryingly, to deny the ambivalence (either by destroying its physical manifestations, or by dismissing its conceptual power). In the case of the five films considered in this chapter (and many more like them), outright prohibition through governmental intervention was the culminating action against the ambivalence presented by these movies.

All five amalgamate principles and practices that just don't fit together, that sabotage a neat concluding interpretation, and that often prompt this sort of ambivalence in their audience. As Maitland McDonagh claims of Argento's oeuvre,

> Obtuse meaning is obtuse precisely because it lies outside of whatever system the reader has adopted in order to make sense of a particular work; it seems unnecessary, excessive. Your mind rebels: the material doesn't fit, doesn't make sense . . . Barthes' radical proposal [to be found in *The Third Meaning*] is that the excess, all the meaning that falls outside the system or systems that determine the work's overall structure, forms its *own* system, one which may exist parallel or tangentially to the others.[7]

While McDonagh and I are plowing up similar terrain here, I wish to distinguish my furrow from hers. First, she immediately identifies the apparent linguistic mish-mash as "outside the system." In contradiction to this, my argument lingers very much "within the system," seeking to comprehend why seemingly acceptable signifying practices become troublesome when they are locked onto other, perhaps even more benign ones. It is mainly in their off-kilter combination of various normally condoned ideas that these films become threatening. The force of these juxtapositions should be measured not through analyzing their various formal components in isolation, or by building them a special avant-garde sphere all their own, but by endeavoring to understand how they destabilize or reconfigure current, more typical (some might say "mainstream") modes of film experience (and a more necessarily restricted definition of this vast field—one which relates to these particular movies—will be put forward presently). Consequently, this essay is less concerned with seeing or hearing the impossible;[8] instead it favors a contemplation of how everyday languages that have been deemed incompatible, for some reason, might be yoked together.

This understanding of ambivalence parts company with similar strategies for the proliferation of meaning (ideas such as polysemy and aporia) in its distinct sense of opposites existing together. Labeling and classification still hold court and rule out any more diffused hermeneutic possibilities. *Ambi-* after all, means *both*, each factor remaining to some extent discrete, pointing out (or propping up) an old order—the choice of action being paramount here. This is not a confusion or—more usually—a creation of something *unheimlich*, but a vacillation between coherent entities. The familiarity of the space in which this locking of horns occurs is something Bauman[9] wishes us to examine closely: "The typically modern practice, the substance of modern politics, of modern intellect, of modern life, is the effort to exterminate ambivalence: an effort to define precisely—and to suppress or eliminate everything that could not or would not be precisely defined. Modern practice is not aimed at the conquest of foreign lands, but at the filling of the blank spots in the *compleat mappa mundi*. It is the modern practice, not nature, that truly suffers no void."[10] Theodor Adorno and Max Horkheimer make a similar observation about our inability to deal with the ambiguous: "The mythic terror feared by the Enlightenment accords with myth. Enlightenment discerns it not merely in unclarified concepts and words, as demonstrated by semantic language-criticism, but in any human assertion that has no place in the ultimate context of self-preservation."[11] Rationality, comprehensibility, and clarity are, these thinkers argue, politically invested and controlled, and I would contend that the hegemonic alignment of all sorts of ideas under the banner of "logic" can be extremely damaging to our perception of the world. One such enforced rallying often occurs at the point at which a film meets its soundtrack. The music within my five chosen films largely refuses to muster in this locale, creating, through its sense of rebellion, an ambivalence within the minds of the films' audiences.

But there are still more ambivalences at work here. Perhaps the most rewarding (or troubling) characteristic of these films is their confusion of fact and fiction, realism and fantasy—distinctions that often support extremely delicate political propositions within the generic domain of the horror film. This determination to tamper with semantic opposition (which is so much the darling of the defenders of these films) creates an intellectual commentary on the role of the horror movie and its constriction within contemporary society.

Of note here is their country of origin, Italy, a place where the bewitchment by and interrogation of the codes of representational realism have been consistent philosophical threads leading from the development of Renaissance perspective through to neorealism, the work of Pier Paolo Pasolini and Mondo documentaries. These more recent cinematic engagements have definitely informed the so-called video nasties. For instance, Deodato (*Cannibal Holocaust*'s director) once worked as an assistant producer for neorealist figurehead Roberto Rossellini. The delight with which *Cannibal Holocaust* and *Cannibal Ferox* concoct lurid fantasies about the non-Western world is not only a commentary on Mondo movies, but also a continuation of the cinematic discussion of how to depict violence and torture that sees Pasolini's *Saló* (1975), itself a film with a long history of prohibition, as a precedent.

These movies extend their deconstructive eagerness into their plotlines as well. *Cannibal Holocaust* follows an NYU research team into the Amazon basin to watch them make a documentary film. They fabricate all manner of horrific events in order to sensationalize not only the film they are making, but also the one we are watching.[12] Similarly self-aware qualities infuse *Cannibal Ferox*, whose protagonist, Gloria, is a doctoral candidate at Brown University intent on wielding what would now be called postcolonial theory to disprove the existence of cannibalism. *Tenebrae* is the story of a crime fiction writer embroiled in murderous situations that seem inspired by his own books. All three of these films assemble a myriad of self-reflexive plot devices and formal witticisms that alert us to how the media manipulate realism. This ranges from *Cannibal Holocaust*'s jokey intertitle "For the sake of authenticity, some scenes have been retained in their entirety" to Deodato's contextualization of his film within a larger media environment: "At the time on television we were always seeing death scenes, they were the years of terrorism and my film was also a condemnation of a certain type of journalism."[13]

Yet, despite this dabbling with the rules and power of realism (perhaps one of the key factors that got these films into such trouble), all of these texts simultaneously delight in their artificiality. *The Beyond*, *Tenebrae*, and *Inferno*, in particular, are awash with irrational, mystifying plot lines; their gore has more in common with spilled ice cream splurted with ketchup than the inner workings of an actual human being. We are to marvel at the aesthetics of these mock-ups, more than we are to "believe in them." Argento's work especially is very much in dialogue with the worlds of fashion, interior design, architecture and (interestingly for a study of music) opera—realms where mutilation and murder are rendered with greater abstraction and where art is less frequently asked to "justify" itself in the way that horror cinema is. This rendition of fantastical and almost ornamental violence does not sit well within the popular and distinctly more literal understanding of cinematic storytelling. In order for the assumptions about the depravity of these films held by the anti-nasties lobbyists to stand firm and for greater numbers of troops to be gathered under their cause, particularly bland, unquestioning ideas about realism were projected onto these movies. Experiencing them on a surface value of what can be seen (but not how and why it is shown) supposedly elicits facile revulsion, identification, and the dread fear of copy-cat behavior erupting out of society's most gullible and vulnerable viewers—or so the tabloids would lead us to believe.[14] Intriguingly, although the soundtracks to these films are often distracting and might knock any confused audience members out of such a detrimental engrossment, the messages their music relays are so wildly removed from the moral agenda of representational realism that the films seem even more abhorrent to those loyal to this aesthetic alone. But to fully comprehend what these soundtracks might be saying, we first need a thorough analysis of what the synthesizer means culturally.

Electronic scoring has a long legacy within films that deal with the unearthly, nonhuman, and supernatural, including Louis and Bebe Barron's entirely electronic compositions for *Forbidden Planet* (dir. Fred M. Wilcox, 1956) and the common usage of the theramin in other sci-fi films of the 1950s. Jeffrey Sconce points out the physical similarity between the theramin's electronic sensors and the antennae that ubiquitously graced the heads of Martians as they were depicted in popular culture of the time. Sconce then traces out how a symbolic allegiance between the two was suggested through their inseparability in contemporary representation: "What antennae ultimately came to stand for in postwar science fiction was the absence of 'humanity'.... Their mission on earth, often executed to the eerie tones of the theremin, was to wholly permeate, slowly occupy, and eventually conquer all of humanity."[15] These film music ancestors, then, proposed a way of thinking about electronic instrumentation that continued into the Italian horror films of the 1980s.

More specifically, synthesizers proper have occupied a position within movies of a more overtly aggressive persuasion since Wendy Carlos's work on *A Clockwork Orange* (dir. Stanley Kubrick, 1971). Throughout the film, we are encouraged to read the instrument as an overtly cold and distancing technology, one expressive of disenfranchisement and even a breakdown of traditional morality—an insinuation that becomes all the more upsetting when Beethoven's extremely emotional and tumultuous orchestral compositions are given the chillingly precise and staid synthesizer treatment. This sense of inappropriate detachment—which mirrors the film protagonist Alex's initial responses to his own actions—is heightened by a startlingly ironic deployment of familiar upbeat music (such as "Singin' in the Rain") during scenes of carnage, a technique that does much to usher into hermeneutic play, by association, this dialectical use of the synthesizer. A related sense of occasional disconnection (albeit more to create a congruent atmosphere of narrative disquiet) is conveyed in the synthesizer scores of other horror flicks such as *The Exorcist* (dir. William Friedkin, 1973), where we hear Mike Oldfield's delicate "Tubular Bells," and the films of John Carpenter, which the director himself scored—American examples that, somehow or other, managed not to get too heavily caught up in the Video Recordings Act furor.[16]

Although the choice of using synthesizers in these films is frequently dismissed as "the cheap option,"[17] this was not really the case. During this particular period, synthesizers were expensive and rather incomprehensible; it took a committed composer with the requisite skills and, usually, an investment in the semantics of the machine to bring about such a score. Also, most of these soundtracks amalgamated more traditional instrumentation—the kind that not only cost money but also demanded a certain compositional aptitude. To label such scores the outcome of corner cutting or bad musicianship (the work of people who did not know how to put together a "proper" horror score) undermines the ingenuity embodied in the sounds of these films and ignores the

FIGURE 2 Scored by Wendy Carlos, Stanley Kubrick's *A Clockwork Orange* (1971) employed the synthesizer to help create its dystopic vision of distance and detachment, an effect made especially profound in Carlos's clinical dissection of Beethoven's *Ninth Symphony*.

lineage of musical pioneers as diverse in makeup as Neu!, Stevie Wonder, and Yes. In response to such prejudice, Dario Argento's explanation of his creative methods can also effectively enlighten us about how his movies were scored: "I love the poetry of technology. For me, technological advances are inspiring. I'll hear of a new camera and it will suggest a story to me."[18]

Perhaps what truly sparks animosity toward such scores, however, is the way in which the new juxtapositions of synthesizer sounds and violent imagery violate many of the rules of horror scoring. Very few violent films are unaccompanied by music, and those that refuse it—such as *Henry: Portrait of a Serial Killer* (dir. John McNaughton, 1986)—are often upsetting to censor and ordinary viewer alike because of their moral ambiguity.[19] The lion's share of horror soundtracks deploys instruments that sound as close as possible to humans in pain: instruments like violins and even the voice that linguistically tag alongside the victim and most pointedly provoke our empathy. Music itself can also function as the perpetrator of brutality, so much so that assertive sonic spasms are commonly known in the scoring trade as "stabs." Dissonance rears its head frequently, although it does so mainly to tell us that things aren't quite right, to provoke an unease, certainly, but one in keeping with our sense of both moral and musical right and wrong. The famous shower scene in *Psycho* (1960) incorporates all of these techniques, leaving us suitably shocked, disoriented, and somewhat violated.

However, synthesizers in the late 1970s and early 1980s (the period when these films were scored) were continually perceived as post- or anti-human/humane, in part because of the implications loaned out to them by the history of sci-fi scoring. Their surface textures were too even to immediately evoke rupture, emotion, or distress, and their workings and histories of technical achievement seemed coldly scientific and futurist rather than bohemian, artistic, and concerned with a sensitivity toward human suffering. For many a listener, the synthesizer's preset predictability (the fact that no matter what the player did physically to a key, the note would still sound the same) would have distanced the instrument from the typical practices of compassionate human input. These were cultural assumptions about what the synthesizer could mean rather than predetermined characteristics, but they were ideas readily played with and promoted by many of its advocates, particularly by deadpan, robot-obsessed bands like Kraftwerk, Tubeway Army, and Devo. Such rationalistic qualities, along with the instrument's association with the nonhuman, did not and does not sit well with how music conventionally functions within the horror genre—and this becomes all the more troubling when a film edges toward more "extreme" obsessions like dismemberment, anthropophagy, and violence toward women, representations that seem to need the clearest of "justifications" for their very portrayal.

The synthesizer's lack of *depth*—in all sorts of senses—complicates its position within horror scoring. A synthesizer of that period produced incredibly even resonances that often cut off abruptly; notes were comprised of much fewer overtones and so sounded emptier than more familiar instruments. This sonic flatness jarred with the ways in which the accompanying images penetrated deep within the victims' bodies, rummaging around protractedly in their innermost recesses. Instead of absorbing the shock of these images or framing them within a consistent sense of three-dimensional depth, the shallow quality of these soundtracks also seems to be reminding the viewer of the fragile and ghostly presence of the flickering cinematic form.[20] The sense of flesh and all

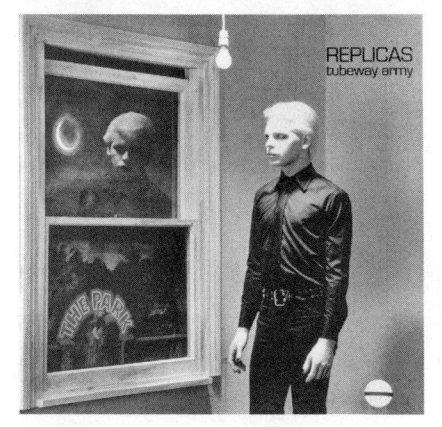

FIGURES 3A, 3B, AND 3C Synth-based recordings of the late 1970s such as Kraftwerk's *Man-Machine*, Devo's *Are We Not Men?*, and Tubeway Army's *Replicas* solidified the instrument's popular association with a dispassionate and at times robotic aesthetic.

the damage that is being done to it is not treated with "appropriate" emotional or spatial responses by the music.

Although the lineage of these scores probably springs from their production teams' affection for the "synth prog" genre,[21] for many a contemporary viewer the sounds of the synthesizer were perhaps more commonly heard in that place of part-time hedonism: the disco. There is often (but not always) a spandex-like [22] effortlessness and a disinterest in pain rather than wailing, pleading, and limbs torn asunder; the obsessive ripping and piercing of flesh is disquietingly matched by high-sheen surface textures. It is almost as if the soundtrack did not care about what it was watching and just wanted to keep on having a good time. Moreover, at the time, synthesizers were, misguidedly, assumed to be easy to play, something that piled an extra sense of work-shy loafing onto these already pleasure-seeking sounds. Nor did the fact that these scores sounded extremely similar to those of coexistent porno movies do anything to extinguish a sense of inappropriate debauchery or a fundamental disrespect toward the evocation of horrific death. A suitable moral tone to comment upon debasement, rape, and torture was not to be found in the persistent clarity and tunefulness of the music.

Goblin's[23] electronic soundtrack for *Tenebrae* perhaps best epitomizes all these values. Upbeat synthesizer music (the kind that easily seduces the body into dance-related movement) surfaces without fail during every violent scene: it enters and exits loudly and abruptly so that we register it and everything it stands for. For example, while a shoplifter is being repeatedly knifed in the neck and pages of Peter Neil's latest novel are being shoved in her mouth, the music is utterly unfaltering in its sleek, laser-like melodies, its even rhythms and resonances. The tune's steady progress and the swift cutouts of its sounds (particularly the hollow "drum" beats) do little to align us with the pain and penetration that is being forced upon this woman's body. Ultimately, to the uninitiated audience member, the music makes no concession to what is happening on screen.

Inferno's soundtrack, composed by Keith Emerson, formulates similarly disjunctive audiovisual arrangements. Despite Emerson's synthesizer prowess, most of *Inferno*'s soundtrack is built out of hyperbolic classical orchestral scoring. However, perhaps the messiest corpse in the film—the one of John, the servant, who is found with his eyeballs gauged out—is introduced to us with ethereal planes of synthesizer layering that seem oblivious of the stomach-churning tableau that we see before us. There is also a striking use of electronic music in the scene where Sara (who is soon to be murdered) rides through the rain in a taxi. While nothing particularly dynamic is happening visually, we hear a complicated and ostentatious synthesizer reworking of Verdi's *Nabucco* (which has been the object of study in Sara's lecture earlier that day) positioned extremely high in the audio mix. Such sonic presences become slightly more tenable—but only slightly—when we later learn that "the architect" (who has designed the three hellish buildings the film explores) is forced to communicate through an electronic voice mechanism by whose flex he is eventually strangled.

This sense that the synthesizer becomes somehow strangely (and often inconsistently) identified with the source of the horror also resonates throughout

FIGURE 4 Director Dario Argento (left) consults with his frequent musical collaborators, the rock group Goblin.

The Beyond, whose soundtrack was composed by Fabio Frizzi. Like *Tenebrae*, the music in *The Beyond* often appears as if from nowhere—it starts and stops at the same volume rather than phasing subtly in and out as many standard soundtracks tend to do, and its quick-fire launching and docking seem somewhat ridiculous (as it does in many of these movies, if one is accustomed to the volume-controlling of mainstream movies). *The Beyond*'s soundtrack is an elaborately flavored gumbo that mixes instruments like bass guitars, flutes, and violins. However, it saves up its more forceful synthesizer deployment for the rendition of zombie attacks and their gruesome outcomes. The synthesizer is thus directly associated with the horror that the film gradually reveals: that Liza's run-down hotel holds within it one of the seven gateways of hell. In the flashback delivered in the opening scenes, the synthesizer lurks in the background as the warlock's face is burned with acid. A synthesizer also readily accompanies Liza during her entry into the accursed room 36. The film oozes, melts, and rips flesh regularly; bodily fluids gush and eyeballs pop, but there is always a smooth synthesizer sound close at hand to confuse our responses to violence and mutilation. Normality, on the other hand, is evoked through older musical styles, such as those heard when John and Liza are safely ensconced in a New Orleans jazz bar.

A similar juxtaposition between musical safety and danger (this time urban New York and the unpredictable Amazon basin) is created in *Cannibal Ferox*.[24] Perhaps the biggest musical jolt comes when we both see and hear a Salvation Army band as the movie cuts back to Manhattan immediately after Mike's castration. However, the film's other regular returns to civilization are more often bluntly marked by funky jazz-infused pieces on horns and bass guitars that contrast with the unusual choice of representing nature (both bountiful and destructive) through the synthesizer. That the most technological instrumentation should stand in for the wilderness ultimately creates a sense of alienation rather than pity as we witness a variety of violent acts in this desolate space. We are left to wonder why this ambivalence has been devised, why a largely pop main theme (which does, admittedly, turn harmonically discordant at various intervals) should befriend such scenes of disorder, chaos, and inhumanity. Perhaps these two sensibilities are closer than we imagine, and it is conceivable that this proposition (and others like it) helped bring about the banning of the film.

Cannibal Holocaust fashions similar musical corollaries between its Amazon location and its score, which was, interestingly, written and conducted by Riz Ortolani, the man behind *Mondo Cane*'s (dir. Paolo Cavara and Gualtiero Jacopetti, 1962)[25] lilting and peaceful rejoinder to the film's various engagements with acts of brutality. The soundtrack is instrumentally, generically and tonally complex, fusing synthesizer sounds with challenging modernist string arrangements[26] and a mawkishly dreamy acoustic guitar-led main theme which is, like *Mondo Cane*'s signature tune, somewhat out of place considering the film's content. However, despite the score's hybridity, it is almost always the synthesizer—in either a wafting and ethereal mode or a jubilant, driving one—which we hear first during the many acts of savagery. Although other instruments are quick to participate in a commentary on the violence depicted, the initial shock of hearing a synthesizer at these moments is scarcely dampened when more linguistically manageable instrumentation joins the fray. There are sections where we hear only synthesizers (for example, when the Amazonians commit their first act of cruelty and near-cannibalism by cutting off a monkey's head and eating its brains), but these are actually fairly rare. The final scene of retribution is perhaps the most elaborate in its interweave of synthesizers and other instru-

FIGURE 5 Riz Ortolani's ambitious score for Deodato's *Cannibal Holocaust* juxtaposes a strangely mawkish theme, modernist string arrangements, and a variety of synthesizers. Yet within this diverse sonic palette, the synthesizer most frequently takes the lead in introducing scenes of violence and savagery.

mentation. During the sequence where one of the documentary crew is castrated, dismembered, decapitated, and devoured, the composition is up-tempo and positively groovy (albeit infringed upon by the occasional discordant string surge). Nothing of the viscera spilling across the screen is captured by the music; the washes of synthesizer resemble buzzing electrical currents rather than anything more corporeal. The soundtrack's signature synthesizer sine y "pow" noises also make a return visit. These flourishes, which are common to disco tracks like Kelly Marie's "Feel Like I'm in Love" (1980), erupt very much like little explosions of pleasure—part of a disco firework display. It is as if the ambivalence of the film wished not only to proclaim the proximity of pleasure to pain, but also to unmask the menacing underbelly of disco hedonism.

In all five of these movies, variations on this kind of music can evidently render their violence gratuitous to certain viewers. Because the tidy, if not somewhat trite, responses of moral condemnation, pity, and identification have been denied us, because the soundtrack we are given is frequently either antithetical or disinterested, these films invite us to ask questions about how appropriate or justified our standard engagement with cinema might be. Philip Brophy (talking about musical dissonance, but in a way that could also relate to synthesizer scoring) makes an astute, rather Brechtian, suggestion: "Perhaps this is why music cues are so neurotically Romantic in their Hanna Barbera reduction of humanist traits: when audiences cannot 'identify' with on-screen characters, they have to delve into themselves to question why they can't. And most people probably seem happy to pretend they can relate to others, when in their social reality they may be totally incapable of such engagement."[27]

These films are so *visually* visceral, so unrelenting in their depiction of Bad Acts (or so the tabloids insisted at the time), that this musical aloofness which would not offer a standard, safe, moral reproof quickly became that worrying incarnation of the ambivalent statement. In this situation, if we were to choose to watch the films at the level of deconstruction—enjoy the camp, remain detached and critical, or even laugh (which it is easy to do when confronted with the hyperbole of the synthesizers and the stylized gore)—then viewers inclined toward the particular investments in realism outlined earlier will find us repugnant. Such an unpredictable set of options, it would seem, was too dangerous for many a Briton, who feared that the coin might land the wrong way up; these movies would have to be dealt with severely, kept out of harm's way, even destroyed. The ambivalence of the films became the pariah, something that just might coax the weak-minded toward an entwined dark side. While many cultural products delight in ambivalence and opacity (indeed derive their revenues from this, in part), the particular location of these films within a seemingly unsurveyable environment (on video, at home) and viewed by certain sections of the population who are habitually considered to be "at risk" (poorly morally educated under-18s whose guardians are frequently out of the picture, for instance) meant that these films were inscribed as unsafe by a host of dynamic campaigners. And so the delicate refusal of these texts to be forthright was left unreported by many tabloid news reports in favor of vehement claims that they embodied unmitigated, uncomplicated reveling in evil and malice—which was so much easier to outlaw. What became manifest was neither the creation of new vocabularies that might incorporate such ambivalences into a more widely acceptable understanding of "logic," or a ferreting among the ideological underpinnings of our old linguistic categories (as someone like Bauman would have hoped for), but utter banishment under the 1984 Video Recordings Act.

While suppressing any serious contemplation of the ambivalence in these films, the contemporary moral assertions made about the movies also gorged on other meanings and agendas, swallowing them up and insisting upon the logical and organic wholeness of an essentially expansionist project—one that also made claims about safety, family, and surveillance. Such engulfing practices were largely made possible because of the new status of film on cassette as a domestic object. As Martin Barker details, "There will now be three standards of assessment for some films: a cinema standard, a TV standard, and the harsher video standard," all of which would be classified by a censorship board appointed by the Home Secretary.[28] With its redefined role in the home, film now occupied a space that was heavily inscribed as a *family* environment with all its concomitant ethical trappings, and its short shrifts for gray areas. In an eagerness to battle for family values, a moral majority sought both to ignore and to wrongly interpret the ambivalence of these movies and to whittle down their suggestiveness by falsely accusing them of a certain literalism. By committing such actions in the name of child protection, the campaigners covered their backs with a *raison d'être* that very few people were likely to want to argue against. Under this guise, a host of other ideas furtively entered the political arena. As Barker argues, "The video nasties issue allowed Thatcherism to become strong again, to present itself as unequivocally on the side of law and order."[29] During an all-important preelection period, the ever-popular cause of child protection allowed the party to drum up mass support that then comfortably buoyed the ensuing legislation.[30]

Of course situations like these, where cinematic matters become contested ground for a wide cross-section of the population, are red rags to the bulls of the cult-film fan world. In they leap (and continue to leap for decades afterward) to defend the subtlety, the intelligence and, most importantly, the liberty of their cherished art form against a manipulative and sanctimonious conservative power structure.[31] While my sympathies lie on the side of the former rather than the latter, I am not interested in validating or excusing these films outright. Fans who do this, I would argue, are often as unequivocal and unremitting as the anti-nasties protesters themselves and are nearly as blinkered and control-hungry—although, admittedly, their desired political end points are entirely different. The fascination in these films for me lies not in whether they are "good" or "bad," "trash" or "art," but in the fact that they are unresolved and nebulous, that they confound the strict notions of hermeneutics which are so easy to politically co-opt. While intriguing work is being done, mainly within the Bourdieu school of thought, on the hegemonic foundations of taste,[32] I am drawn less to the more rarefied stabilities that cult fandom (including the love of video nasties) offers, and more to the riggling chaos that remains if we refuse to neatly pack such films into preexisting pigeonholes, cutting off various of their organs in order that they might fit.

The often confusing audiovisual arrangements of these films encourage us to linger within the not quite sure, to vacillate, and, for me, this is an undervalued dimension of critical thought. First, as Bauman points out, "undecidables brutally expose the artifice, the fragility, the sham of the most vital separations."[33] Through these interactions between soundtrack and image, we are encouraged to question our need for an opposition of dissociation and the representation of death, or to unpick the allegiance between specific realist codes, humanist sympathy, and morality. Second, the urge to achieve a unified, spick-and-span conclusion on what the music, the image, and the narrative are trying to say as a whole often enters into a logic of conquest and eventual domination which fails to ask why such conflicts might have arisen in the first place and how producers and audiences might suffer from so uninquisitive a resolution. Perhaps we should question whether attributing or taking a stance over two opposed debates is always necessarily the most politically judicious action to take.[34] Must we always *belong* (as cult fan academics are often wont to do) to a coherent belief system if we are to present a strong argument or sense of personal identity?

I would like to propose another approach, one that would involve opening up such ideologically laden contradictions in order to help create a different means of rationalizing our world. This would entail not only trying to understand taste, but also endeavoring to reshape it and use it in new ways. The music in these once banned, now heavily cut[35] horror films is stopping us short of a straightforward engagement, but our wavering is intriguing, thought-provoking, and perhaps (eventually) politically fruitful. Yet such contemplation is possible only if academia does not also fall prey to the very wariness of ambivalence I have outlined. This type of film and music analysis can be carried out only if scholarly enquiry relinquishes its frequent supposition that music is simply Mother Image's little helper, colluding with some speciously maintained chimera of narrative univocality and order. If music is seen largely as "backing up" the image track or the storyline, then we are not going to see a way to profit from the ambivalence that erupts out of the clash between these distinct and different languages.

Notes

1. Leon Hunt, "A (Sadistic) Night at the *Opera*," in *The Horror Reader*, ed. Ken Gelder (London: Routledge, 2000), 333.
2. Geoffrey Nowell-Smith, with James Hay and Gianni Volpi, *The Companion to Italian Cinema* (London: Cassell and BFI, 1996), 64–65.
3. According to Martin Barker, the term *video nasties* was first coined in 1982 by the campaigner for "public decency" Mary Whitehouse. It became a catch phrase in tabloid print journalism later on that year and thus had become a familiar concept in the minds of the general British public by 1984. See Martin Barker, ed., "Nasty Politics or Video Nasties?" *The Video Nasties: Freedom and Censorship in the Media* (London: Pluto, 1984).
4. Key authors such as, for example, Irwin Bazelon, Mark Evans, and Royal Brown work almost exclusively in relation to this model, and, although Flinn is critical of classical, after-the-fact systems of scoring, she does not extend her analysis to incorporate different types of soundtrack realization. Even Jeff Smith, who is one of the few theorists to concentrate on pop scores and compilation soundtracks, is driven primarily by a need to understand the harmonious and profitable associations between the music and film industries. See Irwin Bazelon, *Knowing the Score: Notes on Film Music* (New York: Van Nostrand Reinhold Company, 1975); Royal Brown, *Overtones and Undertones: Reading Film Music* (Berkeley: University of California Press, 1994); Mark Evans, *Soundtrack: The Music of the Movies* (New York: Hopkinson and Blake, 1975); Caryl Flinn, *Strains of Utopia: Gender, Nostalgia and Hollywood Film Music* (Princeton, N.J.: Princeton University Press, 1992); and Jeff Smith, *The Sounds of Commerce* (New York: Columbia University Press, 1998).
5. Interestingly, the early days of sound provoked a spate of manifestos and declarations about the creative, dialectical possibilities of attaching sound to the moving image, particularly from Soviet director-theorists such as Sergei Eisenstein and Vsevolod Pudovkin. For instance, in their "Statement," Eisenstein, Pudovkin, and Grigori Alexandrov insisted that "THE FIRST EXPERIMENTAL WORK WITH SOUND MUST BE DIRECTED ALONG THE LINE OF ITS DISTINCT NONSYNCHRONIZATION WITH THE VISUAL IMAGES [sic]. And only such an attack will give the necessary palpability which will later lead to the creation of an ORCHESTRAL COUNTERPOINT of visual and aural images . . . [which] will inevitably introduce new means of enormous power to the expression and solution of the most complicated tasks that now oppress us." See Eisenstein, Pudovkin, and Alexandrov, "Statement on Sound," in *Film Sound:*

Theory and Practice, ed. Elisabeth Weis and John Belton (New York: Columbia University Press, 1985), 84–85. Likewise, Pudovkin's "Asynchronism as a Principle of Sound Film" argues that "the role which sound is to play in film is much more significant than a slavish imitation of naturalism . . . deeper insight into the content of the film cannot be given to the spectator simply by adding an accompaniment of naturalistic sound; we must do more. . . . Only by such counterpoint can primitive naturalism be surpassed and the rich deeps of meaning potential in sound film creatively handled by discovered and plumbed" (ibid., 86, 91). However, very few extended calls to arms of this persuasion have concentrated upon the musical score, a notable exception existing in Theodor Adorno and Hans Eisler's *Composing for the Films*. Since this book's publication in 1947, only small numbers of writers—Michel Chion and Philip Brophy among them—have sought to valorize, or even examine, soundtracks that might contradict other elements of their films' formal organization. See Philip Brophy, "The Secret History of Film Music" series (1997–98), media-arts.rmit.edu.ac/Phil_Brophy/soundtrack-List.html; and Michel Chion, *Audio-Vision: Sound on Screen*, trans. Claudia Gorbman (New York: Columbia University Press, 1994).

6. Zygmunt Bauman, *Modernity and Ambivalence* (Cambridge: Polity, 1991), 3.
7. Maitland McDonagh, *Broken Mirrors/Broken Minds: The Dark Dreams of Dario Argento* (London: Sun Tavern Fields, 1991), 23.
8. As, perhaps, might be the desired end point of such similarly anti-Enlightenment logic projects as Adorno and Horkheimer's. This book is too rich to dwell upon here—it deserves (and has already received) critical attention of a more focused nature. However, Adorno and Horkheimer's image of Odysseus and the sirens is a bleak yet persuasive one to consider at this point and, pertinently, it alludes to the power of music. The writers define the two limited possibilities offered to us under Enlightenment tyranny for encountering new, politically disruptive thought (as symbolically personified by the sirens): we may listen to the sirens' song, as Odysseus did, but remain strapped to the mask—in effect, utterly powerless to move or effect change—or we can block our ears with wax, like Odysseus's crew, and thus entirely relinquish the opportunity of hearing the sirens. Despite the hopelessness of this metaphor, though, Adorno and Horkheimer still cling, as I have already suggested, to the possibility of overthrowing the regime they define and despise. See Adorno and Horkheimer, *The Dialectic of Enlightenment* (London: Verso, 1979).
9. Although Bauman is primarily charting the modernist period, his ideas, as he is quick to acknowledge, continue into contemporary life.
10. Bauman, *Modernity and Ambivalence*, 7–8.
11. Adorno and Horkheimer, *The Dialectic of Enlightenment*, 29.
12. This story line has recently resurfaced in the form of *The Blair Witch Project* (dir. Daniel Myrick and Eduardo Sanchez, 1999), another film that plays with the formal conven-

tions of vérité documentary, updated by the integration of that contemporary "truth-exuding" and "immediate" technology, the handheld digital camera.

13. Interview with Deodato by Gian Luca Castoldi in Castoldi, Harvey Fenton, and Julian Grainger, *Cannibal Holocaust and the Savage Cinema of Ruggero Deodata* (Surrey, UK: FAB Press, 1999), 19.

14. A compelling argument about a different form of identification—one fascinated by deconstructive rather than realist modes of filmic interaction—is developed in Jeffrey Sconce's article "Spectacles of Death: Identification, Reflexivity, and Contemporary Horror," in *Film Theory Goes to the Movies*, ed. J. Collins and H. Radner (London: Routledge, 1993), 103–19. "In both these films [*Freddy's Dead* and *Henry: Portrait of a Serial Killer*, although this argument could be extended to all sorts of horror films], the self-reflexive techniques thought by many theorists to challenge dominant modes of enunciation and identification are used instead as a means of *intensifying* certain forms of viewer identification" (111). Following this line of thought, viewers are not wrapping themselves up in the characters in a traditional realist engagement, but are feeling a special bond with the film because they understand and appreciate the manner in which it is unraveling cinematic trickery. In other words, "the character with whom they [the fans] identify never appears on the screen, but is instead the artistic 'enunciator' whose presence is felt in the text" (117).

15. Jeffrey Sconce, *Haunted Media: Electronic Presence from Telegraphy to Television* (Durham, N.C.: Duke University Press, 2000), 121.

16. One would imagine this was because of the greater clout the American studios had with the British censors, something the Italian producers did not enjoy.

17. This is the first argument that was leveled against my interpretation of these scores on the two occasions when I have delivered conference papers on this topic. Both (nameless!) respondents were keen to contend that the *only* reasons for these films to bear synthesizer soundtracks were those of economic limitation, rather than an appreciation of the synthesizer's semantic richness.

18. Dario Argento, 1991 interview with Maitland McDonagh, in *Broken Mirrors/Broken Minds*, 238.

19. Sconce suggests that the lack of musical soundtrack to *Henry: Portrait of a Serial Killer* enhances the documentary feel created by other formal devices such as the film's cinema vérité–style camerawork. Thus, cumulatively and with the help of the absence of music, the movie is ironically positioned within a more "objective" set of factual discourses. This, in turn, means that firm moral guidelines, so typical of the ways in which violent narratives are framed and distanced, are much less pronounced, and judging the impact upon the audience (ostensibly one of the jobs of the censor) is extremely tricky. See Sconce, "Spectacles of Death."

20. My thanks to Jodi Brooks for pointing this out.

21. Dario Argento, in particular, is known to be a fan of Yes and King Crimson, and he commissioned Keith Emerson to score *Inferno*.
22. The instrument's very name recalls high-tech artificial fibers such as this one.
23. Goblin was a band that focused mainly on producing sound tracks and attained a large amount of album chart success in Italy for their work. Their lineup changed frequently but, for this score, Goblin was comprised of Massimo Morante, Fabio Pignatelli, and Agostino Marangolo.
24. The music to this film was composed by Budy Maglione and arranged by Carlo Cordio.
25. Another film that plays cat and mouse with the standard propositions of documentary filmmaking.
26. It is worth noting here that modernist recourses to atonality are themselves often ambivalent gestures. Consonant and dissonant musical arrangements meet on an equal footing in the work of composers like Schoenberg who refused to adhere to hierarchies which tell us which combinations of notes "sound right." However, to ears that have been tutored according to age-old notions of harmony (and this applies to most of us), these pieces sound confusing, even "wrong." Just like video nasties, then, certain strains of modernist music interrogate cultural oppositions and logics.
27. Brophy, "The Secret History of Film Music."
28. Martin Barker's edited collection *The Video Nasties* provides a very rewarding contemporary discussion of the key debates that accelerated the passing of the Video Recordings Act.
29. Barker, "Nasty Politics or Video Nasties," 11.
30. Ibid., 9–10.
31. See Jeffrey Sconce, "'Trashing' the Academy: Taste, Excess, and an Emerging Politics of Cinematic Style," *Screen* 36 (1995): 371–93.
32. This is a sizable area of scholarship, with key authors such as Henry Jenkins, Sconce, and Sarah Thornton using Bourdieu in their respective studies of the cult texts of television, film, and music. Matt Hills offers a rigorous overview, critique, and development of these theories. See Henry Jenkins, *Textual Poachers: Television Fans and Participatory Culture* (London: Routledge, 1992); Sconce, "'Trashing' the Academy"; Sarah Thornton, *Club Cultures: Music, Media and Subcultural Capital* (Cambridge: Polity); and Matt Hills, *Fan Cultures* (London: Routledge, 2002).
33. Bauman, *Modernity and Ambivalence*, 3.
34. I write in the midst of a war helmed by two men—George W. Bush and Saddam Hussein—whose policies are both abhorrent to me.
35. In the U.K. context.

JOAN HAWKINS

The Sleazy Pedigree of Todd Haynes

In October 2000, the Wexner Art Center invited Todd Haynes, the center's resident visiting artist, to curate a retrospective of his films. The resulting program paired Haynes's own films with films he said had influenced him for a series of double features that ranged from the illuminating to the quirky. *Poison* (1990) was paired with Fassbinder's *Ali: Fear Eats the Soul* (1973). *Safe* (1995) was shown with Max Ophuls's 1949 noir melodrama *The Reckless Moment*. Some early student films were paired with Jean Genet's homage to erotic voyeurism, *Un chant d'amour* (1950). And *Velvet Goldmine* (1998), Haynes's tribute to the glam rock era, played against Russ Meyer's *Beyond the Valley of the Dolls* (1970), the cult film that Meyers claimed was "beyond any film you've ever seen."[1]

On many levels, pairing *Velvet Goldmine* with *Beyond the Valley of the Dolls* makes perfect sense. Thematically, they both deal with the rise and fall of rock musicians against a theatrical backdrop of sex, drugs, and cross-dressing. Formally, they both feature a strong visual style that at times threatens to overwhelm the plot and characters. Both films feature a camp aesthetic. Both narrate a protagonist's fall from innocence. And both rely heavily on rock songs to drive the story. On just the surface level, then, the juxtaposition of these two films invites viewers to interrogate the boundaries between high and low culture and

FIGURE 1 Curating a retrospective of his own work, Todd Haynes paired his glam-rock *Velvet Goldmine* (1998) with Russ Meyer's *Beyond the Valley of the Dolls* (1970), explicitly placing his work in dialogue with the tradition of low trash and high camp.

to consider the ambiguous distinctions between high and low body genre films, which I've discussed at length elsewhere.[2]

What the double bill did not do was demonstrate the influence cult film has had on Haynes's entire oeuvre. One could even argue that the Wexner program was misleading in that it positioned *Velvet Goldmine* as the only Haynes movie indebted to paracinema.[3] In point of fact, almost any Haynes film can be situated within the history of "degraded cultural forms"[4] that make up low popular culture. And if one extends the category of "degraded cultural forms" to include television, which is so often positioned as high culture's binary opposite, then every Todd Haynes film owes a debt to trash and trash aesthetics.

Superstar: The Karen Carpenter Story (1987) uses Barbie dolls to tell the complicated story of Karen Carpenter's rise to stardom and her death from anorexia nervosa. Interestingly, some early scenes of the film invite comparisons to Ed Wood's *Plan 9 from Outer Space*, a film some critics have called the worst movie ever made. *Poison* (1990–91) weaves together three separate stories to comment on the media's portrayal of AIDS. One, a stylized love story between two prison inmates, is equally indebted to the conventions of art cinema and the writings of Jean Genet. One is a modern tabloid news show about a boy who killed his father; and one is a 1950s-style, sci-fi B-movie about a scientist who, after successfully isolating the sex drive, accidentally ingests it and becomes a sex-fiend, mutant, id monster. *Velvet Goldmine* (1998) is indebted to Russ Meyer. *Safe* (1995) uses a dense mediascape (drawn from popular music, infomercials, film, and television clips), as well as pocket book self-help titles, to mount its scathing critique of this society's treatment of gendered and sexed diseases (like environmental illness, chronic fatigue syndrome, and AIDS). *Dottie Gets Spanked* (1994) uses a young boy's obsession with a *Lucy*-style situation comedy to reinvent Freud's "A Child Is Being Beaten." Even *Far from Heaven*—a stately homage to Douglas Sirk—takes on a slightly, over-the-top, B-movie logic at times. The film treats a 1950s couple that seems to have everything—until Frank (the husband, Dennis Quaid) realizes he can no longer deny that he's gay. The scenes in which he cruises men at the local art house cinema and gay bar borrow heavily from the canted-angle aesthetic that characterizes the mad-scientist sequence of *Poison*. In that sense, *Far from Heaven* is as indebted as *Poison* to the 1950s B movies that, as Harry M. Benshoff argues, were always about queer(ed) sex.[5]

The fact that so many low culture references occur within the oeuvre of an acknowledged art director is telling. Haynes made his reputation as an independent, downtown filmmaker,[6] whose work has increasingly crossed over into mainstream art house venues. With the diverse filmography referenced above, Haynes has established himself as a "serious" filmmaker, whose concerns include AIDS, homophobia, adolescent sexual development, female identity, and environmental disease. A stunning film stylist, he has created a body of work that is often beautiful to watch. He has won prizes at Cannes and Sundance and has established himself as an important director in the New Queer Cinema. So the use of sleaze elements and trash style in his work invites the same kind of reading that elsewhere I have ascribed to collector catalogues and fan publications.[7] They enable us to perform a cultural reading strategy similar to the one Fredric Jameson advocates in *Signatures of the Visible*. That is, they invite us to "read high and mass culture as objectively related and dialectically interdependent phenomena, as twin and inseparable forms of the fission of aesthetic production under capitalism."[8]

What I would like to stress in this essay is the "dialectically interdependent phenomena" part of Jameson's quote. That is, "dialectic" has a precise philosophical meaning that Jameson is too theoretically savvy to ignore or to invoke lightly. For Hegel, and later for Marx, "dialectic" refers to the collision of two antithetical terms. As a result of this collision, a new third term is created, one that includes all the elements and contradictions of the original terms, as well as a new possible meaning (the result of synthesis). When I explain this to students—usually as part of a lesson on Sergei Eisenstein—I use the example of parents and their child. That is, two people contribute genetic material that results in the creation of a wholly new, third being. The resultant child contains all the genetic material she has received from her parents (plus a healthy dose of the contradictions anyone who lives within a family experiences), but is still a wholly separate unique individual.

So what I believe Jameson is saying in the above quote is not that we should read high and low culture as twinned, but still essentially separate, terms. Rather I believe he advocates seeing them as mingling in a kind of synthetic union—one from which a new taste culture might ostensibly emerge. The later use of the term *fission* confirms the idea that what Jameson is stressing here is not the coexistence and co-pairing of opposites, but a complex sociochemical reaction that generates a hybrid form (a mutant of its own, if you will).

Many authors claim that postmodernism, with its mixture of high and low culture, its dependence on quotation and pastiche, and its tendency to look for meanings between terms (in the spaces between words, for example) is exactly the kind of third term Jameson is predicting and advocating. But the term *postmodern* has itself become so compromised—so frequently a shorthand reduction of complicated historical and cultural processes into a kind of sound bite, that I am reluctant to use it here (although, if pressed, I would say that yes, Todd Haynes's style is postmodern). I would like, though, to turn to a scholar who frequently writes on postmodern phenomena and borrow one of his terms to describe what I think is going on in the best of Todd Haynes's work.

In *Architectures of Excess,* Jim Collins identifies what he sees as a series of hybrid genre films that emerged in the 1980s—*Road Warrior* (1981), *Blade Runner* (1982), *Blue Velvet* (1986), *Near Dark* (1988), *Who Framed Roger Rabbit* (1988), *Batman* (1989), *Thelma and Louise* (1991), *Last Action Hero* (1993), and *Demolition Man* (1993). These are popular film narratives that, Collins argues, had "become ever more eclectic and citational."[9] While reviews of these films frequently describe their citationality and intertextuality as further evidence of Hollywood's diminishing ability to create new material, Collins reads them as signifiers of "massive, widespread changes within some of the most fundamental categories of filmmaking and film criticism, namely genre, auteur and national cinema."[10] "The eclecticism of contemporary genre films," Collins writes,

> involves a hybridity of conventions that works at cross-purposes with the traditional notion of a genre as a stable, integrated set of narrative and stylistic conventions.... Ultimately, the ubiquity of this hyperconscious quotation and re-articulation suggests a profound change at the most basic level, that of the narrative contract established between text and audience—what films now promise to deliver in terms of "action" and what audiences now conceive of as entertainment has changed so thoroughly that the cultural function of storytelling appears to be in the process of profound redefinition.[11]

As Collins makes clear later in the chapter, the challenge to traditional models of genre mounted by these hybrid texts goes far beyond the blurring of genre boundaries—between horror and sci-fi, for example—that scholars have always noted. In fact, Collins's notion of hybrid genres might be seen as bearing the same relationship to the older notion of blurred (or unstable) generic boundaries that the dialectic bears to binary opposition. That is, the idea of blurred generic boundaries still presupposes the logic of discrete genres (a binary, if you will)—there are elements of horror and elements of sci-fi that are readily identifiable according to their own generic rules and then a gray area where they seem to trip over into one another. Hybrid genres, on the other hand, are new forms that result from the collision of previously stable categories, such that a wholly new synthesis is created. For Collins, this hybridity is a distinctly historical phenomenon, one that emerges in the 1980s and 1990s (the time of Haynes's career). The generic transformations that were previously at work in the 1960s and 1970s, he writes, "may have differed in regard to the degree of respect shown a particular genre, *but in each case the transformation is one that remains within the confines of a specific genre*, whereas the eclectic, hybrid genre films of the eighties and nineties . . . all engage in specific transformations *across genres*" which yield new, synthetic forms.[12]

What Collins believes a film like *Thelma and Louise* does to traditional notions of genre, I believe a film like *Superstar* does to conventional notions of taste culture. In Haynes's movies, elements of low and high culture are so imbricated that they can no longer be seen as inhabiting distinct and separate realms (as in blurred categories).[13] Rather there is a "hybridity of conventions," one that can be seen as operating across traditional notions of taste culture to create a kind of synthesis. To paraphrase Collins, what Haynes's films promise to deliver in terms of "taste" and what his audiences now conceive of as entertainment has changed so thoroughly that the cultural function of taste appears to be in the process of profound redefinition.[14]

Not Exactly Barbie's Dream House

Superstar: The Karen Carpenter Story (1987)[15] is a hybrid text at the levels of both genre and taste culture. The film opens with a date (February 4, 1983). This is followed by a shaky, handheld traveling shot, as Mrs. Carpenter tracks through the house looking for her daughter, Karen. For Barbara Kruger, this sequence is "shot in a tension-laden, cinema-verité-ish style," but for me it's more low-grade and less arty than that, more reminiscent of the opening sequences of low-budget slasher films and the kinds of grainy police crime shoots that Chris Kraus depicts in her 1987 film *How to Shoot a Crime*.[16] While the words that flash on the screen—"A Dramatization" seem largely in keeping with the reality style of a cop show (i.e., a crime shoot), the slasher reference also has strong resonance. One of the key points of the forty-three-minute film is that Mrs. Carpenter bears a great deal of responsibility for her daughter's death. So it's no accident that she's turned into "the slasher" here. But the film also implicates the commodification of women's bodies, the sociopolitical climate of the times, America's investment in consumption as a way of life, and star culture, as well as hetero-normative family life as possible "causes," or at least analogues, of Karen's disease. Throughout the film there are repeated, seemingly unmotivated, inserts—a Barbie doll being spanked, documentary footage of Richard Nixon's Cambodia speech, news footage from the Vietnam War, documentary television footage of the Carpenters performing, Nixon playing the piano, the

Miss America pageant, some interviews with people who assess Karen Carpenter's style, and documentary footage explaining the symptoms and treatment of anorexia nervosa. As one critic noted, it's a "Lilliputian Sirkian movie of the week," shot through with Bruce Conner overtones.[17] I would agree, although—as noted above—I would add grade-Z horror as an important element in the mix.

As the "dramatization" of the first scene gives way to "simulation" (the next intertitle to appear on the screen), the film's style changes from low-budget slasher to an older horror-exploitation model. Focusing for a while on the exterior of the Carpenters' house, Haynes creates a shot that appears very much like a pastiche of the establishing shot in Bela Lugosi's "old man stopping to smell the roses" sequence from *Plan 9*. While the image of the house itself seems general enough—a necessary establishing shot in a film about Barbie dolls—the style of the narration here seems so much a parody of Wood that students often groan and laugh appreciatively when I show the clip in class. The sepulchral timbre, the rhythm, and the intonation of the narrator (Bruce Tuthill) as he asks, "What happened?" match the dread-serious tones of *Plan 9*'s narrator ("The old man . . .") almost beat for beat.

Certainly the admittedly brief intertextual reference resonates with the rest of the project. Working with miniature sets (literally doll-size), on the cheap, with materials commonly found around the home, Haynes seems to have lifted an entire film aesthetic from Wood (the director who painted paper plates to look like flying saucers and used his Zippo lighter to set them on fire for "special effects" shots). In addition, Haynes's position as an important director of the New Queer Cinema movement lends a certain ironic edge to his homage to one of the great transvestite directors in exploitation film history, an edge that also surfaces in *Superstar*'s insinuation that Karen was not the only Carpenter with gender and sexuality issues. At one point in the film, Karen threatens to tell her parents about Richard's "private life" if he tells them about her relapse into anorectic behavior. And in case the audience doesn't get it the first time, she pointedly asks, "Do the Carpenters have something to hide?" We never find out if they do or don't—or what Richard's private life might entail—but students and popular audiences commonly read this scene as a reference to homosexuality.

Finally, the comparison to Wood opens a space for camp in a film that at times—Barbie dolls notwithstanding—risks becoming a little too lugubrious. In fact, for some critics, the "space" opened for camp allows camp to take over completely and threatens to undermine the entire project. Writing for *The Spinning Image*, Graeme Clark asks, "But how seriously are we supposed to take all this? The use of dolls gives the film a campy tone, however sincere Haynes is about his subject matter. And the dramatization of domestic scenes resembles something out of a bad soap opera, complete with corny dialogue. From some angles, *Superstar* looks like a sick joke."[18]

In part, Clark's comment demonstrates the same tendency to split "camp" off from "serious" cinema appreciation that Barbara Klinger observes in Douglas Sirk criticism, where it becomes largely an issue of taste. As Klinger defines it, "the requisite components of camp . . . —a penchant for lowbrow tackiness, hyperbole, and artifice over nature— . . . appears as a specialized mode of interpretation *available primarily to those schooled in culture*. That is, only those who are familiar with a broad range of aesthetic offerings, who understand the conventions of good taste well enough to enjoy deposing them . . . are liable to pursue the highly self-conscious and omnivorous art of camp."[19] Klinger's articulation of camp is closely linked, then, to the "ironic reading strategy," which Sconce identifies as a key element of paracinema fandom. This is a reading strategy whereby those with the right kind of what Bourdieu calls "cultural capital" are able to "valorize all forms of cinematic 'trash'" and "[render] the bad into the sublime."[20]

Superstar's seeming invocation of Ed Wood and the use of a certain Woodsian aesthetic throughout the film draws a parallel, then, between camp and paracinema, one which links the process of postmodern taste hybridization (which I've read into Jim Collins's work) to an overall "queering" of the cinematic process, a "queering" that, some critics maintain, is the crux of Haynes's larger film project.[21] The film's citations and intertextual references should not be read then merely as low-culture moments (or references) within an experimental work, but rather as transformative gestures in the text, gestures that encourage reading across the bounded categories of genre and taste culture to create a new kind of queer synthesis.[22]

This becomes all the more evident when we consider the presence and function of Barbie dolls in the movie. As Chuck Stephens notes, there is an element of "kitsch" that surrounds the dolls, particularly given their presence in an art film (i.e., a film whose audience will be predisposed to read the dolls ironically).[23] That is, there is a degree to which the use of the dolls itself infuses the film with an element of low culture ("kitsch") that can't be easily bracketed off or set apart from the "serious" intent of the film. In fact, the use of Barbie makes sense only when considered against the film's serious attempts at social critique. As Lynn Spigel has pointed out, Barbie's "plastic form is doubled by her equally plastic ability to be molded to almost anyone's desire."[24] It is precisely this malleability, and Barbie's status as the perfect plastic waspwaisted creature onto whom fantasies might be projected, that makes her the ideal analogue for the downside of star culture. The "pressure" of Karen's career—which here is depicted as contributing to her anorexia—is the fear of not measuring up to fan expectations, either of her body or of her voice. In that sense, her anorexia can be read as her attempt to mold herself according to the audience's desires. In the film, this is given a graphic dimension, as the Barbie doll depicting Carpenter is literally whittled away, her little face finally scarred by the necessary "molding" she has attempted both to accommodate and control. Furthermore, the very commodity status of Barbie underscores one of the major threads of social criticism in the film—namely, that the commodification of women's bodies within the larger culture is a necessary precondition to the emergence of a disease that plagues women only in industrialized nations.

Haynes himself has said that he used the dolls to experiment with questions of identification, to see whether audiences could become emotionally connected to dolls onscreen. He learned, he said, "that people will identify at the drop of a hat . . . at almost anything."[25] While I'm not sure that people identify with the dolls in quite the same emotional way that they identify with Rick in *Casablanca*, it is true that the use of dolls *allows* the audience to see the way the process of identification is created (in a way, precisely because we aren't distracted by the presence of "real" people onscreen). As Jeremy Heilman notes, "the use of the dolls . . . allows an opportunity for the viewer to observe the way that editing choices and musical cues can help to create a performance. Haynes's smart use of camera movements [the tilts to mimic POV shots, for example] often lends a bit of emotion to the completely expressionless dolls."[26] Certainly the use of zooms combined with sound distortion succeeds in ren-

FIGURE 2 Haynes's infamous debut, *Superstar: The Karen Carpenter Story*, employed the already highly charged icon of the Barbie doll to anchor its melding of political commentary, experimentalism, and tawdry melodrama.

dering food as threatening and frightening in a way that I haven't seen matched in any other film. In that sense, the film manages to create, if not a sense of identity with and sympathy for Karen Carpenter, at least a sense of identity with and sympathy for people suffering from Karen Carpenter's disease.

Throughout his career, Haynes has been interested in revealing the way in which narrative and traditional processes of cinematic identification work, "without nullifying the process of identification" itself.[27] And, for him, *Superstar* "is the best, cleanest example" of something he's been "drawn to" in all his films; namely, "the way stylistic tropes and conventions of expression can be taken to an extreme point of self-conscious, ironic, highly theatrical, highly worked presentation without losing emotion."[28] That is, the use of dolls provides the "best, cleanest" way of renegotiating (and, Haynes would argue, warming up) the mandates of modernist art cinema (with all its chilly Brechtian distanciation devices), through an emphasis on the reading strategies of camp and paracinema/low culture.

Before closing this section, I'd like to say a few words about the very real hybrid physical nature of the object most of us have come to know as *Superstar*. In

1989, Richard Carpenter and A&M records sued Haynes for unauthorized use of the Carpenters' songs. As a result of this law case, Haynes has been enjoined against further distribution of the film.[29] He is able to show it, in limited circumstances, during complete retrospectives of his work; but he is not allowed to show it in separate, independent screenings. The film is also not legally available for commercial or classroom use. As a result, most people know this film through encounters with pirate videotapes, which may be purchased through paracinema catalogues and Web sites. The effect of this samizdat distribution of what is arguably Haynes's best and boldest work is that viewers frequently watch an experimental film very much through the lens of low culture. The best videotape I've seen of the film is so dark that it completely obscures the date and intertitles at the beginning of the movie and makes reading the surface of the dolls themselves (as they're whittled) almost impossible. A new DVD exists, and while it restores some of the quality of the transfer, it has its own problems, since it's not legible on all DVD machines. As a commodity form, then, *Superstar* enacts transformations across taste cultures, transformations that have been dictated by institutional practices, and—as I have shown elsewhere—the larger hybridization of taste cultures at work in late capitalism.[30]

Kens without Barbies

Like *Superstar*, *Velvet Goldmine* is a hybrid text that invites readings across genres, taste cultures, and even media. The opening title card blends the usual disclaimer of film texts with the acoustic recommendations commonly found on import albums: "Although what you are about to see is a work of fiction it should nevertheless be played at maximum volume."[31] This opening directive to *listen* to the movie as though it were an audio recording establishes a tone that extends throughout the film. Much more than *Superstar*, *Goldmine* plays with the total market saturation of pop culture and the interconnections between media, as album covers open up into music videos and film clips, television appearances segue into concert performances, and so on.

The film deals with an era—the glam rock era—in which the usual order of things was inverted, shaken up. Suddenly, the dandies and the "woofters" were fashionable and it was hip to be bisexual. As *Goldmine*'s female narrator says at the beginning of the film, little did the boys who were being beaten up in the

1960s know that "one day, the whole stinking world would be theirs." As part of this inversion, a certain hybridization of fashion took place—as androgyny emerged as the dominant look, and the historically elegant merged with what formerly had been considered tacky. Furs blended with green nail polish and glitter eye makeup. Fashions previously considered appropriate only for evening were seen on the street in daylight—on men as well as on women. Camp was in, and it brought with it a hybridization of sleaze and glamour, the total theatricality that characterized the era.

As mentioned earlier in the article, camp is closely linked to the "ironic reading strategies" that Sconce identifies as a key element of paracinema fandom, and as a key element of the kinds of hybridity I have discussed throughout the article. Certainly many critics attribute to camp the qualities I attribute to Haynes's hybridization—a fascination with colliding high and low cultural forms, ambiguity of voice, emphasis on performativity and reveling in failed seriousness. Even more striking, though, is the way in which, for some critics at least, the categories of hybridity, paracinema, and camp seem to merge—to become themselves synthetic forms. In his influential "Uses of Camp," Andrew Ross argues, "from an institutional point of view, camp has become the *resident conscience* of a 'bad film' subculture which has its own alternative circuit of festivals, promoters, heroes, stars, and prizes."[32] In the course of the article, he mentions two films that Haynes explicitly notes as influences for *Goldmine*. What's interesting here is that Ross sees these cultural references as belonging to the "decadent and not the vibrant spirit of camp."[33] I say interesting because decadence (both in its sense as a historic cultural movement personified by Oscar Wilde and as a term used to signify the last chapter of a "decaying" era/genre/movement) is precisely *Goldmine*'s topic.

Ross begins his discussion of campy bad movies with a consideration of *Myra Breckinridge* (dir. Michael Sarne, 1970) and Russ Meyer's *Beyond the Valley of the Dolls*, films that were frequently paired in popular reviews and linked in the popular imagination. For Ross, *Myra Breckinridge* becomes yet another example of a good book badly adapted to the screen. "Michael Sarne's much hyped *Myra Breckinridge*," he writes, "based on Gore Vidal's entertaining novel, was a tired, laconic treatment of gay camp fascination with Hollywoodiana, and it evoked a wave of scorn among critics for Rex Reed/Raquel Welch's dual portrayal of transsexualism."[34] It's not clear from Ross's comments (nor, incidentally, from the reviews he cites) whether the scorn was for the actors' performance or for the mere representation of transsexualism onscreen. This was a time, after all, when gay themes were not particularly well received outside gay and camp circles,[35] a fact Ross neglects to adequately address. Similarly, *Beyond the Valley of the Dolls* is dismissed as an example of problematic camp. It "overexposed the keen gluttony of Russ Meyers' earlier exploitation skin flicks," Ross writes, ". . . while Roger Ebert's gilded-trash script for this most synthetic of movies demonstrated how camp deliberately aspires, as Mel Brooks puts it, to 'rise below vulgarity.'"[36]

My quarrel with Ross is not that he points out the vulgar and trash elements of camp, since camp does deliberately embrace both the vulgar and the trashy, but rather that within the hybrid category of popular camp culture he attempts to identify a taste hierarchy (a move that seems antithetical to the consumer practices of both paracinema "bad" film aficionados and followers of popular camp culture). That is he attempts to mark a distinction between a kind of good camp and inferior camp, and this distinction is drawn along rather standard taste-class lines. While the American drive-in/suburban movie theater camp represented by *Myra Breckinridge* and *Beyond the Valley of the Dolls* receives what I consider to be problematic treatment in the essay, another film that greatly influenced *Velvet Goldmine* is extolled as the film that "finally" gave "countercultural camp . . . a run for its money."[37] That film is Nicholas Roeg's *Performance* (1970), a film that played mainly in art houses and appeared as a prestige import film on HBO in the early days of cable television. *Performance* is an extraordinary film whose importance to the era can hardly be underestimated. As Ross correctly points out, it "brought together the working-class criminal subculture and the experimental rock avant-garde within the hallucinogenic milieu of a bad trip."[38] The overarching theme of the film is—as the title suggests—performance, the performative nature of stardom, criminal subculture, and middle-class life. In this film, as in Jenny Livingston's *Paris Is Burning* (1990), every job and every social role becomes a form of drag. But for all the interest it potentially continues to hold for young paracinephiles, *Performance* is also a supremely difficult film for contemporary youth audiences to "read." Certainly my students have more trouble deciphering the codes and

FIGURE 3 *Velvet Goldmine*: a densely intertextual collision of high and low camp.

cultural references of this film than they have in reading any other film (including Haynes's early experimental films) shown in my Todd Haynes class. They complain that even at the level of story, the film is harder to negotiate than films by Godard. Good camp, for Ross then, becomes the kind of camp that requires a very special kind of classed cultural capital to read, one that is foreign to many contemporary youth audiences.

In *Velvet Goldmine* Haynes merges these two strands of camp culture—or rather, shows the way in which glam rock merged these two strands into a hybrid. At the same time, however, he interrogates the very kind of class divisions that Ross, inadvertently perhaps, introduces into camp (the very notion that there *are* two strands of class culture). "There's humour in glam rock," Haynes says, "there's irony and wit, and it's often about its own point of address; it's often about presentation, the inherent artificiality of our so-called natural world. And yet it ends up being very moving with its rhythm, its meter, its colour."[39] In an attempt to convey the irony, the wit, and the rhythm, Haynes

202   JOAN HAWKINS

uses intertextuality to a dizzying degree in this film, so much so that it's hard not only to see where one reference ends and another begins, but also where the boundaries between high culture and low culture actually lie. At the beginning of the film, Oscar Wilde makes an appearance as a space alien who wants to be a "pop icon," and whose emerald green brooch marks and binds glam rockers Jack Fairy, Brian Slade, Curt Wild, and journalist Arthur Stuart into a kind of dandified line of succession. Furthermore, quotes from Wilde and references to his work throughout the film make him one of the key—if mostly unseen— players in the story. In addition, the film makes pointed reference to *Cabaret* (dir. Bob Fosse, 1972), *Citizen Kane* (dir. Orson Welles, 1941), *Lisztomania* (dir. Ken Russell, 1975), David Bowie's *Ziggy Stardust* tour, the bizarre rumor that Paul McCartney was really dead, Leopold von Sacher-Masoch's *Venus in Furs*, Bryan Ferry, Jim Morrison, Kurt Cobain, Kurt Weill, and the artifacts of pop culture (fan magazines, club culture, etc.). At one point, it even pays pointed homage—via a Ken-doll sequence—to *Superstar*.

As though the sheer number of references weren't sufficient to suggest the cultural stew that characterizes postmodern pop culture, the film is organized around a logic of cuts clearly designed to render what Haynes sees as glam rock's "rhythm, its meter, its colour." What Haynes calls "fast cuts" (mainly rapid dissolves) mingle here with what he calls "mad cuts" (rapid dissolves combined with 180-degree pans and swish pans, and competing onscreen motion—during the credits sequence, for example, the letters of the titles move across the screen left to right, while the camera and actors often rush right to left), cuts that blur motion and colour into a kind of kaleidoscopic effect. These punctuate long still scenes, shot at medium to medium-long range, in which theatrical mise-en-scène is put on display, and they are punctuated by "hard cuts," used to visually accentuate moments of rupture, transformation, and closure in the story. Stylistically, it's an exhilarating film to watch, and it plunges us into the world of glam in much the same way that the style of *Superstar* plunges us into the world of eating disorders. The fact that all this is taking place in the past— the film is actually set in 1984, and a journalist is investigating the now-defunct glam era—lends a certain political edge to what Bakhtin might call the carnivalesque atmosphere of the 1970s. The Reagan 1980s are depicted here with a monochromatic gray palette reminiscent of Michael Radford's *Nineteen Eighty-*

Four (1984), a palette that contrasts sharply from the colors and textures of the 1970s. "We wanted to change the world," glam rocker Curt Wild says during one of the 1980s segments, "and ended up . . . just changing ourselves." "What's wrong with that?" the film's hero, Arthur, asks. "Nothing!" Wild replies. "If you don't look at the world."

The jumble of textual references and rhythmic shifts makes it difficult to locate the point of each particular reference or citation (this is not a film whose pointed references can always be read as specific individual analogues or counterpoints to what's going on in the main story—the usual use of such citations in mainstream cinema). Rather it's the mix and hybridity itself that is important. When the references do stand out in a way that invites exegesis (the *Nineteen Eighty-Four* reference, for example), they do so in a way that causes us to read for culture as much as for content. The best example of this is the pointed use of *Citizen Kane*'s structure as the organizing structure of *Goldmine*. As in *Kane*, we have a journalist assigned to investigate the mystery connected with a popular icon's death (in *Kane* the death is real; in *Goldmine* the death itself is a hoax). In each film, the mystery is seen as the key to identity; and in each film the story unfolds as a result of the journalist's interviews and research. Neither story adheres to the strict logic of linear narrative; the interviews often overlap, so that we as viewers find ourselves "rewinding the plot" in order to add additional information or another point of view.

Not only does *Goldmine* borrow the structure of *Kane*, it includes pastiches of at least three scenes from Welles's classic. The newsroom scenes, in which the respective reporters are given their assignments, are remarkably similar. The scene in which Arthur visits Brian Slade's first manager, Cecil, in a hospital or nursing home, looks almost exactly like the scene in *Kane* in which Mr. Thompson interviews Jed Leland. The conversation Arthur has with Brian's ex-wife, Mandy, in a bar, looks almost exactly like the analogous scene in *Kane*, in which Thompson finally gets to talk to Kane's ex-wife, Susan.

While the references to *Kane* lend a certain cultural pedigree to a film (*Goldmine*) that is so heavily obsessed with flash and trash, the inclusion of *Kane* here also invites a reexamination of the classic film, which the American Film Institute named "the greatest American movie ever made."[40] That is, *Citizen Kane* is treated here, in much the same way that it is treated in Michael Chabon's

The Amazing Adventures of Kavalier and Clay (2000), as a work whose natural cultural allies are drawn from the low end of popular culture (comic books in Chabon's novel; fan magazines, rock 'n' roll, and the films of Russ Meyer in *Goldmine*). As in Chabon's novel, the inclusion of *Kane* here denaturalizes it, renders it strange, and for that very reason enables us to read it "outside the box" of its own prestige, to remember that it, too, is a compendium of high and low cultures—one has only to think of the vast storehouse at Xanadu, which houses both jigsaw puzzles and works of European art.

The importance of such taste-culture hybridity is not only that it calls attention to the inherent artificiality and constructedness of our so-called natural or self-evident taste categories (according to which the elements of high and low are presumably always easy to see). It also helps to remind us of what was always truly dangerous about some of the most exciting "high" art. The published screenplay for *Velvet Goldmine* calls for a title card that never made it into the final version of the movie—"For Oscar Wilde, posing as a sodomite." In Haynes's work, all the great artists cited—Rimbaud, Wilde, Genet—are homosexuals whose work and lives were seen as dangerous precisely because they threatened prevailing standards of good taste. What Haynes would like to do, one suspects, is turn them all into "pop idols."

I began this section on *Velvet Goldmine* with a discussion of Andrew Ross's article on camp and class-based taste culture. So, before closing, a more specific discussion of the treatment of class in the film seems warranted. Ross's article "Uses of Camp" invokes class in two ways. On the one hand, it appears to make class-taste distinctions within the broad category of camp—a move that, as I have tried to show, *Velvet Goldmine* pointedly avoids or even subverts. On the other, it invokes camp as "that category of cultural taste, which shaped, defined, and negotiated the way in which sixties intellectuals were able to 'pass' as subscribers to the throwaway Pop aesthetic."[41] Ross is speaking here of a specific use of camp that enabled middle-class intellectuals to overcome a certain bias against popular culture and to find its legitimate cultural use. It is this aspect of camp as a means by which specific classes can negotiate taste and class lines and can gain access to certain classed realms that I want briefly to address here.

One of the key aspects of glam—as represented in *Velvet Goldmine*—is the way in which it opened a space traditionally closed to working-class kids.

Arthur Stuart, the journalist who guides us through the search for Brian Slade, is something of a street kid in the flashback sequences. Forced to leave home because of his sexual preferences, Arthur scrapes together a living, finds a home with a band, and periodically glams it up and goes to concerts. This is not bleak footage. The glam rock concerts give a texture and color to Arthur's life that successfully block out whatever is humdrum and colorless (we don't see him at work, and we don't know how he makes his living, for example). This is in distinct contrast to the "contemporary" 1984 sequences, in which the gray reality of a bleak economy has successfully blocked out whatever vibrancy and pleasure there might be in the world (in fact, if Tommy Stone is an indication, it even blocks good pop music). Part of the point here seems to be that even in a heavily class-based culture (the glam sequences take place in England), camp and glam rock shape, define, and negotiate the way in which working-class kids can "pass" as middle-class kids from good schools (again a comparison to Jenny Livingston's *Paris Is Burning*—in which homeless kids dress up as military officers, fashion models, and Hollywood starlets—seems apt) and can gain access to a world of style, glitter, and seeming privilege. The way in which this surface style becomes linked to real cultural currency for working-class kids is perhaps best emblematized by the green brooch that passes from Oscar Wilde to Jack Fairy to Brian Slade, Curt Wild, and finally Arthur Stuart. Not only does the brooch mark a dandified line of succession, as I argued earlier, it also confers a kind of cultural pedigree on anyone who owns it. Both Brian Slade, whose best ideas initially seem to come from his handlers, and Curt Wild, who initially appears as an inarticulate ex-junkie, begin to speak spontaneously in Oscar Wilde aphorisms and witticisms, once they get the hang of glam style and, incidentally, possess the brooch. That is, in this film, style itself conveys a kind of cultural currency that generally comes only from good middle-class schools (the ability to quote Wilde—and also Shakespeare); one can say, in good camp fashion, that here style *becomes* cultural currency and a potent means of erasing or at least flattening out certain rigid markers of class (education, accent, taste).

All That Sirk and Fassbinder Allow

Andrew Ross ends his discussion of the campy "bad" movies that influenced Todd Haynes with a brief nod to a camp director whose project in some ways mirrors Haynes's own: John Waters. While Waters's films are characterized by a different style and voice than Haynes's, the way that he uses both camp and avant-garde strategies in his films links his project to the one I'm describing here. Most interesting for our purposes, though, is that Waters is a huge fan of Douglas Sirk. In *Shock Value*, Waters acknowledges "Douglas Sirk, a true gentleman who made such great melodramas as *Written on the Wind* and *Magnificent Obsession* that I wanted to fall to my knees when introduced."[42]

In some ways, Haynes did fall to his knees before Sirk when he made *Far from Heaven* (2002), a film that J. Hoberman calls a "supremely intelligent pastiche." Set in 1957, the film is a retelling of Sirk's *All That Heaven Allows* (1955). In Sirk's film, Cary, an attractive widow (Jane Wyman), falls in love with her gardener, Ron (Rock Hudson). Her country club friends and children disapprove of the match, and Cary succumbs to the pressure to stay within her own social class and age group. The film has a happy ending, though. Cary finally realizes that she's made a mistake when she hears that Ron is ill, and the two lovers are reunited at the end.

Haynes's version of the film complicates the basic plot by references to what Hoberman calls the "mirrored scenarios" of Sirk's *Written on the Wind* (1956) and *Imitation of Life* (1959)[43]—that is, by references to homoeroticism and race. In *Far from Heaven*, the woman (Kathy) is not widowed, as she is in Sirk's film, but married, and she becomes aware of Raymond, her African American gardener, at about the same time she learns that her husband Frank is having affairs with other men. There is no happy ending here—at least not in Sirkian terms. After his daughter is attacked in an episode of racial violence (in which he is specifically named as the reason for the assault), Raymond packs up and moves to Maryland. The final scene shows Kathy in the Hartford train station, waving good-bye.

As with the other Haynes films we've discussed, *Far from Heaven* enacts a certain hybridity of taste culture at the level of style. Certain scenes of the film (the opening and the hawthorn in a vase scene, for example) seem to mirror those in *All That Heaven Allows* almost shot for shot, and certain elements of the mise-en-scène, Kathy's station wagon, for example, are so identical to Sirk's that one wonders if Haynes found them at a Universal-International lot sale. Furthermore, during the shooting of the film Haynes very self-consciously restricted actors to a series of conventions associated with the time frame in

FIGURE 4 Rock Hudson and Jane Wyman in a press still for Douglas Sirk's *All That Heaven Allows* (1955). Sirk's celebrated talent for refracting the lowly Hollywood melodrama through the sensibility of the European avant-garde has made him a pivotal figure in a variety of cinematic pantheons, high and low.

which Douglas Sirk was working—the acting style of the 1950s. "There's a sort of vocabulary that comes with that type of acting," Dennis Quaid (Frank) said during a Sundance Channel television special, "which is different from what film acting is today." Haynes echoes that when he says, in the same television special, "We set up a very specific set of restraints in approaching this film, and it began with the writing. It was as if only a certain number of words could be spoken, a certain series of phrases, certain gestures that could take place, and nothing beyond that. It's in a way that still feels like stock dialogue."[44]

This restriction of the acting vocabulary lends a certain campy, theatrical air to the film's entire project. In setting up a distance between what the actors could do and what they were used to being able to do, a distance between what contemporary audiences could see and hear, and what we're used to seeing and hearing, Haynes creates a milieu that enables us to see actors negotiating their roles, in ways that generally remain invisible to us. Interestingly, this is most evident when Dennis Quaid is onscreen in his "queer man trying to pass" persona. In scenes such as the "Do you want another lamb chop?" dinner scene, or the portfolio-week office-montage scenes, we can literally see Quaid negotiate between past and present acting vocabularies as he builds a persona. This adds heightened irony, since the whole problem for Frank, Quaid's character, is how to pass, how to negotiate between queer and heteronormative sexuality, and Quaid's difficulty in negotiating acting codes foregrounds the discomfort of the character (who is himself seen as a kind of actor).

This sense of ironic distance and camp is reinforced by the film's costuming and music, which is in many ways more Sirk than Sirk. Kathy's dresses throughout the film are so startlingly full-skirted and beautiful that at times they threaten to eclipse the actress (Julianne Moore). Certainly, they seem to serve a kind of drag function here, as they continually remind us that Kathy's femininity must be constructed and performed anew every day. It's telling that in the final scenes of the film, when she no longer has a man to dress up for, Kathy wears a simple straight skirt, an outfit that stands in stark contrast to the costumes she wears throughout the rest of the movie. By the time Raymond leaves, it appears, she has given up a little on what Joan Rivière calls "the masquerade."

Just as the acting and costumes in *Far from Heaven* call attention to the artifice of gender-based style (the constructedness and performativity of gender), the drama of the music calls attention to a certain artifice within the genre of melodrama itself, the way the genre is itself literally constructed, as Thomas Elsaesser has maintained, around "problems of style and articulation."[45] As Elsaesser points out, melodrama derives its name from its theatrical use of music, and "in its dictionary sense . . . is a dramatic narrative in which musical accompaniment marks the emotional effects."[46] Certainly, the musical score in Sirk's dramas is theatrical and lush, in ways that are often startling to students (who comment on the use of music to punctuate and drive the story). The lush score here serves the same purpose that it has always served in melodrama—to provide dramatic punctuation and mark emotional effect. But because *Far from*

FIGURE 5 *Far from Heaven* (2002): Haynes's stylization of Sirk's already stylized vision of 1950s America.

Heaven is a contemporary film that uses 1950s codes as much as possible (James Lyons has spoken of the way he even tried to make the editing conform somewhat to 1950s styles), the constructed nature of the genre—the film's adherence to certain modes of articulation and style—become easy to see. This is different from the kind of remake project that translates 1950s codes into analogous contemporary codes, thereby preserving the seeming naturalness of the storytelling device. In that sense, one could argue that Haynes's use of music and his use of costume in this film constitute a kind of drag—and, following Andrew Ross, maintain that a certain "camp meaning" is generated in the text through a sort of historical incongruity and stylistic tension.[47]

At the same time that Haynes engages in a kind of camp channeling of Sirk's style, he also borrows heavily from Rainer Werner Fassbinder's homage to *All That Heaven Allows, Ali: Fear Eats the Soul* (1974). Here an older German working-class woman, Emmi, falls in love with a young Moroccan worker, Ali, and must confront the racial prejudice of her children, colleagues, and neighbors as a result. The mise-en-scène of Fassbinder's film is spare by comparison to either Sirk's or Haynes's. But the framing of the characters—often within door frames or positioned between slats and bars—is visually compelling. As

Haynes himself notes, *Ali* is organized around a visual economy of looks, an economy to which Haynes has consistently returned in his own work. There is a scene early in Fassbinder's film in which Emmi enters the foreign worker's bar, where she meets Ali. There is an intricate interplay of connecting glances, as Emmi looks at the assembled patrons, who each in turn look at her, before the barmaid finally comes to take her order. This relay of glances is repeated several times in the film, and Haynes uses it to remarkable effect in *Far from Heaven*. As J. Hoberman notes, *Far from Heaven* "is a movie about the limbo of petrified desire—most eloquently expressed by a yearning gaze."[48] Both the framing of the characters and the way the yearning gaze is represented in *Far from Heaven* owe more to Fassbinder than they do to Sirk. Certainly the scene in which Kathy meets Raymond at the art show is heavily indebted to a Fassbinder-style social economy of looks, as we literally follow a relay of curious and castigating glances throughout the gallery. In addition, the choice to cast the forbidden relationship as an interracial one is indebted to Fassbinder's retelling of Sirk's story, and even the choice to make homoeroticism explicit in the text seems to be as much a nod to Fassbinder as to Sirk. One of Haynes's few published articles on film aesthetics deals explicitly with homoaesthetics in the films of Fassbinder. And *Far from Heaven* seems to be—at least in part—Haynes's attempt to work out some of the homoaesthetics he attributes to Fassbinder within the context of a Hollywood movie.[49]

At the level of style, then, the film is a hybrid art-house melodrama/serio-camp romance, and as with the other hybrids we have been discussing, it's frequently difficult to separate out influences, to say which shot is influenced by Fassbinder and which by Sirk (and by extension, which is camp and which is straight, which is melodrama and which is art film). In addition, *Far from Heaven* mixes cultural references to create a hybrid taste culture. This is most clearly seen in the scenes involving Raymond—who can discuss modern art and gardening with his white middle-class patrons, and then slip into an entirely different vocabulary as soon as he goes to his favorite club across the tracks. But it's also present in the references to *Poison* and, by extension, to grade-B sci-fi movies, which I cited earlier in the article. It's present in the way in which certain anxieties about popular culture that are present in Sirk's film are smoothed over in Haynes's. The demonization of television, which is so much a part of

All That Heaven Allows (where the final sign of Cary's loveless future arrives in the form of a television set—a Christmas present from her adult children), is largely erased here, as Kathy and Dennis become Mr. and Mrs. Magnatech, and the scenes involving television viewing seem to be reassuringly homey scenes. Similarly, while the action in *All That Heaven Allows* halts at a key moment to allow Cary to read aloud from Henry David Thoreau's *Walden*, the analogous scene in *Far from Heaven* has Kathy's best friend, El, reading to a group of friends an article about Kathy in a popular ladies' magazine.

But while *Far from Heaven*'s effect of mixing high and low cultural forms, art and pop taste cultures, camp and straight performative styles brings it in line with the rest of Haynes's hybrid work, there is something about this film that sets it apart from the rest of the director's project. In *Superstar* and *Velvet Goldmine*, Haynes's hybridization of taste cultures and styles serves to elucidate the politics of the movies and give us real clues as to how the films should be read. The textual and taste-cultural hybridity in *Far from Heaven*, on the other hand, resists opening the text to analysis in quite the same way. For me, at least, *Far from Heaven* remains Haynes's most difficult and least legible film. For a work that outs the homoerotic subtext of Sirkian melodrama and which revels in a kind of camp theatricality, *Far from Heaven* is a movie whose sexual politics are peculiarly hard to decipher. Gay audiences often complain that the film seems to be more about race than about queers, as Kathy's relationship with Raymond is really the compelling nexus of the plot. But even at the level of race, the film can be difficult to decode, since it encourages us both to sympathize with Kathy's attempts to rise above the racial politics of her place in time and to feel superior to her.

There is one scene that has made every audience with whom I've seen this film laugh: the scene in the art gallery, when Kathy meets Raymond with his daughter. Kathy is delighted to see Raymond but surprised that he would know about an exhibit of modern art. "I read the newspaper—like everyone else," he tells her. Caught in a betrayal of her unconscious class prejudice and possibly racism, Kathy is flustered. "I'm not prejudiced," she tells him slowly and carefully, "and my husband and I have always supported equal rights for Negroes and the NAACP." This scene is immediately followed by a shot of everyone looking at Kathy—one of the key scenes in the film where she becomes the object of a critical collective social gaze.

We want to sympathize with Kathy in this scene, and I think we do (since we're aware that she's so much nicer than everyone else in Hartford). Yet the ironic tone of the film here also foregrounds how problematic her "liberalism" is. This strikes me as a different kind of tension than the class tension we see in *All That Heaven Allows* (where, even among contemporary youth audiences, I've never heard anyone laugh at Cary). In the Sirk film, when we as an audience realize that Cary still has the prejudices of her class, we also recognize that she's in real danger of losing contact with her children if she marries Ron. That realization helps to mitigate the superiority we feel over her. Would we really behave any differently? Would we sacrifice our relationship with our kids in order to have a second chance at love? Similarly, in *Ali: Fear Eats the Soul*, we recognize Emmi's racism—her relationship with a man of color notwithstanding. But Fassbinder refuses to let us off the hook as he paints a picture of racism whose very horror lies in its ability to taint even good-hearted people like Emmi. There is no irony here, even when Emmi takes Ali to one of Hitler's favorite restaurants on their wedding day. Racism is such a part of the social landscape, the film seems to suggest, that Emmi can recognize it only when she herself becomes its victim.

In *Far from Heaven*, there is no family pressure (as there is in Sirk) to mitigate against the kind of ironic distance that the film establishes between the audience and Kathy in the art gallery scene. The film does allow us to feel superior to the heroine in ways Fassbinder's film does not. A send-up of white liberalism permeates *Far from Heaven*, emphasized in the improbable scenes of the NAACP canvassing a white, middle-class neighborhood for support and a seemingly overdetermined scene of Kathy herself phoning the NAACP to volunteer her services for their "program." That is, there's a certain irony surrounding Kathy's white liberalism here that colors the depiction of the liberal sensibility available to people living through that time and perhaps undermines our ability to read the film as a comment on social problems we still face.

Part of the problem stems from our desire to read these scenes naturalistically, as though they were meant to be realistic depictions of the true-life scenarios people actually confronted in their suburban homes. But, as Haynes notes, this film is "not really about Hartford, Connecticut, in 1957." Rather it's about the way that life in Hartford gets represented to us, the classic American family scenario, which, as Haynes notes, "we know from the movies more than anywhere else."⁵⁰ From the movies and from television—for while it's true that real people in the 1950s did not see the NAACP routinely canvassing white affluent neighborhoods, they did see scenes very much like this in television dramas of the period (which, like melodrama, often used a certain amount of artifice and heightened drama to create situations of existential choice for the characters). If audiences don't always recognize the media references in *Far from Heaven*, it is perhaps because Haynes did not camp the film up enough, didn't make some of the invisible quotation marks around scenes obvious (the way he does in *Goldmine*).⁵¹

A Final Note on Camp

Throughout this essay I have alluded to the ways in which camp merges with or sheds light upon Haynes's hybridizing project. As Susan Sontag points out in her famous "Notes on 'Camp,'" "camp is not a natural mode of sensibility"; in fact it calls the whole notion of "natural" modes of sensibility into question.⁵² Marked by a love of the unnatural, of artifice and exaggeration, camp is a supremely theatrical category of cultural taste. Related to the cult of the dandy, it is a highly aestheticized mode of viewing the world. It privileges style over content (or shows the absolute inseparability of the two); it privileges irony, stylization, and certain "bad" forms of art. It is, as Sontag tells us, "decadent." As a verb ("to camp it up"), it functions as a mode of seduction. It "dethrone[s] the serious."⁵³

Certainly, these elements are present in Haynes's work. In addition Haynes frequently pays explicit cinematic homage to camp icons: Oscar Wilde in *Goldmine*, Jean Genet in *Poison*, Rimbaud in *The Assassins* (1985). His early essay on Fassbinder, "Homoaesthetics and *Querelle*," can be read as a theoretical attempt to reconcile the aesthetic project of camp with certain strands of feminist film theory. Without putting too fine a point on it, one can argue that reconciling these two modes of knowing (camp and feminist film theory) has been the theoretical underpinning of Haynes's entire film project (certainly, Haynes has returned again and again to movies that he identifies as "feminist"—*Superstar, Safe, Far from Heaven*—movies also heavily indebted to camp). What I have here identified as a project of hybridizing taste cultures can also be read, then, as Haynes's particular inflection on the camp aesthetic.

This is particularly interesting since Haynes sets so many of his films in precise historic moments—1957, 1983, 1984, the Nixon 1970s, the Reagan years—moments of cultural crisis or difficult historic transition. In this context, camp becomes one way (even if only in retrospect) that the culture negotiates difficult moments of social change. George Melly, the English jazz musician and—as Andrew Ross calls him—"pop intellectual," writes that camp is "central to almost every difficult transitional moment in the evolution of pop culture."[54] Haynes takes Melly's assertion and flattens it out, by showing that everything—from the most seemingly serious historic trauma to the most seemingly banal pop music scandal—is part of the pop culture landscape, and camp (or taste-culture hybridity) is one of the most effective means we have for negotiating it all.

All of Haynes's films are hybrid texts, shot through with a camp sensibility. I've chosen *Superstar*, *Goldmine*, and *Far from Heaven* for the main focus of this essay in part because they are overtly about a mediascape that is itself becoming increasingly hybridized. In all Haynes's films, though, elements of high and low not only coexist in a twin relationship but tend to coalesce into a synthetic taste culture, one that we increasingly recognize as the taste culture in which we live.

Notes

Special thanks to Chris Anderson, Margaret Ervin Bruder, Chris Dumas, Skip Hawkins, and Jeffrey Sconce for their help and suggestions.

1. Quoted on the video box, *Beyond the Valley of the Dolls* (Twentieth Century Fox, 1970).
2. See Joan Hawkins, *Cutting Edge: Art-Horror and the Horrific Avant-Garde* (Minneapolis: University of Minnesota Press, 2000).
3. Jeffrey Sconce has defined paracinema as an elastic category that includes splatter films, B movies, government hygiene films, Japanese monster movies, Japanese "pink" movies, old sci-fi and horror, exploitation, sword-and-sandal epics, Elvis flicks, and so on. See Jeffrey Sconce, "'Trashing' the Academy: Taste, Excess, and an Emerging Politics of Cinematic Style," *Screen* 36 (1995): 371–93.
4. This was a term much in use at the 1995 European Cinemas, European Societies conference, held in Bloomington, Indiana. *Cutting Edge* resulted in large part from my irritation over the unproblematic way in which scholars were invoking the notion of an agreed-upon "low" (as in "lesser") culture.

5. See Harry M. Benshoff, *Monsters in the Closet: Homosexuality and the Horror Film* (Manchester: Manchester University Press, 1997).
6. Downtown cinema is a radical form of independent cinema, which for want of a better term I have elsewhere called "avant-garde." See Joan Hawkins, "Midnight Sex-Horror Movies and the Downtown Avant-Garde," in *Defining Cult Movies: The Cultural Politics of Oppositional Taste*, ed. Mark Jancovich, Antonio Lazaro Reboll, James Lyons, Julian Stringer, and Andrew Willis (Manchester: Manchester University Press, 2003), 223–34.
7. See Hawkins, *Cutting Edge*.
8. I used the same quotation from Jameson in a similarly worded passage in *Cutting Edge*, 8. See Fredric Jameson, *Signatures of the Visible* (New York: Routledge, 1992).
9. Jim Collins, *Architectures of Excess: Cultural Life in the Information Age* (New York: Routledge, 1995), 125.
10. Ibid., 126.
11. Ibid., 126–27.
12. Ibid., 131 (first set of italics added).
13. I have purposely avoided using the term *stable* in relation to taste culture. While it is, of course, arguable that genre was ever really a stable category, my previous work on taste culture has attempted to demonstrate that taste itself clearly is not stable. See Hawkins, *Cutting Edge*.
14. Sconce has done some of this work in "'Trashing' the Academy," in which he argues that the notion of cultural capital, expounded by Bourdieu in *Social Distinction*, has become something of an elastic category as paracinephiles have entered the academy.
15. Since the film has been withdrawn from circulation by A&M records and the Carpenter family, copies are difficult to find. Low-grade bootleg videos are available from Video Vamp, 23 Big Spring Circle, Cookeville, Tenn. 38501. A better-quality DVD is available from Anonymous Film Archive.
16. Barbara Kruger, *Remote Control: Power, Culture and the World of Appearance* (Cambridge, Mass.: MIT Press, 1993), 160.
17. Chuck Stephens, "Gentlemen Prefer Haynes," *Film Comment* 31, no. 4 (1995): 76–81.
18. Graeme Clark, "Superstar: The Karen Carpenter Story," *Spinning Image*, www.thespinningimage.co.uk/cultfilms/displaycultfilm.asp?/reviewid=164&aff=13.
19. Barbara Klinger, *Melodrama and Meaning: History, Culture and the Films of Douglas Sirk* (Bloomington: Indiana University Press, 1994), 135, emphasis added.
20. Sconce, "'Trashing' the Academy," 372, 378.
21. See, for example, Norman Bryson, "Todd Haynes's *Poison* and Queer Cinema," *Invisible Culture: An Electronic Journal for Visual Studies*, http://www.rochester.edu/in_visible_culture/issue1/bryson/bryson.html.
22. For more on what such a "queer synthesis" might entail, see Michael Warner, *Fear of a Queer Planet* (Minneapolis: University of Minnesota Press, 1993).

23. Chuck Stephens, "Gentlemen Prefer Haynes."
24. Lynn Spigel, *Welcome to the Dreamhouse: Popular Media and Postwar Suburbs* (Durham, N.C.: Duke University Press, 2001), 311.
25. Justin Wyatt, "Cinematic/Sexual: An Interview with Todd Haynes," *Film Quarterly* 46, no. 3 (spring 1993): 2–8.
26. Jeremy Heilman, "Superstar: The Karen Carpenter Story," November 4, 2002, archived at moviemartyr.com and available at www.rottentomatoes.com/m.Superstar-10002120/reviews.php.
27. Todd Haynes, "Risks of Identity," paper delivered at Knowing Mass Culture/Mediating Knowledge, Center for Twentieth-Century Studies conference, University of Wisconsin, Milwaukee, May 1, 1999.
28. Todd Haynes, *Velvet Goldmine* screenplay (London: Faber and Faber, 1998), xx.
29. The copyright issue—especially within the music industry—has ruined many a good film. *Superstar* can't even be shown in its proper format, as a result of copyright restrictions. *Kurt and Courtney*, Nick Broomfield's 1998 documentary about Courtney Love and Kurt Cobain, suffers from the absence of any of Cobain's songs. And *Velvet Goldmine*, with its many references to David Bowie, would be a better film if some of Bowie's songs had been included on the film sound track.
30. Hawkins, *Cutting Edge*.
31. Interestingly enough, this title card replaces the one called for in the published screenplay, "For Oscar Wilde, posing as a sodomite." See Haynes, *Velvet Goldmine* screenplay, 3.
32. Andrew Ross, "Uses of Camp," in *No Respect: Intellectuals and Popular Culture* (New York: Routledge, 1989), 155, emphasis added.
33. Ibid., 153.
34. Ibid.
35. See the chapter on the 1970s in Vito Russo's *The Celluloid Closet: Homosexuality in the Movies*, rev. ed. (New York: Harper and Row, 1985). When *Sunday Bloody Sunday* (John Schlesinger, 1971) was first released, I went to see it in a suburban California theater. During the scene in which two men kiss, the audience in the balcony stood up and made retching noises.
36. Ross, "Uses of Camp," 153.
37. Ibid.
38. Ibid.
39. Haynes, *Velvet Goldmine* screenplay, xx.
40. American Film Institute, "100 Years, 100 Movies," www.afi.com/tv/movies.asp.
41. Ross, "Uses of Camp," 136.
42. John Waters, *Shock Value* (New York: Thunder's Mouth, 1995), 215.
43. J. Hoberman, "Sign of the Times," *Village Voice*, November 6, 2002.

44. *Anatomy of a Scene: Far from Heaven* (television show), series producer Toby Oppenheimer, first aired Sunday, November 17, 2002, on Sundance Channel.
45. Thomas Elsaesser, "Tales of Sound and Fury: Observations on the Family Melodrama," *Film Theory and Criticism: Introductory Readings*, 4th ed., ed. Gerald Mast, Marshall Cohen, and Leo Braudy (New York: Oxford University Press, 1992), 519.
46. Ibid.
47. Ross, "Uses of Camp," 138.
48. Hoberman, "Sign of the Times."
49. See Haynes, "Homoaesthetics and *Querelle*." *Subjects/Objects* (1985): 71–99.
50. *Anatomy of a Scene.*
51. My undergraduate students tend to talk about the racial politics raised by the film in historical terms, as something we've overcome. In part that has to do with the racial zeitgeist we're experiencing at the moment, but in part it has to do with something in the tone of the film itself which seems to encourage students to read for ironic distance—"we've come a long way."
52. Susan Sontag, "Notes on 'Camp,'" in *Against Interpretation* (New York: Dell, 1966), 275.
53. Ibid., 288–89.
54. George Melly, *Revolt into Style: The Pop Arts in Britain* (London: Allen Lane, 1970), 160–61; see also Ross, "Uses of Camp," 136.

MATT HILLS

Para-Paracinema The *Friday the 13th* Film Series as Other to Trash and Legitimate Film Cultures

I will argue in this chapter that academic accounts of "trash" cinema can be read as overemphasizing trash's opposition to "legitimate" film culture. By excavating a line of argument from foundational work on trash,[1] I will suggest that we need to consider how notions of trash film have worked to exclude certain types of filmic sleaze that have also been simultaneously excluded from, or devalued within, academic discussion. Types of slasher films have, I will suggest, marked one limit to trash's classificatory elasticity. Despite being rejected by legitimate film culture, certain slasher flicks have nevertheless *not* been welcomed into the trash pantheon, becoming intensely problematic in this respect. For example, the *Friday the 13th* franchise—currently running at a total of ten films—seems to have remained resolutely beyond trash revalorization, while also being fixed in many academic accounts as a marker of the "low" and illegitimate slasher film. This piece will thus explore what has and what hasn't been counted as sleazy artistry, taking the *Friday the 13th* films as a case study in fan/academic struggles over the cultural distinctions of trash and legitimate film.

The Limits to Trash

In his influential article outlining the way that certain films and their auteurs have been reclaimed under the classification of trash cinema, Jeffrey Sconce suggests that the "explicit manifesto of paracinematic culture is to valorize all forms of cinematic 'trash,' whether such films have been either explicitly rejected or simply ignored by legitimate film culture."[2] By "paracinema," Sconce means all that exists outside the sacralizing functions of academic film criticism, paracinematic aesthetics being either in excess of, or opposed to, those valued by official, legitimate culture: "For its audience, paracinema represents a final textual frontier that exists beyond the colonizing powers of the academy, and thus serves as a staging ground for strategic raids on legitimate culture and its institutions by those (temporarily) lower in educational, cultural and/or economic capital." Paracinema is a "reading protocol" that is "devoted to all manner of cultural detritus."[3] Note that in these formulations, Sconce repeatedly stresses the inclusiveness of "trash"; its reading protocol (and thus its interpretive community) responds to "*all* forms of cinematic 'trash'" and "*all* manner of cultural detritus." According to this position, trash's coherence as a category lies in its very oppositionality to "legitimate film culture." This account posits a cultural struggle for distinction between two groups: trash fans and academics studying and valuing official film culture. It therefore tends to marginalize struggles for distinction that occur at intragroup levels; that is, between factions of trash fans and also between factions within "the academy."[4]

However, Sconce's foundational study of trash cinema does not only oppose "trash" and "legitimate" film cultures, and it is an alternative interpretation that I want to stress here. Sconce also notes that "in cultivating a counter-cinema from the dregs of exploitation films, paracinematic fans, *like the academy*, explicitly situate themselves in opposition to Hollywood cinema and the mainstream U.S. culture it represents."[5] I want to explore this dimension of Sconce's definition of trash cinema and sleazy artistry by not opposing "trash" and "legitimate" film cultures but rather considering the ways in which they act in concert to exclude certain types of pop culture as "mainstream" sleaze rather than sleazy art.

Considering levels of (sub)cultural struggle within and between different pop culture fandoms, and within the academy, I will argue that paracinema and its reading protocols therefore depend on multiple exclusions. They never merely oppose all "legitimate" film culture, but occasionally come into alignment with aspects of it, tending to discursively construct specific types of trashy, low-cultural film as other to paracinema and its canon. It is this othered, sleazy cinema—not accorded the status of sleazy art—that I will term "para-paracinema" here, since its texts are simultaneously othered by academic fractions of legitimate film culture. Certain "illegitimate" films escape revalorization via trash's reading protocol, while their illegitimacy remains a matter of contention within the academy. Furthermore, such films may not simply represent a "mainstream U.S. culture," as Sconce suggests; they can also be linked to discourses of "cult" film (and can possess their own dedicated cult fandoms) without being revalued either by trash fans or by "the academy."

Exploring the limits to trash, a number of previous writers have sought to amend Sconce's account. In *Cutting Edge: Art-Horror and the Horrific Avant-garde*, Joan Hawkins writes, "Because Sconce is mainly interested in theorizing trash aesthetics, he doesn't take the 'high' aspects of the [paracinema] catalogs' video lists into account. So he does not thoroughly discuss the way in which the companies' listing practices erase the difference between what is considered 'trash' and what is considered 'art,' through a deliberate levelling of hierarchies and recasting of categories."[6] By focusing purely on "trash," Sconce allegedly neglects to consider how "trash" films are transformed in their meaning and their cultural value by virtue of being placed in a paradigm with "art" or "high" cultural film such as avant-garde material directed by Maya Deren, Luis Buñuel, and Salvador Dalí. However, this supposed attack on Sconce's work actually resonates with the aspect of his argument that I have drawn attention to above, since it demonstrates that paracinema can be and has been revalued as film art by placing it in direct cultural proximity to films already deemed aesthetically (and legitimately) valuable. Again, this should remind us that trash film culture often resembles legitimate film culture,[7] especially in its reliance on notions of film art and authorship.[8]

Significantly, Hawkins's assumed corrective to Sconce's work does not simply demonstrate the collapse of cultural hierarchies at work, as Hawkins claims. Operating as a dissemination of cultural value (a case of gilt by association?) this process relies on avant-garde films being paradigmatically valued in order to place trash (however uneasily or insecurely) within this paradigm. Legitimate film culture is supported here, its value-system being used tactically to confer value on sleazy film *art*.

The French sociologist Pierre Bourdieu's work on cultural distinctions has been much used in discussions of trash cinema fans and fan cultures more generally.[9] Bourdieu offers an analysis of cultural hierarchies that allows us to make sense of Hawkins's observations on trash and avant-garde cinema, when he writes:

> One can never entirely escape from the hierarchy of legitimacies. Because the very meaning and value of a cultural object varies according to the system of objects in which it is placed, detective stories, science fiction or strip cartoons may be entirely prestigious cultural assets or be reduced to their ordinary value, depending on whether they are associated with avant-garde literature or music—in which case they appear as manifestations of daring or freedom—or combine to form a constellation typical of middle-brow taste—when they appear as what they are, simple substitutes for legitimate assets.[10]

This appears to precisely capture the aspect of "trash" that Hawkins draws attention to (and which she suggests is absent in Sconce's account). Trash, or paracinema, becomes a "manifestation of daring or freedom" through its association with avant-garde film. But this valorization of trash does not so much collapse cultural hierarchies as presuppose (and reinforce) the cultural value of avant-garde film by way of attempting to contextualize trash within this paradigmatic class of object. Cultural hierarchies are not escaped; instead the lines of cultural demarcation around film as art are stretched as avant-garde legitimacy is discursively borrowed. Trash, in such an analysis, appears to rely more on its legitimate other than on a reading of Sconce's work that would construe trash and legitimate film cultures as oppositional. This line of thought suggests considering trash film culture as always (parasitically) aligned with legitimate film culture, rather than viewing trash as significantly oppositional yet tactically united with legitimate film culture against the Hollywood mainstream. I will explore this issue below with my case study of *Friday the 13th*.

A second line of trash criticism has been forwarded by Mark Jancovich, who has argued that "Sconce's ... account of 'paracinema' ... tends to conflate major differences between the fan cultures that it discusses and so constructs its own sense of the 'real' authentic nature of this fan culture."[11] Jancovich's work and my own earlier discussion of paracinema fans both suggest that fan cultures tend

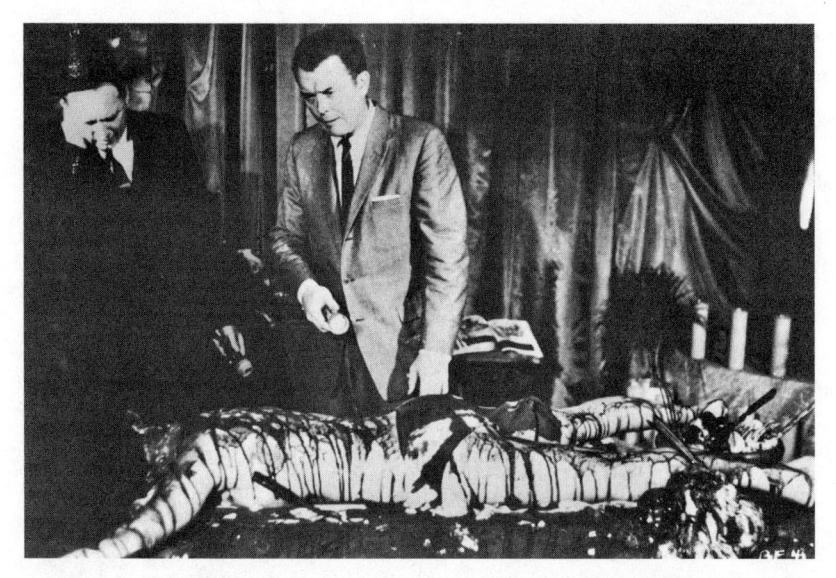

FIGURE 1 Herschell Gordon Lewis's foundational gore film *Blood Feast* (1963): "crude and vicious carnage of the animal innard school."

to struggle for distinction internally and in relation to other fan cultures.[12] For example, Jancovich demonstrates how trash or paracinema fans "often reserve their most direct and vitriolic attacks [for] the tastes of other fans—fans who are dismissed as inauthentic. For example, *Incredibly Strange Films* frequently distinguishes itself from fans of the 1980s slasher film, who are presented, by comparison, as . . . indistinguishable from the conformist masses."[13] This discursive othering proceeds by contrasting the aesthetics of director Herschell Gordon Lewis's *Wizard of Gore* (1970) with those of special effects (SFX) creator Tom Savini, used in the first *Friday the 13th* film and *Friday the 13th: The Final Chapter*: "The *Friday the 13th* series began in neo-horror's late formative period and initially displayed the effects 'wizardry' of Tom Savini (*Friday the 13th*), and Carl Fullerton (*Friday the 13th Part 2*). Both were interviewed in the early issues of the premier horror fanzine, *Fangoria*—Savini in issue 6, and Fullerton in issue 13—where they discussed their craft for these films."[14]

Where Lewis's gore effects are praised in *Incredibly Strange Films* as "crude and vicious carnage of the animal innard school," Savini's work is dismissed as "technically virtuosic [but] slick and facile."[15] In contrast to this trash fan position, Savini's gore effects work—linked to *Friday the 13th*—is frequently applauded by that fraction of horror fans who read the niche U.S. commercial magazine *Fangoria*, as Ian Conrich has demonstrated by quoting from *Fangoria* classified ads:

> "Fangoria is #1, so is *Friday the 13th*. Long Live Horror, Blood and Guts. This is Dr. Blood Signing Off," "Gore: *Friday the 13th* and any other horror movies—I want info. Send to Gore, 1354 . . . ,"*Dawn of the Dead, Friday the 13th* and Tom Savini rule [blood & guts forever]." It is here, where the films function culturally as a modern Grand Guignol [for their fans], that arguably the greatest attraction of the series exists.[16]

What takes place between the *Friday the 13th* fans analyzed by Conrich and the paracinema fans analyzed by Jancovich amounts to an "intrageneric conflict . . . between fans of a particular genre."[17] Fans of trash horror other and devalue slasher-cycle horror as overly commercial or nonunderground. What counts as "real" or "authentic" horror for these paracinema fans is thus defined against "mainstream" horror, but this latter category is a profoundly mobile signifier; the horror texts that are nominated here as "mainstream"—1980s slasher films—have been simultaneously othered in much academic film criticism and in legitimate film culture, but such films are nevertheless not viewed and devalued as mainstream by their cult fans. As Jancovich has argued, addressing slasher-movie fans' knowledge of SFX professionals like Tom Savini and Dick Smith, these are "hardly figures who would be familiar to the majority of moviegoers. The term 'average movie goer' [used in *Incredibly Strange Films* to characterize slasher-movie fans] is therefore an extremely slippery one that operates to conflate a small fan culture with the conformist mass and so produce a clear sense of distinction between the authentic subcultural self and the inauthentic mass cultural other."[18]

Thus, films discursively positioned as "mainstream" by trash and legitimate film cultures may be socially and discursively positioned as "subcultural" by their cult fans. These small fan cultures, and their subcultural contextualization of 1980s slasher films, have to be ignored by trash and legitimate film cultures if they are to sustain their imagined version of slasher movies as irredeemably mainstream. That these attributions of mainstream and authentic status are such highly mobile signifiers is brought home by the fact that Tom Savini's work

FIGURE 2 Special effects guru Tom Savini poses with Jason (Ari Lehman) on the set of *Friday the 13th* (1980).

has been championed by fans of cult horror—especially for his contributions to George Romero's *Dawn of the Dead* (1979) and 1985's *Day of the Dead*[19]—and simultaneously devalued by anti-mainstream slasher fans in relation to the likes of *Friday the 13th*. Although it could thus be argued that Savini—as a figure and as a version of SFX's Foucauldian author-function—mediates and bridges authentic and mainstream genre texts, I would suggest that this point grants a coherence to these differing interpretations and attributions of status that they do not possess. Instead, I view shifting versions of mainstream and cult or authentic horror as emerging through rival (but closely related) interpretive communities.

In a 1993 study of taste and cultural politics, Sconce explored some of these issues around the slasher film, noting the "low critical esteem most film commentators have for the . . . subgenre of the 'slasher' movie. Despite their commercial success and stylistic variety, such films remain a target of indiscriminate ridicule by the film cognoscenti. Often, this derision is aimed as well at the teenage target audience for these films, which critics routinely characterize as a legion of brain-dead pubescent zombies docilely filing into the nation's multiplexes for each new 'teenie-kill' release."[20] Slasher movies have, then, displayed extreme discursive mobility. The slasher flick has represented both "a convenient doormat of popular film criticism [that] provide[s] a formulaic reference point for critics to compare other, more 'worthy' horror films [to],"[21] *and* a point of contrast for fans of horror operating within a paracinematic reading protocol. Hence constituting a form of para-paracinema, slasher movies have been multiply located within the cultural politics of taste, being a "final textual frontier" for legitimate culture's cinephiles/critics and trash's connoisseurs alike.

Even this narrative is overly monolithic: not all slasher films have been equally devalued by critics. Indeed, certain slasher movies have, over time, been accorded a limited respectability within academic film criticism. Sconce's own comparison of the *Nightmare on Elm Street* series with *Henry: Portrait of a Serial Killer* locates the "taste wars" surrounding these films as largely generational[22] but neglects to consider how *Nightmare on Elm Street* can be (and has been) recuperated by academic criticism via the "originality" of auteur Wes Craven.[23] The self-reflexivity of *Wes Craven's New Nightmare* (1994), made a year after the publication of Sconce's essay, has also, arguably, boosted Craven's (sub)cultural capital within legitimate film culture. Sconce relates the critical devaluation of certain horror films to the opposition between "appeals to issues of originality, character, and realism" where these are discursively positioned and valued "over formula, sensationalism, and special effects."[24] Such oppositions have certainly worked to devalue certain slasher movies intensely, while other slashers have been recontextualized as historically significant film art within academic and critical circles. This self-conscious historicization of 1980s slasher movies has provoked and sustained a range of situated shifts in the slasher flick's cultural value. It has allowed contemporary fans of the *Friday the 13th* franchise to discursively locate themselves outside the mainstream by contrasting their enduring love of *Friday the 13th* films with the sheer commercial success of early films in the franchise, making this more of a cult fandom. It has also allowed *Friday the 13th* to be devalued and othered academically via a historical contrast between this film and *Halloween* (dir. John Carpenter, 1978). It is this latter shift that I will focus on in the next section.

The Friday *Franchise and the Formula Fallacy*

Even academic writers who are kindly predisposed to the *Friday the 13th* films, such as Ian Conrich, position themselves slightly apologetically against an assumed weight of critical opinion: "The popular view is that the slasher films of the horror New Wave began with *Halloween* (1978). *The importance of this film is undeniable*, yet the commerciality of *Friday the 13th* (1980) showed that the success of *Halloween* was repeatable and it was only from this position that there was an explosion in the number of slasher films produced."[25]

Halloween is accorded the status of the slasher movie's "origin" here, whereas *Friday the 13th* is linked to discourses of "commerciality." *Halloween* is thus artful and historically significant as the (retrospective) head of a film cycle. It defines and creates a formula, whereas *Friday the 13th* simply repeats this: "*Despite the repetitive nature of these films*, they have acquired a cult following demonstrated perhaps, today, by the number of devoted websites."[26]

Such an opposition—between the valued *Halloween* as "original" and the devalued *Friday the 13th* as a "formulaic repetition"—has stalked through the pages of academic criticism, indicating that the relationship between legitimate culture and slasher films has, over time, become less one of monolithic antagonism and more a case of selective valorization in line with the academy and its dominant aesthetics of realism, originality, and antisensationalism. Toward the end of his excellent survey of horror films and the U.S. movie industry, Kevin Heffernan baldly states that "Paramount's *Friday the 13th* series follows the time-honored 1950s and 1960s tradition of a major studio knocking off the genre success of an independent production (in this case, John Carpenter's . . . *Halloween*)."[27] To take another example, Steven Jay Schneider has remarked that "the revolutionary impact of Carpenter's film can hardly be denied," going on to contrast this with the "bloodier" *Friday the 13th*, which is described as taking "Carpenter's film as a template."[28] This term *template* condenses and carries the logics of cultural distinction at work here, and it recurs in academic criticism, along with the notion of *Friday the 13th* as pure repetition: "Note . . . that the majority of *Halloween*'s many imitators—for example, the . . . *Friday the 13th* films . . . —are somewhat gross in comparison with the original, both in style (their use of subjective camera is laughably obtrusive) and in their increasing emphasis on repellent physical detail."[29]

FIGURE 3 John Carpenter's *Halloween* (1978): The "original" slasher film and perpetual critical foil to the *Friday the 13th* franchise.

As in Andrew Tudor's cultural history of the horror movie quoted above, some critics do not feel the need to distinguish between "the *Friday the 13th* films," assuming that they entirely repeat themselves as well as repeating the template of *Halloween*: "The appealing stability of the monster is worked out formally through the serialization process. The only constant in, say, the *Friday the 13th* films is the psychotic killer. The monster is the norm. It is he, not his victims, to whom the audience finally relates because he will live on into the sequel."[30] *Friday the 13th* films have therefore been powerfully articulated with critically devalued notions of gore over character or narrative (Tudor's "increasing emphasis on repellent . . . detail"), repetition over originality, and commerce over art. Indeed, the nature of the *Friday* franchise's reception in the academy has been, if anything, more formulaic than the films themselves. Despite Paul Budra's allegation that "the only constant . . . is the killer," the franchise's killer has not remained constant. In the first *Friday the 13th* the killer is not Jason Voorhees, it is actually his mother (a point of horror-fan trivia that becomes a matter of life or death in the first *Scream* film). Only in *Part III* does Jason don the hockey mask that becomes his trademark. It could also be argued that once Jason *has* become a constant fixture of the series, he changes significantly across the franchise, developing superhuman strength in *Part III*, becoming more obviously zombie-like after *Part V* and *Part VI*, and displaying a capacity to inhabit other bodies in the "possession horror" reworking of *Part IX, Jason Goes to Hell: The Final Friday*. Recently, the franchise has developed a post-*Scream* self-referential playfulness, evident in the virtual reality sequence of *Jason X*, where the Camp Crystal Lake mise-en-scène of the first film is recreated, and where *Friday the 13th*'s gender representations are critiqued via exaggerated and parodic portrayals of teen bimbos. This increased self-referentiality is also arguably in evidence in the *Freddy vs. Jason* franchise crossover from 2003.

The gender of *Friday the 13th*'s killer has also been rendered more formulaic in academic criticism than it was in the pop cultural text itself, with Jonathan Lake Crane rather bizarrely referring to "Jason" as the first film's slasher: "Jason's spirit has used his mother's body to cleanse the camp of human beings; yet it would be wrong to call Jason a she."[31] Crane ties himself in knots attempting to sustain a critical reading of *Friday the 13th* that marks its killer as male, or at the very least as not female. Failing to do so, Crane eventually falls back on a gender-neutral interpretation, asserting that "Jason is neither male nor female: Jason is really an it. He has no identity beyond the hockey mask that carries no gender markings. The faceless mask . . . is the human face horribly reduced to a plane of purely vicious instrumentality."[32]

Crane's commitment to a *formulaic* semiotic equation of "slasher = male" appears to overwhelm his response to the text. *Friday the 13th*'s denotative level—whereby we would generally agree that Pamela Voorhees, Jason's mother, is the female killer, and that she is motivated by revenge but that she is *not* shown to be possessed by Jason—is displaced by a piece of critical legerdemain which has it that Jason is the killer, and that he is not a she. This entirely overwrites the role played by the character of Pamela Voorhees, as does Crane's torturous conclusion that "Jason is really an it." Although Carol Clover refers to *Friday the 13th*'s "play of pronoun function" as a "visual identity game,"[33] such pronoun confusion appears to be far more pronounced in Crane's critical, formula-sustaining interpretation. Despite the first film offering what will become an unusual equation of (maternal) femininity with the role of slasher (and this actually occurs before the "male = killer" convention becomes firmly fixed in place in the slasher cycle), Crane interprets *Friday the 13th* retroactively as more of the

FIGURE 4 The elusive Jason: perpetually misidentified, degendered, and denigrated.

franchised same, and as more of Jason on the rampage. Pop culture that precedes and *doesn't* fit into a slasher "formula" is here interpreted, and devalued, through the template of just such a formula. Crane's interpretive grid is entirely that of the critic aiming to denigrate and dismiss the *Friday the 13th* franchise. I would therefore argue that most academic criticism circling around the *Friday the 13th* franchise is guilty of a type of formula fallacy—that is, it projects the notion of formula onto these films as an interpretive strategy or activates such a notion through critical intertextuality. Lending an extra poignancy to this fallacy is the fact that readings offered by the academic interpretive community are, empirically and in this instance, more formulaic than the popular cultural texts they denigrate as such.

Whereas Crane concludes by lambasting *Friday the 13th*'s total lack of morality,[34] the following statement by Vera Dika carries almost all of the cultural distinctions that critically surround *Friday the 13th* and thus comes close to being a condensed statement of the formula fallacy: "*Friday the 13th* is a minimalization or reduction of *Halloween*'s essential structure.... What *Friday the 13th* most definitely adds to the stalker formula is a subcultural tone, a quality of exploitation that was not evident in *Halloween*.... *Friday the 13th* has no artistic pretensions, no film-school 'allusions' or 'homages';... its elements have been combined for their maximum impact and profitability."[35] *Friday the 13th* formulaically reduces *Halloween*. Where it adds to the formula (and again, *formula* is the prioritized term here) it does so by a "quality of exploitation" (for which, read the gore and "repellent detail" so disliked by Andrew Tudor), and has "no artistic pretensions" whatsoever. Instead, it's all about "maximum . . . profitability." Unlike Wes Craven's *Nightmare on Elm Street*, his later return to the franchise, and John Carpenter's *Halloween*, *Friday the 13th* has no auteur who can be mobilized, via the cultural work of the author-function, to defend its cultural value within an official/legitimate cultural reading. "Sean S. Cunningham" carries no critical reputation, and thus no subcultural capital as a source of author-based interpretations, as well as being contrasted to "well-known film school graduates (Carpenter, Spielberg, Lucas, Coppola etc)" by virtue of not hailing "from one of the elite filmmaking schools."[36] In terms of cultural distinctions, then, Cunningham's absence as an author-function can be related to accounts of the flesh-and-blood author's relative lack of cultural capital or a scholarly or arty film-school disposition. Either of these could allow film scholars to reclaim Cunningham's work by articulating favored academic theories to his films. Instead, in Vera Dika's account of the slasher cycle, Cunningham's authorial agency is restricted to his plan to imitate *Halloween* and *Dawn of the Dead*.[37] Dika then discusses the work of the director of *Friday the 13th Part II* and *Part III*, Steve Miner (who went on to direct *Halloween H20*) in terms of its approximation to absolute nonstyle. Sean S. Cunningham's direction of *Friday the 13th* was, according to Dika, minimally significant via its construction of a nonlocalized sense of pervasive threat. Even this minor distinction is lost in the sequel: "The gaming process of *Friday the 13th Part II* is also systematized through its changed formal strategies. . . . not only is the story structure identical [to *Friday the 13th*], but most of the formal, narrative and visual elements have been repeated. The most significant variation, however, comes in Miner's direction of the film, and in the tendency toward standardization that it reflects."[38]

This repetitive, formulaic set of critical clichés has produced a situation where, as Reynold Humphries has recently and astutely noted, "*Halloween* is given serious critical treatment, partly because its reflexive nature—the function of the look—lends itself perfectly to an articulation of theory and close analysis, but also because of its status as the first slasher. *Friday the 13th* is considered to lack the intellectual dimension of the earlier film."[39] In fact, Humphries's conclusion is something of an understatement; as I have shown here, *Friday the 13th* has not just been critically positioned as intellectually lacking, it has been othered and devalued in line with the conventional aesthetic norms of the academy and official film culture,[40] said to lack originality and artfulness, to possess no nominated or recognized auteur, and to be grossly sensationalist in its focus on Tom Savini's gory special effects. In contrast, the originality and subtlety of John Carpenter's film-school-educated and theory-alluding, homage-paying *Halloween* have been consistently applauded (although later entries in this *Halloween* franchise are rarely discussed academically, with the exception of *Halloween H20*, legitimated via the authorial role of Kevin Williamson).[41] This extreme contrast in the critical receptions for different slasher films indicates that legitimate film culture does not so much distinguish between genres or cycles (where "slasher movie = bad" *tout court*) as between entries in a genre or cycle that can be valorized through official criteria and those which cannot.

The *Friday the 13th* franchise has thus found itself languishing outside the sanctuary of legitimate film culture as well as outside the trash-as-art revaluations of paracinema. Too obviously a commercial success at the time of its initial release to be feted as underground trash, too historically recent to be recuperated as archival exploitation cinema, too standardized or proficient in its direction to be "bad," and yet possessing its own cult fan following, this reject from legitimate film culture has yet to find a trash revalorization. As para-paracinema—simultaneously other to trash and legitimate film cultures—it indicates that ways in which paracinematic and legitimate film reading protocols can become tactically aligned through a shared revulsion for the untutored, the artless, and the commercial turned cultish.

However, legitimate film culture is, in the case of the *Friday the 13th* franchise, seemingly more elastic in its textual boundaries than is trash cinema's reading protocol. A small number of attempts have been made to academically revalue *Friday the 13th*. Unlike Crane's strained interpretation and attempt to preserve critical distaste, Carol Clover notes that *Friday the 13th* is one of "the most dramatic case[s] of pulling out the gender rug"[42] ever seen in the slasher movie. Clover also notes that it is a matter of some interest that gender representations are visibly adjusted in the slasher movie, a shift thus occurring "at the furthest possible remove from the quarters of theory and showing signs of trickling upward."[43] Like some avant-garde, surreal wound bleeding upward, this imagery positions the slasher movie, *Friday the 13th* included, as a definite source of cultural value for Clover. This bid for cultural distinction is not aesthetic per se. It is, rather, cultural-political, emerging via the very marginality of horror as a "genre that [allegedly] appeals to marginal people (not, by and large, middle-aged, middle-class whites) who may not have quite the same investment in the status quo."[44]

Although I have previously criticized academic culture's tendency to divide popular culture into "good" and "bad" objects or "reactionary" and "progressive" wings,[45] this emphasis adds a degree of complexity to the academic interpretive community's cultural distinctions. Even given a lack of aesthetic criteria, the cultural politics of representation can morally trump and overrule traditionally "aesthetic" concerns, resulting in bids for cultural distinction that are relatively autonomous from the criteria for official valorization identified by Sconce and followed so far in my argument. Of course, in practice, cultural-political bids for cultural distinction can be harnessed to auteurist arguments, and this often proves to be the case in horror criticism, with the films of David Cronenberg challenging gender norms,[46] the films of George Romero radically representing consumers as zombies,[47] the films of James Whale coding queer subtexts,[48] and so on. Yet the logical possibility remains that cultural-political bids for cultural distinction can disturb and reorder cultural hierarchies more radically than stretching art discourses to recontextualize low-cultural objects. Furthermore, such an axis of cultural distinction is specific to academic writing, at least in terms of its potential power to trump other axes of distinction. It has no meaningful analogy in either trash cinema fan culture or film journalism. Perhaps for this reason, academic culture's links to official/legitimate culture, at least within the terrain of cultural and film criticism, are less monolithic than those of other interpretive communities. It is a sense of cultural politics, extending into the capacity to consider bids for cultural value—its own included—as politicized, that acts as academia's community-specific form of distinction.

Academic cultural politics hence operates not only at the level of textual analysis, but also at a metalevel addressing how texts are criticized/canonized, and devalued/distinguished. With regards to trash and horror film, such an emphasis on the political construction of taste is shared by a range of scholarly writers.[49] I have argued here that such a focus must rebound on definitions of trash cinema, such that trash becomes considered not as an inherently inclusive reading protocol that absorbs all that legitimate culture disavows, ignores, or rejects. To the contrary, trash culture presupposes an exclusionary politics of taste that works to expel and marginalize its constructed others, and these others go beyond the officially sanctioned as well as beyond the self-evident mainstream. Although the tawdry detritus of pop culture can be reclaimed as trash, implicit criteria underpin this process, meaning that certain pop cultural texts cannot be readily (anti)canonized as trash, despite being academically devalued. Chief among the criteria for "trashification" would appear to be the ease with which texts can be disarticulated from commercial popularity and thus positioned as "underground" or as sources of subcultural capital. Also significant is the ease with which texts can be recontextualized as trash *art*, meaning that discourses of authorship and avant-gardist aesthetics remain important in the countersacralization of trash art status.

Although not drawing on a Bourdieu-derived theoretical approach to cultural distinction, Ian Conrich has also recently bid for the *Friday the 13th* franchise's recognition and cultural value within academic film criticism. Unlike Clover, Conrich's argument for valorization does not hinge on cultural politics. Instead, Conrich negotiates a discursive position in relation to the conventional norms of official film culture as identified by Sconce, where textual "sophistication" is valued over the visual stimulation of special effects. How, then, does Conrich seek to align the *Friday* films with legitimate culture?

Like many other bids for horror's cultural value within legitimate film culture, Conrich seeks to recontextualize his object of study by intertextually linking it to, and reading it through, cultural texts that are less obviously devalued as low-cultural. This process of recontextualization—already observed by Hawkins in the case of trash—means that horror's academic discussions tend to invoke the "timelessness" of horror, relating horror films to myths as well as to valued theories.[50] Rather than Greek myth, Conrich's valorizing intertext aimed at promoting the *Friday the 13th* series and its cultural value is the late-nineteenth-

and early-twentieth-century theater of Grand Guignol. By reading the series as "modern grand guignol," Conrich recontextualizes its sensationalism, linking it to a historical and theatrical precedent and thus bidding for its increased cultural value. Conrich also emphasizes moments of parody and irony in the series, as well as intertextually relating the first *Friday the 13th* not to *Halloween* as template but rather to the Italian cinema of Mario Bava.[51] Stressing parody has the effect of reading the franchise as self-reflexive, thus aligning it with the aesthetic values of legitimate film culture. Invoking the films of Bava, however, links *Friday the 13th* to films valued as trash art by trash film culture. Hence Conrich attempts to rearticulate *Friday the 13th* intertextually as trash art at the same time as linking it to the norms of legitimate film culture, again indicating that trash and legitimate film cultures cannot always be viewed as opposed to one another. As *Friday the 13th*'s twinned others, trash and legitimate film culture are drawn intertextually together by Conrich in his attempts to reposition and revalue the franchise.

A move to validate *Friday the 13th* as trash art is also made by some *Friday the 13th* fans on the www.fridaythe13thfilms.com message board, where early *Friday* films are repeatedly valued by sections of the fan culture for their display of the killer's gloved hands rather than for showing Jason as a lumbering, masked killer:[52]

> I think the way that the killers aren't shown except for hands and feet until the end in the first five movies is great. It makes it a lot more scary, because the kills weren't so obviously coming.[53]

> I agree, a bit more Italian giallo style in the early films. The later ones are still fun . . . but the fear factor is almost nonexistant [sic].[54]

> For me, less Jason is more. I like the way they played up the tension as best they could in the first 5 *Friday the 13th* films.[55]

By making a similar intertextual link in his academic discussion of the *Friday the 13th* franchise, Conrich combines academic, "legitimate" intertexts (citing theory and positioning the films as "modern grand guignol") with fan intertexts (*Friday the 13th* being read through the trash art *giallo* rather as a "copy" of *Halloween*). Such a hybridized set of intertextualities, contained within the norms of scholarly discourse, suggests that (unusual) bids for the value of popular cultural texts in the academy are more likely to be made by scholar-fans,[56] that is, professional academics who claim fan cultural identities. It is scholar-fans who have put trash cinema on the academic agenda,[57] and it is typically scholar-fans, now well-established in the academy, who continue to challenge separations of trash and legitimate film cultures.[58] Furthermore, it is scholar-fans such as myself and Conrich who have challenged the devaluation of specific texts like *Friday the 13th* in both cultures. Scholars who are also fans are, perhaps, particularly sensitive to the ways in which academia silences or devalues their objects of fandom, as well as being especially alert to the minutiae of cultural distinctions that pervade both academic and fan cultures.

We need to go on investigating the cultural distinctions of trash culture, not only welcoming sleazy film art as an attack on legitimate film culture, but also viewing it, on occasions, as no less exclusionary than its official other. For not all that might be termed popular cultural detritus or sleaze becomes sleazy art. For some texts, the nonactivation of criteria of authorship and trash/legitimate aesthetics can result in a twilight existence beyond academic valorization and trash revalorization. Discursively positioned as lacking an author-function and film-school cultural capital, and viewed as pure, gross commercial repetition (by what I have termed the formula fallacy), the *Friday the 13th* franchise has been one such victim. *Friday* fans track differences across the franchise, analyzing how it "evolved with the times."[59] Yet legitimate film culture has construed the series, sometimes hysterically, as sleazy, artless, formulaic horror, while trash film culture has simultaneously othered *Friday the 13th* and its cult following of fans as mainstream.

Notes

1. Jeffrey Sconce, "'Trashing' the Academy: Taste, Excess, and an Emerging Politics of Cinematic Style," *Screen* 36 (1995): 371–93.
2. Ibid., 372.
3. Ibid., 379, 372.
4. Mark Jancovich interprets Sconce's work as displaying these difficulties. See Jancovich, "Cult Fictions: Cult Movies, Subcultural Capital and the Production of Cultural Distinctions," *Cultural Studies* 16 (2002): 306–22.
5. Sconce, "'Trashing' the Academy," 381, emphasis added.

6. Joan Hawkins, *Cutting Edge: Art-Horror and the Horrific Avant-garde* (Minneapolis: University of Minnesota Press), 16.
7. As noted in Sconce, "'Trashing' the Academy," 381.
8. See Jancovich, "Cult Fictions," 314.
9. As in Sconce, "'Trashing' the Academy," and "Spectacles of Death: Identification, Reflexivity and Contemporary Horror," in *Film Theory Goes to the Movies*, ed. Jim Collins, Hilary Radner, and Ava Preacher Collins (New York: Routledge, 1993); Matt Hills, *Fan Cultures* (London: Routledge, 2002), 46–64; Sarah Thornton, *Club Cultures: Music, Media and Subcultural Capital* (Cambridge: Polity, 1995); and Lyn Thomas, *Fans, Feminisms and 'Quality' Media* (London: Routledge, 2002).
10. Pierre Bourdieu, *Distinction: A Social Critique of the Judgement of Taste* (London: Routledge, 1984), 88.
11. Jancovich, "Cult Fictions," 313.
12. See Hills, *Fan Cultures*, 61–62, and see Mark Jancovich, "'A Real Shocker': Authenticity, Genre and the Struggle for Distinction," *Continuum* 14 (2000): 23–35.
13. Jancovich, "Cult Fictions," 312.
14. Ian Conrich, "The *Friday the 13th* Films and the Cultural Function of a Modern Grand Guignol," *Cinema Journal* (forthcoming).
15. Spainhower quoted in Jancovich, "Cult Fictions," 312–13.
16. Conrich, "The *Friday the 13th* Films."
17. Jancovich, "'A Real Shocker,'" 28.
18. Jancovich, "Cult Fictions," 313.
19. See Tony Williams, *The Cinema of George A. Romero: Knight of the Living Dead* (London: Wallflower Press, 2003).
20. Sconce, "Spectacles of Death," 103.
21. Ibid., 104.
22. Ibid., 106–7.
23. See John Kenneth Muir, *Wes Craven: The Art of Horror* (Jefferson, N.C.: McFarland, 1998).
24. Sconce, "Spectacles of Death," 118.
25. Conrich, "The *Friday the 13th* Films," emphasis added.
26. Ibid., emphasis added.
27. Kevin Heffernan, *Ghouls, Gimmicks, and Gold: Horror Films and the American Movie Business, 1953–1968* (Durham, N.C.: Duke University Press, 2004), 223.
28. Steven Jay Schneider, "Kevin Williamson and the Rise of the Neo-Stalker," *PostScript* 19, no. 2 (2000): 74.
29. Andrew Tudor, *Monsters and Mad Scientists: A Cultural History of the Horror Movie* (Oxford: Blackwell, 1989), 198–99; see also Vera Dika, *Games of Terror: Halloween, Friday the 13th and the Films of the Stalker Cycle* (London: Associated University Presses,

1990), 78; Mark Jancovich, "General Introduction," *Horror: The Film Reader*, ed. Jancovich (London: Routledge, 2002), 8; Darryl Jones, *Horror: A Thematic History in Fiction and Film* (London: Arnold, 2002), 114.

30. Paul Budra, "Recurrent Monsters: Why Freddy, Michael and Jason Keep Coming Back," in *Part Two: Reflections on the Sequel*, ed. Paul Budra and Betty A. Schellenberg (Toronto: University of Toronto Press, 1998), 195.

31. Jonathan Lake Crane, *Terror and Everyday Life: Singular Moments in the History of the Horror Film* (London: Sage, 1994), 151.

32. Ibid., 151.

33. Carol J. Clover, *Men, Women and Chainsaws* (London: BFI, 1992), 56.

34. Crane, *Terror and Everyday Life*, 147.

35. Dika, *Games of Terror*, 64.

36. Ibid.

37. Ibid., 65.

38. Ibid., 78.

39. Reynold Humphries, *The American Horror Film: An Introduction* (Edinburgh: Edinburgh University Press, 2002), 143.

40. See Sconce, "Spectacles of Death," 1993.

41. See Schneider, "Kevin Williamson and the Rise of the Neo-Stalker."

42. Clover, *Men, Women and Chainsaws*, 56.

43. Ibid., 64.

44. Ibid., 231.

45. See Hills, *Fan Cultures*, 30.

46. As argued in Linda Williams, "The Inside-Out of Masculinity: David Cronenberg's Visceral Pleasures," in *The Body's Perilous Pleasures*, ed. Michele Aaron (Edinburgh: Edinburgh University Press, 1999).

47. See Humphries, *The American Horror Film*, 113–18.

48. Harry Benshoff, *Monsters in the Closet: Homosexuality and the Horror Film* (Manchester: Manchester University Press, 1997), 40–51.

49. See, for example, Hawkins, *Cutting Edge*; Jancovich, "General Introduction" and "A Real Shocker"; Sconce, "Spectacles of Death" and "'Trashing' the Academy."

50. For more on this general process in academic writing on horror film, see Matt Hills, "Doing Things with Theory: From Freud's Worst Nightmare to (Disciplinary) Dreams of Horror's Cultural Value," in *Psychoanalysis and the Horror Film: Freud's Worst Nightmares*, ed. Steven Jay Schneider (Cambridge: Cambridge University Press, 2004).

51. See Conrich, "The *Friday the 13th* Films."

52. With the latter being referred to as "Rampage Jason" by "Peter Baker," "Jason Onscreen—How Much Is Too Much?" www.fridaythe13thfilms.com, April 25, 2003.

53. "James M," "Jason Onscreen—How Much Is Too Much?" www.fridaythe13thfilms.com, April 23, 2003.

54. "heh," "Jason Onscreen—How Much Is Too Much?" www.fridaythe13thfilms.com, April 23, 2003.
55. "LilTouchUpWork," "Jason Onscreen—How Much Is Too Much?" www.fridaythe13th films.com, April 25, 2003.
56. For a case study concerning the cult blockbuster, see Hills, *Fan Cultures*, 11–15, and Hills, "*Star Wars* in Fandom, Film Theory, and the Museum: The Cultural Status of the Cult Blockbuster," in *Movie Blockbusters*, ed. Julian Stringer (London: Routledge, 2003).
57. As in Sconce, "'Trashing' the Academy," 377–78.
58. For a more recent example of this, see Walter Metz, "John Waters Goes to Hollywood: A Poststructural Authorship Study," in *Authorship and Film*, ed. David A. Gerstner and Janet Staiger (New York: AFI/Routledge, 2003).
59. "Momma's Boy," "Halloween 1 Discussion," www.fridaythe13thfilms.com, March 4, 2003.

CHRIS FUJIWARA

Boredom, Spasmo, *and the Italian System*

L'ennui, cette consolation *incurable*. E. M. CIORAN

"One is almost never totally bored by a movie," according to Christian Metz. The reason for this, Metz says, is the "affective and perceptual *participation*" that films release in the spectator through their spontaneous appeal to the spectator's "sense of belief." This participation, which produces the experience of the film as a fully realized world, has been given the name "projective illusion" by Richard Allen. Noting that some films promote this illusion more than others, Allen claims that "the rationale of classical Hollywood narration is precisely to maximize the possibilities of filmed drama as projective illusion." Nevertheless, the conventions of narrative cinema are insufficient to ensure that projective illusion will be experienced; they can only make it more likely. Conversely, although films that challenge these conventions (Allen uses Chantal Akerman's *Jeanne Dielman, 23, Quai du Commerce, 1080 Bruxelles* [1976] as an example) "may undermine our capacity to experience projective illusion," they cannot rule out the possibility that the viewer, after making an adjustment to their strategies, will have such an experience.[1]

But does disbelief in the reality of the diegesis (as Metz seems to imply) define filmic boredom? The answer is clearly negative. The boring film may succeed in obtaining my belief in its

FIGURE 1 Italian release poster for *Spasmo* (1974).

"world," but it remains boring nonetheless. To understand this phenomenon, it is necessary to separate "affective and perceptual participation" from the "sense of belief" that allows it to take hold. A sense of belief may be present, but participation may fail to occur or may be withdrawn. The illusion of reality is irrelevant to boredom; it may even encourage it. As for participation, what is it in most cases but the will to be distracted, to accept the film as entertainment commodity on its own terms, and to accept one's place as the subject of consumerist desire? "In boredom there is the lure of a possible object of desire, and the lure of the escape from desire, of its meaninglessness," notes Adam Phillips. To be bored by a film is to reject the offer of, or to collude with the film's failure to offer, a distraction from one's own condition and one's own duration. It's also, as Patrice Petro observes, to "refuse the ceaseless repetition of the new as the always-the-same" that is the hidden logic of commodity fetishism.[2]

By allowing us to suspend desire, boredom films give us an opportunity denied by entertainment films. In such milestones as Andy Warhol's *Sleep* (1963)

FIGURE 2 Andy Warhol's *Empire* (1964): a cinematic landmark of duration and boredom.

and *Empire* (1964), Michael Snow's *La région centrale* (1971), and Akerman's *Jeanne Dielman*, duration radically affects the viewer's experience of the film. After the threshold of discomfort is passed, the viewer enters into a state of pure film watching without identification, in which image and sound are no longer correlated with desire. When director and teacher Mikhail Romm complained that some scenes in Andrei Tarkovsky's diploma film, *The Steamroller and the Violin* (1960), went on for too long, Tarkovsky replied: "If you extend the normal length of a shot, first you get bored; but if you extend it further still you become interested in it; and if you extend it even more a new quality, a new intensity of attention is born."[3]

What happens if this intensity isn't attained, and the viewer remains stuck at the stage of waiting? The viewer undergoes the separation from time that E. M. Cioran identified as the hallmark of boredom. "In boredom, time can't flow. Each instant swells, and the passage from one instant to the other isn't made.... Time is detached from existence and becomes external to us.... We are no longer in time."[4] (These terms resemble those in which Michael Snow described the experience of watching his landmark *La région centrale*: "You are here, the film is there. It is neither fascism nor entertainment.")[5] This experience turns out to be one of pleasure: "One can end up loving this state," Cioran observes.[6]

The less a film seems to change, the more the viewer becomes conscious of her own internal change, and thus of her own duration. (Freud: "In mourning it is the world that has become poor and empty; in melancholia it is the ego itself.")[7] This formula might appear to make the film-as-boring wholly unnecessary, since one could just as well shut one's eyes and plug one's ears to achieve the same result of focusing on an internal object. But in practical film viewing situations, it's impossible to concentrate entirely either on a film or on one's self (by "self" I mean the totality of internal objects of consciousness, including physical comfort or discomfort, reflections, recollections, verbalized thoughts, etc.—what Henri Wallon, in "L'acte perceptif et le cinéma," calls the "proprioceptive series"). There is a continual fluctuation between consciousness of an external object and consciousness of an internal object, between the ideal extremes of 100 percent film/0 percent self and 0 percent film/100 percent self.[8]

The latter type of consciousness, focused on the self, can be identified with what Vivian Sobchack, borrowing terminology from Don Ihde, calls the spectator's "echo focus"—the awareness that the film experience is mediated through an apparatus. According to Sobchack, the "echo" of the apparatus is especially noticeable at two "junctures": that between the spectator's total visual field and the film frame, and that between the place of viewing and the projected visual space of the film. Sobchack notes that "the machine's 'echo' appears quite prominent in the perception of the theoretical or bored spectator."[9] With such theorizing we discover what Metz, in denying filmic boredom, missed: the existence of a world outside the world of the film.

To what extent is boredom a willed action, and to what extent is it a passive experience? Does the subject experience boredom as her own act of rejection, or as a force that she submits to? In being bored, this distinction doesn't come up. A fusion takes place between the experience of something as boring (the "I reject this" of the bored subject) and the boring thing as experienced (the "this bores me").

Boredom is a state of freedom. No one can force me to be bored. I can, in fact, choose to be bored; I can even choose to consider in the light of boredom some object that I once found interesting. Boredom isn't incompatible with a certain excitement; but in being bored, I choose not to be interested in this excitement; I put it at arm's length and see it through a voluntary haze.

As a pointless waiting without explicit content, boredom has sometimes been thematized in films. Some films generate a kind of implicit boredom by focusing on people who are bored or who are in conditions favorable to boredom such as a holiday, a trip, or isolation. Terence Fisher's agreeably mundane *Night of the Big Heat* ([1967] shown in the United States as *Island of the Burning Doomed*) is an excellent example of this type. The proportion and balance in Fisher's framing and the movie's ability to light on something of interest from moment to moment imply an obsessive yet tender concern for a shrunken, demented world about to come to an end. The movie has that sour late-1960s mood of exhaustion and nerves at their limit, perfectly expressed in the recurrent situation of residents of an island off the coast of Britain gathering in the island's only pub to share desultory complaints about the abnormal heat.

British filmmakers weren't alone in becoming interested in boredom during the 1960s. Jean Mitry thought that Antonioni "went as far as it is possible to go" toward thematizing boredom and toward an aesthetic system based "on audience boredom, on the expression of emptiness, the representation of immobility (though it be only moral or mental)."[10] But Antonioni was only one of the more illustrious of the many filmmakers responsible for the tidal wave of boredom that was the Italian cinema of the 1950s, 1960s, and 1970s—a period during which Rome's Cinecittà flourished as, perhaps, the greatest capital of boredom the world has ever known. Not only was boredom made the overt subject of films dealing with the Italian film industry such as Fellini's *La dolce vita* (1960) and Godard's *Le mépris* (1963), but Italian filmmakers also promoted boredom through an exhaustive approach to standardized, sensation-mongering genres, such as the peplum cycle of the late 1950s and early 1960s, the spy films of the mid 1960s, the spaghetti westerns of the mid-to-late 1960s and early 1970s, and the *gialli* of the 1960s and 1970s. I wish to look closely at a film of the latter group, Umberto Lenzi's *Spasmo* (1974).

Before doing so, it may be desirable to spell out my purpose in selecting *Spasmo* to exemplify the promotion of boredom in Italian cinema. First, I'd be unhappy if my claim that certain Italian films, including *Spasmo*, are boring

FIGURE 3 Fellini's *La dolce vita* (1960): a film about boredom and the Italian film industry.

were read as a contemptuous dismissal of these films. On the contrary, it's through being boring that these films—several of them—become interesting to me. Second, in investigating the boringness of *Spasmo* I wish to lay emphasis on those aspects of the film that highlight and comment on the nature of film spectatorship and that disclose the intimate connection between film viewing and boredom. Indeed, the only importance of *Spasmo* to me, for purposes of this essay, lies in its ability to make this link apparent. Third, in alluding to the fact that certain key features of *Spasmo* are shared by other Italian commercial films of its era, I wish to acknowledge that the way in which *Spasmo* discloses the link between viewing and boredom is the way of a certain genre (a "low" one) and to suggest the study of the relationship between film genre, "low culture," and boredom as a path for research.

The beginning of the film is boring. We're given no reason to care about anything. In a high-angle long shot, a motorcycle bearing two young people, a boy and a girl, turns off a main road onto a dirt path along an attractive coastline at night. This shot cuts to a medium-long shot of a parked sedan. The motorcycle pulls up near the sedan. The direct appeal to the spectator is immediate: the boy gets off the motorcycle and approaches the camera, which is inside the car; the boy addresses it (us) through the passenger window. We know nothing of the person whose place we take: only when the car drives away at the end of the scene, after the young couple have had their lovemaking spoiled by the macabre sight of a doll hanging by a cord nearby, can we infer that the driver of the car hanged the doll; it won't be until the end of the film that we can identify this unseen person with a character in the film.

The young couple is marked as "generic young couple." Nothing characterizes them: they merely perform a short series of actions and fulfill a short series of functions. They are present in the film only to be exploited. The camera tilts from the girl's face to her breast as the boy's hand caresses it through her sweater—an automatic and imperious redirection of the viewer's gaze equivalent to a pan that occurs a few moments later, from the girl kissing the boy to the doll's legs hanging in the air. Both camera movements exploit the human figure, treating it as material and implying an equivalence, which the narrative of *Spasmo* will eventually make explicit, between human beings and dolls. The camera movements also exploit the viewer, who is addressed as someone who wants to be titillated, and is capable of being titillated, by images of clothed foreplay and displaced violence against women.

Intercut with the credits, we see a series of shots of dolls. We are bored further. This is to be a film about dolls, apparently—the most boring of things, embodiments of a functionalization of being to which the only possible responses are irritation or melancholy. The music too is somewhat boring, though beautiful: Ennio Morricone's theme, vocalized by a chorus ("ooh-ooh-ooh-ooh-ooh-ooh-ooh-ooooh") over cyclical rhythm-guitar figures, promises a melancholy experience rather than nerve-jangling Argento-esque terror and suspense.

The prologue lies stranded, never to be incorporated into the body of the film. Nothing about an inanimate doll can be an event worthy of a date in the narrative calendar. Only once in the film will the dialogue refer to the dolls, in a line spoken by a nameless character at a gas station.

The story told by the film concerns two brothers, Fritz (Ivan Rassimov) and Christian (Robert Hoffman), sons of a wealthy industrialist (Tom Felleghy). Christian has inherited their grandfather's insanity, and Fritz has long helped Christian, while blaming him for their father's suicide. Hoping to force Christian to recognize his mental disorder and commit himself to a clinic, Fritz hires several people to take part in a strange plot to drive Christian to a mental breakdown. One of the conspirators, Barbara (Suzy Kendall), lures Christian to her motel cabin, where he is attacked by an intruder, Tatum (Adolfo Lastretti). Christian apparently kills Tatum with the latter's gun. Barbara persuades Christian to hide out with her in a supposedly vacant house that proves occupied by two other members of the conspiracy, Malcolm (Guido Alberti) and Clorinda (Monica Monet).

There Fritz's plan goes awry because of the sympathy or attraction that Barbara, Malcolm, and Clorinda all feel toward Christian. Nevertheless, Christian's madness overtakes him, and he kills Clorinda. Tatum returns, kills Malcolm, and tries to kill Christian, but Christian runs over Tatum with his car and fakes his own death. Christian goes on to kill a prostitute-motorist (Rosita Torosh), his ex-girlfriend (Maria Pia Conte), and finally Barbara, before Barbara's lover, Alex (Mario Erpichini), kills Christian in revenge.

The ambiguity of the motives of Fritz and Tatum complicates the story. Why Tatum kills Malcolm, and why he tries to kill Christian, are mysteries the film does not deign to elucidate. Perhaps he's acting under orders from Fritz, who appears scarcely discomfited by the news of his brother's apparent death. It's unclear, in any case, whether the aim of Fritz's plot is to render Christian mentally incompetent for Christian's own good, to avenge their father's suicide, or (as Barbara thinks) to put Christian out of the way so that Fritz can take over the family business.

Even if these questions were answered, the story, as narrated by the film, would still be hard to discern. For most of the film, the plot closely follows the point of view of Christian, who fails to realize that he is insane. Much important information—including the fact that most of the characters, apart from Christian, are conspiring together—is withheld until the last half hour; and it's only in that last half hour that Fritz himself appears. Also, not only does the film delay exposing Christian as a murderer until his last killing, that of Barbara (which comes nearly at the end of the film); but we're not even made aware that his three previous victims have died until their deaths are shown in flashbacks during the scene of Barbara's murder.

Limited by the point of view of a passive and insane character, the plotting of *Spasmo* is as slack as the story is inscrutable. A dissipation of narrative energy becomes especially noticeable after Christian and Barbara arrive at the house, which she says belongs to an absent friend ("she's a Brazilian painter and she left for Rio two weeks ago"). At this point, the film becomes paralyzed by timelessness and emptiness. Christian and Barbara have no apparent incentive to leave the house. The narrative seems to lack the obligation to move in any direction in particular. There is nothing to do.

Immediately on entering the house (by breaking a kitchen window), Christian recognizes that a certain dullness has set in and will overtake them:

CHRISTIAN: You say your girlfriend paints?
BARBARA: Yes, why?
CHRISTIAN: I don't know, everything is so—so dull.
BARBARA: She's got some good booze.

Barbara's last line perfectly manifests the pall of vacation idleness that now hangs over *Spasmo*. The characters have nothing to anticipate and nothing to do but drink. It's unclear when they will be allowed to leave this purgatory. Instead of taking part in a narrative, they are in hiding from it. The decor of the house—including stuffed birds, caged live birds of prey, and a suit of armor—expresses the kind of stifled, frozen time that the characters have entered.

The cinematography plays an important and paradoxical role in instilling this sense of immobility. Shot by Guglielmo Mancori, a busy and accomplished cinematographer who shot many other films for Lenzi and also worked with such directors as Antonio Margheriti, Michele Lupo, Lucio Fulci, and Sergio Sollima, *Spasmo* exemplifies the dominion that the zoom lens held in the Italian commercial cinema of its era. As in other products of the Italian cinematic system, the zoom in *Spasmo* constitutes the characters as static visual patterns. The zoom controls an extended space, but the animate creatures who occupy this space are immobile or suspended, or their movement is annulled: exterior movement is held in abeyance while the movement of consciousness is performed by the zoom.

One moment shows the structural role of the zoom for Lenzi. Barbara and Fritz's lieutenant, Lucas (Franco Silva), arrive at Fritz's office to meet him. The three talk, but we can't hear their dialogue. The camera slowly zooms out to reveal that we're watching them through the window of another office. The widening field of view finally encompasses an intercom on a table in the foreground, on which the camera reframes, zooming into an extreme close-up. Christian's hand reaches in from off camera and flicks a switch. At this point we begin to hear the dialogue in Fritz's office (the first line heard is Fritz's "In other words, you made a mess of things, a complete mess!"). Having through this elaborate visual device justified our ability to hear the dialogue from Christian's auditory point of view, the film now (with its characteristic combination of perversity and opportunism) cuts to a shot inside Fritz's office, as the dialogue continues.

It becomes clear that Lenzi uses the zoom as punctuation, marking the start and end of shots with emphasis; to give structure to his scenes, to give the semblance of movement to dialogues and shapes that lack inner movement: not just the actors who pretend to be corpses (like Barbara in the first postcredits scene and Tatum in the motel bathroom), but also the actors who pretend to be alive but are unable to supply inner movement. The zoom compensates for, but also confirms and celebrates, the tendency of the characters of *Spasmo* to become inanimate and doll-like. (The very faces in *Spasmo* may be taken as boring, in their almost abstract beauty: the faces of Robert Hoffman and Suzy Kendall are perfectly chiseled and defined, that of Ivan Rassimov—the ultimate Italian-system actor?—even more so.)

If Lenzi's preoccupation with the zoom suggests a concern with the external effect of movement at the expense of inner movement, the same can be said of the director's preoccupation with cars. The car is an appropriate analogue to the zoom. Like the zoom, the car is an extension of the body's power to explore the external world. They are comparable in ease of operation: the zoom can be triggered at the push of a button, without the camera or its operator having to displace themselves; typically, for an experienced driver, driving a car requires little strain, only a mostly unremarkable, unacknowledged engagement with the steering wheel, pedals, and other devices.

Both car and zoom lens annul space; they also annul time. Both are technologies of imaginary possession: just as the car makes possible a possession of landscape and scenery (several shots in *Spasmo* revel in the beauty of the seaside environment, as visible from a road), so the zoom facilitates the taking possession of distant visual objects.

The prologue establishes the importance of automobility in *Spasmo*. Over a shot of the young couple staring at the doll, we hear the sound of a car starting up; on the cut, we see the sedan drive away. Cars starting up and driving away are a motif in the film, and often, as in this case, the film insists on the motif by having us hear a car before we see it. In the first scene after the credits, Barbara surprises Christian by taking off abruptly in her car, off-screen. Later, Christian hurries off Alex's yacht to drive away in his car (this time the car is visible in long shot when the engine starts). In a later scene at the painter's house, the sound of a car starting up is heard over a shot of Christian exploring the house, looking for Barbara.

Christian spends much of the film in his car. Twice the camera pans, following his car, only to stop and reframe on a doll attached to a tree. In one scene, Lenzi intercuts close-ups of Christian at the wheel with flashback close-ups of Malcolm and Barbara, repeating dialogue they addressed to him earlier in the film, and with long shots (taken from the front of the moving car) of the road, which, animated by the moving camera and distorted by the wide-angle lens, seems simultaneously to recede into the distance and hurtle toward and past us. Finally, the car is the instrument with which Tatum tries to kill Christian, and by which Christian turns the tables on Tatum, running him over and disposing of his body.

A number of connotations of the car are made explicit in *Spasmo*: namely, its associations with (1) sex, (2) masculinity, (3) economic power, and (4) freedom of movement. (1) Sex: the motorcycling couple at the beginning of the film go in search of a place to make love; Christian and Barbara seduce each other in Christian's car. (2) Masculinity: cars in *Spasmo* are invariably driven by men. In the seduction scene, Christian's imminent possession of Barbara (she has just invited him to her motel) is clinched by a close-up of his hand controlling the phallic gearshift. Women apparently lack direct access to automobility: to leave the yacht and rejoin Christian, Barbara must (at least she claims) get a lift from a truck driver. (3) Economic power: Christian drives a BMW, symbol of wealth and privilege. (4) Freedom of movement: the film is set in a resort area largely configured by automobility; the various locations of the film are separated by distances that can't easily be spanned except by car; several plot points depend on Christian's ability to jump into a car and travel quickly from one place to another.

Cars are vehicles of boredom in *Spasmo*. The car inevitably attracts the notice of the camera, displacing people as objects of visual interest. The relentless attention paid to characters' arrivals and departures by car becomes mechanical; the film seems to say that where the characters go, or merely that they are en route somewhere, is more interesting than why they are going, or who they are.

In the shots of the road taken from the front of Christian's car, Lenzi makes an exceptional effort both to reproduce the visual experience of driving and to infuse it with a psychological element. The shots of the road also activate the familiar analogy between film screen and windshield, although this is complicated by a subtly unnerving aspect of the sequence: the close-ups of Christian are filmed through the windshield, but the road is viewed directly, without the mediation of glass and the concomitant reflections. The mise-en-scène thus delineates Christian's world as private and closed and reminds us that we have access to it, and him, only through reflections, while staging a relatively unmediated confrontation with the external space of the road, which seems to threaten us. Both sides of this shot/reverse-shot pair exemplify Heidegger's description of "the terrifying" in "The Thing": "The terrifying is unsettling.... It shows itself and hides itself in the *way* in which everything presences, namely, in the fact that despite all conquest of distances the nearness of things remains absent."[11]

The film's abrupt transitions between night and day take to a disorienting extreme the film's tendency to collapse time, its foregrounding of the conquest of distances. A straight cut takes Christian and Barbara off Alex's yacht and into Christian's car, but on the yacht it is day, and in the car it is already night. At night, Barbara proposes to Christian that they hide in the painter's house; when they reach the house, it is day. Finally, Christian crawls away through the woods at night, wounded by Alex's gunshot; a straight cut then finds him still crawling, but now on the beach, and in bright sunlight.

Other aspects of the film affirm, in different ways, the inconsequence of space and time, challenging "projective illusion" and the spectator's capacity to believe in the world of the film. The dialogue in *Spasmo* is entirely post-synchronized. From this practice, characteristic of the Italian system, several consequences ensue. One is that there is no original text to reconstitute, whose virtual, potential, or real existence would control readings of the film, to whose authority all interpretations would be referred. What the actors said while being photographed was never meant to be part of the film (Fellini famously told his actors to count, when he was shooting scenes for which the dialogue had not been written); with the international cast of *Spasmo* (the male lead is German, the female lead British, and most of the other actors Italian), the scenes might have been played multilingually (a common practice in Italy).

This means that although the dialogue often sounds like an approximation of what the characters might say, it makes no sense to try to guess what they actually said. Take Christian's remark to Barbara: "I don't know, it's all so absurd, meaningless, and what's absurd is dangerous." The line sounds like a translation from another language. We take such a line as not really spoken. But no really spoken line stands behind it to assure us of a really meant meaning. The meaning of the dialogue isn't anchored to the film.

We have no guarantee that the voices in *Spasmo* are those of the actors who were photographed, nor do we ask for one, if we're familiar with the cinematic system of Italy, in which the movie character is a peculiar construct. But the cinema in general always reserves the option of combining the image of an actor with the voice of another actor (as part of the general arbitrariness of the relationship between image and sound in film), and among many well-known English-language films that exercise this option, we may cite Orson Welles's *Othello* and *The Trial* (though both of these, it may not be irrelevant to point out, are European productions). So it may be more accurate to say of the Italian system that it tolerates as no breach of verisimilitude a somewhat greater obvious discrepancy between voice and image than is usually acceptable in the cinemas of the United States, Britain, or France, that it tolerates disruption between sound and image and the presence of traces of the independence of sound from image (e.g., obviously inexact lip synching) to a greater extent than do other cinematic systems. (An early explicit reference to dubbing in Italian cinema, from the point of view of Hollywood, can be found in Vincente Minnelli's *Two Weeks in Another Town* [1962].)

The Italian system also relies on a certain kind of voice and on actors adept at recording dialogue distinctly while following the lip movements of the on-screen actors. In *Spasmo*, the voices all have that vacuous, colorless, vague quality characteristic of the dubbed voices in standard Italian commercial films of the 1960s and 1970s. Alex's voice is smooth and impersonal. Christian's voice is soft and neutral. Uncommitted to these bodies, these faces, the voices generate boredom.

If, as Merleau-Ponty writes, "the movies are peculiarly suited to make manifest the union of mind and body, mind and world, and the expression of one in the other," the opposite can just as well be said, as *Spasmo* reveals by making manifest the separation of meaning from voice and voice from body, and thus the disunion of mind and world.[12]

One sequence in the film grounds this incoherence in an elaborate primal scene of viewing: the sequence in which Fritz, alone in his office, sits down, turns on a movie projector, and watches a film. The film he watches starts out like a home movie: in a handheld shot of children playing on a lawn, one child, whom we identify as Fritz, runs toward the camera with his hand extended to block its view. But the next scene is shot from a tripod and reveals a vigorous mise-en-scène and decoupage, starting with a shot in which, as Fritz and Christian's father sits on the lawn, reading a newspaper, Fritz enters the shot at right to pick up a glass and take a drink. This shot cuts on Fritz's movement to a striking composition with Fritz in extreme close-up in right foreground, drinking, and Christian framed from the waist up in the middle ground. The camera zooms in on Christian, losing Fritz.

In the next shot, Fritz sits in a chair in the foreground, his back to the camera, while in the right background, the mother approaches; this cuts back to the previous close-up of Christian, looking up and past the camera. This shot cuts to a close-up of the adult Fritz watching the film (the projector's flare aimed at the camera, in the right of the composition), so that Lenzi identifies the two looks at the mother from across twenty years.

If the Kuleshov effect means the imposition of a meaning on shot A through its contiguity with shot B (the meaning consisting in a spatial and psychological contiguity), the cutaways to the adult Fritz watching the film-within-the-film may be considered vacant, meaningless: no transference of meaning through contiguity takes place, only a duplication of looking. We might call this the Lenzi effect. Meaning resides with the film-within-the-film and stays there. The function of the spectator is always only to see, to recognize, to understand. What is seen, recognized, understood is not meaning, but the self-identical.

The next shot in the film-within-a-film zooms in from behind the boy Fritz on the mother as she rushes forward, arms extended. Unexpectedly, Christian enters from off camera right to receive her embrace. This shot is composed, like all the previous shots of the film-within-the-film, so that the projection screen is framed on either side by wood-paneled wall; but now, the camera zooms in on the screen, so that as mother and child embrace, the edges of the screen become lost, and the film-within-the-film engulfs the frame, a visual effect that resembles a blow-up of the 1.33:1 home-movie image into the 2.35:1 Scope image of *Spasmo*. This engulfing of space by the film-within-the-film equals the loss of Ihde's and Sobchack's "echo focus" and a heightening of the spectator's involvement in the film. *Spasmo*'s inscription of this involvement as a cinematic figure linked to the primordial unity of mother and child and to an observing character, Fritz, is both an offer to the viewer to emulate Fritz and a comment on the eviction from reality that befalls any viewer of a film. At the same time as the zoom draws us into the film-within-the-film, the onscreen embrace excludes us.

The film forcefully reminds us of this exclusion by cutting to a close shot of the excluded child, Fritz, looking up from his chair. The camera zooms in on him as he looks down. This shot cuts to a very tight close-up of the mother, looking past the camera and then down as she caresses Christian's head and kisses him. She looks up again past the camera, as if challenging someone, or expecting a challenge.

Unexpectedly, the film now cuts to a high-angle close shot of the father, sitting, looking up past the camera. At the left of the composition, behind him, is a tripod. He turns away slowly (disapproving? resigned?), puts his pipe into his mouth, and resumes reading his newspaper. This cuts to a new shot: a tight close-up of Christian in his mother's embrace, staring fixedly at the camera as her hand caresses the back of his head. Fritz (as spectator in the present time) freezes the frame and looks up at it intensely, then resumes normal projection as the camera zooms in on the boy's blue-gray eyes. In these shots, *Spasmo* links together Fritz, the father, and the film viewer: this passage of the film can be seen as a lesson for the viewer in occupying the paternal role (which Fritz, as the elder son, is to inherit from his father), biding time and waiting for revenge—a lesson whose significance will become apparent later in the film.

The downcast look of the excluded child, Fritz, before his mother's defiant embrace of his brother, repeats what can be called the inaugural gesture of the film. At the end of the prologue, the male motorcyclist watches the mysterious sedan drive off, then looks down. The disappointment apparent on his lowered face, in a close-up extended to a seemingly pointless length, is prophetic of the audience's almost inevitable disappointment with *Spasmo*, and it reveals the profoundly disappointing truth of the film.

Here we must consult Heidegger, who distinguishes being bored *by* a specific object from being bored *with* a certain "passing of time." This second kind of boredom is most relevant. In it, we have "given ourselves time" by entering into a situation "organized in response to an indeterminate emptiness that it is designed to fill."[13] Heidegger's example is an evening out with friends. This kind of passing the time not only fights against boredom, it also "captures" it.[14] We let ourselves "be swept along by whatever is transpiring," in a state of "casualness about joining in." In this state, "any seeking to be satisfied by beings is absent in advance."[15] Furthermore, "our being satisfied, in being there and part of things, manifests itself, if only faintly and indeterminately, as an illusion (a peculiar dissatisfaction!)—as a passing of time which does not so much drive off boredom as precisely *attest* to it and let it be there."[16] In seeking to pass the time, "we have, not wrongly or to our detriment, but legitimately, left our proper self behind in a certain way" and remained in a state of emptiness.[17]

What Heidegger says here can be read as a model of a passive and reserved film viewing that differs radically from Metz's, with its stress on participation. Having left ourselves behind in advance by giving ourselves time to be "entirely present" for "what is present" in the film, "we are cut off from our having-been and from our future." This entails a compression of the present into itself, so that "without the possibility of transition, only persisting remains." The Now ("that peculiar time which is in the present") "stretches itself"—it becomes a "standing Now" that "sets us in place."[18]

The loss of past and future are characteristic of film time. Not only does the viewer willingly leave herself behind to give herself over to the film for its duration, but this duration is a compressed, sealed-off present.

The boredom unleashed by *Spasmo* may force us to confront a truth about cinema: that films—not all films, but those films that we approach as Heidegger approaches his evening out, seeking to pass the time rather than to be deeply satisfied, casual about joining in—are boring. Why is *Spasmo* better able to bring this truth to light than another film? Here I must express a reservation. I don't claim that *Spasmo* is uniquely boring; I take it as a film that exemplifies a boredom that can also be found in other films of its genre. It's the genre that's deeply boring, and that in its way of being boring reveals a truth about cinema. But I have no interest in the problem of constituting the genre and defining its limits, whether historical, national, narrative, thematic, iconographic, or stylistic. It's enough for my purposes that a few qualities that define *Spasmo*, notably as a product of the Italian commercial cinema of a certain period, can also be found in other films that are, perhaps, just as boring. The genre of *Spasmo* is, then, only its way of being boring—a way it shares with certain other films.

Finally, there's something reassuring, comforting, relaxing about *Spasmo*. *Spasmo* is not a deeply troubling film. It doesn't traumatize or attack the viewer. It shows very little blood, and it features only brief moments involving physical pain. The ending of *Spasmo*, which finally explains the prologue and the intermittent shots of dolls throughout the film, is especially reassuring, letting the lover of the *giallo* (a form in which the attractions of violence against women are notoriously blatant) off the hook by portraying a form of violence that could be considered harmless: Fritz, we discover, compulsively mutilates dolls. The viewer of the film is doing something still more innocuous: watching someone mutilate dolls. The escape to which we have given our time gives us back a vision of our own activity as an acting upon the inanimate without consequences for the self, and the society, that we have left behind for ninety-four minutes.

This inconsequentiality reminds us that though boredom offers the antidote to distraction, it can also be recuperated as distraction. *Spasmo* may be boring entertainment, but it is still entertainment. Foreseeing this danger, the Situationists attacked boredom as a dead end, merely the inevitable result of the endless accumulation of images characteristic of the modern, "spectacular" culture against which they mounted their radical critique. It's possible, however, to argue in favor of boredom in situationist terms. The Situationists used two main weapons against the spectacle: *détournement*—the rerouting of existing artworks into new contexts; and *dérive*—a creative drifting through urban environments. Does not the indeterminacy unleashed by the boring film make it an ideal candidate for *détournement*—and even, perhaps, constitute it as pre-

détourné? Can we not, furthermore, conceive of the boring film as an environment for aesthetic *dérive*, in which we wander freely?

If entertainment keeps us waiting, holding out the promise of the new but never fulfilling it, boredom admits waiting to be infinite. It defeats the lie of culture by positing nothingness. As Guy Debord remarks in the penultimate section of *The Society of the Spectacle*: "A critique capable of surpassing the spectacle must know how to bide its time."[19] In boredom, we attend to the indeterminacy of what we are waiting for—in which lies the saving recognition that it does not exist.

Notes

Parts of this article were adapted by the author from his essay "The Force of the Useless," *Hermenaut* 16 (winter 2000): 92–100.

1. Christian Metz, *Film Language: A Semiotics of the Cinema*, trans. Michael Taylor (New York: Oxford University Press, 1974), 4; Richard Allen, *Projecting Illusion: Film Spectatorship and the Impression of Reality* (Cambridge: Cambridge University Press, 1995), 115, 118.
2. Patrice Petro, *Aftershocks of the New: Feminism and Film History* (New Brunswick, N.J.: Rutgers University Press, 2002), 66.
3. Trond S. Trondsen and Jan Bielawski, "Nostalghia.com Looks at *The Steamroller and the Violin*," 2002, www.acs.ucalgary.ca/tstronds/nostalghia.com/TheTopics/Steamroller_and_Violin.html.
4. E. M. Cioran, *Œuvres*, ed. Yves Peyré (Paris: Gallimard, 1995), 1748.
5. Michael Snow, "La Region Centrale," *Film Culture* 52 (spring 1971), quoted in Simon Field, "Michael Snow: A Filmography," *Afterimage* 11 (winter 1982–83), 15.
6. Cioran, *Précis de decomposition*, 1748.
7. Sigmund Freud, "Mourning and Melancholia," in *General Psychology Theory* (1917; New York: Touchstone, 1991), 167.
8. Henri Wallon, "L'acte perceptif et le cinéma," *Revue internationale de filmologie* 13 (1953): 97–100, quoted in Metz, *Film Language*, 10–11.
9. Vivian Sobchack, *The Address of the Eye: A Phenomenology of Film Experience* (Princeton, N.J.: Princeton University Press, 1992), 181.
10. Jean Mitry, *The Aesthetics and Psychology in the Cinema*, trans. Christopher King (Bloomington: Indiana University Press, 1997), 362.
11. Martin Heidegger, *Poetry, Language, Thought*, trans. Albert Hofstadter (New York: Harper and Row, 1971), 166.
12. Maurice Merleau-Ponty, *Sense and Non-Sense*, trans. Hubert L. Dreyfus and Patricia Allen Dreyfus (Chicago: Northwestern University Press, 1964), 58.

13. Martin Heidegger, *The Fundamental Concepts of Metaphysics: World, Finitude, Solitude*, trans. William McNeill and Nicholas Walker (Bloomington: Indiana University Press, 1995), 115.
14. Ibid., 112.
15. Ibid., 117.
16. Ibid., 117–18. Compare Kierkegaard: "A misdirected search for diversion, one which is eccentric in its direction, conceals boredom within its own depths and gradually works it out toward the surface, thus revealing itself as that which it immediately is" (Søren Kierkegaard, *Either/Or*, trans. David F. Swenson and Lillian Marvin Swenson [Garden City, N.Y.: Anchor Books, 1959], 1:286–87).
17. Heidegger, *The Fundamental Concepts of Metaphysics*, 119.
18. Ibid., 124–25.
19. Guy Debord, *The Society of the Spectacle*, trans. Donald Nicholson-Smith (New York: Zone Books, 1995), 154.

GREG TAYLOR

Pure **Quidditas** *or* **Geek** **Chic?** Cultism as Discernment

> The need for a systematic reappraisal of the American cinema, director by director and film by film, has become more pressing in recent years.... The excavations and revaluations must continue until the last worthy director has been rescued from undeserved anonymity. ANDREW SARRIS

> *Switchblade Sisters, Macon County Line, The Warriors*—to you, mere drive-in flicks. To me, *shattering works of art.* MARC EDWARD HEUCK, MOVIE GEEK, BEAT THE GEEKS

How times have changed. Forty years ago, cultist connoisseurship of America's cultural margins could still be considered the rarefied domain of select highbrow critics who hoped to liberate readers from the scourge of middlebrow sterility by trawling the depths of a mass culture that others either ignored or took for granted. But today, cultism is everywhere, and movie geeks (and music geeks, and television geeks) are a dime a dozen—the word *geek* has even been included in the latest edition of the Oxford English Dictionary.[1] This cultural diffusion of cultism is hardly a bad thing, insofar as cultism's canon upheaval and oppositional discernment—the conferring of aesthetic specialness on unlikely artifacts—have essentially transformed the way we interact with cultural products, offering us an elusive promise of authority through an accessible and engaging means of coping with the sheer onslaught of pop artifacts. A great many of us now champion our discernment of *specialness* within the vast field of popular culture as a matter of course—in recreational banter, but also in our engagement with books, fanzines and fan sites, chat rooms, Trivial Pursuit editions, movies (the pastiche frenzy of Tarantino's *Kill Bill: Vol. 1*), television programs (VH1's *The List, I Love the '70s, I Love the '80s, 25 Greatest Commercials,* etc.), the collectibles market (where an original set of *Gilligan's Island* bubble gum cards can fetch $1,500), and *Entertainment Weekly* and *TV Guide* pop-connoisseur lists ("The 100 Greatest Movies of All Time," "The Fifty Funniest Moments of *I Love Lucy*").[2] Today, it seems, we all want (and get) to be oppositional cultists, resistant tastemakers, gloriously marginalized geeks. The startling emergence of oppositional connoisseurship as a mainstream phenomenon obviously raises some important questions, not least concerning the continued validity of the very distinction between mainstream and margin. But cultism's ascendance has also bared some of its inherent limitations as a form of aesthetic discrimination, and it is these limitations that I want to focus on here. In opposing "mainstream" works, cultism's oppositional discernment appears to oppose the very normative criteria by which such works are accorded their normative high cultural status. Yet in reality this is something of a smoke screen. Cultism can hardly eschew normative standards outright, as it provides an alternative canon of marginal works—so it downplays their centrality by subsuming them within a larger oppositional gesture that seems to suffice as an end in itself. That's why, in the midst of a heated musical debate, it seems fun and empowering to single out a marginal/alternative act such as the Stone Roses, but even *more* fun and empowering to single out not the Stone Roses' universally praised self-titled 1989 debut, but their much derided (and much delayed) 1994 follow-up, *Second Coming*. My intuitive sense that the music on *Second Coming* is aesthetically engaging and powerful is still relevant, certainly, but the enjoyment and empowerment of reaching down to rescue this more marginal work depends less on sophisticated analysis than on my willingness to assert my more advanced and daring critical acumen. In fact, sophisticated analysis can even get in the way of the fun, when it starts to cloud the terms of engagement with boring complexities. ("Sure, *The Stone Roses* has some great tracks on it, *but* . . . ; sure, *Second Coming* is overblown and uneven, but . . . .")

This is not to say that pop-cultural works cannot be—or indeed are not—

judged within such traditional evaluative means—all the time. But the dominance of cultist frameworks has not encouraged us to figure out upon which criteria we make our assessments in the first place. Instead, cultist gesturing asserts personal relevance and provides nostalgic good feeling, empowering us by confirming the validity of our own idiosyncratic past and present cultural choices. In truth, cultism was never equipped to handle the complexities of aesthetic analysis, because it originally pitched itself as an alternative to this very sort of traditional discernment. That it did so at least in part by singling out works that actually did not seem to *warrant* such discernment is highly relevant here, as it reminds us that the real nemesis of old-time cultists was not high culture, but the specter of mass-marketed aesthetic complexity offered by the middlebrow text.

Pioneering film cultists such as Manny Farber and Andrew Sarris, like their intellectual brethren Dwight Macdonald, José Ortega y Gasset, and others, pitched their oppositional connoisseurship precisely against this competing form of high pop culture—here epitomized by those Big Important Movies polished with a fake artistic sheen, maudlin piffle gussied with big, important themes or a false air of social conscience. For critic-painter Farber, who toiled for years writing acerbic reviews at the *New Republic* and the *Nation* before penning cultist manifestos such as "Underground Films: A Bit of Male Truth" (1957) and "White Elephant Art vs. Termite Art" (1962), tough-guy action flicks by Anthony Mann and Raoul Walsh beat the pretentious garbage of the Fred Zinnemanns, Sidney Lumets, and Michelangelo Antonionis of this world any day of the week.[3] Similarly, Sarris's much-vaunted "auteur theory" was really just a naked assertion of cult taste, a declaration that "Alfred Hitchcock is artistically superior to Robert Bresson by every criterion of excellence, and further, that, film for film, the American cinema has been consistently superior to that of the rest of the world from 1915 through 1962."[4] For both critics, an oppositional dip into the popular was first and foremost a daring gesture of refusal, a radical insistence that American pop culture was not something to be embarrassed about, and further that the most authentic, vital products of that culture could be found not floating on top, but lurking near the bottom, among the forgotten bits of junk. Becoming a pop culture expert thus meant, first and foremost, acquiring a broad enough awareness of the depths and margins in order to seem not as beholden to normative middlebrow standards as many of one's readers, and not as beholden to normative highbrow standards as one's friends and associates. Obviously enough, it also meant cultivating the ability to spot diamonds in the rough; whether these jewels took the form of forgotten films or neglected directors, they were to be validated as objects of cultural reappraisal by virtue of their virulent stance against the institutional forces of American mediocrity.

This was taking the depths and margins seriously, to be sure. But as a connoisseurship of trash it was always a form of cultural slumming, too—first, in that the rough standards of reappraisal were frequently also those championed in American high art of the postwar period (vitality could now be found in action movies as well as action painting), and second, in that said standards tended to remain vague, obscured behind the oppositional gesture itself, the ardent refusal that always lay at the heart of cultist practice and enabled the celebratory reclamation of cultural authority in the first place. Thus, attempts to delineate the strengths of cult objects in detail have been so rare simply because they are difficult to sustain given the sparseness and even dubious relevance of underlying criteria—as witness the ease with which Sarris's auteur theory was gleefully decimated by his would-be nemesis Pauline Kael.[5] Because cultism is fundamentally gestural and personal, because it is fundamentally about claiming and (less obviously) refusing in order to establish and reinforce one's own personal and cultural identity, discriminatory criteria can prove counterproductive. Cultism is so inextricably bound up with issues of self-definition as to make the critique of any particular cultist gesture tantamount to personal attack.

If anything, this has become only more apparent since the 1970s, when cultism in its various forms emerged as a democratically accessible source of engagement and amusement for literally millions of consumers, even as the highbrow modernist aesthetics that initially spawned it began to wane. Yet what we have been left with is oppositional spectatorship for its own sake, a promise of cultural authority within a larger us-against-them struggle whose terms remain vague at best. Today it seems clearer than ever that the appeal of cultism lies not in marginal aesthetics per se as in the very ability to claim and regulate cultural authority—the ability to claim *that I* like what I like (and know what I know), not *why* I like what I like (and know what I know). Identifying with others who claim similar tastes and expertise, and against others who remain uninitiated, while vigilantly rooting out those profane wannabes who would deign to sully the sacred ground in naked pursuit of their own status, provides more than half the fun.

The centrality and limitations of this sort of identification are captured nicely by author D. B. Weiss in his recent novel of cult/geek obsession, *Lucky Wander Boy* (2003). Here arcade video game junkie Adam Pennyman begins lovingly cataloguing his passions (*Pac-Man*, *Donkey Kong*, *Microsurgeon*) in a "Catalogue of Obsolete Entertainments" before falling headfirst into a dangerously fetishistic and narcissistic affair with the memory of the particularly obscure game referred to in the novel's title. Pennyman's increasing self-absorption is reflected ironically in his writings, which begin as musings on specific games but soon veer toward larger digressions, including a supplementary essay (interestingly enough) "On Geeks." A geek, Pennyman insists, is "a person, male or female, with an abiding, obsessive, self-effacing, even self-destroying love for something besides status" (italics omitted).[6] Indeed, the "heroic pointlessness" of true geekdom actually serves as a sort of "evolutionary door prize" for society's also-rans; for only "when some missing rung prevents a person from climbing their social ladder will they find themselves on a fallow patch of ground where other, more fragile interests can take root." This makes the emergence of the Status Geek and the broader "cultivation of 'geek chic'" a "deeply cynical, pernicious, even nihilistic attempt to plunder lives that are more often than not emotionally destitute already, to steal their sole prized possession and trade it on the open market for a minute of juice with a sexual target, a fleeting hit of superiority in a friendly discussion, the shimmering mirage of depth for an in-flight magazine profile."[7] For Pennyman, then, the Status Geek is thus not simply a fake but a vampire who drains cultism of its very lifeblood while advancing relentlessly toward the very success and recognition that the authentic geek can never hope to attain. In response, the true geek turns his sad fate to his advantage, wearing his marginality on his sleeve while defiantly transcending the very notion of means and ends by encountering "comics or cars or computer games as pure *Quidditas*, whatness, thereness for its own sake."[8] To have to explain why he likes what he likes, and knows what he knows, is to give in to the underlying premise that taste and knowledge must be inherently useful, even pragmatic. In a sense, this makes geeks like the fictional Pennyman cultural renegades in the grand romantic/modern tradition—even as they now operate in the absence of tenable romantic/modern aesthetics. As a result, they must carry the force of their geek resistance almost wholly through the anti-instrumentalism and seeming purposelessness of their cultist obsessions—with the vigorous assertion of distinction from other cultural consumers, notably Status Geek wannabes, sufficing as an end in itself. The ultimate value of this end is another matter: as for Pennyman, he eventually forfeits his job, his girlfriend, and his already tenuous connection with the world that lies beyond his inner memories and fantasies.

An avant-gardist without much of a platform, the geekish Adam Pennyman strikes me as an archetypal victim of the prosperous new cultism, typified by the ascent of Quentin Tarantino, the über–Status Geek whose *Kill Bill: Vol. 1* (2003) represents a veritable orgy of cultist reference to everything from Shaw Brothers martial arts films to spaghetti westerns, Japanese anime, Frankenheimer's *Black Sunday* (1977), *Ironside*, *The Green Hornet*, the Raquel Welch revenge western *Hannie Caulder* (1971), even Trix cereal commercials. What I find particularly interesting, however, is that this new cultism, while apparently antithetically opposed to the ideal of difficult, elitist art, nonetheless secretly clings to its own highbrow bias at least as tenaciously as did the old cultism of Farber and Sarris. Indeed, that bias continues to be obscured so as not to call attention to the nakedly pragmatic nature of cultism's patronizing interest in pop culture as a vibrant (and scandalous) alternative to the stultifying, self-congratulatory safety of middlebrow, the vacuous commercial art of the undiscerning wannabe intelligentsia—whether in the form of a gripping tome from Oprah's book club or a heartwarming Best Picture nominee. In the end, cultists have traditionally been interested less in pop culture per se than in the very ability to gesture toward pop culture in the first place, as to look too closely, or too seriously, at the pop artifact being celebrated is to risk the revelation of embarrassing formal simplicity or self-evidence. This is why placing a premium on being able to claim that I like what I like (and know what I know) is so useful, as it nicely sidesteps the why of aesthetic discernment, even as it also implies a level of condescension that seems oddly out of keeping with cultism's professed ideals. Now that the cultist's focus rests squarely on the assertion and regulation of oppositional knowledge and taste, the specific terms of the cultural distinction and authority he pursues can remain especially fuzzy. Why is this particular expertise valuable? On what basis are these certain works to be privileged? Why is it important to know all this stuff?

The considerable effort it often takes to avoid these questions is nicely foregrounded by Comedy Central's cultist quiz show *Beat the Geeks* (2001–2). Ostensibly a contest in which challengers vie to best resident experts in movie, music, and television trivia—along with assorted guest experts in fields such as horror, *Star Trek*, *The Simpsons*, James Bond, even KISS—*Beat the Geeks* is actually centrally concerned with the assertion, regulation, and continued mystification of cultural authority, including the spectator's own authority as an empowered cultist. An amalgamation of formats pilfered from a number of game/quiz/cooking shows, the program plays out its curious drama of changing reputations and shifting fortunes within the Kitchen Stadium–like Geek Arena, where the mighty geeks ("the finest steel-trap pop-trivia minds in existence," as the host exclaims) stand elevated on an illuminated platform. Robed yet wildly unkempt, they arrogantly yet insecurely tout their own cultist authority in opening pronouncements such as "I've heard a thousand bands perform live, and you've never heard of any of them" and "*Starsky and Hutch, Baa Baa Black Sheep, Mannix*—these are some of the shows I watch . . . in the morning." Then the week's three contestants play the first (*Jeopardy*-styled) "Toss-Up" round. This first round is the program's opportunity to showcase the geeks' privileged status; indeed, in season 1, the geeks sat out this segment entirely, speaking only when asked a casual prompting question designed to showcase their depth of knowledge. (For instance, when asked if he knows what show has won the most Emmys, television geek Paul Goebel carefully notes that *Cheers* has won the most Comedy Series awards, but that *The Mary Tyler Moore Show* has won the most overall, prompting an enthusiastic "Geek! Geek! Geek!" chant from the studio audience.) Even more significantly, our host (initially J. Keith van Straaten, then Blaine Capatch) might now also prompt the geeks to make judgments of aesthetic value: Movie Geek Mark Heuck, for instance, suggests that "Linda Fiorentino is the sexiest and most underused actress in Hollywood," and that "John Cusack . . . is the best actor working right now. He is an

FIGURE 1 The resident geeks and hostess of Comedy Central's *Beat the Geeks* (l–r: Marc Edward Heuck, Andy Zax, Tiffany Bolton, and Paul Goebel).

embodiment of what every man either wishes he was or wishes he knew in a friend. You either want to be him or you want to know somebody just like him. Even when he's played heel characters he's had a humanity about them that he hasn't just been putting on with a handlebar mustache or by cackling weirdly." That the Geeks get to make such judgments is actually really important, if only because the contestants do not—for unlike the Geeks, they have apparently not earned the right to do so through an appropriately prodigious display of cultural knowledge. Initially at least, it seems that the challengers, like the rest of us, might only aspire to legitimate judgment by pitting their modestly geekish obsessions against those of the masters, who even manage to curry the favor of sexy co-host Tiffany Bolton: turning to the camera with "a little advice for all you other co-hosts," she warns, "Stay away from my geeks, bitches!"

Appropriately enough, the obsessions of the contestant pretenders are at first all but ignored by our host, who deigns to chat with them only at the opening of round 2: "You've survived round 1," he announces, "so we might as well get to know you." When he then inquires, "What's the geekiest thing about you?," he is met with typically modest admissions—a waitress is obsessed with New Kids on the Block, a jeweler is addicted to PlayStation. But these admissions are nonetheless crucial, as they suggest a subtle turning point in the proceedings. For now the contestants are being taken a little more seriously, and in the following two "Challenge Rounds," where they first match wits with actual geeks, the geeks themselves will begin to face an uphill battle to retain their dignity. Indeed, they must now literally defend their large gold medals of honor, which must be surrendered to a contestant when they lose a challenge. Everything, it seems, is at stake, and suddenly it doesn't seem quite so fun to be a geek. Not only are these experts now subject to "impossibly difficult" questions (as opposed to the "relatively easy" ones posed of the contestants), it seems clear that the geeks' perversely large pop-cultural expertise is the only thing keeping them from being complete cultural rejects. Given their slobbish appearance and boorish behavior, why else keep them around? The host sternly warns them: "As all you Geeks know, you are being closely monitored—give any indication that you are no longer the Geek we thought you were and you may be replaced. And let's face it: if you begin to suck we really won't like you anymore. So stay on it, guys. I mean, who are we kidding?" Appropriately enough, challenged geek and contestant now trade insults—geek mildly chides challenger for her lack of expertise ("Danielle, I am starting a disco inferno, and I am bringing you down"), while challenger hits geek with a reminder of his looks and/or undesirability ("Don't be jealous that I won't go on a date with you"). The host, for his part, continues to stoke the flames: "Just remember, all the TV geek has is his TV knowledge," he tells a contestant. "You're much better than that, aren't you?"

While Geek success in the Challenge Rounds might be met with the audience "Geek!" chant, failure invites loud boos and shame, and even an excessive display of knowledge or evaluative acumen might prompt a disdainful chant of "Show-Off! Show-Off! Show-Off!" (Even the Iron Chefs don't have it this rough.) Then it's on to the brief "Geek-qualizer," another geek/contestant challenge designed (as the title suggests) to further winnow the field by revealing one contestant to be worthy of a final "Geek-to-Geek Showdown" with the expert of his or her choice. This showdown is what the entire episode has been moving toward: finalist and Geek facing off, literally on the same level now, with the other Geeks rooting lazily from the platform, where they lounge together on a musty couch, eating peanuts out of a yellow plastic bowl. And yet the Geek is still at a disadvantage here, because in this final defense of his honor he is forced to pick a harder (though more valuable) question than the lucky contestant. If he wins, he lives on to be tolerated for yet another day. If he loses, he is, of course, no longer the geek we thought he was.

On the surface, at least, the show appears to level the playing field, gradually stacking the deck in favor of contestant and against geek. As we move along, the sacred cows begin to look less sacred, and we begin to wonder if the geek will even survive another day. This certainly serves to make things more interesting for us spectators, as it complicates and regulates our own empowered involvement by playing with, and dispersing, our potential allegiances with geeks and contestants. The geeks are arrogant underdogs: serious and brilliant but also excessively enamored with their own (illusory) status, marginal and radical but also lonely and subject to ridicule. The contestants, for their part, are comfortably normal but also tediously ordinary, socially acceptable but also dangerously close to being Status Geeks themselves. True Geek life is comically pre-social and even pre-sexual—promo spots show them sharing a shabby (frat?) house, sitting around eating cereal and watching television while cloaked in their ridiculous robes—but then again, it's also *reassuringly* pre-social and pre-sexual. While chances are we too may fancy ourselves as geeks, deep down we also suspect that we are no longer the geeks we thought we were, either, and the program encourages us to feel OK about this by presenting sacred geekdom as a decidedly mixed blessing. You don't *really* want to be a true geek anyhow, do you?

Beat the Geeks sure hopes not. Like more recent cultist nostalgia-fests such as VH1's *I Love the '70s* and *I Love the '80s*, it needs to preserve the weakly grounded specialness of its cultural experts; hence it disperses our allegiances in order to ensure that we do not identify so strongly with the geeks, or with our own geekishness, that cultism's aura of mystery becomes compromised. This is why our geeks must remain odd, removed, and ultimately inaccessible; even if the final contestant manages to beat them, she or he will have a hard time joining them in the habits and odors of authentic geekdom. More important, the play of allegiances also serves to keep us distracted from those larger terms of cultural distinction and authority (the nagging "why" of discernment), obscuring the link between the cultural knowledge elicited by the host's questions, and the cultural authority claimed by the geeks and so prized by the host and audience. We may gather that sufficient range and depth of knowledge is the basis upon which that authority (which includes the authority to discriminate) is conferred, but *Beat the Geeks* consistently fudges the relationship between the two in order to ensure that the latter remains vague and mysterious, the domain of its weird and ultimately untouchable aficionados.

Ultimately, then, the program is founded on a ruse: by keeping our attention so focused on immediate questions of prestige and authenticity (who is the real Status Geek here?), it prevents us from questioning the very standards by which specialized knowledge and cult taste are determined in the first place. Why is it important to be able to identify the director of *Lost Souls* (Janusz Kaminski), or the two stars of the film version of the board game *Jumanji* (Robin Williams and Kirsten Dunst)? *Beat the Geeks* assumes the answer to this question to be self-evident, but of course it has to. The problem, again, is that while cultist discernment still accepts implicit evaluative criteria and the inherent aesthetic value of its chosen objects, it cannot quite fess up to either, as doing so only draws attention away from the gesture itself, and toward aesthetic assumptions which may themselves seem self-contradictory, awkwardly amalgamated, or even inappropriate. This is why cultism's very process serves as a sort of protective veil, naturalizing such implicit criteria within the countercultural gesture's very assertion of rarefied taste. Now one can hope to include an eclectic array of works or artists (André de Toth, Bert I. Gordon, and Linda Fiorentino) in one's own personal pantheon without having to worry about defending the relative merits—as opposed to mere distinctiveness—of each in traditional aesthetic terms.

This veil still serves to maintain the oppositional gesture as a promise of cultural (and more specifically, evaluative) authority over the brave new world of pop entertainment. But this promise necessarily remains a little hollow, to the extent that the means of evaluative assessment remain hidden from view. This actually serves to make the cultism of *Beat the Geeks* seem a little anachronistic, if only because one would think we now live in a climate where one shouldn't have to treat pop culture so gingerly. The truth is that cultists make value judgments all the time; indeed, evaluative assessment is part of the real fun of cultist discourse (think *High Fidelity* [2000]). But cultism has never known quite how to handle aesthetic discrimination, as its grand oppositional gesture is designed to mask evaluative criteria. When Movie Geek Marc Heuck celebrates the talents of John Cusack, he does so using fairly traditional evaluative criteria of subtlety, nuance, and skill of performance, but the show still tries hard to obscure this, elevating and mystifying him, loosely rooting his discrimination in cultist trivia knowledge in order to celebrate his supposed authority while simultaneously shoving him into the margins of resistant spectatorship.

The big secret of Beat the Geeks is that beneath the robes and stringy hair, the geeks are actually very much like us after all. Like them, we make evaluative queries and judgments about pop works all the time; it just doesn't seem so special when we do it. Why was M*A*S*H such a great show? Do the later Star Wars films live up to the original trilogy? Why do CSI: Miami and CSI: NY seem lame compared with the original? These are not aesthetically insignificant questions, and yet our culture is still extremely reluctant even to consider them matters of aesthetic discernment. Why not? I suspect it is because we are still beholden to the same underlying assumptions that fueled cultism to begin with, and that continue to give rise to cultist games like Beat the Geeks. If we cannot quite seem to acknowledge the presence of engagement, fandom, and fun within high culture, we have an equally difficult time acknowledging our routine subjection of pop products to aesthetic criteria such as wholeness, richness, organizational interest, intensity of feeling, and verisimilitude. The countercultural gesture—with its protective veil—still appeals to us, in part because it actually allows us to avoid taking pop culture too seriously. Considering a pop text as "pure Quidditas" lets us off the hook of real comparative discernment by couching evaluation in terms of heroic pointlessness versus crass opportunism, marginality versus mainstream, us versus them. In the end it's not about the work, it's about the empowering nostalgic comforts of the personal past in the face of the looming uncertainties of a collective future.

Now, I am not suggesting that this is in itself a bad thing, or that issues of image and identity are somehow absent from normative evaluative procedures (far from it). Nevertheless, the overwhelming pragmatism of geekish cultism continues to discourage us from facing pop works naked and head-on, and our understanding of culture suffers for it. I see my own difficulty in assessing the merits of the Stone Roses's Second Coming echoed and amplified in the work of Chuck Klosterman, a gifted critic but also a dedicated cultist who, for example, denigrates the "artful" *X-Files* while brazenly elevating the mindless transcendence of *Saved by the Bell* ("I watched it with the same thoughtless intensity I displayed when watching the dryer").[9] But when Klosterman sees true inherent value (richness, affective poignancy, social relevance) in the work of Billy Joel, he seems unsure of how to proceed, because he stubbornly sets his analysis within a cultist framework. So on the one hand, Joel's "subterranean fabulosity" somehow relates to his authenticity, to his not being cool: "unlike Lou Reed or David Bowie, 'Billy Joel' is not a larger pop construct or an expansive pop idea. Billy Joel is just a guy."[10] Yet on the other hand Klosterman also wants to insist that Joel is not "great *because* he's uncool,"[11] but that he's simply great. How ironic then that the work he chooses to epitomize Joel's greatness is *The Nylon Curtain*, "an album that only sold one million copies and was widely seen as a commercial disappointment," but nonetheless includes "six amazingly self-exploratory songs that almost no one except diehard fans are even vaguely familiar with." The problem here isn't that Klosterman wants to praise the heart-wrenching honesty or enigmatic richness of Joel's oeuvre, but that he seems unable to draw the line between more distanced discrimination ("Joel's best work always sounds like unsuccessful suicide attempts") and cultist appreciation ("Granted, I realize that I'm making a trite, superfan-ish argument").[12] This is not because Klosterman is a bad critic, but rather because his (and our) beholdenness to cultist impulses makes the line itself seem woefully uncool and best ignored. Perhaps we still live in an age where we dare not publicly praise Billy Joel's artistry without at least a hint of irony.

If this is true, so much the worse for us—for, like Michael Bérubé, Simon Frith, and Richard Schusterman, I would insist that aesthetic discrimination actually goes hand in hand with an immersion in pop culture.[13] People do take pop works seriously (as art, in effect) all the time; we just cannot or will not talk about it. We might consider jettisoning our old biases in order to begin examining more closely the various and complex aesthetic means by which (and various contexts within which) pop culture's works are commonly assessed, in the living room and the academy alike. But I would also suggest that we continue to examine the various underlying assumptions that have so strongly discouraged us in academia from seeing our own places within this spectrum. After all, who could be more geekish than media scholars?

Notes

1. The revised second edition of the *Compact Oxford English Dictionary of Current English* (Oxford: Oxford University Press, 2003) defines geek as "**1.** an unfashionable or socially inept person. **2.** an obsessive enthusiast."
2. Libby Slate, "Trading Faces: TV Trading Cards Take Their Rightful Place in the Collectibles Market," *TV Guide*, November 15, 2003, 63.
3. Manny Farber, "Underground Films: A Bit of Male Truth," *Commentary* (1957), reprinted in *Negative Space: Manny Farber on the Movies* (Expanded Edition) (Cambridge, Mass.: Da Capo, 1998), 12–24; "White Elephant Art vs. Termite Art," *Film Culture* 27 (1962–63), reprinted in *Negative Space*, 134–44.
4. Andrew Sarris, "Notes on the Auteur Theory in 1962," *Film Culture* 27 (1962–63), 5.
5. See Kael's "Circles and Squares," *Film Quarterly* 16, no. 3 (1963): 12–26, reprinted in *I Lost It at the Movies* (Boston: Little, Brown, 1965), 292–319.
6. D. B. Weiss, *Lucky Wander Boy* (New York: Plume, 2003), 181.
7. Ibid., 182.
8. Ibid., 183.
9. Chuck Klosterman, *Sex, Drugs, and Cocoa Puffs* (New York: Scribner, 2003), 130.
10. Klosterman, *Sex, Drugs, and Cocoa Puffs*, 44–45.
11. Ibid., 43.
12. Ibid., 49.
13. See Michael Bérubé, "Pop Culture's Lists, Rankings, and Critics," *Chronicle of Higher Education*, November 17, 2000, B7–B9; Simon Frith, *Performing Rites: On the Value of Popular Music* (Cambridge, Mass.: Harvard University Press, 1996); Richard Shusterman, *Performing Live: Aesthetic Alternatives for the Ends of Art* (Ithaca, N.Y.: Cornell University Press, 2000).

JEFFREY SCONCE

Movies A Century of Failure

In the distant science-fiction future of 1995, a bored Frenchman decides to spend the afternoon at the cinema. He looks through the ads for the current titles in release: *Dracula versus the Nymphomaniacs*, *Sade, You're a Prude!*, *The Rape of Frankenstein*, *Polyana's Orgy*, *Sodomy on the Bounty*, and *Passport to Lesbos*.

He finally decides to see *The Rape of Frankenstein*, as it seems to have "the largest number of negative guarantees." "It had little chance of disappointing me," observes the jaded narrator. "The fact that it had been breaking box-office records for three weeks meant that it had probably also broken some enviable records for stupidity and lunacy."[1] Arriving at the theater, he is happy that the film's poster confirms his suspicions.

Frankenstein's monster . . . was walking with his hands out in front of him, not in a cemetery this time, or across a bleak moor, but through a horde of naked women writhing with desire, offering themselves to him, arching their bodies toward him, oozing lust from every pore, split all over like walking orifices, stewing in their own hot juices, with their windblown hair brushing against the fleece of their genitalia that seemed to be eagerly reaching out for the whole world; some of them were rubbing their bellies against the monster, who appeared to wonder what was happening to him, while others were on all fours, spread wide, looking defiantly down at the public with an obvious craving for caresses, whips, orgasms, and terror.[2]

The movie itself proves no less disappointing. Diagnosed by a Viennese psychoanalyst as having a "blocked libido," Frankenstein's monster escapes on a two-hour sexual rampage that has him raping a painting, a mannequin, and a corpse before finally turning to the women in the village, all of whom gladly give themselves over to the creature's prodigious sexual assets. In the end, the men of the village disguise themselves as women to lure the creature into a trap and kill him. Leaving the theater, our narrator observes, "When you realize that it took no less than three professional scenario writers, two dialogue writers, and four artistic advisors to turn out that story for retarded adults, it's hard not to feel a little dejected. Then, because you're used to such things, you shrug your shoulders and smile."[3]

This vision of the cinema's future comes from Jacques Sternberg's 1971 novel *Toi, Ma Nuit* (appearing in the United States under the more salacious title *Sexualis '95*). Sternberg's account of a public hungry for the exploits of a rapacious Frankenstein might be dismissed as a standard (though lasciviously exaggerated) mass-elite critique of popular culture, which it certainly is. Yet Sternberg's narrator is not necessarily a high-art snob. He has just as little patience for the avant-garde. "If you want to avoid films made for the mass market," he laments, "you have to put up with abstract films that have no plot or actors and are reduced to cascades of disjointed sounds, fleeting images and shapeless masses."[4] Writing in the late 1960s, Sternberg's disgust with *all* cinema—high and low—expresses a perhaps inevitable endpoint to an elite disaffection stalking the decade's film culture. This is, after all, the same era that saw a revolutionary Jean-Luc Godard pronounce the end of cinema in the closing frames of *Weekend* (1967) and a bored Pauline Kael champion AIP's goofy teen-pic *Wild in the Streets* (1967) over Stanley Kubrick's seriously important *2001: A Space Odyssey* (1968).[5] Musing over the ridiculously sleazy movie titles in the newspaper of the future, Sternberg considers them a statement on where "the cinema has arrived after all its wasted research, honorable bankruptcies, and noble failures: just below the waist. For a long time the cinema has never reached any higher." Terry Southern's *Blue Movie*, also a product of the decade's celluloid ennui, opens with a similar revelation. Bored with his critical and commercial successes in Hollywood, a rudderless director embraces the cinema's last remaining artistic challenge: making a multi-million-dollar hard-core porno film complete with A-list stars, tasteful lighting, and European-style camerawork.

This coalescence of the 1960s' cinematic imagination around tropes of sleaze, boredom, and failure is a fascinating moment in the history of American film culture. While 1968 brought an increasing radicalization of cine-politics in France, the late 1960s saw many critics in the United States raising the white flag of surrender, giving in at last to a long-brooding disillusionment over the gap between film's historical promise and its actual year-to-year practices. This disillusionment continues to haunt contemporary film culture even today, perhaps even more so. Disaffected cinephiles such as Sternberg, Kael, and Southern were once canaries in a cultural coal mine—struggling with a passion for film turned to disappointment turned to derision turned to resignation. Today, however, an entire segment of the culture industry thrives on serving the cinematically dispossessed, a once subterranean but now increasingly visible nation of cinephiles who *love* movies yet *hate* the cinema (or at least what they perceive the cinema as having become). A response, perhaps, to Hollywood's own cynicism in creating increasingly calculated and artless product, a legion of perpetually disgruntled movie critics rant about the state of cinema in contemporary print, broadcasting, and cyberspace, not to mention daily conversation. United in the principle that the cinema has become an unimaginative and perhaps irredeemable sewer of cliché and stupidity, these critics collectively articulate a voice that ranges from the bitterly comic to the comically bitter. In recent years, such ludic cynicism over the state of cinema, the cult of celebrity, and the general fate of popular culture has become known as "snark," an attitude that captures the love/hate relationship of the pop connoisseur to the contemporary media landscape. Cultivated in an ever-growing cultural formation during the 1990s and thriving in our own historical moment, this snark has become a dominant voice in contemporary film criticism, a mock and mocking despair that ranges from Joe Queenan's prankster irony in *Movieline* to the *Onion's* weekly feature, "DVD Commentaries of the Damned." Beth Littleford and Steve Carrell's "We Love Show Business" segments for *The Daily Show* translated this cynicism into an arch parody of entertainment reporting puffery, damning not just Hollywood product but the entire parasitic support industry that keeps such product afloat.

On the Web, movie review sites like RottenTomatoes.com and Mr. Cranky employ an inverse ratings scale. The best *any* film can hope for under Mr. Cranky's ratings system is "one bomb," a designation that equates to "almost tolerable." "Whether it's a comedy, drama or action-adventure film," reads the Web site, "Mr. Cranky can provide myriad detail as to why the movie, to quote the film school term, 'sucks.'"[6] Meanwhile, the Razzies—an awards show for Hollywood's worst achievements of the year—has gone from private party game to international media event. Indeed, recognizing catastrophic cinematic failure has become such a mainstream pursuit that some celebrities actually agree to appear at the Razzies to pick up their awards, all in the hopes of showcasing a sense of self-deprecating humor and thus garnering good press to counteract the horrific buzz about a particularly notorious performance. A more general and increasingly vitriolic disgust with the excess, narcissism, and condescending parochialism of Hollywood, finally, fuels not only the tabloids, but Web sites like defamer.com, television series like *Celebrities Uncensored*, and a growing catalogue of mass market books. Indeed, the culture of Hollywood entitlement has become a convenient populist whipping boy for both the political left and right—not only do the movies "suck" in this worldview, but so too do the amoral, narcissistic, elitist, talentless, navel-gazing suits and stars that keep the entire embarrassing charade going.

Hollywood has always had its critics, of course, ranging from the post-*Day of the Locust* tragedies of innumerable novelists spurned by the film industry to the recurring moral crusades of the religious right. As films like *A Star Is Born* (1937, 1954, 1976), *The Bad and the Beautiful* (1952), and *The Player* (1992) demonstrate, Hollywood itself has for decades rather solipsistically reveled in the self-perceived tragedies of its above-the-line citizenry. Our current era of cinephilic disaffection, however, posits a world where the cinema's unending compromises have finally produced a complete and irreversible artistic collapse, leaving only derisive irony and disengaged contempt as viable modes for engaging the vast majority of contemporary cinematic product. Like Sternberg's misanthropic cinephile, there would seem to be an audience today that appears to go to the movies, not out of an expectation of actually being moved, engaged, or even remotely entertained in any conventional sense, but rather to wallow in the cinema as a faltering medium in a failing culture. Often, the goal is less to

FIGURE 1 Halle Berry in *Catwoman* (2004), a classic in the cinema of "negative guarantees."

watch an individual title than bear witness to an entire cultural institution in collapse. Almost every title is to be met with suspicion, and if there is any pleasure to be had in a day at the theater, it is rooted either in masochism or a radical reframing of what constitutes *interest* in the cinema (or perhaps both). In the summer of 2004, some went to see *Catwoman* because they love loud action movies. Others went because they wanted to see Halle Berry prance around in bondage gear for two hours. And then there were the smirking cine-cynics who could not resist the film's ample "negative guarantees"—Oscar-winning actress reduced, quite literally, to pandering sex kitten, generationally pitted against überbitch Sharon Stone in a spin-off of a sequel to a sequel to a sequel in a supreme testament to the complete creative exhaustion of Hollywood. Advance buzz of production troubles and last-minute recutting only amplified wise-ass anticipation. This last audience, in other words, gleefully went to the theater to see a train wreck. They were not disappointed.

As the cinema enters its second century, we might ask why so many people love to hate the movies. In this new era of snark, negative cinephilia and cine-cynicism, a certain audience no doubt continues to attend dutifully the latest "quality" films that generate art-house buzz yet reserves its true passion for ripping the work of Jerry Bruckheimer, Michael Bay, and other purveyors of spectacular idiocy, a cinema of "negative guarantees" that compels a position of estrangement, alienation, and derision. Such cine-cynicism might be thought of as camp without the empathy or historical distance, a once playful dandyism decayed, through years of despair and disappointment, into the giddy nihilism of the bored libertine. When so few films are capable of surprising you, be they commercial, classic, or experimental, what is the "film lover" to do but give up and engage the institution as a whole in terms of disappointment and failure? For the jaded, bored, and otherwise dispossessed cinephile—a viewer who has spent years chasing even a hint of the faintest possibility of a potential harbinger of something interesting in the cinema—past, present, or future—this final moment of disappointment brings a collapse of all evaluative and affective hierarchies, replacing them with bitter acceptance of a stalemate in the ongoing challenge of "outwitting" the banality of commercial cinema. Considered in this respect, our historical moment's continuing and even growing interest in cinematic failure—be it the doomed blockbuster, the overly precious Sundance winner, or the grindhouse travesty—might best be thought of as a cinematic death wish, a new and terminal aesthetic order where the landmarks of the cinema are not Hitchcock and Welles, neorealism or various new waves, but the delicious implosions of ego-porn like *Full Frontal* (2002) and *Battlefield Earth* (2000), the "screw-you" pre-sold hubris of *Godzilla* (1998) and *Wild, Wild West* (1999) remakes, the midcult pomposity of *American Beauty* (1999) and *Timecode* (2000), and that secret history of sleazy, shitty exploitation cinema that forces all viewers to confront the limits and mortality of the cinema as a whole.

Movie Melancholia

Are there really viewers who love to hate the cinema? To the extent that such self-conscious hostility exists in contemporary film culture, it remains an admittedly esoteric phenomenon, at least in its most bitterly ludic forms. Judging by the opening weekends and eventual DVD sales of *Men in Black 2* (2002), *Van Helsing* (2004), and *Kangaroo Jack* (2003), some people still "love" the movies. Most people probably have no real complaints as to the state of film art. Box-office receipts generally continue to rise, movies are faster and louder than ever, and DVDs allow us all to become idiosyncratic archivists—what could be the problem? No doubt those who continue to find the cinema a source of constant disappointment are the very same people who have (or once had) the highest hopes for the medium: cinephiles—those who do have a profound, even perverse attachment to the movies. As Web pest–turned–Hollywood player Harry Knowles proclaims, "Movies should be better. And someone should be held accountable when they're not." Speaking like generations of movie lovers before him, Knowles declares films "far too important to be left in the hands of those without an emotional stake in them."[7] In this respect, the current quest for a cinema of "negative guarantees," movies that indulge pleasures of alienation over empathy and identification, can only really be understood as part of a larger cinephilic tradition that has long focused on the seemingly perpetual failures of film art. At their core, many cinephiles have long been haunted by a sense of loss and failure in the cinema, making film history, criticism, and theory an often melancholy pursuit.

Reviewing aesthete discourses over the course of the century, the cinema may well be the most disappointing artistic medium in the history of human endeavor—especially the Hollywood cinema that has so dominated film culture since the medium's inception. Whatever period of film history one cares to explore over the past century, one thing is for certain: the cinema has not and is not living up to its potential. Vachel Lindsay's foundational study of 1917, *The Art of the Motion Picture*, is as much a complaint as a celebration. Writing in 1933 about the impact of sound, meanwhile, Rudolph Arnheim warned, "The majority of art-lovers . . . do not see that the film is on its way to the victory of . . . wax museum ideals over creative art."[8] Thirty years later Kael bemoaned a rise of narrative incoherence in film. "I don't think that my own preferences or the preferences of others for coherence or wit and feeling are going to make much difference," she laments. "Movies are going to pieces."[9] Meanwhile, we're all familiar with the depressing critical doxa of today: movies are terrible, audiences are stupid, critics are powerless—all signs point to the cinema devolving into some form of interactive gaming in the next twenty years or so. Bazin's "Myth of Total Cinema" will finally be realized not by immersing audiences in dramas of Dickensian complexity or landscapes of surrealist desire, but instead through endless CGI shots of kickboxing action heroes whirling around and around in the air until even the most hardened PlayStation veteran vomits in ecstasy.

Almost from the origins of "film culture," then, cinephiles have measured film's seemingly unlimited potential against the ceaselessly depressing reality of its achievement. There would seem to be few arts where the stink of failure is so ever present, where more time is spent despairing over lost opportunities, wasted ambition, and abject art. The cinema constantly fails the cinephile, never living up to the imagined ideals of transcendental bliss it once seemed to promise (or more tellingly, actually delivered earlier in life). So, like a spouse in an abusive relationship, the cinephile cannot simply love the cinema, but must constantly try to work through the diabolical mix of pleasure and disappointment that attends that love. Perhaps this is why seemingly all cinephiles have typically had an inordinately tortured relationship to the object of their desire—one of attraction and repulsion, intimacy and estrangement, hope and despair, nostalgia and melancholy. "Why don't people like the right movies anymore?" complains David Denby in the *New Yorker*, putting a new culturalist twist on former colleague Kael's patented aesthetic question, "Why are the movies so bad?" Like many American film critics of his generation, Denby is nostalgic for the 1970s, a period when acknowledged auteurs still put "art" into general release, repertory theaters still unearthed lost gems of the studio era, critics felt they still had some impact on shaping the future of cinematic practice, and the East Coast was still the bastion of taste that kept the philistines of Hollywood in check. Like most people left stranded by the changing eddies of taste, Denby's complaint is more about proles than about practice. Standing alone before a boarded-up rep house, espresso in hand, he might as well be asking where all the right people have gone.

Much of this melancholia is no doubt a function of the unique social position of the film critic in the culture at large. As Greg Taylor argues in his essential history of postwar film criticism, *Artists in the Audience*, "movies have proven surprisingly useful to different groups seeking to bolster widely disparate social identities."[10] Taylor argues that Manny Farber and Parker Tyler, as perhaps the two most influential postwar critics in the United States, turned to movies in the 1950s as "a reactionary retreat from the burgeoning success of abstract expressionism" and were "determined to resist the commodification of modernism and individual expression."[11] In this way, what Taylor terms the "vanguard criticism" of Farber's "cultism" and Tyler's "camp" embraced the cinema less as a legitimate object of artistic interest than as a medium for personal and idiosyncratic critical polemics. "The vulgar medium of motion pictures could become a means to an end," observes Taylor, "offering the vanguard critic an authentic vibrancy against which the studied efforts of the fashionable abstractionists seemed forced and opportunistic."[12] Postwar film criticism as a whole, Taylor seems to suggest, has its foundations in exile, pioneered by aesthetes at odds with the prevailing trends in the world of legitimate art. As cultural elites interrogating a popular medium, film critics frequently bring inordinate amounts of cultural capital to bear on extremely impoverished texts, carrying with them all of the confusion and even contempt of film's ambivalent relationship to prevailing hierarchies of taste.

Strongly indebted to the vanguard criticism of Farber and Tyler, the melancholy resignation of Sternberg, Southern, Kael, and others in the late 1960s seems to issue from a profound moment of self-recognition as to the futility of continuing to critique and encourage cinematic art. This is especially true of Kael's 1968 essay for *Harper's*, "Trash, Art, and the Movies." For Kael circa 1968, the search for serious artistry in the cinema had become a ridiculous project. "We generally become interested in movies because we *enjoy* them," she writes, "and what we enjoy them for has little to do with what we think of as art."[13] She finds in-depth analysis of film technique a laughable pursuit, arguing the available repertoire of film form is by nature limited and by practice positively indistinguishable. Blasting the 1960s vogue for divining serious statements made by important auteurs, Kael writes, "If you could see the 'artist's intention' you would probably wish you couldn't anyway. Nothing is so deathly to enjoyment as the relentless march of a movie to fulfill its obvious purpose."[14] Following Farber, Kael argues viewers must be willing to sift through torrents of movie mud for fleeting nuggets of gold, tiny epiphanies that often have little to do with artistic design or intentionality. Even this, however, may not be enough to save the cinema. She is sympathetic to the many dispirited film critics who have simply given up. "Many film critics quit," she observes, because "they can no longer bear the many tedious movies for the few good moments and the tiny shocks of recognition."[15] In yet another melancholy admission of failure, loss, and defeat, Kael claims that she finds only documentaries to be of interest anymore. "After all the years of stale stupid acted-out stories, with less and less for me in them, I am desperate to know something, desperate for facts, for information, for faces of non-actors and for knowledge of how people live—for revelations, not for the little bits of show-business detail worked up for us by show-business minds who got them from the same movies we're tired of."[16]

This vanguard line of popular criticism trailing back through Kael, Farber, and Tyler all the way to Oscar Wilde is one antecedent for our current climate of cine-cynicism. But this obsession with futility and failure in the cinema is not limited only to popular film criticism, as it has also significantly informed academic film theory's attempts to bolster the cinema's status through ongoing flirtations with continental philosophy. Consider Christian Metz's comments on cinephilia in his canonical contribution to film theory, *The Imaginary Signifier*: "To be a theoretician of the cinema, one should ideally no longer love the cinema and yet still love it: have loved it a lot and only have detached oneself from it by taking it up again from the other end, taking it as the target for the very same scopic drive which had made one love it."[17] Of the cinephile himself, Metz advises, "be him and not be him, since all in all these are the two conditions on which one can speak of him."[18] Small wonder that Lacanian psychoanalysis—with its narratives of lost plenitude and endlessly deferred desire—should so dominate film theory over the past thirty years. Here we see an attempt to theorize the fundamentally deceptive and unsatisfactory exchange in the cinema, a gap once again between promise and execution, fantasy and reality. Work in the Lacanian paradigm typically followed Metz and Raymond Bellour deeper into the mysterious mechanics of film form—but it may well be this body of theory ultimately speaks more to a cultural desire *for* cinema than any hallucinatory psychic structures of desire imagined within cinematic form. Before they are regressed, interpellated, and sutured, what ineffable longing brings people into the theater in the first place? Over the years, why does one's desire for cinema wax and wane? In contemplating the influence and affect of cinema, are the lived anticipations and memories of film content ultimately more meaningful than the occult fantasies of primary and secondary identification? Why, finally, does the cinema remain a source of such constant disappointment for so many, promising much, but ultimately failing over and over again to realize its most transcendental possibilities? In simply accepting the micropolitics of the gaze as the privileged site for understanding the circuits of cinematic desire, Lacanian film theory often overlooked the cinema in its totality as a terrain of libidinal investment, an institution and experience that, for many years at least, seemed always on the verge of realizing some unspoken and yet continually thwarted potential.

In their darkest moments, all cinephiles brood over the final and most profound failure facing their beloved art form—its death. The cinema has died many times now—the advent of sound, the Paramount Decision, the coming of television, the opening frames of George Lucas's *Star Wars* (1977), the proliferation of digital imaging and effects, the triumph of spectacle over narrative, producers over directors, marketing over execution. We should not be surprised, then, that so much writing on film and film culture has been elegiac if not downright funereal. A recent anthology, for example, announces "The End of Cinema as We Know It," concluding with "Twenty-five Reasons Why It's All Over."[19] "We are faced with the inescapable fact," writes Wheeler Winston Dixon, "that 'film' has become an altogether different medium from that imagined and practiced by its pioneers and classicists."[20] Like Denby, Dixon's "end of the line" is to be found in the misguided tastes of youth ("Audiences keep getting younger and more impatient," he laments, as if the Tarzan series of the 1930s and 1940s were kept alive by the philosophy faculty at Princeton).[21] This familiar diagnosis of the cinema's ills betrays the cinephile's anxiety over his or her own mortality, a paranoid and self-pitying fantasy that the object of one's affection is constantly threatening to "move on" and start over, sleeping with younger and more brutish audiences, leaving the spurned lover alone and depressed in bittersweet memories of what once was. Like so much writing on the perpetual crisis of failure, collapse, and death in the cinema, Dixon's piece ultimately assumes the tragic voice of the exiled cinephile ("No, we'll never see the like of *Casablanca* again," he writes), even as he just as inevitably maintains, "despite all this, the cinema will live forever."[22] This last comment is key. All cinephiles, despite their constant depression over a cinema that is lost or never was, ultimately cannot let go, and so continue to animate the body of cinema with regressive dreams of resuscitation and reunion—an act of disavowal much like the serial killer who keeps corpses in the basement for ritualistic abuse and sad comfort.[23]

One might say that all arts have their critics, pessimists, and outright misanthropes—aesthetes nostalgic for representational painting, high modernist fiction, or nineteenth-century tonality. Yet the cinema seems especially cursed in the gap that separates potential from achievement, history from future, and idealization from reality. After all, we rarely critique literature for the novels that should have been written, or the art world for the paintings that should have been painted. We expect television to be crap, so it is never in a position to disappoint us. But movies continue never to live up to their promise, directors never fulfill their potential, producers never seem to understand the artistic possibilities of the medium, "lowbrow" audiences misdirect a profound art into a puerile waste of time, and the cinema as an institution continues to wander in the desert. Thus, in so many tragic scenarios, film history becomes the story of two cinematic planes—a Platonic realm of transcendental synesthesia and the depressing reality of the continuing insults to our cinematic intelligence.

"Film, our most vivacious art, is young enough to remember its first dreams, its limitless promise," wrote Annette Michelson in 1966, "and it is haunted, scarred, by a central, ineradicable trauma of dissociation."[24] This dissociation, of course, is between cinema in a state of pure abstract possibility and its eventual grounding in a corporate economy based on profit. As many have lamented, and will no doubt continue to lament, the cinema is an art form of potentially radical possibility held hostage to the mundane demands of commercial viability. It is the commercial popularity of cinema, after all, that provides both the form's most dynamic engine and most maddening constraints. Born of modernity's new technologies, modes of production, and mass cultural logic, the cinema has always confronted the paradox of linking expanded artistic potential with increasing expenditures of capital. It has thus long been a medium of compromise, reenacting again and again that age-old conflict between directors and studio bosses, screenwriters and producers, geniuses and philistines, art and capital. Unlike most previous forms of aesthetic appreciation, cinephilia has always had to incorporate amateur sociology and cultural history in addition to the usually unsullied realm of poetics. A full appreciation of a benchmark film like Edgar G. Ulmer's *Detour* (1945), after all, requires familiarity with both the historical context of film noir and the production practices of Poverty Row. The film only achieves its true greatness when integrated into a larger metanarrative of popular history, noir literacy, and intrepid directorial perseverance. Without these larger historical frames and fantasies to anchor it, *Detour* remains just a cheap and corny B film.

In its halcyon days, auteurism presented a valiant attempt to organize film art around a more manageable and familiar model of individual creativity, but even here, the emphasis was as much on failure as success. Consider, for a moment, all of the elaborate auteurist mythologies that cinephiles have generated over the years, stories of failure, conflict, and compromise that endlessly rehearse Michelson's "trauma of dissociation," pitting art and capital against one another in a death struggle for the cinema's very soul. Thus, there is the foundational *Welles mythos* of the tortured genius misunderstood and mistreated by Hollywood—a flash of youthful brilliance slowly extinguished by corporate philistines. For many years, classic cinephilia thrived on such recurring tales of injustice and stupidity, as if despotic studio bosses were the colonial oppressors and not the foundational architects of narrative cinema. Welles also figures prominently in what might be called the *mangled masterpiece mythos*, the story of perfect cinematic achievements taken away and destroyed by studio hacks.[25] Mangled masterpieces, it should be noted, are not always purely a function of studio suits recutting a film. Such disasters can also hinge on a single weak link "ruining" an otherwise brilliant achievement. This curse seems to plague Martin Scorsese in particular, with both *The Age of Innocence* (1993) and *Gangs of New York* (2002) impeded by the inclusion of bankable (but less talented) actors in key roles. Perhaps most tragic of all, however, is the *unrealized masterwork mythos*: a production long dreamed of and yet never realized by an auteur (Luis Buñuel's *The Monk*, Orson Welles's *Don Quixote*, and David Lynch's *Ronnie Rocket* come to mind).

Beyond these sagas of unrealized and/or unrecognized genius, there are also a host of stories centering on film as a site of artistic resistance and subterfuge. In the *Sirk mythos*, an artistic genius must labor in lowly genres with insulting scripts but exploits the opportunity to produce thematic or formal critiques of his material, thus casting the director as a subversive trickster creating political art from popular dross. Closely related is the *genre displacement mythos*, a scenario wherein censorship or studio concerns force a filmmaker to "disguise" subversive content in the language of a seemingly unrelated genre (typically westerns, horror, or science fiction).[26] Then there is the *genius of poverty*

FIGURE 2 By very publicly going over budget, encountering numerous difficulties while filming, and running headlong into a growing Kevin Costner backlash, *Waterworld* (1995) helped introduce the idea of the "troubled production" into the popular vocabulary.

mythos, wherein the affronts of low budgets and absurd preselected titles actually present the artist with creative challenges leading to greater experimentation. Ulmer, mentioned above, frequently finds refuge in this mythos, as does Val Lewton's horror cycle at RKO in the 1940s. Cinephiles have also long enjoyed the *hidden drama mythos*, seeing a particular film as symptomatic of some submerged conflict or trauma in the production. *Marnie* (1964) and *The Misfits* (1961) are classic examples at the dawn of New Hollywood. Documentaries like *Hearts of Darkness* (1991), *Burden of Dreams* (1982), and *Lost in La Mancha* (2002), meanwhile, present auteur-centered hagiographies that bring this mythos to the screen.[27] As promotional and behind-the-scenes discourse multiplied in the 1980s and beyond, films like *Heaven's Gate* (1980) and *Waterworld* (1995) created a subgenre of the hidden drama mythos in the guise of the "troubled production"—a term that moves beyond a purely auteurist fascination with the potential for conflict and failure to incorporate a mass "inside dopesterism," one increasingly hip to the rumors of creative and commercial conflicts that can beset a blockbuster production.[28] Though this type of coverage goes back as far as *Cleopatra* (1963), more recent examples often dovetail with larger backlashes against overexposed Hollywood players (e.g., James Cameron, Kevin Costner, and Ben Affleck).

For those wholly invested in the industry's offscreen tragedies of failure, finally, there is the remorse offered by wholly speculative scenarios. What if Kubrick had directed *A.I.* instead of Spielberg? What if Buster Keaton's relatives hadn't sold him out at the end of the 1920s? What if the studio system had survived? What if Woody Allen had never seen a Bergman film? What if Peter Jackson had never read Tolkien? What if Michael Bay's parents had never met? Uniting all of these mythologies in cinephilic lore, from the lone tortured genius to the grand road not taken, is the melancholy and seemingly unwavering idea that film can never be simply what it is but must instead be gauged against some imaginary ideal of a film or cinema that never was or, indeed, could never be. What is on the screen is imperfect, but somewhere else there exists another film, another career, another cinema that is potentially perfect, limitless in its possibility rather than consistently up against the wall of commercial and historical reality. It is a world where Welles doesn't lose final cut on *The Magnificent Ambersons* (1942) or has to settle for Charlton Heston in *Touch of Evil* (1958); a world where Grace Kelly doesn't become the queen of Monaco, leaving us with the simulacrum of Tippi Hedren; a world where Zoetrope studios succeeds and Coppola is not reduced to directing crap like *Jack* (1996);[29] a world where dadaists, surrealists, minimalists, and other assorted modernists had defeated the cinema's plodding turn toward bourgeois realism; a world where the American renaissance doesn't give way to the *Endless Summer of Porky's American Pie, Part 7*.

Exploiter and Exploited

Even before our own era of mass-cult cynicism about the cinema, one group of cinephiles openly embraced the cinema's limitations, failures, and fundamentally disassociative struggle between art and capital. Today's snark and cine-cynicism, an audience entertaining the appeal of negative guarantees, has its foundations in the cults of exploitation, sleaze, and bad cinema that have thrived for over twenty-five years now. As I argued in an earlier article, the appreciation of "bad" cinema followed an interesting trajectory during the 1980s and 1990s, beginning as a simple "so bad it's good" type of derision, but eventually mimicking the esoteric discourses of outsider art to forge a pseudo-populist avant-garde.[30] Ed Wood's transformation from laughably untalented pervert to the idiosyncratic counter-visionary portrayed by Johnny Depp in Tim Burton's bio-fantasy is the most famous example of this impulse, but Doris Wishman, Jess Franco, Mario Bava, and many other fringe filmmakers have enjoyed similar critical reassessment. In the process, many exploitation filmmakers have inspired cults of personality that focus less on their talent or vision, but on the filmmaker's heroic challenge to the fundamental obstacles presented by the cinema itself.

It is a safe bet, for example, that Roger Corman will always be a more beloved and even a more respected figure in film culture than James Cameron. Anyone could sink the Titanic convincingly with $140 million, obsessing for months over every digital extra that spills into the Atlantic, but just try creating a creature worthy of the title *It Conquered the World* (1956) out of $300 in chicken wire and papier-mâché.[31] As anyone who has worked on a film set can attest, Corman stands as patron saint of a bygone era when a filmmaker—despite irritable cameras, questionable film stock, bad sound takes, lousy actors, flubbed lines, or botched continuity—could still take on twenty-five set-ups a day and finish a film in a week. Much of the romance of exploitation cinema stems from this valorization of film production itself as an elemental struggle against the conspiratorial forces of the universe. For many trash cinephiles, this is the essence of the art form, a medium of exploitation that has always been less about realizing some idealized artistic vision than the act of creation itself, transforming the cinema as a whole into an existential metaphor of affirmation in the face of chaotic absurdity.[32] Though aficionados of low-budget science fiction and horror may have first watched these films as objects of ridicule, many also went on to identify with the role of the exploiter in exploitation cinema. Director/producers like Corman, David F. Friedman, William Castle, H. G. Lewis, and others have become folk heroes in this community by acknowledging, indeed embracing, the fundamental hucksterism of all cinema, each in his own way a cynical pragmatist unencumbered by the delusions of art and gravitas that afflict more deluded filmmakers. Echoing P. T. Barnum's archetypically American credo "There's a sucker born every minute," these filmmakers revel in a mutual hostility for an audience of pigeons that ranges from the playful to

FIGURE 3 Promotional still from Roger Corman's *It Conquered the World* (1956): "It" remains an emblem of the courage and creativity involved in low-budget filmmaking.

the downright nasty. Friedman, for example, proudly calls himself "America's most notorious carpetbagger of Cinemadom," while Corman's autobiography appears under the rather confrontational title, *How I Made Over 100 Movies and Never Lost a Dime*. If there is an art here, it is the art of surviving week to week in the fleecing of hix in the stix with pix.

The nostalgic charm of William Castle, in particular, speaks to a mentality that divides everyone into either the exploiter or the exploited. Castle, of course, is revered in film lore for hyping his low-budget horror films with outlandish promotional campaigns and unusual gimmicks, all lovingly recounted in his own aggressively titled memoir, *Step Right Up and I'llScare the Pants off America*. The last great practitioner of the lost art of ballyhoo, Castle's stunts included stationing nurses in the lobby for overwhelmed spectators, fright insurance for those who might die of shock during a screening, and the miracle of E-Mergo, which consisted of a plastic skeleton flying over the audience on a wire.[33] In his most infamous stunt, Castle wired random seats with electrical joy buzzers for screenings of *The Tingler*. To the extent that American popular culture remains infatuated with this era, it is based on a nostalgic fantasy of audiences charmingly naive enough to be taken in by such ridiculous hijinx, a time when a local screening of *Strait Jacket* (1964) could still cut through the media landscape to become a community event, and when one could still zap

FIGURE 4 William Castle's *The Tingler* (1959): the charm of naive exploitation and the melancholy of those who can no longer be exploited.

audience members in the ass with bolts of electricity without getting sued.[34] But, for those cinephiles obsessed with this era and its charmingly dated low-budget fodder, the pleasures of such popular memory are more complex. Balancing this nostalgia, a cultural memory perhaps never even experienced by younger cinephiles, is a metonymic rehearsal of a lifetime's relationship to the cinema, a journey that carries personal memory from the days of giddy matinee expectation to that of growing multiplex disillusionment. Who wouldn't like to re-inhabit, at least for a fleeting moment, the childlike imagination genuinely excited at the sight of a fluorescent skeleton swooping down over the auditorium, to once again surrender to the overwhelming powers of anticipation, desire, and spectacle the cinema once possessed both in our childhoods and in the culture at large, to believe once again, if only for a moment, that *It* might actually conquer the world?[35] When that absolute investment in cinematic magic is no longer possible, there remains only the tragicomic saga of the cinema itself. Film history becomes a mirror to our own mortality, bringing with it the bittersweet recognition that one can never again sit among the screaming yokels below. By reveling in this disjunction between expectations and disappointment, the trashophile is constantly reliving a sadomasochistic fantasy organized around binaries of child and adult, desire and disillusionment, naïveté and cynicism. Like a true sadomasochist, the trashophile enjoys both points of identification—transported one moment to a magical world of skeletons, dinosaurs, vampires, and spaceships, and in the next, laughing at the cheap chicanery that long ago, both culturally and personally, held the power to captivate.

As the most naked battlefield in the cinema's traumatic dissociation between art and capital, the cinemas of trash, sleaze, and exploitation threaten to implode the power of all film by foregrounding yet another fundamental dissociation in the cinema, one even more elemental to debates about the medium's foundations and possibilities. As an art form created from immutable photographic windows on the ever-accelerating culture of the twentieth century, the cinema has always been a paradox: living, immediate, real, and immersive, and yet historical, fading, and obsolescent. Confronting this paradox, trash cinephiles have embraced the valiant yet ultimately doomed attempt of the cinema to transcend not only the eternal struggle between art and capital, but also the medium's foundational anchor in indexical reality.[36]

Once motion pictures lose their ability to transport viewers, to take them to another diegetic time and place, they simply become photography. Diegesis must always eventually yield to documentation as representational codes lose their power, leaving nothing but the naked strategies of shaping reality that only decades, years, or even weeks earlier still held the power to suspend disbelief. By pulling at the stitching that usually binds representation and reality, trash cinephiles live the famous credo of radical documentarians that every film, even the glossiest MGM musical, is ultimately a documentary. They embrace an ethos in stark contrast to the recently publicized efforts of George Lucas and Steven Spielberg to update their back catalogue with new more "convincing" digital effects, as if any amount of digital tweaking could prevent *Star Wars* or *E.T.* (1982) from further deteriorating into archival windows on the late 1970s.[37] By trading in obsolescent trash, exploitation fans stage a continual return of the repressed in film culture generally, lurking at the margins of the art's greatest achievements with a reaper-like reminder of the entire form's inevitable collapse. Consider, for example, the uncontested classics of the cinema, titles regularly vying for the top ten in the esteemed *Sight and Sound* critic's poll: *Sunrise* (1927), *Citizen Kane* (1941), *Vertigo* (1958), *Tokyo Story* (1953). The editors of the magazine say the poll was devised "to show which films stand the test of time in the face of shifting critical opinion." And yet, in its panic to arrest the cinema's decay, the poll just as persuasively demonstrates how no film can stand the test of time. Movies move us, thrill us, scare us, arouse us, scandalize us—but eventually there is only the photographic record of obsolete strategies for moving, thrilling, scaring, arousing, or scandalizing.[38] As they and we get older, it becomes increasingly difficult to sort out artistic power from personal memories of their former power.

As the films of Castle, Wood, Corman, and other B-film luminaries illustrate so vividly, what we typically designate as exploitation—cheap horror, lowly sci-fi, sleazy skin-flicks and other disreputable fare—only compresses this unsatisfactory exchange, accelerating a bait and switch that tricks audiences with promises of exhilarating content but gives them, in the end, only badly rendered spectacle, low-budget genre clichés, or even an asinine plastic skeleton on a wire. While some films require time to dull their affective power, exploitation by its very name implies a gap between promise and practice, ambition, and execution. Titles like *Night of the Bloody Apes* (1969), *The Amazing Transplant* (1970), and *Nude for Satan* (1974) seem to promise so much, and yet can never live up to the images they suggest to the imagination. What film, after all, could possibly live up to the mental theater evoked by the words *Nude for Satan*? Similarly, the poster art for exploitation titles promise a vision that the films themselves can never hope to match. Photographic monsters can never match the ink-and-paint creature on the poster.[39] Hints of sexual abandon lasciviously rendered in advertising translate in the theater into brief and badly exposed moments of nudity. Promises of furiously paced nonstop action that defies time and space are dashed by a few crudely executed and unconvincing fight or chase sequences. No doubt this is why sensationalistic "body genres"—horror and sexploitation especially—remain so central to trash film culture.[40] Nowhere is the gap dividing internal fantasy from public representation more profound. By plumbing the most explosive and taboo recesses of the imagination armed only with impoverished budgets and minimal talent, exploitation trades on that razor's edge dividing desire from disgust and temptation from trash. In the end, the only lasting pleasure is reveling in the chasm dividing expectation and

FIGURE 5 *Satan's Cheerleaders* (1977) promises so much, yet delivers something less.

execution, as well as pondering our own embarrassingly consistent gullibility. Of course *Dr. Butcher, M.D.* (1980) will live up to its title. *Satan's Cheerleaders* (1977) is bound to satisfy even my most appalling fantasies about the intersection of Satanism and cheerleading. Jason or the Leprechaun in outer space— how could that not be unbelievably great?

The New Leavisites

One might argue that today's cinema of "negative guarantees" simply continues this impulse, expanding this sensibility beyond the traditional hunting grounds of trash, sleaze, and exploitation to encompass almost the entirety of the cinema. When the cinema gives you unending lemons, make even more lemonade. And yet today's snarkish cine-cynics—those who would stand in line opening night to witness Alien fight Predator or who are genuinely excited at the prospects of *The Island* (2005) arriving on DVD—present an important shift in the tone and object of such perverse cinephilia. While the "badfilm" and trashophilia cults of previous decades maintained at least one foot in the affectionate tradition of "camp," the new quest for the "bad" replaces camp's tender empathy with a more adversarial engagement of film failure. Ever more sophisticated in the aesthetic and economic foundations of the cinema, today's vanguard cinephile—like Sternberg thirty-five years earlier—adopts an increasingly hostile and confrontational approach to moviegoing. Confronted with increasingly diminished expectations for the cinema, this current film culture mirrors Hollywood's own lack of respect for the movies, attempting to outflank the cynicism of the industry's product with an even more caustically cynical sarcasm and irony. One of the most interesting and influential sites in this regard is the *Onion*, America's premiere repository of collegiate irony and a prime venue in the culture of cine-cynicism. The *Onion* engages movies and pop culture on two fronts, a "fake news" section of satirical comedy and semistraight entertainment section called the A/V Club. A similar sensibility animates both sections, however, especially in relation to mainstream film and television. For example, a front-page story greeted the release of *Catwoman* with a mock headline reading, "Movie Praised for Not Being as Bad as It Could Have Been." The opening copy continues:

> Moviegoers coast to coast hailed *Catwoman*, the new action film starring Halle Barry, as not as much of an unforgivably awful piece of formulaic commercial pabulum as it could have been. "You know, I have to hand it to Warner Brothers," Miami resident Tom Peebles said Monday. "*Catwoman* was terrible, but it actually had one or two decent parts. I really have to say, it could have been a lot worse!" . . . *Catwoman*, loosely based on the DC comics character, has similarly shattered other viewers' bottom-of-the-barrel expectations, offering a small number of redeeming features instead of the expected none.[41]

The article follows the usual comic formula of the *Onion*—translate the minutiae of everyday life into the stilted conventions of journalistic discourse, thus producing an observational humor based on an ironic disjunction between the mundane and the officious. The kernel of truth to be observed here, of course, is the defensive posture so many of us now carry into the multiplex. What had been an esoteric pleasure of slumming for Sternberg in his imaginary screening of *The Rape of Frankenstein* is now increasingly the default sensibility for a much larger audience greeting all cinema. Moreover, the article also captures that momentous shift in adult audiences over the past few decades from more or less neutral spectators in search of entertainment to self-aware targets of marketing hype, an audience that—also like Sternberg—comes to the theater, not so much to "lose themselves" in a thrilling motion picture, but instead to witness the escalating loudness and stupidity of Hollywood's intertwined strategies for marketing and spectacle.

As an instant "bad movie," one requiring absolutely no historical distance to betray the clumsy calculations of its makers, *Catwoman* is a perfect target for such satiric abuse. Nominally related to the hit-and-miss history of the *Batman* franchise, *Catwoman* epitomizes a genre that didn't exist twenty-five years ago, one that at last embraces the cinema's true foundations in an aesthetic *and* economic order. Not so much a science-fiction, fantasy, or crime film, *Catwoman* instead follows the semantic and syntactic protocols of the "summer action blockbuster." Generic markers, in this case, have as much to do with extratextual hype, cross-marketing opportunities, and strategic release schedules—elements that are no longer simply the concern of industry accountants, but are in and of themselves in the foreground of popular cine-culture. Kael observed in 1968 that "we often know much more about both the actors and the characters they're impersonating and about how and why the movie has been made than is consistent with theatrical illusion."[42] If anything, this battle between insider knowledge and theatrical illusion has become even more lopsided, especially as this background knowledge goes beyond long-familiar celebrity gossip to indulge a larger fascination with the production protocols and political economy of the cultural industries in general. Why, for example, are audiences now interested in the weekly horse race of box-office receipts, so much so that these updates have become a staple everywhere in the *Extra–Total Access–Inside Hollywood* culture? How many more thousands of civilians now know such previously "insider" terms as *saturation release, points, word-of-mouth campaign,* and *final cut*? Why is there such an inchoate sense of populist glee when marketing monsters like *Godzilla*, Mariah Carey's *Glitter* (2001), and the infamous *Gigli* (2003) implode into abject failure? Finally, has there ever been a time in film history when more people have more opinions about movies they haven't

FIGURE 6 Ben Affleck and Jennifer Lopez in the infamous *Gigli* (2003), its failure a rich source of populist glee.

actually even seen, evaluating them less on their actual content than on their public profile within a larger cultural field of demographic address and promo-puffery? Indeed, the cinema of "negative guarantees" might more accurately be termed a culture of negative guarantees—a synergistic sarcasm standing in opposition to the synergistic opportunities increasingly exploited by the ever-growing media conglomerates. When yet another Madonna film tanks, it is a cause for celebration on a number of fronts, a small victory in the war against a newly Kabbalahed and Kundalinified persona that will not die, as well as the evil necromancers at Time-Warner who continue to allow Esther-Madonna to sing, act, design, and write children's books.

These tensions between film as art and film as commerce also inform the *Onion*'s entertainment section. In its "straight" interview features, for example, the A/V Club consistently features artists most at odds with the mainstream Hollywood ethos: independent filmmakers, "cult" actors, respected (but little-known) screenwriters. Interspersed with this valorization of marginalized cinematic possibilities are weekly columns that continue an assault of high sarcasm on low objects from a position of cinematic exile. "Movies That Time Forgot," for example, continues the previous decades' interest in trashophilia,

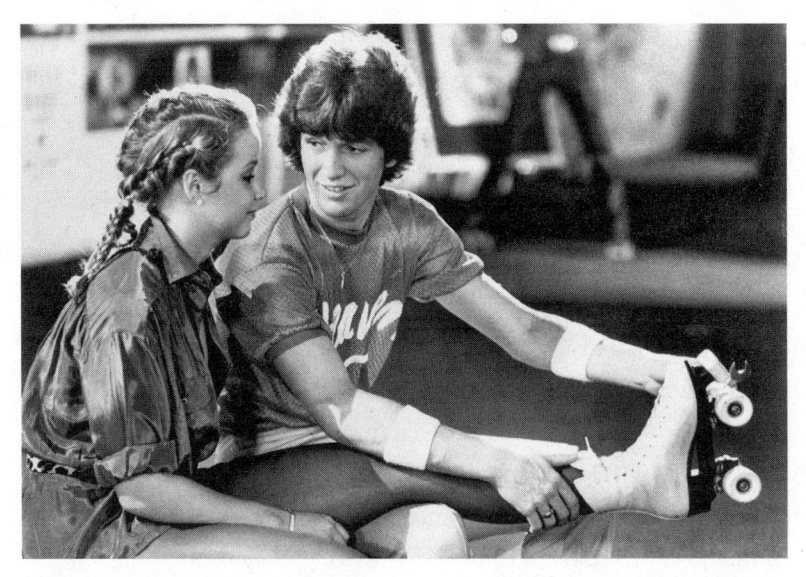

FIGURE 7 Featuring the former star of *The Exorcist*, Linda Blair, and centering on the short-lived late-1970s fad of roller disco, *Roller Boogie* (1979) awaited the bemused derision of future generations.

allowing various staff writers to opine about the detritus of 1970s and 1980s cinema titles like *Roller Boogie* (1979) or *Maniac Cop* (1988).[43] Like most current popular writing on trash and sleaze, the articles are more anthropological than aesthetic—typically engaging the films as strange creatures from a lost and incomprehensible era. Instead of searching for a Farberesque moment of termite activity in these lowly genre titles, the tone is more bemused bewilderment at the social, industrial, and historical confluence that could give rise to a mutant elephant like *Roller Boogie*.

More recently, the *Onion* has responded to the impact of emerging cinematic technologies with a new weekly feature, "DVD Commentaries of the Damned." Here a columnist reviews the commentary track for a recently released and embarrassingly horrible Hollywood feature, standing as mock judge, jury, and executioner for the film's purported crimes against the cinema. The review of the David Spade childhood regression vehicle, *Dickie Roberts: Former Child Star* (2003), lists its crimes:

—Assuming, even after *Lost and Found* and *Joe Dirt*, that inveterate supporting player David Spade somehow qualifies as leading-man material.

—Cannibalizing the premise of *Billy Madison*.
—Creepily giving Spade a love interest . . . who doubles as his mother surrogate.
—Following in the footsteps of *Joe Dirt* by taking cheap shots at a pathetic lead character who embodies a much-abused cultural stereotype, then trying to elicit sympathy for that character's plight.[44]

Importantly, the crimes here almost always involve aesthetic, economic, and ethical misjudgments, illustrating the impulse in this strain of cine-culture to see a motion picture not so much as a rarefied piece of art, but as an overdetermined symptom of a more diffuse cultural logic. In the docket as "The Defendants" for *Dickie Roberts* are David Spade himself and cowriter Fred Wolf, who out of either vanity or masochism have actually agreed to provide an audio commentary on the DVD. Under the recurring categories "Tone of Commentary," "What Went Wrong," "Comments on the Cast," "Inevitable Dash of Pretension," and "Commentary in a Nutshell," the *Onion* skewers that weird yet seemingly ubiquitous mixture of mediocrity and narcissism attending the public profile of so much Hollywood product. As the column mocks Spade and Wolf's attempts to defend the artistic miscalculations of the film, it also implicitly raises a series of potentially disturbing questions about the current state of cultural production. As *Dickie Roberts* was hardly a box-office smash or a critical landmark, why does it merit the "bonus feature" of audio commentary (as if we were listening to Bergman discuss the set-ups in *Persona*)? Beyond writers on deadline in the *Onion*'s staff room, who would sit through a two-hour audio commentary about *Dickie Roberts: Childhood Star*? For that matter, who would want to own (or even rent) *Dickie Roberts* on DVD? Back at the studio, whose taste and sense of the marketplace could be so misinformed as to have allowed this film to be made in the first place? Is every *Saturday Night Live* alumnus, no matter how marginal, uninspired, or unbankable, entitled to a lifetime in feature film production? Is anyone really a David Spade fan? For those who do rent a David Spade film, do they do so to enjoy Spade as a comic performer or to sample the cultural symptom of a David Spade film?[45]

No doubt at the expense of their own comfort and sanity, *Onion* columnists actually rewatch these terrible movies (in the commentary mode, no less!) to harvest little gems of delusion, narcissism, and insincerity for the pleasure of the snarkish audience fascinated by such questions. Obviously, this is a much different approach to close textual analysis than that practiced in the cine-culture of previous decades. It speaks to an interest in the cinema less as a closed textual system than as an open battlefield in an endless struggle between "smart" and "stupid" culture. In opposition to previous forms of mass-elite criticism, however, most of the ire here is directed not at the poor bedraggled audience that must endure such crap, but at the cultural producers complicit in allowing such crap to thrive. Beyond the fatuous artistic self-importance of the creators, other favorite targets of the column include the obligatory and inevitably condescending praise heaped on the crew for its "outstanding commitment to the project," and the endless fawning appreciations of every performance, no matter how inept, horrifying, or downright embarrassing. "DVD Commentaries of the Damned" taps into that strange (and perhaps necessary) sense of denial that permeates the industry, a delusion that once again springs from the cinema's fundamental "trauma of dissociation" between art and capital. When, as in another installment of the column, the director of the *American Idol* quickie knock-off *From Justin to Kelly* (2003), actually claims in all seriousness that his film, while no *Citizen Kane*, is the best summer beach movie since *Where the Boys Are*, he captures tragically and farcically a world where the ego tries desperately to maintain a *Cahiers*-era self-image of a cine-artist, even as one's real existence as a wholly replaceable cog in the Fox empire lurks behind every corner and paycheck.

Humorist Joe Queenan explored similar territory in his columns for *Movieline*, GQ, and *Esquire* in the early 1990s, much of which appears in the collection *Confessions of a Cineplex Heckler*. Like the *Onion*'s, Queenan's approach to film and other arms of the culture industry combines cynical exasperation with a faux-populist call to liberate humanity from the tyranny of studio stupidity. More specifically, Queenan's critical voice combines Kael's urbane resignation as to the state of cinema with the confrontational pranksterism of the legendarily snide *Spy* magazine.[46] In "Matinee Idle," for example, Queenan investigates what lost souls would actually be attending an 11:30 a.m. screening of the Joe Pesci/Danny Glover bomb *Gone Fishin'* (1997). He begins the piece with a classic summation of the "negative guarantee" aesthetic—"Let me confess that I am one of those people who has never lost his childlike belief that the next motion picture he sees could be the worst film ever made. That's why I go to all of them."[47] After he makes a senior citizen's day by refunding his $9 ticket, Queenan anoints himself the "bad movie angel" and begins handing out refunds at theaters across Manhattan. "Wherever there's a movie starring Dan Ackroyd, look around and I'll be there. Wherever there's a movie starring Adam Sandler, Chris Farley, David Spade or Pauly Shore, look around and I'll be there."[48] In "Remains of the Dazed," meanwhile, Queenan returns to the familiar whipping boy of midcult pretension, accepting an editor's challenge to view every single film made by Merchant-Ivory. What does he learn from his experience? "Basically to go a whole lot easier on people like Sylvester Stallone. Movies like *Judge Dredd* may be fascistic and sadistic and evil and stupid, but at least nobody ever says, 'You have your vicar's benediction?' or 'You're a ripping girl' in them."[49] Finally, in "A Complete Lack of Direction," Queenan satirizes the self-importance of B- and C-level directors who insist their names appear as part of the title and marketing of their films, as in "*Dave:* An Ivan Reitman Film" (1993). For this piece, Queenan appeals to old-fashioned American horse sense. "Americans are intelligent, sophisticated people," he writes, "who intuitively understand that the motion picture industry is a glorified form of manufacturing, not unlike the canning industry, where a bunch of interchangeable packagers with interchangeable skills compete to see who can produce the most serviceable, durable merchandise, and who can do it in the most timely and cost-effective fashion. The American people do not know or care who Ridley Scott or Adrian Lyne are, and they haven't the faintest idea which one of them directed *Indecent Proposal*."[50] Queenan might be thought of as a liberal version of Michael Medved or Ben Stein, equally convinced that the cinema is "out of touch" with any reality beyond Sunset Boulevard, and yet attacking the culture industries for their uninspired artistic ambitions rather than any perceived moral irresponsibility.

Bringing the snarkish sensibility of the negative guarantee to the blogosphere (where it thrives in its most unadulterated forms), Defamer.com announces in its masthead, "L.A. is the world's cultural capital. This is the gossip rag it deserves." A twenty-first-century version of the old tabloid rags of classic Hollywood, *Defamer* balances embarrassing tidbits about celebrities and industry executives, most often gathered by a string of disaffected gophers, PAs, interns, and hangers-on, with more sweeping condemnations as to the state of the motion picture business. Reporting on the Labor Day box office for 2004, for example, the editors note, "Unlikely second place finisher *Without A Paddle* is redefining the term 'late summer blockbuster.' This new definition includes 'screaming thirteen year olds needing something to do,' 'not actually making much money,' and 'Matthew Lillard hilariously playing off a strong homoerotic subtext.' Watch for the lessons learned from WAP in next year's crop of late August releases."[51] As with Queenan and the *Onion*, the critique is of art and industry interpenetrated, approaching *Without a Paddle* not as a good or bad comedy, but as strategically dumped bomb strategically spun by studio flacks into the illusion of a moderate success. As is befitting a blog manned by aspiring above and below the line talent living in Hollywood, Defamer is particularly insider in its approach, its collective voice capturing the alienated self-loathing of writers, directors, and actors who aspire to make it in the industry and yet recognize that making it will require the complete and utter surrender of their artistic integrity: *Without a Paddle* sucks. But I would kill for the opportunity to be involved in its sequel.

The caustic irony and derision of the *Onion*, Queenan, Defamer, and many other burgeoning voices in contemporary cine-cynicism continue an ongoing fascination with the contradictions and failures attending the cinema's schizoid identity as art and commodity, even as they offer significantly new iterations of this theme. Moving beyond the often narrow concerns of formal analysis and aesthetic value, they instead present a more politicized engagement of the cinema as a cultural institution. Film criticism, of course, has always been political in some sense, be it implicitly or explicitly. As veterans of the Seventh Art debates, for example, the earliest film critics sought to encourage the cinema to realize its potential, to eschew the theatrical and novelistic and exploit the promise of its own media specificity. Later critics sought to define and defend the battle lines between art and capital, reveling in the autobiographies of those intrepid artists laboring within or against the hegemony of the Hollywood studios. Camp and cultism, as we see in Taylor's work, empowered the critic to sift through film history and create his or her own idiosyncratic standards for "true" or great cinema, criteria that rarely had anything to do with artistic intention or even audience enjoyment. Today's increasingly prominent strand of caustic, cynical, and otherwise "negative" film culture, however, like so much other contemporary pop cult criticism, revels in both high irony and a ludic nihilism—seeing the cinema not so much as an art form that one might valiantly defend from clueless moneymen or that might be mined creatively for individual epiphanies, but rather, as an occupied cultural field that must be continually attacked, resisted, and mocked in guerrilla skirmishes of wit, snark, and sarcasm.

Many have observed that irony, sarcasm, and satire are often employed as tools of the dispossessed, providing a strategy for confronting power indirectly. In this respect, the insider cynicism of so much contemporary writing on film and popular culture might best be approached as a form of elitist populism—elitist in that it speaks from a position of privilege on the terrain of cultural capital, inheriting the vanguard critic's aesthetic pedigree and an accompanying reflexive disdain for middlebrow pap,[52] populist in that it attempts (or feigns) to speak for a vast audience that might be liberated from the venal stupidity of those who hold the culture industries hostage. One might describe this mode of ironic derision as a new form of Leavisism, a term that critics, fairly or unfairly, have come to attach to any mass elite agenda of cultural custodianship. Unlike the criticism practiced by the *Scrutiny* group at the beginning of last century, however, cine-cynics do not seek to snuff out an emerging popular art so as to defend the standards of an existing elite; rather, they write from within a position of popular discrimination as cinephiles who feel dispossessed of their own beloved popular medium.[53] It is a Leavisism, in other words, born of a century's worth of experience, both good and bad, with the possibilities and limitations of the culture industries. Moreover, it is a Leavisism that incorporates both popular experience with mass art and an acceleration of information about the practices of the culture industries. As the *Onion*, Queenan, and Defamer make clear, when the cinema is increasingly less about the possibilities of art and affect and becomes more the decipherment of predictable architectures, witless formulas, and achingly obvious attempts at "exploitation" in all of its guises, the actual viewing of films is no longer all that important or even necessary. These writers epitomize an ironic cine-subculture that now thrives in the absence of any actual cinema. To the delight of Oscar Wilde, Roland Barthes, and an entire intellectual tradition devoted to creating criticism that is more interesting, lively, and engaging than its nominal object, this latest strand of cine-culture demonstrates that having a position *on* the cinema is often more rewarding than actually viewing cinema.

Our Dismal Yet Delirious Future

Writing on the threshold of Hollywood's attempt to exploit the camp/trash aesthetic in titles like *Barbarella* (1968), *Modesty Blaise* (1966), *In Like Flint* (1967), *Myra Breckenridge* (1970), *Rocky Horror* (1975), *The Valley of the Dolls* (1967), and *Beyond* (1970), Sternberg, Kael, and other cinematic misanthropes of the late 1960s anticipated a moment when film's formal limitations, cultural fissures, and accidental absurdities would become more interesting than its consistently unimaginative artistic ambitions. Assessing Kael's broadside on the possibilities of "film art," Taylor observes skeptically, "Now the crazy vitality of one small scene could make even the most terrible picture worthwhile, reminding us that Art is first and foremost about enjoyment, not boredom or pedagogy."[54] After meticulously detailing the history and legacy of the "vanguard criticism" practiced by Farber, Tyler, and Kael, Taylor ends *Artists in the Audience* with a somewhat unexpected plea for restoring more objective criteria of "value" as a legitimate pursuit in film criticism. For Taylor, it would seem, the cinema is once again in danger of perishing, and the vanguard critics' legacy of elitist repurposing devolved into smirking irony is a chief culprit. As Taylor argues, vanguard camp and cultism "has always pitched itself against the very possibility of popular movie art, assuming that Hollywood's 'centrifugal collective' militates against formal unity and integrity, and that business interests, marketing campaigns, and popular fashion foreclose any real possibility of judicious gatekeeping within the commercial realm."[55] Taylor ends his book by calling for a retreat from the vanguard beachhead, hoping to restore a certain equilibrium between artist, critic, and audience.

> In warping key conceptions of aesthetic value and critic-artist relations, cultism and camp have risked consigning an entire medium to the scrap heap of cultural detritus. In privileging the marginal or derided, in claiming formal or symbolic intricacy where none exists, we prove again and again that *we* are more inventive and more profound than the guardians of the culture industry, that we ultimately exercise (aesthetic) control over the consumption

of their trash. But we do so at the expense of engaging the larger possibilities of movie art and the larger obligations of criticism.[56]

No doubt the positions taken by Farber, Kael, and Tyler were extraordinarily elitist at times, and faced with the prospect of vanguard criticism's dumbing down in the endless mockery of a post–*Mystery Science Theater 3000* universe, Taylor's turn to a quasi-Arnoldian, semi-Kierkegaardian stance on film aesthetics certainly has some appeal. Rather than bring sweetness and light to the cinema and its audience, Taylor implies, camp and cultism can only approach issues of artistic merit with discomfort, confusion, and denial. Having retreated into wholly idiosyncratic criteria of excellence, the pop cult connoisseur (of any and all media) finds it difficult to engage in any meaningful debate over aesthetic power and worth, instead playing the endless one-upsmanship of his or her superior sensitivity to embodiments of "true" cinema, rock 'n' roll, *manga*, *roman noir*, and so on.

And yet as critics, fans, and general audiences become increasingly self-aware, fragmented, and cynical as consumers of cultural product, one might ask if it is possible (much less desirable) to return to an era where "aesthetic values," "critic-artist relations," "movie art," and "the obligations of criticism" could be seen as stable categories. Taylor calls for nurturing the fragile art of cinema, sheltering it from a culture of corrosive irony and competitive connoisseurship. But what if the "mass audience" for cinema has now come to realize what so many writers of film history and criticism have either known or suspected for many years now: the cinema is not really an art at all, but an industrial and cultural circus masquerading behind obsolescent discourses and impossible expectations about art. At best, the cinema is, as Kael describes it, a "tawdry corrupt art for a tawdry corrupt world."[57] Perhaps our current moment of snarkish cine-cynicism, in turn, is exactly the tawdry, corrupt critical voice the movies deserve. As the culture of film production becomes increasingly about fame rather than art, as corporate interests continue to solidify in shaping the possibilities of movies big and small, as the avant-garde remains stranded in the solipsistic hinterland of gallery and museum distribution—perhaps the movies should be resisted, mocked, and discouraged on all fronts.

A half-century ago Theodor Adorno lamented, "every trip to the cinema leaves me, against all my vigilance, stupider and worse."[58] Thirty years ago Kael observed "cinephiles have always recognized each other at once because they talk less about good movies than what they love in bad movies."[59] Our current climate of cine-cynicism might be thought of as an attempt to merge these two seemingly immutable truths, an attempt to synthesize camp and critical theory in a new sociological poetics that views the supreme "obligation of criticism" to be the *continued* cultivation of an audience more "inventive and profound than the guardians of the culture industry." Even today, many still enjoy discussing what they love in bad movies more than debating if there really is a new way, after all of these years, to position a camera, edit a scene, light a set, or unfurl a narrative. Increasingly, what we love in "bad movies" is less the isolated continuity error or over-the-top performance, but instead the richly over-determined moments of excess that invoke the vertiginous breakdown of sanity and logic across our entire culture. The slow-motion shots of children running with American flags at the end of *Armageddon* (1998). A hyperbolically homophobic ex-Marine killing a martyred Kevin Spacey at the end of *American Beauty*. A rappin' kangaroo that in fact doesn't actually rap in his own movie. Vin Diesel's mysteriously inconvenient fur action coat in *xxx* (2002). A murderous Leprechaun smokin' chronic with his army of zombie hos in *Leprechaun 5* (2000). The exceedingly obvious collection of character-defining modernist paintings on display in *Titanic* (1997). Bruce Willis and Matthew Perry mugging their way through a sequel to a film that no one saw in the first place. A sexy heroine walking through a postapocalyptic landscape armed with an Uzi and yet modestly holding a bath towel around her naked body in *Resident Evil 2* (2004). Jar Jar. *Gigli*. *Josie and the Pussycats* (2001). These are the great moments in our current cinema—symptoms of a cultural imagination unfettered in exploring the depths of its own confusion and bankruptcy. We need a poetics up to the task of engaging the profoundly bizarre, disturbing, inane, and epiphinal moments that characterize our current cinematic plight, a poetics that no longer brackets off the cinema from the entire field of cultural production but instead integrates the incomplete (and often arbitrary) object on the screen with the strategic beauty of a well-executed billboard campaign, the demographic chicanery of a misleading trailer, the reinscription and retextualization of the DVD release, the ineffable mechanisms of "buzz" that situate films, performers, and audiences in seemingly random empathetic and adversarial relationships. We need a poetics that follows every moment of every film back through its fleeting diegetic illusions to the profilmic nexus of strategies that give shape to every frame. Cultism we can probably do without. But camp in all its various incarnations, including today's snarkish cine-cynics, has always been its own form of deconstructive critical theory and thus remains a crucial tool to help us redouble our Adornoesque vigilance against our own impending mass stupidity and worseness. If the cinema is to be "saved," it will be by finally and forever reframing it as *practice*. At this point in its frustrating history of perpetual failure, the cinema is far too important to still be hamstrung by accusations of being simply an "art."

Notes

1. Jacques Sternberg, *Sexualis '95*. (New York: Berkley, 1967), 17. Originally published in France as *Toi, Ma Nuit*.
2. Ibid., 17.
3. Ibid., 19.
4. Ibid., 16.
5. Pauline Kael, "Trash, Art, and the Movies," in *Going Steady: Film Writings, 1968–1969*. New York: Marion Boyars, 1994.
6. See www.mrcranky.com.
7. Harry Knowles (with Paul Cullum and Mark Ebner), *Ain't It Cool? Hollywood's Redheaded Stepchild Speaks Out* (New York: Warner Books, 2002), 13.
8. Rudolph Arnheim, *Film as Art*. (Berkeley: University of California Press, 1967), 213.
9. Pauline Kael, "Zeitgeist and Poltergeist," in *I Lost It at the Movies* (New York: Marion Boyars, 1994).
10. Greg Taylor, *Artists in the Audience: Cults, Camp, and American Film Criticism* (Princeton, N.J.: Princeton University Press, 1999), 19.
11. Ibid., 20.
12. Ibid.
13. Pauline Kael, "Trash, Art, and the Movies," in *Going Steady: Film Writings, 1968–1969* (New York: Marion Boyars, 1994), 102.
14. Ibid., 93.
15. Ibid., 93.
16. Ibid., 128–29. In his most recent films, Werner Herzog seems to have taken up this aesthetic as well, increasingly turning his back on the "fiction" film for a series of essayistic and idiosyncratic documentaries.
17. Christian Metz, *The Imaginary Signifier: Psychoanalysis and the Cinema* (Bloomington: Indiana University Press, 1982), 15.

18. This comment, in particular, is worth relishing for its logical circularity and dissociative conflict.
19. See Jon Lewis, ed., *The End of the Cinema as We Know It* (New York: New York University Press, 2002).
20. Wheeler Winston Dixon, "Twenty-five Reasons Why It's All Over," in *The End of Cinema as We Know It*, ed. Jon Lewis (New York: New York University Press, 2002), 356.
21. Ibid., 365.
22. Ibid., 366.
23. As a product of the tail end of hard-core 1970s-era avant-populist cinephilia, I only have the most vague and repressed memories now of the cruel moment when I finally realized and accepted that Jerry Lewis would never direct another film.
24. Annette Michelson, "Film and the Radical Aspiration," in *Film Theory and Criticism*, 2nd ed., ed. Gerald Mast and Marshall Cohen (New York: Oxford University Press, 1979), 618.
25. Ironically, an always resourceful Hollywood has become very savvy at turning even this artistic "outrage" into a marketing strategy by releasing the director's cut version for video and DVD consumption by "in-the-know" cinephiles.
26. A classic example is Renee Daalder's *Massacre at Central High* (1976)—a Holocaust allegory expressed in the conventions of the teensploitation revenge flick.
27. Before turning to hobbits and Kong, Peter Jackson parodied this particular type of film history in his mockumentary for New Zealand television, *Forgotten Silver* (1995).
28. The "troubled production" also contains the occult subgenre of the "cursed production." *The Exorcist* and *Poltergeist* have been accompanied by stories of cursed cast members and unexplainable accidents on the set. More recently, advance press for Mel Gibson's *The Passion of the Christ* claimed James Caviezel, the actor portraying Jesus, was hit by lightning during the filming!
29. And where heir apparent Sofia does not become romantically involved with every film-geek's ego un-ideal, Quentin Tarantino.
30. Jeffrey Sconce, "'Trashing' the Academy: Taste, Excess, and an Emerging Politics of Cinematic Style," *Screen* 36 (1995): 371–93.
31. Frank Zappa, of all people, extols the virtues of this film and its "cheesy" monster in the song "Cheepnis" on *Roxy and Elswhere* (1974).
32. Tim Burton captures this attitude perfectly in the sequence of *Ed Wood* where the director, previously depressed at not finishing *Plan 9*, pulls it together in a whirlwind of "can-do" creativity to finish the film.
33. Eric Schaefer's *"Bold! Daring! Shocking! True!": A History of the Exploitation Film, 1919–1959* (Durham, N.C.: Duke University Press, 1999) documents the use of many of these practices well before Castle adopted them in the 1950s.

34. This nostalgic approach prevails in *Matinee* (1993), Joe Dante's valentine to B-cinema loosely based on Castle's career.
35. In "Trash, Art, and the Movies," Kael writes, "When you're young the odds are very good that you'll find something to enjoy in almost any movie. But as you grow more experienced, the odds change" (127).
36. This might explain why there is no "camp" animation.
37. Such desperation is the celluloid equivalent to the larger Hollywood ethos that believes immortality lies in the right combination of yoga, publicity, and plastic surgery.
38. This anxiety over film's ties to indexical reality has been a recurring theme of classical film theory. As early as 1938, Rudolph Arnheim wrote, "I would venture to predict that film will be able to reach the heights of the other arts only when it frees itself from the bonds of photographic reproduction and becomes a pure work of man, namely, as animated cartoon or painting" ("A New Lacoon: Artistic Composites and the Talking Film," in *Film as Art* [Berkeley: University of California Press, 1967], 213).
39. No doubt this truism is at the heart of that philosophy of horror that maintains it is best to suggest the monster, as in *Cat People* or *The Blair Witch Project*, rather than show it directly.
40. Linda Williams, "Film Bodies: Gender, Genre, and Excess," *Film Quarterly* 44, no. 4 (1991): 2–13.
41. *The Onion* 40, no. 31 (August 4, 2004).
42. Kael, "Trash, Art, and the Movies," 88.
43. In an interesting generational shift, writers for the *Onion* seem much more fascinated with schlock from the 1970s and 1980s, as opposed to the previous generation of trashophiles interest in cinematic detritus of the 1950s and 1960s.
44. *Onion*, August 5–11, 2004.
45. Spade's career, it should be noted, began as one of the vanguard practitioners of snark. His "Hollywood Report" segments on *Saturday Night Live* (1990–1995) are emblematic of the snark sensibility in its formative moments. Somewhat ironically, in the time since I wrote this paragraph, Spade's less-than-stellar film career has brought him back to television, where he has translated his *SNL* snarkdom into a half-hour entertainment show for Comedy Central titled *The Showbiz Show*.
46. In many respects, *Spy* was truly a magazine ahead of its time. Snarkish in the extreme, its inability to translate beyond its NYC-centric Gen-X audience prevented the magazine from surviving into the golden age of snark it helped create.
47. Joe Queenan, "Matinee Idle," *Confessions of a Cineplex Heckler* (New York: Hyperion, 2000), 101.
48. Ibid., 105.
49. Queenan, "Remains of the Dazed," in *Confessions of a Cineplex Heckler*, 92. Updating the piece for his book, Queenan adds as an epilogue, "Since this piece appeared in 1995,

Ismail Merchant and James Ivory have continued to make Merchant-Ivory movies, as there is no law against it" (93).

50. Queenan, "A Complete Lack of Direction," in *Confessions of a Cineplex Heckler*, 58.
51. Defamer.com, September 4, 2004.
52. The foundational work in this area remains Pierre Bourdieu's *Distinction: A Social Critique of the Judgement of Taste* (Cambridge, Mass.: Harvard University Press, 1987).
53. Stuart Hall and Paddy Whannel employed the concept of "popular discrimination" in *The Popular Arts* (New York: Pantheon, 1965) to complicate the era's typically binary divide between mass and elite culture, arguing that audiences of popular culture always make discriminating choices of value within "mass cultural" offerings.
54. Taylor, *Artists in the Audience*, 123.
55. Ibid., 151.
56. Ibid., 157.
57. Kael, "Trash, Art, and the Movies," 87.
58. Theodor Adorno, *Minima Moralia* (London: Verso, 1974), 25.
59. Kael, "Trash, Art, and the Movies," 89.

Selected Bibliography

Adams, Henry E., Lester W. Wright Jr., and Bethany A. Lohr. "Is Homophobia Associated with Homosexual Arousal?" *Journal of Abnormal Psychology* 105 (1996): 440–45.

Adorno, Theodor. *Minima Moralia*. London: Verso, 1974.

———, and Max Horkheimer. *The Dialectic of Enlightenment*. London: Verso, 1979.

Allen, Richard. *Projecting Illusion: Film Spectatorship and the Impression of Reality*. Cambridge: Cambridge University Press, 1995.

"An Advertising Code for Motion Pictures." In *The 1961 Film Daily Yearbook for Motion Pictures*. New York: Film Daily, 1961.

Arnheim, Rudolph. *Film as Art*. Berkeley: University of California Press, 1967.

Bakhtin, Mikhail. *Rabelais and His World*. Bloomington: Indiana University Press, 1984.

Barker, Martin, ed. "Nasty Politics or Video Nasties?" *The Video Nasties: Freedom and Censorship in the Media*. London: Pluto, 1984.

Barthes, Roland. *The Pleasure of the Text*. New York: Hill and Wang, 1975.

Bauman, Zygmunt. *Modernity and Ambivalence*. Cambridge: Polity, 1991.

Bazelon, Irwin. *Knowing the Score: Notes on Film Music*. New York: Van Nostrand Reinhold, 1975.

Benshoff, Harry M. *Monsters in the Closet: Homosexuality and the Horror Film*. Manchester: Manchester University Press, 1997.

Berenstein, Rhona J. *Attack of the Leading Ladies: Gender, Sexuality, and Spectatorship in Classic Horror Cinema*. New York: Columbia University Press, 1996.

Berg, Charles Ramírez. *Cinema of Solitude: A Critical Study of Mexican Film, 1967–1983*. Austin: University of Texas Press, 1992.

———. "The Cinematic Invention of Mexico: The Poetics and Politics of the Fernández-Figueroa Style." In *The Mexican Cinema Project*, edited by Chon A. Noriega and Steven Ricci. Los Angeles: UCLA Film and Television Archive, 1994.

Berube, Allan. *Coming Out under Fire: The History of Gay Men and Women in World War II*. New York: Penguin, 1990.

Bourdieu, Pierre. *Distinction: A Social Critique of the Judgment of Taste*. Translated by Richard Nice. Cambridge, Mass.: Harvard University Press, 1984.

Bowen, Michael. "Embodiment and Realization: The Many Film-Bodies of Doris Wishman." *Wide Angle* 19, no. 3 (1997): 64–90.

Bronksi, Michael. *Pulp Friction: Uncovering the Golden Age of Gay Male Pulps*. New York: St. Martin's Griffin, 2003.

Brophy, Philip. "The Secret History of Film Music." 1997–98, media-arts.rmit.edu.ac/Phil_Brophy/soundtrackList.html.

Brown, Royal S. *Overtones and Undertones: Reading Film Music*. Berkeley: University of California Press, 1994.

Bryson, Norman. "Todd Haynes's *Poison* and Queer Cinema." *Invisible Culture: An Electronic Journal for Visual Studies*, no. 1 (winter 1998), www.rochester.edu/in_visible_culture/issue1/bryson/bryson.html.

Budra, Paul. "Recurrent Monsters: Why Freddy, Michael and Jason Keep Coming Back." In *Part Two: Reflections on the Sequel*, edited by Paul Budra and Betty A. Schellenberg. Toronto: University of Toronto Press, 1998.

Carroll, Noël. "Nightmare and the Horror Film: The Symbolic Biology of Fantastic Beings." *Film Quarterly: Forty Years—A Selection*, edited by Brian Henderson and Ann Martin with Lee Amazonas. Berkeley: University of California Press, 1999.

Castoldi, Gian Luca, Harvey Fenton, and Julian Grainger. *Cannibal Holocaust and the Savage Cinema of Ruggero Deodata*. Surrey, UK: FAB Press, 1999.

Chion, Michel. *The Voice in Cinema*. Translated by Claudia Gorbman. New York: Columbia University Press, 1999.

Cioran, E. M. *Œuvres*. Edited by Yves Peyré. Paris: Gallimard, 1995.

Clark, Graeme. "Superstar: The Karen Carpenter Story." *Spinning Image*. www.thespinningimage.co.uk/cultfilms/displaycultfilm.asp?/reviewid=164andaff=13.

Clark, James M. *The Dance of Death in the Middle Ages and Renaissance*. Glasgow: Jackson, Son, and Company, 1950.

Clover, Carol. *Men, Women, and Chainsaws: Gender in the Modern Horror Film*. Princeton, N.J.: Princeton University Press, 1993.

Collins, Jim. *Architectures of Excess: Cultural Life in the Information Age*. New York: Routledge, 1995.

Conrich, Ian. "The *Friday the 13th* Films and the Cultural Function of a Modern Grand Guignol." *Cinema Journal* (forthcoming).

Crane, Jonathan Lake. *Terror and Everyday Life: Singular Moments in the History of the Horror Film*. London: Sage, 1994.

Debord, Guy. *The Society of the Spectacle*. Translated by Donald Nicholson-Smith. New York: Zone Books, 1995.

De Grazia, Edward and Newman, Roger K., *Banned Films: Movies, Censors and the First Amendment*. New York: R. R. Bowker, 1982.

Delaney, Samuel R. *Times Square Red, Times Square Blue*. New York: New York University Press, 1999.

Dever, Susan. *Celluloid Nationalism and Other Melodramas: From Post-Revolutionary Mexico to* fin de siglo *Mexamérica*. Albany: State University of New York Press, 2003.

Dika, Vera. *Games of Terror: Halloween, Friday the 13th and the Films of the Stalker Cycle*. London: Associated University Presses, 1990.

Dixon, Wheeler Winston. "Twenty-five Reasons Why It's All Over." In *The End of Cinema as We Know It: American Film in the Nineties*, edited by Jon Lewis. New York: New York University Press, 2002.

Druss, Richard G. "Cases of Suspected Homosexuality Seen at an Army Mental Hygiene Consultation Service." *Psychiatric Quarterly* 41 (January 1967): 62–70.

Dyer, Richard. *Now You See It: Studies on Lesbian and Gay Film*. New York: Routledge, 1990.

Eisenstein, Sergei, Vsevolod Pudovkin, and Grigori Alexandrov, "Statement on Sound." In *Film Sound: Theory and Practice*, edited by E. Weis and J. Belton. New York: Columbia University Press, 1985.

Elsaesser, Thomas. "Tales of Sound and Fury: Observations on the Family Melodrama." In *Film Theory and Criticism: Introductory Readings*, 4th ed., ed. Gerald Mast, Marshall Cohen, and Leo Braudy. New York: Oxford University Press, 1992.

Evans, Mark. *Soundtrack: The Music of the Movies*. New York: Hopkinson and Blake, 1975.

Faderman, Lillian. *Odd Girls and Twilight Lovers: A History of Lesbian Life in Twentieth-Century America*. New York: Penguin, 1991.

Farber, Manny. *Negative Space: Manny Farber on the Movies (Expanded Edition)*. Cambridge, Mass.: Da Capo, 1998.

Fielding, Raymond. *The March of Time, 1935–1951*. New York: Oxford University Press, 1978.

Flinn, Caryl. *Strains of Utopia: Gender, Nostalgia and Hollywood Film Music*. Princeton, N.J.: Princeton University Press, 1992.

Fowles, Jib. *Advertising and Popular Culture*. Thousand Oaks, Calif.: Sage Publications, 1996.

———. "Advertising's Fifteen Basic Appeals." In *American Mass Media: Industries and Issues*, 3rd ed., edited by Robert Atwan, Barry Orton, and William Vesterman. New York: Random House, 1984.

Freud, Sigmund. "Mourning and Melancholia." In *General Psychology Theory*. 1917. New York: Touchstone 1991.

———. *Jokes and Their Relation to the Unconscious*. Translated by James Strachey. New York: Norton, 1960.

Friedman, David F. "Wages of Sin." Interview by David Chute. *Film Comment* 22, no. 4 (1986): 32–39; 42–48.

Frith, Simon. *Performing Rites: On the Value of Popular Music*. Cambridge, Mass.: Harvard University Press, 1996.

Gaines, Jane. "Everyday Strangeness: Robert Ripley's International Oddities as Documentary Attractions." *New Literary History* 33 (2002): 781–801.

Gans, Herbert J. "Urbanism and Suburbanism as Ways of Life: A Re-evaluation of Definitions." In *Human Behavior and Social Processes: An Interactionist Approach*, edited by Arnold M. Rose. Boston: Houghton Mifflin Company, 1962.

Gastaldi, Ernesto. *Voglio entrare nel cinema: Storia di uno che ce l'ha fatto*. Milan: A. Mondanori, 1991.

Gioscia, Nicolai. "The Gag Reflex and Fellatio." *American Journal of Psychiatry* 107 (May 1950): 380.

Goodwin, Sarah Webster. *Kitsch and Culture: The Dance of Death in Nineteenth-Century Literature and Graphic Arts*. New York: Garland and Company, 1988.

———, and Jean Wirth. *La Jeune fille et la morte: Recherches sur les thèmes macabres dans l'art germanique de la Renaissance*. Geneva: Librairie Droz, 1979.

Gordon, Margaret T., Stephanie Riger, Robert K. LeBailly, and Linda Heath, "Crime, Women, and the Quality of Urban Life." In *Women and the American City*, edited by Catherine R. Stimpson, Elsa Dixler, Martha J. Nelson, and Kathryn B. Yatrakis. Chicago: University of Chicago Press, 1981.

Hall, Stuart, and Paddy Whannel. *The Popular Arts*. New York: Pantheon, 1965.

Hardy, Phil, ed. *The Overlook Film Encyclopedia: Horror*. Woodstock, N.Y.: Overlook, 1995.

Harries, Dan. *Film Parody*. London: BFI, 2000.

Harris, Neil. *Humbug: The Art of P. T. Barnum*. Boston: Little, Brown, 1973.

Hawkins, Joan. *Cutting Edge: Art-Horror and the Horrific Avant-Garde*. Minneapolis: University of Minnesota Press, 2000.

———. "Midnight Sex-Horror Movies and the Downtown Avant-Garde." *Defining Cult Movies: The Cultural Politics of Oppositional Taste*, edited by Mark Jancovich, Antonio Lazaro Reboll, James Lyons, Julian Stringer, and Andrew Willis. Manchester: Manchester University Press, 2003.

———. *Todd Haynes*. Urbana: University of Illinois Press, forthcoming.

Haynes, Todd. *Velvet Goldmine* (screenplay). Great Britain: Faber and Faber, 1998.

———. "Homoaesthetics and *Querelle*." *Subjects/Objects* (1985): 71–99.

Heffernan, Kevin. *Ghouls, Gimmicks, and Gold: Horror Films and the American Movie Business, 1952–1968*. Durham, N.C.: Duke University Press, 2004.

Heidegger, Martin. *Poetry, Language, Thought*. Translated by Albert Hofstadter. New York: Harper and Row, 1971.

———. *The Fundamental Concepts of Metaphysics: World, Finitude, Solitude*. Translated by William McNeill and Nicholas Walker. Bloomington: Indiana University Press, 1995.

Hershfield, Joanne. "Race and Ethnicity in the Classial Cinema." In *Mexico's Cinema: A Century of Film and Filmmakers*, edited by Joanne Hershfield and David R. Maciel. Wilmington, Del.: Scholarly Resources, 1999.

———. *Mexican Cinema/Mexican Woman, 1940–1950*. Tucson: University of Arizona Press, 1996.

Hills, Matt. *Fan Cultures*. London: Routledge, 2002.

———. "Doing Things with Theory: From Freud's Worst Nightmare to (Disciplinary) Dreams of Horror's Cultural Value." In *Psychoanalysis and the Horror Film: Freud's Worst Nightmares*, edited by Steven Jay Schneider. Cambridge: Cambridge University Press, 2004.

———. "*Star Wars* in Fandom, Film Theory, and the Museum: The Cultural Status of the Cult Blockbuster." In *Movie Blockbusters*, edited by Julian Stringer. London: Routledge, 2003.

Hocquenghem, Guy. *Homosexual Desire*. Translated by Daniella Dangoor. Durham, N.C.: Duke University Press, 1993.

Howarth, Troy. *The Haunted World of Mario Bava*. London: FAB, 2001.

Humphries, Reynold. *The American Horror Film: An Introduction*. Edinburgh: Edinburgh University Press, 2002.

Hunt, Leon. "A (Sadistic) Night at the *Opera*." In *The Horror Reader*, edited by Ken Gelder. London: Routledge, 2000.

Jameson, Fredric. *Signatures of the Visible*. New York: Routledge, 1992.

Jancovich, Mark. "Cult Fictions: Cult Movies, Subcultural Capital and the Production of Cultural Distinctions." *Cultural Studies* 16, no. 2 (2002): 306–22.

———. "'A Real Shocker': Authenticity, Genre and the Struggle for Distinction." *Continuum* 14, no. 1 (2000): 23–35.

———, ed. *Horror: The Film Reader*. London: Routledge, 2002.

Jenkins, Henry. *Textual Poachers: Television Fans and Participatory Culture*. London: Routledge, 1992.

Johnston, Claire. "Women's Cinema as Counter-Cinema." In *Movies and Methods*, vol. 1, edited by Bill Nichols. Berkeley: University of California Press, 1985.

Jones, Darryl. *Horror: A Thematic History in Fiction and Film*. London: Arnold, 2002.

Kael, Pauline. "Circles and Squares." *Film Quarterly* 16, no. 3 (1963): 12–26.

———. *I Lost It at the Movies*. Boston: Little, Brown, 1965.

———. "Trash, Art, and the Movies." In *Going Steady: Film Writings, 1968–1969*. New York: Marion Boyars, 1994.

Kemp, Earl, ed. *The Illustrated Presidential Report of the Commission on Obscenity and Pornography*. San Diego: Greenleaf Classics, 1970.

Kierkegaard, Søren. *Either/Or*. Translated by David F. Swenson and Lillian Marvin Swenson. Garden City, N.Y.: Anchor Books, 1959.

Kleinhans, Chuck. "Taking Out the Trash: Camp and the Politics of Irony." In *The Politics and Poetics of Camp*, edited by Moe Meyer. New York: Routledge, 1994.

Klinger, Barbara. *Melodrama and Meaning: History, Culture and the Films of Douglas Sirk*. Bloomington: Indiana University Press, 1994.

Klosterman, Chuck. *Sex, Drugs, and Cocoa Puffs*. New York: Scribner, 2003.

Knight, Alan. "Racism, Revolution, and *Indigenismo*: Mexico, 1910–1940." In *The Idea of Race in Latin America, 1870–1940*, edited by Richard Graham. Austin: University of Texas Press, 1990.

Knowles, Harry, with Paul Cullum and Mark Ebner. *Ain't It Cool? Hollywood's Redheaded Stepchild Speaks Out*. New York: Warner Books, 2002.

Kruger, Barbara. *Remote Control: Power, Culture and the World of Appearance*. Cambridge, Mass.: MIT Press, 1993.

Lasch, Christopher. *The Culture of Narcissism: American Life in an Age of Diminishing Expectations*. New York: Norton, 1991.

Lewis, Jon, ed. *The End of the Cinema as We Know It*. New York: New York University Press, 2002.

Lucas, Tim. *Mario Bava: All the Colors of the Dark*. Cincinnati: Video Watchdog, 2005.

Maltin, Leonard, ed. *Leonard Maltin's 2003 Movie and Video Guide*. New York: Plume, 2003.

Mangravite, Andrew. "Once upon a Time in the Crypt." *Film Comment* 29, no. 1 (1993): 50–53; 59–60.

Martinet, Pascal. *Mario Bava: Filmo n. 6*. Paris: Edilig, 1984.

McDonagh, Maitland M., *Broken Mirrors/Broken Minds: The Dark Dreams of Dario Argento*. London: Sun Tavern Fields, 1991.

Melly, George. *Revolt into Style: The Pop Arts in Britain*. London: Allen Lane, 1970.

Merleau-Ponty, Maurice. *Sense and Non-Sense*. Translated by Hubert L. Dreyfus and Patricia Allen Dreyfus. Chicago: Northwestern University Press, 1964.

Metz, Christian. *Film Language: A Semiotics of the Cinema*. Translated by Michael Taylor. New York: Oxford University Press, 1974.

———. *The Imaginary Signifier: Psychoanalysis and the Cinema*. Bloomington: Indiana University Press, 1982

Metz, Walter. "John Waters Goes to Hollywood: A Poststructural Authorship Study." In *Authorship and Film*, edited by David A. Gerstner and Janet Staiger. New York: AFI/Routledge, 2003.

Michelson, Annette. "Film and the Radical Aspiration." In *Film Theory and Criticism*, 2nd ed., edited by Gerald Mast and Marshall Cohen. New York: Oxford University Press, 1979.

Mitry, Jean. *The Aesthetics and Psychology in the Cinema*. Translated by Christopher King. Bloomington: Indiana University Press, 1997.

Moller, David. "Nuderama." *Vision* 1, no. 2 (1962): 19.

Monsiváis, Carlos. "Cantinflas: That's the Point!" In *Mexican Postcards*. London: Verso, 1997.

Muir, John Kenneth. *Wes Craven: The Art of Horror*. Jefferson, N.C.: McFarland, 1998.

Nestle, Joan. *A Restricted Country*. Ann Arbor, Mich.: Firebrand Books, 1987.

Nichols, Bill. *Introduction to Documentary*. Bloomington: Indiana University Press, 2001.

———. *Representing Reality: Issues and Concepts in Documentary*. Bloomington: Indiana University Press, 1991.

———. "The Voice of Documentary." *Film Quarterly* 36, no. 3 (1983): 17–29.

Nietzsche, Friedrich. *The Gay Science: With a Prelude in German Rhymes and an Appendix of Songs*. Edited by B. Williams, translated by J. Nauckhoff and A. del Caro. Cambridge: Cambridge University Press, 2001.

Noriega, Chon. "'SOMETHING'S MISSING HERE!': Homosexuality and Film Reviews during the Production Code Era, 1934–1962." *Cinema Journal* 30, no. 1 (1990): 20–41.

Nowell-Smith, Geoffrey, with James Hay and Gianni Volpi. *The Companion to Italian Cinema*. London: Cassell and BFI, 1996.

Packard, Vance. *The Hidden Persuaders*. New York: David McKay Company, 1957.

Parish, James Robert. *Gays and Lesbians in Mainstream Cinema*. Jefferson, N.C.: McFarland, 1993.

Petro, Patrice. *Aftershocks of the New: Feminism and Film History*. New Brunswick, N.J.: Rutgers University Press, 2002.

Pilcher, Jeffrey M. "Cantinfladas of the PRI: (Mis)Representations of Mexican Society in the Films of Mario Moreno." *Film Historia* 9, no. 2 (1999): 189–206.

———. *Cantinflas and the Chaos of Mexican Modernity*. Wilmington, Del.: Scholarly Resources, 2000.

Podalsky, Laura. "Disjointed Frames: Melodrama, Nationalism, and Representation in 1940s Mexico." *Studies in Latin American Popular Culture* 3 (1984): 57–73.

Poselli, Stefano, and Riccardo Morrocchi, eds. *Horror all'italiana, 1957–1979*. Florence: Glittering Images, 1996.

Quarles, Mike. *Down and Dirty: Hollywood's Exploitation Filmmakers and their Movies*. Jefferson, N.C.: McFarland, 1993.

Queenan, Joe. *Confessions of a Cineplex Heckler*. New York: Hyperion, 2000.

Randall, Richard S. *Censorship of the Movies: The Social and Political Control of a Mass Medium*. Madison: University of Wisconsin Press, 1970.

Riera, Emilio García. *Historia documental del cine mexicano: 1983–1942*. Guadalajara: Universidad de Guadalajara, 1992.

Ross, Andrew. "Uses of Camp." *No Respect: Intellectuals and Popular Culture*. New York: Routledge, 1989.

Russo, Vito. *The Celluloid Closet*, rev. ed. New York: Harper and Row, Publishers, 1987.

Sarris, Andrew. "The American Cinema." *Film Culture* 28 (1963): 1–51.

———. "Notes on the Auteur Theory in 1962." *Film Culture* 27 (1962–63): 35–51.

Schaefer, Eric. *"Bold! Daring! Shocking! True!": A History of Classical Exploitation Films, 1919-1959*. Durham, N.C.: Duke University Press, 1999.

———. "Gauging a Revolution: 16mm Film and the Rise of the Pornographic Feature." *Cinema Journal* 41, no. 3 (2002): 3–26.

———, and Eithne Johnson. "Quarantined! A Case Study of Boston's Combat Zone." In *Hop on Pop: The Politics and Pleasure of Popular Culture*, edited by Henry Jenkins, Tara McPherson, and Jane Shattuc. Durham, N.C.: Duke University Press, 2002.

Schneider, Steven Jay. "Kevin Williamson and the Rise of the Neo-Stalker." *PostScript* 19, no. 2 (2000): 73–87.

Schusterman, Richard. *Performing Live: Aesthetic Alternatives for the Ends of Art*. Ithaca, N.Y.: Cornell University Press, 2000.

Sconce, Jeffrey. *Haunted Media: Electronic Presence from Telegraphy to Television*. Durham, N.C.: Duke University Press, 2000.

———. "Spectacles of Death: Identification, Reflexivity and Contemporary Horror." In *Film Theory Goes to the Movies*, edited by Jim Collins, Hilary Radner, and Ava Collins. London: Routledge, 1993.

———. "'Trashing' the Academy: Taste, Excess, and an Emerging Politics of Cinematic Style." *Screen* 36 (1995): 371–93.

Sedgwick, Eve Kosofsky. *Epistemology of the Closet*. Los Angeles: University of California Press, 1990.

Sitney, P. Adams. *Visionary Film: The American Avant Garde*. New York: Oxford University Press, 1974.

Smith, Jeff. *The Sounds of Commerce*. New York: Columbia University Press, 1998.

Snow, Michael. "La Region Centrale." *Film Culture* 52 (spring 1971). Quoted in Simon Field, "Michael Snow: A Filmography." *Afterimage* 11 (winter 1982–83), 15.

Sobchack, Vivian. *The Address of the Eye: A Phenomenology of Film Experience*. Princeton, N.J.: Princeton University Press, 1992.

Sontag, Susan. "Notes on Camp." *Against Interpretation*. New York: Dell Publishing, 1966.

Southern, Terry. *Blue Movie*. New York: World Publishing, 1970.

Spigel, Lynn. *Welcome to the Dreamhouse: Popular Media and Postwar Suburbs*. Durham, N.C.: Duke University Press. 2001.

Stephens, Chuck. "Gentlemen Prefer Haynes." *Film Comment* 31, no. 4 (1995): 76–81.

Sternberg, Jacques. *Sexualis '95*. New York: Berkley Publishing, 1967.

Taylor, Greg. *Artists in the Audience: Cults, Camp, and American Film Criticism*. Princeton, N.J.: Princeton University Press, 1999.

Thibaut, Frédéric. "Une affaire de femme." *Cineastes* 8 (2002): 44.

Thomas, Lyn. *Fans, Feminisms and 'Quality' Media*. London: Routledge, 2002.

Thornton, Sarah. *Club Cultures: Music, Media and Subcultural Capital*. Cambridge: Polity, 1996.

Tittle, Charles R. and Mark C. Stafford, "Urban Theory, Urbanism, and Suburban Residence." *Social Forces* 70 (1992): 725–44.

Tudor, Andrew. *Monsters and Mad Scientists: A Cultural History of the Horror Movie*. Oxford: Blackwell, 1989.

———. "Why Horror? The Peculiar Pleasures of a Popular Genre." In *Horror: The Film Reader*, edited by Mark Janovich. London: Routledge, 2002.

Turan, Kenneth, and Stephen F. Zito. *Sinema: American Pornographic Films and the People Who Make Them*. New York: Praeger, 1974.

Tyler, Parker. *Screening the Sexes: Homosexuality in the Movies*. New York: Da Capo, 1993.

Upchurch, Alan. *Barbara Steele, an Angel for Satan*. Cahors: G. Noël Fanéditions, 1991.

———. "The Dark Queen." *Film Comment* 29, no. 1 (1993): 53.

Vale, V., and Juno, Andrea. *Incredibly Strange Films*. San Francisco: V/Search, 1985.

de la Vega Alfaro, Eduardo. "The Decline of the Golden Age and the Making of the Crisis." In *Mexico's Cinema: A Century of Film and Filmmakers*, edited by Joanne Hershfield and David R. Maciel. Wilmington, Del.: Scholarly Resources, 1999.

———. "Origins, Development and Crisis of the Sound Cinema (1929–1964)." In *Mexican Cinema*, edited by Paulo Antonio Paranaguá. London: BFI, 1995.

Wallon, Henri. "L'acte perceptif et le cinéma." *Revue internationale de filmologie* 13 (1953): 97–100.

Warner, Michael. *Fear of a Queer Planet*. Minneapolis: University of Minnesota Press, 1993.

Waters, John. *Shock Value*. New York: Thunder's Mouth, 1995.

Weiss, D. B. *Lucky Wander Boy*. New York: Plume, 2003.

West, Louis Joylon, William T. Doidge, and Robert L. Williams. "An Approach to the Problem of Homosexuality in the Military Service." *American Journal of Psychiatry* 115 (1958): 392–401.

Williams, Linda. "Film Bodies: Gender, Genre, and Excess." *Film Quarterly* 44, no. 4 (1991): 2–13.

———. *Hardcore: Power, Pleasure and the "Frenzy of the Visible."* Berkeley: University of California Press, 1999.

———. "The Inside-Out of Masculinity: David Cronenberg's Visceral Pleasures." In *The Body's Perilous Pleasures*, edited by Michele Aaron. Edinburgh: Edinburgh University Press, 1999.

———, ed. *Porn Studies*. Durham, N.C.: Duke University Press, 2004.

———. "When the Woman Looks." In *Revision: Essays in Feminist Film Criticism*, edited by Mary Ann Doane, Patricia Mellencamp, and Linda Williams. American Film Institute Monograph Series, vol. 3. Frederick, Md.: University Publications of America, 1984.

Williams, Tony. *The Cinema of George A. Romero: Knight of the Living Dead*. London: Wallflower Press, 2003.

Winick, Charles. "Some Observations on Characteristics of Patrons of Adult Theaters and Bookstores." *Technical Report of the Commission on Obscenity and Pornography*, vol. 4. Washington, D.C.: U.S. Government Printing Office, 1971.

Wood, Robin. *Hollywood from Vietnam to Reagan*. New York: Columbia University Press, 1986.

Wyatt, Justin. "Cinematic/Sexual: An Interview with Todd Haynes. *Film Quarterly* 46, no. 3 (spring 1993): 2–8.

Zeeland, Steven. *Sailors and Sexual Identity: Crossing the Line between "Straight" and "Gay" in the U.S. Navy*. New York: Harrington Park, 1995.

———. *Military Trade*. New York: Harrington Park, 1999.

Žižek, Slavoj. *Enjoy Your Symptom! Jacques Lacan in Hollywood and Out*. New York: Routledge, 1992.

Contributors

Harry M. Benshoff is an associate professor in the Department of Radio, Television, and Film at the University of North Texas. He is the author of *Monsters in the Closet: Homosexuality and the Horror Film* (Manchester University Press, 1997) and coauthor (with Sean Griffin) of *Queer Images: A History of Gay and Lesbian Film in America* (Rowman and Littlefield, 2006), *Queer Cinema: The Film Reader* (Routledge, 2004), and *America on Film: Representing Race, Class, Gender, and Sexuality at the Movies* (Blackwell, 2004). He has also published many essays on topics such as *Dark Shadows* fan cultures, blaxploitation horror films, Hollywood LSD films, and *The Talented Mr. Ripley*.

Kay Dickinson lectures in Media and Communications at Goldsmiths College, University of London. She is the editor of *Movie Music, The Film Reader* (Routledge, 2003) and coeditor, with Glyn Davis, of *Teen TV: Genre, Consumption and Identity* (BFI, 2004). Her articles can be found in *Popular Music, Screen, Camera Obscura*, and in many anthologies on film, television, and music. Her contribution to this volume is part of a larger project titled *Off Key: When Film and Music Won't Work Together* (Oxford University Press, forthcoming).

Chris Fujiwara is the author of *Jacques Tourneur: The Cinema of Nightfall* (Johns Hopkins University Press, 2001) and of forthcoming books on Otto Preminger and Jerry Lewis. A film critic for the *Boston Phoenix* and a former contributing editor of *Hermenaut*, Fujiwara has also written articles and reviews for *Film Comment, Cineaste, InterCommunication, Osian's Cinemaya, Film International, positions*, and other publications, and he has contributed essays to such anthologies as *The X List: The National Society of Film Critics' Guide to the Movies That Turn Us On* (ed. Jami Bernard, Da Capo, 2005), *The Film Comedy Reader* (ed. Gregg Rickman, Limelight Editions, 2004), *The Science Fiction Reader* (ed. Rickman, Limelight Editions, 2004), *The 1,001 Films You Must See Before You Die* (ed. Steven Jay Schneider, Quintet/Barron's, 2005), and *Ozu 2003* (ed. Shigehiko Hasumi, Asahi Shimbun,

2003). Fujiwara has taught and lectured on film studies and film history at Yale University, Rhode Island School of Design, and Emerson College and has served on juries at many international film festivals.

Colin Gunckel is a PhD student in the critical studies program of the Department of Film, Television, and Digital Media at the University of California at Los Angeles. Drawing from undergraduate studies in media arts and Latin American literature, his research has focused on low-budget and exploitation genres produced in Mexico, contemporary Mexican cinema, Spanish-language film exhibition in the Southwest, and Chicano art.

Joan Hawkins is an associate professor in the Department of Communication and Culture at Indiana University. She is the author of *Cutting Edge: Art-Horror and the Horrific Avant-garde* (University of Minnesota Press, 2000).

Kevin Heffernan is an associate professor in the Division of Cinema-Television at Southern Methodist University and the author of *Ghouls, Gimmicks, and Gold: Horror Films and the American Movie Business, 1953–1968* (Duke University Press, 2004). He is the coauthor of *My Son Divine* and coscreenwriter and associate producer of the documentary *Divine Trash*, winner of the Filmmakers Trophy at the 1998 Sundance Film Festival. He is currently writing a book on East Asian cinema after 1997.

Matt Hills is a senior lecturer in Media and Cultural Studies at Cardiff University. He is the author of *Fan Cultures* (Routledge, 2002), *The Pleasures of Horror* (Continuum, 2005), and *How to Do Things with Cultural Theory* (Hodder-Arnold, 2005). Current works in progress include *Key Concepts in Cultural Studies* (Sage), and *Triumph of a Time Lord: Regenerating Doctor Who in the Twenty-First Century* (I. B. Tauris).

Chuck Kleinhans has pursued disreputable subjects since writing a dissertation on the low form of comedy, farce. He has written articles on the change from film to video pornography, the Pamela Anderson pirated sex tape, trash and camp aesthetics, and the work of George Kuchar and John Waters. He also made films on tacky subjects such as the Jerry Lewis Labor Day Telethon and juvenile amusements in the Wisconsin Dells. When not moonlighting in Chicago's offbeat urban wonders, he pursues his day job at Northwestern University's program in screen cultures.

Tania Modleski teaches in the English Department at the University of Southern California and has long written about topics considered sleazy in the academic world. Her books include *The Women Who Knew Too Much: Hitchcock and Feminist Theory* (Methuen, 1988), a second edition of which has just appeared and includes a lengthy new afterword; and *Loving with a Vengeance: Mass-Produced Fantasies for Women*, a new edition of which is forthcoming from Routledge.

Eric Schaefer is an associate professor and associate chair in the Department of Visual and Media Arts at Emerson College in Boston. He is the author of *"Bold! Daring! Shocking! True!": A History of Exploitation Films, 1919–1959* (Duke University Press, 1999) and has published articles on exploitation and sexploitation film in *Cinema Journal*, *Film History*, *Film Quarterly*, and other journals and anthologies. He is working on *Massacre of Pleasure: A History of Sexploitation Film, 1960–1979*.

Jeffrey Sconce is an associate professor in the Screen Cultures Program at Northwestern University and the author of *Haunted Media: Electronic Presence from Telegraphy to Television* (Duke University Press, 2000). His work on disreputable media product has appeared in many anthologies and journals, including *Screen* and *Science as Culture*. His article "'Trashing' the Academy: Taste, Excess, and an Emerging Politics of Cinematic Style" has recently been reprinted in the third edition of Leo Braudy and Marshall Cohen's *Film Theory and Criticism* (Oxford University Press, 2004).

Greg Taylor is associate professor of film in the Conservatory of Theatre Arts and Film at Purchase College, SUNY. He is the author of *Artists in the Audience: Cults, Camp, and American Film Criticism* (Princeton University Press, 1999) and a number of articles on film criticism, cinematic modernism, and the avant-garde.

Index

A&M Records, 199, 216 n.14
Abductors, The, 32
Abominable Dr. Phibes, The, 153
Acapulco Uncensored, 26, 27
Ackroyd, Dan, 300
Adorno, Theodor, 167, 171, 186 nn.5, 8, 304, 306
Adult Film Association of America (AFAA), 39
Adventures of Lucky Pierre, The, 22
Advertising Code for Motion Pictures, 20
Advise and Consent, 79
Affleck, Ben, 287, 296
Age of Innocence, The, 285
Ahí está el detalle, 136
A. I., 287
Akerman, Chantal, 240, 242
Alazraki, Benito, 136
Albertazzi, Giorgio, 154
Alberti, Guido, 247
Alda, Robert, 144, 156
Alexandrov, Grigori, 185 n.5
Ali: Fear Eats the Soul, 189, 210, 213
Allá en el Rancho Grande, 128
Allen, Richard, 240
Allen, Woody, 162 n.19, 287

Allied Artists, 155, 156, 157, 158, 160
All That Heaven Allows, 207, 208, 210, 211, 213
Amanti d'oltretomba. See *Nightmare Castle*
Amazing Adventures of Kavalier and Clay, The, 205
Amazing Transplant, The, 55–58, 66, 292
American Beauty, 278, 305
American Broadcasting Company (ABC), 157
American Film Distributing (AFD), 22, 30
American Film Institute (AFI), 205
American Idol, 299
American International Pictures (AIP), 1, 4, 21, 144, 145, 152, 153, 155, 157, 159, 274
American Pie, 99
Anger, Kenneth, 73
Animal, The, 32
Annie Hall, 162 n.19
Antonioni, Michelangelo, 244
Anything Once, 32
Archibald, William, 81
Arenas, Rosa, 137
Are We Not Men?, 177
Argento, Dario, 167, 168, 170, 173, 175, 179, 188 n.21

Arkoff, Sam, 145, 153, 155, 157
Armageddon, 305
Arnheim, Rudolph, 279, 308 n.38
Arnold, Matthew, 304
Art Forum, 3
Art:21, 3
Assassins, The, 214
Atamian, Armand, 26
At War with the Army, 73
Audubon Productions, 24, 31
Auteurism, 3, 159
Avant-Garde, 9, 73, 99, 123, 170, 207, 208, 221, 222
Azteca Distribution, 25

Baa Baa Black Sheep, 265
Babuscio, Jack, 71
Baby Doll, 21, 75
Bad and the Beautiful, The, 276
Bad Girls Go to Hell, 52–54, 55, 66, 68
Baker, Carroll, 21
Bakhtin, Mikhail, 64, 204
Bamboo House of Dolls, 157
Barbarella, 303
Bare Hunt, The, 21
Barker, Martin, 183, 185 n.3, 188 n.28
Barnum, P. T., 100, 106, 107, 117 n.7, 288
Baron Blood, 144, 155, 156, 160
Barron, Bebe, 173
Barron, Louis, 173
Bartco, 25–26
Barthes, Roland, 8–9, 170, 302
Batman, 192, 295
Battlefield Earth, 278
Baudry, Jean-Louis, 64
Bauman, Zygmunt, 169, 170, 171, 184
Bava, Mario, 12, 144, 145, 146, 148, 151, 153, 155, 156, 158, 159, 235, 288
Bay, Michael, 278, 287

Bazelon, Irwin, 185 n.4
Bazin, André, 279
Beat the Geeks, 14, 259, 265–270
Beatty, Warren, 35
Beethoven, Ludwig von, 174, 175
Bell, Bare, and Beautiful, 21
Bellour, Raymond, 282
Benshoff, Harry, 11, 191
Berenstein, Rhona, 125
Berg, Charles Ramirez, 129, 130, 137
Bergman, Ingmar, 287, 298
Bern, Gus, 158
Berry, Halle, 277, 294
Bérubé, Michael, 271
Bestia magnifica, La, 137
Best Man, The, 79
Bethview Amusement Corporation, 39
Beyond, The, 168, 173, 179
Beyond the Door, 162 n.19
Beyond the Green Door, 35
Beyond the Valley of the Dolls, 189, 190, 200, 201, 303
Big Snatch, The, 26–27
Billy Budd, 11, 72, 77, 78, 79, 92 n.21
Billy Madison, 298
Black Sabbath, 149
Black Sunday (1960), 148
Black Sunday (1977), 264
Blade Runner, 192
Blair, Linda, 297
Blair Witch Project, The, 186, 187 n.12, 308 n.39
Blanc, Erika, 148
Blanco, Jorge Ayala, 137
Blaze Star Goes Nudist, 52
Blood and Black Lace, 151
Blood Feast, 223
Blue Velvet, 192
Bobbit, Lorena, 47

Body of a Female, 30
Boin-n-g!, 21
Bolton, Tiffany, 266
Bonanza, 103
Bond, James, 59, 265
Bourdieu, Pierre, 6, 8, 28, 99, 184, 188 n.32, 196, 216 n.14, 221, 222, 234, 309 n.49
Bowen, Michael, 65–68, 119 n.20
Bowie, David, 203, 217 n.29, 271
Boxoffice International, 24, 27
Brackage, Stan, 118 n.13
Brainiac, The, 15 n.5
Brando, Marlon, 81, 82
Braunsberg, Andrew, 161 n.6
Brecht, Bertolt, 181, 198
Brennan, William J., 43 n.6
Bresson, Robert, 261
Briggs, Joe Bob, 60
Broidy, Steve, 155
Bronski, Michael, 73
Brontë, Charlotte, 68
Brontë, Emily, 68
Brooks, Mel, 201
Broomfield, Nick, 217 n.29
Brophy, Philip, 181, 186 n.5
Brown, Royal, 185 n.4
Bruckheimer, Jerry, 278
Brutes, The, 32
Bucket of Blood, 153
Budra, Paul, 228
Buñuel, Luis, 118 n.16, 221, 285
Bunny & Clod, 35, 36
Burden of Dreams, 286
Burlesque, 21, 29
Burns, John Horne, 73
Burstyn v. Wilson, 20, 42–43 n.3. *See also* Supreme Court
Burton, Tim, 288
Bush, George W., 188 n.34

Cabaret, 155, 157, 160, 203
Cabinet of Dr. Caligari, 154
Cady, Dan, 35
Cahiers du Cinéma, 159
Cameron, James, 287, 288
Camille 2000, 31
Canby, Vincent, 84
Cannes Film Festival, 12, 144, 145, 152, 155, 158, 191
Cannibal Ferox, 168, 172, 180
Cannibal Holocaust, 168, 172, 180, 181
Cantinflas, 123, 124, 125, 131, 133, 134, 135, 136
Capatach, Blaine, 265
Capote, Truman, 81
Captain, The, 73
Cárdenas, Lázaro, 128
Cardona, René, 137
Carey, Mariah, 295
Carlos, Wendy, 174, 175
Carpenter, John, 174, 226, 227, 228, 231, 232
Carpenter, Karen, 190, 195, 198
Carpenter, Richard, 199
Carrell, Steve, 275
Carroll, Nöel, 125, 129, 130, 139
Casablanca, 197, 283
Case, Sue-Ellen, 64
Casey, Larry, 88
Castañeda, Luis Aceves, 138
Castle, William, 5, 288–290
Castle of Blood, 149, 150, 151
Cathouse, 97
Cat on a Hot Tin Roof, 75
Cat People, 308 n.39
Catwoman, 277, 294–295
Caught in the Act—Naked, 32
Cavara, Paolo, 180
Caviezel, James, 307
Celebrities Uncensored, 276

Chabon, Michael, 205
Chambers, Marilyn, 35
Champlin, Charles, 83
Chandler, Otis, 41
Cheers, 265
Chernoff, Sam, 40, 41
Children's Hour, The, 82
Chimes at Midnight, 157
Chion, Michel, 186 n.5
Cinecittà, 244
Cinéfantastique, 159
Cinephilia, 1, 2, 3, 6, 7, 8, 15, 160, 274–306
Cioran, E. M., 240, 242
Citizen Kane, 105, 203, 204, 292, 299
City and the Pillar The, 73
Clark, Graeme, 196
Cleopatra, 286
Clift, Montgomery, 82
Clinton, Bill, 71, 116
Clockwork Orange, A, 40, 174, 175
Cloister of the Innocents, 150
Clover, Carol, 47, 62, 229, 232, 233, 234
Clover Films, 37
Cobain, Kurt, 203, 217 n.30
Coleman, Lonnie, 73
Collins, Jim, 192, 193, 194, 196
Columbia Pictures, 39
Come Play With Me, 31
Comedy Central, 14, 265, 266, 308 n.45
Coming Out Under Fire, 89
Commission on Obscenity and Pornography, 34
Committee for the Freedom of Homosexuals, 87
Conner, Bruce, 195
Conrich, Ian, 224, 234, 235, 236
Consolidated, 25
Conte, Maria Pia, 247
Cook, Pam, 10, 69

Copley, James S., 37
Coppola, Francis Ford, 81, 287
Coppola, Sofia, 307 n.29
Cordio, Carlo, 188 n.24
Corman, Roger, 288, 289, 292
Correll, Matilde, 123
Costner, Kevin, 286, 287
Cotton, Joseph, 144
Counter-cinema, 10, 62, 70 n.11
Counterphobic cinema, 63
Country Hooker, 27
Crane, Jonathan Lake, 229, 230, 232
Craven, Wes, 226, 231
Cresse, Bob, 26
Cronenberg, David, 233
CSI: Miami, 270
CSI: New York, 270
"Cultism," 6, 14, 259–271, 301
Cunningham, Sean S., 231
Curious Female, The, 32
Cusak, John, 265–266, 270

Daalder, Renee, 307 n.26
Daily Show, The, 275
Daisy Chain, The, 27
Dali, Salvador, 221
Damn the Defiant, 79
"Danse macabre," 146, 150, 151
Dante, Joe, 308
Danza Macabra, 151, 152. See also *Castle of Blood*
Daughter of the Sun, 19, 20
Dave, 300
David, Zorro, 81
Dawn of the Dead, 224, 225, 231
Day of the Dead, 225
Deadly Weapons, 59, 64, 66
Debauchers, The, 32
Debord, Guy, 257

Deep Throat, 44–45 n.30
Defamer.com, 276, 300–301, 302
Defilers, The, 32, 50–52
Delany, Samuel R., 44 n.29, 120 n.21
De la Vega Alfaro, Eduardo, 136, 143 n.35
Del Río, Dolores, 135
Demolition Man, 192
Denby, David, 280, 283
Deodato, Ruggero, 168, 172, 181
Depp, Johnny, 288
Deren, Maya, 221
Dérive, 14, 256–257
Detective, The (1968), 80
De Toth, André, 269
Detour, 284
Détournement, 14, 256–257
Dever, Susan, 136
Devil's Cleavage, The, 114
Devil's Nightmare, 152
Devo, 176, 177
Dickie Roberts, Former Child Star, 297–298
Dickinson, Emily, 68
Dickinson, Kay, 12–13
Diesel, Vin, 305
Dika, Vera, 230, 231
Di Lazzarro, Dalia, 161 n.6
Direct Cinema, 103, 115
Distribpix, 30
Dixon, Wheeler Winston, 283
Doane, Mary Beth, 63
Dolce vita, La, 244, 245
Do Me! Do Me! Do Me!, 32
Don Quixote, 285
Donna & Lisa, 31
D'Orgaz, Elena, 123
Dottie Gets Spanked, 191
Double Agent '73, 59–60, 66
Dracula, 148
Dr. Butcher, M.D., 293

Drive-in cinema, 42
Dumb and Dumber, 99
Dunaway, Faye, 35
Dynasty, 98

Ebert, Roger, 201
Ed Wood, 288
8½, 162 n.15
Eisenstein, Sergei, 185 n.5, 192
Eisler, Hans, 186 n.5
Elders, Jocelyn, 116
Elsaesser, Thomas, 209
Emerson, Keith, 178, 188 n.21
Empire, 242
End as a Man, 76
Entertainment Ventures, Inc. (EVI), 25, 26
Erpichini, Mario, 247
Escalera, Rudy, 25
E.T., 291
Euripides, 104
Eve and the Handyman, 21
Excited, 32
Exorcist, The, 12, 145, 148, 174, 297, 307 n.28
Exotic Dreams of Casanova, The, 29
Evans, Mark, 185 n.4
Exploitation cinema, 10, 24, 99–100, 114, 278

Fadiman, William, 81
Fajardo, Eduardo, 146
Fangoria, 224
Farber, Manny, 6, 261, 264, 280, 281, 282, 303
Far From Heaven, 13, 191, 207–215
Farley, Chris, 300
Fassbinder, Rainer Werner, 189, 210, 211, 213, 214
"Feel Like I'm in Love," 181
Felleghy, Tom, 246

Fellini, Federico, 162 n.15, 244, 252
Fernández, Emilio, 121, 135
Ferry, Bryan, 203
Fiorentino, Linda, 265, 269
Fireworks, 73
First Amendment, 20
Fisher, Terence, 244
Flateau, Joel, 80
Flesh for Frankenstein, 161 n.6
Flinn, Caryl, 185 n.4
Flipper, 31
Flynn, Hazel, 92 n.22
Forbidden Planet, 173
Forbidden Pleasure, 32
Ford, John, 2
Forgotten Silver, 307
For Single Swingers Only, 32
Forster, Robert, 81, 82
Fortune and Men's Eyes, 73, 95 n.74
Fosse, Bob, 203
Foucault, Michel, 58, 225
Fowles, Jib, 28
Franco, Jess, 159, 288
Frankenstein, 123–124
Freda, Riccardo, 149
Freddy's Dead, 187 n.14
Freddy vs. Jason, 229
Frederick's of Hollywood, 105
Frenzy, 52
Freud, Sigmund, 107, 108, 127, 191, 243
Friday the 13th, 13, 219, 222, 224, 225, 226, 227, 228, 230, 231
Friday the 13th, Part II, 223, 231
Friday the 13th, Part III, 229, 231
Friday the 13th, Part VI: Jason Lives, 229
Friday the 13th: The Final Chapter, 223
Friedkin, William, 174
Friedman, David F., 22, 24, 25, 26, 32, 34, 50, 61, 288

Frith, Simon, 271
Frizzi, Fabio, 179
From Justin to Kelly, 299
Frusta é il corpo, La. See *Whip and the Body*
Fujiwara, Chris, 14
Fulci, Lucio, 168, 248
Fullerton, Carl, 223
Full Frontal, 278

Gaines, Jane, 118 n.10
Galán, Alberto, 135
Gallery, The, 73
Gangs of New York, 285
Garber, Marjorie, 64
Garland, Judy, 87
Gastaldi, Ernesto, 161 n.5
Gay, Ramón, 137
Gay Deceivers, The, 11, 72, 85–89
Gays and Lesbians in Mainstream Media, 79
Gazarra, Ben, 76–77
Genet, Jean, 189, 191, 205, 214
Gibson, Mel, 307 n.28
Gigli, 295–296
Gilligan's Island, 260
Ginzberg v. United States (1966), 26. See also Supreme Court
Girls Gone Wild, 107
Girl with Hungry Eyes, The, 31
Glen or Glenda, 114, 115
Gli Orrori del Castello di Noremburga. See *Baron Blood*
Glitter, 295
Glover, Danny, 299
Goblin, 178, 179, 188 n.23
Godard, Jean-Luc, 53, 202, 244, 274
Godzilla, 7
Godzilla (1998), 278, 295
Goebel, Paul, 265

Goldilocks and the Three Bares, 21
Gone Fishin', 299
Good Man is Hard to Find, A, 28
Gordon, Bert I., 269
Gorky, Maxim, 96
"Grand Guignol," 224, 235
Great White, 162 n.19
Greene, Lorne, 103
Green Hornet, The, 264
Greer, Michael, 86, 88
Gunckel, Colin, 12

Hall, Stuart, 14, 309 n.53
Halloween, 226, 227, 228, 230, 231, 232, 235
Halloween H20, 231
Hamilton, George, 80
Hanna-Barbera, 181
Hannie Caulder, 264
Harries, Dan, 123, 124
Harris, Julie, 81
Hawkins, Joan, 13, 221, 222, 234
Haynes, Todd, 13, 189–215
Hearts of Darkness, 286
Heaven's Gate, 286
Hedren, Tippi, 287
Heffernan, Kevin, 12, 227
Hegel, Georg Wilhelm Friedrich, 192
Heidegger, Martin, 14, 251, 255
Heilman, Jeremy, 197
Henry: Portrait of a Serial Killer, 175, 187 nn.14, 19, 226
Hentai, 29
Hepburn, Audrey, 82
Hermanaut, 14
Hershfield, Joanne, 131, 132
Herzog, Werner, 306 n.16
Heston, Charlton, 287
Heuck, Marc Edward, 259, 265, 266, 270
Hidden Persuaders, The, 21

Hideout in the Sun, 23
High Fidelity, 269
Hills, Matt, 13, 188 n.32
Hitchcock, Alfred, 5, 51–52, 66, 68, 162 n.15, 261, 278
Hoberman, J., 207, 211
Hocquenghem, Guy, 90, 91 n.11
Hodges, Charles, 34
Hoffman, Robert, 246
Home Box Office (HBO), 96, 97, 201
Homicidal, 5
Horkheimer, Max, 167, 171, 186 n.5
Horowitz, Gad, 127
Horrible Dr. Hitchcock, The, 149
Hot Erotic Dreams, 29
House of Exorcism, 12, 144, 145, 154, 157, 158, 162 n.19. See also *Lisa and the Devil*
How I Made a Million Dollars and Never Lost a Dime, 289. See also Roger Corman
How to Shoot a Crime, 194
Howarth, Troy, 156
Hudson, Rock, 207, 208
"Humbug Effect," 100, 106, 107
Humphries, Reynold, 231
Hungerford Chapel, 150
Hunt, Leon, 167
Hurdes, Las, 118 n.16
Hussein, Saddam, 188 n.34
Huston, John, 81, 82

I Am Curious Yellow, 108
I, A Woman, 35
I Crave Your Body, 32
If . . ., 73
I Love the '80s, 260, 268
I Love the '70s, 260, 268
I tre volti della paura, 149, 151. See also *Black Sabbath*
Ihde, Don, 243, 254

Image Entertainment, 160
Imitation of Life, 207
Immoral, The, 32
Immoral Mr. Teas, The, 20, 21, 23, 49
Importance of Being Earnest, The, 98
Incredibly Strange Films, 8, 223, 224
Indecent Desires, 58
Indecent Proposal, 300
Independence Day, 89
Inferno, 168, 173, 178, 188 n.21
In Like Flint, 303
Ironside, 264
Isherwood, Christopher, 81
Island, The, 293
Island of the Burning Doomed, 244
It Conquered the World, 288, 289

Jack, 287
Jackson, Peter, 287, 307 n.27
Jacobellis v. Ohio, 43 n.6. See also Supreme Court
Jacopetti, Gualtiero, 117 n.6, 180
Jaeger, Andy, 155, 157
Jameson, Fredric, 191, 192
Jancovich, Mark, 222, 223, 224, 236 n.4
Janitzio, 121
Jason Goes to Hell: The Final Friday, 229
Jason X, 229
Jaws, 157
Jeanne Dielman, 23 Quai du Commerce, 1080 Bruxelles, 240, 242
Jenkins, Henry, 188 n.32
Jerry Springer Show, The, 106–107
Joe Dirt, 297, 298
Joel, Billy, 271
Johnson, Claire, 10, 62, 69
Johnson Administration, 119 n.19
Josie and the Pussycats, 305
Jumanji, 269

Juno, Andrea, 8
Jurassic Park 2: The Lost World, 6, 7
Justine ou les Infortunes de la Vertu, 53, 67

Kael, Pauline, 1–9, 14, 15, 67, 262, 274, 275, 279, 281, 282, 295, 299, 303–305
Kaminski, Janusz, 269
Karloff, Boris, 149
Kauffmann, Stanley, 84
Kazan, Eliza, 6
Keaton, Buster, 287
Keith, Brian, 81
Kelly, Grace, 287
Kendall, Suzy, 247
Kessler, Bruce, 95 n.71
Key Club Wives, 29–30
Kier, Udo, 161 n.6
Kierkegaard, Søren, 258 n.16, 304
Kill, Baby, Kill, 148
Kill Bill, Vol. 1, 260, 264
King Crimson, 188 n.21
"Kinkies," 49. See also "Roughies"
Kinsey, Alfred, 108
Kinsey Report, The, 29
KISS, 265
Kiss, The, 96, 97
Klein, Melanie, 59
Kleinhans, Chuck, 11
Klinger, Barbara, 196
Klosterman, Chuck, 14, 270–271
Knowles, Harry, 279
Koschina, Sylva, 146
Kraftwerk, 176, 177
Kraus, Chris, 194
Kruger, Barbara, 194
Kubrick, Stanley, 40, 175, 274, 287
Kuchar, George, 99, 114
Kuleshov effect, 253
Kurt and Courtney, 217 n.30

Lacan, Jacques, 57, 64, 282, 283
Landeta, Matilde, 136
Lasch, Christopher, 31
Lasky, Gil, 95 n.71
Last Action Hero, 192
Lastretti, Adolfo, 247
Last Year at Marienbad, 153
Law, John Philip, 83, 85
Leather Boys, The, 73
Leavisism, 302
Lehman, Ari, 225
Lenzi, Umberto, 168, 244, 249, 253
Leone, Alfredo, 12, 144, 148, 153, 155, 156, 158, 160
Leone, Sergio, 161 n.5
Leprechaun 5, 305
Let Me Die a Woman, 61, 113–115, 119–120 n.21
Let's Go Native, 24–25
Let's Play Doctor, 32
Lewis, Herschell Gordon, 5, 22, 223, 288
Lewis, Jerry, 73, 307 n.23
Lewton, Val, 286
Libertine, The, 37
Lillard, Matthew, 301
Lindsay, Vachel, 279
Lippert, Robert, 154
Lisa and the Devil, 12, 144–146, 148–158, 160
Lisztomania, 203
Littleford, Beth, 275
Living Head The, 137
Livingston, Jenny, 201–202, 206
Llorona, La, 137
Locke, John, 117 n.7
Lola Cassanova, 136
Lolita, 21
Lonesome Cowboys, 84
Lopez, Jennifer, 296
Lorna, 52

Lorre, Peter, 76
Lost and Found, 297
Lost in La Mancha, 286
Lost Skeleton of Cadavra, The, 2–3
Lost Souls, 269
Love and Anarchy, 157
Love Camp 7, 52
Love Thy Neighbor and His Wife, 31
Lucas, George, 283
Lucas, Tim, 156, 291
Luchadoras contra la momia, Las, 137
Lucky Wander Boy, 14, 263–264
Lugosi, Bela, 195
Lupo, Michele, 248
Lusty Neighbors, 32
Lynch, David, 285
Lyne, Adrian, 300
Lyon, Sue, 21
Lyons, James, 210

Macdonald, Dwight, 261
MacLaine, Shirley, 82
Madison Avenue, 75
Madonna, 296
Maglione, Budy, 188 n.24
Magnificent Ambersons, The, 287
Magnificent Obsession, 207
Maltin, Leonard, 144, 145, 148, 160
Mancori, Guglielmo, 248
Mangravite, Andrew, 148
Maniac Cop, 297
Man Machine, 177
Mannix, 265
Mantis in Lace, 4
Many Ways to Sin, 32
Man Who Would Be King, The, 155, 157
March of Time, 104–105
Marcuse, Herbert, 127
Margheriti, Antonio, 149, 159, 161 n.6, 248

Maria Candelaria, 121, 135, 136
Marie, Kelly, 181
Marinet, Pascal, 153
Marnie, 286
Marriage Drop-Outs, The, 32
Martin, Dean, 73
Marx, Karl, 192
Mary Tyler Moore Show, The, 265
Maschera del demonio, La. See *Black Sunday*
*M*A*S*H*, 270
Massacre at Central High, 307 n.26
Massacre of Pleasure, 30
Masters and Johnson, 108
Mati, Tia, 131
Matinee, 308 n.34
Maus, Pedro, 136
McCartney, Paul, 203
McCullers, Carson, 73, 81
McDonagh, Maitland, 170
McNaughton, John, 175
Medel, Mañuel, 123, 125, 134
Medved, Michael, 300
Melly, George, 215
Melville, Herman, 77, 92 n.21
Men in Black 2, 278
Men, Women, and Chainsaws, 62
Mépris, Le, 244
Merchant-Ivory, 300, 309 n.49
Merleau-Ponty, Maurice, 253
Messiah of Evil, 162 n.19
Metro-Goldwyn-Mayer, 291
Metz, Christian, 240, 282
Metzger, Randy, 24
Mexican Revolution, 121, 128
Meyer, Russ, 8, 21, 49, 52, 189, 190, 191, 200, 201, 205
Michelson, Annette, 284, 285
Michigan State Court of Appeals, 36

Midnight Cowboy, 73
Mier, Felipe, 136
Miner, Steve, 231
Minnelli, Vincente, 75
Mini-Skirt Love, 29
Misfits, The, 286
Miss America pageant, 195
Mitam, 30
Mitry, Jean, 244
Modleski, Tania, 10
Moeller, David, 23
Molesters, The, 32, 33, 34
Mom and Dad, 60–61
Momia azteca contra el robot humano, La, 138
Mondo Bizarro, 99, 102, 105, 106, 108
Mondo Cane, 99, 100, 180
Mondo Cane 2, 117 n.6
Mondo cinema, 11–12, 99–103, 105, 172
Mondo Freudo, 99, 100, 102, 106, 107, 108
Monet, Monica, 247
Monk, The, 285
Monogram Studios, 6, 155
Monsivás, Carlos, 143 n.26
Moon is Blue, The, 75
Moonlighting Wives, 32
Moore, Julianne, 209
Morangolo, Agostino, 188 n.23
Morante, Massimo, 188 n.23
Moreno, Mario. *See* Cantinflas
Morgan, Chesty, 59, 60, 68
Morricone, Ennio, 246
Morrisey, Paul, 161 n.6
Morrison, Jim, 203
Motion Pictures Association of America (MPAA), 20, 24, 35, 40, 80
"Mr. Cranky," 276
Mr. Peter's Pets, 21
MTV, 96

Mulvey, Laura, 63
Mutiny on the Bounty, 79
Mutual v. Ohio, 42 n.3. *See also* Supreme Court
My Bare Lady, 21
Myra Breckinridge, 200, 201, 303
Myrick, Daniel, 186 n.12
Mystery Science Theater 3000, 2, 304

Naked Fog, 30
Naked Paradise, 21
National Catholic Organization of Motion Pictures, 84
National Film Board, 103
National Screen Service, 25
Nature Camp Confidential, 52
Navarro, Carlos, 121
Near Dark, 192
Nestle, Joan, 48
Neu!, 175
New Kids on the Block, 266
New Queer Cinema, 195
Nietzsche, Friedrich, 167
Nightmare Castle, 148
Nightmare on Elm Street, 226, 231
Night of the Big Heat, 244
Night of the Bloody Apes, 292
Nineteen Eighty-Four, 204
Nixon, Richard, 119 n.19, 194, 215
Noriega, Chon, 75
Notorious Big City Sin, 26
Novak, Harry, 24, 25, 26
Novo, Salvador, 123, 124, 128
Nowell-Smith, Geoffrey, 167
Nude for Satan, 292
Nude on the Moon, 49, 50
"Nudie Cuties," 20, 21, 22, 23, 24, 29, 49
Nudist Camp Films, 20, 23, 49–50, 52
Nylon Curtain, The, 271

Obscenity, 23, 26, 100
Odd Tastes, 32
Offers, Steve, 24–25
Oklahoma Publishing Company, 39
Oldfield, Mike, 174
Ophuls, Max, 189
Olympic International, 29, 30
Once Upon a Time in America, 161 n.5
Onion, The, 275, 294–299, 301, 302, 308 n.43
Only Angels Have Wings, 73
Oona, 31
Operazione paura. *See Kill, Baby, Kill*
Orano, Alessio, 146
Orellana, Carlos, 122
Orgy at Lil's Place, 32
Oro, Juan Bustillo, 136
Ortega y Gasset, José, 261
Ortolani, Riz, 180, 181
Oscars, 87, 277
Othello, 252

Packard, Vance, 21
Papillon, 155, 157, 160
"Paracinema," 8, 13, 15 n.5, 200, 215 n.3, 220, 221, 222, 224
Paramount Decision, 283
Paramount Studios, 157, 227
"Para-paracinema," 13, 219
Paris Is Burning, 201–202, 206
Paris Ooh-La-La!, 22
Pasolini, Pier Paolo, 172
Passion of the Christ, The, 307 n.27
Peeping Tom, 59
Peppard, George, 80
Peppercorn-Wormser, 145, 157, 158
Performance, 201, 202
Perkins, Anthony, 146
Perrin, Tomás, Jr., 123

Perry, Matthew, 305
Persona, 298
Pesci, Joe, 299
Petro, Patrice, 241
Phillips, Adam, 241
Photon, 159
Pignatelli, Fabio, 188 n.23
Pilcher, Jeffrey M., 123, 124, 126, 128, 134, 143 n.26
Pink Flamingoes, 3, 114
Plan 9 from Outer Space, 190, 195
Playboy, 34, 85, 106
Player, The, 276
Plus longue nuit du diable, La. See *Devil's Nightmare*
Podalsky, Laura, 135
Poe, Edgar Allan, 117 n.7, 149, 150
Poison, 189, 190, 191, 211, 214
Polsky, Abe, 95 n.71
Poltergeist, 307 n.28
Polyester, 3
Ponce, Manuel Barbachano, 136
Pornography, 4, 19, 34, 40, 41, 49, 58, 96, 97, 109, 110
Porter, Cole, 98
Portillo, Rafael, 122
Postgraduate Course in Sexual Love, The, 110–112, 115
"Poverty Row," 155, 284
Powell, Michael, 59
Price, Vincent, 153
Prince and the Nature Girl, The, 52
Production Code, 20, 75, 76, 78, 79, 80
Production Code Administration (PCA), 75, 77, 79, 80, 82, 92 nn.16, 17
Psycho, 4, 53, 146, 176
Public Broadcasting System (PBS), 3
Pudovkin, Vsevolod, 185–186 n.5
Pussycat Theater, 41, 42

Quaid, Dennis, 191, 208, 209
Queenan, Joe, 275, 299–300, 301, 302
Quetzalcoatl, 125

Rachel, Rachel, 79
Radford, Michael, 204
Radio-Keith-Orpheium (RKO), 286
Raíces, 136
Randall, Dick, 22
Rassimov, Ivan, 246
"Razzie" awards, 276
Reagan, Ronald, 204, 215
Reali, Carlo, 156
Real Sex, 96, 97
Reckless Moment, The, 189
Redes, 121
Red Lips, 31
Reed, Lou, 271
Reed, Rex, 201
Reflections in a Golden Eye, 11, 72, 80, 81, 82, 84, 85
Reflections on Black, 118 n.13
Région centrale, La, 242
Reich, Wilhelm, 116
Reitman, Ivan, 300
Replicas, 177
Republicans, 116
Resident Evil 2, 305
Resnais, Alain, 153
Revueltas, Silvestre, 123
Riera, Emilo Garcia, 124
Rimbaud, Arthur, 205, 214
Rio Escondido, 121
Rivera, Diego, 121, 124, 128
Road Warrior, 192
Robot Monster, 15 n.5
Robot vs. the Aztec Mummy, The, 122, 137, 138, 139, 140
Rocky Horror Picture Show, The, 303

Rodrigo, Joaquin, 147
Rodríguez, Ismael, 137
Roeg, Nicholas, 201
Roller Boogie, 297
Romero, George, 225, 233
Romm, Mikhail, 242
Ronnie Rocket, 285
Rophie, Katie, 48
Rosemary's Baby, 148
Ross, Andrew, 200–202, 205, 207, 210, 215
Rossellini, Roberto, 172
Rossi-Stuart, Giacomo, 148
Roth decision, 23, 38. *See also* Supreme Court
RottenTomatoes.com, 276
"Roughies," 5, 49
Ruined Bruin, The, 21
Russell, Jane, 21
Russell, Ken, 203
Russo, Mary, 64
Russo, Vito, 87
Ryan, Anthony-James, 21–22
Ryan, Robert, 78

Sacher-Masoch, Leopold von, 203
Safe, 189, 191, 215
Saló, 172
Sanchez, Eduardo, 186 n.12
San Fernando, Miguel, 137
San Francisco International Film Festival, 84
Santoni, Espartaco, 146
Sarne, Michael, 200, 201
Sarris, Andrew, 95 n.74, 260, 261, 262, 264
Satan's Cheerleaders, 293
Saturday Night Live, 298, 308 n.45
Savalas, Telly, 144, 146, 153
Saved by the Bell, 271
Savini, Tom, 223, 224, 225, 232

Schaefer, Eric, 10
Scheingarten, Louis, 25
Schindler's List, 6, 7
Schneider, Steven Jay, 227
Schoenberg, Arnold, 188 n.26
Schusterman, Richard, 271
Sconce, Jeffrey, 173, 187 nn.14, 19, 188 nn.32, 196, 200, 215 n.3, 216 n.14, 220, 221, 222, 225, 234, 236 n.4
Scorsese, Martin, 285
Scott, Ridley, 300
Scream, 228
Scrutiny, 302
Scum of the Earth, 32–33
Sedgwick, Eve Kosofsky, 79
Sei donne per l'assassino, 151
Sensual Encounters, 32
Sergeant, The, 80, 83–85
Serving in Silence: The Margarethe Cammermeyer Story, 89
Sex, Drugs, and Cocoa Puffs, 14
Sexploitation, 10, 19–46, 108–116
Sex Shop, Le, 157
Sexual Freedom in Denmark, 108–110, 115
Seyrig, Delphine, 154
Sgt. Matlovich vs the U.S. Air Force, 89
Shakespeare, 206
Shaw Brothers, 264
She's . . . 17 and Anxious, 32
Ship's Company, 73
Shore, Pauly, 300
Showbiz Show, The, 308 n.45
Shurlock, Geoffrey, 82, 92 n.16
Sight and Sound, 291, 292
Signo de la Muerte, El, 12, 121–135, 136, 137, 140, 141
Silva, Carmen, 156
Silva, Franco, 248
Simpsons, The, 265

Siqueiros, David, 121
Sirk, Douglas, 191, 196, 207, 209, 210, 211, 213, 285
Situationists, 14, 256–257
Slasher film, 194, 223, 224, 225, 226, 232
Sleaze, 4, 5, 6, 98–99, 114, 115
Sleep, 214
Sleep With Me, 89
Smith, Dick, 224
Smith, Jack, 99
Smith, Jeff, 185 n.4
Smut Peddler, The, 32
Snow, Michael, 242
Snyder, Marjorie, 82
Sobchack, Vivian, 243, 254
Sollima, Sergio, 248
Solomon, Joe, 95 n.71
Some Like it Violent, 32
Something Weird Video, 119 n.20
Sommer, Elke, 144, 146, 156, 160
Sontag, Susan, 6, 98
Southern, Terry, 274, 275, 281
Space Thing, 29
Spacey, Kevin, 305
Spade, David, 297, 298, 300, 308 n.45
Spasmo, 14, 240–257
Spiegel, Sam, 92 n.16
Spielberg, Steven, 6, 7, 287, 291
Spigel, Lynn, 197
Springer, Jerry, 107
Spy Magazine, 299, 308 n.46
"Stag films," 23
Stallone, Sylvester, 300
Stamp, Terence, 78, 92 n.22
Star is Born, A, 276
Starsky and Hutch, 265
Star Trek, 265
Star Wars, 270, 283, 291
Steamroller and the Violin, The, 242

Steele, Barbara, 148, 149
Steiger, Rod, 80, 83
Stein, Ben, 300
Steinman, Joe, 24–25
Stephens, Chuck, 197
Sternberg, Jacques, 274, 275, 276, 281, 294, 303
Stone, Sharon, 277
Stone Roses, The, 260, 270
Straight Jacket, 289
Strange One, The, 11, 72, 76–77, 79
Streamers, 89
Streetcar Named Desire, A, 75
Streible, Dan, 118 n.17
Substitution, 28
Suburban Confidential, 29
Suddenly Last Summer, 75
Sundance Channel, 208
Sundance Film Festival, 191, 278
Sunrise, 292
Superstar, The Karen Carpenter Story, 13, 190, 194–199, 203, 212, 215
Supreme Court, 20, 23, 26, 42 n.3, 43 n.6, 49
Swappers, The, 32
Switchblade Sisters, 259

Take Me Naked, 29–30
Tales of Terror, 153
Tarantino, Quentin, 90, 260, 264, 307 n.29
Tarkovsky, Andrei, 242
Taste, 7, 8, 13, 28
Taylor, Elizabeth, 81, 82
Taylor, Greg, 6, 14, 280, 301, 303–304
Tea and Sympathy, 75
Tenebrae, 168, 172, 173, 178, 179
Terror at the Opera, 167
Terzano, Ubaldo, 161 n.6
Test Pilot, 73

Thar She Blows, 26
Thatcher, Russell, 73
Thatcherism, 183
Thelma and Louise, 192, 194
Thibaut, Professor, 66, 68
Thomas, Kevin, 39
Thomas Crown Affair, The, 4
Thoreau, Henry David, 212
Thornton, Sarah, 188 n.32
Timecode, 278
Times Square, 44 n.29, 67
Time-Warner, 296
Tingler, The, 289, 290
Tinti, Gabriele, 146
Titanic, 305
Tizoc, 137
Together, 35
Toi, Ma Nuit, 274
Tokyo Story, 292
Tolkien, J. R. R., 287
Too Young, Too Immoral!, 32
Top Gun, 90
Torosh, Rosita, 247
Touch of Evil, 287
Trader Hornee, 26
Trial, The, 252
Troma Films, 5
Tubeway Army, 176, 177
"Tubular Bells," 174
Tudor, Andrew, 125, 228
Tuthill, Bruce, 195
25 Greatest Commercials, 260
Twilight Girls, The, 20, 24
2001: A Space Odyssey, 1, 274
Two Weeks in Another Town, 252
Tyler, Parker, 6, 72, 90, 280, 281, 282, 303

Ulmer, Edgar G, 6, 284, 286
Ultra Volume Photo, 26

Un chant d'amour, 189
Underwater, 21
United Theatrical Amusement (UTA), 26
Universal Studios, 123–124, 138, 157, 208
Unlawful Entry, 5
Urueta, Chano, 121, 122, 123, 137
Ustinov, Peter, 77, 78, 79

Vale, V., 8
Valenti, Jack, 40, 41
Valley of the Dolls, The, 303
Valli, Alida, 146
Van Straaten, J. Keith, 265
Van Voorhis, Westbrook, 104–105
"Vanguard Criticism," 6, 281
Velde, Donald, 25–26
Velvet Goldmine, 13, 189, 190, 191, 199–206, 212, 214, 215
Venus in Furs, 203
Verdi, Giuseppe, 98, 178
Vertigo, 292
VH-1, 96, 260, 268
Victim, 80
Victors, The, 80
Vidal, Gore, 73, 201
Video formats, 42, 159
"Video Nasties," 13, 168, 172, 183, 185 n.3
Video Recordings Act, 168, 182, 188 n.28
Video Watchdog, 159
Vietnam Conflict, 89, 111, 194
Vixen, 35

Wallon, Henri, 243
Wanda, the Sadistic Hypnotist, 4
Warhol, Andy, 67, 241, 242
Warner Brothers, 40, 81, 82, 294
Warriors, The, 259
Waters, John, 3, 13, 99, 207
Waterworld, 286

Waugh, Tom, 120 n.21
Weekend, 84, 274
Weill, Kurt, 203
Weiss, D. B., 14, 263
Welch, Raquel, 201, 264
Welles, Orson, 104, 157, 203, 204, 205, 252, 278, 285, 287
Wertmuller, Lina, 157
Wes Craven's New Nightmare, 226
Wexner Art Center, 189
Whale, James, 123–124, 233
Whannel, Paddy, 14, 309 n.53
Whip and the Body, 151
Whitehouse, Mary, 185 n.3
Who Framed Roger Rabbit?, 192
Wilcox, Fred M., 173
Wild, Raymond, 37
Wilde, Oscar, 6, 200, 203, 205, 206, 214, 282, 302
Wild in the Streets, 1–2, 4, 7
Wild, Wild West, 278
Williams, Linda, 49, 51
Williams, Robin, 269
Williams, Tennessee, 75
Williamson, Kevin, 232
Willingham, Calder, 76
Willis, Bruce, 305
Winfrey, Oprah, 264
Wings, 73

Wish, Jerome, 88, 95 n.71
Wishman, Doris, 2, 10–11, 47–69, 112–113, 288
Without a Paddle, 301
Without a Stitch, 31
Wizard of Gore, 223
Wolf, Fred, 298
Wonder, Stevie, 175
Wood, Ed, 114, 115, 159, 190, 195, 196, 288, 292
Wood, Robin, 12, 127, 131
World without Shame, 23
Written on the Wind, 207
Wyman, Jane, 207, 208

X-Files, The, 271
XXX, 305

Yellow Submarine, 84
Yes, 175, 188 n.21
You, 31

Zappa, Frank, 307 n.31
Zax, Andy, 266
Ziggy Stardust tour, 203
Zinnemann, Fred, 121
Žižek, Slavoj, 64
Zoetrope Studios, 287

Library of Congress Cataloging-in-Publication Data

Sleaze artists : cinema at the margins of taste, style, and politics / Jeffrey Sconce, ed.

p. cm.

Includes bibliographical references and index.

ISBN 978-0-8223-3953-3 (cloth : alk. paper)

ISBN 978-0-8223-3964-9 (pbk. : alk. paper)

1. Sensationalism in motion pictures. 2. Sex in motion pictures. I. Sconce, Jeffrey, 1962–

PN1995.9.S284S54 2007

791.43'653—dc22   2007014128